CLIMATE CHANGE

As frustration mounts in some quarters at the perceived inadequacy or speed of international action on climate change, and as the likelihood of significant impacts grows, the focus is increasingly turning to liability for climate change damage. Actual or potential climate change liability implicates a growing range of actors, including governments, industry, businesses, non-governmental organisations, individuals and legal practitioners. *Climate Change Liability* provides an objective, rigorous and accessible overview of the existing law and the direction it might take in seventeen developed and developing countries and the European Union. In some jurisdictions, the applicable law is less developed and less the subject of current debate. In others, actions for various kinds of climate change liability have already been brought, including high-profile cases such as *Massachusetts* v. *EPA* in the United States. Each chapter explores the potential for and barriers to climate change liability in private and public law.

RICHARD LORD QC is a London-based commercial litigator with over twenty-five years' experience, particularly of international disputes in the Commercial Court and in arbitration, and with a particular interest in private law aspects of climate change.

SILKE GOLDBERG is a Paris-based senior associate in Herbert Smith's global energy practice and a researcher in energy law at Rijksuniversiteit Groningen, The Netherlands.

LAVANYA RAJAMANI is a Professor at the Centre for Policy Research, New Delhi, where she writes, teaches and advises on international environmental law, in particular international climate change law and policy.

JUTTA BRUNNÉE is Professor of Law and Metcalf Chair in Environmental Law at the University of Toronto.

CLIMATE CHANGE LIABILITY

Transnational Law and Practice

Edited by

RICHARD LORD

SILKE GOLDBERG

LAVANYA RAJAMANI

JUTTA BRUNNÉE

CAMBRIDGE
UNIVERSITY PRESS

CAMBRIDGE UNIVERSITY PRESS
Cambridge, New York, Melbourne, Madrid, Cape Town,
Singapore, São Paulo, Delhi, Tokyo, Mexico City

Cambridge University Press
The Edinburgh Building, Cambridge CB2 8RU, UK

Published in the United States of America by Cambridge University Press, New York

www.cambridge.org
Information on this title: www.cambridge.org/9781107017603

First published 2012

Printed in the United Kingdom at the University Press, Cambridge

A catalogue record for this publication is available from the British Library

Library of Congress Cataloguing in Publication data
Climate change liability : transnational law and practice /
[edited by] Richard Lord ... [et al.].
p.   cm.
Includes bibliographical references and index.
ISBN 978-1-107-01760-3 (hardback) – ISBN 978-1-107-67366-3 (paperback)
1. Liability for climatic change damages.   2. Climatic changes–
Law and legislation.   3. Conflict of laws–Liability for environmental damages.
I. Lord, Richard, 1959–
K955.C557   2012
344.04′6342–dc23
2011041581

ISBN 978-1-107-01760-3 Hardback
ISBN 978-1-107-67366-3 Paperback

CONTENTS

v

CONTRIBUTORS AND EDITORIAL BOARD MEMBERS

Contributors

ROSS ABBS B.A. (HONS), LL.B. (HONS) (NEWCASTLE), B.C.L. (OXON) is a Research Assistant at the Faculty of Law, University of Sydney.

DR MYLES ALLEN is Professor of Geosystem Science in the School of Geography and the Environment and Department of Physics, University of Oxford. He has served on the Intergovernmental Panel on Climate Change and leads the climateprediction.net project, using computing time donated by the public for climate research. His interests focus on uncertainty in climate analysis and prediction, particularly the challenge of attributing harm to human influence on climate.

RIFQI SJARIEF ASSEGAF is the head of the research division of the Presidential Task Force to Combat Corruption in the Enforcement System and senior researcher at the NGO Indonesian Institute for Judicial Independence (LeIP). He specialises in judicial reform, anti-corruption and access to information and is actively involved in research, legal drafting and policy advocacy in those areas. In 2005, he received The Asia Foundation 50th Anniversary Award in Recognition of Outstanding Contribution to Law Reform in Indonesia.

JUTTA BRUNNÉE is Associate Dean of Law (Graduate) and Professor of Law and Metcalf Chair in Environmental Law, University of Toronto. Her teaching and research interests are in the areas of Public International Law and International Environmental Law. She is co-author of *Legitimacy and Legality in International Law: An Interactional Account* (Cambridge University Press, 2010), which was awarded the American Society of International Law's 2011 Certificate of Merit for pre-eminent contribution to creative scholarship.

viii

DR PETER CASHMAN is a barrister and Professor of Law (Social Justice) at the University of Sydney. He holds a degree in law and a diploma in criminology from the University of Melbourne and a Master of Laws degree and a Ph.D. from the University of London. He has practised law in the United Kingdom, the United States and Australia and is the author of numerous publications, including *Class Action Law and Practice*.

DR DEBBIE COLLIER B.A., LL.B. (RHODES UNIVERSITY), LL.M., PH.D. (UNIVERSITY OF CAPE TOWN) is an Attorney of the High Court of South Africa, a Senior Lecturer in the Department of Commercial Law at the University of Cape Town, and the Deputy Director of the Institute of Development and Labour Law.

PROFESSOR MEINHARD DOELLE, B.SC. (CHEMISTRY), LL.B. (DAL.), LL.M. (OSGOODE HALL), J.S.D. (DAL.), is an Associate Professor at Dalhousie University's Schulich School of Law. He serves as the Associate Director of the Marine and Environmental Law Institute and has written books on a variety of environmental law topics, of which his most recent are *Environmental Law: Cases and Materials* (2009) and *The Federal Environmental Assessment Process: a Guide and Critique* (2008).

DALIA FAROUK is a qualified lawyer registered at the Egyptian Bar Association and works as Pro Bono Counsel with law firm Sharkawy & Sarhan. She works on providing legal consultations to NGOs, social ventures, public interest projects and to eligible low-income individuals on various subjects of the law. She has also worked on general corporate issues.

MICHAEL B. GERRARD is Andrew Sabin Professor of Professional Practice at Columbia Law School in New York, where he teaches courses on environmental and energy law and directs the Center for Climate Change Law. He is Senior Counsel to Arnold & Porter LLP and has written or edited nine books, including *Global Climate Change and US Law* (2007) and *The Law of Clean Energy: Efficiency and Renewables* (2011).

SHIBANI GHOSH is a practising public interest lawyer specialising in environmental and access-to-information laws. She has litigated, among others, cases challenging environmental clearances granted to infrastructure projects. Shibani is also a Research Associate at the Centre for

Policy Research, New Delhi, and a member of the Legal Initiative for Forest and Environment (LIFE), New Delhi. She has previously worked as a legal consultant with the Central Information Commission, a quasi-judicial body set up under the Right to Information Act, 2005. Shibani holds the following degrees: B.A., LL.B. (Hons), B.C.L. (Oxon) and M.Sc. in Environmental Change and Management (Oxon).

JAN GLAZEWSKI is Professor in the Institute of Marine and Environmental Law at the Faculty of Law, University of Cape Town. He holds postgraduate degrees in law and Environmental Studies from the University of Cape Town, and a postgraduate law degree from the University of London. He is an Advocate of the High Court of South Africa and a member of the Cape Bar.

SILKE GOLDBERG, M.A., PG.D.L. is a Paris-based Senior Associate in Herbert Smith's Global Energy practice and a Research Fellow in Energy Law at Rijksuniversiteit Groningen (Netherlands). Silke has experience in advising on energy and climate change transactions internationally as well as in European energy law and policy. She has published on issues of European energy law, emission trading and supply security.

PROFESSOR JOSE JUAN GONZALEZ, holds a degree in law (Mexico, 1981), an LL.M. in Economic Law (Mexico, 1984) and a Ph.D. in Environmental Law (Spain, 1999). He is a full Professor and Researcher at the Metropolitan Autonomous University in Mexico and head of its Environmental Law Ph.D. Among numerous other roles, he chairs the Mexican Institute for Environmental Law Research and is Director of the *Mexican Environmental Law Journal*. He has written several books and drafted the current Environmental Act of Mexico City.

MAX GUTBROD has been a Partner in the Moscow office of Baker & McKenzie for fifteen years and co-heads the firm's Russian Climate Change and Energy Efficiency Practice. In 2004, he started advising major foreign companies and Russian and foreign regulators on various climate change and energy efficiency matters (including Kyoto Protocol-related issues).

DENG HAIFENG is an Associate Professor of the law school of Tsinghua University, China, and General Secretary of its Centre for Environmental, Natural Resource and Energy Law. He is a Director of both the

Environmental Law Research Society of the China Law Science Society and the Environmental Law Research Society of Beijing Law Science Society, and the Associate General Secretary of the Environmental Law Society of the China Environmental Science Society.

PATRICIA KAMERI-MBOTE is a Professor of Law at Strathmore University. She studied law in Nairobi (LL.B., 1987), Warwick (LL.M. in Law and Development, 1989), Zimbabwe (Post-graduate Diploma in Women's Law, 1995) and Stanford (J.S.M., 1996 and J.S.D., 1999). Among other roles, she is an Advocate of the High Court of Kenya and Director of the International Environmental Law Research Centre. She has published widely on environmental law, women's rights and property rights.

JOSI KHATARINA has been working in the field of environmental law for twelve years and is a senior researcher at the Indonesian Center for Environmental Law (ICEL). She was the coordinator of the civil society coalition which shaped the development of the Indonesian Freedom of Information Act 2008. She is currently an Assistant of the Presidential Task Force to Combat Corruption in the Enforcement System.

PROF. DR HANS-JOACHIM KOCH is Professor at the University of Hamburg (Emeritus, 2010) and is a founder of the Research Centre for Environmental Law at the University of Hamburg. From 2002–08 he was Chairman of the German Advisory Council on the Environment (SRU) and, since 2005, has been Chairman of the Association for Environmental Law (*Gesellschaft für Umweltrecht e. V*).

LUDWIG KRÄMER studied law and history in Kiel, Munich and Paris and has an LL.D. from Hamburg University. Until 2004, he was both a Judge at the Landgericht, Kiel and an Official of the Commission of the European Communities. He is a Visiting Professor at University College London and was, until 2010, Lecturer at the College of Europe, Bruges. He has published some twenty books and more than two hundred articles on EU environmental law.

BARTOSZ KURAŚ, LL.M. is a lawyer in the Environmental Law Practice Group and M & A Group at Wardyński & Partners. He graduated from the Faculty of Law and Administration at the Adam Mickiewicz University in Poznań (2006) and the Faculty of Law at the Albert-Ludwigs-Universität in Freiburg (2008) and is currently working to obtain a Ph.D. in the

Agricultural Law Department at the Adam Mickiewicz University in Poznań.

RICHARD LORD QC is a commercial litigator with over twenty-five years' experience, particularly of international disputes in the Commercial Court and in arbitration. His specialist subjects are insurance and maritime law, and he has also developed a particular interest in private law aspects of climate change. He acts as a mediator and arbitrator, and has written textbooks on Bills of Lading and the Arbitration Act.

MICHAEL LÜHRS studied law in Berlin and is an Attorney at Law. He specialised in emissions trading and planning law and is currently working on his Ph.D. on climate liability in German civil law.

DENNIS MAHONY is the head of Torys' Environmental, Health and Safety Practice Group and Co-Chair of the firm's interdisciplinary Climate Change and Emissions Trading Practice. He is the International Vice-Chair of the Energy and Environmental Markets and Finance Committee of SEER and the editor and one of the principal authors of *Law of Climate Change in Canada*. He is certified by the Law Society of Upper Canada as a Specialist in Environmental Law.

FIONA MUCKLOW CHEREMETEFF is an English solicitor and a non-resident Research Associate at the TMC Asser Institute in The Hague. Fiona's practice focuses primarily on banking, finance, environmental (climate change) and public international law matters. She is co-editor of *Environmental Finance and Socially Responsible Business in Russia: Legal and Practical Trends* (2010).

DR COLLINS ODOTE holds LL.B., LL.M. and Ph.D. degrees in law from the University of Nairobi. He teaches environmental jurisprudence, land use and international environmental law at the University of Nairobi and is currently engaged as a postdoctoral research fellow at Strathmore University. He also chairs the Board of The Institute for Law and Environmental Governance (ILEG), a Nairobi-based NGO.

LAVANYA RAJAMANI is a Professor at the Centre for Policy Research, New Delhi. She was previously a university Lecturer in Environmental Law, and Fellow and Director of Studies in Law at Queens' College, Cambridge. She is author of *Differential Treatment in International Environmental Law* (2006), co-editor of *Promoting Compliance in an Evolving Climate Regime*

(Cambridge University Press, 2011), *Implementation of International Environmental Law* (2011) and numerous articles. She has worked as a Consultant to the UN Framework Convention on Climate Change Secretariat, the Indian Ministry of Environment and Forests, the Danish Ministry of Climate Change and Energy, the UNDP, the World Bank and the Alliance of Small Island States.

DARIA RATSIBORINSKAYA is an environmental lawyer who has experience in both European and national environmental law in Moscow, Brussels and Amsterdam. She read law at the MGIMO-University of Moscow and was awarded an LL.M. in International and European Environmental Law from the University of Amsterdam. She currently combines lecturing and doctorate research at the Erasmus University of Rotterdam.

ISSI ROSEN-ZVI teaches Environmental Law, Local Government Law, Administrative Law and Civil Procedure at the Faculty of Law, Tel Aviv University. He obtained his LL.B. (*magna cum laude*) from Bar-Ilan University, his LL.M. in law and sociology (*summa cum laude*) from Tel Aviv University and his J.S.D. from Stanford Law School. He has published several articles and a book entitled *Taking Space Seriously* (2004).

MAS ACHMAD SANTOSA is a founder and Board Chairperson of the Indonesian Center for Environmental Law (ICEL) and has been a Senior Lecturer in Environmental Law in the law school, University of Indonesia since 1990. In 2010 he was appointed by the President of the Republic of Indonesia as Acting Commissioner for the Corruption Eradication Commission. He is a member of the Presidential Task Force to Combat Corruption in the Enforcement System and the Commission on Environmental Law of IUCN, and is Senior Advisor for Human Rights, Legal Reform and Access to Justice of UNDP Indonesia.

SERGEI SITNIKOV co-heads the Russian Climate Change and Energy Efficiency Practice in Baker & McKenzie's Moscow office. He regularly participates in Russian and international conferences and advises clients on issues relating to the development of energy efficiency related projects and the implementation of the Kyoto Protocol. He has written numerous journal articles and is co-author of *Trading in Air: Mitigating Climate Change through the Carbon Markets* (2010).

ALEX SMITH is a Litigator at Torys LLP in Toronto and a contributing author to *The Law of Climate Change in Canada*.

PEDRO LUCAS DE MOURA SOARES is an independent environmental lawyer in Natal-RN, Brazil.

DR TIM STEPHENS B.A. (HONS), LL.B. (HONS) (SYD.), M.PHIL. (CANTAB), PH.D. (SYD.) is a Senior Lecturer at the Faculty of Law, University of Sydney, Co-Director of the Sydney Centre for International Law and co-editor of the *Asia Pacific Journal of Environmental Law*. He has published widely, including *International Courts and Environmental Protection* (Cambridge University Press, 2009). He received the 2010 IUCN Academy Junior Scholarship Prize for his environmental law research.

MACIEJ SZEWCZYK is a lawyer in the Environmental Law Practice Group and M & A Group at Wardyński & Partners, specialising in environmental protection law as well as M & A transactions. He graduated from the Faculty of Law and Administration at the Adam Mickiewicz University in Poznań (2007).

YUKARI TAKAMURA is a Professor in international law at Nagoya University, Japan, specialising in international environmental law and climate law and policy. She has published many books and articles, including the recently published 'Do markets matter? The role of markets in the post-2012 international climate regime' in T. Sawa, S. Iai and S. Ikkatai (eds.), *Achieving Global Sustainability* (2011).

DR. RODA VERHEYEN is a practising Attorney at Law in the Hamburg law firm Rechtsanwälte Günther and former Director of the Climate Justice Programme. She has experience of and is bringing cases arguing climate change in planning law (road construction, waterways, municipal land-use plans), licensing of coal plants, and under coastal protection and water law.

DOMINIK WAŁKOWSKI is a lawyer in the Environmental Law Practice Group at Wardyński & Partners, specialising in environmental protection law. He graduated in International Relations (majoring in European Law, Economy and Culture) from the Adam Mickiewicz

University in Poznań (2003) and from the university's Faculty of Law and Administration (2004), and is currently working to obtain a Ph.D. in the Department of International Public Law at the Adam Mickiewicz University in Poznań.

GREG WANNIER is a Post-doctoral Research Scholar and Deputy Director of the Center for Climate Change Law (CCCL) at Columbia Law School. He received his J.D. from Stanford Law School, where he served as President of the Environmental Law Society and editor-in-chief of the *Stanford Journal of Law, Science & Policy*. He also graduated *summa cum laude* from UCLA with a joint B.A./B.S. in International Politics and Evolutionary Biology, and earned a Master's degree in Environmental Policy from the E-IPER program at Stanford University's School of Earth Sciences.

TOMASZ WARDYŃSKI, CBE, is an *adwokat* and founding partner of Wardyński & Partners. He is listed as an Arbitrator at the Polish Chamber of Commerce's Court of Arbitration, the Arbitration Court at the Polish Confederation of Private Employers Lewiatan, and the International Arbitral Centre of the Austrian Federal Economic Chamber (VIAC) in Vienna. He is a member of the Warsaw Bar. Tomasz Wardyński is active in the International Bar Association, in particular its Legal Practice Division.

YANKO MARCIUS DE ALENCAR XAVIER is full Professor, Faculty of Law, Universidade Federal do Rio Grande do Norte-UFRN, Natal-RN, Brazil, Chair of the Natural Resources and Energy Law Research Group and Member of the Academic Advisory Group of the International Bar Association's section on Energy, Environment, Natural Resources and Infrastructure Law.

LAMIAA YOUSSEF is an admitted Egyptian attorney and heads the Pro Bono Department of law firm Sharkawy & Sarhan. She is currently en-rolled in the LL.M. in International and Comparative Law at the American University in Cairo.

IZABELA ZIELIŃSKA-BARŁOŻEK is a legal adviser and Partner, lead-ing the Environmental Law Practice Group at Wardyński & Partners and specialising in environmental protection law as well as corporate and commercial transaction law. She is a Vice Chair of the Environmental Law Practice for Europe/Middle East/Africa in Lex Mundi.

Editorial Board members

BEN BOER is Emeritus Professor in Environmental Law at the University of Sydney. Formerly, he was Professor in Environmental Law. He continues to teach in various units of study in the Master's programme. He has published widely in the area of environmental and natural resources law and policy, and is currently focusing his research on biodiversity, climate change and protected areas law. For further information and publications see http://sydney.edu.au/law/about/staff/BenBoer/.

JAMES CAMERON is the founder and Vice Chairman of Climate Change Capital. A barrister, entrepreneur and pre-eminent expert in developing policy response to climate change, James represents the firm at the highest levels of business and government. He is a member of the Prime Minister's Business Advisory Group, GE's Ecomagination Advisory Board and Pepsico UK's Advisory Board, and Chairman of the World Economic Forum's Agenda Council on Climate Change.

DANIEL FARBER is the Sho Sato Professor of Law and Chairman of the Energy and Resources Group at the University of California, Berkeley. He is also the Faculty Director of the Center for Law, Energy, and the Environment. Professor Farber is a member of the American Academy of Arts and Sciences and a life member of the American Law Institute.

SIR SYDNEY KENTRIDGE QC was admitted as an Advocate of the Supreme Court of South Africa in 1949 and appointed Senior Counsel in 1965. He was called to the English Bar (Lincoln's Inn) in 1977, joining 1 Brick Court (now Brick Court Chambers) and took Silk in 1984. He has been Chairman of the Johannesburg Bar (1972–89), a Judge of Appeal in Botswana (1981–89), a Judge of the Courts of Appeal of Jersey and Guernsey (1988–92) and an Acting Justice in the South African Constitutional Court (1995–6). His practice covers all fields of constitutional law, human rights law and commercial law.

RICHARD MACRORY QC is a barrister and Professor of Law at University College London where he is Director of the Centre for Law and the Environment and the UCL Carbon Capture Legal Programme. Professor Macrory has been a board member of the Environment Agency in England and Wales, and a member of the Royal Commission on

Environmental Pollution. He was first Chairman of the UK Environmental Law Association and is currently a Patron of the Association.

M. C. MEHTA is a noted environmental lawyer in the Supreme Court of India. He has been successful in obtaining landmark judgments and orders for the protection of the environment, human rights and the cultural heritage of India. He has been instrumental in the advancement of the Right to a Healthy Environment, the Public Trust Doctrine, the principle of Strict and Absolute Liability, and the Exemplary Damages, Polluter Pays and Precautionary principles through Environmental Public Interest litigation. He also believes in working at the grassroots level in order to create awareness of the environment, conservation and protection of natural resources through peoples' movements. He has been presented with many awards, including the UNEP Global 500 Award, the Ramon Magsaysay Award for Asia and the Goldman Environmental Prize for Asia.

PHILIPPE SANDS QC is a barrister at Matrix Chambers, practising in public international law. He appears regularly before English and international courts. He is a Professor of Laws and Director of the Centre of International Courts and Tribunals at University College London. He is author of *Torture Team: Rumsfeld's Memo and the Betrayal of American Values* (2008) and *Lawless World: America and the Making and Breaking of Global Rules* (2005, 2006).

SONG YING is Associate Professor of Public International Law at the School of Law of Peking University, China. She is a member of the editorial board of the *Chinese Yearbook of International Law*. Her main research areas are international environmental law and the external relations law of the European Union. She acts as expert and counsel for China and various international organisations.

JAAP SPIER obtained his Mag. Iuris from Erasmus University, Rotterdam and his Ph.D. (Doctor iuris) from Leyden University (1981). He is Attorney-General in the Supreme Court of The Netherlands, Honorary Professor of Comparative Insurance Law at Maastricht University and founder and Honorary President of the European Group on Tort Law. He is the author and editor of various books and articles, including in the field of climate change.

Mary Robinson, Honorary President Oxfam International and President of Mary Robinson Foundation – Climate Justice

Climate justice links human rights and development to achieve a human-centred approach, thus safeguarding the rights of the vulnerable and sharing the burdens and benefits of climate change and its resolution equitably and fairly. As such, climate justice incorporates the principle of corrective justice – the idea that those who have contributed most to the global stock of greenhouse gas emissions have a moral obligation to make significant emissions reductions in order to avoid dangerous climate change. This is necessary as the countries and people who are most vulnerable to climate change are those who contributed least to the problem.

Climate justice can also be used to assign liability for past and projected contributions to climate change. This can assist the most marginalised and disenfranchised in our global community to find justice through the courts, thus paving the path for financial reparations through distributive justice. It can also be used, along with moral suasion and multi-lateral political and legal agreements, to insist on equitable burden-sharing and greater equality through financial assistance and technology transfer.

However, assigning climate change liability for those seeking redress or basic compensation from corporations or governments who refuse to act and who are seen to have violated basic human rights creates a number of problems. First, it is difficult to establish causality between the harm done or tortious act and the direct damage suffered. Secondly, it is difficult to establish liability and apportion damages accordingly. Thirdly, it may be difficult to establish legal standing or *locus standi* for petitioners before the courts.

This book sets out the legal principles underpinning climate change liability. It offers an extensive and comprehensive overview of national climate change policies and legislation as well as different rights-based legal arguments in various jurisdictions that could be used to achieve climate justice at a national level. Notwithstanding the climate justice opportunities potentially afforded by litigation, the need for a new legally binding agreement under the United Nations Framework Convention on Climate Change (UNFCCC) remains vital. Only a legally binding international framework can ensure that actions will be taken to reduce emissions and to protect the most vulnerable from the potentially catastrophic impacts of climate change.

ACKNOWLEDGEMENTS

We acknowledge with gratitude the support and assistance which we, and this book, have received from so many quarters. All those associated with this project have given generously of their time and their wisdom. Some deserve particular recognition.

We owe a debt of gratitude to those who first conceived the idea of a comparative study of national laws pertaining to climate change liability, and especially to Jaap Spier, Advocate-General in the Supreme Court of the Netherlands and Honorary Professor of comparative insurance law at Maastricht University. We are pleased to have Professor Spier as an Editorial Board member, providing continuity between the first seeds of an idea and the current book.

Whilst the book is a rigorous academic study independent from any political influence by any organisation, we would like to thank Jasper Teulings, General Counsel of Greenpeace International, Joss Saunders, General Counsel of Oxfam and Niall Watson, Programmes Legal Adviser at WWF-UK for their continued support and encouragement.

Special thanks are also due to Oxfam for funding a conference in January 2011 which enabled authors and editors of this book to exchange ideas and which sowed the seeds for a very fruitful cooperation between authors across various jurisdictions.

All of the authors and Editorial Board members have toiled diligently, and without complaint or reward, to create what we hope is a rich store of information and learning and distil it into a book which, if not quite pocket size, will be portable and accessible to many.

Cambridge University Press, our publishers, have been supportive and understanding of the difficulties in finalising within a short timeframe a book to which so many have contributed. We are grateful to them in making possible our ambition to publish the book in time for COP 17 in Durban.

Finally, and in a class of her own, it is impossible to overstate the importance of the pivotal role in this book played by Pascale Bird, our

project manager. She has spent uncounted and uncountable hours in keeping the project and its numerous participants on track, with unfailing patience, good humour and dedication, and has engaged in a huge variety of tasks from the almost sublime to the immensely tedious. Without Pascale, there would have been no book.

We have endeavoured to ensure that the law and factual material stated is correct as at 31 March 2011 except where otherwise stated in the relevant chapter.

Each editor and contributing author is acting solely in their individual private capacity. Any information presented, and any views or opinions expressed, do not represent the views of any employing institution and should not be ascribed to the same.

ABBREVIATIONS

AAU:	Assigned Amount Units
ACESA:	US American Clean Energy and Security Act
AF(B):	Adaptation Fund (Board)
AGF:	Advisory Group on Climate Change Financing
AIJ:	Activities Implemented Jointly
ALBA:	Bolivia, Cuba, Ecuador, Nicaragua and Venezuela
Annex I Parties:	Australia, Austria, Belarus, Belgium, Bulgaria, Canada, Croatia, Czech Republic, Denmark, Estonia, European Union, Finland, France, Germany, Greece, Hungary, Iceland, Ireland, Italy, Japan, Latvia, Liechtenstein, Lithuania, Luxembourg, Malta, Monaco, Netherlands, New Zealand, Norway, Poland, Portugal, Romania, Russian Federation, Slovakia, Slovenia, Spain, Sweden, Switzerland, Turkey, Ukraine, United Kingdom and the United States of America.
AOSIS:	Alliance of Small Island States
AWG-KP:	Ad Hoc Working Group on Further Commitments for Annex I Parties under the Kyoto Protocol
AWG-LCA:	Ad Hoc Working Group on Long Term Co-operative Action under the Framework Convention on Climate Change
BAP:	Bali Action Plan 2007
BASIC:	Brazil, South Africa, India and China
BAU:	Business As Usual
BRIC:	Brazil, Russia, India and China
CACAM:	Central Asia, Caucasus, Albania and Moldova
CAN:	Climate Action Network
CBD:	Convention on Biological Diversity
CBDR:	Common But Differentiated Responsibilities
CC:	Compliance Committee
CCL:	Climate Change Levy
CCS:	Carbon Capture and Storage
CDE:	Carbon Dioxide Equivalent (in g/kg/t)
CDM:	Clean Development Mechanism
CDP:	Carbon Disclosure Project

CERs:	Certified Emission Reductions (issued by CDM)
CGE:	Consultative Group of Experts on National Communications from Parties not included in Annex I Parties
CMP:	Conference of the Parties serving as the Meeting of the Parties to the Kyoto Protocol
COP:	Conference of the Parties to the Kyoto Protocol
CRF:	Common Reporting Format (for all Annex I Parties)
CRPs:	Conference Room Papers
CTCN:	Climate Technology Centre and Network
DER:	Direct Emission Reduction
DNA:	Designated National Authority
ECBI:	European Capacity Building Initiative
ECHR:	European Convention on Human Rights
ECJ:	European Court of Justice
EGTT:	Expert Group on Technology Transfer
EIA:	Environmental Impact Assessment
EIA:	Environmental Investigation Agency
EIT:	Countries with Economies in Transition
EPA:	US Environmental Protection Agency
ERPA:	Emission Reduction Purchase Agreement
ERRs:	Emission Reduction Rights
ERU:	Emission Reduction Unit
ETS:	Emissions Trading System
EU ETS:	European Union ETS
EUA:	European Union Allowances
G-77/China:	Coalition of 77 developing nations and China
GCF:	Green Climate Fund/Global Climate Fund/Governors' Climate and Forest Task Force
GEF:	Global Environmental Facility
GHG:	Greenhouse Gas
GNI:	Gross National Income
GWP:	Global Warming Potential
ICA:	International Consultation and Analysis
ICAO:	International Civil Aviation Organisation
ICSTD:	International Centre for Trade and Sustainable Development
IET:	International Emissions Trading
IIED:	International Institute for Environmental Development and Policy
IIGCC:	Institutional Investors Group on Climate Change
IISD:	International Institute for Sustainable Development
IMO:	International Maritime Organisation
INCR:	Investor Network on Climate Risk
IPCC:	Intergovernmental Panel on Climate Change

ITL:	International Transaction Log
JI:	Joint Implementation
LDCF:	Least Developed Countries Fund
LDCs:	Least Developed Country Parties
LEG:	Least Developed Countries Expert Group
LRI:	Legal Response Initiative
LRTAP:	Convention on Long Range Transboundary Air Pollution
LU:	Land Use
LULUCF:	Land Use, Land Use Change and Forestry
MDB:	Multilateral Development Bank
MRV:	Monitoring, Reporting and Verification
MVC:	Most Vulnerable Country
NAI:	Non-Annex I Countries
NAMAs:	Nationally Appropriate Mitigating Actions
NAPAs:	National Adaptation Programmes of Action (for LDCs)
NWP:	Nairobi Work Programme
ODA:	Official Development Assistance
OECD:	Organisation for Economic Co-operation and Development
OLCA:	Overseas Low Carbon Aid
PLO:	Public Liaison Officer
QELRC:	Quantified Emissions Limitation or Reduction Commitments
QELRO:	Quantified Emissions Limitation and Reduction Objectives
REDD+:	Reducing Emissions from Deforestation and Forest Degradation in developing countries (Supporting forest conservation, sustainable management of forests and enhancement of forest carbon stocks)
ROC:	Renewal Obligation Certificate
SBI:	Subsidiary Body for Implementation
SBSTA:	Subsidiary Body for Scientific and Technological Advice
SCCF:	Special Climate Change Fund
SICA:	Central American Integration System
SIDS:	Small Island Developing States
TEC:	Technology Executive Committee
UNCCD:	United Nations Convention to Combat Desertification
UNDRIP:	United Nations Declaration on Rights of Indigenous Peoples
UNEP:	United Nations Environment Programme
UNEPFI:	United Nations Environment Programme Finance Initiative
UNFCCC:	United Nations Framework Convention on Climate Change
VCUs:	Voluntary Carbon Units
VER:	Voluntary Emission Reductions
WBCSD:	World Business Council on Sustainable Development

PART I

Legal, scientific and policy aspects

1

Introduction

JUTTA BRUNNÉE, SILKE GOLDBERG,
RICHARD LORD QC AND LAVANYA RAJAMANI

1.01   Climate change presents to society as a whole a wide range of threats, and a narrower range of opportunities, on the political, economic and social level. It also poses questions and challenges for the law. These legal questions and challenges are relevant not just to lawyers; the law affects all members of society to a greater or lesser extent, whether as policymakers, businesspeople, campaigners of all hues or individual citizens. All of these actors are subject to a complex and much disputed matrix of rights and obligations: legal rights and obligations, political and moral rights and obligations, owed by and to individuals, corporations and States, and, in some cases, to future generations. The law is a tool; it may variously be a sword, a shield and the rock on which societies are built.

1.02   Climate change itself is multifaceted in many respects; it raises physical, scientific, economic, social, political and cultural issues along with legal ones. The web connecting the various causes and effects of climate change is complex. Possible legal solutions to climate change problems are likewise complex and difficult to classify. They encompass a wide range of international and national law. The law exists to serve society, and has accordingly evolved to meet the changing needs and challenges of society. With climate change, this evolution involves – and will, we believe, increasingly involve – both the application of existing legal concepts, including some ancient doctrines generally seen as dormant if not extinct, to new factual issues, and the development of new legal concepts.

1.03   The attempts to address climate change through international regulation are well known and ongoing. As frustration mounts in some quarters at the perceived inadequacy or speed of this process and as the likelihood of significant climate change impacts grows, focus turns increasingly to what might be termed 'liability' for climate change. By 'liability' we mean the concept that the law may provide redress or remedy to those who are or may be adversely affected by climate change, and control (or provide compensation for) the behaviour of those public or private actors who may be directly or indirectly responsible for it.

1.04   There is no clear line between the law of 'regulation' and that of 'liability'; the two are inexorably intertwined. This book however focuses on climate change 'liability'. It is a comparative study, giving an overview of what the law is and what direction it might take in eighteen countries. We have tried to select a representative sample of countries. In some, the applicable law is less developed and less the subject of current debate; in others actions for various kinds of climate change liability have already been brought. Both categories of countries are of interest for the purposes of this volume, as their examples illustrate the potential for and barriers to liability for climate change.

1.05   The aim of this book is to provide a readable work relevant to a range of different people all over the world. In casting the net wide, we cannot make all of the book essential reading for everyone. The opening sections outline at a high-level of generality some of the problems and actual or possible legal solutions to climate change. The national chapters discuss these in more detail. The book is aimed at lawyers, both practising and academic, but also at policymakers, educators, campaigners on all sides of the climate change debate, companies, business people, NGOs and civil society at large. The focus of several of the chapters is on the developing world, where many of the effects of climate change may be most keenly felt, and where some of the most creative legal solutions to climate change problems have emerged.

1.06   We are not looking to replicate the various works on national climate change law and liability. Rather, we hope that the comparative outlook of this volume will enable a migration and cross-fertilisation of ideas across national and regional boundaries. We have tried to bring together concepts of 'liability' arising in very different contexts. These contexts include the liability of national and local governments in relation to what they do (or do not do) about climate change, the liability of private individuals or corporations for the effects of climate change, as well as human rights law, competition regimes and some 'soft law'.

1.07   We want to emphasise that, while international law is part of the background against which climate change liability law develops, the focus of this volume is firmly on national law. We address public international law only to the extent that it impacts on relevant national law. Similarly, while our authors often draw on general environmental or liability law to tease out options for climate change liability, this book is not a textbook on environmental law as such. Whilst the chapter on the European Union gives an overview of the overall EU climate policy and describes the relevant Directives, their transposition into national law and application by the relevant national courts is discussed in the chapters on individual EU Member States.

1.08   A much debated issue is whether direct liability will be imposed on those 'responsible' for climate change to pay compensation to those who suffer its consequences. The definitive answer to this question may not appear for years or decades. If it is in the affirmative, it will have immense consequences. But it is important to bear in mind that, in the meantime, climate change liability is daily being established in less glamorous and less globally significant ways, especially in an administrative law context. The daily grind of climate change liability, in a local administrative law context or as a factor in a simple negligence claim, deserves as much attention as direct liability claims.

1.09   The debate about climate change itself remains as vigorous as ever. The overwhelming scientific consensus is that it is occurring, that it is potentially very damaging, and that its cause is largely anthropocentric in nature. But how acute will climate change be? How quickly will it occur? What will be its effect? It is obvious that the legal response to climate change will depend in very large measure on the answers to these questions, which science may enable us to predict and history will ultimately judge.

1.10   This book assumes that the IPCC's current (2007) report is well-founded. We do not consider that this background assumption renders the book irrelevant to 'climate sceptics' – those who doubt that the climate is changing, or that climate change is caused by human activity or presents a significant problem. Regardless of one's belief in or doubts about climate change, this book shows that liability arising related to climate change is developing apace and, in some jurisdictions, on a large scale. As Chapter 20 (on the USA) illustrates, the substantial recent increase in litigation about climate change has occurred not despite but because of the highly polarised opinions on the issue. Climate change liability affects everyone, from those who suffer loss and damage that is directly related to climate change, to taxpayers, voters of all political persuasions and corporations.

1.11   It may appear paradoxical for an Editor to hope that a work to which so many have contributed so much will never be put to practical use. Still, we want to be clear that our purpose in this book is not to advocate for climate litigation. Indeed, we share the widespread belief that an international regime that involves all States and that provides for the action that science tells us is needed to avert dangerous climate change, would be the preferred approach. In the event that such a regime is agreed within the next year or so, the role of litigation lawyers will be minimal, with actions being limited to disputes over interpretation, enforcement and breach. A number of climate change court claims to date have been met with the defence that the claims are either non-justiciable, as being concerned with issues exclusively in the political arena, or are preempted by existing regulations. Such defences would increase in strength in the event of comprehensive agreement which was capable of achieving the objectives of the UNFCCC.

1.12   Such an outcome appears unlikely at present. As is well known, the current international regime reflects what is politically possible and not what is considered scientifically essential or even desirable. The gap between these different indicia is immense, and it is not clear even whether it is currently closing or opening wider (but see Chapter 4 for a discussion of the policy contexts). The world is faced with a number of other possibilities including an international agreement, but one reached only after many years and/or of relatively weak content, or the degeneration of the international regime into a series of initiatives confined to specific topics or specific States or regions. Just as the last few decades have seen a widening, in many respects, of economic inequalities both as between developing and industrialised countries and within many countries even in the industrialised world,[1] so there is a real danger of a widening of climate change inequalities – in vernacular terms between the 'victims' and those who are 'sitting pretty' because they are unaffected by, or even benefiting from, climate change. If the central premise is accepted that the purposes of the law include serving society, reflecting its attitudes and providing redress for injustices, the prospect of a marked increase in climate change liability is a very real one. Furthermore, the class of 'victims' extends well beyond residents of Alaskan villages, Pacific Islands, and the Bangladeshi coastline (to name but a few obvious ones). The economic, social and cultural consequences of climate change are very wide-ranging.

1.13   The key commitments of this book are to be objective, balanced and rigorous in analysis. In short, it is intended as nothing more than a modest addition to the store of knowledge, with the hope that it is accessible and of interest to a wider audience than those whose bookshelves are already full of legal textbooks.

1.14   The nature and extent of the 'liability' under discussion is addressed in Chapter 3. It is sufficiently broad that knowledge of it will be a tool for many, but a different tool in different hands. We hope that campaigners on climate change, from whatever standpoint, will find it informative and of practical use. We hope that lawyers will find inspiration from the ideas and concepts developed in other States and systems of law different from their own. We hope that policymakers, and industrialists and their insurers and shareholders, will be guided by insight into the actual and potential consequences of their decisions.

---

[1] See, for instance, Giovanni Arrighi, Beverly J. Silver and Benjamin D. Brewer, 'Industrial Convergence, Globalization, and the Persistence of the North-South Divide', *Studies in Comparative International Development*, 38(1) (2003), 3–31 for a discussion on the continuing North-South divide.

2

The scientific basis for climate change liability

MYLES ALLEN

2.01   The aim of this chapter is to provide an overview of the science of 'detection and attribution' as applied to the global climate system and explain how it relates to events that actually cause harm, such as instances of extreme weather.[1] Detection and attribution are scientific terms for tools for the lawyer's task of showing the existence, causes and effects of climate change. Lawyers do not always mean the same things as scientists do when using words such as 'evidence', 'proof' and 'cause'. Climate change lawyers need not be scientists, but they need to understand the application of science, in terms of its uses and limits. This is likely to be crucial in considerations of liability for climate change, which often entails enquiry into two closely related matters: first, 'proof' of causes of climate change itself, in terms of large-scale temperature rise; and second, 'proof' of its effects in terms of specific weather events (storms, floods, heatwaves) or localised climate changes (temperature change, precipitation, wind and so on).

2.02   The chapter discusses: the relationship between weather and climate; the nature of the evidence for external influence, both natural and anthropogenic, on large-scale average temperatures; the implications of these changes for local extreme weather events; and the kind of evidence that might potentially be available to a court should the issue of causation arise. To avoid the discussion becoming too abstract, I will use as an example a recent study[2] quantifying the role played by increased greenhouse

---

[1] A more detailed study, by the author and others, of the science of detection and attribution as relevant to issues of liability and the lawyers' approach to causation is 'Scientific Challenges in the Attribution of Harm to Human Influence on Climate', *University of Pennsylvania Law Review*, 155 (2007), 1353.

[2] P. Pall *et al.*, 'Anthropogenic Greenhouse Gas Contribution to Flood Risk in England and Wales in Autumn 2000', *Nature*, 470 (2011), 382–5.

gases ('GHG') in the floods that occurred in England and Wales in autumn 2000, but the emphasis is on the basic principles rather than the details of that particular study.

2.03   The relationship between weather and climate is central to the issue of liability, so it helps to begin by clarifying what they are: climate has traditionally been defined by the World Meteorological Organisation (WMO) as the average weather and the statistics of its variability over a period of thirty years.[3] This definition is clearly problematic when considering the impact of an external driver of climate (in lay terms a cause of change or potential cause of change) like rising GHGs, which current evidence suggests are causing significant changes in climate on timescales shorter than thirty years. It is even less relevant if we consider the impact of other climate drivers like anthropogenic aerosols, which could in principle cause changes on even shorter timescales, particularly if artificial aerosol injection were to be contemplated as part of a programme of deliberate geo-engineering.

2.04   In any discussion of timescales, it is worth noting that the climate responds to the levels of GHGs present in the atmosphere relative to pre-industrial levels, not to rates of change in these levels, which complicates the link between emissions and impact for the most important GHG (in terms of current and projected impact), carbon dioxide. Carbon dioxide has a very long effective atmospheric lifetime, such that emissions today will continue to affect the climate for many centuries[4] unless active measures are taken in the future to remove them.[5] Hence any reasonably foreseeable change in carbon dioxide emissions will take some decades to have any discernible effect on climate, and carbon dioxide emitted a hundred years ago is continuing to affect the climate

[3] World Meteorological Organization, *Calculation of Monthly and Annual 30-Year Standard Normals*, WCDP-No. 10, WMO-TD/No. 341 (1989); *The Role of Climatological Normals in a Changing Climate*, WCDMP-No. 61, WMO-TD/No. 1377 (2007) (Geneva: World Meteorological Organization).

[4] S. Solomon *et al.*, 'Irreversible Climate Change due to Carbon Dioxide Emissions', *Proceedings of the National Academy of Sciences of the United States of America*, 106(6) (2009), 1704–9; DOI:10.1073/pnas.0812721106 (2009).

[5] Although possible in principle, active carbon dioxide removal is currently considered prohibitively expensive even if it could be done on a sufficient scale to have a global impact: see J. Shepherd *et al.*, *Geoengineering the Climate: Science, Governance and Uncertainty* (London: Royal Society, 2009) (http://royalsociety.org/Geoengineering-the-climate/).

today. A second popular misconception is that, because roughly
half current carbon dioxide emissions are taken up by the oceans
and land biosphere, if global emissions were reduced by a factor of two or more, atmospheric concentrations would stop rising or begin to fall. This is incorrect: our current understanding
of the carbon cycle is that even a very substantial reduction in
emissions would simply cause atmospheric concentrations to rise
more slowly.[6] Concentrations are only projected to fall after carbon dioxide emissions are reduced close to zero, and even then, it
would be centuries to millennia before the climate would return
to anything close to its pre-industrial state. This clearly impacts
on what constitutes 'relief' of climate change: reducing emissions
alleviates the rate at which the problem worsens, but does not
'solve' it in the conventional sense.

2.05   A more precise definition of climate than the traditional WMO
        definition is the 'expected' weather, and its variability, given the
        boundary conditions (in lay terms the parameters governing the
        climate system, including atmospheric composition, levels of
        solar and volcanic activity and so on) that apply to the atmos-
        phere-ocean system at any given time. This means the statistics
        of weather compiled not over a long period of time but by a large
        number of hypothetical realisations of the atmosphere-ocean
        system ('possible worlds', in lay terms) with identical boundary
        conditions. An immediate implication of this is that climate,
        precisely defined, cannot be directly observed. Only in a closed
        stationary system, in which the boundary conditions do not
        change over a long period of time, would it be possible to 'observe'
        climate directly. In the real climate, boundary conditions change
        all the time, so the idea of 'pure' observations of climate or cli-
        mate change is impossible in principle: its properties can only
        be inferred through a combination of observations, theory and
        computer simulation models.

2.06   This point is important, since the use of computer simulation
        models in climate research is controversial, given the acknowl-
        edged flaws in all currently available climate models. We will see
        the critical role played by simulation when we come to consider

---

[6] M. R. Allen *et al.*, 'Warming Caused by Cumulative Emissions of Carbon Dioxide Towards
the Trillionth Tonne', *Nature*, 458 (2009), 1163–6.

the link between climate and weather. Critics of mainstream climate science often argue that model-based results are intrinsically inferior to 'direct observations', so it is important to understand that there is no such thing as a model-free observation of climate. What we observe is the weather, which is only one realisation of the many possible weathers that make up the distribution we call the climate. Conversely, since it is impossible to simulate climate directly purely on the basis of fundamental physical principles, there is also no such thing as an observation-free climate model. All scientific inferences about climate involve a combination of models and observations.[7]

2.07   A more subtle implication of this point is that external drivers of climate can only manifest themselves through changing probabilities.[8] When the concept of probabilistic event attribution was first proposed,[9] quantifying the contribution of human influence to the probability of an event occurring was seen as something of a novelty, whereas it should in fact be seen as a simple extension of other attribution questions, such as quantifying the impact of GHGs on the warming (or, more precisely, the increase in expected global mean temperature) observed over the past fifty years. The expected global mean temperature in a given year is one property of the so-called 'climate attractor'; the probability of a flood occurring in Oxfordshire in that year is another. The second may be harder to estimate, but there is no difference between them in principle.

2.08   It is often said that it is impossible to attribute a single weather event to human influence on climate, since all of the weather events we currently observe could have occurred at some level of probability in a pristine climate unaffected by human influence. This fact is important for the issue of liability, since actual harm is often associated with localised extreme weather events. If the only quantities for which causal attribution statements could be

---

[7] For an excellent deeper discussion, see P. Edwards, *A Vast Machine: Computer Models, Climate Data and the Politics of Global Warming* (Cambridge, MA: MIT Press, 2010).

[8] The law has been much troubled by causation in disease cases where the precise cause of the disease cannot be proved by science. Because of the chaotic nature of weather, it is not possible to reconstruct an exact model of past events nor to predict with precision what will happen in the future.

[9] M. R. Allen, 'Liability for climate change', *Nature*, 421 (2003), 891–2.

made were very large-scale, low-frequency variations like the trend in global mean temperature, then attribution of harm to human influence on climate would be impossible in principle, since these large-scale changes do not, in themselves, necessarily cause harm.[10]

2.09   In fact, there is no difference in principle between attributing causes for a single weather event and attributing causes for the observed trend in global mean temperature. In both cases, an event is observed (the 'event', in the latter case, being the increase in recorded temperatures over the past fifty years) that could have occurred, at some level of probability, in a pristine climate. What causal attribution means, in both cases, is that human influence on climate substantially increased the probability of occurrence of the event in question.

2.10   When assessments like that of the Intergovernmental Panel on Climate Change report,[11] for example, that it is 'very unlikely' that the global patterns of warming during the past half-century are due to known natural causes, they mean specifically that the 'null-hypothesis' that the warming is natural can be rejected at or below the 10 per cent level. This statement accounts for a range of sources of uncertainty, including in the size of the warming itself due to uncertainties in observations. A substantial contributor to the uncertainty (the fact that the null-hypothesis of no human influence cannot be ruled out entirely) is internal climate variability: the chaotic fluctuations that occur naturally in the atmosphere-ocean system. One implication of the IPCC statement, therefore, is that there is a less than 10 per cent chance of a global pattern of warming of the magnitude observed over the past few decades occurring in the absence of human influence on climate. In fact, most of the studies on which the IPCC statement was based assign a substantially lower probability to this eventuality.[12]

---

[10] No attempt is made here to address legal definitions of 'harm' or 'damage' in contrast to simple 'change', nor to consider as such the important issues of long-term 'damage' such as increased disease, precipitation pattern shift, desertification/salination or inundation of islands or coastal zones.

[11] S. Solomon *et al.*, *Climate Change 2007: The Physical Science Basis* (Cambridge University Press, 2007).

[12] See references in Hegerl *et al.*, Chapter 9 of Solomon *et al.*, *ibid.*

2.11   Given that the actual observed warming is very similar in magnitude to the warming expected if human influence is taken into account, it could be said (although the IPCC does not put it this way) that with human influence included there is a roughly 50 per cent chance of a warming as large or larger than that which has been observed. Hence, on this interpretation, the IPCC statement implies that human influence on climate has increased the probability of occurrence of a warming trend as large as that observed over the past fifty years by at least a factor of five (from <10 per cent to around 50 per cent). Individual studies suggest a much higher increase. This is not the standard interpretation of the IPCC statement, but it serves to illustrate how even conventional attribution statements about large-scale climate changes can be couched in probabilistic terms. Hence there is no difference in principle between the challenge of attributing causes for a flood in Oxfordshire to attributing causes for the observed trend in global mean temperature. Both represent weather events that may have been made more likely by anthropogenic changes in the underlying climate attractor, and the scientific challenge is to establish how much their probability of occurrence has changed as a result of human influence.

2.12   In discussing global temperature trends, the IPCC goes further, addressing the question of 'how much' of the warming is 'due' to human influence. It is meaningful, in the context of global temperature changes, to say that x per cent may be due to carbon dioxide, y per cent to solar variability and so on, because the impacts of these different factors add up. To a very good approximation, if a climate model is run with changing carbon dioxide alone, and subsequently run with changing solar activity alone, the sum of the impact of these two changes, imposed individually, is equal to their impact when imposed together. The concept of 'contributions from different factors' is much more problematic when we are considering a single extreme weather event. Since a weather event must be considered as a single, self-reinforcing and indivisible whole, it makes no more sense to ask 'how much of this flood was due to human influence?' than to ask, when a loaded die is thrown and lands as a six, how many of the dots were due to the loading. What can be done is to ask how different factors may have contributed to the probability of an event occurring, a point we return to below.

2.13   The evidence for human influence on global temperatures over
        the past fifty years provides an illustration of how all causal attri-
        bution statements rely on a combination of observations and
        modelling. To illustrate this point, I will present a simple analysis
        following Lockwood (2008) quantifying the role of natural and
        anthropogenic drivers in recent global temperature changes.[13]
        This example will also allow me to explain, incidentally, how the
        fact that 1998 remains the warmest year on record over a decade
        on does not provide any concrete evidence for a deceleration in
        anthropogenic warming.

2.14   The black line in the top panel of Figure 2.1 shows observed
        global temperatures since the 1950s (systematic monitoring only
        began with the 1957–58 International Geophysical Year for many
        regions of the globe). The grey line shows modelled temperatures
        assuming a very simple, but still physically coherent, empirical
        model in which global temperatures are assumed to be the sum of
        responses to individual forcing factors, with the response to each
        forcing represented by a simple equation representing the fact
        that temperatures do not respond instantly to external forcing,
        through the heat capacity of that atmosphere-ocean system.[14]
        Hence the cooling effect of a volcanic eruption may persist for
        several years after the volcanic ash has dissipated. Comparing
        temperatures directly with these potential external climate driv-
        ers would therefore be misleading. Even the simplest analysis of
        global mean temperatures requires some form of climate model:
        there is no such thing as a model-free analysis, just as there is no
        such thing as an observation-free model.

2.15   The contributions from the three main natural drivers of global
        temperature changes are shown in the next three panels: the El
        Niño/Southern Oscillation (ENSO) phenomenon (represented by
        sea-surface temperature fluctuations in the Equatorial Pacific);

---

[13] M. Lockwood, 'Recent Changes in Solar Outputs and the Global Mean Surface
    Temperature. III. Analysis of Contributions to Global Mean Air Surface Temperature
    Rise', *Proceedings of the Royal Society A*, 464 (2094) (2008), 1387–1404; doi:10.1098/
    rspa.2007.0348.
[14] The 'model' in question is given by $\tau dT/dt + T = \alpha F$ where T is the temperature departure
    from its long-term equilibrium value, t is the time, τ is a time-constant representing the
    'sluggishness' of the response and α is a constant of proportionality, both estimated from
    data.

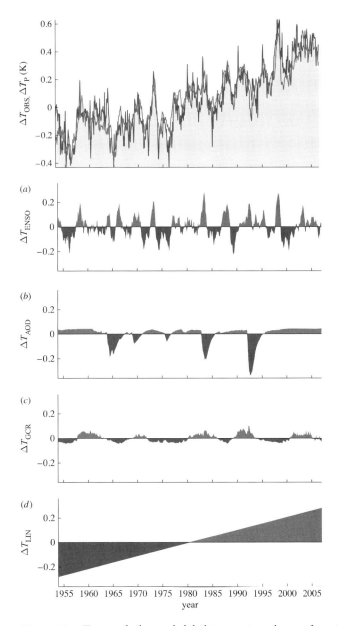

Figure 2.1:   Top panel: observed global temperature changes from 1953 to 2008 (black line) and empirical reconstruction based on the sum of contributions shown in lower panels (grey line). Lower panels: estimated contributions from (a) ENSO, (b) volcanic eruptions, (c) solar variability and (d) the warming trend. Reproduced from Lockwood (2008); see source (bibliographical information at note 13) for further details.

explosive volcanic eruption (represented by stratospheric aerosol load); and solar variability (represented by fluctuations in galactic cosmic ray flux). The final panel shows the estimated trend, for which there is no explanation other than the combined effect of rising anthropogenic GHGs and sulphate aerosols. The temperature changes in the bottom four panels, when added together, give the grey line in the top panel.

2.16   This figure serves to illustrate two important points: first, these three natural factors and an anthropogenic trend of approximately 0.1°C per decade on average are sufficient to account for observed global temperature changes over the past half-century: there is no evidence for a substantial residual contribution from other modes of decadal variability such as the Pacific Decadal Oscillation. Since the timescales associated with ENSO and volcanic eruptions are relatively short, and the contribution from solar variability is relatively small, this suggests the overall picture of a sustained background anthropogenic warming trend with superimposed sub-decadal variability is likely to continue.

2.17   This brings us to the second point: a number of papers have speculated recently whether the lack of a warming trend over the decade 2000–2009 might indicate that more than previously thought of the warming prior to 2000 was due to some natural multi-decadal variation which has now reversed.[15] The figure indicates that there is no need to invoke such a process to explain the temperature changes since the exceptionally warm ENSO year of 1998: what we are seeing can be explained as the combined effect of ENSO and solar variability acting to mask the background anthropogenic trend within this decade. While it remains a hypothetical possibility that natural variability might halt or reverse the anthropogenic trend over the coming decade, we should recognise that this remains hypothetical: there is no clear evidence to suggest it will happen. On the basis of the evidence available today, average temperatures in the 2010s are likely to be warmer than the 2000s, just as the 2000s were warmer than the 1990s, the 1990s warmer than the

---

[15] See, for example, T. DelSole *et al.*, 'A Significant Contribution of Unforced Multidecadal Variability in the Recent Acceleration of Global Warming', *J. Climate*, 24 (2011), 909–26.

1980s, and the 1980s warmer than the 1970s. Although we will continue to see interannual temperature fluctuations within a decade, the warming trend from decade to decade is proceeding very much as expected based on predictions made back in the 1990s.[16]

2.18   So what are the implications of this warming trend? A gradual increase in global mean temperatures of 0.1–0.2°C per decade is barely perceptible. Some impacts of this warming, such as the sea level rise caused by thermal expansion of the oceans, take the form of a gradual and predictable trend. In many locations, however, the global average rise of 15–20 cm over the twentieth century is masked by local variations in relative sea level, many of which might be caused by factors such as the draining of aquifers causing land subsidence as much as by global sea level rise. In any case, instances of actual harm in coastal regions due to flooding or saline contamination of ground water are typically associated with storm surge events during which local relative sea levels might vary by metres rather than centimetres. Hence quantifying harm due to human influence on climate is primarily a matter of understanding its impact on extreme weather. This presents particular challenges for both the science of climate change and the communication of results to policymakers and the public and has so far been attempted for a relatively small number of specific events, including the UK floods of autumn 2000,[17] the European summer heatwave of 2003[18] and the Russian heatwave of 2010.[19]

2.19   Many of the most extreme and damaging weather events occur because a self-reinforcing process amplifies an initial weather anomaly. This has two important implications. First, predicting the statistics of such extreme weather events by extrapolating the statistics of less extreme events requires caution, since the governing physical processes may change in these most extreme

---

[16] M. R. Allen *et al.*, 'Quantifying the Uncertainty in Forecasts of Anthropogenic Climate Change', *Nature*, 407 (2000), 617–20.

[17] Pall *et al.*, *ibid.*

[18] P. A. Stott *et al.*, 'Human Contribution to the European Heatwave of 2003', *Nature*, 432 (2004), 610–14.

[19] R. Dole *et al.*, 'Was there a Basis for Anticipating the 2010 Russian Heatwave?', *Geophysical Research Letters*, 38 (2011), L06702.

cases. Second, it will often be impossible in principle to say how much human or any other external influence on climate contributed to the magnitude of a particular event, in the sense of trying to quantify how much smaller the event would have been in the absence of human influence. Instead, it is necessary to consider the event as a single, self-reinforcing whole, and ask how external drivers contributed to the probability of that event occurring.[20] No regional weather event has yet been reported that was only made possible by human influence on climate, in the sense that there was only a negligible chance of it occurring in the absence of human influence.[21]

2.20   Quantifying the absolute probability of an event occurring in a hypothetical world without human influence on climate is necessarily very uncertain: hence studies have tended to focus on quantifying relative probabilities, or specifically the Fraction Attributable Risk (FAR), defined as the FAR = 1 – P0/P1, where P0 is the probability of an event occurring in the absence of human influence on climate, and P1 is the corresponding probability in a world in which human influence is included. The ratio between P0 and P1 is generally better known than either of these quantities individually.

2.21   Much of the informal discussion of the role of human influence in specific extreme weather events focuses on the question of whether an event may have a precedent in the early instrumental or paleo-climate record before a substantial human influence on climate occurred. Under this probabilistic approach to event attribution, it is clear that this discussion is beside the point: if an

[20] D. A. Stone and M. R. Allen, 'The End-to-End Attribution Problem: From Emissions to Impacts', *Climatic Change*, 71(3) (2005), 303–18; and D. A. Stone *et al.*, 'The Detection and Attribution of Human Influence on Climate', *Annual Reviews of Resources and the Environment*, 341 (2009), 16–40.

[21] C. Schär *et al.* (2004) assigned an extremely long return-time to the temperatures observed in summer 2003 under pre-industrial conditions (that is they estimated that it would happen only once in a very long period). Fischer *et al.* (2008) show how, in a regional climate modelling study, warm temperatures in central Europe in the summer of 2003 were amplified by dry soil-moisture conditions. In a normal European summer, rising temperatures increase the evaporation of soil moisture, which absorbs energy, providing a negative feedback. In 2003, the soil became so dry this process was suppressed along with the usual vertical mixing by clouds, allowing surface temperatures to rise rapidly. This is an example of a self-reinforcing event for which estimated return-times based on the distribution of normal summer temperatures are irrelevant.

event occurred in a pre-industrial climate, we can conclude that human influence was not necessary for that event to occur (so P0 is non-zero, and FAR is not unity), but human influence may still have increased the probability of that event occurring (P1 greater than P0, so FAR greater than zero).

2.22   For events that occur relatively frequently, or events for which statistics can be aggregated over a large number of independent locations, it may be possible to identify trends in occurrence-frequency that are attributable to human influence on climate through a single-step procedure, comparing observed and modelled changes in occurrence-frequency.[22]

2.23   For events with return-times of the same order as the timescale over which the signal[23] of human influence is emerging (thirty to fifty years, meaning cases in which P0 and P1 are of the order of a few per cent or less in any given year), such single-step attribution is impossible in principle: it is impossible to observe a change in return-time taking place over a timescale that is comparable to the return-time itself. For these events, attribution is necessarily a multi-step procedure. Either a trend in occurrence-frequency of more frequent events may be attributed to human influence and a statistical extrapolation model then used to assess the implications for the extreme event in question; or an attributable trend is identified in some other variable entirely, such as surface temperature, and a physically based weather model is used to assess the implications. Neither approach is free of assumptions: no weather model is perfect, but statistical extrapolation may also be misleading for reasons given above.

2.24   Pall *et al.* (2011) provide a demonstration of multi-step attribution using a physically based model, applied to the floods that occurred in the UK in the autumn of 2000. The immediate cause of these floods was exceptional precipitation, this being the wettest autumn to have occurred in England and Wales since records began. To assess the contribution of the anthropogenic increase in GHGs

---

[22] This is the approach taken, for example, in S. K. Min *et al.*, 'Human Contribution to More-Intense Precipitation Extremes', *Nature*, 470 (2011), 378–81.

[23] 'Signal' and 'noise' are used to denote the 'noise' in terms of background non-human factors influencing climate and the ability to detect over a specific period the 'signal' of a specific factor such as human activity.

to the risk of these floods, the period April 2000 to March 2001 was simulated several thousand times using a seasonal-forecast-resolution atmospheric model with realistic atmospheric composition, sea-surface temperature and sea-ice boundary conditions imposed. This ensemble was then repeated with both composition and surface temperatures modified to simulate conditions that would have occurred had there been no anthropogenic increase in GHGs since 1900. The change in surface temperatures was estimated using a conventional detection and attribution analysis using response-patterns predicted by four different coupled models, allowing for uncertainty in response amplitude. Simulated daily precipitation from these two ensembles was fed into an empirical rainfall-runoff model and severe daily England and Wales runoff used as a proxy for flood risk.

2.25　　Results are shown in Figure 2.2, which shows the distribution of simulated runoff events in the realistic autumn 2000 ensemble in dark grey, and in the range of possible 'climates that might have been' in various shades of lighter grey. Including the influence of anthropogenic greenhouse warming increases flood risk at the relevant threshold by around a factor of two in the majority of cases, but with a broad range of uncertainty: in 10 per cent of cases the increase in risk is less than 20 per cent. This is significant in the context of legal doctrines, discussed elsewhere in this book, to the effect that in appropriate cases if factor X more than doubles the risk of event Y occurring, it may be said that Y has been proved to be 'caused' by X.

2.26　　Pall *et al.*'s conclusions pertained to the particular flood diagnostic they considered. Kay *et al.* (2011),[24] analysing the same ensembles but using a more sophisticated hydrological model with explicit representation of individual catchments, found that GHG increase has more likely than not increased flood risk in the October to December period, with best-estimate increases also around a factor of two for the risk of peak daily runoff exceeding the relevant threshold. The increased noise resulting from smaller catchments and the impact of re-evaporation of rainfall, however, increased uncertainty to the extent that the null-hypothesis of no

[24]　A. Kay *et al.* (2011), 'Attribution of Autumn/Winter 2000 flood risk in England to anthropogenic climate change: a catchment-based study', *J. Hydrology*, 406 (2011), 97–112.

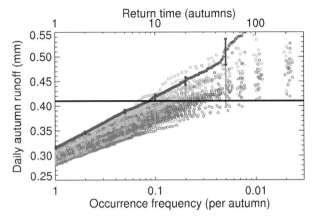

Figure 2.2:   Return times for precipitation-induced floods aggregated over England and Wales for conditions corresponding to October to December 2000 with boundary conditions as observed (dark grey) and under a range of simulations of the conditions that would have obtained in the absence of anthropogenic greenhouse warming over the twentieth century (lighter shades) – different shades correspond to different climate models used to define the greenhouse signal, black horizontal line to the threshold exceeded in autumn 2000. Reproduced from Pall *et al.* (2011); see source (bibliographical information at note 2 above) for further details.

    attributable increase in risk could no longer be rejected at the 10 per cent level for any individual catchment.

2.27   More significantly, Kay *et al.* also showed that the change in flood risk over the entire October to March period was substantially lower, due to a reduction in the risk of snow-melt-induced flooding in spring, such as occurred in 1947, compensating for the increased risk of precipitation-induced flooding in autumn. This illustrates an important general point: even if a particular flood event may have been made more likely by human influence on climate, there is no certainty that all kinds of flood events have been made more likely.

2.28   With the science of event attribution still confined to isolated case studies, no systematic survey exists of the impact of human influence on the risk of damaging weather events across the world. Many, perhaps the majority, of observed extreme weather events currently remain in the category of the 2010 Russian heat-wave: not made substantially more nor less likely by human

influence on climate.[25] Rising GHGs are likely to have contributed substantially to an increased risk of some events, such as
precipitation-induced flooding in autumn 2000 in the UK, while
others, such as snow-melt-induced spring UK floods, may have
been made less likely.

2.29   In our 2007 article (see note 1 above) we concluded by asking a
number of questions of lawyers. As these questions remain relevant in facilitating the meaningful interaction of lawyers and scientists on these issues, I repeat some of them here, in summary
form. First, what is the 'natural' climate against which the actual
climate should be compared: the climate of 200 years ago, or the
climate that would have obtained today in the absence of human
influence? Second, in evaluating actual and potential harm and
what constitutes 'relief' of climate change, are we primarily interested in impacts over the next quarter-century or so, or longer
timescales? Third, if one accepts that 'proof' of causation is likely
to be in terms of probability and risk, is the Fractional Attribution
of Risk model discussed above the most useful approach for the
lawyers and courts who are charged with questions of liability
for climate change? The answer to these questions and others
discussed above will be vital in addressing 'liability' in various
different forms, whether this is in terms of alleged 'responsibility' of one State or group of corporations for damage caused by
climate change, the scientific justification for regulatory action
(or inaction) when challenged in the courts, or otherwise.

[25] R. Dole *et al.*, *ibid.*

3

Overview of legal issues relevant to climate change

JUTTA BRUNNÉE, SILKE GOLDBERG,
RICHARD LORD QC AND LAVANYA RAJAMANI

(A) Introduction

What is 'climate change liability'?

3.01   By its nature, climate change gives rise to myriad potential forms of liability. It is global in geographic terms. Arguments rage about its extent, causes and effects. It potentially affects nearly everyone, and may do so for tens or hundreds of years. It requires addressing at State, regional and individual levels. All feasible responses are complex and costly. It is hard to conceive of a more effective recipe for spawning liabilities of all kinds.

3.02   What do we mean in this book, by 'climate change liability'? The concept of legal liability is well understood. Liability is not usually an absolute, intransitive concept. Liability is usually 'to' or 'in respect of' another person, so whenever a liability is under discussion one must also consider the corresponding rights. In this book, in one sense we focus on 'liability' as something narrower than any obligation arising as a matter of law or legal principle. This book is not about liability arising under treaties or public international law, neither is it concerned with contractual obligations, such as those that might arise under emissions trading schemes or clean development mechanism projects under the Kyoto Protocol. We do however use 'liability' in a broader sense than litigation, and also consider 'liability' which may fall short of enforceable legal liability. It includes liability to do something or refrain from doing it, as well as liability for compensation. We have sought to focus on liabilities arising from or directly related to climate change and its effects, and not from all activities which may themselves have an impact on, or be impacted by, climate change. This is not a book on environmental law more generally.

Who will use the law?

3.03   Those most obviously interested in questions of climate change liability are those who may be under such a liability, or those who assert corresponding rights as a result of being adversely affected by climate change. But an increasingly important category of liability is that said to arise as a result of responses to climate change. The regulatory responses to climate change, whether international, regional, national or local, are often controversial and costly. As discussed in Chapter 20 (on the USA), it is not only environmentalists and civil society who bring claims relating to climate change. Increasingly, industry is challenging attempts to regulate climate change. For example, the US Environmental Protection Agency (EPA), mandated by the seminal *Massachusetts* v. *EPA* Supreme Court decision to regulate greenhouse gas (GHG) emissions under the US Clean Air Act,[1] now faces numerous legal challenges to its attempts to do so. Furthermore, it is artificial to classify people into those for and against responses to climate change or into industry or environmental lobbies. Projects intended to combat climate change, such as dams constructed or Reducing Emissions from Deforestation or Degradation (REDD) measures, may be highly controversial in terms of effect on the local environment or indigenous peoples.

3.04   The likely effects of climate change are summarised in the IPCC Fourth Assessment Report (FAR).[2] The physical effects are those on people, property and ecosystems, as a result of global mean increase in temperature, and associated effects in terms of regional climate variation. These include change in weather events within the climate such as changing patterns of precipitation, changes in frequency of extreme weather events (temperature, wind, precipitation) and sea level rise. Some physical effects are obvious, such as inundation of coastal areas, or subsidence of buildings constructed on previously frozen ground. Others are less so, such as

---

[1] See Chapter 20 (on the USA), para. 20.23.
[2] *IPCC Fourth Assessment Report: Climate Change 2007*, available at: www.ipcc.ch/publications_and_data/publications_and_data_reports.shtml.

floods caused by the collapse of dams which have been weakened by subsidence caused by drought. Personal 'injury' may involve increased exposure to disease. In short an almost limitless set of permutations of causal chains can be envisaged.

3.05   These physical phenomena have economic effects, not only on those physically affected, but more widely, extending to those whose livelihoods and financial wellbeing depend on those who are directly affected. It is the type of loss and not its amount, which is likely to be relevant to liability, but it is notable that on any mainstream view the figures are very large. Whilst methodology and quantification are controversial, the Stern Review considers costs of 5, 10 or even 20 per cent of GDP[3] and an August 2009 report by the IIED and the Grantham Institute[4] suggested that the 2007 FCCC estimates of adaptation costs of $40–170 billion per annum were significant underestimates.[5] Even if only a fraction of these sums are the subject of disputes over liability, the stakes are high.[6]

3.06   Even where there is no physical damage or direct economic loss, adverse effects may be suffered in terms of loss of security, enjoyment amenity or national identity, and one of the ongoing legal debates is the extent to which climate change engages human rights, whether economic, social or cultural as enshrined in various laws, declarations, charters and constitutions.

3.07   As also indicated in the FAR, the effects are not uniform. Some States or regions will at least in direct terms benefit from climate change. Instances of adverse impacts are summarised in the national chapters of this book, but by way of examples only, from different parts of the world:
    (1)   The allegations in the celebrated and ongoing US case of *Connecticut* v. *AEP* include heatwaves, smog, coastal erosion,

---

[3] Global GDP being currently of the order of US$ 70 trillion (i.e. 70×10^{12}). See www.cia.gov/library/publications/the-world-factbook/geos/xx.html.

[4] Martin Perry *et al.*, *Assuming the Costs of Adaptation to Climate Change* (August 2009). See http://pubs.iied.org/pdfs/11501IIED.pdf.

[5] In a similar vein, a few months later the International Energy Agency estimated that the cost of failing to curb emissions so as to limit temperature rise to 2°C would cost $500bn per annum.

[6] The cost of relocation of the 400 villagers of Kivalina in the eponymous case was estimated at $95–$400m (*Native Vill. of Kivalina* v. *Exxon Mobil Corp.*, 663 f. Supp. 2d 863 (N.D. Cal. 2009). See Chapter 20, para. 20.63).

droughts, fires, harm to hardwood forests and a reduction in biodiversity.

(2) The Inuit Circumpolar Conference Petition of 2005 to the Inter-American Commission on Human Rights alleged 'slumping, landslides, coastal erosion, loss of sea ice, loss of igloo quality snow, loss of wetlands, inability to pursue traditional hunting and food gathering, change in precipitation, increasingly violent storms, changes in animal and plant species, and health problems due to increased temperatures and sun intensity'.

(3) The 2009 report of the Bangladesh and UK All Party Parliamentary Climate Change Groups[7] referred to effects of climate change including coastal erosion and inundation leading to displacement of up to 30 million people, salination, change in Himalayan glacier melt leading to floods and droughts, change in precipitation patterns and intensity, and reduction in wheat (32 per cent) and rice (8 per cent) crops.

(4) Micronesia has commented:[8] 'We are not certain if our biggest threat is from ocean acidification that will erode our islands from underneath, or from sea level rise that could submerge our islands under the sea, or from changes in weather and typhoon intensity that could make inhabiting our islands impossible. But we know that our continued peaceful existence is totally at risk.'

3.08   Climate change is often seen as an environmental issue, but it is not easy to classify, and differs from many classic environmental problems in a number of respects that are relevant to liability. Specifically: (i) GHGs, and especially CO_2, are not pollutants in the conventional sense, with CO_2 being an inert gas with little direct effect on the environment other than acidification of water; its effect is indirect in terms of radiative forcing; (ii) the effect of CO_2 is not localised so that, on the one hand, every tonne of CO_2 contributes to every instance of climate change anywhere in the world

---

[7] *Climate Change Equity: is it a Plan, an Aspiration or a Fashion Statement? A Report of a Joint Inquiry by Bangladesh Parliament's All Party Group on Climate Change and Environment and The UK All Party Parliamentary Climate Change Group* (December 2009). See http://www.gci.org.uk/Documents/APPCCG%20Climate%20Change%20 Equity%20Report.pdf.

[8] In the address of its President Mori to COP 15 in Copenhagen in December 2009: http:// climatepasifika.blogspot.com/2009/12/fsmcop15-seal-deal-to-save-humanity.html.

and, on the other hand, the contribution of that tonne is very small; (iii) a consequence of this delocalised effect is that physical proximity between emission source and 'victim' is neither a necessary nor a sufficient condition in terms of showing causal connection; and (iv) CO_2 has a long-term effect and there is a significant time lag between emission and its effect in climate change terms.

3.09   Thus a wide range of claimants may seek to invoke rights or allege liabilities. They include:

(1)   Individuals who are adversely affected by a decision of a public body or who have allegedly suffered loss or damage of one or more of the above kinds, or an infringement of their rights. Individuals may in certain circumstances join together to bring 'class' or 'collective' actions where claims of persons with common or similar interests may be heard in one action.

(2)   Corporations are likely to suffer many of the same types of damage (especially to property) as individuals. Indeed because of the longevity and wealth of large corporations compared to ordinary individuals, corporations who suffer several instances of damage, perhaps to different properties and over a long period, may most easily be able to prove damage arising from climate change.

(3)   NGOs and charities may also have claims. Some, such as the (English) National Trust or the 'land trust' plaintiffs in *Connecticut* v. *AEP*,[9] may do so as property owners. Others may do so from political motivations, and be able to show sufficient interest to bring actions. It is not a surprise to find that a large number of public law actions are brought by environmental organisations such as Friends of the Earth, Greenpeace, and the Sierra.

(4)   Local and national governmental bodies may be claimants for the same reasons as corporations. Their actions may also have an added 'public interest' element, and they may sue on behalf of their citizens (e.g. public nuisance cases).

(5)   All of the above are likely to have 'first party' insurance, against property damage and/or business interruption. Insurers who have paid such claims are often subrogated to the rights which their insureds have against third parties,

---

[9]   *AEP* v. *Connecticut*, 10-174, 2011 WL 2437011 (US June 20, 2011), discussed in Chapter 20 (on the USA), paras. 20.64ff, and in section C below.

'stepping into their shoes' to act as claimants. The insurance industry has enormous economic power, and a strong vested interest in climate change. It represents to it both a threat and an opportunity. The opportunity is primarily seen by the industry in commercial terms, but an effective insurance mechanism is important in the range of measures that enable adaptation to climate change.

(6) All of the above potential claimants are legal personalities in the usual sense. However, climate change is not limited in its impact to humans, but on the contrary poses a serious threat to animal and plant species, biodiversity and ecosystems. This fact raises the possibility of certain legal systems either allowing 'the environment' or some aspect of it access to justice in itself, or allowing interested bodies to represent natural resources, flora and fauna affected by climate change.[10] Thus the 2008 Ecuador constitution grants rights to Nature or 'Pacha Mama' itself, and in April 2010 Bolivia hosted the making of a 'Universal Declaration of Mother Earth Rights'.[11]

(7) A concept which resonates with the public law concept of 'intergenerational equity', which is a key principle in the FCCC process,[12] is that of the rights of future generations. For example, this right, potentially relevant in public trust/global commons type claims, was recognised in the *Oposa* v. *Factoran* case.[13]

Who may be liable in relation to climate change?

Public bodies

3.10 State and public bodies are likely to face allegations of legal liability in relation to climate change, over and above those made in a political context of 'responsibility' for past GHG emissions and 'climate debt'. They include national governments and

---

[10] See also Christopher Stone's classic 'Should Trees Have Standing? Toward Legal Rights for Natural Objects', 45 S. Cal. L. Rev. 450 (1972).

[11] World People's Conference on Climate Change and the Rights of Mother Earth, People's Agreement of Cochabamba (April 2010). See http://pwccc.wordpress.com/2010/04/24/peoples-agreement/.This document has however no legal status, although at Bolivian instigation debate is currently taking place in the UN General Assembly on these issues (see www.un.org/en/ga/64/meetings/).

[12] See for example Article 3.1 of the FCCC itself.

[13] *Oposa* v. *Factoran*, Philippine Supreme Court (1993) G.R. 101083.

departments/ministries, as well as equivalent bodies at local level. Two types of potential liability must be distinguished, which might be termed 'public law' and 'private law' liability. Under the domestic public (or administrative) law branches of most national systems of law, decisions of public bodies or of bodies performing a public function are reviewable by the courts in specified circumstances. The private law liability of public bodies may arise where they fail to discharge a duty to take appropriate steps to avoid loss or damage (for example to construct flood defences in a specific area) and are held liable to compensate those affected. These liabilities are separate from the possible public international law liabilities of a State for being the source of GHG emission and contributing to climate change, and are also separate from those which may attach to a State in its capacity as owner of State industries (see below).

Industry

3.11 Anthropogenic GHG emissions are caused largely by activities carried out in certain industry sectors. The most important are: (i) what is loosely termed the 'energy' sector, responsible for provision of fuel, power, heating etc; (ii) the transport sector; and (iii) the agriculture/forestry sector. Other manufacturing sectors (such as cement) are also important. As most significant industrial activity is carried out through corporations, these are obvious targets for actions claiming that they are responsible for climate change. The distinction between government and industry is blurred where, as in some countries, the relevant industries are owned or controlled by the State.[14] This factor may cut both ways in legal terms, as a State-controlled industry may claim a species of sovereign immunity from liability for some purposes, but (for example) utility companies may be regarded as public bodies or agents of the State for others (for example judicial review, human rights and 'public trust' purposes).

Ancillary commercial entities

3.12 Whilst corporations are the most obvious targets for private law actions, liability may also attach to those who promote, support and advise them, including their shareholders, lenders and

---

[14] As in the case of China where the State controls much of the coal industry; China is by some way the leading producer of coal in the world.

professional advisers (auditors, lawyers, actuaries) and liability as between these entities in relation to climate is also a possible scenario.

Insurers

3.13   Insurers' status in a commercial context is discussed briefly in Chapter 4. They have been mentioned as potential claimants above. However, insurers are also potentially liable in respect of climate change in their capacity of liability insurers of other potentially liable parties and their officers or directors. Even where the allegation against the insured is unsuccessful, insurers (who typically pay costs of the underlying legal action) are exposed. Usually their liability is in direct terms under the policy and to indemnify the insured, although in some jurisdictions direct action by an injured third party against the insurer of the party liable is possible. The liability of insurers in this way depends in part on the liability of the insured and in part on what risks are underwritten, and on what basis. Depending on policy terms, the risks potentially have a 'long tail' where, as with asbestos, liability arises long after the action or inaction complained of. An exploration of policy wordings and coverage arguments is beyond the scope of this book,[15] but the issue of coverage for liability alleged in the *Kivalina* case (see Chapter 20 (on the USA) and section C below) has already been litigated in *Steadfast* v. *AES*, in which on 2 August 2010 the Supreme Court of Virginia denied coverage on the grounds that there was no 'occurrence' as required by the policy. Argument on appeal took place in April 2011. The seriousness with which insurers take the possibility of liability of all kinds in relation to climate change is demonstrated by the volume of material on it published by them and alluded to in Chapter 4.

TYPES OF LIABILITY

3.14   In this book types of liability are divided broadly into 'public', 'private' and 'other'. These types of liability potentially overlap.

---

[15] But see Jeffrey W. Stempel, 'Insurance and Climate Change Litigation' in William C. G. Burns and Hari M. Osofsky (eds.), *Adjudicating Climate Change* (Cambridge University Press, 2009) for a full discussion.

(B)   'Public' liability

3.15   Most national laws provide for the review of decisions of public authorities. The principles of course vary from country to country but some themes emerge. Inaction or omission is generally reviewable as well as 'positive action and decisions', as exemplified in the *Massachusetts* v. *EPA* case, where the EPA was compelled to regulate CO_2 as a pollutant within the meaning of the Clean Air Act. Common grounds of review of a decision include: (i) unlawfulness; (ii) excess of powers, jurisdiction or 'vires'; (iii) unreasonableness or irrationality; and (iv) procedural deficiency. In addition, it is ordinarily necessary for the applicant in such case to show that: (i) the decision is of a type amenable to review; and (ii) he/she has sufficient interest or 'standing' to be allowed to bring the application. Remedies may include the quashing of the decision or a positive order compelling specific action. The breadth of the potential review of this kind is illustrated by the national law chapters, but the cases fall into two broad types. The first concerns laws or regulations themselves, and specifically whether, in making these, the body concerned has complied with its obligations under some superior legislative or constitutional provision. Thus if a law requires the Minister of the Environment to draw up plans to reduce GHG emissions in a certain sector, a failure to do so may be reviewable, as may be plans which do not comply with the relevant statutory duty. The second type is concerned with administrative decisions made under a regulatory scheme, and typically concerns decisions to grant or refuse licences or permits for a particular activity.

3.16   National administrative law can only be considered properly in the context of the relevant substantive national law. Thus the scope of public law action depends not simply on the administrative law, but on the extent to which the law provides for climate change and its consequences. Such law may be found in the constitution, possibly in human rights legislation, and possibly in national environmental law generally. A number of countries have legislated specifically for climate change, either in direct terms (such as in the UK) or indirectly in terms of regulations to reduce GHG emissions and/or increase energy efficiency.

3.17   Climate change liability may be engaged in relation to laws or regulations which do not have climate change control as their primary object. As the national chapters illustrate, administrative decisions on planning and permits for projects of many kinds, from mines to dams to power plants, may be subject to litigation on the grounds that climate change considerations have not been taken into account. An innovative example is the case of *FSM* v. *Prunerov* where the Federated States of Micronesia compelled the undertaking of an environmental impact assessment of a Czech coal-fired power plant by initiating a complaint in January 2010.[16] Other examples are challenges in the USA under Acts such as the Endangered Species Act in relation to species threatened by climate change, for example the polar bear.[17]

(C)   'Private' liability

3.18   Private law claims envisage one person, C, who alleges he/she has suffered damage from climate change, suing D, who is allegedly responsible in part for it, for compensation, or for an order to make D change his/her behaviour. C might be a person who suffered in a heatwave, or had his/her house flooded. D might be an oil company or power generator. The claim will be brought in 'tort' or 'delict'. In common law systems a specific tort has to be alleged, and those most commonly discussed in this context are 'nuisance' and 'negligence'.[18] Establishment of this type of liability has been seen as a kind of holy grail by

---

[16] A summary in English of the claim is at www.pohodacez.cz/press/english-summary-of-the-prunerov-case-53.

[17] Chapter 20 (on the USA), paras. 20.37ff.

[18] The possibilities of this type of claim are discussed in the national chapters, but also in greater depth in the following: David A. Grossman, 'Warming Up to a Not-So-Radical Idea: Tort-Based Climate Change Litigation', *Colum. J. Envtl. L.*, 28(1) (2003); David Hunter and James Salzman, 'Negligence in the Air: The Duty of Care in Climate Change Litigation', 155 *University of Pennsylvania Law Review* (2007); Burns and Osofsky (n. 15 above), Ch. 9; Roda Verheyen, *Climate Change Damage and International Law* (Martinus Nijhoff, 2005); Giedré Kaminskaité-Salters, *Constructing a Private Climate Change Lawsuit under English Law* (Kluwer Law International, 2010); James Burton, Stephen Tromans QC and Martin Edwards, 'Climate Change: What Chance a Damages Action in Tort?', *UKELA e-law*, 55 (2010), 22; and Joseph Smith and David Shearman, *Climate Change Litigation* (Presidian, 2006). A very recent addition to this collection is Michael Faure and Marjan Peeters (eds.), *Climate Change Liability* (Edward Elgar, 2011) focusing on tort in European law.

environmental campaigners and as an unacceptable disaster scenario by sectors of industry which might have to bear the cost. The numbers of potential claimants and defendants in this type of action, and the scale of potential compensation, are all huge, and indeed the very wide scope of such claims is one policy factor against their being permitted. No action of this type has yet succeeded. Few have been brought, almost all in the USA. The four most important US cases to date, including the recent decision of the Supreme Court in *AEP* v. *Connecticut*, are analysed in Chapter 20. The prospects of success of any private law claim are of course heavily dependent on the facts and on the relevant law, but a number of themes have emerged in litigation.

Damage

3.19   A claimant will normally have to prove that he/she has actually suffered damage, and that the damage is of a type which the law regards as recoverable. A simple definition of damage is adverse change, but proof of this will not necessarily suffice for the purpose of establishing liability. In some cases, where an injunction is sought as well as or instead of compensation, it may be sufficient to prove that he/she will suffer future harm.

Causation

3.20   This is often seen as the most serious obstacle to private law claims. The claimant must first prove that any damage results from an event or situation caused by climate change. For the reasons discussed in the national chapters, this proof may not be difficult in the case of damage caused by mean temperature rise, or sea level rise, or other long-term climate change, but is more difficult for damage caused by specific extreme weather events, although a statistical approach may still provide sufficient proof in some cases. As discussed in Chapter 17 (on English law), recent studies have suggested that anthropogenic climate change has at least doubled the risk of certain events occurring, which may be legally significant. In any case, even greater difficulties arise in attributing climate change or its effects to a specific defendant or group of defendants. This attribution problem arises partly because damage occurring now is a result of emissions in the past and particularly because any individual emitter will only be responsible for a very small percentage of overall GHGs. The claimants in the US direct liability cases have countered this point both with arguments of law on 'material contribution' and 'traceability' and with evidence that a relatively small number of corporate groups are 'responsible' for a disproportionately large share of emissions.[19] The figures of course depend on methodology, but in the *Connecticut* v. *AEP* litigation it is said that the five defendant power company corporate groups were together responsible for about 10 per cent of all anthropogenic GHG emissions in the USA, and it has been alleged by environmental groups that Exxon Mobil alone is 'responsible' for about 5 per cent of post-industrial global anthropogenic CO_2 emissions.[20]

Fault

3.21   Some torts require C to show that not only did D cause damage, but that D acted wrongly or unreasonably.[21] This requirement engages the debate as to whether emitters could have carried on business in a different way, whether it was unreasonable for them not to do so, and what difference this would make or would have made. This debate arises since GHG emissions are a necessary consequence of the basic way of life of the majority of people, especially in developed countries, the main question being whether alternative technologies could or should have been adopted.

Foreseeability

3.22   A closely related question is whether a GHG emitter can foresee or could have foreseen that a particular conduct would or might have an effect on climate change. Whilst foreseeability could not be seriously denied in relation to a period after (say) 1990, it is

[19] In English law there has been much recent debate about causation and statistical evidence, albeit not in a climate change context (see Chapter 17, section C).

[20] Friends of the Earth International, *Exxon's Climate Footprint: the Contribution of Exxon Mobil to Climate Change since 1982* (January 2004). See www.foe.co.uk/resource/reports/exxons_climate_footprint.pdf.

[21] Others impose 'strict' liability regardless of fault. There is also a trend towards strict liability (the polluter pays) in the imposition of liability by law such as in the European Environmental Liability Directive 2004/35/EC.

open to debate how much earlier the possible consequences of GHG emission could be foreseen. The complaint in the *Kivalina* case gives a detailed chronology of the alleged state of knowledge on GHG emission risks, starting in 1896.[22]

Justiciability

3.23   In the USA there are ongoing arguments about whether this type of claim is 'justiciable' at all, on the basis that some issues, which involve questions of policy and international relations, are exclusively the preserve of the executive or legislature and not subject to adjudication in the courts.

Pre-emption, displacement and statutory authority

3.24   A related question is that of pre-emption or statutory authority. A defendant may raise as a defence to any claim a national law or international treaty which he/she alleges authorises, explicitly or implicitly, his/her conduct. Such a defence might invoke national laws directed at climate change on emission standards generally,[23] or multilateral environmental agreements, such as the FCCC or the Kyoto Protocol.[24]

Long-term view

3.25   It is difficult to form a view as to the prospects of this type of liability being established. There are many obstacles to bringing a successful suit. The recent decision of the US Supreme Court in *AEP* v. *Connecticut* presents a major setback to claimants in the US courts but has not altogether killed off the prospect of liability being established in the USA or elsewhere in

---

[22] See *Kivalina*, n.6 above, para. 134ff.

[23] For example the basis on which the claim in *AEP* v. *Connecticut* was dismissed by the US Supreme Court (10-174, 2011 WL 2437011 (US June 20, 2011)) was that federal common law nuisance claims were displaced by the *Clean Air Act* which authorised the EPA to regulate GHG emissions, because the statute 'speaks directly to the question at issue' (see Chapter 20).

[24] However the emission limits under the Kyoto Protocol are expressed not to be a licence or permit to emit up to those amounts. Decision 2/CMP.1 provides: 'Further recognizing that the Kyoto Protocol has not created or bestowed any right, title or entitlement to emissions of any kind on Parties included in Annex I …'.

a private law tort claim. In the opinion of the Editors, much depends on developments on two potentially related fronts. The first is the evolving regulatory framework, whether national, regional or international. Few would dispute that regulation is a more appropriate response to climate change than litigation. At present, however, there is a huge gap between what is politically possible to deliver and what science tells us is necessary to avoid significant and long-term damage. The more progress is made on the regulatory front, the less need and the less scope for private liability. The second factor is how climate change and consequential damage actually develops. One can envisage a failure of the regulatory approach and a 'business as usual' scenario over ten, twenty or fifty years, with major emitters carrying on in the knowledge of likely consequences in terms of contribution to climate change, and serious progressive climate change damage becoming manifest. In such a case, the defences discussed above against private law claims based on well-established tort principles may turn out to be ineffective against arguments made in the second half of this century that: (i) serious damage has occurred; (ii) it was known that it would occur (as per the IPCC reports) and could have been prevented (as per the Stern review); and (iii) the principal emitters chose not to act effectively, primarily for reasons of short-term economic benefit.

Secondary/ancillary liability

3.26   Although of less general public interest than the direct liability cases exemplified by the *Kivalina* and *AEP* v. *Connecticut* type cases, the ancillary type of private liability described above is likely to be of increasing practical importance. This is where a defendant is found liable for failing to take into account climate change factors in a variety of contexts, resulting in damage, or more damage, than would have been the case had the defendant acted with due care and diligence.[25]

---

[25] So for example the US Army Corps of Engineers was found liable in November 2009 for damages of over $700,000 suffered by five plaintiffs as a result of Hurricane Katrina, on the basis of negligence in relation to maintenance of the New Orleans flood defences, with: *In Re Katrina Canal Breaches Consolidated Litigation*. New Orleans is on a part of the US coastline generally acknowledged to be vulnerable to the effects of climate change,

3.27   Commercial entities that may be held to be under liabilities in respect of climate change, albeit in a less direct manner, are those responsible, whether under the general law of tort, a statutory duty, or otherwise, for preventing its effects. Typically, these entities will be architecture, engineering or similar firms that design, build and maintain infrastructure which is either designed to reduce the effects of climate change or is vulnerable to its effects. Buildings which crack, flood or blow over, dams, flood defences and firebreaks which fail, roads or railways which buckle in extremes of heats or droughts – these are all likely to be sources of climate change liability.

3.28   Another potentially important source of private law liability arises from the increasing requirement, discussed in Chapter 4, for businesses to make disclosure of climate change related information. A failure to do so properly may incur liability to related parties such as shareholders, lenders or insurers, or to independent third parties.

(D)   'Other' liability

3.29   There are a number of other respects in which climate change liability may be engaged. They fall into numerous disparate categories and are not mutually exclusive.

Constitutional rights

3.30   An increasing number of countries, especially developing countries, are providing in their constitution or otherwise the right of citizens to a clean and/or healthy environment.[26] This right may be used as a means of alleging a liability on the part of those who fail to ensure such an environment. Whether such liability arises is highly dependent on the facts and the national law concerned,

---

and the essence of the unsuccessful claim in *Comer* v. *Murphy* was that GHG emitters had contributed to the ferocity of Hurricane Katrina (see Chapter 20, para. 20.63).

[26]   These include India (see Chapter 7) and, according to the *AIDA Environmental Defense Guide* (2010), twenty Caribbean and Latin American States. Examples in Africa include Kenya and South Africa (see Chapter 12 and Chapter 13). The constitutional right to this effect in the Philippines was relied upon in the classic case of *Oposa* v. *Factoran* in the Philippine Supreme Court (1993), n.13 above, which held that rights extended to future generations (see also Chapter 7 at para. 7.20).

but issues which will be relevant are: (i) whether climate change damage which is different in cause from traditional environmental problems, comes within the scope of the right at all; and (ii) whether the right, even if infringed, is amenable of corresponding remedy. This is primarily because (iii) a right may only be exercisable against public bodies. Despite these difficulties, activities which might contribute to or increase the effect of climate change may fall foul of such rights.

Human rights

3.31   The issue of human rights has a place in a discussion of 'liability' because of the potential liability on relevant persons or bodies to prevent or abate, or provide compensation for breaches of them. Climate change has obvious human rights implications and so what Stephen Humphreys describes as 'the silence' on human rights may at first sight appear puzzling.[27] Humphreys suggests five reasons: (i) difficulty of enforcement; (ii) difficulty of establishing extraterritorial responsibility; (iii) difficulty of establishing local accountability; (iv) difficulty caused by emergency conditions; and (v) conflict with other rights. To this one might add that environmental rights have only recently moved to centre stage as 'third generation' rights.[28] It is perhaps no coincidence that modern constitutions (such as Ecuador (2008) and Kenya (2010)) almost invariably contain references to environmental rights and there is a close link between human rights and domestic constitutional law.

3.32   Increasing attention is now being paid to the idea of climate change being a Human Rights ('HR') issue, with the effects of climate change infringing HR.[29] This follows from the nature of damage that may directly result from climate change (see above), whether on individuals or whole sectors of society. In addition to

---

[27] In Stephen Humphreys (ed.), *Human Rights and Climate Change* (Cambridge University Press, 2009).

[28] After first generation political rights and second generation economic and social rights, third generation rights may include environmental rights and rights to natural resources (see Burns and Osofsky, n. 15 above, p. 181).

[29] See, for example, Lavanya Rajamani, 'The Increasing Currency and Relevance of Rights-Based Perspectives in the International Negotiations on Climate Change', *Journal of Environmental Law*, 22(3) (2010), 391–429.

national human rights laws, addressed in the national chapters, there are important international and regional human rights regimes, and rights under national, regional and international regimes may overlap.[30]

3.33   At an international level the key instruments are the United Nations Declaration on Human Rights of 1948, the International Covenant on Civil and Political Rights and the International Covenant on Economic Social and Cultural Rights (both adopted in 1966). Neither of these, however, gives a specific environmental right. The issue of climate change was raised expressly in the UN Human Rights Council Resolutions 7/23 of March 2008 and 10/4 of January 2009,[31] after a request to this effect by the Maldives.[32] Also relevant is the UN Declaration of the Rights of Indigenous Peoples, adopted by General Assembly Resolution 61/295 on 13 September 2007.

3.34   At a regional level, regimes include: (i) the European Convention on Human Rights (discussed in the national chapters); (ii) the Inter-American System for Promotion and Protection of Human Rights; the San Salvador Protocol (to which some twenty-six American States but not including the USA are Parties) provides a right to a healthy environment in Article 11; and (iii) the African Charter on Human and People's Rights which provides (by Article 24) for a right to a satisfactory environment favourable to development.[33]

3.35   A right is only of use if there is a corresponding duty on another person or body to respect or enforce that right, an effective tribunal and a remedy. Despite the difficulties faced in these respects

---

[30] For detailed studies of HR issues in relation to climate change, see Humphreys (n. 27 above), *Climate Change in the Work of the Committee on Economic, Social and Cultural Rights* (CIEL, 2010), *Environmental Defense Guide* (AIDA, 2010), and Burns and Osofsky (see n. 15 above), Ch. 8.

[31] With this resolution being expressly referred to in the Cancun text on long-term Cooperative Action.

[32] See John H. Knox, 'Linking Human Rights and Climate Change at the United Nations', *Harvard Environmental Law Review*, 33 (2009), 477.

[33] In the *Ogoni* case it was held by the Commission that Nigeria was in breach of Article 24 (amongst others) in relation to Shell gas flaring and other activities in the Ogoni delta (155/96 (2001)). See also the *Endorois Community* case where the Commission found breaches of rights of indigenous people by the Kenyan government when the complainants were displaced for the purposes of creating a game reserve (276/2003 (2009)).

by many climate change 'victims', human rights jurisprudence and the related issue of liability for breaches of human rights are likely to become increasingly important. Apart from the continued development of rights expressly cast in terms applicable to climate change, more traditional rights may be interpreted as covering climate change consequences:[34]

- the right to life/survival may be engaged, especially in the cases of increase in frequency or severity of extreme weather events;
- the right to health is potentially very relevant with the potential for increased incidence of disease as well as many other problems;
- the right to subsistence/adequate standard of living;
- the right to peace and security (with possible implications for the engagement of the Security Council);
- the right to private and family life (as in Article 8 ECHR) as interpreted broadly in cases such as *López Ostra* v. *Spain* (see Chapter 17 on English law);
- the right to information (for example under Article 10 ECHR or Article 19 of the ICESCR);
- cultural and social rights as expounded in Chapter V of the petition of the Inuit Circumpolar Conference;[35]
- the rights of indigenous peoples generally (see the African Commission *Endorois* case (above) and the Inter-American cases of *Yanomami*[36] and *Saramaka*,[37] as well as the Inuit Petition).

Public trust

3.36　　There is a well-established common law doctrine, of considerable antiquity, of 'public trust', under which national resources may be regarded as trust property, held on trust by the State for the people as beneficiaries.[38] The State as trustee would be liable for breaches of trust. Though traditionally applied to resources

---

[34] See Humphreys (n. 27 above), pp. 76–83.
[35] http://inuitcircumpolar.com/files/uploads/icc-files/FINALPetitionICC.pdf.
[36] *Yanimami* v. *Brazil*, Report No. 12/85, Case 7615, March 5, 1985.
[37] *Saramaka People* v. *Suriname*, Series C, No. 196, November 28, 2007.
[38] For full discussion of this doctrine and its resurgence and potential application in a climate change context, see Burns and Osofsky (n. 15 above), Ch. 5.

such as fishing or water rights, it could be applied to the atmosphere or the environment more generally, especially in the context of the atmosphere as public goods or global commons or 'a common heritage of mankind'.[39] A revival of use of the doctrine has occurred in Canada and India,[40] as well as in the Philippines where in *Oposa* v. *Factoran* the Supreme Court stated that the government's obligation to protect natural resources for present and future generations was said to exist 'from the inception of humankind'.[41] It remains to be seen however if the renaissance of this ancient doctrine will extend to climate change, and how its application might conflict with other rights and obligations.[42] It has however been argued that it could extend beyond a purely domestic citizens/government arena, on the basis that all nations are co-trustees of global commons, and potentially liable as such, at least to other co-trustees for breach of that duty. A possible aspect of this doctrine that has been suggested is actions, against States or public utilities to be regarded as agents of the State, based on committing or procuring breaches of fiduciary duty. However to date there has been no successful invocation of the doctrine in a climate change context.

Competition/supply chain

3.37   As discussed in Chapter 4, in political and scientific terms the real debate on climate change policy is not so much as to the nature or cause of the problem, or even the nature of the remedy, but more as to who pays for it, both geographically (who pays and how much now?) and temporally (should current generations pay to save future ones?). Competition and anti-trust law operate at a number of levels to attempt to eliminate anti-competitive practices, and include the WTO regime and US and EU competition laws, which may offer scope for imposition of liability on States or corporations who continue to operate in a carbon-intensive environment and thereby gain an unfair competitive advantage.

---

[39] See Humphreys (n. 27 above), p. 199.
[40] See Chapters 7 and 19.
[41] G.R. No. 101083, 30 July 1993, Supreme Court of the Philippines, para. 1.
[42] In May 2011 there was coordinated filing, by 'Youth' in fifty states of the USA, of legal and administrative actions against the states invoking the public trust doctrine in order to compel action to reduce GHG emissions, as detailed at www.ourchildrenstrust.org/.

These issues resonate with considerations in relation to trade underlying the FCCC negotiations.

3.38   Humphreys suggests that the failure of States to honour FCCC obligations might be viewed as a subsidy.[43] Lord Stern has suggested in an interview that 'nations that were taking strong action on emissions could start imposing restrictions on "dirty" US exports by 2020'.[44] On a different aspect of this issue, the Committee on Economic Social and Cultural Rights in 1999 urged the WTO to undertake a review of the full range of international trade and investment policies which would address as a matter of the highest priority the impact of WTO policies on the environment.[45]

3.39   Although not directly connected with climate change, the US Lacey Act[46] provides an interesting illustration of 'long-arm' legislation, seeking to legislate in State A to address a problem in State B which may have laws but be unable or unwilling to enforce them. The Act, passed in 2008 to combat illegal logging, essentially makes illegal, as a matter of US law, trade in plants and plant products which were harvested or produced in breach of the laws of the country of origin (or any US law).

Criminal law

3.40   This area merits only passing mention for present purposes. Nonetheless, in many jurisdictions acts which contravene laws or policies on the environment generally or climate change specifically may attract criminal liability, for example on the part of public officials or directors or officers of private corporations.

Soft law – non-legal 'liability'

3.41   Lawyers often underestimate the importance of 'soft law' or non-legal forms of liability. As a result, they may miss the enormous potential effect, in political, reputational and other terms of a

---

[43] See Humphreys (n. 27 above), p. 56.
[44] As reported in the UK *Times* and *Guardian* on 19/20 November 2010.
[45] *CESCR Statement to the Third Ministerial Conference of the WTO* (E/C.12/1999/9 26, November 1999).
[46] Passed in 1900, Ch. 53 of Title 16, USC, but amended in May 2008, inserting s. 8204.

finding of breach of standards, codes or rules even if those standards were not 'law' in the conventional sense. Examples from the great variety of processes that might lead to such findings include:

- Complaints that may be brought for breach of OECD guidelines on the conduct of business, as discussed in Chapter 15 (on German law).
- The World Heritage Convention 1972 provides an obligation on States to protect World Heritage sites, many of which are potentially vulnerable to climate change. Further, the World Heritage Committee is obliged to list sites which are in danger from various threats.[47]
- Receipt and dissemination of information is vital. Access to information is discussed below, but an adverse finding by a body overseeing advertising (such as the UK Advertising Standards Authority), in relation to claims about climate-related products or services may have significant impact. At a time when pressure from regulators, investors and advocacy groups requires disclosure by corporations and public bodies of an increasing amount of information on climate change, the ability to challenge the adequacy or accuracy of disclosure is important. A recent example is the two complaints filed in 2010 by Client Earth to the UK Financial Reporting Review Panel about the annual reports (required under the UK Companies Act) of BP and Rio Tinto in relation to climate change related information.[48]
- There are a large number of codes, guidelines and panels of varying status, regarding conduct of business. Breach of these codes or guidelines, or adverse findings by a relevant body may be said to constitute a kind of liability, and climate change considerations are potentially relevant to the World Bank Inspection Panel, the Equator Principles,[49] the United Nations Principles for Responsible Investment,[50] and the UN Global Compact (Principles 7–9).[51]

[47] See generally Burns and Osofsky (n. 15 above), Ch. 11.
[48] ClientEarth – Justice for the Planet. See www.clientearth.org/testing-the-law-and-the-regulator.
[49] Equator Principles. See www.equator-principles.com/.
[50] United Nations Global Compact, The Ten Principles. See www.unpri.org/principles/.
[51] Principles for Responsible Investment. See www.unglobalcompact.org/AboutTheGC/TheTenPrinciples/index.html.

(E)   Ancillary matters

Founding jurisdiction

3.42   One of the features of climate change is that the most serious damage caused is often in developing countries whereas potential defendants are generally corporations in developed countries. Thus the ability of claimants to found jurisdiction for their claim is fundamental – a right is of little use unless a tribunal can be found to uphold and enforce it. Each nation or region (for example the EU) has its own regime and rules as to the basis on which a defendant can be sued. These are usually based either on presence of the defendant within the territory concerned or other factors connecting the claim with that territory. There has been widespread dissatisfaction with the lack of an appropriate international tribunal to address environmental claims, and consequent attempts to set up an International Court of the Environment.[52]

Applicable law

3.43   It is sometimes assumed that because climate change is an international problem, 'international law' governs climate change liability. In fact, this is rarely likely to be the case and in nearly all public and private liability cases the court or tribunal seised of the matter has to determine, as well as its own jurisdiction, what the applicable law is. For private claims, all States have their own 'conflict of law' rules for this purpose. In tort cases, the rules usually focus on which system of law the claim has the closest connection with, which may be where the act complained of occurs, or where the damage complained of occurs, or some other place.

Remedies

3.44   Public law remedies usually involve 'quashing' an order or decision, or requiring a government body to act. In private law claims,

---

[52] Led by the English lawyer Stephen Hockman QC (see his article of January 2011 at www.6pumpcourt.co.uk/publication/publicationList.aspx).

the remedy sought is usually compensation or damages, but may be an injunction or declaration. Courts are well used to assessing the value of conventional claims based on personal injury, property damage or economic loss. Courts may also have to engage in the climate change context with the 'new metrics' of human, social and natural capital (as well as financial and manufactured capital)[53] and valuation of ecosystems and human rights.

Obtaining information

3.45   Many legal battles are won or lost not on the substantive law but on the ability of one side to obtain information which the other wants to be kept secret. A fundamental requirement of a fair legal or political system is an appropriate process for obtaining (or resisting) disclosure of information, and the practical importance of this in terms of a study of climate change liability can hardly be overstated. A great deal of national law (discussed in the national chapters) has developed on the rights to information, whether in the context of litigation or in the broader context of a right to information which is held by public bodies and/or in relation to the environment. A related issue is the existence and enforcement of any duty (which is statutory, imposed by professional/regulatory bodies or otherwise) on holders of information to retain it. Again the scope of this duty is dependent on national laws, but it is a trite observation that many successful attempts to establish liability might have foundered but for the retention and ultimate disclosure of documentation of other information.

Enforcement

3.46   Enforcement of judgments and awards is in theory easy in many international contexts, under various bilateral agreements, domestic laws and, in the case of arbitrations, the 1958 New York Convention.[54] In practice this is often more difficult, either because the right to enforce a judgment from a court in State A is resisted on various legal grounds in State B, or simply because the

---

[53] See Jonathon Porritt, *Capitalism as if the World Matters* (Earthscan, 2006).
[54] The 1958 Convention on the Recognition and Enforcement of Foreign Arbitral Awards.

defendant has no assets to enforce against where the judgment can legally be enforced.[55]

Costs/access to justice

3.47   The cost of establishing or resisting liability may be a significant barrier to an effective legal system. In addition to costs issues specific to national laws, two matters of more general importance merit brief reference.

3.48   The first is the 2001 Aarhus Convention on Access to Justice in Environmental Matters. Whilst only of European application it is important in its imposition of a requirement on States to ensure access to justice in such matters which is 'fair, equitable, timely and not prohibitively expensive'.[56]

3.49   The second is the use of 'collective redress' or class actions which enable large numbers of people who individually lack resources to bring (they are invariably claimants, not defendants) legal actions which they could not otherwise do. Class actions are well established in the USA. Where one action can be brought on behalf of many claimants, it both spreads the cost and risk of proceedings among many claimants, and multiplies the potential exposure of the defendant. The potential power of collective redress has led to the leading insurance company Swiss Re: publishing (with specific reference to climate change liability) a report in 2009 entitled *The Globalisation of Collective Redress – Consequences for the Insurance Industry*,[57] which surveys on a global basis the current and possible future provisions for such class actions.

Relationship between private and public international law

3.50   A discussion of public international law is outside the scope of this book. One of the notable features of climate change liability

---

[55] The paradigm recent example is the Ecuadorian court judgment in February 2011 in the *Ecuador* v. *Chevron* litigation, where it remains to be seen whether all or any of the judgment for over US$ 18 billion against Chevron will ever be satisfied.

[56] Article 9(4).

[57] See http://media.swissre.com/documents/Globalisation_of_Collective_Redress_en.pdf.

is the degree of convergence and crossover between public international law and private international law, and private law liability may increasingly borrow from public law principles, including for example the precautionary principle and the 'no harm' principle. Some commentators have raised the possibility of liability as between claimant (C) and defendant (D), on the basis of C and D both as States (pure public law), C and D both as private entities (usually seen as pure private law) and C as a State and D as a private entity (or vice versa).[58]

(F)   Concluding thoughts

3.51   Drawing together some of the threads woven in the national chapters, what conclusions can be drawn about overall trends in climate change liability? The Editors have no crystal ball but suggest the following possible developments:

- An overall rise in importance of climate change liability, both in terms of types of liability and numbers of cases. This is illustrated by the national chapters, and especially Chapter 20 (on the USA).[59]
- A hiatus in private law damages claims. The Supreme Court decision in *Connecticut* v. *AEP* by no means signals the end of the concept of private law liability, but it may well end the run of cases on this issue in the USA.
- A sharp rise in domestic public law claims, both in terms of cases seeking to require regulatory action on climate change and of cases seeking to restrain it.
- A rise in 'indirect' or 'ancillary' private liability cases. These arise not from any development in the law but in the increase in incidence of damage actually or allegedly caused or exacerbated by climate change.

---

[58] See, for a discussion of these issues, Michael Faure and Andre Nollkaemper, 'International Liability as an Instrument to Prevent and Compensate for Climate Change' (2007) at http://ssrn.com/abstract=1086281, the FIELD report of October 2010 and Peter Roderick and Roda Verheyen, 'Beyond Adaptation' (WWF, 2008).

[59] See also the review by Professors David L. Markell and J.B. Ruhl of all 201 climate change liability cases filed in the USA in 2010, 'An Empirical Assessment of Climate Change in the Courts: A New Jurisprudence or Business as Usual?' (February 2011). See http://papers.ssrn.com/sol3/papers.cfm?abstract_id=1762886.

- An increased use of lateral thinking and legal innovation, whereby laws or regulations existing for primary purposes other than in relation to climate change are used in an attempt to impose or avoid liability in respect of it or its effects. Examples to date include the *FSM* v. *Prunerov* case discussed above and The Endangered Species Act cases in the USA, as well as the 'Rainwater Collection' case filed in 2010 in the Philippines. In this case the claimants relied on a twenty-one-year-old law, largely forgotten and ignored, to compel the government to take action to address the flooding risk said to be seriously increased due to climate change.[60]
- An increasing flexing of the muscles of developing country courts in terms of findings of liability for climate change.
  - This could well occur for a number of reasons, including the increase of damage in such countries, the changes in the law in those countries to facilitate findings of liability and the increased willingness of the courts to meet the challenge of climate change with appropriate legal responses. These may include enactment of specific laws directed to climate change or more general rights to a clean environment. For clues as to the future one only has to look towards India. Whilst there is no current trend there specifically as far as climate cases are concerned, there is the potentially potent combination of the following: (i) well developed law and activist judiciary; (ii) its status as a potentially serious 'victim' of climate change; and (iii) at the same time its large population, economic power and growth rate, and status as a 'top ten' (in cumulative terms) GHG emitter.
  - The effect of such a trend is of course not confined to the States in which the courts pronounce. The nature of climate change adds a strong international dimension. The traditional view in some quarters was that 'victims' of environmental damage in developing countries look to sue transnational corporations in the USA or Europe and that in a developing country court a claimant would suffer from lack of developed law and/or a low level of damages and/or an inability to enforce any judgment. A number of factors suggest that this may change. Whilst it remains to be seen

---

[60] *Oposa and others* v. *Philippine Government* (action 191806).

whether the Ecuadorian court judgment in the well-known claim against Chevron can be enforced, the history of this case to date may provide a pointer to the future, and one to which both developed and developing countries need to pay close attention.

4

Policy considerations

JUTTA BRUNNÉE, SILKE GOLDBERG,
RICHARD LORD QC AND LAVANYA RAJAMANI

Context

4.01　This chapter examines briefly the political, economic and regulatory contexts in which liability for climate change may be relevant, and seeks to provide a short summary of key national and international policy considerations, in so far as these are relevant to the existence of various bases for climate change liability.

4.02　Climate change liability does not exist in a vacuum. There are two related aspects of context. The first is the inherent nature of climate change, which has come in little more than twenty years from political obscurity to occupy centre stage as 'the defining human development challenge for the 21st century'.[1]

4.03　The second is that climate change is a 'cross-cutting' issue. The complexity of climate change as an issue in its own right, as outlined in Chapter 3, is compounded by its interrelationship with other contemporary issues and phenomena. These (which are not homogenous in type) include: (i) population growth; (ii) economic development and increased resource consumption; (iii) patterns of land use; (iv) food, water and energy security, including 'peak oil'; (v) the imperative for sustainability in its various senses; (vi) human rights, including rights to life/survival and health, a clean environment, peace and security, and culture; (vii) the struggle between States and 'blocs' for economic and political supremacy or advantage, and concerns over competition issues

---

[1] UNDP, Human Development Report 2007–8, *Fighting Climate Change: Human Solidarity in a Divided World.*

between low- and high-carbon economies; (viii) the blurring of the lines between North/South or developed/developing countries, with the growing political and economic power, relative to the traditionally 'developed' OECD States, of countries such as Brazil, China and India; (ix) the renewable or clean-energy debate, including the debate as to the roles of carbon capture and storage, nuclear power and biofuels respectively, the technical and economic viability of renewable sources of energy and the question of whether this debate is a threat or opportunity for business and its interrelation with existing competition regimes; and (x) the problems of intragenerational and intergenerational equity and the balance between them.

4.04   There is thus considerable scope for overlap and interaction between measures addressing climate change and those addressing other contemporary issues. A study of these is beyond the scope of this book, but the UN Framework Convention on Climate Change ('FCCC') and its underlying policy cannot properly be considered in isolation from other declarations or multilateral agreements, and the policies underlying them or bodies overseeing them. Examples include the UN Convention on Biodiversity, the UN Convention to Combat Desertification, the UN Convention on the Law of the Sea, the Montreal Protocol on Substances that Deplete the Ozone Layer, the Universal Declaration of Human Rights, the International Covenant on Civil and Political Rights, the International Covenant on Economic, Social and Cultural Rights, the UN Declaration on the Rights of Indigenous Peoples, the UN Security Council, and (in a different category) the World Trade Organization.

4.05   Positioned within this contextual matrix are the actors at international, regional, national, sub-national and individual levels:
- States, which may have a conflict between international legal/ethical obligations and national economic interest, as well as conflicts between national development and resource conservation imperatives, especially in developing countries.
- Cities, municipalities, and local governments.
- Civil society, including environmental advocacy groups, prospective 'victims' of climate change damage, or citizens in neither camp but who consider action to address climate change desirable for ethical and environmental reasons.

- Indigenous peoples and local communities.
- Industry and business, for whom climate change can be a threat or an opportunity, and sometimes both. Businesses are subject to the same physical risks of climate change as others, and business models and strategy may need to adapt to assess and address them. Industry faces increasing pressure from a number of different sources, including: (i) regulators/ legislatures;[2] (ii) lenders and shareholders, including investors who push climate change up the corporate agenda for social responsibility or economic reasons;[3] and (iii) environmental activists. For much of industry, certainty of regulatory environment is as important as the substance of regulations.
- Insurers, who have a key role. Some leading companies, such as Swiss Re, Munich Re and Zurich have put climate change high on their agenda.[4] As for other businesses, for insurers too climate change can be a threat and an opportunity, and they will bear the economic consequences of much of the loss and damage from climate change.[5] The insurance industry has enormous power and is uniquely positioned to drive behavioural change. It is exposed to climate change damage both as a 'first party' property insurer and as a 'third party' liability insurer.

---

[2] For example, on 2 February 2010 the US Securities and Exchange Commission issued interpretive guidance on the need for corporations to make climate change related disclosure in required regulatory filings. Whilst this did not introduce any actual new disclosure requirements, it was widely seen as a wake-up call for industry as to the costs and risks of climate change and the need to assess these.

[3] Such as Carbon Credit Rating, Carbon Disclosure Project, Investor Network on Climate Risk (www.incr.com); IIGCC (www.IIGCC.org).

[4] There is a vast body of literature on insurance and climate change, but in a liability context see particularly: Carol Zacharias, *Climate Change is Heating Up D&O Liability* (ACE Insurance, 2009); *The Insurance Industry and Climate Change – Contribution to the Global Debate* (The Geneva Association, 2009); and *The Globalisation of Collective Redress – Consequences for the Insurance Industry* (Swiss Re, 2009). This last report drew comparison between climate change litigation and asbestos litigation and predicted that climate change related liability could develop more quickly than asbestos related liability did.

[5] With the caveats first that much property, especially in developing countries, is uninsured, and second that the cost is ultimately borne by industry, not the insurers, who are private profit-making corporations, and reflect risk in premiums charged. The role of insurers in adaptation and in addressing long-term damage through 'Cat Bonds' and other innovative devices is a topical issue but one beyond the scope of this book.

International climate change law and policy:
the FCCC, 1992 and Kyoto Protocol, 1997

4.06   It is less than twenty years since the FCCC came into being in 1992. One hundred and ninety-four States, including all major States, are Parties. The Convention's preamble acknowledges both the right of States to exploit their own resources and the responsibility of States not to cause damage to the environment of other States or areas beyond their boundaries ('no harm' principle).

4.07   The objective of the FCCC is to prevent 'dangerous anthropogenic interference with the climate system' (Article 2). The FCCC does not determine what constitutes 'dangerous anthropogenic interference', leaving it instead to be determined politically. The key principles that guide the achievement of this objective are set out in Article 3 and include inter- and intra-generational equity, common but differentiated responsibilities ('CBDR'), the precautionary principle, and the right of developing countries to develop and the requirement to do so in a sustainable manner.[6] All Parties are charged under Article 4.1 to take action to mitigate climate change, and cooperate in preparing for adaptation. Article 4.2 obliges Parties listed in Annex I to the Convention (developed countries and economies in transition) to do so by limiting and reducing anthropogenic emissions of greenhouse gases ('GHGs'). It further requires Parties listed in Annex II (broadly, OECD countries) to provide financial and technological assistance to developing countries. The FCCC endorses the value of targets set to timetables and requires developed countries to take the lead on mitigation. The burden-sharing arrangement underpinning this division of responsibilities, and the nature, content and extent of CBDR in the climate regime, has been disputed since the ink dried on the FCCC. These disagreements led, in part, to the US rejection of the subsequent Kyoto Protocol.

4.08   The philosophy underpinning the FCCC is that appropriate action would mitigate (i.e. avoid) most or all 'dangerous' climate change and that what cannot be mitigated could be adapted to.

---

[6] Neither 'developing' nor 'developed' countries are categories that are defined in the Convention. The latter, however, are often equated with OECD countries.

Since the adoption of the FCCC, it is becoming increasingly evident that such mitigation may not in fact be possible. For example, according to a recent assessment,[7] the mitigation pledges under the Copenhagen Accord,[8] even if fulfilled, would probably lead to a global mean temperature rise significantly in excess of the 2°C limit referred to in the Copenhagen Accord and reiterated in the Cancun Agreements.[9] Hence, increasingly, attention has been focused on adaptation and, looking beyond adaptation, on how to address unavoidable long-term damage.

4.09   The mitigation battleground was (and in part remains) how much reduction Annex I countries will commit to. But the debate has moved increasingly to issues of mitigation by large developing countries and, specifically, to nationally appropriate mitigation actions and related measurement, reporting and verification obligations for these countries.

4.10   The adaptation battleground was (and remains) funding, and specifically who should provide it and in what shares, but there is also a developing battle between most vulnerable countries for their respective share of the cake.

4.11   These issues are inextricably linked with the battleground on finance issues. Although there is emerging agreement on the scale of finances required, there is little agreement on whether finances will be 'provided' or 'mobilised', where the finances will come from, how much of a role the market will play, and on the governance structures and accessibility of the new financing bodies. The current commitment by developed countries to provide finance of $30 billion in the period 2010–12 and mobilise $100 billion per year by 2020 to address adaptation and mitigation issues in developing countries is

---

[7] United Nations Environment Programme (UNEP), *The Emissions Gap Report* (November 2010), available at http://hqweb.unep.org/publications/ebooks/emissionsgapreport/ (estimating a rise of between 2.5 and 5°C).

[8] Decision 2/CP.15, 'Copenhagen Accord', FCCC/CP/2009/11/Add.1 (30 March 2010), 4.

[9] Decision 1/CP.16, 'The Cancun Agreements: Outcome of the Work of the Ad Hoc Working Group on Long-term Cooperative Action under the Convention', FCCC/CP/2010/7/Add.1 (15 March 2011); and Decision 1/CMP.6, 'The Cancun Agreements: Outcome of the Work of the Ad Hoc Working Group on Further Commitments for Annex I Parties under the Kyoto Protocol at its Fifteenth Session', FCCC/KP/CMP/2010/12/Add.1 (15 March 2011).

ambitious and, despite progress in Cancun, short on detail for implementation.[10]

4.12   The positions of the various States and groupings in the FCCC negotiations are neither static nor simple. The position of vulnerable States, such as small island nations, is readily comprehensible – maximum mitigating and adaptation action. The position of the USA, the largest developed GHG emitter, is often seen as equally simple – a refusal to commit to more than limited unilateral emission reductions in the absence of what it perceives as necessary action by certain developing countries. There are a large number of groupings in the negotiations, some of which have member States that are not at first sight natural bedfellows. For example, the 'G-77 + China' includes the small island States, the least developed countries and the OPEC (oil producing) States. Recently emerged groups include BASIC (Brazil, South Africa, India and China) and ALBA (Bolivarian Alliance for the Americas – Bolivia, Cuba, Ecuador, Nicaragua and Venezuela). Space does not permit a detailed discussion of these groupings. Suffice it to say that the diverse range of interests and ideologies represented across these negotiating coalitions has made for intractable and laboured negotiations. So much so that, in Cancun, the Chair was compelled to redefine 'consensus' and overrule an objection by one State to enable the adoption of the Cancun Agreements.[11]

4.13   As implicit in the preceding discussion, the main milepost after the FCCC was the Kyoto Protocol of 1997, which committed Annex I countries to quantified reduction of GHG emissions in a first commitment period of 2008–12. Market mechanisms, including emissions trading between Annex I countries and the clean development mechanism between Annex I and non-Annex I countries, were provided for to assist Parties in reaching their commitments. The Kyoto targets represent the first and thus far only legally binding commitments to GHG emission reductions.[12]

---

[10]   Decision 1/CP.16, *ibid.*, paras. 95–101.

[11]   See L. Rajamani, 'The Cancun Climate Change Agreements: Reading the Text, Subtext and Tealeaves', *International & Comparative Law Quarterly*, 60(2) (2011), 499–519.

[12]   Both the FCCC and the Kyoto Protocol are legally binding. Decisions taken by Conferences of Parties, absent explicit treaty authorisation, are not legally binding; but they have significant operational and political importance. See J. Brunnée, 'Coping with

The Kyoto Protocol, however, has numerous shortcomings. First, the Kyoto targets are inadequate in themselves to achieve the objective of the Convention. Current Kyoto commitments, even if met, will not limit temperature increase to acceptable levels. In addition, the targets are inadequately implemented in a number of jurisdictions. Emissions decreases thus far in evidence are linked to countries' economic fortunes, such as, for example, economic decline in countries of the former Soviet Union ('hot air'), rather than to rigorous GHG mitigation policies and measures. In addition, the targets do not extend to non-Annex I countries, such as China, India and Brazil, that are among the top ten emitters in cumulative terms.[13] Further gaps include: (i) the omission of sectors including aviation and shipping; (ii) problems with 'hot air', 'leakage' of emissions-intensive activities to non-parties, and the accounting rules on land use, land-use change and forestry ('LULUCF');[14] and (iii) inadequate protection of forests. Although Russia joined the Protocol, the USA did not, which left the treaty weakened, perhaps fatally, as the flagship international instrument to combat climate change.

4.14   The IPCC published its Fourth Assessment report in 2007. This report, with its conclusions on the existence,[15] likely effects[16] and likely causes[17] of climate change, gave new impetus to the negotiation process.[18]

4.15   The Bali Action Plan ('BAP') is a further milestone, but also marked a fork in the road, with the possibility, on some interpretations, of moving away from a Kyoto-style approach with its

Consent: Law-Making under Multilateral Environmental Agreements', *Leiden Journal of International Law*, 15 (2002), 1–52.

[13] According to UNEP: see http://maps.grida.no/go/graphic/top-20-greenhouse-gas-emitters.

[14] With the effect that certain GHG 'reductions' were more apparent than real.

[15] Warming is 'unequivocal'.

[16] Including impacts on Water, Ecosystems, Food, Health and Coasts.

[17] Very likely that most of the observed increase since the middle of the twentieth century is caused by the increase in anthropogenic GHG emission.

[18] The previous year the 2006 Stern report, commissioned by the UK government, concluded that prompt action on CC, at a cost of about 1 per cent of GDP, could prevent much larger future costs of CC, perhaps up to 20 per cent of GDP. It thus made an economic case for action in CC, and was instrumental in securing support for the 2008 UK Climate Change Act. See also for data leading to similar conclusions the United Nations Development Programme 2007/8 Human Development Report.

quantified legally binding reductions.[19] The BAP launched a process to advance the climate change regime through long-term cooperative action on climate change, with the aim of reaching an 'agreed outcome' by Copenhagen, 2009. This process is one of two parallel negotiating tracks in the negotiations. The other is the process that was launched under the Kyoto Protocol in Montreal, 2005, to negotiate Annex I targets for the second commitment period. The BAP initiated discussions on Nationally Appropriate Mitigating Actions ('NAMAs') for developing countries, Measurement, Reporting and Verification ('MRV'), Reduced Emissions from Forest Deforestation and Forest Degradation ('REDD'), response measures, and long-term damage. Paragraphs 1(b)(i) and (ii) were especially significant, providing for a potentially fundamental realignment in the balance of commitments between developed and developing countries, with a number of possible tools to achieve the objective of the climate regime other than legally binding quantified emission reduction commitments.

4.16   As is well known, COP 15 in Copenhagen in December 2009 failed to achieve a legally binding outcome. It merely resulted in the aforementioned 'Copenhagen Accord', which was reached among only twenty-eight nations, at the heads of State level, and then 'noted' by the COP.[20] The COP suffered from problems of process and procedure as well as from more fundamental divisions, especially between the US and China, over substantive issues, including the developed/developing country balance of responsibility in mitigation, and related issues of MRV. Progress on mitigation and adaptation was very limited, although reference was made to developed countries providing US$ 30 billion funding in 2010–12 and mobilising $100 billion per year by 2020. Despite the weaknesses and limitations of the Accord, it is significant that none of the major players disputed the essential IPCC conclusions on the need for urgent action on both mitigation and adaptation. One hundred and forty-four States have associated themselves with the Accord, and many of these States have submitted targets and actions under its appendices.[21]

---

[19]   Decision 1/CP.13, 'Bali Action Plan', FCCC/CP/2007/6/Add.1 (14 March 2008).
[20]   Decision 2/CP.15, n. 8 above.
[21]   A list of associated States is available at http://unfccc.int/meetings/cop_15/copenhagen_accord/items/5262.php.

4.17   COP 16 in Cancun in December 2010, in sharp contrast to COP 15 in Copenhagen, started from a low base of expectation and garnered praise for the effective management of the process, restoring some trust in the utility of multilateral environmental agreements as a solution to a global environmental problem. However, in substantive terms, Cancun's main achievement was to provide a significant stepping stone towards a comprehensive, agreed outcome, in particular by integrating the compromises contained in the Copenhagen Accord into the FCCC process, and by operationalising the institutional promises of the Accord.[22]

4.18   The LCA and KP tracks remain alive with ingenious use of a bridging device to link the two, in the form of an information document containing targets and actions noted by the COP. There was also deliberate ambiguity as to whether this document was referable to the LCA or KP tracks. Across the LCA and KP tracks, the Cancun Agreements effectively took note of documents that did not exist at the time, as pledges on mitigation had been provided under the Copenhagen Accord, and they had yet to be compiled into the information documents that the COP took note of. The pledges so far received fall well below what is necessary to limit temperature rise to 2°C (the so called gigatonne gap).[23]

4.19   There were also some process concerns at Cancun. The COP decision was arrived at on a rather strained use of the term 'consensus'. Bolivia objected strenuously and expressly to the decisions but was overruled. The decisions themselves do little to resolve the three fundamental questions left after Copenhagen: (i) the fate of the Kyoto Protocol; (ii) the legal form and architecture of any future regime; and (iii) the extent of differential treatment between developed and developing States. Many see the system of pledge and review, that now appears to have been endorsed, as markedly less effective in achieving the FCCC objective than legally binding commitments.

4.20   Positive achievements included scaled-up Adaptation Finance (Adaptation Framework and Adaptation Committee), the launch

---

[22] For the Cancun Agreements, see n. 9 above.
[23] See UNEP, n. 7 above.

of the Green Climate Fund, the launch of REDD+ and the inclusion of CCS in CDM.

4.21 Issues for COP 17 in Durban will thus include:
- The future of the Kyoto Protocol, with Japan, Canada and Russia likely to join the USA outside any future commitment period.
- The extent of differentiation between developed and developing States in relation to mitigation, and related issues on MRV.
- The legal form of any agreement – whether it will be legally binding, and whether it will replace or complement the Kyoto Protocol.
- The architecture of the new agreement – whether it should embody a Kyoto-style prescriptive architecture setting targets to timetables, backed by a compliance system for developed countries, or a Copenhagen Accord style architecture permitting all States to select targets and actions, but requiring transparency in relation to those targets and actions.
- The ambition of the new agreement, given the 'gigatonne gap' between actual pledges and those needed to achieve a rise of only 2°C, let alone 1.5°C.
- A host of other issues, such as:
  - REDD between market mechanisms and human rights/ UNDRIP issues.
  - Agriculture.
  - Bunkers.
  - Finance for adaptation.
  - Loss and damage.

Regional and national initiatives

4.22 The failure to reach any international agreement to address climate change, let alone in a timely manner, has inevitably led to much activity outside the FCCC process. The existence of regulatory or voluntary schemes outside the international framework may at the same time weaken the development of a comprehensive global agreement[24] and be valuable initiatives in their own right.

---

[24] This may resonate, however, with those who believe the appropriate approach is one that focuses on incremental steps in multiple fora in the right direction. In the words of Harvard economist Robert N. Stavins, 'smaller, practical steps – some of which are

Numerous initiatives exist at regional, national, sub-State and local levels, some complementary to the FCCC and some independent of it. Most interest has been focused on the USA, partly because of its global significance as an emitter, partly because it did not join the Kyoto Protocol and partly because of the intense political and legal battles over the legality or appropriateness of attempts to regulate GHG emissions, exacerbated by deep political policy divisions between the Presidency and Congress.

4.23   Examples of regional or similar schemes include:

(1) The Asia Pacific Partnership on Clean Development.[25] Its focus is expanding private sector investment in clean technology and its partners are the USA, Australia, Canada, India, China, Japan and Korea.

(2) The Regional Greenhouse Gas Initiative ('RGGI'),[26] whereby ten northeastern and mid-Atlantic States of the USA seek to use a cap-and-trade market mechanism to reduce emission in the power sector.

(3) The Western Climate Initiative,[27] involving Canadian provinces and states in the west of the USA, seeking to implement climate change policies at regional level.

(4) The EU Emissions Trading Scheme ('ETS'),[28] which will continue to address climate change even in the absence of an international legally binding agreement.

(5) Of a rather different nature, the Mexico City Pact,[29] a voluntary initiative between 180 cities with a combined population of over 300 million, seeking to implement city-appropriate climate change measures.

The role of markets

4.24   Debate remains intense about the role of markets in the response to climate change, and in particular mitigation. Kyoto provided

occurring outside the United Nations climate process – are going to be more easily achievable, and thus more effective, than holding out for some overarching thunderclap in a global accord'. See Robert N. Stavins, 'Why Cancun Trumped Copenhagen: Warmer Relations on Rising Temperatures', available at http://belfercenter.ksg.harvard.edu/analysis/stavins/?p=913.

[25] www.asiapacificpartnership.org/english/default.aspx.

[26] www.rggi.org/home.

[27] www.westernclimateinitiative.org/.

[28] See Chapter 14, para. 14.08.

[29] www.worldmayorscouncil.org/the-mexico-city-pact.

for market mechanisms as a means to achieve emission reduction, under the clean development mechanism, joint implementation and emissions trading mechanisms. The ETS, which the EU developed around the requirements of the Kyoto Protocol and which is discussed in some detail in Chapter 14, has been beset with difficulties, including in the use of a baseline methodology that created the temptation of overstating past emissions and that, at the first verification date, then created a market crash in May 2006. Recently, the issues have been more about the security and hence integrity of the system in the wake of cyber attacks on national registries. In turn, in the USA, the recent and ongoing battle over the legality of California's cap-and-trade scheme[30] is symptomatic of underlying policy battles over whether regulation is needed at all, and if so whether a carbon tax, trading schemes or other options are the better approaches. The involvement of the market in other aspects of climate change regulation, such as REDD, is opposed by some environmentalists.[31] Nonetheless, the market is generally recognised as having an important part to play in the field of climate change, which has itself been described as 'the greatest and widest-ranging market failure ever seen'.[32]

4.25   The approaches of 'markets' and 'regulation' are highly interdependent. One of the main drivers underlying policy differences on mitigation in the FCCC negotiations are fears that transition to a low-carbon economy in developed nations will give high-carbon economies in developing countries an unfair competitive advantage. The question of incentives for 'clean' technology has as its reverse side the issue of subsidies for fossil fuel use. Whilst the distinction between an investment and a subsidy lies largely in the eye of the beholder, authorities such as the IAEA have advocated the saving of up to $300 billion per annum by abolishing

[30] On 18 March 2011, the San Francisco Superior Court issued its decision in *Association of Irritated Residents* v. *California Air Resources Board*, setting aside and enjoining implementation of the Scoping Plan developed by the California Air Resources Board (CARB) under California's landmark Global Warming Solutions Act of 2006 (AB 32). New Hampshire and New Jersey are just two examples of states which have in 2011 seen legal battles over GHG reduction measures.

[31] Essentially on the grounds that REDD does not adequately protect either forests or indigenous peoples dependent upon them: see 'Forests and REDD', Friends of the Earth, November 2010, available at www.foe.co.uk/resource/briefings/climate_justice_brief_9.pdf.

[32] Stern Review 2006.

fossil fuel subsidies, said to be on course to reach $600 billion by 2015.[33]

4.26   It is sometimes thought that industry as a whole is opposed to climate change regulation on grounds of cost; this is however an over-generalisation. Many sectors of industry and many individuals and corporate players see change to a low-carbon economy as not only a moral imperative but a business opportunity. In this sense their time horizons and ability to innovate and react are much more conducive to change than those of politicians in developed countries. Industry is however generally united in its desire to have a clear and long-term regulatory framework on the basis of which its strategy and investment policy can be shaped.[34] In this it has to date been sorely disappointed.

4.27   It should be noted that trading schemes are not limited to developed countries. For example, in April 2011 China announced plans to introduce emissions trading schemes in six regions by 2013, expanding to a national scheme in 2015 as it attempts to control its rapidly increasing emissions.[35]

Technology cooperation and transfer

4.28   Technology is for obvious reasons key in terms of both mitigation and adaptation, and technological progress is clearly dependent on a number of policy driven factors such as: (i) incentives to invest in relevant technology; (ii) public funding for or investment in such technology; (iii) financial incentives for use of the technology (including renewable energy sources); and (iv) the regulatory 'playing field'.

4.29   A key element in the international negotiations is technology transfer and in particular cooperation and facilitation of transfer from developed to developing countries, although the more 'developed' developing countries are themselves in the forefront

---

[33] IAEA World Energy Outlook 2010.

[34] See for example *Business Leadership on Climate Change – Encouraging Engagement and Action* (PwC, December 2010).

[35] Reuters, 11 April 2011, citing Sun Cuihua, the vice-director of the climate change department at China's National Development and Reform Commission. Kenya opened Africa's first carbon exchange in March 2011 and Taiwan reportedly intends to launch a carbon trading platform in September 2011.

of technological progress. The main barriers to transfer are funding and intellectual property rights.

The thesis of this book

4.30 'Time and Tide wait for no man'; and neither will they, nor the world's lawyers, await the results of the ponderous FCCC process.

4.31 Of much potential significance is the so-called risk quadrant, whose axes are the future extent of climate change damage and the effectiveness of regulatory response, which may determine whether climate change liability continues to increase in importance. The quadrant is itself 'iterative', as liability or the prospect of liability will drive behaviour and thus influence the content of the risk quadrant. In this regard, 'liability' looks both backwards for redress and forward in terms of its effect on future behaviour.

4.32 Climate change liability has many uses and is relevant to many players. Though in traditional manner it is seen as either a financial liability for industry or a string to the bow of environmentalists, knowledge of liability is a corporate and policy tool, relevant to risk management, valuations and business planning. It is relevant to policymakers as they strive for an informed view of consequences of action or inaction on various issues. And, to conclude this policy chapter with a celebrated legal quote, applicable to all the actors referred to above: 'Be you ever so high, the law is above you.'[36]

---

[36] Thomas Fuller, as quoted in *Gouriet v. Union of Post Office Workers* [1977] QB 729, per Lord Denning (decision reversed on appeal).

PART II

National laws

Asia and Pacific

Australia

ROSS ABBS, PETER CASHMAN AND
TIM STEPHENS

(A) Introduction

The Australian legal system

5.01   The Commonwealth of Australia is a federal State with three
levels of government comprising a national government, the
governments of six states and two territories, and local government. The federal government, the Commonwealth, has no
direct constitutional power to legislate with respect to environmental matters. Nevertheless, several heads of power contained
in section 51 of the Commonwealth Constitution provide
a basis for wide-ranging climate change legislation. These
include the corporations power and the external affairs power,
the latter of which enables the Commonwealth Parliament to
pass laws implementing treaties to which Australia is a Party.[1]
As Australia is a Party to the United Nations Framework
Convention on Climate Change ('FCCC')[2] and its Kyoto
Protocol,[3] the Commonwealth may legislate to meet its obligations under these agreements.

5.02   The states and territories also have the constitutional capacity to
pass laws with respect to climate change and have done so as the
Commonwealth has been unwilling or unable to regulate greenhouse gas ('GHG') emissions. However, to the extent that state
laws are inconsistent with federal legislation addressing the same

---

[1] See especially *Commonwealth* v. *Tasmania* (1983) 158 CLR 1.
[2] New York, 9 May 1992, in force 21 March 1994, 1771 UNTS 165.
[3] Kyoto Protocol to the United Nations Framework Convention on Climate Change, Kyoto,
11 December 1997, in force 16 February 2005, (1998) 37 ILM 22.

subject matter they are invalid.[4] The Commonwealth's efforts to establish a comprehensive emissions trading scheme ('ETS') were thwarted in 2010 when the upper house of the Commonwealth Parliament, the Senate, voted against a package of eleven Bills that would have established the Carbon Pollution Reduction Scheme ('CPRS').[5]

5.03   Environmental matters, including climate change cases, are adjudicated in federal, state and territory courts and administrative tribunals, with most cases being brought before specialist environmental courts or tribunals at state level.[6]

The governmental stance on climate change

5.04   Australia's per capita GHG emissions are among the highest in the world, with only Bahrain, Bolivia, Brunei, Kuwait and Qatar ranking higher.[7] Around half of Australia's emissions are produced by the stationary energy sector, which is heavily reliant on coal-fired power plants. Emissions from agriculture and transport comprise the other main sources of Australia's carbon footprint.

5.05   Australia signed the Kyoto Protocol in 1998 after winning significant concessions in the negotiation of the Protocol text. It was permitted an emissions increase (to 108 per cent of 1990 levels) rather than bound to a reduction like most other States, and the so-called 'Australia clause' allowed countries with net emissions from land use change and forestry to include such emissions in their 1990 baseline. Because land clearing was being brought under control in Australia in the 1990s, this meant that Australia could meet its Kyoto target relatively easily, with major smokestack industries such as power generation and aluminium and cement production given room to increase their emissions.

[4] Australian Constitution, s. 109.
[5] These included the Carbon Pollution Reduction Scheme Bill 2010 (Cth) and the Australian Climate Change Regulatory Authority Bill 2010 (Cth).
[6] See L. Pearson, 'Australia' in L. Kotzé and A. Paterson (eds.), *The Role of the Judiciary in Environmental Governance: Comparative Perspectives* (Kluwer Law International, 2009), p. 321.
[7] R. Garnaut, *The Garnaut Climate Change Review: Final Report* (Cambridge University Press, 2008), p. 153.

Despite this preferential treatment, the Australian government decided in 2002 not to ratify the Kyoto Protocol. This decision was overturned following the election of the Labor government in 2007.

5.06 Australia's Fifth National Communication on Climate Change, submitted to the FCCC Secretariat in March 2010, indicated that Australia was on track to meet its Kyoto target without relying on the Protocol's flexibility mechanisms, with emissions projected to reach 106 per cent of 1990 levels over the first commitment period (2008–12).[8] However, emissions are projected to increase sharply, to 121 per cent of 2000 levels by 2020, unless abatement measures are taken.[9]

5.07 In January 2010, Australia submitted emissions reduction targets to the FCCC Secretariat in connection with the Copenhagen Accord. These involved an unconditional pledge to cut emissions by 5 per cent on 2000 levels by 2020, with additional reductions of up to 15 per cent and 25 per cent contingent upon the level of action taken by other States. The 25 per cent reduction will apply if there is 'an ambitious global deal capable of stabilising levels of [GHGs] in the atmosphere at 450 ppm CO_2-eq or lower'.[10] The government has also committed to an emissions reduction target of at least 60 per cent below 2000 levels by 2050. Although the upper-range mid-term 2020 target follows the recommendation of the Garnaut Review,[11] the long-term target falls well short of the 90 per cent reduction that Professor Garnaut found was consistent with a global contraction and convergence approach.[12]

[8] Department of Climate Change, *Australia's Fifth National Communication on Climate Change* (2010), p. 86.

[9] *Ibid.*, p. 87.

[10] Letter from P. Wong (Minister for Climate Change and Water) to Y. de Boer, 27 January 2010, available at http://unfccc.int/files/meetings/application/pdf/australiacphaccord_app1.pdf.

[11] The Garnaut Review was commissioned in 2007 by then Leader of the Federal Opposition Kevin Rudd along with the governments of the Australian states and territories. It was required to 'examine the impacts of climate change on the Australian economy, and … recommend medium- to long-term policies and policy frameworks to improve the prospects of sustainable prosperity' (see Garnaut, *Garnaut Climate Change Review*, p. xiii).

[12] *Ibid.*, p. 209.

National climate change risks

5.08   Australia is one of the developed countries most vulnerable to the impacts of climate change. As the driest inhabited continent on earth, with already high levels of climate variability, Australia can expect a range of severe impacts if there is no mitigation of global emissions. Under a business-as-usual scenario it is expected that by 2100 drought will be increasingly frequent; there will be severe stress on urban water supplies; irrigated agricultural production in the Murray Darling Basin, Australia's main 'food bowl', will have declined by more than 90 per cent; the Great Barrier Reef will effectively have been destroyed; and many coastal areas including the Kakadu wetlands will have been transformed by rising sea levels.[13]

The CPRS

5.09   The Commonwealth, state and territory governments have implemented a range of initiatives to address climate change, but to date these have fallen short of a comprehensive regime to reduce Australia's GHG emissions.

5.10   The National Greenhouse and Energy Reporting Act 2007 (Cth) established a mandatory system for the reporting by corporations of their GHG emissions and energy consumption, and the Labor government elected in 2007 pledged to introduce a cap-and-trade ETS by 2010. Following an extensive process of consultation, which involved the release of Green and White Papers, and exposure drafts of legislation, Bills to establish the CPRS were introduced into Parliament in 2009.

5.11   These Bills were rejected by the Senate, where the government did not command a majority. In April 2010, the government announced that it would delay the implementation of the CPRS until the end of the first commitment period of the Kyoto Protocol. The 2010 election then saw the Labor Party form government with the support of a number of independents and a Greens member of the House of Representatives. The government established a Multi-Party Climate Change Committee

---

[13]   *Ibid.*, Ch. 6.

to explore options for the development of a national carbon price.

5.12   In December 2010, the Committee released a communiqué outlining eleven policy principles to 'guide' deliberations on a carbon price mechanism.[14] These principles are: environmental effectiveness; economic efficiency; budget neutrality; competitiveness of Australian industry; energy security; investment certainty; fairness; flexibility; administrative simplicity; clear accountability; and fair contribution to global efforts. In February 2011, it released a 'proposal' setting out the 'broad architecture' for a potential carbon pricing scheme.[15] The proposal envisages the initial imposition of a carbon tax, with provision being made for 'conversion' to a cap-and-trade ETS after a set period of time. However, two members of the Committee reserved their position on the proposal, and significant details were left at large. Carbon pricing is currently the subject of intense political controversy. However, it remains likely that many elements of the CPRS will feature in whatever regulatory scheme is ultimately adopted.[16]

5.13   Had it been implemented, the CPRS would have constituted one of the world's broadest emissions trading schemes. It would have applied to the six GHGs covered by the Kyoto Protocol and to around 75 per cent of Australia's emissions, including emissions from stationary energy production, industrial processes, waste, and – most notably – transport, as well as fugitive emissions from oil and gas production. Agricultural emissions were excluded. The CPRS would have directly applied to around 1,000 enterprises.

5.14   Under the CPRS (and in contrast to the situation obtaining under the European Union ETS), the majority of emissions permits were to be auctioned. Controversially, free permits and transitional assistance were to be provided to emissions-intensive and trade-exposed industries in order to prevent 'carbon leakage'.

[14] Multi-Party Climate Change Committee, 'Communiqué', 21 December 2010, available at www.climatechange.gov.au/government/initiatives/multi-party-committee/meetings/third-meeting/communique.aspx.

[15] Multi-Party Climate Change Committee, 'Carbon Price Mechanism', 24 February 2010, available at www.climatechange.gov.au/~/media/Files/minister/combet/2011/media/february/mr20110224.pdf.

[16] See R. Briese, 'Climate Change Mitigation Down Under: Legislative Responses in a Federal System', *Asia Pacific Journal of Environmental Law*, 13 (2010), 75.

Free permits were also to be issued to coal-fired power plants. Other features of the CPRS included a transitional price cap mechanism involving an unlimited number of non-tradeable and non-bankable permits that could be purchased from the government at a fixed price, and an assistance package to ensure that low and middle income families were given offsets for increasing household costs.

National Renewable Energy Target

5.15   The Renewable Energy Target ('RET') scheme was implemented in 2009, replacing the Mandatory Renewable Energy Target introduced in 2001. Following amendments that came into effect on 1 January 2011, the RET is now divided into two parts: the Large-Scale Renewable Energy Target and the Small-Scale Renewable Energy Scheme. These are administered by the newly established Office of the Renewable Energy Regulator, and enable households and industry with renewable energy systems to generate certificates that can be sold to purchasers such as electricity retailers, which are required to acquire certificates to meet an annual target.[17] The goal of the RET is for 20 per cent of Australia's electricity to be generated by renewable means by 2020.

(B)   Public law

5.16   In the absence of a comprehensive regulatory framework to limit GHG emissions, litigants have turned to the courts in an effort to enforce environmental laws bearing on climate change. The courts have also been called upon to review administrative decisions in which climate change issues have not been appropriately or adequately considered.

Standing to seek public remedies[18]

5.17   In order to enforce existing laws, or to seek judicial review or merits review of administrative decisions, a litigant must first

---

[17] See Renewable Energy (Electricity) Act 2000 (Cth).
[18] For a more comprehensive treatment of the law of standing in Australia, see e.g. G. Bates, *Environmental Law in Australia*, 7th edn (LexisNexis Butterworths, 2010), Ch. 15; R. Douglas, *Douglas and Jones's Administrative Law*, 6th edn (The Federation Press, 2009), Ch. 22.

establish that he/she has standing to do so. Rights of access to civil enforcement mechanisms[19] and formal merits review procedures arise from legislation, whereas rights to seek judicial review derive either from statute or from the Commonwealth Constitution.

5.18   Historically, Australian courts took a narrow view of the rights of persons seeking to attack the validity of decisions or legislation. Such persons had no standing to litigate unless they were more particularly affected than other people,[20] or would derive some benefit or advantage over and above that to the ordinary citizen,[21] or had a 'special interest' beyond a 'mere intellectual or emotional concern'.[22] The traditional approach has given way in recent years to a somewhat more 'flexible' attitude.[23] Nonetheless, it continues to be said that standing at common law depends upon the demonstration of some 'interest' surpassing an abstract desire to enforce norms of public administration.[24] The Australian Law Reform Commission ('ALRC') has observed that the resolution of issues of standing on this footing tends to be 'cumbersome and confusing',[25] a criticism which has been amplified by subsequent academic commentary.[26] Although standing requirements have rarely impeded public environmental litigation in recent years,[27]

[19]   For example, section 475 of the Environment Protection and Biodiversity Conservation Act 1999 (Cth) permits 'interested' persons, including persons or incorporated organisations involved in recent activities for the protection or conservation of, or research into, the environment, to seek an injunction in the Federal Court to prevent contravention of the Act. Some state and territory planning and environmental statutes go further, incorporating 'open standing' provisions (see e.g. Environmental Planning and Assessment Act 1979 (NSW), s. 123; Protection of the Environment Operations Act 1997 (NSW), s. 252).

[20]   *Anderson* v. *Commonwealth* (1932) 47 CLR 50.

[21]   *Robinson* v. *Western Australian Museum* (1977) 138 CLR 283.

[22]   *Australian Conservation Foundation* v. *Commonwealth* (1980) 146 CLR 493.

[23]   See e.g. *North Coast Environment Council Inc.* v. *Minister for Resources* [1994] FCA 1556; *Environment East Gippsland Inc.* v. *VicForests* [2010] VSC 335.

[24]   Where common law constraints on standing are insurmountable, the Attorney-General may enable a judicial review action either ex officio or by way of a relator action, but this is highly unlikely in the environmental context (see Bates, *Environmental Law in Australia*, [15.29]–[15.30]).

[25]   Australian Law Reform Commission, *Beyond the Doorkeeper – Standing to Sue for Public Remedies* (Report No. 78, 1996), [4.12].

[26]   See e.g. P. Cane and L. McDonald, *Principles of Administrative Law: Legal Regulation of Governance* (Oxford University Press, 2008), p. 191.

[27]   See R. Douglas, 'Uses of Standing Rules 1980–2006', *Australian Journal of Administrative Law*, 14 (2006), 22, 36.

their continued vagueness ensures that they remain a source of uncertainty.

5.19   Legislation has adjusted the common law rules on standing in certain areas. Many Commonwealth statutes rely on the generic judicial review machinery supplied by the Administrative Decisions (Judicial Review) Act 1977 (Cth) ('ADJR Act'). Section 5(1) of the Act specifies that a person who is 'aggrieved by' a decision[28] under prescribed Commonwealth legislation may seek judicial review by the Federal Court or the Federal Magistrates Court on enumerated grounds. In practice, the 'person aggrieved' criterion leads to inquiries comparable to those undertaken in respect of the common law 'special interest' requirement,[29] and thus to similar problems.

5.20   The ADJR Act test may itself be modified for particular statutory contexts. For example, where a decision made under the Environment Protection and Biodiversity Conservation Act 1999 (Cth) ('EPBC Act') is sought to be reviewed, an applicant who has engaged in recent activities for the protection or conservation of or research into the environment will be taken to be a 'person aggrieved'.[30]

Enforcement of environmental laws

5.21   There have been a number of cases in which private individuals and non-governmental organisations have sought to utilise open standing provisions of environmental legislation to address asserted contraventions of the legislation in relation to climate change matters.

5.22   For instance, in *Gray* v. *Macquarie Generation*,[31] the applicants, climate change activists, argued that CO_2 produced from a coal-fired power station constituted waste requiring a valid environment protection licence, and that the failure to acquire such a

---

[28] To be reviewable under the ADJR Act a decision generally needs to be 'final or operative and determinative' and not just a 'step along the way', and 'substantive' rather than 'procedural': *Australian Broadcasting Tribunal* v. *Bond* (1990) 170 CLR 321, 337 (Mason CJ).

[29] R. Douglas, 'Standing' in M. Groves and H. Lee (eds.), *Australian Administrative Law: Fundamentals, Principles and Doctrines* (Cambridge University Press, 2007), p. 158, at p. 164.

[30] EPBC Act, s. 487.   [31] [2010] NSWLEC 34.

licence gave rise to an offence under section 115 of the Protection of the Environment Operations Act 1997 (New South Wales). On an application by the respondent for summary dismissal, the New South Wales Land and Environment Court ('NSWLEC') held that CO_2 was not a waste in the relevant sense.

Review of government decisions having climate change impacts

5.23   The opportunities for judicial review and merits review of governmental decisions connected to climate change policy are limited in so far as relatively few statutory provisions directly relate to or specifically mention climate change issues.[32] By way of example, a 2008 review of Commonwealth and New South Wales ('NSW') legislation concerning the responsibilities of coastal councils for climate change risks found that of 137 relevant instruments, only 16 contained the words 'climate change', 'sea level rise' or 'greenhouse'.[33] None placed any direct obligations on decision-makers in relation to coastal adaptation.

5.24   The relative paucity of laws directly addressing climate change concerns has sometimes compelled litigants to ventilate such concerns by circuitous means. For example, unsuccessful efforts have been made to link GHG emissions to a disparate assortment of 'protected matters' in order to ensure that they are accounted for in certain processes under the EPBC Act.[34] It stands to reason that opportunities to seek review of government decisions bearing on climate change issues may increase as regulation connected to climate change proliferates.

Judicial review of administrative decisions

5.25   Judicial review of the legality of administrative decisions may be sought on various grounds.[35] Most climate change related cases

[32] See the discussion in R. Ghanem, K. Ruddock and J. Walker, 'Are Our Laws Responding to the Challenge Posed to Our Coasts by Climate Change?', *University of New South Wales Law Journal*, 31 (2008), 895, 901.

[33] See Environmental Defender's Office, *Coastal Councils and Planning for Climate Change: An Assessment of Australian and NSW Legislation and Government Policy Provisions Relating to Climate Change Relevant to Regional and Metropolitan Coastal Councils* (2008).

[34] See below at [5.32]–[5.35].

[35] See ADJR Act, s. 5(1). The ADJR Act is substantially declaratory of the common law in this respect.

have primarily concerned the alleged failure by a decision-maker to take proper account of relevant considerations. Such a failure can only be made out if a decision-maker has failed to attend to a consideration which is expressly or implicitly *required* by a statute to be addressed in making the decision in question. However, where such a matter is so insignificant that a failure to consider it could not have materially affected the decision, a court will not intervene.[36]

5.26   Other possible grounds of review – involving, for example, error of law, procedural irregularity or impropriety – are likely to be less frequently available. Opportunities for review of the rationality of decisions are ordinarily limited due to the stringency of relevant tests.[37] The law as to legitimate expectations is similarly confined, and effective only to safeguard certain process rights.

Mitigation case law

5.27   In *Gray* v. *Minister for Planning*,[38] the applicant sought to challenge decisions of the Director-General of the Department of Planning in connection with an environmental assessment prepared in support of a proposed coal mine. The assessment gave consideration to direct emissions from the project and indirect emissions in respect of its use of electricity. However, emissions from third party burning of coal were not examined in detail. Pain J concluded that:

> there is a sufficiently proximate link between the mining of a very substantial reserve of thermal coal in NSW, the only purpose of which is for use as fuel in power stations, and the emission of [GHGs] which contribute to climate change/global warming, which is impacting now and likely to continue to do so on the Australian and consequently NSW environment, to require assessment of that GHG contribution of the coal when burnt in an environmental assessment under Pt 3A [of the Environmental Planning and Assessment Act 1979 (NSW) ('EPAA')].[39]

---

[36] See *Minister for Planning* v. *Walker* [2008] NSWCA 224, [34] (Hodgson JA) ('*Walker*').
[37] See e.g. *Kennedy* v. *NSW Minister for Planning* [2010] NSWLEC 129, [102]–[103] (Biscoe J) ('*Kennedy*').
[38] [2006] NSWLEC 720 ('*Gray*'). See further A. Rose, '*Gray v Minister for Planning*: The Rising Tide, of Climate Change Litigation in Australia', *Sydney Law Review*, 29 (2007), 725.
[39] *Gray* [2006] NSWLEC 720, [100].

5.28   Pain J held that the Director-General's failure to take into account principles of ecologically sustainable development ('ESD')[40] (and in particular the principle of intergenerational equity and the precautionary principle) in considering the public interest[41] served to invalidate his 'view' as to the sufficiency of the assessment.[42] However, the assimilation of ESD principles to the public interest was criticised as premature in a subsequent case, discussed below.

5.29   *Drake-Brockman* v. *Minister for Planning*[43] also concerned an alleged failure to address ESD principles in light of the GHG emissions associated with a proposed development. However, in the circumstances of the case, Jagot J concluded that the Minister had in fact considered all relevant matters. Her Honour emphasised that the EPAA neither dictated that ESD concerns should override other relevant considerations, nor demanded 'any particular method of analysis of a potentially relevant subject matter'.[44]

5.30   The relationship between climate change, principles of ESD and the general public interest under the EPAA has again been put in issue in *Haughton* v. *Minister for Planning*,[45] in which the applicant is contesting ministerial approval of concept plans for two new power stations in NSW. The decision of Craig J was awaited at the time of writing.

5.31   In *Australian Conservation Foundation* v. *Latrobe City Council*,[46] the operator of a large brown-coal power station in Victoria sought approval to develop a new coalfield. A panel appointed by the Minister to consider the proposal was instructed not to consider matters relating to GHG emissions from the power station. Nonetheless, a submission to the panel from the Australian

---

[40] On the nature and function of ESD principles in Australian environmental and planning law, see e.g. J. Peel, 'Ecologically Sustainable Development: More than Mere Lip Service?', *Australasian Journal of Natural Resources Law and Policy*, 12 (2008), 1; Bates, *Environmental Law in Australia*, [7.16]–[7.22]. On the treatment of ESD principles in climate change litigation, see e.g. N. Durrant, *Legal Responses to Climate Change* (The Federation Press, 2010), pp. 225–230.

[41] See *Gray* [2006] NSWLEC 720, [42]–[44] (Pain J).

[42] *Ibid.*, [143].   [43] [2007] NSWLEC 490.

[44] *Ibid.*, [132].   [45] 10/40423, 10/40424 (NSWLEC).

[46] [2004] VCAT 2029.

Conservation Foundation addressed that issue. In proceedings before the Victorian Civil and Administrative Tribunal ('VCAT'), the Foundation contended that the panel's failure to take account of its submission contravened a legislative requirement that it consider all submissions. Morris P concluded that the environmental impacts of GHG emissions were relevant, and should have been considered. In effect, Morris P 'rejected the notion that [GHG] emissions from the [power station were] trivial in comparison to total global [GHG] emissions, and should therefore be disregarded in planning processes'.[47]

5.32   On a federal level, challenges of a similar nature have been brought in respect of decisions made under the EPBC Act. The Act designates as 'protected' certain matters of national environmental significance.[48] In general, proposed 'actions' (including developments) that are expected to 'impact'[49] on protected matters are prohibited in the absence of ministerial approval. Upon being referred such an 'action', the Minister (or a delegate of the Minister) must determine whether its expected impacts render it a 'controlled action', and as such subject to special approval and assessment procedures.[50] Whilst an action's expected contribution to climate change is not effective to enliven the 'controlled action' regime of itself,[51] 'conservationists have argued that the regime should apply to emission-intensive projects on the grounds that they [will] contribute to climate change, which in turn [is] likely to threaten [protected] matters'.[52]

[47] C. Berger, 'Hazelwood: A New Lease on Life for a Greenhouse Dinosaur' in T. Bonyhady and P. Christoff (eds.), *Climate Law in Australia* (The Federation Press, 2007), p. 161, at p. 170.

[48] See EPBC Act, Pt. 3. 'Protected matters' include, inter alia, certain World Heritage values; the character of 'declared' wetlands; and prescribed threatened species or communities.

[49] See EPBC Act, s. 572E.   [50] EPBC Act, s. 75.

[51] It is worth noting that calls for a 'greenhouse trigger' to be incorporated into the EPBC Act have thus far been to no effect. Such a trigger would render 'actions' expected to generate GHG emissions in a prescribed amount liable to 'control' on that basis alone (see A. Macintosh, 'The Greenhouse Trigger: Where did it Go and What of its Future?' in Bonyhady and Christoff, *Climate Law in Australia*, p. 46). A recent independent review of the EPBC Act recommended that an 'interim' trigger be introduced, stressing the need to re-evaluate the utility of such a mechanism in light of any future comprehensive emissions regulation regime (A. Hawke, *The Australian Environment Act – Report of the Independent Review of the Environment Protection and Biodiversity Conservation Act 1999* (Commonwealth of Australia, 2009), [4.86]–[4.110]).

[52] A. Macintosh, 'The Commonwealth' in T. Bonyhady and A. Macintosh (eds.), *Mills, Mines and Other Controversies: The Environmental Assessment of Major Projects* (The

5.33   In *Wildlife Preservation Society of Queensland Proserpine/
Whitsunday Branch Inc.* v. *Minister for the Environment and
Heritage*,[53] the applicant challenged determinations to the effect
that two proposed coal mines were not 'controlled actions'. It contended that the Minister's delegate had failed to take into account
adverse impacts on protected matters from GHG emissions
resulting from the construction and operation of the mines, and
from the burning of coal thus extracted. Dowsett J held that the
delegate had, in fact, considered these issues. However, Dowsett J
went further, questioning whether climate change as attributable
to the mines could be considered to impact upon matters 'protected' under the Act at all:

> I am far from satisfied that the burning of coal at some unidentified
> place in the world, the production of [GHGs] from such combustion, its
> contribution towards global warming and the impact of global warm-
> ing upon a protected matter, can be so described … The applicant's
> case is really based upon the assertion that [GHG] emission is bad, and
> that the Australian government should do whatever it can to stop it
> including, one assumes, banning new coal mines in Australia.[54]

5.34   Peel has observed that the *Wildlife Whitsunday* case 'suggests the need for applicants to provide detailed information
to the Court as to the likely extent of climate change impacts
and feasible means of measuring GHG emissions in order to be
successful'.[55]

5.35   *Your Water Your Say Inc.* v. *Minister for the Environment,
Heritage and the Arts*[56] also involved a claim that a delegate of the
Minister had failed to take account of climate change impacts in
determining whether a proposed action was 'controlled' under
the EPBC Act. In that case, the relevant 'action' had to do with
the construction of a desalination plant in Victoria. It was held
in the circumstances that climate change impacts attributable to
the proposed action were not required to be taken into account
as a matter of law, and that in fact the Minister's delegate had

---

Federation Press, 2010), p. 224, at p. 231. See also Durrant, *Legal Responses to Climate
Change*, pp. 243–4.

[53] [2006] FCA 736 ('*Wildlife Whitsunday*').

[54] *Ibid.*, [72].

[55] J. Peel, 'Climate Change Litigation' in *Climate Change Law and Policy in Australia*
(LexisNexis Butterworths, 2009), [8–075].

[56] [2008] FCA 670.

considered them nonetheless.[57] The delegate had concluded that 'linkages between specific additional [GHG] emissions and potential adverse impacts on matters [protected under] the EPBC act are uncertain and conjectural'.[58]

5.36   Other proceedings concerning the EPBC Act have alleged juris-dictional error. In *Anvil Hill Project Watch Association* v. *Minister for Environment and Water Resources*,[59] the applicant challenged a determination that the construction and operation of an open-cut coal mine was not a controlled action. The Minister's delegate had decided that the project, including downstream GHG emissions from the burning of coal from the mine, would not have signifi-cant, identifiable, impacts on protected matters. The Full Federal Court agreed with the judge at first instance that the Act did not require an objective factual determination as a condition prece-dent to the exercise of the power to designate an action as 'con-trolled'. The question as to whether there were significant impacts did not give rise to a jurisdictional fact that could be challenged.

5.37   Objectors to carbon-intensive projects can invoke other grounds of review in order to ensure that relevant assessment and approval procedures are carried out in a manner conform-able to law. In *Queensland Conservation Council Inc.* v. *Xstrata Coal Queensland Pty Ltd*,[60] the Council ('QCC') had made representations to the Queensland Land and Resources Tribunal in respect of Xstrata's application to expand the coverage of an existing mining lease. QCC had contended that climate change impacts flowing from the development of a new mine on the rele-vant site required that certain conditions be imposed. In pro-ceedings before the Tribunal, it was common ground between the parties that anthropogenic climate change was occurring and that GHG emissions associated with the mine would contribute to it. Despite this, the Tribunal held that QCC had failed to link the mine's GHG emissions to 'discernible harm',[61] and refused

---

[57]   *Your Water Your Say Inc.* v. *Minister for the Environment, Heritage and the Arts* [2008] FCA 670, [22] (Heerey J).

[58]   *Ibid.*, [15].   [59]   (2008) 166 FCR 54.

[60]   [2007] QCA 338 ('*QCC*').

[61]   *Re Xstrata Coal Pty Ltd* [2007] QLRT 33, [21] (Koppenol P). Peel has opined that the judg-ment of Koppenol P was 'in its conclusions and tone, an exemplar of climate change scep-ticism' (Peel, 'Climate Change Litigation', [8–085–5]).

to impose the conditions sought. The Tribunal's reasoning relied on material said to cast doubt on whether climate change is a function of GHG emissions. This material had been drawn to the attention of QCC at a late stage of the proceedings, with no indication given as to the use to which the Tribunal proposed to put it. In review proceedings before the Queensland Court of Appeal, it was held that the Tribunal had denied QCC natural justice:

> The Tribunal relied on the Carter-Byatt critique which contended, contrary to the facts accepted by the parties at the hearing, that there was no scientific evidence demonstrating anthropogenic [GHG] induced global warming, to ultimately conclude that it was not appropriate to impose the conditions sought by QCC … There was nothing in the statutory or factual matrix of this case that made it unreasonable for the Tribunal to inform QCC that having read the critique it was inclined to accept and act on it, so that QCC had an opportunity to respond.[62]

Adaptation case law

5.38   The alleged failure to consider climate change impacts *on* proposed developments (as distinct from the climate change impacts *of* such developments) has been used as a foundation for opposing developments in general or their scale in particular.

5.39   In *Walker* v. *Minister for Planning*,[63] it was contended that the Minister should have considered flood risk as a result of climate change before approving a concept plan for a major residential and retirement development on coastal land at Sandon Point, south of Sydney. The NSWLEC held at first instance that failure to consider whether flood risk may be compounded by climate change invalidated the Minister's decision to approve the concept plan under Part 3A of the EPAA.[64] The Court reasoned that ESD principles were part and parcel of the public interest, and in the circumstances required climate change flood risk to be assessed. However, this decision was reversed on appeal, on the basis that at the relevant time, principles of ESD were not so plainly an element of the public interest as to necessarily have

---

[62] *QCC* [2007] QCA 338, [47] (McMurdo P).
[63] [2007] NSWLEC 741. See also the later proceedings in *Kennedy* [2010] NSWLEC 129, [83]–[91] (Biscoe J).
[64] [2007] NSWLEC 741, [161].

demanded consideration.[65] However, it was noted that ESD principles *would* need to be addressed in similar cases in the future, and that failure to do so could be considered evidence of failure to take account of the public interest.

5.40 This came to pass in *Aldous* v. *Greater Taree City Council*,[66] which was concerned with whether a local council had neglected to consider principles of ESD when approving the construction of a new house in a beachfront area on the mid-north coast of NSW. It was argued that the Council had failed to take into account the public interest as required by section 79C of the EPAA. The NSWLEC distinguished *Walker*, concluding that as a consequence of increasing public concern with ESD, it was now a component of the public interest. However, the Court concluded that there had been no failure to take ESD principles into account, as the Council had considered relevant climate change impacts.

Merits review of administrative decisions

5.41 When empowered to engage in merits review, a court or tribunal stands in the shoes of the original decision-maker[67] and may take account of fresh evidence where necessary. In the context of Australian environmental law, rights to seek merits review are typically conferred on persons who have themselves sought to invoke statutory processes. It is less common for third party objectors to be afforded such rights, although exceptions often exist in connection with approval processes for major developments.[68]

5.42 The first Australian climate change case, *Greenpeace Australia Ltd* v. *Redbank Power Co. Pty Ltd*,[69] involved an application by Greenpeace for merits review of a decision to grant development consent under Part 4 of the EPAA for the construction of a coal-fired power station in NSW. It was contended that the operation of the plant would result in a net increase in CO_2 emissions from power stations in the state, and thus contribute to the greenhouse effect. The Court was invited to apply the precautionary principle and refuse development consent. Although Pearlman J

---

[65] *Walker* [2008] NSWCA 224. [66] [2009] NSWLEC 17.

[67] See e.g. Land and Environment Court Act 1979 (NSW), s. 39(2).

[68] Bates, *Environmental Law in Australia*, [18.2].

[69] (1994) 86 LGERA 143.

found that the proposed plant's CO_2 emissions would contribute to climate change, she considered that there was uncertainty as to their significance. After taking into account alleged environmental benefits of the development, Pearlman J approved the application. However, approval was made subject to various conditions, including a requirement to plant trees to offset emissions.

5.43   There have been numerous more recent merits review cases relating to climate change across Australian jurisdictions. Most have concerned whether climate change risks were adequately addressed when granting development approvals.[70] Litigants have been most active in Victoria, and VCAT has now developed a substantial climate change jurisprudence.

5.44   Initial cases such as *Gippsland Coastal Board* v. *South Gippsland Shire Council*[71] sought to address climate change risks in a context in which planning instruments made no specific mention of climate change impacts such as sea level rises and increasingly frequent severe storms. The Victorian government has since adopted the Victorian Coastal Strategy and the State Planning Policy Framework, with clause 13 of the latter setting out a detailed framework for planners in identifying and managing the coastal impacts of climate change. These matters are now explicitly considered in merits review.[72]

5.45   Another category of merits review case connected to climate change has concerned development applications for renewable energy projects, principally wind farms. In some instances, local residents have objected to such proposals because of adverse impacts such as damage to aesthetic values and noise. In *Taralga Landscape Guardians Inc.* v. *Minister for Planning*,[73] the NSWLEC sought to balance the concerns of local residents regarding a large wind farm in the Southern Tablelands of NSW

[70] See e.g. *Charles & Howard Pty Ltd* v. *Redland Shire Council* [2006] QPEC 95; *Northscape Properties Pty Ltd* v. *District Council of Yorke Peninsula* [2007] SAERDC 50; *Gippsland Coastal Board* v. *South Gippsland Shire Council (No. 2)* [2008] VCAT 1545; *Myers* v. *South Gippsland Shire Council* [2009] VCAT 1022; *Ronchi* v. *Wellington Shire Council* [2009] VCAT 1206; *Owen* v. *Casey City Council* [2009] VCAT 1946; *Myers* v. *South Gippsland Shire Council (No. 2)* [2009] VCAT 2414; *Cooke* v. *Greater Geelong City Council* [2010] VCAT 60; *Taip* v. *East Gippsland Shire Council* [2010] VCAT 1222.

[71] [2008] VCAT 1545.

[72] See e.g. *Kala Developments Pty Ltd* v. *Surf Coast Shire Council* [2010] VCAT 2106.

[73] [2007] NSWLEC 59. See also *Perry* v. *Hepburn Shire Council* [2007] VCAT 1309.

with the broader public interest in the increased generation of renewable energy. The Court resolved the case in favour of the latter, finding that the public benefits outweighed any detriment to the local community and particular landholders, and making particular reference to the principle of intergenerational equity.

Remedies

5.46   Success in challenges based on environmental protection and planning laws in Australia may be pyrrhic. Where matters have not been considered at first instance, they may subsequently be taken into account to no substantive effect. Moreover, further administrative or judicial consideration of the relevant issue may be pre-empted by legislative intervention.[74]

Assessment of public law litigation

5.47   The experience of litigants who have raised climate change concerns under the auspices of Australian public law has been mixed. However, it is worth bearing in mind that even 'unsuccessful' challenges may generate benefits of some kind.[75] Litigation may serve to draw attention to the likely impacts of proposed developments, and to related regulatory deficits. It may disrupt the assumptions on which GHG emitters base relevant planning and operational decisions. It may also oblige governments to publicly address considerations of policy that would otherwise be avoided.[76] Finally, litigation may draw into sharper focus judicial thinking on the causation of, and responsibility for, climate change impacts. Peel has commented that 'the primary contribution of the case law has been in developing a legal culture more

---

[74] For example, the effect of the decision in *QCC* [2007] QCA 338 was overturned by specific legislation passed by the Queensland Parliament (see C. McGrath, 'The Xstrata Case: Pyrrhic Victory or Harbinger?' in Bonyhady and Christoff, *Climate Law in Australia*, p. 214, at pp. 226–227; cf. *Australians for Sustainable Development Inc.* v. *Minister for Planning* [2011] NSWLEC 33; see also J. Smith, 'Special Cases: Planning and the Law in Australia', *Australian Environment Review*, 26 (2011), 66).

[75] See T. Bonyhady, 'The New Australian Climate Law' in Bonyhady and Christoff, *Climate Law in Australia*, p. 8, at pp. 20–4.

[76] See e.g. K. Ruddock, 'The Bowen Basin Coal Mines Case: Climate Law in the Federal Court' in Bonyhady and Christoff, *Climate Law in Australia*, p. 180, at pp. 182–3.

aware of the need to factor climate change considerations into environmental decision-making'.[77]

5.48   Overall, however, it is hard to avoid the conclusion that public law litigation provides at best an inefficient means of obliging governmental attention to climate change impacts. That concerned parties have resorted to it at all reflects the failure of governments to ensure that such impacts are balanced in relevant decision-making processes as a matter of course.

(C)   Private law[78]

5.49   Having considered various forms of litigation directed to compelling governmental action, Hsu (writing in the North American context) contends that 'seeking direct civil liability against those responsible for [GHG] emissions' is the only litigation strategy 'that holds out any promise of being a magic bullet'[79] in connection with climate change. Hsu observes:

> By targeting deep-pocketed private entities that actually emit [GHGs] … a civil litigation strategy, if successful, skips over the potentially cumbersome, time-consuming, and politically perilous route of pursuing legislation and regulation. The civil litigation strategy is potentially a means of regulation itself, as a finding of liability could have an enormous ripple effect and send [GHG] emitters scrambling to avoid the unwelcome spotlight.[80]

5.50   Despite the potential efficacy of private law action against entities associated with GHG emissions, the legal context in Australia provides reasons for circumspection, and no such action has been initiated to date. The discussion that follows will be framed around the prospects of negligence or nuisance proceedings against such entities, although it is important to note that private law litigation having a connection to climate change may take

[77] Peel, 'Climate Change Litigation', [8–215].

[78] Parts of this section have been adapted from an earlier publication by two of the authors: P. Cashman and R. Abbs, 'Liability in Tort for Damage Arising from Human Induced Climate Change' in R. Lyster (ed.), *In the Wilds of Climate Law* (Australian Academic Press, 2010), p. 235.

[79] S. Hsu, 'A Realistic Evaluation of Climate Change Litigation through the Lens of a Hypothetical Lawsuit', *University of Colorado Law Review*, 79 (2008), 701, 716–717.

[80] *Ibid.*, 717.

many other forms.[81] The range of potential plaintiffs reflects the multiplicity of direct and indirect harms that may be attributable to climate change impacts, although limitation issues will likely restrict the class of viable claims. For the purposes of illustration, we will refer to the law applicable in NSW, but endeavour to draw attention to different rules from other Australian jurisdictions where the circumstances warrant it.[82]

Negligence

5.51   Broadly speaking, negligence may be established where a defendant has breached a duty of care owed to a plaintiff, thereby causing harm to the plaintiff.

Duty of care

5.52   Despite numerous attempts,[83] no general formulation as to when a duty of care will exist has been deemed satisfactory.[84] Whilst in many circumstances a duty is recognised as a matter of course, difficulties arise when considering novel situations, particularly where the relationship between the plaintiff and a defendant is unfamiliar or tenuous.

5.53   It is necessary, but not sufficient, to show that harm to the plaintiff was a reasonably foreseeable consequence of a defendant's negligence,[85] and the courts can frequently be seen to be reaching for some additional factor said to justify or exclude the imposition of a duty in a particular case or class of cases. However, the jurisprudence has not crystallised into anything resembling a

---

[81] For example, Durrant considers the potential for legal action against: (a) local authorities responsible for adaptation initiatives; and (b) professionals who provide advice or services connected to climate change impacts (see Durrant, *Legal Responses to Climate Change*, Chs. 20, 21).

[82] The common law of torts is uniform throughout Australia, and the statutory regimes applicable in different states and territories are identical in many respects.

[83] See e.g. *Anns* v. *Merton LBC* [1978] AC 728; *Jaensch* v. *Coffey* (1984) 155 CLR 549, 578–587 (Deane J). See also Chapter 17, at para. 17.48.

[84] Cf. *Berrigan Shire Council* v. *Ballerini* (2005) 13 VR 111, 115 [8] (Callaway JA) (observing that '[t]he search for principle is worse than looking for a needle in a haystack. The needle is not there') ('*Ballerini*').

[85] See e.g. *Sutherland Shire Council* v. *Heyman* (1985) 157 CLR 424, 481 (Brennan J); *Sullivan* v. *Moody* (2001) 207 CLR 562, 576 [42], 583 [64] (Gleeson CJ, Gaudron, McHugh, Hayne and Callinan JJ) ('*Sullivan*').

neat checklist of factors to which it may be profitable to advert in circumstances of novelty. In *Sullivan* v. *Moody*,[86] the High Court of Australia noted that:

> Different classes of case give rise to different problems in determining the existence and nature or scope, of a duty of care. Sometimes the problems may be bound up with the harm suffered by the plaintiff, as, for example, where its direct cause is the criminal conduct of some third party. Sometimes they may arise because the defendant is the repository of a statutory power or discretion. Sometimes they may reflect the difficulty of confining the class of persons to whom a duty may be owed within reasonable limits. Sometimes they may concern the need to preserve the coherence of other legal principles, or of a statutory scheme which governs certain conduct or relationships. The relevant problem will then become the focus of attention in a judicial evaluation of the factors which tend for or against a conclusion, to be arrived at as a matter of principle.[87]

5.54   The 'factorial' approach affirmed in *Sullivan*[88] provides little guidance as to when a duty of care will be imposed in a case having no clear precedent, and may operate as a disincentive to path-breaking litigation. Some judges have candidly acknowledged that decision-making in this area is a product of 'trade-offs and value judgments',[89] in turn informed by 'questions of fairness, policy, practicality, proportion, expense and justice'.[90] The climate change context is particularly problematic because

---

[86] (2001) 207 CLR 562. See also *Roads and Traffic Authority of NSW* v. *Dederer* (2007) 234 CLR 330, 345 [43]–[44] (Gummow J); *Brodie* v. *Singleton Shire Council* [2001] 206 CLR 512.

[87] (2001) 207 CLR 562, 579–580 [50] (Gleeson CJ, Gaudron, McHugh, Hayne and Callinan JJ) (footnotes omitted).

[88] See also *Perre* v. *Apand Pty Ltd* (1999) 198 CLR 180 ('*Perre*'). Factors identified in *Perre* as being relevant to whether the defendant was subject to a duty to avoid causing purely economic loss to the plaintiff included: (a) whether the plaintiff was particularly 'vulnerable' to suffering harm by reason of the defendant's conduct; (b) whether the defendant had 'actual knowledge' of the risk of harm that eventuated, and of its magnitude; (c) whether the imposition of such a duty would raise the spectre of indeterminate liability, or burden the defendant 'out of all proportion to his wrong'; and (d) whether the harm that materialised would have been 'relatively easy to avoid'. See R. Mulheron, 'The March of Pure Economic Loss … but to Different Drums', *Canberra Law Review*, 7 (2003), 87, 89–95.

[89] *Ballerini* (2005) 13 VR 111, 115 [8] (Callaway JA).

[90] *Swain* v. *Waverley Municipal Council* (2005) 220 CLR 517, 547 [79] (McHugh J); cf. *Caparo* [1990] 2 AC 605, 618 (Lord Bridge of Harwich); *Sullivan* (2001) 207 CLR 562, 580 [53] (Gleeson CJ, Gaudron, McHugh, Hayne and Callinan JJ).

plaintiffs and defendants may be linked only by the fact that relevant harm has come to pass as a matter of fact.

5.55   In the first place, it may be very difficult to show that the harm alleged was a reasonably foreseeable consequence of the activities of a particular defendant. If a plaintiff cannot rely on any direct or specific relationship with such a defendant as supporting the existence of a duty,[91] a suit would presumably be founded on the latter's conduct with respect to the world at large, and such conduct may be both geographically and temporally divorced from any adverse consequences for the plaintiff.

5.56   Moreover, satisfying the court that it would be *appropriate* to recognise a duty as a matter of legal policy would likely be difficult. The *Sullivan* approach is inherently conservative. Recognising that negligence may consist in the fact of emitting GHGs that feed into a global phenomenon with worldwide effects would have unpredictable consequences, and raise the very real prospect of indeterminate liability. The cases suggest extreme reluctance to impose a duty in such circumstances.[92] Moreover, the diversity of agents to whose activities climate change may be attributed renders it arguable that to impose any significant measure of liability on a particular defendant would be to burden that defendant disproportionately.[93]

5.57   The significance of any lack of proximity between plaintiff and defendant is likely to be heightened where the harm alleged comprises purely economic loss.[94]

Standard of care/breach of duty

5.58   Even if it could be established that a relevant duty existed in a particular case, it might be difficult, if not impossible, to establish that a defendant has actually breached that duty. The issue

---

[91] See *Agar* v. *Hyde* (2000) 201 CLR 552, 578 [66]–[67] (Gaudron, McHugh, Gummow and Hayne JJ) ('*Agar*').

[92] Cf. e.g. *Agar* (2000) 201 CLR 552, 563 [19] (Gleeson CJ); *Sullivan* (2001) 207 CLR 562, 582 [61] (Gleeson CJ, Gaudron, McHugh, Hayne and Callinan JJ). See also *Perre* (1999) 198 CLR 180.

[93] Cf. *Perre* (1999) 198 CLR 180, 221–2 [108] (McHugh J).

[94] *Perre* (1999) 198 CLR 180.

of breach is now governed primarily by section 5B of the Civil Liability Act 2002 (NSW) ('CLA'),[95] which provides that:

(1) A person is not negligent in failing to take precautions against a risk of harm unless:

    (a) the risk was foreseeable (that is, it is a risk of which the person knew or ought to have known); and

    (b) the risk was not insignificant; and

    (c) in the circumstances, a reasonable person in the person's position would have taken those precautions.

(2) In determining whether a reasonable person would have taken precautions against a risk of harm, the court is to consider the following (amongst other relevant things):

    (a) the probability that the harm would occur if care were not taken;

    (b) the likely seriousness of the harm;

    (c) the burden of taking precautions to avoid the risk of harm;

    (d) the social utility of the activity that creates the risk of harm.

5.59   Section 5B appears in general to be affirmative of the antecedent common law,[96] albeit that some of its language differs slightly from that used in *Wyong Shire Council* v. *Shirt*,[97] previously regarded as the leading authority on breach of duty in Australia.[98] The Ipp Report, which provided the bedrock for much of the CLA, had expressed concern that the mere fact of foreseeability of risk was being taken as giving rise to a breach of duty without reference to the countervailing considerations now enumerated in section 5B(2).[99]

5.60   Thus, a court is required to consider whether a reasonable person in the defendant's position would have foreseen that his/her conduct created a 'not insignificant'[100] risk of injury to the plaintiff

---

[95] Similar provisions have been adopted in most other Australian jurisdictions.

[96] Cf. *Waverley Council* v. *Ferreira* [2005] NSWCA 418, [27] (Ipp JA); *Council of the City of Liverpool* v. *Turano* [2008] NSWCA 270, [362] (McColl JA) ('*Turano*'); *Bostik Australia Pty Ltd* v. *Liddiard* [2009] NSWCA 167, [94] (Beazley JA), [158] (Basten JA).

[97] (1980) 146 CLR 40 ('*Shirt*').

[98] See *New South Wales* v. *Fahy* (2007) 232 CLR 486.

[99] D. Ipp *et al.*, *Review of the Law of Negligence* (2002), 105 [7.14] ('Ipp Report').

[100] On the meaning of this phrase, see Ipp Report, 105 [7.15]; cf. B. McDonald, 'Legislative Intervention in the Law of Negligence: The Common Law, Statutory Interpretation and Tort Reform in Australia', *Sydney Law Review*, 27 (2005), 443, 465–6.

or a class of persons including the plaintiff. If so, the court must then consider what a reasonable person would have done by way of response to that risk. As Mason J commented in *Shirt*:

> The perception of the reasonable man's response calls for consideration of the magnitude of the risk and the degree of probability of its occurrence, along with the expense, difficulty and inconvenience of taking alleviating action and any other conflicting responsibilities which the defendant may have.[101]

5.61   In the context of climate change litigation, a court would be required to address itself to the risk that the particular type of harm concerned would come to pass as a result of climate change, rather than the risk of climate change occurring in its generality. Specifically, the court would need to consider whether a reasonable person in the position of the defendant should have anticipated the creation of such a risk. Self-evidently, this would present a variety of case-specific problems, differing according to the species of harm in question. Durrant has noted that climate change is an area in which 'knowledge of the risk of harm has developed over time',[102] and as such the relevant standard of care may have heightened as scientific knowledge has increased and awareness of the potential consequences of climate change has become more widespread. The position and character of the defendant(s) may also be of relevance. The fact that the damage in issue may have resulted from an unpredictable chain of events need not bar a finding of breach of duty; if the general species of risk that ultimately materialised should have been anticipated, the unlikelihood of the actual damage involved is not necessarily problematic. This may be of particular relevance to litigation dealing with extreme weather events.

5.62   The issue of whether a defendant ought to have taken precautions against the risk of harm is required to be addressed prospectively, that is, by 'look[ing] forward to identify what a reasonable person would have done, not backward to identify what would have avoided the injury'.[103] It is in this context that

---

[101]   *Shirt* (1980) 146 CLR 40, 47–48.

[102]   See Durrant, *Legal Responses to Climate Change*, pp. 274–5 (noting that a series of international agreements and reports might have significance in this connection).

[103]   *Turano* [2008] NSWCA 270, [364] (McColl JA) citing *New South Wales* v. *Fahy* (2007) 232 CLR 486, 505 [57] (Gummow and Hayne JJ).

the factors identified in section 5B(2) would be considered, with a focus on the reasonableness of the conduct of the defendant. The idea that 'the social utility of the activity that creates the risk of harm' should be taken into account may be particularly problematic in climate change litigation. It is difficult to know how a court is generally expected to go about evaluating such utility.[104] However, it would presumably be arguable that many, if not most, activities resulting in the emission of GHGs have some degree of usefulness, and the real issue would be whether precautions should have been taken to reduce their adverse effects at the relevant time. The reasonableness of taking particular precautions will be critical in this context. In some areas, it is conceivable that the only 'precaution' actually open to a defendant would have been to cease certain activities altogether. In other cases, it may be arguable that by failing to moderate or modify those activities (e.g. by making use of available technological improvements), a defendant failed to adhere to an acceptable standard of care.

5.63   One significant issue may relate to the degree to which society has become dependent on particular GHG-emitting activities. A court may be reluctant to hold that an emitter should have taken steps to reduce GHG emissions where doing so would have caused detriment or inconvenience to large sections of the population. Durrant points out that it may also be necessary to consider 'any relevant statutory or customary standards', observing that '[i]ndustries worldwide have *historically* emitted unabated [GHGs] since the time of the industrial revolution'.[105] Moreover, where a particular sector has been subject to relevant government regulation, it may be difficult to argue that an entity which complied with the applicable regime has breached any duty of care. This point is likely to have particular salience if litigation is brought with respect to emissions generated in a jurisdiction subject to a comprehensive regime along the lines of the CPRS.[106]

---

[104] McDonald, 'Legislative Intervention in the Law of Negligence', 466.
[105] N. Durrant, 'Tortious Liability for Greenhouse Gas Emissions? Climate Change, Causation and Public Policy Considerations', *Queensland University of Technology Law and Justice Journal*, 7 (2007), 404, 413 (emphasis in original).
[106] See above at [5.09]–[5.14].

Causation

5.64   From a plaintiff's point of view, causation is likely to raise two distinct problems. The first is doctrinal, and concerns the attribution of causal responsibility to a particular defendant in accordance with legal principle. The second is practical, and concerns the establishment *by evidence* of some kind of causal link between relevant negligence and the damage suffered. The difficulties likely to arise in the latter connection should not be underestimated. Even in the context of ordinary toxic tort litigation, the question of whether there is a factual connection between exposure to a particular product or substance and the harm suffered by a plaintiff may be complex, and the subject of conflicting, wide-ranging and expensive expert evidence. Climate change is likely to be significantly more complicated from an evidentiary point of view, and a defendant could be expected to commit significant resources to challenging the scientific foundation of any claim made against them. The science of climate change is complex, and in some respects uncertain.[107] A plaintiff may be forced to rely upon evidence said to establish a statistical association between the negligence alleged and the harm said to have been suffered.[108] Mank has observed that:

> Because climate is affected by several factors interacting in complex ways, it is difficult for scientists to tease out what percentage of any climate change is affected by GHGs, and it is even more difficult to determine what percentage is affected by a specific polluter or group of polluters ... Climate is a chaotic system affected by natural fluctuations in frequency and severity, so it is difficult to determine to what extent human activities, such as producing GHGs, affect those frequencies or variations.[109]

---

[107] Cf. Durrant, *Legal Responses to Climate Change*, pp. 279–281. However, scientific uncertainty is often exaggerated by vested interests (see N. Oreskes and E. Conway, *Merchants of Doubt* (Bloomsbury Press, 2010), Ch. 6).

[108] Cf. e.g. *Seltsam Pty Ltd* v. *McGuiness* (2000) 49 NSWLR 262.

[109] B. Mank, 'Civil Remedies' in M. Gerrard (ed.), *Global Climate Change and US Law* (American Bar Association, 2007), p. 183, at p. 201 (footnotes omitted). However, attribution studies are becoming more sophisticated (see e.g. Q. Schiermeier, 'Increased Flood Risk Linked to Global Warming', *Nature*, 470 (2011), 316).

The 'elements' of causation

5.65 In NSW,[110] section 5D of the CLA provides that:

'(1) A determination that negligence caused particular harm comprises the following elements:[111]

(a) that the negligence was a necessary condition of the occurrence of the harm (factual causation) and

(b) that it is appropriate for the scope of the negligent person's liability to extend to the harm so caused (scope of liability).

(2) In determining in an exceptional case,[112] in accordance with established principles, whether negligence that cannot be established as a necessary condition of the occurrence of harm should be accepted as establishing factual causation, the court is to consider[113] (amongst other relevant things) whether or not and why responsibility for the harm should be imposed on the negligent party.[114]

…

(4) For the purpose of determining the scope of liability, the court is to consider (amongst other relevant things) whether or not and why responsibility for the harm should be imposed on the negligent party.'

5.66 Precisely how these provisions alter the common law is yet to be completely resolved. Previously, causation in negligence revolved around a holistic 'commonsense' approach, described in *March* v. *Stramare (E & MH) Pty Ltd*[115] in terms specifically rejecting recourse to a structured, two-stage inquiry such as that

---

[110] Similar provisions have been enacted in other Australian jurisdictions (see Wrongs Act 1958 (Vic.), s. 51; Civil Liability Act 2002 (WA), s. 5C; Civil Liability Act 2003 (Qld), s. 11; Civil Liability Act 2002 (Tas.), s. 13; Civil Liability Act 1936 (SA), s. 34; Civil Law (Wrongs) Act 2002 (ACT), s. 45).

[111] The onus of proving 'any fact relevant to the issue of causation' is explicitly placed on the plaintiff: Civil Liability Act 2002 (NSW), s. 5E.

[112] In some jurisdictions, the relevant legislation refers to an 'appropriate' case: Wrongs Act 1958 (Vic.), s. 51(2); Civil Liability Act 2002 (WA), s. 5C(2).

[113] In Western Australia, the corresponding legislation also specifically obliges the court to consider 'whether and why the harm should be left to lie where it fell': Civil Liability Act 2002 (WA), s. 5C(2).

[114] Corresponding provisions in South Australia and the ACT are quite different in form (see Civil Liability Act 1936 (SA), s. 34(2); Civil Law (Wrongs) Act 2002 (ACT), s. 45(2)).

[115] (1991) 171 CLR 506 ('*March*').

now apparently compelled by section 5D.[116] Despite this, a series of decisions in NSW courts has taken the principles 'embodied' in section 5D to accord with the common law.[117] In light of comments by various members of the High Court,[118] this position may be untenable. The extent to which section 5D should be taken to signal something more than a semantic shift in the law of negligence remains unclear.[119] Aside from the fundamental issue of how the existence of 'elements' of causation affects the shape of the relevant inquiry, the provision also gives rise to particular uncertainty with respect to the domain and parameters of section 5D(2).

Factual causation

5.67   Because the individual agents responsible for the increased atmospheric concentration of GHGs are so numerous and dispersed, it is difficult to imagine that a plaintiff could *ever* show that the negligence of one such agent was a precondition to the realisation of particular climate change impacts.[120] Even a large-scale, long-term emitter of GHGs should be able to construct a compelling argument to the effect that its activities had made but a marginal relative contribution. This being the case, a plaintiff would likely be required to establish the fact of an 'exceptional case' in accordance with section 5D(2).

5.68   Problematically, section 5D(2) is extremely ambiguous.[121] It establishes that the 'but for' test can be circumvented, but does not speak to when or why. The provision was 'explained' prior to its enactment as follows:

---

[116] *March* (1991) 171 CLR 506, 515. See also *Bennett* v. *Minister of Community Welfare* (1992) 176 CLR 408, 412–413 (Mason, Deane and Toohey JJA).

[117] See in particular *Ruddock* v. *Taylor* (2003) 58 NSWLR 269.

[118] See *Travel Compensation Fund* v. *Tambree* (2005) 224 CLR 627, 643 [46]–[48] (Gummow and Hayne JJ), 653–4 [79]–[82] (Callinan J); *Adeels Palace Pty Ltd* v. *Moubarak* (2009) 239 CLR 420, [42]–[44] (French CJ, Gummow, Hayne, Heydon and Crennan JJ). See also McDonald, 'Legislative Intervention in the Law of Negligence', 474; S. Bartie, 'Ambition Versus Judicial Reality: Causation and Remoteness Under Civil Liability Legislation', *University of Western Australia Law Review*, 33 (2007), 415, 420–2.

[119] *Zanner* v. *Zanner* [2010] NSWCA 343, [11] (Allsop P).

[120] Cf. M. Allen and R. Lord, 'The Blame Game: Who Will Pay for the Damaging Consequences of Climate Change?', *Nature*, 432 (2004), 551, 552.

[121] See e.g. D. Mendelson, 'Australian Tort Law Reform: Statutory Principles of Causation and the Common Law', *Journal of Law and Medicine*, 11 (2004), 492, 503–4.

The rules for factual causation are set out, including the very limited exception to the 'but for' test. This exception was developed by the court for those rare cases, often in the dust diseases context, where there are particular evidentiary gaps. By including this exception in the bill it is not intended that the bill extend the common law in any way. Rather, it is to focus the courts on the fact that they should tread very carefully when considering a departure from the but for test.[122]

5.69   In general, an 'evidentiary gap' has been said to exist where two (or more) putative tortfeasors are implicated in particular loss or damage but the evidence is incapable of establishing the nature or extent of their respective causal contributions. The Ipp Report identified two distinct species of case in which such a gap might be bridged:

- a case in which harm 'is brought about by the *cumulative* operation of two or more factors, but … is indivisible in the sense that it is not possible to determine the relative contribution of the various factors to the total harm suffered', such as *Bonnington Casting* v. *Wardlaw*,[123] which was said to establish that one such factor 'can be treated as a cause of the total harm suffered, provided it made a "material contribution" to the harm';[124] and

- a case in which harm has resulted from one (or more) of two (or more) separate acts of negligence, but it cannot be determined which caused the harm as a matter of fact. In *Fairchild* v. *Glenhaven Funeral Services Ltd*,[125] the House of Lords held that in an appropriate case, any defendant whose conduct 'materially increased the risk' of the harm could be held liable.[126]

5.70   Whether or not the *Bonnington* principle should be regarded as 'exceptional' is debatable. Mendelson notes that whatever the specificity of its origins, the 'material contribution' idea 'has … been applied indiscriminately in any legal context'.[127] Indeed, explanations of causation at common law often eschewed reference to the

---

[122] New South Wales, *Parliamentary Debates*, Legislative Assembly, 23 October 2002, 5764.

[123] [1956] AC 613.   [124] Ipp Report, p. 109 [7.28].

[125] [2003] 1 AC 32 ('*Fairchild*'). See also *Barker* v. *Corus UK Ltd* [2006] 2 AC 572 ('*Barker*'); *Sienkiewicz* v. *Greif (UK) Ltd* [2011] UKSC 10 ('*Sienkiewicz*').

[126] Ipp Report, p. 110 [7.30].

[127] Mendelson, 'Australian Tort Law Reform', 500.

'but for' test altogether and instead used language evocative of *Bonnington*. For example, in *Henville* v. *Walker*, McHugh J said:

> If the defendant's breach has 'materially contributed' to the loss or damage suffered, it will be regarded as a cause of the loss or damage, despite other factors or conditions having played an even more significant role in producing the loss or damage. As long as the breach materially contributed to the damage, a causal connection will ordinarily exist even though the breach without more would not have brought about the damage.[128]

5.71   Despite this, recognition that a non-decisive 'material contribution' to harm amounts to a legal cause would now appear to be contingent on successful invocation of the 'exceptional case' mechanism contained in section 5D, with its broadly framed 'whether or not and why' inquiry. If this obstacle could be overcome, a critical question would concern the meaning of materiality in the circumstances of the case.[129] Much would presumably depend upon how close an analogy could be drawn between climate change and the medical phenomena in issue in cases like *Bonnington*.[130]

5.72   The decision in *Fairchild* has been extensively analysed elsewhere.[131] For present purposes, it will suffice to say that it may be of limited relevance in the climate change context. *Fairchild* was a case in which the plaintiff's injuries could have been caused by either or both of two different agents, but it was impossible to separate out their respective causal contributions. Crucially, each agent's conduct was sufficient to have caused those injuries of itself, and all relevant sources of risk to the plaintiffs were tortious.[132] By way of contrast, in a climate change case, a defendant could only (subject to evidentiary issues) be shown to have contributed in some finite degree to a generalised global process, which in turn could be shown to have caused harm to the

---

[128] (2001) 206 CLR 459, 493 [106] (footnote omitted); see also e.g. *Roads and Traffic Authority* v. *Royal* [2008] HCA 19, [85] (Kirby J), [143] (Kiefel J) ('*Royal*').
[129] Cf. *Amaca Pty Ltd v Ellis* (2010) 240 CLR 111, 136 [68] (French CJ, Gummow, Hayne, Heydon, Crennan, Kiefel and Bell JJ) ('*Amaca*'); *Sienkiewicz* [2011] UKSC 10, [107]–[108] (Lord Phillips).
[130] Cf. *Amaca* (2010) 240 CLR 111, 136 [67] (French CJ, Gummow, Hayne, Heydon, Crennan, Kiefel and Bell JJ).
[131] See e.g. J. Stapleton, 'Lords A'Leaping Evidentiary Gaps', *Torts Law Journal*, 10 (2002), 1, 11.
[132] See *ibid.*, 17 citing *Fairchild* [2003] 1 AC 32, 40 [2], 66–7 [33].

plaintiff, or at least increased the risk that such harm would be inflicted. It could never be established or assumed that the activities of that particular defendant were of themselves sufficient to that process in motion, even in theory.

5.73 The question of causation would, therefore, revolve around whether making some definite contribution to a process resulting from the cumulative effect of a multitude of such contributions (as well as extrinsic causes) could or should be regarded as a legal cause – not whether a *possible* cause of harm should be deemed to be a cause-in-fact for reasons of justice and fairness.[133] It would not be a case, like *Fairchild*, in which the defendant *may* have caused the harm by itself, *may* have caused the harm in conjunction with another party, or *may* not have contributed to the harm at all. This would seem to affirm the centrality of the materiality question alluded to above. That said, an approach based on *Fairchild* could potentially find some application in the specific factual context of extreme weather events.[134]

Scope of liability

5.74 Section 5D(1)(b) of the CLA directs attention to the normative aspect of causation. The requirement that a decision-maker consider whether it is 'appropriate' to impose liability on a particular defendant would appear, on its face, to leave an extraordinary variety of factors in play. The Ipp Report observed that the kind of 'policy' matters going to 'scope of liability'[135] tend to require evaluation 'case-by-case rather than by the application of detailed rules and principles'.[136]

5.75 Some considerations which may be relevant to the 'scope of liability' in climate change litigation include:
  - the significance of the causal contribution of the defendant to climate change relative to other causative factors (both

---

[133] Cf. *Fairchild* [2003] 1 AC 32, 68 [36] (Lord Nicholls of Birkenhead).

[134] See Chapter 17, at para. 17.61.

[135] The Ipp Report specified that such matters included considerations typically discussed by reference to such concepts as 'legal cause', 'real and effective cause', 'commonsense causation', 'foreseeability' and 'remoteness of damage', although its treatment of these issues has been criticised (see McDonald, 'Legislative Intervention in the Law of Negligence', 474).

[136] Ipp Report, 115 [7.45].

anthropogenic and natural). If the defendant's negligent activities have made but a minor contribution, a court might conclude that those activities were not a 'real' or 'effective' or 'commonsense' cause of the particular damage alleged. It might also be said that natural phenomena ought to be taken to have 'broken' whatever chain of causation exists as a matter of fact;

- the degree to which the end result of the chain of causation (that is, the damage) is removed from the defendant's negligent conduct. If the damage is distant in space or time, or has been produced in an unpredictable or improbable manner, a court might decline to make the defendant responsible for it;
- other policy considerations, including some of those which might also arise in connection with whether there has been a breach of duty, particularly those concerned with the broader consequences of imposing liability in the specific type of case in issue.

5.76   In the result, even if a plaintiff could find a means of establishing what section 5D of the CLA calls 'factual causation', we agree with Durrant that 'it is highly probable that the Court would conclude that it is *not* appropriate to impose liability for the emission of [GHGs] and the resulting … harm'.[137]

Nuisance

5.77   The tort of private nuisance is concerned with serious and unreasonable interference with the use of, or rights over, land. By contrast, public nuisance is addressed to conduct causing general affront to a broader section of the population.[138] Both heads of nuisance may be enlivened by adverse effects associated with 'emissions', and in one sense public nuisance seems particularly apposite to the climate change context. However, broadly speaking, the law is poorly adapted to dealing with the consequences of large-scale industrial activity, and has rarely ventured beyond cases involving close geographical propinquity:

---

[137]   Durrant, 'Tortious Liability for Greenhouse Gas Emissions?', 421 (emphasis in original).
[138]   See Chapter 17, at para. 17.43.

> Nuisance law plays its most characteristic role in the resolution of small-scale local disputes between neighbouring landowners into which regulators cannot or will not intervene.[139]

5.78 Considerations of space preclude a comprehensive examination of the principles underpinning the law of nuisance, but several general theoretical problems would seem to present themselves:

- nuisance cases concerning emissions have typically involved their direct transmission to affected locations. In a climate change case, emissions would have fed into a global phenomenon having incidental regional effects. Whether the law would accommodate a situation in which the activities of the defendant are not proximate to the pleaded interference in a conventional sense, and the defendant lacks genuine control over the interference, is open to question. It is probable that considerations of remoteness would come into play;[140]

- the requirement that interference said to amount to nuisance be 'unreasonable' calls for a value judgement in the circumstances of the case.[141] It is likely that many of the policy considerations referred to above in connection with negligence would also deter a court from holding GHG-emitting activities to be 'unreasonable' in the nuisance context;

- inherent in the 'unreasonableness' test is the idea that individuals must show a degree of tolerance for interferences or inconveniences that are endemic to a particular area. The law does not recognise an absolute right to protection from bothersome activities. Subjection to local manifestations of a phenomenon like climate change is in one sense a normal incident of human existence.

5.79 Thus, while the law of nuisance might have the potential to short-circuit some of the complications associated with the law of negligence, it has severe limitations and raises a number of doctrinal hurdles of its own. Moreover, an action in nuisance would

---

[139] F. Trindade, P. Cane and M. Lunney, *The Law of Torts in Australia*, 4th edn (Oxford University Press, 2007), p. 167. See also J. Conaghan and W. Mansell, *The Wrongs of Tort*, 2nd edn (Pluto Press, 1999), p. 132.

[140] See R. Balkin and J. Davis, *The Law of Torts*, 4th edn (LexisNexis Butterworths, 2008), [14.57].

[141] See Trindade *et al.*, *The Law of Torts in Australia*, pp. 169–173, 195–6.

not permit a plaintiff to evade the kind of scientific difficulties and problems of proof that a negligence suit would raise.

Further issues

5.80   Difficulties in dealing with substantive law do not exhaust the problems that would face the proponent of a tort-based climate change lawsuit.[142]

Remedies

5.81   It is important to note that for all of the effort likely to be expended in pursuing a claim in respect of climate change impacts, any redress potentially available may be relatively nominal and/or ineffective to check the activities of GHG emitters. Of course, the significance of this concern will depend upon the objectives of the plaintiff in bringing proceedings.

5.82   In relation to damages, the CLA provides that in so far as a civil claim for economic loss or damage to property is concerned, a proportionate liability regime applies, such that:

> the liability of a defendant who is a concurrent wrongdoer in relation to that claim is limited to an amount reflecting that proportion of the damage or loss claimed that the court considers just having regard to the extent of the defendant's responsibility for the damage or loss.[143]

5.83   Given that any individual emitter's causal contribution to climate change would probably be considered relatively nominal, it is difficult to imagine a court awarding any significant monetary damages to a plaintiff under such a provision. In any event, precisely how a court would go about determining the extent to which a defendant should be held responsible by reason of such contribution is less than clear. Some commentators have suggested that something resembling the 'market share' theory of liability that has been used by some courts in the United States to 'approximate' the responsibility of defendants in causally intractable drug liability cases[144] could be adapted to the climate

---

[142]   See also below at [5.91]–[5.98] (dealing with costs in litigation).

[143]   Civil Liability Act 2002 (NSW), s. 35(1)(a).

[144]   See e.g. *Brown* v. *Superior Court (Abbott Laboratories)* 75 1 P 2d 470 (1988) and *Hymowitz* v. *Eli Lilly & Co*, 539 NE 2d 1069 (1989), cited *Barker* [2006] AC 572, 593 [45] (Lord Hoffmann).

change context.[145] However, aside from raising significant practical problems, it is arguable that such a solution would operate to distort defendants' relative culpability, and thereby offend basic principles of justice.[146]

5.84   It may be that a plaintiff would be more interested in seeking to restrain GHG-producing activities by means of a prohibitory injunction. The jurisdiction of a court to grant an injunction is discretionary. It would probably be difficult to persuade a court to grant any kind of interlocutory injunction in proceedings against a GHG emitter given that the plaintiff would need to show that his or her prospects of ultimate success were sufficient to justify restraining relevant activities in the meantime, taking account of the (probably significant) practical consequences of doing so.[147] Moreover, a plaintiff seeking interim relief would ordinarily be required to provide an undertaking as to damages in connection with the effects of any prohibitory order sought.

Civil liability of government bodies

5.85   Government bodies, and particularly local authorities, may face claims in tort as a result of their action or inaction in response to risks arising from climate change impacts.[148] However, the potential liability of such bodies is narrowed significantly by a patchwork of statutory exemptions and protections.[149] As

[145] E. Penalver, 'Acts of God or Toxic Torts? Applying Tort Principles to the Problem of Climate Change', *Natural Resources Journal*, 38 (1998), 563, 592; cf. J. Smith and D. Shearman, *Climate Change Litigation: Analysing the Law, Scientific Evidence and Impacts on the Environment, Health and Property* (Presidian Legal Publications, 2006), pp. 110–111.

[146] See Cashman and Abbs, 'Liability in Tort', pp. 258–9.

[147] *Beecham Group Ltd* v. *Bristol Laboratories Pty Ltd* (1968) 118 CLR 618; *Australian Broadcasting Corporation* v. *O'Neill* (2006) 227 CLR 57.

[148] See e.g. Z. Lipman and R. Stokes, 'Shifting Sands: The Implications of Climate Change and a Changing Coastline for Private Interests and Public Authorities in Relation to Waterfront Land', *Environmental and Planning Law Journal*, 20 (2003), 406; J. McDonald, 'The Adaptation Imperative: Managing the Legal Risks of Climate Change Impacts' in Bonyhady and Christoff, *Climate Law in Australia*, p. 124; P. England, 'Heating Up: Climate Change and the Evolving Responsibilities of Local Government', *Local Government Law Journal*, 13 (2008), 209; B. Preston, 'Climate Change Litigation' (Paper presented at the 'Climate Change Governance after Copenhagen' Conference, Hong Kong, 4 November 2010), 10; Durrant, *Legal Responses to Climate Change*, Ch. 20.

[149] See Durrant, *Legal Responses to Climate Change*, Ch. 20.

Durrant concludes, the ambit of liability of government bodies in Australia is closely confined and diminishing further as these continue to expand.[150]

A class or representative action?

5.86   In theory, proceedings seeking compensation for climate change harms would seem ideally suited to commencement under class or representative action rules.[151] However, this may be unattractive where the extraction of money from the defendant is not the primary aim of the proponent. In particular, the commencement of the proceedings in class or representative form would compound their complexity, inflate the costs bound up in their outcome, present the defendant with additional non-substantive grounds of attack and increase the likelihood of inordinate interlocutory delay.[152]

5.87   On the other hand, it may be that a public interest organisation would see strategic benefit in vesting proceedings with a 'participatory' character. Moreover, the aggregation of a large number of claims may have the effect of raising the stakes for the defendant, although it is difficult to say whether this would be of any net benefit to a plaintiff.

Assessment of private law litigation

5.88   It would be premature to conclude that tort litigation seeking to prevent or redress climate change impacts in Australia is bound to fail. However, as the foregoing discussion demonstrates, it is reasonable to expect that such litigation will raise a host of practical problems and prove difficult to accommodate under existing substantive law. Indeed, it is arguable, on a general level, that private law processes are ill-adapted to dealing with a problem in the nature of climate change. There is considerable force to the comment of Boutrous and Lanza that relevant issues:

> must be confronted at the national and international levels by [government]. They cannot rationally be addressed through piecemeal

---

[150] *Ibid.*, p. 297.
[151] See e.g. Supreme Court Act 1986 (Vic.), Pt. 4A; Uniform Civil Procedure Rules 2005 (NSW), rr. 7.4–7.5.
[152] See generally P. Cashman, *Class Action Law and Practice* (The Federation Press, 2007).

and ad hoc tort litigation seeking injunctive relief – or, even worse,
billions of dollars in retroactive and future money damages – against
targeted industries for engaging in lawful and comprehensively-regu-
lated conduct.[153]

5.89   Nonetheless, in the near term, carefully targeted private law litigation may have value as part of broader efforts to draw public
notice to aspects of climate change, stimulate political responses
and influence corporate behaviour. Such litigation may, even if
only indirectly, play an important role in deterring hazardous
conduct.[154]

(D)   Practicalities: litigation costs

5.90   The costs involved in maintaining climate change litigation in
Australia are liable to present an immense problem, even for
well-resourced litigants. The expense involved in mounting an
action is likely to be significant, particularly where a substantial volume of scientific and other expert evidence is called for.
Moreover, a party is also ordinarily at risk of being ordered to pay
the legal costs of his or her opponent if unsuccessful.[155] Such costs
may far exceed that party's pecuniary interest, if any, in the outcome of the case. Accordingly, it is hardly surprising that costs
have been identified by the Environment Defenders Office (Vic.)
as 'the major barrier to environmental litigation in Australia'.[156]

5.91   In most Australian jurisdictions, the ordinary rule that 'costs follow the event' may be displaced at the discretion of the court.[157]

---

[153] T. J. Boutrous Jr. and D. Lanza, 'Global Warming Tort Litigation: The Real "Public
Nuisance"', *Ecology Law Currents*, 35 (2008), 80, 81; cf. Peel, 'The Role of Climate Change
Litigation', 103.

[154] Cf. *Royal* [2008] HCA 19, [114] (Kirby J).

[155] The risk may be lessened by particular statutory regimes, notably in the merits review
context (see e.g. Bates, *Environmental Law in Australia*, [18.7]). In some jurisdictions
(e.g. VCAT) costs are not awarded as a matter of course.

[156] Environment Defenders Office (Victoria), 'Costing the Earth? The Case for Public
Interest Costs Protection in Environmental Litigation' (September 2010), 6.

[157] On the principles relevant to the exercise of costs discretion in the Federal Court, see
Ruddock v. *Vadarlis (No. 2)* (2001) 115 FCR 229, at 234–5 [11] (Black CJ and French J)
('*Vadarlis*'). In proceedings before the NSWLEC, a recent amendment to the rules spe-
cifically provides that the Court may exercise its discretion not to order costs in public
interest litigation (see Land and Environment Court Rules 2007 (NSW), r. 4.2; *Gray* v.
Macquarie Generation (No. 2) [2010] NSWLEC 82; *Delta Electricity* v. *Blue Mountains
Conservation Society Inc.* [2010] NSWCA 263, [203] (Basten JA) ('*Delta*').

However, courts have typically been cautious in circumventing that rule in favour of litigants claiming to represent the public interest,[158] and in practice such litigants are rarely insulated from the risk of having to pay other parties' costs if they lose. In *Oshlack* v. *Richmond River Council*, Kirby J noted that:

> Courts, whilst sometimes taking the legitimate pursuit of public interest into account, have also emphasised, rightly in my view, that litigants espousing the public interest are not thereby granted an immunity from costs or a 'free kick' in litigation.[159]

5.92   The reluctance of the courts to grant costs concessions to public interest litigants would appear partly to arise from the amorphous quality of the public interest concept, which makes it difficult to consistently justify exceptions to the ordinary rule.[160] It has often been noted that many cases involve a public interest of some kind.[161] It has also been emphasised that even where a litigant has genuinely and conscientiously sought to pursue a public interest, regard must be had to the position of any defendant unwillingly dragged into court. In *Oshlack*, McHugh J pointedly observed that 'sympathy is not a legitimate basis to deprive a successful party of his or her costs'.[162]

5.93   In general, only a confluence of special circumstances[163] is likely to convince a court to depart from the ordinary costs rule, where it

---

[158] Australian Law Reform Commission, *Costs Shifting – Who Pays for Litigation* (Report No. 75, 1995), [13.3]–[13.4]. See e.g. *Oshlack* v. *Richmond River Council* (1998) 193 CLR 72 ('*Oshlack*'); *Vadarlis* (2001) 115 FCR 229; *Save the Ridge Inc.* v. *Commonwealth* [2006] FCAFC 51 ('*Save the Ridge*').

[159] (1998) 193 CLR 72, 123 [134] (footnote omitted).

[160] Cf. *Oshlack* (1998) 193 CLR 72, 100 [75] (McHugh J); *Buddhist Society of Western Australia (Inc.)* v. *Shire of Serpentine-Jarrahdale* [1999] WASCA 55, [11] (Kennedy, Wallwork and Murray JJ); *QAAH of 2004* v. *Minister for Immigration and Multicultural and Indigenous Affairs* [2004] FCA 1644, [5] (Dowsett J).

[161] See e.g. *Oshlack* (1998) 193 CLR 72, 98–9 [71] (McHugh J); *Ruddock* (2001) 115 FCR 229, 238 [19] (Black CJ and French J); *Northern Territory* v. *Doepel (No. 2)* [2004] FCA 46, [11] (Mansfield J).

[162] *Oshlack* (1998) 193 CLR 72, 106 [90] (McHugh J).

[163] See e.g. *Save the Ridge* [2006] FCAFC 51; *Wilderness Society Inc.* v. *Turnbull* [2007] FCA 1863; *Your Water Your Say Inc.* v *Minister for the Environment, Heritage and the Arts (No. 2)* [2008] FCA 900 ('*YWYS No 2*'). In *Engadine Area Traffic Action Group Inc.* v. *Sutherland Shire Council (No. 2)* [2004] NSWLEC 434, [15], Lloyd J referred to five factors to be taken into account in determining whether litigation was in the public interest: (1) the public interest said to be served by the litigation; (2) the size and nature of the group of people said to be affected; (3) whether the case involves enforcement of public

applies.[164] The fact that particular climate change litigation raises issues of some novelty may not suffice to compel such departure. Although Australian courts have sometimes chosen to make no orders as to costs in public environmental law cases,[165] anticipating when a court will be receptive to the claim that a litigant has acted in the public interest remains difficult. Uncertainty as to the costs consequences of bringing particular proceedings may of itself ensure that they are never seriously contemplated,[166] especially when it is likely that success at first instance will simply trigger appeal proceedings that magnify the proponent's costs exposure. Mechanisms by which the attitude of a court to the issue of costs may be anticipated are presently very limited.[167]

5.94   The *Wildlife Whitsunday* case[168] provides a vivid illustration of the costs implications of environmental litigation. As Ruddock observes:

> The … case [only] occurred because the client was prepared to risk their organisation to run the litigation. As an organisation with no paid staff or recurrent funding, they were able to take this risk. It was also possible because they obtained a fee waiver for the Federal Court fees, and pro bono … legal assistance …
>
> As a result of the adverse costs order that resulted from the unsuccessful litigation, Wildlife Whitsunday voluntarily agreed to wind up their organisation.[169]

---

law obligations; (4) whether the 'prime motivation' is to uphold the public interest and the rule of law; and (5) whether the proponent has a pecuniary interest in the outcome.

[164] Cf. Victorian Law Reform Commission, *Civil Justice Review*, Report No. 14 (2008), p. 670. It should be noted that the question of costs does not require 'all or nothing' decision (see e.g. *Mees* v. *Kemp (No. 2)* [2004] FCA 549, [20]–[21] (Weinberg J)).

[165] See e.g. *Oshlack* (1998) 193 CLR 72; *Blue Wedges Inc.* v. *Minister for Environment, Heritage and the Arts* (2008) 165 FCR 211; *Minister for Planning* v. *Walker (No. 2)* [2008] NSWCA 334. In other cases, courts have declined to depart from the usual rule (see e.g. *YWYS No. 2* [2008] FCA 900; *Hastings Point Progress Association Inc.* v. *Tweed Shire Council (No. 3)* [2010] NSWCA 39). In some proceedings, costs have been apportioned (see e.g. *Wilderness Society Inc.* v. *Hon Malcolm Turnbull, Minister for Environment and Water Resources* [2008] FCAFC 19; *Lansen* v. *Minister for Environment and Heritage (No. 3)* [2008] FCA 136/.

[166] See Environment Defenders Office, 'Costing the Earth?', 20.

[167] Cf. e.g. *British Columbia (Minister of Forests)* v. *Okanagan Indian Band* [2003] 3 SCR 371; *R (Corner House Research)* v. *The Secretary of State for Trade and Industry* [2005] EWCA Civ 192. See also Australian Law Reform Commission, *Costs Shifting*, Ch. 13; Victorian Law Reform Commission, *Civil Justice Review*, pp. 667–676.

[168] *Wildlife Whitsunday* [2006] FCA 736. See above at [5.33].

[169] Ruddock, 'The Bowen Basin Coal Mines Case', p. 184.

5.95   In sum, even with a respectable substantive case and exemplary motives, the proponent of climate change related proceedings will frequently be required not only to foot the considerable expense of assembling an arguable claim, but also to accept the real risk of an adverse costs award in the event of failure. The difficulties are likely to be acute where the use of private law against private parties is contemplated.

Costs limiting orders and security for costs

5.96   In order to mitigate the deterrent effect of a potential costs order, a 'public interest' litigant may seek an order, early in the proceedings, imposing a limit on any costs which may be ordered at their conclusion.[170] In the Federal Court, such an order has been held to also limit the costs able to be recovered by such a litigant in the event of success.[171]

5.97   On the other hand, a defendant may seek an order that the plaintiff provide an amount of money or guarantee by way of security to meet some or all of the defendant's costs at the conclusion of the proceedings.[172] Although security for costs orders are not normally made against individual litigants who are impecunious, a corporate litigant which is unlikely to be able to meet any order for costs made against it may be ordered to provide security. Where an order for security for costs is made against a public interest litigant, it may have the (no doubt sometimes intended) effect of terminating or staying the litigation. In the NSWLEC, a security for costs order was recently made against a conservation group in a pollution case.[173]

---

[170] See e.g. Federal Court Rules, O. 62A; cf. *Woodlands* v. *Permanent Trustee Company Ltd* (1995) 58 FCR 139; *Corcoran* v. *Virgin Blue Airlines Pty Ltd* [2008] FCA 864 ('*Corcoran*'). Similar orders can be sought from the NSWLEC pursuant to Uniform Civil Procedure Rules 2005, r. 42.4: cf. *Blue Mountains Conservation Society Inc.* v. *Delta Electricity* [2009] NSWLEC 150; *Delta* [2010] NSWCA 263. In *Caroona Coal Action Group Inc.* v. *Coal Mines Australia Pty Ltd* [2009] NSWLEC 165, Preston CJ declined to make a costs limiting order.

[171] See e.g. *Corcoran* [2008] FCA 864, [5] (Bennett J); cf. *Delta* [2010] NSWCA 263, [187]–[188] (Basten JA) (noting that 'the language of the [Uniform Civil Procedure Rules 2005 (NSW)] imposes no such constraint').

[172] See e.g. Uniform Civil Procedure Rules 2005 (NSW), r. 42.21; Corporations Act 2001 (Cth), s. 1335; Land and Environment Court Rules 2007 (NSW), r. 4.2(2).

[173] *Blue Mountains Conservation Society Inc.* v. *Delta Electricity (No. 2)* [2009] NSWLEC 193. Leave to appeal was refused: *Delta Electricity* v. *Blue Mountains Conservation Society Inc. (Security for Costs)* [2010] NSWCA 264.

(E)   Other law

5.98   Climate change has supplied the impetus for, or the backdrop to, legal proceedings in a range of other contexts, and it is reasonable to assume that different kinds of cases with climate change connections will continue to appear.

Trade practices law

5.99   The Australian Consumer Law allows 'any person' to seek injunctive and/or declaratory relief in respect of misleading or deceptive conduct, or conduct likely to mislead or deceive, in trade or commerce.[174]

5.100   The Australian Competition and Consumer Commission ('ACCC') is the federal body charged with supervising compliance with trade practices law, and has examined a range of claims made by businesses to the effect that their products or services have low or neutral climate change impacts.[175] For example, the ACCC took action against GM Holden Ltd, the distributor of Saab vehicles in Australia, which claimed in its advertising that Saab cars offered 'carbon neutral' motoring. The Federal Court granted declarations that GM Holden had made false and misleading statements, contravening sections 52 and 53(c) of the Trade Practices Act 1974 (Cth).[176] The ACCC has recently indicated that enforcement action in respect of 'greenwashing' in advertising remains a priority.[177]

Criminal law

5.101   Climate change is likely to intersect with the criminal law in a variety of ways, which may multiply if concern about climate change

[174] See Competition and Consumer Act 2010, Sch. 2. The ACL came into force on 1 January 2011, superseding provisions found in twenty Commonwealth, state and territory laws. These laws will continue to apply to transactions and conduct that occurred before the coming into force of the ACL. See www.consumerlaw.gov.au.

[175] See Durrant, *Legal Responses to Climate Change*, pp. 321–5; Preston, 'Climate Change Litigation', 12–16.

[176] *Australian Competition and Consumer Commission* v. *GM Holden Ltd (ACN 006 893 232)* [2008] FCA 1428. The Trade Practices Act 1974 (Cth) was the federal precursor to the ACL.

[177] Australian Competition and Consumer Commission, *Annual Report 2009–10* (Commonwealth of Australia, 2010), p. 191.

becomes more widespread, climate change impacts become more severe or relevant regulatory schemes proliferate. A recent report produced by the Australian Institute of Criminology observes, for example, that carbon offsetting and emissions trading schemes create new opportunities for fraud and corruption.[178] The report further notes that climate change impacts may spur an increase in crimes such as water theft, illegal fishing and wildlife poaching.[179]

5.102   Increasing concern about climate change may also see a rise in civil unrest.[180] Criminal proceedings have already been brought against climate change activists for activities involving alleged damage to, or interference with, private property and public infrastructure (such as ports and railways used to transport coal for export).[181] In the United Kingdom, such activists have sometimes been able to invoke lawful justification as a defence.[182] Defendants in Australia have typically had less success in avoiding conviction, except in cases where there has been no demonstrable physical interference with, or alteration to, property.[183]

Public international law

5.103   It is possible to identify three types of international proceedings in which Australia may become involved. The first are what might be termed 'progressive' proceedings designed to bring positive outcomes for global climate policy by enforcing emissions cuts in an international court or tribunal like the International Court of Justice or the International Tribunal for the Law of the Sea. Australia could conceivably be an applicant or a respondent in such proceedings. The second category of international litigation is 'regressive' in the sense that it may be brought to prevent

---

[178] S. Bricknell, *Environmental Crime in Australia* (Australian Institute of Criminology, 2010), p. 6.

[179] *Ibid.*

[180] See A. Bergin and R. Allen, *The Thin Green Line: Climate Change and Australian Policing* (Australian Strategic Policy Institute, 2008), p. 5.

[181] Protesters may also be the target of less conventional legal proceedings (see e.g. T. Anthony, 'Quantum of Strategic Litigation – Quashing Public Participation', *Australian Journal of Human Rights*, 14(2) (2009), 1).

[182] See Chapter 17, at paras. 17.79–17.80.

[183] *Director of Public Prosecutions* v. *Fraser and O'Donnell* [2008] NSWSC 244.

Australia or other States from implementing policies to reduce emissions if these have the effect of interfering with other norms such as those relating to trade liberalisation. A third, more likely, category of international proceedings comprises 'administrative' proceedings such as those available under the Kyoto Protocol compliance regime to ensure that Australia adheres to its obligations.[184]

5.104   In relation to the first category, there are several norms of both customary and conventional character that could be used by States impacted by climate change as a basis for proceedings against States that have failed to take steps to limit GHG emissions. Several Pacific island States specifically declared on signing and ratifying the FCCC and Kyoto Protocol that joining the climate regime in no way constituted a renunciation of any rights under international law concerning State responsibility for the adverse effects of climate change.[185] As with domestic tort law proceedings, international proceedings based on State responsibility for transboundary damage are unlikely to be successful, primarily due to the difficulty of determining causation of specific climate change impacts.

5.105   Potentially more promising 'progressive' litigation is that making specific reference to treaty provisions that have a bearing on climate change policy. An example is the 1972 World Heritage Convention,[186] which imposes obligations upon States Parties such as Australia to protect and transmit to future generations outstanding world cultural and natural heritage. The two world heritage sites in Australia most vulnerable to climate change are the Great Barrier Reef (which has already experienced widespread coral bleaching as a result of elevated water temperatures) and Kakadu National Park (which is threatened by rising sea levels). Other 'progressive' proceedings could be pursued before human rights complaints bodies such as the UN Human Rights

---

[184] See further T. Stephens, 'International Courts and Climate Change: "Progression", "Regression" and "Administration"' in Lyster, *In the Wilds of Climate Law*, p. 53.

[185] See http://unfccc.int/essential_background/convention/items/5410.php (UNFCC); http://unfccc.int/kyoto_protocol/status_of_ratification/items/5424.php (Kyoto Protocol).

[186] Opened for signature 16 November 1972, [1975] ATS 47 (entered into force 16 December 1975), arts. 4, 5.

Committee, which Australia has recognised as having competence to examine individual human rights communications.[187]

5.106   'Regressive' proceedings through the World Trade Organization
('WTO') dispute settlement system appear increasingly likely
if States lose patience with the slow pace of negotiations on the
climate change regime and seek to take unilateral measures to
impose trade restrictions on the import of carbon-intensive products. Although the WTO has developed an important body of
jurisprudence accepting the legitimacy of certain unilateral trade
measures designed to protect exhaustible natural resources,[188]
how it would address a measure such as a border tax arrangement
implemented as part of a national ETS remains highly uncertain.
The attitude of the Australian government to such measures is
also unclear, as it has generally been a strong and active supporter
of the global trade liberalisation agenda, and has participated as
a third party in proceedings in the WTO supporting challenges
to measures such as the European Union's moratorium on the
import of genetically modified agricultural products.[189]

5.107   Finally, Australia could be the target of 'administrative' proceedings within the climate change regime itself if it fails to meet its
procedural or substantive obligations under the Kyoto Protocol
or its successor. The Kyoto Protocol compliance procedure has
begun to be utilised to deal with a number of what are termed
by the regime to be 'questions of implementation', with alleged
or actual non-compliance with procedural obligations by four
States (Greece, Canada, Croatia and Bulgaria) considered by the
Enforcement Branch of the compliance system.

(F)   Conclusion

5.108   Bonyhady has observed that despite the heterogeneity of the
Australian public law cases, it is possible to discern a nascent body

---

[187] See further O. Cordes-Holland, 'The Sinking of the Strait: The Implications of Climate
Change for Torres Strait Islanders' Human Rights Protected by the *ICCPR*', *Melbourne
Journal of International Law*, 9 (2008), 405.
[188] See T. Stephens, *International Courts and Environmental Protection* (Cambridge
University Press, 2009), Ch. 10.
[189] *European Communities – Measures Affecting the Approval and Marketing of Biotech
Products*, WTO Doc WT/DS291/R, WT/DS292/R, WT/DS293/R (2006) (Report of the
Panel).

of 'climate law', with the science of climate change and issues of causation and proof being drawn into sharper focus.[190] It is likely that aspects of the public law jurisprudence will influence the approach of courts to private law climate change litigation, if and when it materialises. However, climate change as a legal subject matter raises formidable substantive and practical problems, and it is difficult to predict the direction in which the relevant law will develop.

[190] See T. Bonyhady, 'The New Australian Climate Law' in Bonyhady and Christoff, *Climate Law in Australia*, pp. 8, 13.

6

China

DENG HAIFENG

(A) Introduction

The Chinese legal system

6.01   The People's Republic of China ('PRC'/'China') is situated in
Eastern Asia, bounded by the Pacific in the East. The third largest country in the world, after Canada and Russia, it has an area
of 9.6 million square kilometres, or one-fifteenth of the world's
landmass. China is a united and multi-ethnic country, with a
unitary system of government yet a multi-tiered legal system.
The development of the current legal system began in the early
1980s. China has a long tradition of civil law systems dating back
to the Qing Dynasty. This tradition has to a large extent been
maintained to the present day. There is a vast network of laws and
regulations in China. As of 2010, there are a total of 236 national
laws, more than 690 administrative regulations and more than
8,600 local laws and regulations.[1]

6.02   The main sources of the law in China include the laws enacted
by the National People's Congress ('NPC'), which have the highest authority, administrative regulations enacted by the State
Council, which cannot be in conflict with statutes, and local
laws and regulations enacted by provincial legislatures and
governments. The case law of courts and tribunals are not official sources of law, although decisions of the Supreme People's
Court are used in practice to guide lower courts when the law is
unclear.

---

[1] The Information Office of the State Council White Paper, 'China's Efforts and Achievements in Promoting the Rule of Law', available at www.scio.gov.cn/zfbps/ndhf/2008/
200905/t307866_2.htm.

6.03   Under the Organic Law of the People's Courts (1983), judicial power is exercised by the courts at four levels: (i) basic people's courts: courts at county or district level; tribunals may also be set up in accordance with local conditions; (ii) intermediate people's courts: prefecture-level courts; (iii) higher people's courts: provincial-level courts; and (iv) the Supreme People's Court (also known as the National Supreme Court, or Supreme Court).[2]

6.04   The highest court in the judicial system is the Supreme People's Court in Beijing, directly responsible to the NPC and its Standing Committee. It supervises the administration of justice by the people's courts at various levels. Cases are decided within two instances of trial in the people's courts. This means that, from a judgment or order of first instance of a local people's court, a party may bring an appeal only once to the people's court at the next highest level, and the people's procuratorate may appeal a court decision to the people's court at the next highest level. Additionally, judgments or orders of first instance of the local people's courts at various levels become legally effective if, within the prescribed period for appeal, no party makes an appeal. Judgments and orders rendered by the Supreme People's Court as court of first instance become effective immediately.[3]

The governmental stance on climate change

6.05   As a responsible country, China has paid and continues to pay great attention to its responses to climate change, in part by incorporating it as an important strategic goal in its economic and social development. This has entailed adopting a series of active policies and actions that, coupled with perfection of the relevant laws and regulations, has produced outstanding results. Climate change is not only a scientific, political and economic issue, but also a legal issue. Therefore China has tried its best to perfect its laws and regulations on climate change. This has resulted in the current legal regime, where the liabilities caused by climate change are enumerated in the relevant laws and regulations.

---

[2] www.lawinfochina.com/Legal/Display_1.asp.
[3] www.lawinfochina.com/Legal/Display_1.asp.

6.06   In order to address climate change effectively, the Chinese gov-
        ernment established in June 2007 a National Leading Committee
        on Climate Change based on the former National Coordination
        Committee on Climate Change. It is led by the Prime Minister,
        Wen Jiabao, and involves twenty ministries and government
        departments.[4] Amongst these twenty ministries, the National
        Development and Reform Commission (NDRC) is the key
        member:

> The Department of Climate Change of the NDRC is responsible for
> comprehensively analyzing the impact of climate change on social-
> economic development; organising and coordinating the formulation
> of key strategies, plans and policies dealing with climate change; tak-
> ing the lead in the implementation of the United Nations Framework
> Convention on Climate Change, and in collaborating with other inter-
> ested Parties in international climate change negotiations; coordinat-
> ing and carrying out international cooperation in response to climate
> change and related capacity building; organising and implementing
> the work relating to clean development mechanism ('CDM'); and
> undertaking concrete work assigned by the National Leading Group
> Dealing with Climate Change, Energy Conservation and Emission
> Reduction.[5]

        The NDRC can use all the administrative measures at its disposal
        such as issuing orders or commands, implementing national
        plans or drafting policies, etc., for addressing climate change.

6.07   Currently, there is no law directly aimed at climate change.
        However, this chapter examines existing rules and regulations in
        three clusters. The first cluster relates to policies such as China's
        National Climate Change Programme. The second encom-
        passes legislations covering a broad spectrum of issues ranging
        from environmental protection, climate change and energy

---

[4] The member organisations include: State Council; Ministry of Foreign Affairs; National
Development and Reform Commission; Ministry of Science and Technology; Ministry
of Industry and Information Technology; Ministry of Finance; Ministry of Land and
Resource; Ministry of Environment Protection; Ministry of Housing and Urban-
Rural Development; Ministry of Transport; Ministry of Water Resources; Ministry of
Agriculture; Ministry of Commerce; Ministry of Health; National Bureau of Statistics;
State Forest Administration; China Academy of Science; China Meteorological
Administration; National Energy Bureau; Civil Aviation Administration of China; State
Oceanic Administration.
[5] A list of the Main Functions of Departments of the NDRC is available at http://en.ndrc.
gov.cn/mfod/t20081218_252201.htm.

conservation to emissions reduction. These laws are grounded in constitutional law, basic and specific laws of environmental protection and laws on energy utilisation, and they find their expression in government rules and regulations. Legal liability arising from their infraction can be divided into public law and private law liability. While private law liability manifests itself in terms of tortious liability, public law liability is divided into administrative liability, governed by the laws on energy utilisation and specific laws of environmental protection, and criminal liability. The third and final cluster relates to initiatives from civil society.

National '11th Five-Year Plan' on
environmental protection

6.08   In November 2007, the State Council issued the National '11th Five-Year Plan' reflecting the growing awareness of climate change issues in China. The 11th Five-Year Plan specifies targets for the development of the environmental industry and provides the policy orientations for the legislations addressing climate change. It focuses on greenhouse gas ('GHG') emission control and aims to strengthen energy conservation – optimise the structure of energy consumption and enhance energy efficiency; control and mitigate GHG emissions, especially in industrial production; develop renewable resources; strengthen methane popularisation in rural areas; capture and reuse landfill gas emissions in urban areas, control the speed and rate at which methane emissions are increased; improve forests coverage, thereby enhancing carbon sinks; build capacity to address climate change, and strengthen the capacity to monitor and statistically analyse GHG emissions.[6] In March 2011, the State Council issued the National '12th Five-Year Plan', which continues the measures listed in the 11th Five-Year Plan to address climate change. The Proposal of the State Council of China concerning the 12th Five-Year Plan for National Economic and Social Development specifically mentions 'actively addressing climate change', and 'taking significant reduction of energy consumption and CO_2 emission as restrictive indexes, so as to effectively control GHG emissions'.

---

[6] The National 11th Five-Year Plan on Environmental Protection is available at www.gov.cn/zwgk/2007–11/26/content_815498.htm.

The target of the energy consumption per unit of GDP reduction in the 12th Five-Year Plan is 16 per cent.[7]

National Plan for Addressing Climate Change

6.09   Also in 2007, China formulated the National Plan for Addressing Climate Change (the 'National Plan'),[8] which is the first overall policy document addressing climate change. It is also the first national plan on climate change to be issued by a developing country. The National Plan requires China to closely coordinate its response to climate change and the implementation of its sustainable development strategy with building a resource-efficient, environment-friendly and innovative society. This entails focusing on GHG mitigation on the one hand and on enhancing the capability to address climate change by clearly prescribing targets on the other. The National Plan can therefore be seen as the fundamental framework document for China's response to climate change. It plays a direct role in China's implementation of the FCCC and the Kyoto Protocol.[9] Following the adoption of the National Plan, the provinces, autonomous regions and municipalities directly under the Chinese Central Government adopted their own plans and programmes along with the industries concerned, adapting the national strategy on addressing climate change to the political and practical realities prevalent in those areas.

White Paper on China's Policies and Actions on Addressing Climate Change

6.10   In 2008, China issued a White Paper on China's Policies and Actions on Addressing Climate Change,[10] which discusses the impact of climate change on the country, as well as its responses to climate change: it outlines strategies and objectives for addressing climate change, policies and actions for mitigation of and adaptation to climate change, and building institutions and mechanisms for coping with climate change. In 2009 and

---

[7] See http://news.sina.com.cn/c/2010–10–27/204721364515.shtml.

[8] Available at www.ccchina.gov.cn/WebSite/CCChina/UpFile/File189.pdf.

[9] Guo Dongmei, *Research on Legal Systems for Addressing Climate Change* (Beijing: Law Press, 2010), p. 142.

[10] 'China's Climate Change Policies and Actions', published on 4 June 2007 in Beijing, available at www.gov.cn/zwgk/2008–10/29/content_1134378.htm.

2010, the NDRC issued Annual Reports on China's Policies and Actions on Addressing Climate Change.[11]

Basic framework of legislation relevant to climate change

Overview

6.11   China is yet to enact a dedicated law on climate change. Only the policies as articulated in the Plans and documents discussed above exist. However, there are several provisions in existing laws that have a bearing on climate change. These can be found mainly in the relevant sections of environmental, administrative and economic laws, and to a lesser extent in civil and criminal laws. In actual fact, before the adoption of the FCCC and the Kyoto Protocol China had adopted a number of laws and regulations with a bearing on climate change, but these were not incorporated into the legal framework on climate change at that time.[12] The laws that have a bearing on climate change include the following:

Constitution

6.12   China's Constitution of 1982, which embodies the fundamental guiding principles according to which China is governed, is the basis for formulating other laws. Although the Constitution is silent on the issues of climate change or GHG emission reduction, Article 26 states:

> The State protects and improves the living environment and the ecological environment, and prevents and controls pollution and other public hazards. The State organises and encourages afforestation and the protection of forests.[13]

6.13   The protection and improvement of the environment and the prevention and control of pollution and other public hazards will have an impact on GHG emissions either directly or indirectly. Afforestation will also be critical to reducing GHG emissions.

---

[11] The 2009 Annual Report can be found at www.ccchina.gov.cn/WebSite/CCChina/ UpFile/File572.pdf; for the 2010 Annual Report, see http://qhs.ndrc.gov.cn/gzdt/ t20101126_382695.htm.

[12] Guo Dongmei, *Research on Legal Systems*, p.144.

[13] Article 26, the Constitution of the People's Republic of China, 1982.

Basic law on environmental protection

6.14   The Environmental Protection Law (1989) ('EPL') is the basic law
        on environmental protection in China, establishing the frame-
        work and legal basis for environmental protection. It clearly spe-
        cifies 'air' as one of several environmental factors thus bringing
        air under the regulatory and protective framework of environ-
        mental law. Article 24 of the EPL deals with prevention from
        waste, air and dust pollution, and damage to the environment.
        As provided by the EPL, a unit which is likely to cause envir-
        onmental pollution and other public hazards shall incorporate
        environmental protection measures into its plans. These include
        establishing responsibilities for environmental protection, and
        adopting effective measures to prevent and control the pollution
        and harms caused to the environment by waste (whether gas,
        water or residues), dust, radioactive substances, noise, vibration
        and electromagnetic radiation generated in the course of produc-
        tion, construction or other activities.[14] Article 24 provides a legal
        basis for the control of air pollution, which could be used in a
        climate change context.

Laws on utilisation of energy

6.15   The reasonable utilisation of energy plays an important role in
        energy conservation and emission reduction in China. Therefore,
        the laws on energy utilisation constitute the most important part
        of the climate change legislation. These laws include the Electricity
        Law of 1995, the Coal Law of 1996, the Energy Conservation Law
        of 1997 (amended in 2007) ('ECL') and the Renewable Energy
        Law of 2005. In addition, an 'Energy Basic Law' to unify China's
        four energy laws is being prepared. These laws establish a dense
        system of rules that help control GHG emission. For example, the
        ECL states:

> the State implements a system of accountability for energy conserva-
> tion targets and a system for energy conservation evaluation under
> which the fulfilment of energy conservation targets is one element
> taken into consideration in the evaluation of the local people's govern-
> ments and their responsible persons.[15]

---

[14] Article 24, Environmental Protection Law of the People's Republic of China, 1989.
[15] Article 6, Energy Conservation Law of the People's Republic of China, 2007.

And Article 7 of the ECL states:

> the State implements an industrial policy conducive to energy conservation and environmental protection, restricts the development of industries of high energy consumption and high pollution, and develops energy-saving and environmentally friendly industries.[16]

Articles 68 and 86, which deal with the imputation of legal liability, are also of interest.[17]

Specific laws on environmental protection

6.16   Some provisions in China's Law on the Prevention and Control of Environmental Pollution by Solid Waste (2004) (the 'Solid Waste Law') have a bearing on GHG emission reduction and control. For instance, Article 43 of the Solid Waste Law states:

> Urban people's governments shall, in a planned way, improve the fuel mix and develop coal gas, natural gas, liquefied gas and other clean energy for use in cities. The relevant departments of an urban people's government shall arrange for the supply of clean vegetables in cities, in order to reduce the quantity of urban household waste. The relevant departments of an urban people's government shall make overall plans to rationally establish networks for purchasing household waste, in order to promote the recycling of such waste.[18]

The use of clean energy is certain to reduce GHG emissions effectively.

6.17   China's Law on the Prevention and Control of Atmospheric Pollution (2000) ('APL') takes the development and utilisation of clean energies as the focal point of air pollutant emission controls and therefore plays an important role in changing China's energy structure and in controlling GHG emission. According to the APL, 'the State shall encourage and support the development and

---

[16] Article 7, *ibid.*

[17] Article 68, *ibid.*: 'Where any organs in charge of approving or verifying fixed assets investment projects approve or verify the construction of projects not in compliance with statutory standards for energy conservation in violation of this Law, the personnel directly in charge and other directly responsible personnel shall be given disciplinary sanctions.'

   Article 86, *ibid*: 'If any State functionary abuses his power, is derelict in his duties, or practices graft in energy conservation administration, which constitutes a criminal offence, criminal liability shall be pursued. If such act is not serious enough to constitute a criminal offence, disciplinary sanctions shall be imposed according to law.'

[18] Article 43, Solid Waste Law.

utilisation of clean energies such as solar energy, wind energy and water energy',[19] and 'the relevant departments under the State Council and the local people's governments at various levels shall adopt measures to improve the urban energy structure and popularise the production and utilisation of clean energy'.[20]

6.18   China's adoption of the Promotion of Clean Production Law of 2002 ('Clean Production Law') shifted the emphasis from traditional end-of-pipe pollution control to the prevention of pollution. Clean production refers to the continued application of the environmental strategy of prevention to energy utilisation, production process and product design for all industrial enterprises. The emphasis is on improving the utilisation rate of resources and energies simultaneously with reducing the generation, discharge and toxicity of pollutants, so as to reduce the risks for human beings and the environment.[21] The provisions on utilisation of clean energy and clean production in this law may effectively control GHG emissions. For example, this law establishes a duty on the governments at all levels to purchase products conducive to energy and water conservation, waste reuse, environmental protection and resource conservation.[22]

6.19   In 2008, China adopted the Law on Circular Economy Promotion ('CEPL'). The CEPL aims to improve the efficiency of resource utilisation, protect and improve the environment and realise sustainable development. It targets the activities conducted in the processes of production, circulation and consumption, by promoting reuse, recycling and related measures, thereby helping to reduce GHG emissions. The specific legal provisions on the control of GHG emissions can be found in Article 17 dealing with the system of labelling resource efficiency, and Article 18 pertaining to the system of eliminating the outdated production technologies, techniques, equipment and products.[23]

[19] Article 9, APL.   [20] Article 25, *ibid*.

[21] Wang Mingyuan, *Theory on Clean Production* (Beijing: Tshinghua University Press, 2004), p. 13.

[22] Article 16, Clean Production Law.

[23] Article 18, CEPL: 'The general administration for promoting circular economy under the State Council shall promulgate the catalogue of technologies, processes, equipment, materials and products that are encouraged or restricted or abandoned by the government. The production, import and sale of equipment, materials and products under the catalogue of abandonment shall be prohibited; and the use of technologies, processes, equipment and materials under the catalogue of abandonment shall be prohibited.'

6.20   Forests play an important role in regulating the climate by trapping and storing CO_2 and generally protecting the environment. Consequently, China's Forests Law of 1998, dealing with the administration and protection of forests, forest cutting and planting and the relevant legal liabilities, constitutes an important part of the legal regime relevant to climate change in China. Better forest management, including the control of deforestation, can play a key role in controlling climate change.

6.21   In the current legal system, all the above laws fall under the rubric of environmental law. Although these laws are implemented by different administrative entities, they have similar legal aims and adopt similar methods in implementation and enforcement. Several provisions of these laws have an indirect bearing on climate change, inter alia through strengthening forest protection, promoting the development of a circular economy, and encouraging clean production methods to enhance environmental quality.

Administrative regulations and rules

6.22   China has adopted many administrative rules and regulations on energy conservation and emission reduction in pursuance of its commitment towards fighting climate change. These regulations aimed at controlling GHG emissions include the Measures for Administration of Efficient Use of Electricity (2000), the Measures for Administration of Energy Efficiency Labelling (2004) and the Provisions on Administration of Energy Conservation in Civil Construction (2008). For example, according to Article 3 of the Measures for Administration of Energy Efficiency Labelling (2004), the country is required to adopt a nationwide unified energy-efficiency labelling scheme for energy-consuming products that are widely used and have greater energy-saving potential. The government is required to develop and issue a list of energy-efficiency labelled products of the PRC (the 'List') and publish national energy-efficiency standards, implementation rules, and label patterns and specifications.[24]

6.23   In addition, the NDRC, in conjunction with the Ministry of Science and Technology and the Ministry of Foreign Affairs,

---

[24] Article 3, The Measures for Administration of Energy Efficiency Labelling, 2004.

issued the Measures for Administration of Operation of Clean Development Mechanism Projects[25] ('Measures for Administration') in 2005 as the special administrative regulation on GHG emissions. The core of the Clean Development Mechanism ('CDM') is to allow developed countries to acquire the certified emission reductions by cooperating with developing countries at project level. The Measures for Administration designate the NDRC as the competent authority to develop CDM projects on behalf of the Chinese government. Additionally, the National Coordination Committee on Climate Change has been designated as the review and coordination authority for important CDM policies.

6.24   CDM projects in China are primarily focused on the improvement of energy efficiency, development and utilisation of new and renewable energy and the reclamation of methane and coal-bed methane. To further develop the CDM in China, the Measures for Administration stipulate the license conditions, specific enforcement procedures and the principles guiding the relationship between the Measures for Administration and the FCCC or the Kyoto Protocol.

6.25   In addition to State and administrative rules and laws, local rules have been formulated to address local conditions. Some instances are the Provisions of Tianjin City on Administration of Energy Conservation in Construction (2006), the Regulations of Shanxi Province for Energy Conservation (2000) and the Measures of Anhui Province for Encouragement of Energy Conservation (2008). These local rules, as part of China's legislation on climate change, prescribe a series of policies and measures aimed at GHG emission reduction.

6.26   The above five sections together constitute the basic framework of China's legislation on climate change. To these domestic rules, one needs to add the FCCC, the Kyoto Protocol and other international instruments relating to climate change and GHG emission reduction and to which China is a Party. Other international instruments concluded by China include the China-EU Joint

---

[25] http://cdm.ccchina.gov.cn/UpFile/File579.pdf. The Measures for Administration were issued after amendment on the basis of the Provisional Measures for Administration of Operation of Clean Development Mechanism Projects published on 30 June 2004.

Declaration on Climate Change (2005),[26] the Joint Statement on CDM Cooperation between the Chinese and French Governments (2007)[27] and the Memorandum on Climate Change Cooperation between the Chinese and Australian Governments (2004).[28] These documents define the rights and entitlements of, as well as obligations placed on, countries.

Emissions sources and energy mix

6.27   The National GHG Inventory for China in the year 2005 includes estimated net anthropogenic GHG emissions from the energy sector, industrial processes, agriculture, land-use change and forestry, and waste, and identifies these gases as carbon dioxide (CO_2), methane (CH_4) and nitrous oxide (N_2O).[29]

6.28   The energy activities inventory mainly covers emissions of CO_2 and N_2O from the combustion of fossil fuels, emissions of CH_4 from coal mining and post-mining activities, fugitive emissions of CH_4 from oil and natural gas systems, and emissions of CH_4 from the burning of biomass fuels.

6.29   The industrial processes inventory includes emissions of CO_2 in the production processes of cement, lime, iron and steel, and calcium carbide, as well as emissions of N_2O in the production process of adipic acid.

6.30   The agricultural activities inventory covers emissions of CH_4 from flooded rice paddy fields, animal enteric fermentation and manure management as well as emissions of N_2O from croplands and animal waste management.

6.31   The land-use change and forestry activities inventory mainly covers changes in the stocks of forests and other ligneous plants

[26] This Declaration was signed on 5 September 2005. In the Declaration, the two Parties emphasise their commitment to the objectives and principles of the FCCC and Kyoto Protocol and, under this framework, agreed to establish a climate change partnership. 'The partnership will strengthen the climate change including clean energy, cooperation and dialogue to promote sustainable development.' The text of the Declaration can be found at http://industry.oursolo.net/data/development-change-climate-energy-2/.

[27] The Joint Statement was signed on 26 November 2007 in Beijing. It is available at www.amb-chine.fr/chn/zfgx/zzgx/t384507.htm.

[28] The Memo was signed on 16 August 2004 in Beijing. See Guo Dongmei, *Research on Legal Systems*, p. 148.

[29] www.ccchina.gov.cn/cn/NewsInfo.asp?NewsId=22684.

as well as emissions of CO_2 due to the conversion of forests to non-forest land. The waste treatment inventory mainly covers emissions of CH_4 from treating municipal solid waste and that from treating municipal domestic sewage and industrial wastewater.[30]

China's climate risks

6.32   Climate change deeply affects and influences China and its actions. China's temperature rise has basically kept pace with global warming. The latest information released by the China Meteorological Administration shows that the average temperature of the Earth's surface in China rose by 1.1°C between 1908 and 2007, and that China experienced twenty-one warm winters in the period 1986 to 2007, the latter being the warmest year since the beginning of systematic meteorological observations in 1951.[31] China experienced grave climate damage in 2009 and 2010. In 2009, it suffered from extremely high temperatures in summer and very low temperatures in winter, temperatures it had not witnessed for decades. An extraordinarily severe drought occurred in 2009–10 in southwest China, the most serious drought in recorded history. In 2010, fourteen rounds of rainstorm continuously attacked south China and regions south of the Yangtze River after entering the flood season; ten rounds of rainstorms continually attacked north China and west China and temperatures were high beyond historical extremes in many

---

[30] National Development and Reform Commission, 'The PRC Initial National Communications on Climate Change', available at www.ccchina.gov.cn/en/NewsInfo.asp?NewsId=7111.

[31] The national distribution of precipitation in the past half-century has undergone marked changes, with increases in western and southern China and decreases in most parts of northern and northeast China. Extreme climate phenomena, such as high temperatures, heavy precipitation and severe droughts, have increased in frequency and intensity. The number of heatwaves in summer has grown, and droughts have grown worse in some areas, especially northern China; heavy precipitation has increased in southern China; and the occurrence of snow disasters has risen in western China. In China's coastal zones, the sea surface temperature and sea level have risen by 0.9°C and 90mm, respectively, over the past thirty years. The text of the White Paper can be found at: National Development and Reform Commission, 'White Paper: China's Policies and Actions on Climate Change', at http://bbs.pkucat.com/viewthread.php?tid=763.

places.[32] Cumulatively, these caused major casualties and economic loss to China.

Legal liabilities for climate change in China

6.33 Legal liabilities, as the safeguard of legal operations, are an indispensable part of the rule of law.[33] Briefly, legal liabilities refer to circumstances where persons (whether individuals, public bodies or others) are held responsible by law for their actions/inactions or decisions. Sanctions that may be imposed include requiring the person responsible to indemnify or compensate for the loss caused, compulsory performance or acceptance of punishment. The laws with a bearing on climate change impose certain duties and responsibilities on persons and any violation or breach, manifested by a failure to perform or conform, result in legal liabilities. These liabilities can be divided into public law and private law liability.

(B)   Public law

Law on the Environmental Impact Assessment

6.34 China's Environmental Impact Assessment ('EIA') Law ('EIA Law') defines EIA as the process (including the institutions involved) whereby the impacts of planning and construction projects are analysed, predicted and appraised, after which countermeasures for preventing or mitigating the negative impacts identified are proposed and follow-up monitoring is ensured.[34] The EIA Law can arguably be used in a climate change context where projects have an impact on the climate and consequently, Articles 29 to 35, which define the relevant liabilities including administrative and criminal liability, may be relevant.

---

[32] National Development and Reform Commission, the Foreword of 'China's Policies and Action for Addressing Climate Change – 2010 Annual Report', available at http://qhs.ndrc.gov.cn/gzdt/t20101126_382695.htm.

[33] Zhang Wenxian, *Research on Category for Philosophy of Law* (Beijing: China University of Political Science and Law Press, 2001), p.116.

[34] Article 2, EIA Law.

6.35   Generally speaking, an EIA will lead to the planning application being obtained or rejected, and the entity in charge of the project obtaining (or not) the necessary permit. If the EIA reveals that an illegal act has occurred, the EIA Law includes administrative remedies (such as disciplinary measures or penalties) and, if the act constitutes a crime, criminal sanctions. For instance, the planning permit may be revoked or the licence previously granted may be declared void.

6.36   The EIA Law mandates public participation in the conduct of the assessment process. In February 2006, the former State Administration of Environmental Protection (the Ministry of Environmental Protection) adopted the Provisional Measures for the Public Participation in EIA,[35] which aim to achieve effective public participation through consideration and securing of public rights such as the right to access information, the right to participate and the right that opinions or suggestions put forward be properly considered. If such public rights are infringed, the public may seek legal remedies. For example, the public may report to the competent administrative authority as stipulated in Article 18 of the Provisional Measures for Public Participation in EIA, and access administrative review procedures.[36]

6.37   Public Participation in EIA is an important aspect of the process. In a developing country citizens' environmental concerns can only be addressed gradually, but democratic participation of the public in the EIA process is in keeping with the times. Public participation in the EIA process was introduced relatively recently in China compared to developed countries. Although some progress has been made there are still many problems, such as limited awareness of public participation provisions, limited availability of information on construction projects, time lag in public participation, unreasonable design of questionnaires, unscientific statistical results and ineffective feedback as well as supervision of public participation. These problems have a serious impact on the effectiveness of public participation in the

---

[35] The Environmental Protection Agency issued 'Interim Measures on Public Participation in Environmental Impact Assessment' on 18 March 2006, available at www.gov.cn/jrzg/2006–02/22/content_207093_2.htm.

[36] www.gov.cn/jrzg/2006–02/22/content_207093_2.htm.

EIA process, as well as on the quality of the EIA and its ability to catalyse long-term improvements in the environmental protection policies and systems of the nation. The continuous development of public participation in the EIA process in China should draw on experiences both at home and abroad but be tailored to national conditions. At the very least, the legislator should place prime importance on public participation in environmental protection and establish the principle of public participation as a fundamental law of China.

Energy conservation and emission reduction

Overview

6.38   As evidence that resources conservation is now a basic national policy, China has rebalanced its strategic priorities in relation to conservation and development and prioritised conservation in the development of energy.[37] This is reflected in the 11th Five-Year Plan, which sets energy consumption per unit of GDP targets at 20 per cent less than 2010 levels. In order to achieve these targets, there has been a significant focus on energy conservation all over China, with the aim of promoting scientific development. This progress in energy conservation is achieved through a number of policies and measures, which include: (i) perfecting laws, regulations and standards; (ii) strengthening supervision and accountability; (iii) improving technological progress and eliminating outdated production capacities; (iv) implementing key projects; (v) reinforcing policy incentives; and (vi) developing nationwide actions. Based on the statistics issued by the State, energy consumption per unit of GDP dropped by 4 per cent in 2010, with a cumulative drop of 19.6 per cent[38] for the five-year period up to the end of 2010 (the '11th Five-Year period').[39] The above illustrates how energy conservation and emission reduction measures form important constituent elements in China's fight against climate change since their primary focus is on controlling GHG emissions and mitigation of climate change.

[37]   Article 4, Energy Conservation Law of the People's Republic of China, 2007.
[38]   The target of the energy consumption per unit of GDP reduction in the 11th Five-Year Plan is 20 per cent. See http://news.ifeng.com/mainland/detail_2011_02/10/4606571_0.shtml.
[39]   NDRC 2010 Annual Report (see n. 32 above).

Legal liability under the ECL

6.39   As mentioned above, China has put in place a system of accountability for energy conservation targets in the 11th Five-Year
period.[40] It has also introduced a system for energy conservation
evaluation, which will be discussed below. The ECL encompasses,
in addition to these systems, procedures for eliminating outdated
products, equipment and processes; and systems reporting on
the energy utilisation of key energy-intensive entities and energy
efficiency labelling. It also contains specific provisions on energy
conservation for industries in the construction and transport
sectors, public organisations and key energy-intensive entities
and simultaneously promotes and encourages technological progress on energy conservation. Chapter 6 of the ECL covers liabilities related to energy conservation and includes the following:

6.40   First, administrative liabilities: these comprise the bulk of legal
liabilities arising under the Law on Energy Conservation and
include the following three categories:

(i)   Liabilities on the administrative authorities which involve
disciplinary measures. For instance, Article 68(1) states:
'Where any organ in charge of approving or verifying fixed
assets investment projects approves or verifies a project that
does not comply with statutory standards for energy conservation in violation of this Law, the personnel directly
in charge and other directly responsible personnel shall be
given disciplinary sanctions.'

(ii)   Liabilities on construction companies, energy-intensive
product manufacturers and energy-intensive entities for
breach of the relevant provisions of the ECL, in particular
Article 68(2), Articles 69 to 75, Article 77 and Articles 79 to
84. The available remedies include warnings, fines, an order
to suspend operations so as to permit rectification and revocation of business licences.

(iii)   Liabilities of other entities such as those borne for the provision of false information under Article 76 by service entities
engaging in energy conservation consultancy, design,
assessment, test, audit and certification or for contravening the provisions of the ECL, borne by an enterprise for

40   http://news.sina.com.cn/c/2006–03–16/16158457479s.shtml.

transmission-line system of electric power. Remedies include rectification orders,[41] the confiscation of illegal earnings and the imposition of fines.

6.41   Second, criminal liability: the relevant provisions are Articles 85 and 86. They are, however, general provisions imputing criminal liability for actions only indirectly concerned with climate change.

Legal liability under the Renewable Energy Law

6.42   Renewable energy refers to wind, solar, water, biomass, geothermal and ocean energy.[42] Article 4 of China's Renewable Energy Law (2005) ('REL') reflects the prioritisation given to the development and use of renewable energy in the energy sector in China: 'The Government encourages economic entities, whether public or private, to participate in the development and use of renewable energy and protects the legal rights and interests of the developers and users of renewable energy on the basis of law.' With regard to the use of renewable resources, the REL outlines a system to ensure that a certain target on renewable energy is met; it also provides for grid-connected power for renewable energy, grid-connected power price and expenses distribution for renewable energy and special funds for renewable energy.[43] This is evidence again of China's active support for the development and use of renewable energy and a contravention of the same will give rise to the following administrative and criminal liabilities:

6.43   Administrative liability, which is broadly divided into two constituent parts:
  (i) Failure to perform or the inappropriate performance of its duty by the administrative authority which may result in disciplinary measures under Article 28 of the REL.
  (ii) Departure by the enterprises concerned from their legal obligations. Examples include cases where 'the power grid enterprises fail to purchase renewable power in full' or

---

[41] This is a form of administrative remedy which requires the entity which is in breach of the regulations to terminate the wrongful behaviour.
[42] Article 2, Renewable Energy Law of the People's Republic of China, 2005.
[43] Articles 7, 14, 19 to 22 and 24, *ibid*.

'enterprises involved in natural gas pipeline network and heat pipeline network fail to make the connection of natural gas and heat that conform to the grid connection technical standard into the network' or 'gas-selling enterprises fail to include biological liquid fuel that conforms to the national standard into their fuel-selling system'. The administrative liabilities are prescribed in Articles 29, 30 and 31 respectively. Remedies include orders to make corrections within the stipulated time period, and fines.

6.44   Criminal liability, in accordance with Article 28 of the REL, in cases where the action of the authorities constitutes a crime in the administration and supervision of the development and use of renewable energy. As under the ECL, the criminal liabilities at issue here are only indirectly concerned with climate change.[44]

The legal liabilities under the Plan for Implementation of Energy Consumption per Unit of GDP Evaluation System

6.45   The above-mentioned system of energy conservation evaluation is specifically set out in the ECL. During the period of the 11th Five-Year Plan, the responsibility for energy conservation and emissions reduction was assigned to governmental authorities at all levels. This resulted in the establishment of a system of target accountability that held local government officials accountable for the failure to complete target tasks. In order to assist with the evaluation of energy conservation and emissions reduction, China adopted the Plan for Implementation of Energy Consumption per Unit of GDP Evaluation System[45] ('Evaluation System Plan') in 2007, which included specific provisions for governments and enterprises. In 2009 and 2010, the Chinese government assessed the attainment of these energy conservation targets and the fulfilment of energy conservation measures for thirty-one provincial governments and thousands of key enterprises across the country.[46]

---

[44] For an example of enforcement of criminal liability under this situation, see para. 6.56 below.
[45] The State Council Approved Energy Saving Statistics Monitoring and Assessment Inform the Implementation of Programmes and Approaches, available at www.gov.cn/zwgk/2007–11/23/content_813617.htm.
[46] NDRC 2010 Annual Report (see n. 32 above).

6.46   In accordance with the provisions of the Evaluation System Plan, the objects of energy conservation evaluation are the people's governments at the provincial level and thousands of key energy-intensive enterprises.[47] The Evaluation System Plan also contains evaluation measures, results and procedures, and measures to encourage conservation and penalise failure.

6.47   Under the provisions in the Evaluation System Plan:

> a provincial people's government which is deemed to have undera-chieved, shall, within one month after the publication of the evaluation results, report to the State Council in writing, stating the measures it intends to take to remedy the situation within a stipulated period of time, and send a copy to the NDRC. In the event of failure to remedy the situation, the supervisory department will investigate and assign responsibility to the relevant responsible person.[48]

> In practice, the results of the energy conservation evaluation at provincial level provide an important basis for comprehensively evaluating the leadership of the provincial people's government and leader cadres.

6.48   Another Evaluation System Plan provision provides that:

> an enterprise which is deemed to have underachieved, shall, within one month after the publication of the evaluation results, commu-nicate to the local provincial people's government the measures it intends to take to remedy the situation and make the rectification within a stipulated period of time.[49]

> The evaluation results in State-owned enterprises or State-holding enterprises in thousands of key industries provide an important basis for the State-owned assets supervisory commis-sion to assess the performance of company managers. These pro-visions suggest that the evaluation results of energy conservation and emissions reduction measures will act as a source of internal incentive and form the basis of sanctions for public servants.

6.49   In addition to the State, provinces have also adopted their own evaluation plans for energy conservation and emissions

---

[47] This refers to enterprises whose annual overall energy consumption is more than 180,000 tons of standard coal in nine key energy-intensive industries including steel, non-ferrous metals, petrol and petrochemicals, chemicals, construction materials, coal, electricity, papermaking, textile industries – in total 998 enterprises.
[48] NDRC 2010 Annual Report (see n. 32 above).   [49] *Ibid.*

reduction, adapted to local conditions. Instances abound such as the Plan of Shanxi Province for Implementation of Energy Consumption per Unit of GDP Evaluation System[50] or the Plan of Nanchang City for Implementation of Energy Consumption per Unit of GDP Evaluation System[51], with similar incentive and penalty provisions.

Legal liability on climate change in the specific laws on environmental protection

6.50   The laws referred to earlier, such as the Solid Waste Law, the APL, the Clean Production Law and the CEPL, although concerned with mitigation and GHG emission reduction, were not formulated directly to combat climate change.

6.51   On the face of it, the prevention and control of air pollution can have an impact on climate change. According to the Fourth Assessment Report[52] on climate change issued by the Intergovernmental Panel on Climate Change in 2007, there is a 90 per cent probability that global warming is caused by an increase in anthropogenic GHG emissions. The GHGs defined under the Kyoto Protocol include six gases, namely CO_2, CH_4, N_2O, HFCs, PFCs and SF_6. If these GHGs were listed as air pollutants, their emissions would be subject to the APL. However, at present China does not list these GHGs as air pollutants under the APL and thus their emission is not regulated under the climate change framework. Hence, no liability under this framework will arise.

Climate change liability and procedural law

6.52   Litigation is an important channel for the crystallisation of liabilities. China provides for civil, administrative and criminal

[50] Provincial People's Government of Shanxi Province on the Issuance of Emission Reduction Monitoring and Assessing the Implementation of Statistical Programmes and Methods of Notification, available at www.shanxigov.cn/n16/n8319541/n8319612/n8321663/n8322659/n8335621/n8337437/8683192.html.

[51] People's Government on the Issuance of the Implementation Plan of Energy Consumption Per Unit of GDP Evaluation System of Nanchang City was published on 11 September 2009, and is available at http://xxgk.nc.gov.cn/fgwj/qtygwj/200909/t20090927_165493.htm.

[52] IPCC (2007), IPCC Fourth Assessment Report: *Climate Change 2007* (AR4). For the full text of this report, see www.ipcc.ch.

litigation; all of which may, theoretically, be relevant to an action on climate change.

6.53   This is best explained by way of an example: an enterprise discharges a large amount of CO_2. CO_2 is one of the main gases responsible for creating the 'greenhouse effect' and an increased concentration of CO_2 in the atmosphere is believed to cause climate change, which in turn could conceivably cause, through flooding for instance, damage to local residents' properties. The residents should then be able to bring a civil lawsuit and claim compensation from the enterprise for the losses they sustained. Another instance would be the discharge of great quantities of GHGs by a government-approved plant. The result could be an administrative lawsuit brought about by residents living near the plant demanding the revocation of the government approval pursuant to which the plant was built. By way of further example, if a company discharged such amounts of CO_2 as to aggravate climate change, and the resulting disaster and environmental harm killed countless precious lives, the public prosecution body would file a criminal lawsuit. But these are hypothetical scenarios. The problems arising hereunder are listed as follows:

6.54   First, GHGs causing climate change are not listed in China's laws as pollutants. Therefore, their emissions do not infringe any law. Second, causation is difficult to prove. Third, the harmful effects of GHG emissions on the climate may not become apparent until long after they are released into the atmosphere. Thus, they often do not adversely affect contemporary interests, although they set in motion long-term environmental damage. This makes the identification of the *locus standi* for a court or tribunal problematic.

6.55   The problems raised by the third point can possibly be addressed by bringing public welfare lawsuits, which would include civil and administrative environmental public welfare lawsuits. Generally speaking, this kind of lawsuit enables a plaintiff without a direct interest to file a claim in the interest of public welfare. However, this does not solve the first two problems mentioned above, and there is no provision for bringing a public welfare lawsuit in the procedural rules. China's procedural rules stipulate strict limitations on the standing of claimants and require them to have a legal interest in the case.[53] This suggests that the existing legal framework, in particular the procedural rules, including those on *locus standi*, presents an obstacle to a successful claim based on harm or damage from climate change.

Climate change liability and environmental criminal law

6.56   Chinese criminal law recognises environmental crimes as part of its legal framework. Hence, a chapter of 'the Crime of Disrupting the Order of Social Administration'[54] recognises fifteen kinds of crimes and establishes, inter alia, the 'crime of violating the protection of the environment and resources'. Liability under the above fifteen categories of crime arises only if any national laws or regulations have been infringed. This includes three categories: first, the crime of discharging environmental pollutants; second, the crime of importing solid waste; and third, the crime of destroying natural resources. Thus, under the aegis of environmental crimes, there is no specific crime on climate change. Since China's Criminal Law (1997) ('Criminal Law') applies the strict principle of 'a legally prescribed punishment for a specified crime', GHG emissions cannot be subject to liabilities and responsibilities arising out of criminal law, and the existing criminal liabilities in other environmental laws are not relevant in this context. For example, Article 45 of the EPL states that:

> any person conducting supervision and management of environmental protection who abuses his power, neglects his duty or engages in malpractices for personal gains shall be given administrative sanction by the unit to which he belongs or the competent higher authorities;

[53] Article 3, Civil Procedure Law of the People's Republic of China, 2007. In dealing with civil litigation arising from disputes on property and personal relations between citizens, legal persons or other organisations and between the three of them, the people's courts shall apply the provisions of this Law.

Article 2, Administrative Procedure Law of the People's Republic of China, 1989. If a citizen, a legal person or any other organisation considers that his/her or its lawful rights and interests have been infringed by a specific administrative act of an administrative organ or its personnel, he/she or it shall have the right to bring a suit before a people's court in accordance with this Law.

[54] The 'Crime of Undermining Protection of Environment or Resources' is listed as one of the crimes in the category of crimes 'Disrupting the Order of Social Administration' in China's Criminal Law (1997). The text is available in English at www.procedurallaw.cn/english/law/200807/t20080724_40992.html.

if his act constitutes a crime, he shall be investigated for criminal responsibility according to law.[55]

In the case of specific application, the punishment shall be subject to the provisions of the Criminal Law as well as to Article 45 of the EPL. Moreover, such criminal liability is indirectly related to, and not directly caused by, climate change. Therefore, generally speaking, there is no crime specific to climate change in the Criminal Law, although some crimes related to climate change might indirectly entail criminal legal liability.

(C)   Private law

6.57   The climate tort is part of environmental torts, which are directly recognised under Article 124 of the General Principles of the Civil Law, Articles 41 and 42 of the EPL, Chapter 8 of the Tort Law and other specific laws on environmental protection.[56] These laws directly prescribe the legal liability for environmental torts.

6.58   Environmental torts encompass conduct or activities (industrial or from other anthropogenic sources) which cause harm or damage to personal, property or environmental rights and interests or to public property.[57]

6.59   The essential ingredients of environmental torts are threefold: (i) there is an act causing the injury, but such act is not required

---

[55] Article 45, EPL.

[56] Article 124, The General Principles of the Civil Law, 1986: 'Any person who pollutes the environment and causes damage to others in violation of state provisions for environmental protection and the prevention of pollution shall bear civil liability in accordance with the law.'

Article 41, EPL: 'A unit that has caused an environmental pollution hazard shall have the obligation to eliminate it and make compensation to the unit or individual that suffered direct losses. A dispute over the liability to make compensation or the amount of compensation may, at the request of the Parties, be settled by the competent department of environmental protection administration or another department invested by law with power to conduct environmental supervision and management. If a party refuses to accept the decision on the settlement, it may bring a suit before a people's court. The party may also directly bring a suit before the people's court.'

Article 65, Tort Law of the People's Republic of China, 2009: 'Where any harm is caused by environmental pollution, the polluter shall assume the tort liability.'

[57] Wang Mingyuan, *Legal Remedy System on Environmental Tort* (Beijing: China Legal Publishing House, 2001), p.13.

to be illegal; (ii) there is a harmful result, which includes actual harm or the risk of possible harm; and (iii) there is causation between such act and the harmful result. As the principle of causation presumption[58] is applicable to environmental torts, the burden of proof is reversed, i.e. the party causing the injury shall bear the burden of proving that there is no causality between the act causing the injury and the harmful result. The principle of strict liability[59] is applicable to environmental torts in China, which means that liability will be imposed on the person legally responsible for the loss or damage without a finding of fault being necessary.

6.60   The remedies available in cases of environmental torts, in accordance with China's laws, include ceasing the infringement, removing the hindrance, eliminating the danger, *restitutio in integrum*, compensating for loss and offering an apology. The most common remedies are cessation of the infringing act and compensation for the loss caused.

6.61   Climate change may, in theory, give rise to liability under private law, usually in the form of infringement liabilities. When a person's actions harm the climate and thereby cause harm or damage to others' rights and interests (whether life, body, property or environment), that person may become liable.

6.62   However, there are several obstacles to the crystallisation of such liability. First of all, liabilities are predicated on existing legal provisions and their contravention. If GHG emissions are not brought under the legal framework, there can be no liability for emitting GHGs. Secondly, it is very difficult to prove causation in the context of climate change, in so far as establishing a direct link between the damage caused and the actions of the person allegedly responsible is problematic. For instance, it is hard to

---

[58] Article 66, Tort Law of the People's Republic of China, 2009: 'Where any dispute arises over an environmental pollution, the polluter shall assume the burden of proving that it should not be held liable or that its liability could be mitigated under certain circumstances as provided for by law, or of proving that there is no causation between its conduct and the harm.'

[59] Article 7, Tort Law of the People's Republic of China, 2009: 'The party who is legally responsible for infringing upon a civil right or interest of another person, whether he is at fault or not, as provided for by law, shall be subject to legal provisions on strict liability.' Under the law, the liability for environmental pollution is one of these situations.

establish a causal connection between the immersion of a house in Tuvalu due to sea level rise and the excessive discharges of CO_2 by a big plant in Houston. If the principle of presumption of causation is applied without due consideration, the person responsible for the GHG emissions may be wrongly held liable. This is exacerbated by the hidden nature of the harmful effects of climate change, which often become apparent long after the event, at a time when the person allegedly responsible for the harmful activity may no longer be alive (in the case of a natural person) or trading (in the case of a company bankruptcy). If the person allegedly responsible is no longer there, pursuing a claim seems pointless.

6.63 Since there is no provision in China for private law liability directly caused by climate change, GHG emissions will not give rise to tort liability.

(D) Conclusion

6.64 Climate change is a major global challenge. It is the common mission of all of mankind to curb global warming and save our planet. China was the first developing country to adopt and implement a National Climate Change Programme. In the past twenty years, in order to face the challenge of climate change, China has formulated or revised about twenty laws, including the Forest Law (in 1998), the Clean Production Law (in 2002), the REL (in 2005), the ECL (in 2007), the CEPL (in 2008) and the Regulations on Administration of Energy Conservation in Civil Construction (in 2008). Laws and regulations have been an important means to address climate change. However, at present China does not have a specific law on climate change. Climate change issues are dealt with at policy level, through these laws as well as civil society initiatives. Similarly, the issue of climate change liability (whether civil, criminal or administrative) tends to arise through provisions in other fields that are indirectly related to climate change. Looking to the future, the question of the integration of climate change liability within the Chinese legal system is likely to be dictated by the Chinese government's stance in the climate change negotiations, and the actual responsibility of China under the FCCC.

6.65   Finally, it is worth highlighting that the National Development and Reform Commission, the key member of the National Leading Committee on climate change, announced on 23 March 2011 (World Meteorological Day) that the Chinese government has decided to enact a specific climate change law.[60] One hopes that the legislation will be fully committed to achieving and even exceeding the GHG mitigation goals that China has adopted. This will instil confidence in not only the Chinese people but also the world. However it is worth bearing in mind that even if a specific climate change law is adopted, the many difficulties in implementation and enforcement identified in this chapter are likely to stand in the way of an effective response to climate change.

6.66   There are two distinct but related aspects to addressing climate change: mitigation by stabilising GHG concentrations in the atmosphere, and adaptation by reducing vulnerability or improving adaptive capacity to climate change. Although adaptation has recently featured high on the international and national climate change law-making agendas, adaptation is less developed and researched than mitigation. As a direct way to prevent and reduce climate change damage, adaptation is especially important for those who are suffering most from the current and expected climate change impacts.[61] The proposed climate legislation in China should focus on establishing systems and regulations to address adaptation needs, in particular through the use of market mechanisms.[62] The use of market mechanisms both for adaptation and mitigation will likely address the implementation concerns, as well as incentivise voluntary GHG reductions.

[60] www.chinalawinfo.com/fzdt/NewsContent.aspx?ID=28758.
[61] Zhang Zitai, 'Legal Approaches to Climate Change Adaptation', *Global Law Review*, 5 (2008), 57.
[62] Deng Haifeng, 'Review on Administrative Command and Control Approach in Environmental Law', *Hebei Law Science*, 23 (2005), 52.

7

India

LAVANYA RAJAMANI AND SHIBANI GHOSH

(A)   Introduction[1]

Legal system

7.01   India is a parliamentary democracy governed by a lengthy written constitution widely perceived to be a 'living instrument', having been amended over a hundred times since its adoption in 1950.[2] India has, in part, a common law legal system, a legacy of its colonial past. The principal sources of law are: (i) legislation, including statutes passed by the Parliament and state legislatures, and subordinate legislation such as rules, notifications and orders passed under the statutes; and (ii) common law to be found in decided cases developed by courts through a reliance on precedent. Much of the law of tort and administrative law is common law based.

7.02   The Indian judicial system consists of a Supreme Court that sits in Delhi, and has original, appellate and advisory jurisdiction, and twenty-one High Courts spread across the territory of India.[3] In addition, there are several specialised tribunals including the recently constituted National Green Tribunal. The law declared by the Supreme Court is binding on all courts within the territory of India.[4]

---

[1] This section draws on L. Rajamani, 'India and Climate Change: What India Wants, Needs and Needs to Do', *India Review*, 8(3) (2009), 340–74.

[2] The Constitution of India, 1950, available at http://indiacode.nic.in/coiweb/welcome. html.

[3] See for further information on the Indian Court system www.indiancourts.nic.in/index. html.

[4] Article 141, The Constitution of India, 1950.

Policy context

7.03   India is on a mission to develop. Economic growth, and with it, poverty eradication, energy security and provision of universal access to energy, are central and enduring preoccupations of the Indian government. Justifiably so: India is placed 134th on the Human Development Index,[5] 41.6 per cent of its population lives on less than US$ 1.25 a day,[6] and an estimated 44 per cent does not have access to electricity.[7] India's developmental mission, as framed, however, may well leave large carbon footprints, and ultimately weaken its ability to develop.

7.04   If India's current growth rate continues,[8] energy demand will more than double by 2020.[9] In addition, if India's targets on poverty, unemployment and literacy in its 11th five year plan[10] – some more ambitious than the Millennium Development Goals ('MDGs')[11] – are to be met, and energy provided to the nearly 500 million Indians without access to electricity, this will lead to much greater energy use.[12] India will soon be a significant contributor to climate change.[13] India is predicted by some estimates

---

[5] *Human Development Report: Overcoming Barriers* (2009), available at http://hdr.undp.org/en/statistics/.

[6] *Ibid.*

[7] *Human Development Report: Fighting Climate Change*, 2007, available at http://hdr.undp.org/en/reports/.

[8] See *Economic Surveys*, Ministry of Finance, Government of India for current growth rate, available at www.finmin.nic.in.

[9] See *India Country Presentation*, Dialogue on Long-term Cooperative Action to Address Climate Change by Enhancing Implementation of the Convention, First Workshop, 15–16 May 2006, available at www.unfccc.int/meetings/dialogue/items/3669.php.

[10] *Towards Faster and More Inclusive Growth: An Approach to the 11th Five Year Plan*, Planning Commission, Government of India (2006), p. 98, available at www.planning-commission.nic.in. An approach to the 12th Five Year Plan set to commence in 2012–13 is currently under preparation.

[11] *India's Initial National Communication to the United Nations Framework Convention on Climate Change*, Ministry of Environment and Forests, Government of India (2004), Table 6.1, pp. 192–3, available at www.unfccc.int.

[12] See *Integrated Energy Policy*, Planning Commission, Government of India (August 2006), pp. xiii and 18–32, noting that to sustain 8 per cent growth through 2031 India would need to increase its energy supply by 3–4 times, and its electricity supply by 5–7 times. Available at www.planningcommission.nic.in.

[13] The rate of growth of GHG emissions in India is approximately 4.6 per cent annually as compared to a world average of 2 per cent. See Subhodh Sharma, Sumona Bhattacharya

to become the third largest emitter by 2015,[14] and with the United States, European Union, China and Russia, to account for two-thirds of global greenhouse gases ('GHGs').[15]

Emissions profile and energy mix

7.05   India's energy use is currently at a low per capita emissions rate of 1.5 metric tons annually,[16] and a cumulative share of 4.6%.[17] Of India's net CO_2 Eqv emissions, 58% can be sourced to the energy sector, 22% to industry, 17% to agriculture and 3% to waste. Of the emissions from the energy sector, 37.8% can be sourced to electricity, 7.5% to transport and 7.2% to residential uses.[18]

7.06   Coal is the mainstay of India's energy supply, accounting for 53% of installed generation capacity.[19] Hydro accounts for 22.8%, gas for 10.3%, wind for 7.2%, nuclear for 2.8% and other renewables for 2.9%.[20] Coal, not surprisingly, also accounts for 40% of India's energy consumption, combustible renewables and waste for 27%, oil for 24%, natural gas for 6%, hydroelectric power for 2% and nuclear for 1%.[21] India has large reserves of coal, but limited reserves of oil. The majority of India's substantial oil requirements is imported from the Middle East.[22]

and Amit Garg, 'Greenhouse Gas Emissions from India: A Perspective', *Current Science*, 90 (2006), 326–33.

[14] Executive Summary, *World Energy Outlook* (2007), p. 49, available at www.iea.org/Textbase/npsum/WEO2007SUM.pdf.

[15] Executive Summary, *World Energy Outlook* (2008), p. 12, available at www.worldenergy-outlook.org/docs/weo2008/WEO2008_es_english.pdf.

[16] *India: Greenhouse Gas Emissions 2007*, Indian Network for Climate Change Assessment, Ministry of Environment and Forests, Government of India (May 2010), p. i. All Ministry of Environment and Forests documents on climate change are available at http://moef.nic.in/modules/about-the-ministry/CCD/.

[17] The global average per capita rate is 4.5 metric tons, India's per capita rate is low compared to most industrialised countries and less than half of China's 3.8 metric tons rate. The USA has a per capita emissions rate of 20.6, Australia of 16.2 and Canada of 20 (see n. 7 above).

[18] See n. 16 above.

[19] R. Tongia, M. Saquib, H. S. Ramakrishna, *Indian Power Supply Position 2010*, CSTEP Working Paper, WP 1–30.8.2010 (Bangalore, 2010), p. 6, available at www.cstep.in/node/213.

[20] *Ibid.*

[21] *Country Analysis Briefs: India, 2010*, Energy Information Administration (2010), available at www.eia.doe.gov/emeu/cabs/India/Full.html.

[22] *Ibid.*

7.07   The Indian government, recognising electricity supply as central to sustained growth, global competitiveness and rural development, set itself the targets of providing electricity to all by 2010, and meeting full demand by 2012.[23] To meet these targets, the National Electricity Policy advocates 'maximum emphasis' on feasible hydro potential, significant increase in nuclear capacity, full exploitation of feasible non-conventional energy resources, but with recognition, however, that coal will continue 'to remain the primary fuel'.[24]

Climate risks

7.08   In the words of India's Environment Minister, Jairam Ramesh, 'no country in the world is as vulnerable, on so many dimensions, to climate change as India. Whether it is our long coastline of 7000 kms, our Himalayas with their vast glaciers, our almost 70 million hectares of forests (which incidentally house almost all of our key mineral reserves) – we are exposed to climate change on multiple fronts'.[25] The Indian Network for Climate Change Assessment ('INCCA'), a network of 120 institutions and 220 scientists across India, predicts that: the annual mean surface air temperature in India is likely to rise by 1.7°C and 2.0°C in the 2030s; melting glaciers will increase flood risk and decrease water supply; sea level rise (rate of 1.3 mm/year) will threaten coastal regions; monsoons, on which agriculture depends, will become more erratic and rain less plentiful; and incidence of malaria and other vector-borne diseases will increase, as will heat-related deaths and illnesses.[26] The INCCA also highlights prospective threats to food and water security: by 2080–2100, there is a probability of 10–40 per cent loss in crop production, and before 2025 India is likely to reach a state of water stress.[27]

7.09   India's economy is also likely to be significantly impaired by the impacts of climate change. The Stern Review notes that even a

---

[23] *National Electricity Policy*, Ministry of Power, Government of India (2005), s. 2, available at http://powermin.nic.in/whats_new/national_electricity_policy.htm.

[24] *Ibid.*

[25] Indian Network for Climate Change Assessment, *Climate Change and India: A 4X4 Assessment – A Sectoral and Regional Analysis for 2030s*, Ministry of Environment and Forests, Government of India (16 November 2010), p. 3.

[26] See generally *Ibid.*   [27]   *Ibid.*

small change in temperature could have a significant impact on the Indian monsoon, resulting in up to a 25 per cent reduction in agricultural yield.[28] A 2–3.5°C temperature increase could cause as much as a 0.67 per cent loss in GNP, and a 100 cm increase in sea level could cause a loss of 0.37 per cent in GNP.[29] Recent Indian research found that southwest monsoon rainfall had decreased by 4.7 per cent between 1965 and 2006, as compared to 1931–64.[30] A quarter of the Indian economy is dependent on agriculture, and any impact on this sector will fundamentally impair India's ability to meet its development goals. Climate change, therefore, is an issue that is increasingly being taken seriously by India.

International negotiating position, actions and partnerships

7.10   In international fora, India, a Party to the Framework Convention on Climate Change ('FCCC')[31] and its Kyoto Protocol,[32] has consistently rejected legally binding quantitative GHG mitigation targets.[33] India argues that, given its limited role in contributing to the problem, its overriding development needs, and the historical responsibility of developed countries, India cannot be expected to take on mitigation targets.[34] India is also opposed to establishing a quantitative long-term global goal or a peaking year, unless it is accompanied by an appropriate burden-sharing arrangement based on equity and differential treatment for developing countries.[35]

---

[28] Executive Summary, *Stern Review on the Economics of Climate Change* (2006), p. 6, available at www.hm-treasury.gov.uk.

[29] J. Roy, 'A Review of Studies in the Context of South Asia with a Special Focus on India: Contribution to the Stern Review' (2006), available at www.hm-treasury.gov.uk/media/5/0/roy.pdf.

[30] Ministry of Earth Sciences, Government of India, Press Release, 11 August 2010, available at www.pib.nic.in/release/release.asp?relIbid=64577.

[31] United Nations Framework Convention on Climate Change, 29 May 1992, *International Legal Materials*, 31 (1992), 849.

[32] Kyoto Protocol to the United Nations Framework Convention on Climate Change, 10 December 1997, *International Legal Materials*, 37 (1998), 22 (the 'Kyoto Protocol').

[33] See for a representative sample, *Climate Change Negotiations: India's Submissions to the UNFCCC*, Ministry of Environment and Forests, Government of India (August 2009).

[34] *Ibid.*

[35] See Letter by Jairam Ramesh, Minister of State for Environment and Forests, Letter to the Members of Parliament: Cancun Agreements, 20 December 2010, on file with authors.

7.11   Nevertheless, in 2007, India promised that its per capita emissions would not exceed the levels of developed countries.[36] India believes that this will incentivise developed countries to achieve timely reductions in their per capita emissions.[37] The OECD average per capita emissions is 13.2.[38]

7.12   India has also offered to embark on a path of decarbonisation. Decarbonisation, according to India, refers to an economy with lower carbon intensity over time.[39] Decarbonisation includes enhanced energy efficiency, a shift in primary energy use from fossil fuels to renewable energies (including hydropower) and nuclear energy, and changes in production and consumption patterns.[40] In 2010, India crystallised its offer to decarbonise into a voluntary undertaking under the non-binding Copenhagen Accord[41] to 'endeavour to reduce the emissions intensity of its GDP by 20–25 percent by 2020 in comparison to the 2005 level'.[42] This undertaking has been mainstreamed into the FCCC process through an information document taken note of[43] by the Cancun Agreements, 2010.[44]

7.13   India is an enthusiastic participant in the Clean Development Mechanism;[45] 21.2 per cent of all registered projects are from India (second only to China at 44.4 per cent, and followed by Brazil at 6.2 per cent); 10.8 per cent of all expected certified

---

[36] PM's Intervention on Climate Change at Heiligendamm, Meeting of G8 + 5, Heiligendamm, Germany, 8 June 2007, available at www.pib.nic.in.

[37] PM's address at the 95th Indian Science Congress, 3 January 2008, available at www.pib.nic.in.

[38] *Human Development Report: Fighting Climate Change* (see n. 7 above).

[39] 'Dealing with the Threat of Climate Change', India Country Paper, the Gleneagles Summit, 2005.

[40] *Ibid.*

[41] Decision 2/CP.15, Copenhagen Accord, FCCC/CP/2009/11/Add.1 (30 March 2010), p. 4 ('Copenhagen Accord').

[42] India – Letter to the Executive Secretary, 30 January 2010, available at www.unfccc.int/files/meetings/application/pdf/indiacphaccord_app2.pdf.

[43] See 'Compilation of Information on Nationally Appropriate Mitigation Actions to be Implemented by Parties Not Included in Annex I to the Convention', FCCC/AWGLCA/2011/INF.1 (18 March 2011), p. 26.

[44] Decision 1/CP.16, 'The Cancun Agreements: Outcome of the Work of the Ad Hoc Working Group on Long-term Cooperative Action under the Convention', FCCC/CP/2010/7/Add.1 (15 March 2011), at para. 49.

[45] Article 12, the Kyoto Protocol.

emissions reductions (CERs) are from India (as compared to 63.7 per cent from China and 4.7 per cent from Brazil).[46]

7.14 India is part of several bilateral and plurilateral arrangements on climate change and energy. India is a part of the Asia Pacific Partnership on Clean Development and Climate,[47] the Carbon Sequestration Leadership Forum,[48] the Methane to Markets Partnership[49] and the International Partnership for a Hydrogen Economy.[50] India has bilateral partnerships with the European Union (EU),[51] the United States (USA)[52] and the United Kingdom (UK)[53] on climate research and technology. India also participates in meetings of the G20, G8+5 and the Major Economies Forum[54] that seek to resolve political issues and provide stimulus to the climate negotiations. In the negotiations, India is part of the BASIC (Brazil, South Africa, India and China) group,[55] which itself is part of the G77/China, a large coalition of developing countries.[56]

Domestic policies and measures

7.15 India launched its National Climate Change Action Plan in 2008 bringing together existing and proposed efforts at decarbonisation under eight national missions: solar energy; enhanced energy efficiency; sustainable habitats; water; the Himalayan ecosystem; 'Green India'; sustainable agriculture; and strategic knowledge for climate change.[57] These missions are intended to assist India

[46] CDM Statistics, available at www.cdm.unfccc.int.
[47] Further details available at www.asiapacificpartnership.org/.
[48] Further details available at www.cslforum.org/.
[49] Further details available at www.methanetomarkets.org/.
[50] Further details available at www.iphe.net/.
[51] 'India-EU Strategic Partnership Joint Action Plan', available at www.ec.europa.eu.
[52] 'Overview of the US-India Climate Change Partnership', US Department of State, available at www.state.gov.
[53] 'Working with Developing Countries – India', Department for Environment, Food and Rural Affairs, Government of the UK, available at www.defra.gov.uk.
[54] Further details available at www.majoreconomiesforum.org/.
[55] India hosted the Sixth BASIC Ministerial Meeting, 26–27 February 2011; further details available at http://moef.nic.in/downloads/public-information/BASIC-Stat-6.pdf.
[56] Further details available at www.g77.org/.
[57] *National Action Plan on Climate Change*, Prime Minister's Council on Climate Change, Government of India (2008), available at http://www.pmindia.nic.in/Pg01–52.pdf.

in adapting to climate change, as well as in launching its economy on a path that 'would progressively and substantially result in mitigation through avoided emissions'.[58] The Plan, an initial cut at addressing the issue, does not contain any mechanisms to estimate the cost of climate change impacts or compliance. Neither does it mainstream climate change factors into development planning, as evidenced by the fact that no reference is made to how this Action Plan is qualified by, or qualifies, India's Integrated Energy Policy.[59]

7.16   In the years since the release of the Plan, there have been several developments. The Indian government is in the process of developing a 'roadmap for low carbon development'.[60] The relevant Ministries have developed comprehensive mission documents detailing objectives, strategies, plans of action, timelines, and monitoring and evaluation criteria.[61] There are several noteworthy initiatives contained in these missions, including: the creation of a market – a perform, achieve and trade mechanism – in energy savings certificates; the adoption of a target to generate 20,000 MW of solar power by 2022; and a commitment to double the area to be afforested in the next ten years, taking the total to 20 million ha.[62] In addition, the Indian government has announced a levy – a clean energy tax – of US$ 1 per ton on coal.[63] State-level action plans on climate change are also in preparation.

7.17   India's domestic climate policy interventions can be located squarely within the logic of a co-benefits approach – an approach that seeks to exploit synergies between development and climate change. Given India's development imperatives, it has chosen to channel its limited resources into areas that have significant co-benefits. Hence the emphasis in India's domestic policy interventions on energy efficiency, conservation, and diversification of energy sources (with the promotion of renewable energies as an element). These interventions deliver climatic benefits, but

---

[58] *Ibid*, p. 6.   [59] See n. 12 above.
[60] See generally *India: Taking on Climate Change – Post-Copenhagen Domestic Actions*, Ministry of Environment and Forests, Government of India (30 June 2010).
[61] *National Action Plan on Climate Change* (see n. 57 above), pp. 2 and 47; see also Press Information Bureau Release, Ministry of Environment and Forests, Finalisation of the Eight National Missions, 11 August 2010.
[62] See n. 60 above, p. 5.   [63] *Ibid*, p. 2.

also enhance energy security, lead to greater energy availability and access, and accelerate development.

(B)   Public law

The constitutional framework, environmental rights and international law[64]

7.18   The Constitution of India, in Part III, titled 'Fundamental Rights', creates a regime of protection for a privileged set of rights. Laws inconsistent with or in derogation of these rights are void to the extent of their inconsistency.[65] The centrepiece of these fundamental rights is the right to life and liberty.[66] This right has over the years been extended through judicial creativity to cover unarticulated but implicit rights such as the right to live with human dignity,[67] the right to livelihood,[68] the right to education,[69] the right to health and medical care of workers,[70] and most importantly for current purposes, the 'right of enjoyment of pollution-free water and air'.[71]

7.19   Although, thus far, no climate-related claim has been brought before the Supreme Court, it is likely, should such a claim be brought – given the Court's jurisprudence and its expansionist proclivities – that it would either interpret the environmental right to include a right to climate protection or apply a human rights optic to climate impacts.

---

[64]   This subsection draws from L. Rajamani, 'The Right to Environmental Protection in India: Many a Slip between the Cup and the Lip?', *Review of European Community And International Environmental Law*, 16 (2007), 274.

[65]   Article 13(2), The Constitution of India, 1950.

[66]   Article 21, *Ibid.*

[67]   *Francis Coralie Mullin* v. *The Administrator, Union Territory of Delhi* (1981) 1 SCC 608, at paras. 7 and 8.

[68]   *Olga Tellis* v. *Bombay Municipal Corporation* (1985) 3 SCC 545, at para. 32.

[69]   *Mohini Jain* v. *State of Karnataka* (1992) 3 SCC 666, at para. 12, and *J. P. Unni Krishnan* v. *State of Andhra Pradesh* (1993) 1 SCC 645, at para. 166, before the introduction of Article 21A.

[70]   *Consumer Education and Research Centre* v. *Union of India* (1995) 3 SCC 42, at paras. 24 and 25.

[71]   *Subash Kumar* v. *State of Bihar* (1991) 1 SCC 598, at para. 7. See also *M. C. Mehta* v. *Union of India* (1992) 3 SCC 256, at para. 2, and *Virender Gaur* v. *State of Haryana* (1995) 2 SCC 577, at para. 7.

7.20   There are many different formulations of the constitutionally protected environmental right in India. Some of these formulations are expansive in that they can readily encompass protection against new forms of environmental harm. Other formulations are more limiting. The less expansive definitions define the environmental right in the context of either pollution or health. So, for instance, in relation to pollution, the environmental right has been characterised as the right to 'pollution-free air and water',[72] 'fresh air, clean water',[73] 'pollution-free environment'[74] and 'clean environment'.[75] It has been defined in the context of human health, as for instance, the right to a 'humane and healthy environment',[76] a 'hygienic environment'[77] and 'sanitation'.[78] It may be difficult in the context of these formulations to argue for an expansion of the environmental right to include climate protection, given that GHGs are not generally considered pollutants and do not typically contribute to localised pollution resulting in identifiable health impacts.

7.21   However, the constitutionally protected environmental right has also been characterised as the right to: 'environmental protection and conservation of natural resources';[79] 'live in a healthy environment with minimal disturbance of [the] ecological balance';[80] a 'decent environment';[81] and a 'living atmosphere congenial to human existence'.[82] These formulations leave ample scope for value judgements and judicial discretion, and hence admit the possibility of protecting against threats to the climate. Climate

---

[72] *Charan Lal Sahu* v. *Union of India* (1990) 1 SCC 613, at para. 137.

[73] *Narmada Bachao Andolan* v. *Union of India* (2000) 10 SCC 664, at para. 244.

[74] *Vellore Citizens Welfare Forum* v. *Union of India* (1996) 5 SCC 647, at paras. 16 and 17.

[75] *Ibid.*

[76] *K. M. Chinnappa and T. N. Godavarman Thirumulpad* v. *Union of India* (2002) 10 SCC 606, at para. 18, and *State of MP* v. *Kedia Leather and Liquor Ltd* (2003) 7 SCC 389, at para. 9.

[77] *Virender Gaur and Ors* v. *State of Haryana and Ors* (1995) 2 SCC 577, at para. 7.

[78] *K. M. Chinnappa and T. N. Godavarman Thirumulpad* v. *Union of India* (2002) 10 SCC 606, at para 18.

[79] *Intellectuals Forum, Tirupathi* v. *State of AP* (2006) 3 SCC 549.

[80] *Rural Litigation and Entitlement Kendra* v. *State of UP* (1985) 2 SCC 431, at para. 12. See also *Narmado Bachao Andolan* v. *Union of India* (2000) 10 SCC 664, at para. 120, and *Virender Gaur and Ors* v. *State of Haryana and Ors* (1995) 2 SCC 577, at para. 7.

[81] *Shantistar Builders* v. *Narayan Khimala Totame and Ors* (1990) 1 SCC 520, at para. 9.

[82] *Virender Gaur and Ors* v. *State of Haryana and Ors* (1995) 2 SCC 577, at para. 6.

change will undoubtedly disturb the ecological balance, however that term is defined. It will also render the atmosphere less 'congenial' to human existence. The inhabitants of the Sundarbans, at the frontline of climate change, can testify to this.

7.22   Even if the Supreme Court is reluctant to extend the environmental right to cover climate protection, it will likely be impressed with an approach that applies a human rights (in the Indian context, a 'fundamental rights') optic to climate impacts. A host of rights and progressive realisation towards them, such as the rights to life, health and water, among others, will be at risk from climate impacts. There is a burgeoning and ever-persuasive literature arguing the case.[83] These rights – to life, health and water – are, as we have seen, constitutionally protected in India. The Supreme Court would need but little persuasion to read climate impacts as threatening these rights.

7.23   The environmental right is complemented by relevant provisions of the Directive Principles of State Policy,[84] in particular Articles 47[85] and 48A[86] which articulate the duties of the State with respect to public health and environmental protection. Although the Directive Principles of State Policy are not intended to be 'enforceable by any court', they are nevertheless 'fundamental in the governance of the country' and it is 'the duty of the State to apply these principles in making laws'.[87] In addition to the relevant Directive Principles of State Policy, the Constitutional schema also includes Article 51A(g) which imposes a duty on citizens to protect and improve the environment.[88]

7.24   India, one of the first jurisdictions to embrace an environmental right, is perceived as having 'fostered an extensive

---

[83] See e.g. S. Mcinerney-Lankford, M. Darrow and L. Rajamani, *Human Rights and Climate Change: A Review of the International Legal Dimensions* (World Bank, 2011); Stephen Humphreys, *Climate Change and Human Rights: A Rough Guide* (The International Council on Human Rights Policy, 2008); C. Bals, S. Harmeling and M. Windfuhr, *Climate Change, Food Security and the Right to Adequate Food* (Bonn: Germanwatch e.V., 2008); *Climate Wrongs and Human Rights: Putting People at the Heart of Climate Change* (OXFAM Report, 2008); and *Protecting Health from Climate Change* (World Health Organization, 2008).

[84] Part IV, Articles 36–51, The Constitution of India, 1950.

[85] Article 47, *ibid.*   [86] Article 48A, *ibid.*

[87] Article 39, *ibid.*   [88] Article 51A(g), *ibid.*

and innovative jurisprudence on environmental rights'.[89] The courts have fleshed out the environmental right by integrating into Indian environmental jurisprudence numerous principles of international environmental law.[90] These include the polluter pays principle,[91] the precautionary principle,[92] the principle of inter-generational equity,[93] the principle of sustainable development[94] and the notion of the State as a trustee of all natural resources.[95] The Supreme Court has held these principles to be 'essential features of sustainable development',[96] 'imperative for preserving ecology'[97] and 'part of environmental law of India'.[98] The Court requires these principles to be 'applied in full force for protecting the natural resources of this country'.[99] The constitutionally protected environmental right complemented by these principles of international environmental law provides a fertile breeding ground for ambitious rights-based climate claims.

7.25   The principles, in particular, of precaution, public trust and inter-generational equity, as interpreted by the Indian courts, will prove useful to prospective rights-based climate claimants. The precautionary principle requires the State to take environmental measures 'to anticipate, prevent and attack' the causes of

---

[89] Michael R. Anderson, 'Individual Rights to Environmental Protection in India' in A. Boyle and M. R. Anderson (eds.), *Human Rights Approaches to Environmental Protection* (Oxford University Press, 1996), p. 199.

[90] For instance principles that are contained in Principles 3, 4, 15 and 16, Rio Declaration on Environment and Development, 1992.

[91] *Indian Council for Enviro-legal Action* v. *Union of India* (Bichhri Case) (1996) 3 SCC 212. See also *M. C. Mehta* v. *Kamal Nath* (2000) 6 SCC 213, at 220.

[92] *Vellore Citizens' Welfare Forum* v. *Union of India* (1996) 5 SCC 647. See also *Narmada Bachao Andolan* v. *Union of India* (2000) 10 SCC 664, at 727.

[93] *State of Himachal Pradesh* v. *Ganesh Wood Products* (1995) 6 SCC 363. See also *Indian Council for Enviro-legal Action* v. *Union of India* (CRZ Notification case) (1996) 5 SCC 281.

[94] *M. C. Mehta* v. *Union of India* (Taj Trapezium Case) (1997) 2 SCC 353, at 381. See also *Narmada Bachao Andolan* v. *Union of India* (2000) 10 SCC 664, at 727.

[95] *M. C. Mehta* v. *Kamal Nath* (1997) 1 SCC 388.

[96] *Vellore Citizens' Welfare Forum* v. *Union of India* (1996) 5 SCC 647, at para. 11.

[97] *Karnataka Industrial Areas Development Board* v. *C. Kenchappa and Ors* (2006) 6 SCC 371, at para. 32.

[98] *Research Foundation for Science Technology & National Resource Policy* v. *Union of India and Anor* (2005) 13 SCC 186, at para. 24.

[99] *Intellectuals Forum, Tirupathi* v. *State of AP* (2006) 3 SCC 549, at para. 63.

environmental degradation.[100] It posits further that, 'where there are threats of serious and irreversible damage, lack of scientific certainty should not be used as a reason for postponing measures to prevent environment degradation'.[101] Finally, it lays the onus of proof on the actor or the developer/industrialist to demonstrate that the proposed action is 'environmentally benign',[102] an unusual and controversial interpretation of the principle. Climate change falls neatly into the category of threats that it would be wise to take early action on. This principle could be used to argue the case for ambitious mitigation and adaptation intervention, and to challenge State action that falls short.

7.26   The doctrine of public trust would add further weight to the argument. This doctrine places an affirmative duty on the State as a trustee of certain public resources to protect resources like air, sea, water and the forests for the enjoyment of the general public.[103] The Court envisages that this doctrine would be equally appropriate 'in controversies involving air pollution, the dissemination of pesticides, the location of rights of ways for utilities, and strip mining of wetland filling on private lands in a state where governmental permits are required'.[104] The issue of climate change could well engage the duty of a state as trustee to protect the atmosphere from indiscriminate GHG emissions.

7.27   The principle of inter-generational equity may also be of assistance.[105] The principle, formulated originally in the context of forest resources, holds that 'the present generation has no right to deplete all the existing forests and leave nothing for the next and future generations'.[106] Climate change presents the ultimate

---

[100]   *Vellore Citizens' Welfare Forum* v. *Union of India* (1996) 5 SCC 647, at para. 11, and *S. Jagannathan* v. *Union of India* (1997) 2 SCC 87, at para. 41. See also *Karnataka Industrial Areas Development Board* v. *C. Kenchappa and Ors* (2006) 6 SCC 371, at para. 32.

[101]   *Ibid.*, at para. 11.   [102]   *Ibid.*

[103]   *M. C. Mehta* v. *Kamal Nath* (1997) 1 SCC 388, at para. 25; see also *Intellectuals Forum, Tirupathi* v. *State of AP* (2006) 3 SCC 549, at paras. 59 and 60, and *Karnataka Industrial Areas Development Board* v. *C. Kenchappa and Ors* (2006) 6 SCC 371, at paras. 32–7.

[104]   Citing Joseph Sax, *ibid.*, at para. 22.

[105]   *State of Himachal Pradesh* v. *Ganesh Wood Products* (1995) 6 SCC 363, at para. 46.

[106]   *Ibid.* See also *Indian Council for Enviro-legal Action* v. *Union of India* (1996) 5 SCC 281, at para. 26; *AP Pollution Control Board* v. *M. V. Nayudu and Ors* (1999) 2 SCC 718, at para. 52; *T. N. Godavarman Thirumulpad* v. *Union of India and Ors* (2006) 1 SCC 1, at paras. 88, 89.

'inter-generational' problem. Current generations inherited the problem, are exacerbating it, and will likely leave a legacy that imposes severe burdens of protection and sacrifice on future generations. All three principles – precaution, public trust and inter-generational equity – are to varying degrees recognised in the FCCC as well.[107] These principles offer powerful building blocks in a rights-based claim seeking more aggressive State action on climate change. The Indian courts would likely provide a nurturing environment for such claims.

7.28   Rights-based claims relating to mitigation, however, may prove difficult to sustain. The principal hurdle in sanctioning State action relating to mitigation as insufficient or requiring the State to take further action will be in identifying benchmarks. How much action is appropriate for a country like India, given its, thus far, limited contribution to the problem, and its limited ability, on its own, over time, to resolve the problem? If the international regime had reached an equitable and effective burden-sharing agreement, and the Indian government was falling short of its just share of the burden, a claim may lie. However, in the absence of such an agreement, the Court would need to substitute its judgement for that of the international community, as well as that of the executive, which it may be reluctant to do. The reluctance may stem from concerns about intervening in an intensely political and polarised North-South climate debate as well as, albeit less so, stepping on the executive's toes. In the Court's jurisprudence, '[a]n excessively political role identifiable with political governance betrays the court into functions alien to its fundamental character, and tends to destroy the delicate balance envisaged in our constitutional system between its three basic institutions'.[108]

7.29   Rights-based claims relating to adaptation may fare better. A claim may lie for instance where the government is not taking the necessary action to adapt to predicted climate change in particularly vulnerable areas such as the Sunderbans, and the resulting climate impacts breach the claimant's protected rights to life, health, water etc.[109] In the case of adaptation, since core human

---

[107] Article 3, FCCC.
[108] *Bandhua Mukti Morcha* v. *Union of India* (1984) 3 SCC 161, at 232.
[109] See e.g. 'Sunderbans' Stoic Settlers Bear Witness to Climate Change', *The Pioneer*, 25 April 2011.

rights are implicated, rather than the right to environment, which is subject to limits in the service of development, claims may prove more successful.

7.30   Rights-based claims relating to adaptation may also be able to press international law into service. Article 51(c) of the Indian Constitution requires the State to 'foster respect for international law and treaty obligations'.[110] Implicit in this Article, according to the Supreme Court, is that '[a]ny International Convention not inconsistent with the fundamental rights and in harmony with its spirit must be read into these [Article 21 etc] provisions to enlarge the meaning and content thereof, to promote the object of the constitutional guarantee'.[111]

7.31   The core human rights threatened by climate impacts are protected under several human rights treaties that India is a Party to, including the International Covenant on Civil and Political Rights[112] and the International Covenant on Economic, Social and Cultural Rights.[113] India has an obligation under these treaties to respect, protect and fulfil the rights contained in them. This obligation is binding on every State Party, India included, and must be given effect to in good faith.[114] India is, also, as we have seen, a Party to the FCCC and its Kyoto Protocol.

7.32   India's treaty commitments read together arguably require it to approach climate change not just as a global environmental problem but also as a human rights issue. Such an approach would have substantive and procedural implications. Substantively, India may be required to devote greater resources to adaptation so as to lessen the human cost of climate impacts. Procedurally, India may be required to integrate the human rights implications of climate impacts into its planning and policy-making processes. India's treaty obligations could be thus interpreted by the Supreme Court to 'enlarge the

---

[110]   Article 51(c), The Constitution of India, 1950.

[111]   *Vishaka* v. *State of Rajasthan* (1997) 6 SCC 241, at para. 7.

[112]   International Covenant on Civil and Political Rights, 1966, reprinted in *International Legal Materials*, 6 (1967), 368.

[113]   International Covenant on Economic, Social and Cultural Rights, 1966, reprinted in *International Legal Materials*, 6 (1967), 360.

[114]   Article 26, Vienna Convention on the Law of Treaties, 1969, reprinted in *International Legal Materials*, 8 (1969), 679. See also CCPR General Comment 31, CCPR/C/21/Rev.1/Add.13.

meaning and content' of the constitutional guarantees, inter alia to life, health and water.

Judicial activism and public interest litigation[115]

7.33   The Indian judiciary is an extraordinary institution. It is, unlike in societies more deferential to separation of powers, a dynamic actor that shapes law, evolves policy, and plays a central determinative role in the governance of modern India. The Court plays this role primarily through the exercise of its self-fashioned public interest jurisdiction.

7.34   The origins of public interest jurisdiction in India can be traced to the late 1970s, early 1980s, and in particular the case of *S. P. Gupta* v. *Union of India* in which Justice Bhagwati relaxed the rule of *locus standi* and opened up the doors of the Supreme Court to public-spirited citizens – both those wishing to espouse the cause of the poor and oppressed (representative standing) and those wishing to enforce performance of public duties (citizen standing).[116]

7.35   Public interest litigation in India can be pursued either in the High Court or Supreme Court. If the complaint is of a legal wrong, Article 226 of the Constitution permits recourse to the High Court of the state. If the complaint alleges a violation of fundamental rights, Article 32 of the Constitution permits direct recourse to the Supreme Court. For violations of fundamental rights, the Supreme Court may issue an order, direction or writ, including a writ in the nature of *habeas corpus*, *quo warranto*, *mandamus*, prohibition or *certiorari*.[117] The High Courts can pass similar orders for enforcement of fundamental rights as well as of other legal rights.[118]

7.36   At the behest of public-spirited individuals, the courts have passed (and continue to pass) orders in a range of cases. In the

---

[115]   This subsection draws on L. Rajamani and A. Sengupta, 'The Supreme Court' in N. G. Jayal and P. B. Mehta (eds.), *Oxford Companion to Politics in India* (Oxford University Press, 2010), p. 80, and L. Rajamani, 'Public Interest Environmental Litigation in India: Exploring Issues of Access, Participation, Equity, Effectiveness and Sustainability', *Journal of Environmental Law*, 19 (2007), 293–321.

[116]   *S. P. Gupta* v. *Union of India*, 1981 Supp SCC 87, at 233.

[117]   Article 32, The Constitution of India, 1950.

[118]   Article 226, *ibid*.

environmental field the Supreme Court, for instance, has passed hundreds of orders inter alia to protect the Taj Mahal from corrosive air pollution,[119] rid the river Ganges of trade effluents,[120] address air pollution in Delhi and other metropolitan cities,[121] protect the forests and wildlife of India,[122] and clear cities of their garbage.[123]

7.37   The power of public interest litigation in India lies in its freedom from the constraints of traditional judicial proceedings. Public interest litigations in India have come to be characterised by a collaborative approach, procedural flexibility, judicially supervised interim orders and forward-looking relief. Judges in their activist avatar reach out to numerous parties and stakeholders, form fact-finding, monitoring or policy-evolution committees, and arrive at constructive solutions to the problems flagged for their attention by public-spirited citizens. Judges have tremendous power, in particular in public interest litigations, to design innovative solutions, direct policy changes, catalyse law-making, reprimand officials and enforce orders.

7.38   The Supreme Court is constitutionally empowered to 'make such order as is necessary for doing complete justice in any cause or matter pending before it'.[124] Judges are not hesitant to exercise this power in what they perceive as the public interest. The discretion and flexibility that the courts have arrogated to themselves in the context of public interest jurisdiction will enable them, when faced with a climate case, to tailor solutions to problems, evolve policy where a vacuum exists, and govern when they perceive a governance deficit. The case of *T. N. Godavarman* v. *Union of India* is a case in point. The Supreme Court defined a 'forest' in the absence of a definition in the Forest (Conservation) Act, 1980,[125] and in so doing, the Court extended the protective framework of the statute to *all* forests, irrespective of the nature of their ownership or classification.[126] It has since taken over the

---

[119] *M. C. Mehta* v. *Union of India* (Taj Trapezium Case), W.P. No. 13381/1984.
[120] *M. C. Mehta* v. *Union of India* (Ganga Pollution Case), W.P. No. 3727/1985.
[121] *M. C. Mehta* v. *Union of India* (Delhi Vehicular Pollution Case), W.P. No. 13029/1985, and *M. C. Mehta* v. *Union of India* (Delhi Industrial Relocation Case), W.P. No. 4677/1985.
[122] *T. N. Godavarman Thirumulpad* v. *Union of India*, W.P. No. 202/1995.
[123] *Almitra Patel* v. *Union of India*, W.P. No. 888/1996.
[124] Article 142, The Constitution of India, 1950.
[125] (1997) 2 SCC 267, at 269.
[126] *Ibid.*

governance of the forests in India and passed numerous significant orders, including: that no forest, national park or wildlife sanctuary can be de-reserved without its explicit permission; and no non-forestry activity will be permitted in a national park or wildlife sanctuary even if prior approval under the Forest (Conservation) Act, 1980 has been obtained. It has also imposed complete bans on the movement of cut trees and timber from some states, and on felling of trees in 'any forest, public or private' in various hill regions.[127]

7.39   In the recent past, the judiciary, has, however, struck a cautionary note. In *Divisional Manager, Aravalli Golf Club and Anor* v. *Chander Hass*, the Court chastised the judiciary for overreach, and advocated judicial self-restraint.[128] In *State of Uttaranchal* v. *Balwant Singh Chaufal*, the Supreme Court directed the High Courts to formulate rules to encourage genuine public interest litigations, and discourage those filed for extraneous reasons.[129] Although some limits to the use of public interest litigations may be in the offing, these will likely only weed out those claims that are filed for private reasons, personal gain and such like. The public interest culture, although straining the judicial system to its limits, is still alive and well.

Environmental law and regulation

7.40   India has a wide array of environmental laws,[130] and an extensive network of Central and State Pollution Control Boards, among other regulatory authorities, to govern them.[131] The laws most relevant for current purposes are: the National Green Tribunal Act, 2010; the Environment (Protection) Act, 1986; the Air (Prevention and Control of Pollution) Act, 1981; and the Forest (Conservation) Act, 1980. Together these laws offer liberal access to litigants, a principled and environmentally benevolent framework, and numerous hooks for climate liability.

---

[127] Orders in n. 122 above.   [128] (2008) 1 SCC 683.
[129] (2010) 3 SCC 402.
[130] All environmental legislations are available at http://envfor.nic.in/legis/legis.html.
[131] See e.g. the website of the Central Pollution Control Board, Government of India, www.cpcb.nic.in/.

7.41   The newly constituted National Green Tribunal has jurisdiction over 'all civil cases where a substantial question relating to environment (including enforcement of any legal right relating to environment) is involved' and arises in the context of a defined set of environmental laws, including those listed above.[132] The Tribunal is empowered to hear appeals brought by 'any person aggrieved' by the decisions or orders of authorities under the air, water, biodiversity, environment and forest legislations.[133] In addition to the customary extension of 'person' to artificial juridical persons,[134] there is reason to believe that the courts, as they have in the past, will read 'aggrieved person' expansively. In *Prafulla Samantara* v. *Union of India*[135] the Delhi High Court held that the term 'aggrieved persons' includes 'public spirited interested persons, environmental activists or other such voluntary organisations working for the betterment of the community as a whole'.[136] A range of actors will in theory be able to approach the National Green Tribunal. It is worth noting, however, that the National Green Tribunal (Practices and Procedures) Rules, 2011, impose various burdensome procedural requirements, which may in practice deter claimants from appearing in person.[137] Nevertheless, dedicated climate litigants are likely to bring their claims before the Tribunal. Appeals lie from this Tribunal to the Supreme Court.[138]

7.42   The Tribunal, while passing an order, is required to apply the principles of sustainable development, precaution and polluter pays.[139] These principles, discussed earlier, have been fleshed out in case law, and are considered part of the law of the land. The application of the precautionary principle, in particular, may prove beneficial to climate litigants. The Tribunal also has far-ranging powers to order relief and compensation to victims of pollution or environmental damage, for restitution of damaged property, and even for restitution of the damaged environment.[140]

[132]   Section 14, National Green Tribunal Act, 2010.
[133]   Section 16, *ibid.*   [134]   Section 2(j), *ibid.*
[135]   W.P.N. 3126/2008, Order dated 6 May 2009.   [136]   *Ibid.*
[137]   See e.g. Rules 8 and 13, National Green Tribunal (Practices and Procedures) Rules, 2011, available at http://moef.nic.in/modules/recent-initiatives/NGT/.
[138]   Section 22, National Green Tribunal Act, 2010.
[139]   Section 20, *ibid.*   [140]   Section 15, *ibid.*

7.43   The Environment (Protection) Act, 1986, empowers the Central
         Government to take all necessary measures for protecting and
         improving the environment, and preventing, controlling and
         abating environmental pollution.[141] The central government
         has issued several pieces of secondary legislation to regulate dif-
         ferent aspects of the environment, including the Environment
         Impact Assessment notifications that may prove useful to climate
         litigants.

7.44   The Environment Impact Assessment regime in India requires
         a certain defined set of projects to obtain environmental clear-
         ances from either the Ministry of Environment and Forests or the
         state-level Environment Impact Assessment Authority, depend-
         ing on the size of the project, before commencing operations.[142]
         These authorities rely on data gathered and scrutinised by expert
         appraisal committees.[143] The expert appraisal committees are
         required to take account inter alia of the outcomes of public con-
         sultations in arriving at their recommendations.[144] Such public
         consultations provide avenues for civil society to introduce cli-
         mate considerations into the decision-making process. Expert
         appraisal committees are also permitted to consider documents
         other than those submitted by the project proponent while mak-
         ing recommendations.[145] These documents could include evi-
         dence relating to the potential climate impacts of the project.

7.45   Any 'aggrieved person' can challenge the grant or denial of envir-
         onmental clearances before the National Green Tribunal.[146]
         Clearances have been quashed before other fora on grounds
         such as: 'crucial impacts' were not taken into account;[147] public

---

[141] Section 3, Environment (Protection) Act, 1986.
[142] Gazette Notification for Environmental Impact Assessment, Ministry of Environment
       and Forests, Order, New Delhi, 14 September 2006. The following categories of projects,
       some if of a certain scale, require environmental clearances: mining, extraction of nat-
       ural resources and power generation, primary processing, materials production and
       processing, building/construction/area/township development projects, oil/gas trans-
       portation, hazardous waste, manufacturing/fabrication and physical infrastructure.
[143] Section IV, *ibid.*   [144] Section III, *ibid.*   [145] Section IV, *ibid.*
[146] Section 16(h) and (i), National Green Tribunal Act, 2010.
[147] *Vimal Bhai* v. *Union of India*, Appeal Nos. 8, 9 and 10 of 2007, National Environmental
       Appellate Authority, Order dated 15 September 2010; *Pratap Singh Thakur* v. *MoEF*,
       Appeal No. 34 of 2009, National Environmental Appellate Authority, Order dated 30
       August 2010. NEAA orders available at http://ercindia.org/neaa.php.

consultation procedure was improperly followed;[148] environmental impact was too great;[149] information submitted was false;[150] decision-granting clearance was not reasoned;[151] and data provided was inadequate to judge the environmental impact.[152] In cases where clearances have been granted without due consideration of GHG intensity or footprints of particular projects, litigants could challenge the clearance on the grounds that these 'crucial impacts' were not taken into account. It is worth noting that notwithstanding this seemingly progressive framework, only 1 per cent of applications for environmental clearances are currently rejected.[153] To take an example, of the fifty-eight coal mining projects seeking environmental clearances in 2009–10, thirty-one were approved, none were rejected, and the rest are pending.[154]

7.46   The Air (Prevention and Control of Pollution) Act, 1981, defines air pollutant as 'any solid, liquid or gaseous substance including noise present in the atmosphere in such concentration as may be or tend to be injurious to human beings or other living creatures or plants or property or environment'.[155] Although this has yet to be done, arguably, GHGs could be covered, through judicial interpretation, under this definition, and regulated. The American Environment Protection Agency, following the landmark case of *Massachusetts* v. *EPA*,[156] found that GHG emissions from moving vehicles are 'reasonably likely' to threaten public health and welfare, therefore certified six GHGs as pollutants, and proceeded

---

[148] *Prafulla Samantra* v. *Union of India*, Appeal No. 18 of 2009, National Environmental Appellate Authority, Order dated 15 September 2010.

[149] *Gomantak Shetkari Sangathana* v. *Union of India*, Appeal No. 30 of 2009, National Environmental Appellate Authority, Order dated 15 July 2010.

[150] *T. Mohana Rao* v. *Union of India*, Appeal Nos. 1–6 of 2010, National Environmental Appellate Authority, Order dated 14 July 2010.

[151] *Utkarsh Mandal* v. *Union of India*, W.P. No. 9340/2009 & C.M. Appl. Nos. 7127/09, 12496/2009, Decision dated 26 November 2009.

[152] *Balachandra Bhikaji Nalwade* v. *Union of India & Others*, W.P. No. 388/2009, Decision dated 18 July 2009.

[153] Tabulated based on information provided to Shibani Ghosh by the Ministry of Environment and Forests in response to a series of Right to Information applications filed in 2010. See Press Note, 'There is Still Only One in a Hundred Chance of Having Your EC Rejected', available at www.ercindia.org.

[154] *Ibid.*, Ministry of Environment and Forests Letter dated 15 November 2010.

[155] Section 2(a), Air (Prevention and Control of Pollution) Act, 1981.

[156] *Massachusetts* v. *EPA*, 549 US 497 (2007); see Chapter 20.

to regulate these under the Clean Air Act, 1970.[157] A similar interpretation to 'air pollutants' under the Air (Prevention and Control of Pollution) Act, 1981, would permit relevant authorities under this legislation to inter alia lay down 'standards for emission of air pollutants into the atmosphere from industrial plants and automobiles or for the discharge of any air pollutant into the atmosphere from any other source whatsoever not being a ship or an aircraft'.[158]

7.47   The Forest (Conservation) Act, 1980,[159] restricts the conversion of forestland to non-forest use. State governments have to seek prior approval from the central government before de-reserving forestland, permitting non-forest use, or assigning it for private use.[160] The Supreme Court has carved a role for itself in forest conservation.[161] State governments are required to obtain permission from the Supreme Court for de-reserving forestland.[162] The central government relies on the recommendations of a government-appointed Forest Advisory Committee in making decisions relating to such approvals.[163] The Committee can consider, inter alia, the potential climate impacts caused by the diversion of forest land to non-forest purposes, for instance the impacts attributable to the submergence of forest land by a hydro power project. 'Aggrieved persons' can challenge approvals, possibly on climate-related grounds, granted by the Central Government, before the National Green Tribunal.[164]

Judicial review

7.48   Public bodies take numerous decisions, in the course of exercising their functions, that will likely have an impact, direct or indirect, on climate change. They may take decisions approving the setting-up of coal-based power plants or permitting forestland

---

[157] See Chapter 20.

[158] Section 17(g), Air (Prevention and Control of Pollution) Act, 1981.

[159] For a comprehensive study of the Supreme Court's interventions in the area of forest regulation, see generally R. Dutta and B. Yadav, *Supreme Court on Forest Conservation*, 3rd edn (Delhi: Universal Law Publishing, 2011).

[160] Section 2, Forest (Conservation) Act, 1980.

[161] *T. N. Godavarman Thirumulpad* v. *Union of India*, W.P. No. 202/1995.

[162] *Ibid.*   [163] Section 3, Forest (Conservation) Act, 1980.

[164] Section 16(e), National Green Tribunal Act, 2010.

to be cleared for mining. Climate litigants may wish to challenge such decisions by seeking judicial review of administrative action. There are various techniques available to do so – writs, appeals for review, references to courts, injunctions, declarations, suits for damages for tortious actions (of government bodies/employees), etc. Of these, the technique most favoured is that of writs.[165] The two most relevant, for current purposes, would be that of *mandamus*[166] and *certiorari*.[167] A writ of *mandamus* may be issued to compel the performance of a public legal duty by a public authority[168] while the writ of *certiorari* may be issued to quash a decision of a body, administrative or quasi-judicial, that affects the rights or interests of any person.[169]

Grounds for judicial review

7.49 Judicial review of administrative action can be sought on several grounds, including:[170] illegality; irrationality; proportionality; and procedural impropriety.

7.50 *Illegality*: The decision of an administrative body or the exercise of its discretionary powers may be considered illegal if the body acted without jurisdiction, failed to exercise its jurisdiction, or abused its jurisdiction or discretionary powers.[171] In the climate context, abuse of discretionary power due to non-inclusion of relevant considerations and non-application of mind by the administrative body may prove useful. If the statute lays down considerations, express or implied, which have to be taken into account by an administrative body while exercising its discretionary powers, the non-inclusion of such relevant considerations would render the decision illegal.[172] Even if the statute does

---

[165] G. P. Singh and A. Aradhe, *M. P. Jain & S. N. Jain: Principles of Administrative Law*, 6th edn (LexisNexis Butterworths Wadhwa Nagpur, 2010), p. 495.

[166] *Comptroller and Auditor-General of India* v. *K. S. Jagannathan* (1986) 2 SCC 679.

[167] *T. C. Basappa* v. *T. Nagappa* AIR 1954 SC 440.

[168] M. P. Jain, *M. P. Jain & S. N. Jain: Principles of Administrative Law*, 6th (enlarged) edn, 2 vols. (LexisNexis Butterworths Wadhwa Nagpur, 2007 (reprinted 2010)), vol. II, p. 2149.

[169] *Ibid*, p. 2177.

[170] *Tata Cellular* v. *Union of India* (1994) 6 SCC 651.

[171] I. P. Massey, *Administrative Law*, 7th edn (Lucknow: Eastern Book Company, 2008), pp. 394–6.

[172] *Ranjit Singh* v. *Union of India* AIR 1981 SC 461; *K. Shanmugam* v. *SKVS (P) Ltd* AIR 1963 SC 1626; *Sachidananda Pandey* v. *State of West Bengal* AIR 1987 SC 1109.

not lay down such considerations but provides general powers to the body, the courts may still read in relevant considerations and quash the decision of the body.[173] Relevant considerations may also be gauged from the facts and circumstances of the case, the aims and objectives of the statute and the impact of the decision/action.[174] In the context of decisions affecting the environment, the latest scientific data and technical reports testifying, for instance, to adverse environmental impacts of a project are relevant considerations that the decision-making authority is required to take account of.

7.51   An administrative decision can also be challenged when the authority has not applied its mind to relevant considerations,[175] when it acts mechanically,[176] or it acts under dictation.[177] If the government mechanically permits an industry or process without applying its mind to the potential climate impacts, its decision may be challenged before the courts as illegal.

7.52   *Irrationality* (or *Wednesbury* unreasonableness): A further ground on which an administrative decision can be challenged is irrationality. For an administrative decision to be considered irrational, the court has to hold, on material, that the decision is so outrageous as to be in total defiance of logic or moral standards.[178] The intervention of the court in such cases is limited to an examination of the decision-making process, not the decision. If the court finds that the administrator acted illegally, did not perform his/her primary role well, either omitted relevant factors or took irrelevant factors into consideration, or his/her view is one which no reasonable person could have taken, then the court may quash the decision as being arbitrary and in violation of Article 14 of the Constitution.[179] In a climate context, if it can

---

[173] *Siddharam Satlingappa Mhetre* v. *State of Maharashtra* AIR 2011 SC 312.

[174] G. P. Singh and A. Aradhe, *M. P. Jain & S. N. Jain: Principles of Administrative Law*, p. 640.

[175] *Kanchanlal Maneklal Chokshi* v. *State of Gujarat* AIR 1979 SC 1945.

[176] *Chairman, Board of Mining Examination* v. *Ramjee* (1977) 2 SCC 256, at 262.

[177] *State of NCT of Delhi* v. *Sanjeev* (2005) 5 SCC 181, at 190.

[178] *Indian Railway Construction Co. Ltd* v. *Ajay Kumar* (2003) 2 SCC 579, at 591 (following Lord Diplock in *Council of Civil Service Unions* v. *Minister for the Civil Service* [1984] 3 All ER 935); *Chairman, All India Railway Rec. Board* v. *K. Shyam Kumar* (2010) 6 SCC 614.

[179] *Om Kumar* v. *Union of India* (2001) 2 SCC 386, at 411.

be shown that the authority, despite enjoying the discretion, did not consider relevant climate change policies and reports while granting regulatory approvals or making policy choices, a case for irrationality could be made.

7.53   *Proportionality*: The test of proportionality permits the courts to undertake a closer scrutiny of the administrative decision-making process than that merited by the *Wednesbury* test. Since this necessarily leads to a greater intervention in what is otherwise the executive's domain, the courts apply the test of proportionality principally in the context of fundamental rights.[180] The Supreme Court explains 'proportionality' as 'whether, while regulating exercise of fundamental rights, the appropriate or least restrictive choice of measures has been made by the legislature or the administrator so as to achieve the object of the legislation or the purpose of the administrative order, as the case may be'.[181] In recent years, the Supreme Court has held in some cases that the *Wednesbury* test has given way to the proportionality test.[182] But this position remains contested.[183] As climate-related claims are likely to be founded on the fundamental right to life, the courts are likely to apply the proportionality test.

7.54   *Procedural impropriety*: A decision of an administrative body can be reviewed on the ground that the procedure as stated in the law has not been followed. If a statute prescribes a procedure for exercise of power, the statutory authority must exercise its power in a manner prescribed or not at all.[184] Even if there is no statutory requirement, administrative bodies are expected to be just, fair and reasonable in their dealings or they could fall foul of Articles 14, 19 and 21 of the Constitution which have been read together to provide protection to the principles of natural justice.[185]

---

[180]   *Union of India* v. *G. Ganayutham* (1997) 7 SCC 463.
[181]   *Om Kumar* v. *Union of India* (2001) 2 SCC 386, at 399.
[182]   *State of UP* v. *Sheo Shanker Lal Srivastava* (2006) 3 SCC 276; *Indian Airlines Ltd* v. *Prabha D. Kanan* (2006) 11 SCC 67; *State of Madhya Pradesh* v. *Hazarilal* (2008) 3 SCC 273.
[183]   *Chairman, All India Railway Rec. Board* v. *K. Shyam Kumar* (2010) 6 SCC 614.
[184]   *Indian Banks' Association, Bombay* v. *M/s Devkala Consultancy Service* AIR 2004 SC 2615.
[185]   *Maneka Gandhi* v. *Union of India* AIR 1978 SC 597.

Other aspects of judicial review

7.55   Writs are commonly dismissed on the ground that the plaintiff lacks standing, there is unreasonable delay, or that an alternative efficacious remedy exists. Cases raising climate claims are unlikely to be affected by these grounds. First, Indian courts take, as we have seen, a liberal approach to standing.[186] Second, Articles 32 and 226 of the Constitution do not prescribe a reasonable timeframe within which a case must be brought before the court. Besides, in climate and environmental claims, the cause of action will likely be ongoing, and if there is illegality it is likely to be continuing.[187] Third, as one of the issues in a climate claim is likely to be the violation of the fundamental right to life, the existence of an alternative efficacious remedy is not a ground for the court to reject a writ before it.[188]

(C)   Private law

7.56   There have been no significant private law claims in India based on allegations of actual or anticipated damage from climate change. However, should claimants be inclined to bring such claims, the two torts that offer promise are nuisance and negligence. The essential elements of both torts are drawn from the common law principles of tort evolved by the courts in England, and applied to the extent of their suitability and applicability to Indian conditions.[189]

Nuisance

7.57   Although there is no strict definition of the tort of nuisance, it may be defined as 'an inconvenience that materially interferes with the ordinary physical comfort of human existence'.[190] The

---

[186] G. P. Singh and A. Aradhe, *M. P. Jain & S. N. Jain: Principles of Administrative Law*, pp. 550–3.

[187] *H. D. Vora* v. *State of Maharashtra* AIR 1984 SC 866.

[188] *Mumtaz Post Graduate Degree College* v. *Vice Chancellor* (2009) 2 SCC 630.

[189] *Rajkot Municipal Corporation* v. *Manjulben Jayantilal Nakum* (1997) 9 SCC 552; *Gujarat State Road Transport Corporation* v. *Ramanbhai Prabhatbhai* (1987) 3 SCC 238.

[190] *Vasant Manga Nikumba* v. *Baburao Bhikanna Naidu (Deceased) by LRs.* 1995 Supp. (4) SCC 54, at 56.

Supreme Court has identified the essential elements of nuisance as an unlawful act, and damage, actual or presumed.[191]

7.58   There are two kinds of nuisance – public nuisance and private nuisance. Public (or common) nuisance according to the Indian Penal Code, 1860 is an act or illegal omission which 'causes any common injury, danger or annoyance to the public or to the people in general who dwell or occupy property in the vicinity, or which must necessarily cause injury, obstruction, danger or annoyance to persons who may have occasion to use any public right'.[192] Private nuisance affects one or more individuals rather than a large group.

7.59   Public nuisance may offer some (limited) hope to climate litigations. For a claim to be successful the damage need not already have occurred. It is sufficient if there is an imminent danger to the health or the physical comfort of the community in the locality in which the trade or occupation causing the nuisance is conducted.[193] In *Kuldip Singh* v. *Subhash Chander Jain*, the Supreme Court held that '… a future nuisance to be actionable must be either imminent or likely to cause such damage as would be irreparable once it is allowed to occur …'.[194] This will prove useful in climate-related litigation, as the damage, while not imminent, is potentially irreparable.

7.60   Both civil and criminal remedies are available in public nuisance cases. The Code of Civil Procedure, 1908, provides that the Advocate General or, with the permission of the court, even persons to whom no damage has been caused, can file a suit.[195] This may prove useful to civil society in filing climate-related claims. However, this provision is not widely used in this fashion due to the lengthy delay in bringing civil proceedings to a close, and the liberal access provided to higher courts in India. Cases of public nuisance can also be pursued and addressed under criminal law.[196]

---

[191] *Rafat Ali* v. *Sugni Bai* AIR 1999 SC 283 (quoting from *Halsbury's Laws of England*).
[192] Section 268, Indian Penal Code, 1860. The texts of all Indian laws are available at http://indiacode.nic.in/.
[193] *Suhelkhan Khudyarkhan* v. *State of Maharashtra* (2009) 5 SCC 586.
[194] AIR 2000 SC 1410.   [195] Section 91, Code of Civil Procedure, 1908.
[196] Chapter XIV, Indian Penal Code, 1860; Sections 133–144, Code of Criminal Procedure, 1973; and special or local laws. See *Suhelkhan Khudyarkhan* v. *State of Maharashtra* (2009) 5 SCC 586.

7.61 In a landmark case on nuisance, the Supreme Court directed a municipality to remove the public nuisance caused due to lack of sanitation and drainage facilities and improper disposal of factory effluents.[197] The municipality pleaded lack of funds but the Supreme Court held that financial inability did not exonerate the municipality from statutory liability.[198]

7.62 The law of public nuisance may therefore offer some promise for climate litigants. While it may be difficult to prove imminent danger related to GHG emissions, it may be possible to demonstrate irreparable damage. It could also be argued that since emission of pollutants constitutes a nuisance, by logical extension emission of GHGs can also be construed to be a nuisance.

Absolute liability

7.63 The Supreme Court in a landmark decision in 1987 fashioned a new rule of tortious liability that has come to be characterised as 'absolute liability'.[199] The court held that where an enterprise is engaged in a hazardous or inherently dangerous industrial activity and harm results on account of an accident in the operation of such hazardous or inherently dangerous activity, the enterprise is strictly and absolutely liable to compensate all those who are affected by the accident.[200] Unlike the principle laid down in *Rylands* v. *Fletcher*, the absolute liability principle does not require an 'escape' of the thing (causing the harm) from the premises. Further, the enterprise is held liable irrespective of the care taken by it to prevent the accident.[201] Indeed none of the exceptions allowed by the rule of strict liability in *Rylands* apply in the case of absolute liability.[202] The justification for this type of liability is that a non-delegable duty is owed to the community to ensure that highest standards of safety are maintained.[203] In addition, the enterprise alone is in a position to prevent and discover any harm and send out warning signals against potential

---

[197] *Municipal Council, Ratlam* v. *Vardichan* (1980) 4 SCC 162, at 163–4.
[198] *Ibid.*, at 170.
[199] *M. C. Mehta* v. *Union of India* (1987) 1 SCC 395.
[200] *Ibid.*, at 421.   [201] *Ibid.*
[202] *Ibid.*   [203] *Ibid.*, at 420–1.

harm.[204] The court, to achieve deterrence, also held that the quantum of compensation should depend on the 'magnitude and capacity' of the enterprise.[205]

7.64   In *Indian Council for Enviro-Legal Action* v. *Union of India*[206] the Supreme Court held chemical industry units absolutely liable for discharging waste in the surrounding areas, polluting the soil and water, and thereby adversely affecting people living in the vicinity. The Supreme Court also, for the first time, relied on the principle of 'polluter pays' and held the industries responsible not only for compensating the victims but also for repairing the damage caused to the environment and restoring the water and soil to the condition it was in before the units commenced their operations.[207] In *Deepak Nitrite* v. *State of Gujarat*, the Court broadened the basis of compensation and held that 'compensation to be awarded must have some broad correlation not only with the magnitude and capacity of the enterprise, but also with the harm caused by it'.[208]

7.65   These cases, and concepts – both of absolute liability and polluter pays – are useful tools in the arsenal of public interest environmental litigants. However, since claims can only be brought once the damage has been caused, they may prove useful only in a subset of climate-related claims.

Negligence

7.66   Negligence is both a tort and a crime (some forms of it are offences under the Indian Penal Code).[209] As a tort, it has been defined as the breach of duty caused by the omission to do something that a reasonable man, guided by those considerations that ordinarily regulate the conduct of human affairs, would do, or doing something that a prudent and reasonable man would not

---

[204] *Ibid.*   [205] *Ibid.*

[206] (1996) 3 SCC 212, at 246; see application of the principle in *Jaipur Golden Gas Victims* v. *Union of India* 164 (2009) DLT 346; *Nagrik Sangarsh Samiti and Ors* v. *Union of India and Ors*, W.P. No. 3499/2005 MANU/DE/0965/2010; *State of J & K* v. *Zarda Begum and Ors* 2003 (1) JKJ 706.

[207] *Indian Council for Enviro-Legal Action* v. *Union of India* (1996) 3 SCC 212, at 247–8.

[208] (2004) 6 SCC 402, at 407.

[209] Sections 269, 284–289 and 304A, Indian Penal Code, 1860.

do.[210] The Supreme Court has identified the elements of negligence as:

> … whether the defendant owed a duty of care to the plaintiff, whether the plaintiff is a person or a class of persons to whom the defendant owed a duty of care, whether the defendant was negligent in performing that duty or omitted to take such reasonable care in the performance of the duty, whether damage must have resulted from that particular duty of care which the defendant owed to the particular plaintiff or class of persons.[211]

7.67   The plaintiff has to establish that the defendant owes a duty of care. This requires the plaintiff to demonstrate foreseeability of the damage, a sufficiently proximate relationship between the parties, and that it is just and reasonable to impose such a duty.[212] In addition there ought not to be any policy considerations that negative the existence of such a duty. The courts have held the concept of duty of care to be a fluid one, 'influenced and transformed by social, economic and political development'.[213]

7.68   The breach of the duty of care has to lead to some damage – whether in the form of economic loss or damage to person or property. A cause of action for negligence only arises when damage occurs[214] and not on the date on which the negligent act took place.[215]

7.69   The defendant's negligent act must have caused the damage. However, the defendant does not have to be wholly responsible for the damage. The courts have relaxed the causal rules in some instances. In the case of *Jaipur Golden Gas Victims* v. *Union of India*,[216] the Delhi High Court, relying on English[217]

---

[210] G. P. Singh, *Ratanlal & Dhirajlal: The Law of Torts*, 26th edn (LexisNexis Butterworths Wadhwa Nagpur, 2010), p. 474.

[211] *Rajkot Municipal Corporation* v. *Manjulben Jayantilal Nakum and Ors* (1997) 9 SCC 552, at 597–8.

[212] *Ibid.*, at 579–80.

[213] *Jay Laxmi Salt Works (P) Ltd* v. *State of Gujarat* (1994) 4 SCC 1, at 12.

[214] *Kishorilal* v. *Chairman Employees State Insurance Corpn* (2007) 4 SCC 579.

[215] *Jay Laxmi Salt Works (P) Ltd* v. *State of Gujarat* (1994) 4 SCC 1, at 17.

[216] *Jaipur Golden Gas Victims* v. *Union of India* 164 (2009) DLT 346.

[217] *Bonnington Castings Ltd* v. *Wardlaw* [1956] AC 613; and *McGhee* v. *National Coal Board* [1973] 1 WLR 1, HL.

and Canadian cases,[218] held that the claimant does not have to prove that the defendant's breach of duty was the sole, or even the main, cause of damage, provided he/she can demonstrate that it made a material contribution to the damage. Although the Court borrowed and applied concepts from foreign law, it did not analyse these in sufficient detail or depth to permit sensible predictions on the direction in which causal rules will evolve. Suffice to say that the cases that the Court borrowed from find causation where a material contribution to the damage exists. They also equate a 'material contribution to the damage' to a 'material increase in the risk' of the damage occurring. This might prove helpful in climate claims, where proof of causation, given multiple contributory factors and difficulties in attribution, hamstrings litigation. For instance, claims against power plants arguing that their indiscriminate GHG emissions, among other causes, have materially increased the risk of climate change and extreme weather events occurring, may, in the event of such events occurring, help locate liability and obtain compensation for victims.

7.70   For a climate claim based on negligence to be successful, the claimant would first have to establish proximity and foreseeability of damage. The person causing the GHG emission would have to be aware of the foreseeable damage that could be caused due to increased GHG emissions. Although the damage suffered by the plaintiff as a result of climate change (higher risk of disease, rising sea level, increases in extreme weather conditions etc.) may have several contributory factors, the relaxed causal rules in operation may allow the claim of the plaintiff to proceed.

7.71   Where negligence is proven, the courts can award damages that could be nominal, substantial or exemplary.[219] An injunction may also be sought to prevent the further infringement or disturbance of a right or prevent continued breach of duty of care leading to negligence.[220]

---

[218] *Jon Athey v. Ferdinando Leonati & Kevin Johnson* [1996] 3 SCR 458; and *Resurfice Corp. v. Hanke* [2007] 1 SCR 333.

[219] G. P. Singh, *Ratanlal & Dhirajlal: The Law of Torts*, pp. 209–11.

[220] Governed by provisions of the Specific Relief Act, 1963 and the Code of Civil Procedure, 1908.

(D) Other law

Criminal law

7.72 The Indian Penal Code, 1860, imposes a punishment on any person (including company, association etc.) who voluntarily vitiates the air in a manner which makes it harmful to the health of persons residing or carrying on business in the area.[221] This provision may be of limited use to climate litigants, for not only is there a requirement of physical proximity, but the fine that can be imposed is a mere 500 Rupees (approximately US$ 10).

Competition law

7.73 Although the Competition Act was passed by Parliament in 2002, significant provisions of the Act such as Sections 3 (prohibition of anti-competitive agreements) and 4 (prohibition of abuse of dominant position) came into force only in 2009. The legislation is therefore recent and is yet to reach a stage when it can be creatively interpreted so as to prohibit competitive advantage that might be enjoyed by industries that are emission-intensive.

World heritage

7.74 India has twenty-three cultural sites and five natural sites that are part of the list of World Heritage Sites.[222] Changes in temperature and rising sea levels will likely have an adverse impact on historical monuments as well as the floral and faunal diversity of the heritage sites.[223] One of the natural sites in India is the Sunderbans in West Bengal, featured on the cover of this book. Projected sea level rise due to climate change is the single largest threat to it.[224] The mangroves forests of Sunderbans are known for their biodiversity, and increased salinity in the water would threaten their continued existence.[225] The World Heritage

---

[221] Section 278, Indian Penal Code, 1860.
[222] A list of properties in India inscribed in the World Heritage List is available at http://whc.unesco.org/en/statesparties/in.
[223] UNESCO, *Case Studies on Climate Change and World Heritage* (2007), pp. 12–14.
[224] Note 25 above, at 97.
[225] UNESCO, *Case Studies on Climate Change and World Heritage* (2007), p. 36.

Convention, 1972, ratified by India in 1977, obliges States to protect and conserve the identified heritage sites.[226] This arguably
includes action to reduce the impact of climate change on these
sites.[227]

Unfair trade practices

7.75   Under Indian law, if any false or misleading statement about
the standards, quality, composition, quantity etc. of a product
is made orally, verbally or through visible representation, then
it constitutes an unfair trade practice.[228] A complaint against
unfair trade practices can be made at specialised fora constituted under the Consumer Protection Act, 1986, by a consumer
to whom such a good was sold, by a recognised consumer association, or even by the central or state governments.[229] Orders can
be issued by the competent forum for discontinuation of such
practices.

7.76   There is no special law relevant to the field of advertising.
However, the Advertising Council of India, a voluntary organisation of the advertising sector, has formulated a Code for Self-
Regulation in Advertising.[230] The Code states, inter alia, that:
advertisements cannot distort facts or mislead consumers; they
cannot abuse the lack of knowledge or experience of a consumer;
and should not contain anything that is in breach of the law or
omit anything that the law requires. Violation of the Code can
be challenged before the Consumer Complaints Council set up
under the Code. If the Council upholds a complaint against an
advertiser and the advertiser does not comply with the Council's
decision, the Council can report to the concerned government
agency.[231]

---

[226] Articles 4, 5, World Heritage Convention, 1972.
[227] Presentation by Janhwij Sharma, 'ASI and World Heritage', International Conference on
Asian World Heritage Cities, 18–20 April 2010.
[228] Section 2(1)(r)(1), Consumer Protection Act, 1986.
[229] Section 12(1), *ibid.*
[230] Available at www.ascionline.org/regulation/ASCI_Code_of_Self_Regulation.pdf.
[231] The procedure for processing a complaint against an advertisement, for contravention
of the Code, is available at www.ascionline.org/procedure/procedure_1.htm.

7.77   The provisions of the Consumer Protection Act and the Code can be relied on in cases where companies such as those selling automobile as well as electrical and electronic equipment make claims with regard to their emissions, fuel/energy efficiency or their impact on the climate that may be false or misleading.

(E)   Practicalities

7.78   This section provides an overview of the procedural aspects of the law and analyses whether the current state of law is procedurally amenable to climate claims.

Founding jurisdiction for a claim

7.79   The Civil Procedure Code, 1860, is the principal procedural legislation with regard to civil suits in India and therefore any tort-based climate change claim would be governed by it. For a person to be made a party to a civil suit, residence or domicile in India is not necessary. If the cause of action has arisen in India, the immoveable property with regard to which a compensation claim has been made is situated in India or if the defendant carries on business in India,[232] the suit can be brought before the appropriate civil court in India irrespective of the nationality or domicile of the defendant.

7.80   Criminal offences under the Indian Penal Code, 1860 can be tried either at the court in whose local jurisdiction the cause of action has arisen or at the court in whose local jurisdiction the consequences have been suffered.[233] Therefore offences such as public nuisance and criminal negligence can be tried in Indian courts, if the act causing the nuisance or the criminally negligent act has been committed in India or if the impact of the act is felt in India. The residence, domicile and citizenship of the person responsible for the act are not relevant. The provisions of the Indian Penal Code, 1860, are equally applicable if the offences are committed outside India by an Indian citizen.[234]

---

[232] Section 19, Code of Civil Procedure, 1908.
[233] Section 179, Code of Criminal Procedure, 1973.
[234] Section 4, Indian Penal Code, 1860.

Enforcement

7.81 There are many ways in which a civil decree can be enforced in India – delivery of property; attachment and sale of property; appointment of receiver; arrest and detention in prison (if certain conditions are met).[235] Decrees passed by foreign courts can be executed by Indian courts as if they were decrees passed by an Indian court if the foreign court is of a 'reciprocating territory'.[236] However, if the decree is not conclusive the Indian courts can refuse to execute it.[237] An arbitral award can be executed in the same way as any other civil decree.

7.82 Foreign arbitral awards can be enforced in India under the Arbitration and Conciliation Act, 1996. The court can refuse to enforce an award on certain grounds such as the enforcement of the award is contrary to public policy, the agreement for arbitration is not valid in law or the subject matter is not capable of settlement through arbitration in India. If the court makes a finding that the arbitral award is enforceable, then it is deemed to be a decree of the court.[238]

Ancillary orders

7.83 The Code of Civil Procedure, 1908 recognises the inherent power of courts to issue such orders as are necessary to meet the ends of justice.[239] Among other orders, Indian courts have the power to issue temporary injunctions[240] to restrain a defendant from causing any injury to the plaintiff or breach of contract during the continuance of suit proceedings.[241] They can issue injunction orders to restrain the commission of any act that is likely to damage property that is the subject matter of a suit.

---

[235] Section 51 read with Order XXI, Code of Civil Procedure, 1908.

[236] Section 44A, *ibid.*

[237] Section 13, *ibid.* (explaining that a foreign decree can be found to be inconclusive on grounds such as incompetence of the decreeing court, violation of principles of natural justice, etc.).

[238] Sections 49, 58, Arbitration and Conciliation Act, 1996.

[239] Section 151, Code of Civil Procedure, 1908.

[240] Sections 37–42, Specific Relief Act, 1963, and Order XXXIX, Code of Civil Procedure, 1908.

[241] Order XXXIX, Rule 2, *ibid.*

Courts can also pass interlocutory orders preserving property that is the subject matter of a suit or for inspecting and authorising a person to enter any property to take samples or undertake experiments necessary to bring to light full information and evidence.[242]

Litigation costs

7.84   Costs of litigation are generally borne by the litigants unless a person is entitled to legal services from the State.[243] The courts have discretion to award costs.[244] In case the court decides not to award costs then it has to state the reasons in its order.[245] The court can also impose costs in cases of proven false and vexatious claims[246] and deliberate delay.[247]

Obtaining information

7.85   In a civil suit, parties have to file copies of documents relied on by them to the court.[248] The court has the power to order discovery either on its own or in response to an application filed with it. It can issue necessary directions with regard to delivery and answering of interrogatories (set of questions filed by either party), inspection, production, impounding and return of documents or other objects.[249] It can even issue summons to a person required to give evidence or produce documents.[250] In a criminal case, whenever the court or the officer in charge is of the opinion that certain documents or any other things are necessary for the case, summons or order may be issued.[251] Electronic records can also be summoned by the court.

7.86   The Indian Evidence Act, 1872 imposes certain restrictions on the disclosure of information derived from unpublished official records relating to affairs of the State and communication made

---

[242] Order XXXIX, Rule 7, *ibid*.
[243] The Legal Services Authorities Act, 1987, in Section 12, lays down the criteria for providing legal services.
[244] See Order XXA and Section 35, Code of Civil Procedure, 1908.
[245] *Ibid*.   [246] Section 35A, *ibid*.
[247] Section 35B, *ibid*.   [248] Order VII, Rule 14, *ibid*.
[249] Section 30 read with Order XI, *ibid*.
[250] *Ibid*.   [251] Section 91, Code of Criminal Procedure, 1973.

in official confidence.[252] However, if there is a conflict between the provisions of the Right to Information Act, 2005[253] and the Indian Evidence Act, 1872, the former will override the latter.[254]

7.87   The Right to Information Act, 2005 provides statutory recognition to a hitherto uncodified fundamental right to information.[255] This legislation is intended to promote transparency and accountability in the governance of the country.[256] Citizens can file Right to Information applications seeking information from public authorities, i.e. government bodies and bodies that are owned, controlled or substantially financed by the government.[257] Information can also be obtained from private bodies as long as these can be lawfully accessed by a public authority.[258] Certain types of information are exempt from disclosure such as trade secrets, intellectual property etc.[259] However, even exempt information can be provided if public interest warrants disclosure.[260] The Right to Information Act, 2005 lays down a strict timeline within which the information has to be provided,[261] and non-compliance with the timeline, without reasonable cause, can lead to individual liability of the concerned official.[262]

7.88   The Right to Information Act, 2005 can be a useful mechanism to obtain information on actions initiated by government agencies to respond to climate change;[263] on reasons, if on record, for governmental inaction; on decisions taken by such agencies which may result in GHG emissions or reduction in carbon sink, etc. This information would be admissible as evidence in litigation, and as the source would be the government, it would be difficult for the government to challenge its authenticity/accuracy.

---

[252] Sections 123, 124, Indian Evidence Act, 1872.
[253] See paras. 7.87–7.90, below.
[254] Section 22, Right to Information Act, 2005.
[255] *State of Uttar Pradesh* v. *Raj Narain* AIR 1975 SC 865.
[256] Preamble, Right to Information Act, 2005.
[257] Section 2(h), *ibid.*   [258] Section 2(f), *ibid.*
[259] Section 8(1)(d), *ibid.*   [260] Section 8(1)(d), (2), *ibid.*
[261] Section 19(1), (3), *ibid.*   [262] Section 20(1), (2), *ibid.*
[263] The Right to Information Initiative of the Climate Revolution, a Gurgaon-based organisation, has filed several applications with the Ministry of Environment and Forests, the Prime Minister's Office and other government departments seeking information relating to the government's policy on climate change. The information received is publicly available at http://climaterevolution.net/rti/.

7.89   Government bodies are under an obligation to retain documents for a certain period of time. Each department is expected to formulate 'weeding out' rules clearly stating the length of time a type of record is to be maintained.[264] Companies are also required to retain certain records for a stipulated length of time.[265]

7.90   Under the Right to Information Act, 2005, public authorities are under an obligation to *suo moto* disclose information relating to them – such as details about their organisation, functions, work practices, budget, remuneration of employees, recipients of concessions, minutes of meetings etc.[266] The Companies Act, 1956 and other provisions of corporate law require companies to disclose certain information about the company.[267] For instance, when there is a public issue of shares, the offer document would include important up-to-date information about the company – its history and corporate structure, shareholders agreements, details about the management etc. According to the disclosure requirements, the corporate structure must include information about environmental issues.

Conclusion

7.91   Climate-related claims have yet to be litigated in India. There are a few cases in which climate change is referred to, but only in passing. This situation may, however, be set to change. Climate change and its impacts are rapidly capturing the popular imagination in India. There is a growing recognition of the importance and urgency of the climate challenge, and a slew of climate policies and initiatives have been launched in response. India has an engaged and proactive civil society, an activist judiciary, a progressive body of enviro-legal jurisprudence and an unparalleled culture of public interest litigation.

7.92   There are several hooks in Indian law for climate-related claims to be litigated. It is but a question of time before these hooks are raised and explored before the courts. Of these hooks however,

---

[264] The Public Records Act, 1993.
[265] Companies (Preservation and Disposal of Records) Rules, 1966.
[266] Section 4, Right to Information Act, 2005.
[267] Securities and Exchange Board of India (Issue of Capital and Disclosure Requirements) Regulations, 2009.

the constitutional rights-based ones – whether in relation to an environmental right, or core rights to life, health, etc. – are most likely to be explored first. Not least because other cases can take up to fifteen years to be disposed of.[268] Constitutional rights-based avenues, given the rich culture of judicial activism and public interest litigation prevalent in India, offer the most promise, and are therefore well worth tracking.

---

[268] National Litigation Policy, Ministry of Law and Justice, Government of India (23 June 2010). There are currently 54,600 cases pending before the Supreme Court, and 41,83,731 cases before the High Courts (*Court News*, July–September 2010, available at http://supremecourtofindia.nic.in/courtnews/2010_issue_3.pdf).

8

Indonesia

MAS ACHMAD SANTOSA, JOSI KHATARINA
AND RIFQI SJARIEF ASSEGAF

(A) Introduction: climate change risk, sources and government policies and measures

Climate change risk

8.01 Climate Change has a significant negative impact on Indonesia. The combination of sea level rise and an increased occurrence of extreme weather, i.e. La Nina and El Nino,[1] will cause higher intensity of erosion and abrasion. In turn it will further negatively affect the changes in the coastline that is already losing ground to higher sea level.[2] This negative impact is reflected in Indonesia's capital Jakarta. It is estimated that by 2100 Jakarta's coastline will be reduced by 15 km, thereby directly affecting the central business district.[3] The erosion also contributed to the loss of twenty-four Indonesian islands in two years (2005–07).[4] Extreme weather also causes a significant negative impact on the lives of the population that lives along the coastline. This population is often subject to maritime accidents[5] and disasters caused by extreme weather, diseases[6], drought and flood. These factors also have a severe impact on

---

[1] It is predicted that from 2001–30 La Nina and El Nino will occur every year. By comparison, from 1870–1999 they only happened once in every four years. Bappenas, 'ICCSR: Scientific Basis; Analysis and Projection of Sea Level Rise and Extreme Weather Event' (March, 2010), pp. 38–41.
[2] ICCSR, p. 47.   [3] ICCSR, p. 59.
[4] GoI, 'National Action Plan Addressing Climate Change' (NAPACC) (2007), p. 5.
[5] Because of the extreme weather caused by anomalies in the climate, an accident happened on 29 December 2006 in the Java sea that caused the deaths of more than 200 people. ICCSR, p. 46; NAPACC (2007), pp. 3–5.
[6] NAPACC (2007), pp. 5–6.

the agricultural sector.[7] It should be noted that agriculture is a source of income for 40 per cent of the Indonesian workforce.[8]

Sources of greenhouse gases

8.02   The majority of Indonesia's GHGs come from land use change and the forestry sector (46%), followed by energy (24%), peat fire (12%), waste (11%), agriculture (5%) and industry (2%).[9]

Governmental stance on climate change

8.03   Indonesia is party to the FCCC and Kyoto Protocol. Both were ratified through Act No. 6/1994 and Act No. 17/2004 respectively.

8.04   The President has announced Indonesia's commitment to reduce GHG emissions by up to 26% by national effort and 41% with international support by 2020.[10] The plan for emissions reduction is explained in the table below.

8.05   The National Council on Climate Change (DNPI), headed by the President, was established in 2008.[11] The Council is tasked with developing policies, strategies and programmes to address climate change, coordinating climate change activities and strengthening Indonesia's position in international negotiations.[12] Initiatives are also taken at the regional level through the establishment of a Regional Council on climate change,[13] a green development strategy[14] and adaptation plan.[15]

---

[7] For example, drought will cause a decrease of palm oil production of up to 6 per cent per year. GoI, ICCSR; *Sektor Pertanian* (ICCSR Agriculture Sector) (March 2010), pp. 18–25.

[8] ICCSR Agriculture Sector, p. 1.

[9] The total amount is 1,415,988 Gt CO_2e. Summary for Policy Makers: Indonesia Second National Communication Under UNFCCC (November 2009) ('2nd National Communication'), pp. 6–7.

[10] This commitment was first announced on 25 September 2009 before the G20 meeting in Pittsburgh, USA.

[11] This Council is established through Presidential Regulation 46/2008.

[12] Article 3, Presidential Regulation 46/2008.

[13] 'Kaltim Bentuk Dewan Perubahan Iklim Daerah', available at www.kaltimprov.go.id/kaltim.php?page=detailberita&id=4231.

[14] East Kalimantan and Aceh, for example, have stated themselves as Green Provinces. See for instance www.kaltimprov.go.id/kaltim.php?page=detailberita&id=4474.

[15] See www.antaramataram.com/berita/?rubrik=5&id=11456.

Table 1: *Action Plan to reduce emissions*

Issue	Planned emissions reduction		Action Plan	Responsible party
	26%	41%		
Forestry and peat land	0,672	1,039	Control of fire on forest and peat land, management of water, rehabilitation of forest and peat land, combating illegal logging, deforestation prevention, public empowerment	Ministry of Forestry, Ministry of Environment (MoE), Ministry of Agriculture (MoA), Ministry of Public Works (MPW).
Agriculture	0,008	0,011	Introduction of low emission of Paddy variety, irrigation efficiency, use of organic fertiliser	MoA, MoE
Energy and transportation	0,038	0,056	The use of biofuel, higher standard of machine in using more efficient fossil fuel, demand side management, energy efficiency, and expansion of renewable energy	Ministry of Transportation, Ministry of Energy, MPW.
Industry	0,001	0,005	Energy efficiency, use of renewable energy	Ministry of Trade
Waste	0,048	0,078	Closure of open dumping and develop integrated final dumping	MPW, MoE
	0,767	1,189		

Source: Adapted from National Action Plan Reduction of Green House Gas Emission, draft per August 2010

8.06   The Indonesian Government entered into a Letter of Intent ('LoI') with the Norwegian Government on 26 May 2010. This represents an important development in the area of reducing emissions from deforestation and forest degradation.[16] Under the terms of the LoI, the Norwegian Government has pledged to contribute funds to Indonesia's REDD+ efforts to the tune of US$ 1 billion. As part of this initiative, the Indonesian government has established a Presidential Task Force to lay the groundwork for the introduction of a new institution tasked with, inter alia:[17]

- implementing REDD+ activities;
- introducing a moratorium on new concession licences on the primary forest and peat land areas;
- developing an instrument for financing; and
- developing a draft national strategy on REDD+.

(B)   Legal system and practice

Source of law and hierarchy of legislations

8.07   Indonesia inherited its civil law system from the Dutch. In addition to written laws, other sources of Indonesian law are custom, case law, treaty and doctrine. Indonesian law acknowledges the rank or hierarchy of legal norms. According to Law 10/ 2004 on Legislation Making, the hierarchy, from the highest to the lowest, is: *Undang-undang Dasar 1945* (the 'Constitution'); *Undang-undang* (the 'Statutes' or 'Laws', enacted by Parliament and Government) or *Peraturan Pemerintah Pengganti Undang-undang* (the 'Government Regulation in Lieu of Law'); *Peraturan Pemerintah* (the 'Government Regulation'); *Peraturan Presiden* (the 'Presidential Regulation'); and *Peraturan Daerah* (the 'Local Regulations').[18] Lower-level norms should not contradict higher-level norms. The law also acknowledges legal norms made by other arms of government, ministerial or public bodies, as

---

[16] LoI between the Government of the Kingdom of Norway and the Government of the Republic of Indonesia on 'Cooperation on Reducing Greenhouse Gas Emissions from Deforestation and Forest Degradation', signed 26 May 2010.

[17] Presidential Decree 19/2010 concerning Working Group to Prepare Institutional Development of REDD+.

[18] Article 7, Law 10/ 2004.

long as they are mandated to do so by the law (although their positions in the hierarchy are still in dispute).[19]

Law enforcement

8.08   Generally, criminal law is enforced by the police and the public prosecution service. There are several government agencies and independent bodies that can investigate (and prosecute) special crimes – such as the Civil Servant Investigation Unit ('PPNS') in the area of forestry and environment.

8.09   Law enforcement agencies, aside from some independent bodies, are perceived as far from effective. Their integrity, commitment, competency and professionalism – including enforcement of environmental-related crimes – are often questioned.[20]

8.10   The government has a significant role in supervising and enforcing administrative law in relation to private sector activities on environmental issues. However, due to the points raised above, notwithstanding many alleged violations, that power is seldom used.[21]

The judiciary

Structure and jurisdiction

8.11   The judiciary is divided into four main jurisdictions: General Courts, Religious Courts, Military Courts and Administrative Courts. The law also allows the establishment of special courts/chambers under each of the four jurisdictions. *Mahkamah Agung* (the 'Supreme Court') has the power to hear appeals from every jurisdiction and to review the compliance of lower-level regulations with higher-level regulations, including statutes – but not their compliance with the Constitution.[22]

---

[19] For example when a ministerial regulation contradicts a local regulation. In practice, normally the former will be recognised as higher law if it gets its mandate from the law to regulate the disputed matter.

[20] See for instance, Satuan Tugas Pemberantasan Mafia Hukum (Satgas PMH), *Modus Operandi, Akar Masalah dan Penanggulangannya* (Jakarta: Satgas PMH, 2009).

[21] Mas Achmad Santosa, *Good Governance dan Hukum Lingkungan* (Jakarta: ICEL, 2001).

[22] Article 24 A (1), 1945 Constitution.

8.12   In addition to these 'traditional courts', Indonesia has a newly established *Mahkamah Konstitusi* (the 'Constitutional Court'). Its main authority is to review the constitutionality of a statute passed by the parliament and the government.[23]

Judicial independence, impartiality, competence, accountability and culture[24]

8.13   While judicial independence from the legislative and executive branches is no longer a serious issue in 'traditional courts',[25] issues around judicial impartiality, competence, accountability and culture still persist. Generally, judges do not perceive case law as an important factor in deciding similar cases, thereby making it difficult for parties to predict the outcome of a case. Moreover, court decisions usually do not provide in-depth legal grounds/arguments. Similarly, discussions/reviews of the court's decisions are rare.

8.14   Many judges tend to decide according to a strict interpretation of the letter of the law and only when the law is clear and explicit. As a consequence, they refrain from entertaining legal arguments that are based on the intent or spirit of the law or general provisions in the law such as those that make reference to human rights – not to mention international principles or case law from other jurisdictions. Some judges take the position that general provisions of the law that require implementing regulations do not produce legal consequences until such regulations are passed.

---

[23] *Ibid.*

[24] For this part, see generally Satgas PMH, *Modus Operandi*, 2009; Sebastiaan Pompe, *The Indonesian Supreme Court: a Study of Institutional Collapse* (Cornell University, Southeast Asia Program, 2005); Adriaan Bedner, *Administrative Courts in Indonesia: A Socio-Legal Study* (Kluwer Law International, 2001); David Nicholson, *Environmental Dispute Resolution in Indonesia* (Leiden: KITLV Press, 2009); Rifqi S. Assegaf, 'Judicial Reform in Indonesia, 1998–2006' in Naoyki Sakumoto and Hikmawanto Juwana (eds.), *Reforming Laws and Institutions in Indonesia: an Assessment* (Jakarta: FHUI, 2007); Rifqi S. Assegaf and Josi Khatarina, *Keterbukaan Informasi di Pengadilan* (Jakarta: LeIP, 2006).

[25] Before the so-called Reform Era, judicial independence was fragile due to government intervention, especially in big cases involving the government, the elites or corporations connected with the elites. After the Reform Era there were several reform initiatives which significantly minimised direct intervention into the judiciary.

8.15   At the same time, an established legal doctrine, case law or legal expert's witness argument is occasionally referred to by the judges when interpreting some basic/common legal issues.

Litigation culture

8.16   Indonesians are not litigious people.[26] This is primarily due to the state of the judiciary (as mentioned above), limited access to justice and limited legal awareness, various cultural issues and, in some cases (including environmental cases), imbalance of power between the perpetrator and the victim. Public interest litigation is relatively common. It is normally brought to court or is supported by non-governmental organisations which unfortunately have limited resources at their disposal.

(C)   Legal framework for climate change related issues

Laws and regulations

8.17   Indonesia has no specific law on climate change. However, there is a framework of laws that govern environmental issues. These laws can be divided into three main categories according to their scope of application: General Environmental Law; Sectoral Environmental Law; and Provincial and Local Environmental Legislation.

General environmental law

8.18   General Environmental Law includes the Environmental Management and Protection Act ('EMPA') of 32/2009, the Waste Management Act of 18/2008 and the Spatial Planning Act of 26/2007.

8.19   EMPA explicitly acknowledges that climate change is happening and makes several references to it. For example, the State is obliged to have a mitigation and adaptation plan as part of its Environmental Protection and Management Plan ('EPMP').[27]

---

[26] The Asia Foundation, 'Survey Report on Citizen's Perception of The Indonesian Justice Sector' (2001), shows that 62 per cent of Indonesians will avoid taking their dispute to court at all costs.

[27] Article 10 (4), EMPA.

The EPMP has therefore to be developed at national, regional and local levels in the form of a government regulation and a provincial/local regulation.[28] The EMPA also regulates the government's obligation to establish criteria for environmental damage caused by climate change and stipulates clearly that the breach of it by intention or negligence would result in criminal prosecution.[29]

8.20 The EMPA also introduces a Strategic Environmental Study ('SES'), which should be used as a guide in policy-making – such as in developing a spatial plan or in evaluating programmes.[30] The SES is developed based on an analysis of the carrying capacity of the environment, risks to the environment – including risks caused by climate change and the capacity to adapt to climate change, efficiency in the utilisation of natural resources, vulnerability and adaptability to climate change, resilience and the prospect of biological diversity utilisation.[31]

8.21 A new characteristic of EMPA is the introduction of an integrated environmental licence/permit. The EMPA states that an environmental licence should be acquired prior to the issuance of the operational licence for projects requiring an environmental impact assessment ('EIA').[32] The law also stipulates that if an environmental licence is revoked, then the business licence is automatically annulled.[33]

8.22 One of the aims of the Waste Management Act is to put an end to the practice of open dumping that is very common in Indonesia.[34] The law states that open dumping should be discontinued by 2013.[35] However, to date no implementing regulation has been passed even though the law states that it should be completed by 2009.

8.23 The Spatial Planning Act is important as it strengthens environmental capacity, i.e. by defining the minimum amount of forest and open-space area in each province.

---

[28] Article 10 (3), EMPA.
[29] Articles 98 and 99 *junto* Article 21 (2), EMPA.
[30] Article 19 (1), EMPA.   [31] Articles 15–17, EMPA.
[32] Article 40 (1), EMPA.   [33] Article 40 (2), EMPA.
[34] Open dumping releases methane into the atmosphere.
[35] Article 44, DWMA.

Sectoral environmental law

8.24   Sectoral Environmental Law consists of laws that regulate sectors that have an impact on the environment, or in this case, on climate change. These laws are: Industry Act of 5/1984; Forestry Act of 41/1999; Oil and Gas Act of 22/2001; Plantation Law of 18/2004; Energy Act of 30/2007; Mining of Mineral and Coal Law of 4/2009, and Electricity Law of 30/2009.

8.25   The Industry Act only provides minimum and normative environmental considerations but none are operational.[36] The Act does not provide adequate encouragement to cleaner production, including emission reductions.

8.26   The Forestry Act of 41/1999 is very important in the Indonesian context since most of Indonesia's emissions come from the forestry sector. This law provides a framework for different uses of forests, forest delineation, business activity in the forest area and criminal sanctions for illegal activities within the forest.[37] However, the law and its implementing regulation still have many loopholes, for instance those that permit conversion of protected forests into other uses. Forest delineation is critical to ensuring legal certainty in forest areas since, for example, all criminal sanctions under the Forestry Act are only applicable to forest areas. At the implementation level, forest delineation has only been completed for around 11 per cent of the whole forest area.[38] Problems caused by weak legislation and numerous implementation problems contribute to the current rate of deforestation of around 1 million ha per year.[39]

8.27   Indonesian emissions from the agriculture sector (including plantations) are low, while climate change impact on it is significant. Unfortunately, the Agriculture Act does not provide a framework for adaptation to climate change. However, the Act acknowledges the impact of the agriculture sector on the environment, thus

---

[36] See Articles 2, 3 and 9 for normative provisions.
[37] See ICEL's research on Climate Friendly Legal Framework on forestry sector (forthcoming).
[38] Marcus Colchester, Martua T. Sirait and Boedhi Wijardjo, *The Application of FSC Principles Number 2 and 3 in Indonesia: Obstacles and Possibilities* (Jakarta: Walhi, 2003), p. 141.
[39] Ministry of Forestry, Statistik Kehutanan Indonesia, 2008, p. 15.

requiring an EIA for agricultural businesses.[40] It is important to note that one of the highest pressures for forest conversion comes from the agricultural sector, particularly palm oil plantations.[41] The Act also mentions the role of agriculture as a carbon sink.[42] Unfortunately, there is no further explanation on the carbon sink role in the Act.

8.28   The Energy Act does not provide a strong framework for encouraging the use of renewable energy. Nonetheless, Presidential Regulation No. 5 of 2006 gives clearer direction by stipulating that by the year 2025, the proportion of renewable energy should be more than 15 per cent to ensure the fulfilment of national energy demand.[43] At the same time, the President released an instruction to enhance the supply and use of biofuel.[44] Currently there is a policy that obliges the government to buy geothermal energy from producers.[45]

8.29   The Mining of Mineral and Coal Law and Oil and Gas Act basically do not address emission reductions from these sectors.

8.30   The *Majelis Permusyawaratan Rakyat* ('People's National Assembly') and the government have identified problems embedded in the natural resources related legal framework.[46] Some of these are: the natural resources related legislation provides too much discretion in granting concession permits and in taking decisions on forest areas, with few checks and balances; the relevant legislations have many flaws and loopholes which are often used to justify unsustainable practices; and the legislation is not supportive of indigenous people and forest-dependent people.

[40] Article 25, Law 18/2004.

[41] Resosudarmo, *et al.*, National Country Profile on REDD+ (Jakarta: CIFOR, forthcoming).

[42] Article 4, Agriculture Act.

[43] That comes from geothermal, biofuel, and other renewable energies, each for more than 5 per cent.

[44] Presidential Instruction 1/2006.

[45] Based on Article 6 of the Electricity Act which is further regulated by Ministry of Energy Regulation 2/2011. Press Release of the Ministry of Energy and Mineral Resources, 21 February 2011 concerning socialisation of the new Minister Regulation in www.esdm. go.id/siaran-pers/55-siaran-pers/4173-sosialisasi-peraturan-menteri-esdm-no-2-ta-hun-2011.html.

[46] Ketetapan Majelis Permusyawaratan Rakyat No. IX/MPR/2001, 9 November 2001. The decree obligates the government and the parliament to address the issue in the natural resources related legislations.

Therefore, the strategy calls for the development of a national climate-friendly legal framework to support effective mitigation and adaptation measures to address climate change. Five main elements of this climate-friendly legal framework are:[47] (i) legislation should be based on environmental inventory, environmental protection and management plan, and strategic environmental study – three of the environmental management instruments provided for in the EMPA; (ii) legislation related to major drivers of GHGs should orientate to reduce GHGs; (iii) legislation should give adequate protection of the rights of the marginalised people, particularly indigenous and forest-dependent people; (iv) legislation should be able to contribute to the creation of strong deterrent effects; and (v) legislation related to mitigation and adaptation should seriously consider civil and political rights as well as economic, social and cultural rights, particularly for the marginalised people as guaranteed by the Constitution.

(D)   Climate change litigation

Public law

Overview

8.31   There are four avenues for bringing a climate-related action in the area of public law: (i) constitutional review before the Constitutional Court; (ii) judicial review (of legislation) before the Supreme Court; (iii) challenge of administrative decision before the Administrative Court; and (iv) administrative enforcement through regulatory compliance.

Constitutional review

8.32   The human rights provisions under the Constitution, particularly the right to a healthy environment, can be used as grounds to challenge statutes which are not supportive of GHG reductions before the Constitutional Court. Article 28 H (1) reads: 'Every person shall have the right to … enjoy a good and healthy environment …' Other provisions, such as the right to work (Article 28 D) and the right to property (Article 28 G) also can

---

[47] Mas Achmad Santosa, *Role of Governance in Addressing Climate Change*, unpublished paper prepared for Democratic Governance Unit, UNDP-Indonesia (December, 2010).

be used.[48] Furthermore, Article 33 acknowledges the sustainable development principles.[49]

8.33   While the interpretation of right to a healthy environment was never tested, in the *Water Act* case the Court used environmental arguments in its reasoning. Although the main legal issue in the case related to the question of deciding who can utilise technology to modify the weather by making artificial rain (private sector or State), the Court also maintained that such activity can only be undertaken 'after an in-depth study and experiment, including by developing capacity to prevent negative impacts on the environment and humans'.[50] This decision bears witness to the progressive character of the Constitutional Court,[51] and we can expect the public to use this forum in similar cases on climate change related statutes.

8.34   To bring a legal action before the Constitutional Court, one must prove the potential damage that he/she might be exposed to as a result of the enactment of the statute.[52] In the *Water Act* case the Court argued that practically everybody has the right to a healthy environment, thus allowing a wide interpretation of legal standing in related cases.[53]

Judicial review of regulations

8.35   Generally, a legal action can be brought before the Supreme Court, for instance to review ministerial or local regulations on permits and planning, provided that such regulations clearly violate a statute (e.g. EMPA) or a government regulation. There will be wider grounds to review ministerial or local regulations once the Environmental Protection and Management Plan (EPMP)

---

[48] Climate change could also create loss of jobs (e.g. due to long droughts) as well as private property.

[49] Jimly Asshiddiqie, *Green Constitution: The Green Nuance in the 1945 Constitution* (Jakarta: Rajawali Press, 2009).

[50] Constitutional Court Decision 058–059–060–063/PUU-II/2004 and 008/PUU-III/2005, at 511.

[51] Simon A. Butt, *Judicial Review in Indonesia; between Civil Law and Accountability?: A Study of Constitutional Court Decisions 2003–2005* (unpublished D.Phil. thesis, Melbourne University, 2006), pp. 171–240.

[52] Constitutional Court Decision 006/PUU-III/2005.

[53] Constitutional Court Decision 058–059–060–063/PUU-II/2004 and 008/PUU-III/2005, at 479.

has been passed[54] and provided substantive guidance on how to mitigate and adapt to climate change. As has been discussed, the EPMP should be enacted in the form of a government regulation which is superior in the hierarchy of legal norms.

8.36   It is important to note that, according to the Supreme Court Regulation No. 1/2004, a judicial review application should be submitted no later than 180 days after a regulation has been passed (Article 2 (4)). This provision inevitably limits the right of a third party whose claim may emerge after the period has expired. In the *Head of Local Government's Election, Appointment and Dismissal* case a panel of Supreme Court justices allowed a judicial review application from a third party even though it was submitted after the time limit had expired.[55] However, it seems that the above decision has not been followed by other justices.[56]

Challenging administrative decisions

Jurisdiction

8.37   Aside from the judicial review mechanism above, government liability for its actions/inactions can be enforced in two other jurisdictions: Administrative Courts and General Courts. The Administrative Courts only have jurisdiction to settle disputes arising in the field of administration as a consequence of the issuance (or non-issuance) of an administrative decision. The law identifies the elements of an 'administrative decision' as:[57]

- a written determination;
- issued by an administrative organ/official;
- containing an administrative act based on the law and regulation;

---

[54] See discussion on this matter in the environmental framework section, at para. 8.19 above.

[55] They argue, among other things, that since such limitation is restricting human rights, it should be regulated by statute, not lower-level regulations. See Supreme Court Decision 41/P/HUM/2006.

[56] In latter decisions, the Supreme Court normally rejected judicial review applications submitted after the time limit.

[57] Article 1 (3), Law 5/1986. Some of the elements are controversial in practice. See Bedner, *Administrative Courts* and P. M. Hadjon, 'Judicial Review of Administrative Action and Government Liability in Indonesia' in Yong Zhang (ed.), *Comparative Studies on Governmental Liability in East and South East Asia* (Kluwer Law International, 1999), pp. 118–120.

- that is concrete (i.e. not abstract or of a general nature) and pertaining to an individual (i.e. concerning a person/legal person);
- that is final (can be applied without approval from another agency or official); and
- that creates legal consequences for a person/legal person.

Other claims related to liability for unlawful governmental activities fall under the jurisdiction of the General Courts.[58]

8.38   With this limited jurisdiction, we can anticipate that only legal actions concerning the issuance of a permit can be raised in climate change litigation.[59] Nonetheless, this is a big issue because research shows that many permits issued by government for mining and agriculture corporations in forest areas violate forestry and spatial planning regulations – thus contributing to the ongoing massive destruction of forest areas.[60]

Grounds for challenge and timing

8.39   There are two grounds on which an administrative decision can be challenged:[61]

- the administrative decision is contrary to law and regulations; and
- the administrative decision is contrary to good governance practices (which are narrowly interpreted as: legal certainty, supremacy of law, transparency, proportionality, professionalism and accountability).

8.40   To successfully challenge a permit, the plaintiff needs to establish an explicit violation of the law or regulation caused by the issuance of that permit. There is a risk when using good governance principles as the legal basis for the challenge due to the narrow interpretation of those principles in the current

---

[58] See also the elucidation of Law 5/1986.
[59] In theory such actions offer a strong chance of success in climate-related cases, unless there is 'extra judicial involvement' as in the case of *Transgenic Cotton* where the court argued that the Ministry of Agriculture decision authorising restricted planning of transgenic cotton in several areas to Monsanto was actually not a permit, thus it did not have to complete an EIA.
[60] Satgas PMH, *Report on Modus Operandi of Illegal Activities in Judiciary Sector* (2011, unpublished).
[61] Article 53 (2), Law 9/2004.

law as compared to the principles already established and practiced.[62]

8.41   The law stipulates a time limit by which individuals who are the subject of the administrative decision must submit their application (no later than ninety days after the decision was received or published).[63] There is no such provision for any third party affected by the decision. Such third party can refer to the Supreme Court Guidance which allows judges to decide the time limit on a case-by-case basis – which normally goes in favour of the applicant.[64]

Legal standing

8.42   In order to have standing before the Administrative Court, an individual applicant must have suffered loss as a result of the contested decision (Article 53 [1]). However, environmental NGOs have been granted legal standing by law and in the case law.[65]

Remedy

8.43   The main remedy in an Administrative Court is the annulment of administrative decisions and rehabilitation. Monetary compensation is available, only as pro forma, up to around US$ 600.

---

[62] Prior to the amendment of Law 5/1986 some judges already applied good governance principles – such as principles of prudence and justification of decision – as grounds to review an administrative decision despite there being no explicit provision in Law 5/1986 allowing the use of those principles. In the new amendment (Law 9/2004) some, but limited, good governance principles are incorporated. The new law, for instance, does not include the principles of prudence and justification of decision. Thus there is a risk the judges may not apply those principles or other principles that are not explicitly acknowledged in the new law. See Anna Erlyana, 'Administrative Court and Legal Reform since 1998 in Indonesia' in Sakumoto and Juwana (eds.), *Reforming Laws*, p. 95. It is important to note that in the controversial *Transgenic Cotton* case, the judges found that the Minister of Agriculture had carried out the necessary checks (e.g. public announcement, expert review and laboratory test) before issuing the decision – which was thus in line with the precautionary principle. The failure to perform EIA was not considered a violation of that principle.

[63] Article 55, Law 5/1986.

[64] According to the Supreme Court Circular Letter 2/1999, enforced in, e.g., Supreme Court Decision 41K/TUN/1994, the application should be lodged no later than ninety days after the third party became aware of the existence of the contested decision. See Bedner, *Administrative Court*, p. 115.

[65] Article 92, Law 32/2009. See also Mas Achmad Santosa and Sulaiman N. Sembiring, *Hak Gugat Organisasi Lingkungan* (Jakarta: ICEL, 1997) and *Walhi v. Inti Indorayon Utama* (South Jakarta District Court Decision 820/Pdt./G/1988/PM.Jkt.Pst).

Nonetheless, based on the Court's Specific Guidance No. 223/
Td.TUN/X/1993 and the case *Lindawati* v. *Bupati Gianyar*, the
plaintiff can seek material compensation in a General Court as a
follow-up to his/her victory in the Administrative Court.[66]

Administrative enforcement through regulatory compliance

8.44   The central and local governments are responsible for promot-
       ing regulatory compliance following the issuance of permits. In
       doing so, they have extensive powers, such as entering premises,
       taking samples, checking equipment, etc.[67] They can also impose
       sanctions on corporations that violate regulations by, inter alia,
       issuing warnings or revoking permits.[68] However, as mentioned
       earlier, those powers are seldom used by the responsible officers
       despite many alleged legal violations by corporations.

Private law

Unlawful action: Introduction

8.45   Civil proceedings deal with, among other things, any unlaw-
       ful action (*perbuatan melawan hukum*) by person, legal per-
       son or government – excluding those instances that fall within
       the jurisdiction of Administrative Courts as discussed earlier.
       Consequently, it is civil proceedings that are likely to be brought
       in relation to climate change issues.

8.46   There are two grounds for legal actions in relation to unlawful
       activities in a climate change context. These can be found in
       Article 1365 of the Civil Code and Article 87 of the EMPA.
           Article 1365 states that:

   Every unlawful action which causes loss to another person, obliges
   the person by whose fault the loss has resulted, to compensate that
   loss.

   Article 87 reads:

   Every party responsible for the enterprise and/or activity committing unlawful action in the form of pollution and/or environmental

---

[66] Bedner, *Administrative Courts*, p. 174.
[67] Article 74 (1), Law 32/2009.   [68] Article 76 (2), Law 32/2009.

damage causing loss to another person or the environment shall be obliged to pay compensation and/or carry out certain actions.

8.47   Elements of an unlawful action that must be established, as well as other important related aspects, are elaborated below.[69]

Unlawful action

8.48   The term 'unlawful' is usually defined widely, to include actions that contravene:[70]

- another's subjective right (e.g. freedom, reputation or property);
- lawful obligations of persons;
- public decency; and
- principles of propriety/appropriateness, prudence and reasonable care.

8.49   Article 1365 is wider than Article 87 since the action that can be challenged under that Article is not limited to those who cause environmental pollution or damage as in Article 87. Furthermore, the subject of the law in Article 1365 is everybody (including the government),[71] while in Article 87 the subject is limited to the party responsible for the enterprise and/or activity. Thus, to challenge the government's unlawful action, we can only use Article 1365 as our legal basis.

Fault

8.50   In general, fault includes subjective and objective elements. Subjectively, a person must have understood the meaning and the nature of the action and must have acted with deliberate intention or negligence in carrying out the unlawful action. Objectively, the measure is whether a reasonable person in the same circumstances would have foreseen the potential damage and would have acted differently.[72] Both of these elements must be fulfilled to establish fault. Although elements of fault are not

---

[69] Rosa Agustina, *Perbuatan Melawan Hukum* (Jakarta: Program Pasca Sarjana FH UI, 2003), p. 36.

[70] Setiawan, 'Empat Kriteria Perbuatan Melawan Hukum Yurisprudensi', *Varia Peradilan*, 16(II) (January 1987), 716.

[71] Wirjono Prodjodikoro, *Perbuatan Melanggar Hukum* (Bandung: Sumur Bandung, 1976), p. 84.

[72] Moegni Djojodirdjo, *Perbuatan Melawan Hukum* (Jakarta: Pradnya Paramita, 1982), p. 66.

explicitly listed in Article 87, in practice plaintiffs must be able to prove the existence of both these elements.[73]

8.51 The EMPA provides for strict liability (liability without faults) for activities that use hazardous materials, produce hazardous waste or 'create serious threat to the environment'.[74] Under the previous law, strict liability implicitly applied to any activity that required an EIA.[75] However, in the new EMPA the language has been changed to provide for strict liability for actions that cause a 'serious threat to the environment'.[76] It remains to be seen how the courts will interpret this provision.

Damage or loss

8.52 Article 1365 only recognises damage or loss to a person, including both material and immaterial loss. Examples of the latter include damage to one's health, enjoyment of life or feeling of security. Article 87 also acknowledges damage or loss to the environment.

Causality

8.53 The causality element is one of the most important aspects of this law, as the action in question has to be the most proximate and actual cause of the claimed loss.[77]

Remedies

8.54 There are several remedies available in civil litigation, including provision of compensation and an order to perform a certain action. The EMPA provides several examples of 'certain actions', which include: installing or improving waste management units; restoring environmental functions or eliminating causes of environmental pollution and/or damage.[78]

---

[73] Nicholson, *Environmental Dispute Resolution*, p. 74.

[74] Article 88, Law 32/2009.

[75] Suparto Wijoyo, 'Penyelesaian Sengketa Lingkungan Menurut UUPLH', *Jurnal Hukum Lingkungan*, V(I) (1999), 32–3; and Koesnadi Harjasoemantri, 'Strict Liability (*Tanggung Jawab Mutlak*)', 8 (paper presented at the Lokakarya Legal Standing & Class Action, Hotel Kartika Chandra, Jakarta, 7 December 1998) in Nicholson, *Environmental Dispute Resolution*, p. 83 (see also pp. 82–5). However, courts are not demonstrating progress in the application of this concept. Nicholson, pp. 82–5, based on the *Laguna Mandiri Case* and *PT Walhi v. PT Pakerin*.

[76] Article 88, EMPA.

[77] Djojodirdjo, *Perbuatan Melawan Hukum*, p. 35

[78] Elucidation of Article 87, Law 32/2009.

8.55   There do not appear to be any cases where a court has granted a remedy in the form of an order for the government to initiate a policy to minimise a similar risk in the future.[79] Nonetheless, there are cases where the court has ordered companies to repair the environmental damage and take actions necessary to prevent or reduce future negative impact.[80]

Burden of proof

8.56   The plaintiff bears the burden of proof in respect of Article 1365 and Article 87 although, at least in the law, judges have a discretion to extend the burden of proof to the defendant under certain conditions.[81]

Who may claim and who can be a defendant?

8.57   Anyone who can prove that he/she suffered damage/loss can claim compensation, especially for material loss. Environmental NGOs can bring claims for certain actions only in the context of environmental preservation. Principally, anyone 'responsible' for the damage/loss can be sued. Normally, the court will interpret 'responsible' narrowly, targeting the main actors.

Standing and representations

8.58   Standing to bring civil proceedings in General Courts is similar to standing in Administrative Courts. NGOs are also given legal standing.[82] The main difference is the recognition of a class action

---

[79] In the *Nunukan* case the court found that the Government was not conducting an unlawful activity in protecting a migrant worker while acknowledging that the protection currently afforded to migrant workers is not satisfactory. It therefore instructed the Government to enact all necessary laws, ratify relevant convention(s) and generally take concrete steps to reform the status of migrant workers (South Jakarta District Court Decision 28/PDT/G/2003/PN.JKT.PST). This decision was rejected by the High Court (480/PDT/2005/PT.DKI).

[80] *Wahli v. PT Freeport Indonesia* (South Jakarta District Court Decision 399/PDT.G/2000/PN.Jaksel) and the *Mandalawangi Landslide* case (Supreme Court Decision 1794K/Pdt/2004) where the court ordered the defendants in a class action to reclaim the landslide areas through forest and land rehabilitation programmes.

[81] Article 163, HIR and Article 1865, Civil Code. Nonetheless the judge may shift the burden of proof to the defendant under certain conditions. However, this is seldom done. See Yahya Harahap, *Hukum Acara Perdata* (Jakarta: Sinar Grafika, 2006), pp. 518–34.

[82] According to Law 32/2009, there are three requirements for a NGO to have standing before the court: (a) it should be formed as a legal person; (b) its statute must clearly state that it was established to preserve/protect the environment; and (c) it has to have been actively involved in environmental preservation/protection for no less than two years.

procedure in the general court.[83] Supreme Court Regulation No. 2/2002 provides clear guidance on how to administer a class action, in response to controversy in past practice.[84] Citizen's lawsuits are also beginning to be recognised.[85]

Potential cases: government liability

Overview

8.59   To date there has not been a single case brought to the courts using the climate change arguments. Thus, in this section we will try to elaborate potential for climate change litigation in the context of Indonesian private law, as discussed above.

8.60   Apart from cases where strict liability applies, elements of fault and causation in environmental disputes generally are difficult for plaintiffs to prove. Loss resulting from pollution, for instance, involves a complex chain of causality. In many cases, pollution may originate from multiple sources, thus making it difficult to prove that a particular action by the defendant caused the loss in question although joint responsibility is acknowledged in several cases.[86] Even more difficult problems may be faced in climate-related litigation, especially direct climate change litigation in Indonesia. First, Indonesia is not the main contributor to GHGs. Second, defendants can argue (and this will most likely be in line with the courts' interpretation) that it is nature (weather, climate, etc.) that caused the loss, not them.

8.61   It seems more likely that indirect rather than direct challenges on climate change issues will succeed. Nevertheless, it may be possible to directly challenge the government's unlawful actions related to climate change since the government has several obligations under the law.

---

[83] Article 91, Law 32/2009.

[84] Indro Sugianto, *Class Action; Membuka Akses Keadilan Bagi Masyarakat* (Malang: Intranss Press, 2005), pp. 119–121.

[85] In *J. Sandyawan Sumardi, el* v. *Government of Indonesia*, for instance, the District Court accepted for the first time an application using the citizen lawsuit procedure. Nonetheless, there were critics of the decision since it did not provide clear qualification to bring citizen lawsuits (see District Court Decision 28/PDT.G/2003/PN.Jkt.Pusat). As discussed earlier, there is a tendency for many judges not to entertain new concepts in the absence of guidance from the Supreme Court. Thus it is safer to say that since there is still no guidance from the Supreme Court concerning this matter, there will be cases where citizen lawsuits will be rejected by the courts.

[86] See for instance *Walhi* v. *Pt Pakerin et al.* (District Court Decision 8/Pdt.G/1998/PN.Plg).

8.62   Article 1365 stipulates that there are at least three occasions where government liability in the context of climate change is enforceable, that is if the government: (i) fails to conduct its specific obligation under the environmental legal framework related to climate change; (ii) fails to take necessary action under human rights or other relevant laws to prevent climate change impact; or (iii) acts in contravention to its plan, policy or obligation. The following illustrate these three scenarios.

Failure to conduct obligation under environmental legal framework

8.63   As discussed, environmental law and regulations impose several obligations on the government in relation to mitigation and adaptation. Among others, these obligations include the obligation to develop an Environmental Protection and Management Plan, a Strategic Environmental Study and criteria for environmental damage caused by climate change, and to complete the delineation of forest areas and spatial plan and prohibit open dumping. Some, if not all, of these obligations can be challenged in court on the basis of unlawful action.

8.64   As an example, the government has acknowledged that some parts of Jakarta will be impacted by climate change[87] and that it should develop adaptation plans. If such plans are absent and people in that area suffer losses attributable to climate change, they could argue that the government should be held liable for the failure to comply with its stipulated obligation. This challenge, however, may be difficult to sustain as it would be difficult to establish the causal link between the absence of an adaptation plan and the loss suffered. In addition, scientific expert opinion is also required to prove cause and effect.

8.65   The government's obligation to put an end to open dumping so as to minimise the release of GHGs into the air as well as prevent smell and other negative consequences, is on a different plane. When the government does not comply with its stipulated obligation to put an end to open dumping practices and there is a loss, e.g. there is a landslide that causes loss to property or life, the causal link is clearer – improving the plaintiff's chances in court.

[87] ICCSR, p. 59 and 2nd National Communication, p. 17.

Failure to implement an obligation under human rights or other relevant laws

8.66   Human rights provisions, such as the right to life, property or the right to environment or right to health as stipulated in the Health Act[88] can be used as a basis to challenge the government's failure to properly adapt to climate change by minimising climate change impacts on health. Due to the change of climate, for example, there is a higher risk that the public will suffer from dengue fever. Consequently, if the government failed to initiate the necessary policy and take the relevant actions to minimise the risk and loss/damage occurs, grounds may be available to take legal action. There is a significant probability of success. In *Gun Subasri, el* v. *Government of Indonesia cq Governor of Jakarta* the court assessed the adequacy of the local government's system to prevent and respond to (regular) floods in Jakarta and found that the Mayor was indeed engaging in an unlawful inaction in failing to implement the system correctly.[89]

8.67   Indigenous people can also claim that their right over land in the forest areas[90] has not been respected by a REDD or a forest conservation project.[91] Nonetheless, this particular issue is related to other causes – such as the unfinished task of delineating forest areas, and conflicts between the laws of forestry and land law (both topics would require specific attention that is beyond the scope of this chapter).[92]

8.68   The most readily available legal ground to raise claims is in relation to a government failure to inform the public on the impact of climate change. The Public Access to Information Law clearly states that a public body, including the government,[93] should

---

[88] Article 4, Law 39/2009.

[89] Unfortunately the Mayor was not the party in the case, thus the court rejected the claims due to *error in person* reasons.

[90] Indigenous people rights are acknowledged in some laws, including the Human Rights Law and Land Law.

[91] See for example disputes over forest area between PT REKI and Indigenous People of Anak Dalam Tribe in Jambi TempoInteraktif: 'Berebut Hutan Jambi', available at www.tempointeraktif.com/hg/nusa_lainnya/2011/03/07/brk,20110307–318193,id.html.

[92] See, inter alia, Myrna Safitri, 'Forest Tenure: Thesis on Socio-Legal Challenges of Securing Communities Rights' (unpublished D.Phil. thesis, Leiden University, 2011).

[93] The Law applies to a 'private body' if it is a State-owned company (which is financially supported, entirely or in part, by State budget), political party or non-governmental

publish information relating to public harm, including natural or man-made disaster.[94] As mentioned above, the government is already in possession of data related to areas in Jakarta that will be impacted by climate change. Thus, if the government does not provide this information to those who live in or have property that will most likely be damaged or destroyed due to sea level rise, then such entities should have standing to claim compensation from the government when the actual damage/loss takes place. Although the right to information under the Public Access to Information Law has never been tested, in *David Tobing* v. *Minister of Health* the Supreme Court confirmed that the government's failure to publish information concerning the existence of harmful bacteria in baby milk is an unlawful inaction as it demonstrates carelessness on the part of the government in conducting its public-service duty.[95]

Failure by the government to implement its plan/policy or action contrary to the government's plan/policy or obligation

8.69   As discussed, the government has adopted policies related to climate change, such as measures to increase the use of renewable energy or to put an end to open dumping practices at certain times. While the government's failure to achieve its plan/target is difficult to challenge,[96] a member of the public can challenge the government's level of effort in implementing its policies. The likelihood of success is low, however, especially due to the difficulty in linking such failure to the loss that might occur. Nevertheless, such an action can be used as a means to pressure the government to take climate change more seriously.

8.70   Government action that contravenes its own plan/policy is a different story. In West Sumatera for instance, the government developed infrastructure (roads) despite the fact that, based on research, the area is likely to be impacted by climate change

---

organisation that gets financial support from the State, public donation or an international grant. Thus, private corporations are not subject to the Law (Article 1 (3), Law 14/2008).

[94] Article 10, Law 14/2008 and Article 12 [2] point a and b, Information Commission Regulation 1/2010.

[95] Supreme Court Decision 2975 K/Pdt/2009.

[96] Indroharto, *Perbuatan Pemerintah Menurut Hukum Publik dan Hukum Perdata* (Jakarta: LPP-HAN, 1995), pp. 87–93.

(sea level rise).[97] When such infrastructure is damaged (and in this case, it was), a member of the public can make a claim against the government for wasting public funds.[98] Similarly, if there is damage to private property in such an area, the property-owner can challenge before an Administrative Court the government's act in permitting houses or businesses to be built in this area.

Prospective bases: business liability

8.71   Businesses may also be held liable for their indirect activities that contribute to climate change. For example, if they breach a logging licence (by, e.g., logging outside the designated area) or start fires and burn land for the purpose of land-clearing. In such cases, there is no need to prove the activity's relation to climate change as the breach itself is an unlawful action. Thus if such actions result in damage to a person or to the environment (as in *Walhi* v. *P. T. Pakerin et al*[99]), the businesses concerned can be held liable.

8.72   Another possibility is that a business can be challenged for conducting an activity without a proper licence. An environmental NGO wishing to bring a lawsuit on this basis would only need to prove that such unlawful activity is damaging the environment.

Criminal law

8.73   There are several provisions of criminal law that can be used in the context of climate change; for example under the EMPA a person whose activity exceeds the standard criteria for environmental damage, or who is burning land (for land clearing) or conducting an activity without an environmental licence, can be prosecuted. The EMPA also recognises corporate criminal liability including corporate directors' liability. The EMPA, Forestry,

---

[97] See www.klhsindonesia.org/file_share/ESP23_SEA_Padang.pdf; plan to develop waterfront city, 34–5; and http://jurnal.pdii.lipi.go.id/admin/jurnal/61081222.pdf (riset ttg kondisi geografis pantai padang).

[98] Jawa Pos Nasional Network, 'Abrasi Pantai Meluas; 86 Bangunan Hanyut', available at www.jpnn.com/read/2010/11/05/76320/Abrasi-Pantai-Meluas,-86-Bangunan-Hanyut.

[99] The case is about a corporation which burnt land for land clearing which contributed to a significant forest fire.

Spatial Planning and Access to Information Acts also envisage sanctions for: (i) officials granting an operational licence without prior approval and an environmental licence; (ii) officials granting an environmental licence without an Environmental Impact Statement; (iii) officials intentionally not performing their supervisory work, which results in environmental damage; (iv) persons cutting and transporting logs without a proper licence; (v) officials granting permits that are not in accordance with spatial plans; and (vi) any public body failing to disclose information relating to public harm.

8.74   While the law is relatively adequate in terms of providing legal protection in the climate change context, law enforcement, as discussed earlier, remains an issue. Furthermore, most people who have been convicted of crimes under the Forestry Act (for instance, for cutting and transporting logs without a proper licence) are field actors (physical perpetrators), not intellectual actors (functional perpetrators).

Practicalities

Orders and enforcement

8.75   Courts can issue protective orders, such as freezing orders. They can also issue orders to inspect the disputed object so as to gather enough information to be able to decide the case.

8.76   General Court decisions are mostly enforceable, for instance by seizing the defendant's assets, although problems have occurred in such instances.[100] Administrative Court decisions used to be difficult to enforce, unless the losing party (the government) was willing to enforce it voluntarily. The new law seeks to resolve this issue by stipulating that sixty days after a court has declared that the administrative decision challenged is unlawful, it is automatically null and void and the court can, inter alia, order the government to pay a mandatory sum (*dwangsom*). [101]

---

[100] Yahya Harahap, *Ruang Lingkup Permasalahan Eksekusi Bidang Perdata* (Jakarta: Sinar Grafika, 2005), pp. 389–438.
[101] Article 116, Law 51/ 2009.

8.77 Foreign court decisions do not have any legal effect. Only foreign arbitration awards concerning commercial matters can be legally enforced (by submitting a request to the court).[102]

Litigation costs

8.78 Plaintiffs are required to pay a certain amount of estimated court fees (for the administration of the case) to initiate civil and administrative litigation. However, the court will order the losing party to pay the fees at the end of the process.[103] This does not include legal fees and costs of gathering evidence, such as laboratory test or expert witness fees – both of which are more substantial. Impecunious plaintiffs are entitled to have court fees waived and to free legal assistance.[104] There are no fees levied to lodge a claim before the Constitutional Court.

Access to information

8.79 A party can request the judge to order the other party to provide information as long as he/she can convince the court of the importance of that information to the litigation.

8.80 According to the EMPA, EIA contents, government reports and evaluation of environmental observation/monitoring concerning the compliance and quality change in environmental conditions and spatial plans are all considered as public information. However, there are no grounds for a member of the public to access documents submitted by corporations to the government, besides EIA-related documents. With the new Freedom of Information Act (see below) such documents do not form part of the information that can be exempted from public access, and therefore should be accessible.

---

[102] Article 67 (1), Law 30/1999. Other conditions are: reciprocity principles and enforcement are not against public policy. There are notorious cases where courts have refused to recognise and enforce or even annul international awards without reasonable arguments, although that is not the majority position of courts. See S. R. Luttrell, 'Lex Arbitri Indonesia – The Law, Practice and Place of Commercial Arbitration in Indonesia Today', available at www.srluttrell.com/articles/Lex_Arbitri_Indonesia_(Int_A_L_R-%20 Dec-2007).pdf.

[103] Article 181 (1), Civil Procedural Law.

[104] Article 144 C, Law 51/ 2009 and Article 68, Law 49/ 2009. See also Supreme Court Circular 10/2010.

8.81   Since Law 14/2008 regarding Public Access to Information came into force in 2010, there are stronger legal guarantees to access to information from a public body (either State or private). Public body decisions, policies (and supporting documents), project planning as well as correspondence of head/officers are all available for public information. There is also an obligation for a public body to publish information relating to public harm.

(E)   Conclusion

8.82   To date there is no strong legal framework to address climate change in Indonesia. Although there have been some advances, particularly through the Environmental Management and Protection Act, in general environmental governance is plagued by weak law enforcement. Law enforcement agencies and the judiciary are perceived as far from effective and their integrity, commitment and professionalism are often called into question. Nonetheless, the government stance on climate change is positive and there are some positive developments in government policies and law.

8.83   The commitment by President Susilo Bambang Yudhoyono to reduce GHGs by 26 per cent with self-financing and by up to 41 per cent with international support by 2020 has attracted national stakeholders – government and non-government – and the international community to develop ways to implement climate change mitigation in Indonesia, particularly in relation to reducing deforestation and forest degradation as a major source of GHGs. The LoI between the Government of Indonesia and the Royal Norwegian Embassy has induced Indonesia to take concrete steps to resolve longstanding problems on reforestation and forest degradation through REDD+ including instituting a moratorium policy to suspend new licences in primary and secondary forests and peat land, and to accelerate and improve enforcement practices so as to create a strong deterrent. At the end of May 2011, the long-anticipated Presidential Instruction on moratorium was issued.[105] This Instruction basically stated that all new

---

[105] Presidential Instruction 10/2011 on Suspension of Issuance of New Licences and Improvement of Governance in Primary Forest and Peat Land.

licences on primary forest and peat land should be suspended in two years' time. During this time improvement of governance in the forest and peat land is required.

8.84   The strengthening of enforcement practices in the area of natural resources has begun through the establishment of a joint enforcement team initiated by the Ministry of Forestry consisting of the Ministry of Forestry, Ministry of Environment, police, and public prosecutors. The joint enforcement team could be viewed as a positive step to develop synergised efforts in promoting strong and effective environmental enforcement instead of a sectoral approach in an uncoordinated fashion.

8.85   The Supreme Court and the Ministry of Environment, in cooperation with the Indonesian Centre for Environmental Law and the Asian Environmental Compliance and Enforcement Network, have developed the practice of environmental certification of judges, which authorises only certified judges to handle environmental and natural resources related cases. To be certified, judges require special training and continuous evaluation. With this, judges' knowledge and expertise in handling natural resources related cases, including climate change cases, should be improved.

8.86   The current involvement of the Corruption Eradication Commission in working with the Ministry of Forestry in preventing potential corruption in the forestry sector could also be seen as a concrete step in promoting sound and good governance in Indonesia's forestry management. This initiative should be an important beginning for further work to address a potential risk of corruption in mitigation of and adaptation to climate change. As reiterated by UNDP, corruption will potentially affect the REDD+ readiness, implementation and distribution phases.[106]

---

[106] *Staying On Track: Tackling Corruption Risks in Climate Change* (UNDP, 2010).

9

Japan

YUKARI TAKAMURA

(A) Introduction

The Japanese legal system

9.01   Contemporary Japanese law[1] is primarily based on statute law, which underlies the present Constitution ('*Nihonkoku kenpo*') enacted in 1946[2] as the 'Supreme Law of the Nation'.[3] Although the Constitution and some laws had been revised under the influence of US law during the period of the Allied occupation after the Second World War, major codes, including the Civil code and the Criminal code, were modelled on the French and German codes and are still heavily influenced by the Civil law system.

9.02   The main sources of the law, in addition to the Constitution, are (i) legislation, which is enacted by the Diet (Parliament), (ii) cabinet orders and ministerial ordinances, which are enacted by the central government, and (iii) local regulations enacted by local authorities within their power under legislation. While there has been debate on whether or not judgments of courts are to be considered as sources of law, judgments, especially those of the Supreme Court, are in most cases respected and followed as precedent by lower courts. The courts have played a critical role in the development of Japanese law, especially in areas such as environmental law.

---

[1] For Japanese legal system, see H. Oda, *Japanese Law*, 3rd edn (Oxford University Press, 2009).

[2] See www.kantei.go.jp/foreign/constitution_and_government/frame_01.html.

[3] Article 98 of the Constitution: 'This Constitution shall be the supreme law of the nation and no law, ordinance, imperial rescript or other act of government, or part thereof, contrary to the provisions hereof, shall have legal force or validity.'

Constitution

9.03   The Constitution provides for a list of fundamental rights. While there is no explicit provision relating to environment, some rights, especially 'personal rights' based on Articles 13[4] and/or 25[5] of the Constitution, have been often invoked in environmental litigation.

The governmental stance on climate change

9.04   Japan is a Party to the United Nations Framework Convention on Climate Change ('FCCC') and its Kyoto Protocol. As a Party to the Kyoto protocol, Japan is required to reduce its Greenhouse Gas ('GHG') emissions by 6 per cent below 1990 levels in the period 2008–12[6].

9.05   The Global Warming Prevention Headquarters established by the Cabinet's decision just after the Third Session of the Conference of Parties (COP3) of FCCC is responsible for promoting national climate policies and measures and implementation of the Kyoto Protocol. It is composed of all ministers and chaired by the Prime Minister. Following the 1998 Guidelines of Measures to Prevent Global Warming, in October 1998, the Law Concerning the Promotion of the Measures to Address Global Warming ('1998 Law')[7] was adopted by the Parliament. The 1998 Law provides a legal framework for Japanese policies and measures to tackle climate change (see paras. 9.13–9.20 below).

9.06   Despite the early response after the adoption of the Kyoto Protocol, it was not until the adoption of the Marrakesh Accords, the detailed rulebook of the Kyoto Protocol, in 2001,

---

[4] Article 13 of the Constitution: 'All of the people shall be respected as individuals. Their right to life, liberty, and the pursuit of happiness shall, to the extent that it does not interfere with the public welfare, be the supreme consideration in legislation and in other governmental affairs.'

[5] Article 25 of the Constitution: 'All people shall have the right to maintain the minimum standards of wholesome and cultured living. In all spheres of life, the State shall use its endeavours for the promotion and extension of social welfare and security, and of public health.'

[6] See Article 3.1 and Annex B of the Kyoto Protocol.

[7] See www.japaneselawtranslation.go.jp/law/detail/?id=97&vm=04&re=oi.

that concrete policies and measures to achieve the Japanese 6 per cent reduction target were decided, in 2002, through revision of the 1998 Guidelines and amendment of the 1998 Law. Based on the amended 1998 Law, a new Global Warming Prevention Headquarters was established and has gained official regulatory status. The amended 1998 Law also obliges the government to establish the Kyoto Protocol Target Achievement Plan ('KPTAP') to meet its 6 per cent reduction commitment under the Kyoto Protocol.

9.07   While the government stance to achieve a 6 per cent reduction target under the Kyoto Protocol has been continuously affirmed, there are few mandatory measures to implement this target. Japanese climate policy is based principally on voluntary initiatives, such as voluntary action plans for industries. Each industrial association and sectoral organisation is encouraged to fix a voluntary target and implement it. The voluntary action plan that was originally initiated by the Nippon Keidanren (national economic organisation) has become a national scheme with annual governmental review under the Kyoto Protocol Target Achievement Plan. Mandatory measures, especially the imposition of a carbon tax and a national emissions trading scheme, have been strongly resisted by most of the business sector, in particular the Nippon Keidanren.

9.08   As regards mitigation commitments beyond 2012, all political parties including the party currently in government, the Democratic Party ('DP'), recognise that, based on scientific findings, especially from the Intergovernmental Panel on Climate Change ('IPCC'), vigorous efforts are needed to address climate change. Global long-term reduction targets such as at least 50 per cent global emission reduction by 2050 are supported by all political parties in Japan.

9.09   However there are dramatic differences between political parties when it comes to mid-term targets. The former Prime Minister Yukio Hatoyama made a statement at the United Nations Summit on Climate Change held on 22 September 2009:

Based on the discussion in the Intergovernmental Panel on Climate Change (IPCC), I believe that the developed countries need to take the lead in emissions reduction efforts. It is my view that Japan should positively commit itself to setting a long-term reduction target. For its mid-term goal, Japan will aim to reduce its emissions by 25 per cent by 2020, if compared to the 1990 level, consistent with what the science calls for in order to halt global warming.[8]

He also announced the need to introduce national policies and measures including a domestic emissions trading mechanism and a feed-in tariff for renewable energy, as well as the consideration of a global warming tax. He added the promise of a 25 per cent target in 2020: 'However, Japan's efforts alone cannot halt climate change, even if it sets an ambitious reduction target. It is imperative to establish a fair and effective international framework in which all major economies participate. The commitment of Japan to the world is premised on agreement on ambitious targets by all the major economies.'

9.10   This 25 per cent reduction target was criticised by the Japanese business sector for fear of possible increase in carbon price and loss of international competitiveness vis-à-vis emerging economies, especially China. Although most parts of his statement at the UN were derived from a public pledge that the DP had made in its election manifesto, this announcement caused debate even within the party. At the end of 2010, the current DP government in fact suspended its initiative to introduce an emissions trading scheme, while it decided to introduce feed-in tariffs with moderate price-setting and to increase slightly tax on fossil fuels over the next five years.

9.11   Under these circumstances, the government has been arguing in the climate negotiations for a new single legally binding instrument covering all major emitters to replace the Kyoto Protocol post-2012. As Japan announced in Cancun: 'we will never inscribe our target in the Annex B to the Kyoto Protocol under any circumstances and conditions' since the 'Kyoto second commitment period will never constitute a fair and effective single framework with the participation of all major emitters'.[9] While

---

[8] Statement by Prime Minister Yukio Hatoyama at the United Nations Summit on Climate Change, 22 September 2009, New York, available at www.kantei.go.jp/foreign/hatoyama/statement/200909/ehat_0922_e.html.

[9] Statement by Japan at the Fifteenth Session of the Ad-hoc Working Group on Further Commitments for Annex I Parties under the Kyoto Protocol (AWG-KP) on 29 November 2010, held in Cancun, Mexico.

this stance has attracted strong criticism from developing countries and environmental groups, it has received support in Japan, especially from the business sector.

9.12   The earthquake on 11 March 2011 and nuclear incident in Fukushima is likely to change national and governmental debate on future energy and climate policy. The 25 per cent reduction target is premised on construction of fourteen new nuclear plants, which might now be impractical with public opposition. Increased dependency on thermal power plants would be inevitable for a shorter period, and a drastic shift from nuclear to renewable energy has been gaining increased support. However the governmental stance on future energy policy and climate policy will take considerable time to finalise. At the Bangkok climate talks in April 2011 Japan announced that 'it is too premature to assess how the recent developments will influence energy supply and demand, Japanese economy as a whole or our climate change policy in the future' while assuring that Japan will continue its serious efforts to tackle climate change.[10]

1998 Law Concerning the Promotion of the Measures to Address Global Warming

9.13   The 1998 Law Concerning the Promotion of the Measures to Address Global Warming ('1998 Law') is the centrepiece of Japanese climate policy, providing a general framework, including an institutional one, for measures to address climate change. This Law refers to the stabilisation objective provided in Article 2 of the FCCC,[11] but does not set legally binding national targets in response.

9.14   The 1998 Law obliges the government to elaborate and implement measures to tackle climate change;[12] to take necessary measures to implement Japan's international commitments, including

---

[10] Presentation made by Japan in the pre-sessional workshop on assumptions and conditions related to the attainment of quantified economy-wide emission reduction targets by developed country Parties, as requested by decision 1/CP.16, paragraph 38, held on 3 April 2011 under the Ad Hoc Working Group on Long-term Cooperative Action under the Convention (AWG-LCA).

[11] Article 1 of the 1998 Law.   [12] Article 3.1, *ibid.*

measures facilitating its participation in international emissions trading;[13] and to promote international cooperation for reducing emissions.[14] The 1998 Law provides for a Kyoto Protocol Target Achievement Plan, which the government is required to elaborate and, where necessary, revise.[15]

9.15   Local authorities have an obligation to reduce emissions according to natural and social conditions.[16] The government and local authorities are required to reduce and/or limit their own emissions.[17]

9.16   Companies and citizens have a duty to make efforts to reduce and/or limit their emissions, and to cooperate on measures taken by the government and local authorities.[18]

9.17   The government is obliged to estimate national emissions and removals by sinks to implement its reporting and inventory requirements under the FCCC and the Kyoto Protocol. It is also required to make these emission and removal data public on an annual basis.[19]

9.18   Designated large-emitter companies have an obligation to report their emissions annually.[20] The 'large-emitter company' means 'designated energy management factories' and 'designated transportation companies and cargo owners' under the Act concerning rational use of energy, 1979 ('the 1979 Energy Conservation Act') (see paras. 9.21–9.29 below) for energy-related CO_2 emissions, as well as for emissions of GHG other than energy-related CO_2 emissions, designated installations of which total annual emission is equal to/more than 3,000tCO_2 equivalent.[21] For installations that submit their report under the 1979 Energy Conservation Act, the portions of their report regarding matters pertaining to CO_2 emissions shall be deemed as reports under the 1998 Law.[22] Any person may request the disclosure of these submitted data.[23] These designated companies, when considering that disclosure

[13] Article 3.4, *ibid.*   [14] Article 3.6, *ibid.*
[15] Articles 8 and 9, *ibid.*   [16] Article 4.1, *ibid.*
[17] Articles 3.2 and 4.2, *ibid.*   [18] Articles 5 and 6, *ibid.*
[19] Article 7, *ibid.*   [20] Article 22–1, *ibid.*
[21] Articles 5 and 5–2 of Order for Enforcement of the Law Concerning the Promotion of the Measures to Address Global Warming.
[22] Article 21–10.   [23] Article 21–6.

might impede their 'rights, competitive position and other legitimate interest', may request the government to disclose only total emissions and not to disclose detailed emission data by sources.[24] The minister in charge (in most cases, the Minister of Economy, Trade and Industry) decides whether such requests should be allowed or not.[25] In cases of non-reporting or false reporting, a financial penalty (up to 200,000 yen) is to be imposed on companies concerned.[26]

9.19　　There are several possibilities for climate litigation related to the 1998 Law. A first possible type of litigation is that a citizen and/or a civil society organisation brings an action requesting the government and/or local authority to implement their obligation or impose or confirm their obligation to take more aggressive mitigation action under the Law. Besides difficulties in standing surrounding judicial review as mentioned below, another specific difficulty exists relating to the 1998 Law. This Law imposes weak obligations on government and local authorities, permitting them considerable discretion. In most cases their obligations are limited to elaborating measures and making all efforts, obligations that are difficult to enforce.

9.20　　This is also true for the obligations imposed on private entities. The only exception is the mandatory obligation placed on large-emitting companies to report their emission data. In the case of non-compliance with these reporting obligations, and if there is no enforcement action by the government, a suit may be brought by a citizen before the court in order to request the government to take the necessary measures to address such non-compliance. If the government decides not to disclose emission data upon request of disclosure, a claimant requesting disclosure has the right to institute an action against such an administrative order of non-disclosure on the basis of the Act on Access to Information Held by Administrative Organs enacted in 1999.[27] Three cases of this nature related to the 1979 Energy Conservation Act are currently pending before the courts (see paras. 9.78–9.80 below).

---

[24] Article 22–3.1.　　[25] Article 21–3.　　[26] Article 50.

[27] The Act on Access to Information Held by Administrative Organs was enacted in 1999 and has become effective since 1 April 2001. The Act provides for the right of any person to request disclosure of information held by governmental organs and procedure for such request. In principle, local authorities are out of the scope of the Act: many but not all

The Act concerning the rational use of energy

9.21   The Act concerning the rational use of energy was enacted in 1979 ('the 1979 Energy Conservation Act'),[28] after the oil crisis in the 1970s. The 1979 Act is significant for two reasons. First, it tackles CO_2 emissions from energy use, which constitute 90 per cent of GHG emissions in Japan. Second, while most existing measures in Japan are not mandatory, the 1979 Act provides for mandatory measures. While the Act itself does not contain any references to climate change (only its ordinances refer to it), this legislation has been one of the core measures to tackle climate change.

9.22   The 1979 Act mainly provides for four categories of measures. The first category of measures is for factories and installations with large energy consumption (annual consumption is equal to/more than 1,500kl of crude oil) ('designated energy man-agement factories').[29] These installations have an obligation to make all efforts to reduce their energy used per unit of through-put by 1 per cent annually. To do so, they have to appoint energy managers, submit their planned measures and periodically report on their energy use. About 13,000 factories are currently covered.

9.23   The second category of measures is for buildings.[30] Owners of buildings larger than or equal to 2,000 m^2 of total floor space ('designated buildings') have an obligation to report on the energy efficiency measures taken on new constructions and large-scale repair works and to make a periodic report on maintenance.

9.24   The third category of measures is for machinery and equip-ment.[31] Producers and importers of electrical appliances, such as computers and domestic appliances specified by the Ordinance, are obliged to keep the energy efficiency of their products not lower than that of the most efficient energy products commer-cially available on the market. This is known as the Top Runner Method.

---

local authorities have enacted local regulations to similar effect. See www.japaneselaw-translation.go.jp/law/detail/?id=99&vm=04&re=01&new=1.

[28] Act Concerning the Rational Use of Energy, 1979 (1979 Energy Conservation Act). See www.japaneselawtranslation.go.jp/law/detail/?id=1855&vm=04&re=01&new=1.

[29] Chapter III of the 1979 Act.   [30] Chapter V, *ibid.*   [31] Chapter VI, *ibid.*

9.25   From April 2007, measures for consigners and carriers are also introduced.[32] Transportation companies and cargo owners with 200 automobiles or more are obliged to submit long- and medium-term plans and to periodically report on their energy use.

9.26   In addition, energy suppliers are obliged to make efforts to disseminate highly energy efficient equipment and publish information on the implementation and effects of such efforts. Further, retailers have an obligation to make efforts to display the energy efficiency performance of their products in order to provide the consumer with information on annual electricity consumption, fuel cost, etc.[33]

9.27   If there is non-compliance with such obligations, the Minister of Economy, Trade and Industry and other competent ministers who have jurisdiction over business pertaining to installations, buildings etc. may take measures such as recommendations, orders and public announcements of non-compliance.[34]

9.28   The government shall endeavour to take fiscal, financial and taxation measures necessary to promote the rational use of energy.[35] Public financial institutions such as the Development Bank of Japan furnish companies wishing to invest in energy conservation promotion with funds at a preferential rate.

9.29   In the context of climate litigation, although the 1979 Act and related ordinances stipulate more specific obligations and standards than the 1998 Law, these obligations are in principle to submit data concerning energy use and to report on measures taken. Some indicative targets, however, have been provided by the Ministry of Economy, Trade and Industry as guidelines for business to take measures. While it should be relatively simple for a citizen to challenge the omission of the government to enforce non-compliance by business with its reporting obligations, difficulties remain in determining whether or not mitigation efforts by business are sufficient or whether the government has taken

---

[32] Chapter IV, *ibid.*   [33] Article 86, *ibid.*
[34] Articles 16 (for designated energy management factories); 57 (for carriers); 64 (for consigners); 75, 75–2 and 76–6 (for designated buildings); and 79 and 81 (for machinery and equipment).
[35] Article 82.

adequate measures to oblige business to make more appropriate levels of mitigation efforts.

National climate change risks

9.30   *Global Warming Impacts on Japan*, report from a research project funded by the Ministry of the Environment ('MOE'), presented projections for three scenarios: 450 ppm stabilisation scenario, 550 ppm stabilisation scenario and business-as-usual ('BaU') scenario. These three scenarios project an average temperature increase of 2.1°, 2.7° and 3.8° respectively in 2100 compared to pre-industrial levels.

9.31   Although provided projections are not comprehensive, major findings are the following: the cost of damage by floods will increase up to about 5 trillion yen per year by 2050, and will increase beyond 2050. Rice production will likely increase by 2050 but production areas and pattern will likely change drastically. Risk of death by heat stress will double in all scenarios by 2050 and beyond that, the risk might triple. The report concludes by projecting more severe impacts in various areas even with a 450 ppm stabilisation scenario, but noting that a drastic cut of global emissions could significantly mitigate damage caused by climate change.[36]

Industrial and natural resources (emissions sources and energy mix)

9.32   In 2008, crude oil accounted for 41.9% of total primary energy supply; coal for 22.8%; natural gas for 18.6%; nuclear for 10.4%; hydro for 3.1% and renewables for 3.1%.[37]

9.33   In 2008, coal-fired generation accounted for 26.8% of total electricity generation; gas-fired generation for 26.3%; oil-fired generation for 13.0%; nuclear for 24.0%; hydro for 7.1% and renewables and others for 2.8%.[38]

---

[36] See www.nies.go.jp/s4_impact/pdf/s-4_report_2009eng.
[37] Agency for Natural Resources and Energy, *White Paper on Energy 2010* (in Japanese), available at www.enecho.meti.go.jp/english/index.htm. For another reference, Agency for Natural Resources and Energy, *Energy in Japan* 2010 (English).
[38] See www.fepc.or.jp/present/jigyou/shuyoukoku/sw_index_03/index.html. The above report *Energy in Japan* provides slightly different numbers but the trends are similar.

9.34   Until the 1960s, Japanese energy depended on domestically
        produced coal and hydro that accounted for about 60% of pri-
        mary energy supply. Due to the shift from coal to cheap oil, the
        ratio has drastically declined since then. In 2007, the Japanese
        self-sufficiency ratio of energy was as low as 4%, including hydro
        power. This is very low compared to other countries.[39]

9.35   According to figures published by the MOE and the Greenhouse
        Gases Inventory Office of Japan, National Institute of
        Environmental Studies ('NIES'),[40] the following were the main
        sources of GHG emissions in Japan in 2008: 34.0% from the
        power sector; 28.0% from industries; 18.8% from transport; 8.1%
        from commercial and service sectors; 4.9% from households;
        4.1% from industrial processes; and 2.1% from waste. It is clear
        that as much as 62% comes from the power and industrial sec-
        tors, which are the main sources of emissions in Japan.

9.36   Since the adoption of the Kyoto Protocol, Japanese emission has
        been consistently about 4–8% above the 1990 level. However,
        due to the financial crisis experienced since mid-2008, Japanese
        emissions have recorded significant decreases. Emissions in 2009
        were 4.1% below the 1990 level without counting removals from
        national sinks (expected to be 3.8% in the Kyoto Protocol Target
        Achievement Plan) and Kyoto mechanisms units.[41] This decline
        can be traced to a decrease in industrial activities, for instance
        steel production.

(B)   Public law

Overview of judicial review system

9.37   The Constitution stipulates that: 'The whole judicial power is
        vested in a Supreme Court and in such inferior courts as are estab-
        lished by law. No extraordinary tribunal shall be established, nor
        shall any organ or agency of the Executive be given final judicial

---

[39] See n. 37 above.
[40] Ministry of the Environment, Japan, Greenhouse Gas Inventory Office of Japan (GIO),
     CGER, NIES, *National Greenhouse Gas Inventory Report of JAPAN*, April, 2010, available
     at www-gio.nies.go.jp/aboutghg/nir/2010/NIR_JPN_2010_v4.0E.pdf.
[41] *Ibid.*

power.' (Article 76). The Supreme Court and lower courts have all the judicial power. The courts are the final adjudicators and deal with all legal actions against public bodies and private persons.

9.38 There are five types of courts in the Japanese judicial system: Supreme Court; 8 High Courts (with 6 branches and Intellectual Property High Court); 50 District Courts (with 203 branches); 438 Summary Courts; and 50 Family Courts (with 203 branches and 77 local offices).[42] The jurisdiction of each court is provided for in the Law, starting with the Law on Courts enacted in 1947. There are no administrative or constitutional courts.

9.39 Article 81 of the Constitution stipulates: '[t]he Supreme Court is the court of last resort with power to determine the constitutionality of any law, order, regulation or official act'. On the basis of the provision, not only the Supreme Court but also lower courts may determine the constitutionality of any law, ordinance and administrative decision. In practice, it is rare that the courts, including the Supreme Court, judge a law unconstitutional except cases concerning discrepancies in the value of votes.

9.40 It should be noted that judicial review including review of the constitutionality of any law is only possible when it is necessary to render judgment on a specific case. Abstract normative control on constitutionality without a specific dispute, as in the German Constitutional Court, is not allowed in Japan.[43]

9.41 Besides these courts, there are several administrative commissions, which are part of the government but operate independently from it. One of these commissions is the Environmental Dispute Coordination Commission ('EDCC') (see paras. 9.97–9.100 below).

9.42 In the context of climate litigation, judicial review on administrative litigation and civil procedure are the most likely potential types of legal actions. There is also a possibility of recourse to the EDCC.

---

[42] See www.courts.go.jp/english/system/system.html#01.
[43] Oda, *Japanese Law*, pp. 32–3.

Administrative litigation

9.43   The Administrative Case Litigation Act ('ACLA')[44] provides for
        different types of actions to be brought for the purpose of judi-
        cial review: (i) Actions for the Revocation of Administrative
        Dispositions (Articles 8–35); (ii) Other Actions for the Judicial
        Review of Administrative Dispositions (Articles 36–38) contain-
        ing four sub-categories; (iii) Public Law-Related Actions (Articles
        39–41); (iv) Citizen Actions (Article 42); and (v) Interagency
        Actions (Article 43). Each category of actions has its own scope
        and conditions under the Act. To be filed effectively, an action
        needs to fall into and meet the requirements of the relevant
        category.

        Actions for the Revocation of Administrative
        Dispositions

9.44   Actions for the Revocation of Administrative Dispositions
        ('*Torikeshi sosho*') are actions seeking the revocation of an admin-
        istrative disposition and any other act constituting the exercise of
        public authority by an administrative agency (Article 3.2). This
        category is considered the most typical administrative litigation.

9.45   Before going into judgment on merits, courts examine three
        main requirements by which the action could be admitted by the
        court. First, actions shall target an administrative 'disposition'.
        The 'disposition' subject to this type of actions does not cover
        all administrative acts but the ones that in law directly establish
        rights and obligations of nationals and/or which directly deter-
        mine their scope.[45] This by implication excludes some types of
        administrative acts such as acts internal to the administration,
        administrative guidance (which has been often used in Japan by
        the government to guide private persons), and intermediate acts
        in a series of acts.

9.46   What might constitute an administrative 'disposition'? The
        Supreme Court decided that while a decision on urban planning
        constitutes the exercise of public authority by an administra-
        tive agency, the elaboration of a re-zoning plan prior to urban

---

[44] See www.japaneselawtranslation.go.jp/law/detail/?id=1922&vm=04&re=01&new=1.
[45] Judgment of the Supreme Court, 29 October 1964, *Minshu* 18(8), 1809.

planning is only a 'blueprint' which does not determine rights and obligations of persons concerned[46] and therefore does not constitute an 'administrative disposition' subject to this category of actions.

9.47   In a recent case related to a re-zoning plan, however, the Supreme Court set a new precedent by stating that once a re-zoning plan is decided, it would be possible to foresee what kind of effect might be caused to the rights of landowners in the area concerned; it would also be possible to foresee that they would be subject to a relocation decision as a next step, and therefore, a decision on a re-zoning plan would have direct effect on their legal status and constitutes an administrative disposition within the meaning of the Act. The Supreme Court added that although landowners may have recourse to actions for revoking a relocation decision, it would be less likely that the Court would nullify the decision and that claimants could not enjoy effective remedies after the project had actually started.[47]

9.48   Despite this decision of the Supreme Court in the context of a re-zoning plan, there is no similar judgment of the Court that recognises urban planning as a 'disposition' within the meaning of the Act.

9.49   The second requirement is a standing to sue (Article 9). The Act limits the standing to file actions for the revocation of administrative dispositions to *persons who have a 'legal interest'*. The person to whom the disposition is addressed clearly falls within this definition.

9.50   The question is to what extent the third parties (who are not an addressee) of the disposition enjoy such standing. Courts have interpreted 'legal interest' as an 'interest protected by law'.[48] While criticising this interpretation as too narrow to provide appropriate remedies to claimants, the majority of scholars interpret it as 'interests deserving protection by law'. Under this interpretation, whether to have a standing or not will be determined on a case-by-case basis, taking into account the nature

---

[46] Judgment of the Supreme Court, 23 February 1966, *Minshu* 20(2), 271.
[47] Judgment of the Supreme Court, 10 September 2008, *Minshu* 62(8), 2029.
[48] Judgment of the Supreme Court, 14 March 1981, *Minshu* 32(2), 211.

and extent of the interests injured and whether or not the interests injured are distinguishable from those of the general public.

9.51   While the Supreme Court has maintained its interpretation of 'interest protected by law', it has shown some flexibility in interpreting standing by considering the concrete damage suffered by claimants especially when there is direct damage to life and the person[49] (for example, the Nigata Airport case[50]). In a similar vein, the Supreme Court recognised that inhabitants of the area within 58 km of MOX plant 'Monju' may have a standing to file an action for revocation of a decision on a construction permit.[51]

9.52   This interpretation was incorporated into the Act by an amendment in 2004 which inserted Article 9.2:

9.53   When judging whether or not any person, other than the person to whom an original administrative disposition or administrative disposition on appeal is addressed, has the legal interest prescribed in the preceding paragraph, the court shall not rely only on the language of the provisions of the laws and regulations which give a basis for the original administrative disposition or administrative disposition on appeal, but shall consider the purposes and objectives of the laws and regulations as well as the content and nature of the interest that should be taken into consideration in making the original administrative disposition. In this case, when considering the purposes and objectives of said laws and regulations, the court shall take into consideration the purposes and objectives of any related laws and regulations which share the objective in common with said laws and regulations, and when considering the content and nature of said interest, the court shall take into consideration the content and nature of the interest that would be harmed if the original administrative disposition or administrative disposition on appeal were made in violation of the laws and regulations which give a basis therefor, as well as in what manner and to what extent such interest would be harmed.

---

[49] T. Otsuka, *Environmental Law*, 3rd edn (Yuhikaku, 2010), pp. 700–01.

[50] Niigata Airport case, Judgment of the Supreme Court, 17 February 1989, *Minshu* 43(2), 56. The Niigata Airport case was raised by those living in the area surrounding the airport. Claimants requested the revocation of a licence permitting regular air service by defendants in order to bring to an end the significant noise pollution caused by the air service operations. The Supreme Court recognised standing for those, in terms of general social norms, who suffer significantly from noise caused by aircraft activity permitted by the licence.

[51] Monju Mox Plant case, Judgment of the Supreme Court, 9 April 1993, *Minshu* 46(6), 571.

9.54   The Supreme Court has passed judgments respecting the effects of the amendment. In the Odakyu case, for instance, in the context of a rail expansion project, it accepted the standing of inhabitants and landowners within the area covered by the ordinance on environmental impact assessment issued by the Metropolis of Tokyo.[52]

9.55   The third requirement is that actions can only be filed when the legal interest can be 'recovered by revoking the original administrative disposition'.

9.56   For this category of actions, the filing of an action in principle does not preclude the effect of the administrative disposition, the execution of the disposition or the continuation of any subsequent procedure (Article 25.1). The court may, upon petition, by an order, stay the whole or part of the effect of the administrative disposition and the execution of the administrative disposition. It may also stay the continuation of any subsequent procedure if there is an urgent necessity in order to avoid any serious damage that would be caused by the disposition, the execution of the disposition or the continuation of any subsequent procedure. However, the court may not stay the effect of an administrative disposition if the purpose can be achieved by staying the execution of the disposition or staying the continuation of any subsequent procedure (Article 25.2).

9.57   For instance, the government authorised the construction of a coal-fired power plant that will significantly increase CO_2 emissions. Citizens want to challenge this authorisation. In such a case, to whom and to what extent will standing be admitted? Courts have shown some flexibility in interpreting standing for such actions. In interpreting under Article 9.2 of the Act, courts consider (i) the purposes and objectives of the laws and regulations and of any related laws and regulations that share a common objective; and (ii) the content and nature of the interest in making the administrative disposition. The extent to which courts take into account related laws and regulations depends on a consideration of the above items by courts. References in the objectives and purposes of these laws and regulations to the

---

[52] Odakyu case, Judgment of the Supreme Court, 7 December 2005, *Minshu* 59(10), 2645.

interest of citizens in protecting the climate system might help to further expand the standing.

Action for the declaration of nullity

9.58   The category (ii) of Other Actions for the Judicial Review of Administrative Dispositions (Articles 36–38) contains four types of action. The first type of action is an 'action for the declaration of nullity, etc.' ('*Muko kakunin sosho*'). This is an action seeking the declaration of the existence or non-existence of, or validity or invalidity of, an administrative disposition (Article 3.4). Standing for this type of action is provided for in Article 36 with the understanding that its standing is similar to the one for actions for revocation. Therefore a similar problem might be raised (see paras. 9.49–9.54 above).

Action for the declaration of illegality of inaction

9.59   The second type of action is an 'action for the declaration of illegality of inaction' ('*Fusakui no iho kakunin sosho*'). This is an action seeking the declaration of illegality of an administrative agency's failure to make an administrative disposition which it should have made within a reasonable period of time in response to an application filed under laws and regulations (Article 3.5). This type of action may be filed only by a person who has filed an application for an administrative disposition, and therefore it would have a relatively small role in the context of climate litigation.

Mandamus action

9.60   The third type of action is a '*mandamus* action' ('*Gimuzuke sosho*'). This is an action seeking an order to the effect that an administrative agency should make an administrative disposition (see para. 9.45 above) in the following cases: (i) where the administrative agency has not made a certain administrative disposition which it should make (excluding the case set forth in the following item); (ii) where an application for administrative review for requesting the administrative agency to make a certain administrative disposition has been filed or made under laws and regulations, but the administrative agency has not made the administrative disposition which it should have made

(Article 3.6). While the latter case (ii) is brought before the court on the basis of failure by administration to respond to an application, the former case (i) is not premised on such failure. In the context of environmental litigation, the former type of action has been often brought before courts. For instance, a citizen might bring an action in order to seek an order obliging the government to introduce more stringent mitigation measures in accordance with the objective of the 1998 Law and/or the 1997 Act. Another example is the actions for disclosure of emission data brought by Kiko network as introduced below.

9.61   Requirements for a *mandamus action* are relatively stringent compared to other types of actions. Article 37–2 (1) states: 'a *mandamus* action may be filed only when any serious damage is likely to be caused if a certain administrative disposition is not made and there are no other appropriate means to avoid such damage'.

9.62   The Act thus requires 'seriousness of damage caused' and 'supplementarity' for actions to be filed. When judging whether or not any serious damage would be caused, the court shall consider the degree of difficulty in recovering from the damage and shall take into consideration the nature and extent of the damage as well as the content and nature of the administrative disposition.

9.63   As for standing, a *mandamus* action may be filed only by a person who has a legal interest in seeking an order to the effect that an administrative agency should make a certain administrative disposition. For interpretation of 'legal interest', Article 9.2 on standing for revocation of an administrative disposition shall apply *mutatis mutandis*.

9.64   Kiko Network, the national centre of climate NGOs in Japan, has brought three actions of this type before the courts in order to compel the government to disclose emission data of large-emitting companies (see 9.78–9.80 below).

Action for an injunctive order

9.65   The action for an injunctive order is an action seeking an order, in cases where an administrative agency is about to make a certain administrative disposition which it should not make, to the effect that the administrative agency should not make the administrative disposition (Article 3.7).

9.66   An action for an injunctive order may be filed only in cases where any serious damage is likely to be caused if a certain administrative disposition is made; provided, however, that this shall not apply if there are any other appropriate means to avoid such damage (Article 37–4.1).

9.67   These requirements of 'seriousness of damage' and 'supplementarity' mean that claimants should substantiate the existence of threat of serious damage impossible to be recovered by action for revocation of administrative disposition or for suspension of disposition. With these requirements, it is rare that courts admit this type of action for an injunctive order to be filed.

Public law related action

9.68   A public law related action is an action relating to an administrative disposition that confirms or creates a legal relationship between parties, wherein either party to the legal relationship shall stand as a defendant pursuant to the provisions of laws and regulations, an action for a declaratory judgment on a legal relationship under public law and any other action relating to a legal relationship under public law (Article 4). With the 2004 amendment of the Act, the latter part of Article 4 was added, recognising formally substantive public law related action.

9.69   A recent case of this type of action, the Henoko assessment case,[53] has been brought before the court to confirm the governmental obligation to go through an appropriate environmental impact assessment (EIA) in case there is a defect in the EIA procedure. To what extent this type of action contributes to environmental litigation depends on how the interpretation of terms such as 'legal relationship under public law' might evolve.

Citizen actions

9.70   A citizen action ('*Jumin sosho*') is an action seeking a correction of an act conducted by an agency of the State or by a public entity

---

[53] The Henoko Assessment Case is the one that relates to the relocation project of a US military base to the Henoko area in Okinawa where there are important habitats for dugongs.

which does not conform to laws, regulations and rules, which is filed by a person based on his/her status as a voter or any other status that is irrelevant to his/her legal interest (Article 3.8).

9.71 Citizen actions do not only target an administrative disposition but any act conducted by an administrative agency or by a public entity when they do not confirm to laws and rules. Importantly, citizen actions do not require a person to show his/her legal interest.

9.72 However, these actions are to be filed only by persons specified by the relevant Acts in cases specifically provided for in these Acts. At present, citizen actions may only be filed to seek corrections of financial and budgetary acts by local authorities under the Local Autonomy Law (Articles 242 and 242–2 of Local Autonomy Law).

9.73 According to the Local Autonomy Law, an injunctive order against an illegal financial act may be issued provided that such an act significantly impedes prevention of serious danger to human life and body and other public welfare. Therefore, such an injunctive order is rarely issued.

9.74 The most crucial element of citizen actions lies in determining when a financial and budgetary act of an administrative body can be construed as illegal. The judgments of courts are diverse. Some courts limit the scope of citizen actions purely to financial and budgetary acts (meaning that the acts aim directly at financial administration); others admit that acts subject to citizen actions are not only purely financial and budgetary ones but also acts constituting the grounds for financial payment. Payment for dredging ooze was accepted as a financial and budgetary act in the Tagonoura hedoro (ooze) case,[54] while payment for maintaining and conserving a forest reserve was not accepted in the Kyoto City forest reserve case.[55]

9.75 In the context of climate change, citizen actions have the potential to indirectly control administrative acts through budgetary

---

[54] Tagonoura hedoro (ooze) case, Judgment of the Supreme Court, 13 July 1982, *Minshu* 36(6), 970.

[55] Kyoto City forest reserve case, Judgment of the Supreme Court, 12 April 1990, *Minshu* 44(3), 431.

and financial control, especially if 'financial and budgetary act' is broadly construed. However, disappointingly, the current scope allowed for citizens' actions is very narrow since it is not local authorities but the government that has the jurisdiction over most climate-related areas, starting with energy policy. It would play a significant role in climate protection if citizens' actions are allowed for budgetary and financial acts by the government. For instance, it would contribute to emission reduction if subsidies for import of coal by the government could be challenged and then suspended through citizen actions. Another example is that citizens might challenge through citizen actions the legality of payments for overseas development assistance that would increase CO_2 emissions, such as funding for an inefficient coal-fired power plant.

Action under the State Redress Act, 1947

9.76　The State Redress Act enacted in 1947[56] provides the following: 'When a public officer who exercises the public authority of the State or of a public entity has, in the course of his/her duties, unlawfully inflicted damage on another person intentionally or negligently, the State or public entity shall assume the responsibility to compensate therefor.' (Article 1)

9.77　Action under the State Redress Act is brought to correct illegality of acts by the administration. Recently, an increased number of actions to seek correction of unlawfulness in the context of failure to use administrative power, and compensation therefore, have been brought before the courts. A significant case is that of the public nuisance one of the Minamata disease (poisoning caused by industrial mercury pollution). The Supreme Court held that when the failure to exercise administrative power is manifestly unreasonable, such inaction is unlawful.[57]

Cases with direct relevance to climate change

9.78　In 2005, the Kiko Network brought three actions before the courts seeking a revocation of the decisions not to disclose emission

---

[56] The State Redress Act, 1947. See www.japaneselawtranslation.go.jp/law/detail/?id=1933&vm=04&re=01&new=1.

[57] Judgment of the Supreme Court, 24 November 1989, *Minshu* 43(10), 1169; Judgment of the Supreme Court, 23 June 1996, *Minshu* 49(6), 1600.

data of large-emitting installations, and an order of disclosure by the government. In 2004 the Kiko Network began requesting the Directors of Regional Bureaux to disclose reports submitted by designated installations under the 1979 Act. They did this on the basis of the 1999 Act on Access to Information Held by Administrative Organs.[58] The Act provides that any person may request from the head of an administrative organ the disclosure of administrative documents held by the administrative organ concerned (Article 3). When there is a disclosure request, unless it is for information protected by non-disclosure, the head of an administrative organ shall disclose said administrative documents to the applicant (Article 5).

9.79   Emission data for the year 2000, for which disclosure was rejected, amounted to around 20 per cent of total emissions of Japan, from 17 per cent of designated installations including steel manufacturing plants. In the course of these three actions brought by the Kiko Network, decisions not to disclose emissions data relating to 340 installations (out of 753) were modified to permit disclosure.

9.80   The defendants argued that the requested information falls into Article 5 (ii) (a): 'Information which when disclosed is likely to cause harm to the rights, competitive position, or other legitimate interests of the said juridical persons, etc. or of the said individual.' District courts of Nagoya, Osaka and Tokyo accepted requests from Kiko Network and ordered the disclosure by stating that in order to justify non-disclosure it is necessary to demonstrate the probability of causing harm to legitimate interests of concerned juridical persons, and that the abstract possibility of such harm is not sufficient to justify non-disclosure.[59] In October 2007 the Osaka High Court revoked the judgment of the Osaka District Court by stating there had been no abuse of discretion by administrative organs.[60] The Kiko Network then appealed to the Supreme Court. The Nagoya High Court, on the other hand, in

---

[58] See n.27 above.

[59] Judgment of Nagoya District Court, 5 October 2006; Judgment of Osaka District Court, 30 November 2007, available at www.kikonet.org/theme/archive/kaiji/decision-osaka20070130.pdf; and Judgment of Tokyo District Court, 28 September 2007, available at www.kikonet.org/theme/archive/kaiji/decision-tokyo20070928.pdf.

[60] Judgment of Osaka High Court, 19 October 2007, available at www.kikonet.org/theme/archive/kaiji/decision-osaka20071019.pdf.

November 2007 maintained the judgment of the Nagoya District Court and ordered disclosure.[61]

(C)   Private law – civil litigation

9.81   The Civil Code[62] enacted in 1896 contains a general provision on tort liability. Article 709 states: 'A person who intentionally or negligently violates the rights of others shall be liable for the loss caused by the act.' Despite the dramatic social changes since 1896, this provision on tort liability has remained unchanged. On the basis of this provision, a claimant may seek compensation for loss and an injunction of the act causing the loss. Neither a specific area of nor a special body of rules dealing with public and private nuisances exists: Article 709 of the Civil Code deals with all the cases involving tort liability and the courts have developed a flexible interpretation of this provision so as to deal with environmental litigation by considering the unique features and specifics of such litigation.

Negligence

9.82   For a person to be liable for the loss caused by his/her act, the person should have violated the rights of others intentionally or negligently. In the context of environmental litigation, negligence has been interpreted in two different ways. The first interpretation is that if a person can foresee the occurrence of the damage, he/she is liable. The second interpretation is that if a person can avoid foreseeable damage, but does not do so, he/she is liable. Scholars advocate the first while courts maintain the second. Some lower courts dealing with pollution cases have passed judgments to the effect that when there is a threat to life and body, costs to avoid the damage should not be considered and defendants should be obliged to cease operations.[63]

---

[61] Judgment of Nagoya High Court, 15 November 2007, available at www.kikonet.org/ theme/archive/kaiji/decision-nagoya20071115.pdf.

[62] Civil Code, 1986. For Parts I, II and III, see www.japaneselawtranslation.go.jp/law/detail /?id=1928&vm=04&re=01&new=1; for Parts IV and V, see www.japaneselawtranslation. go.jp/law/detail/?id=2&vm=04&re=01&new=1.

[63] First Kumamoto Minamata disease case, Judgment of Kumamoto District Court, 20 March 1973, *Hanrei jiho* 696, 15.

9.83 Operators who engage in hazardous activities involving significant risks have an obligation to avoid the damage resulting from the risk occurring. For instance, operators of mining and of nuclear plants owe liability without fault under specific legislations.

Causation

9.84 One of the greatest difficulties in the context of environmental litigation is to establish the causal link between the act causing the loss and the occurrence of damage. In theory, the burden of proof of factual causation primarily falls on victims (claimants). As it is difficult for victims to bear this burden in most cases, scholars and courts try to mitigate their burden of proof. Some lower courts admit indirect evidence to prove causation.[64] For instance, the Niigata District Court in the First Niigata Minamata Disease Case allocated the burden of proof between the claimants and the defendant. The claimants had to identify and show reasonable grounds for what the substance causing damage was, and how the substance reached the victims, and the defendant had to demonstrate that it did not release the substance in question. Other courts still require claimants to prove a high probability of causation, but admit epidemiologic proof in order to mitigate the burden of proof for claimants.[65]

9.85 Even in the case of diseases that do not show a particular relationship between the pollutant in question and the disease, such as bronchitis, the Osaka District Court in the Second to Fourth Nishiyodogawa air pollution cases[66] admitted claims by accepting epidemiologic evidence of factual causation between collective acts and the disease, stating that as proving causation between the individual act and the disease is extremely difficult, it would therefore be socially and economically inappropriate that claimants assume the burden of proof, and to such extent, it would be appropriate that burden of proof would fall on defendants.

---

[64] For instance, First Niigata Minamata disease case, Judgment of Niigata District Court, 29 September 1971, *Kamin* 22 (9–10), 1. See Otsuka, *Environmental Law*, pp. 669–74

[65] For instance, Itai Itai disease case, Toyama District Court, 30 June 1971, *Hanrei jiho* 635, 17.

[66] Judgment of Osaka District Court, 5 July 1996, *Hanrei jiho* 1538, 17.

9.86   Recently, some lower courts have begun to award compensa-
        tion tailored to the degree of probability.[67] In an action brought
        by victims of a relatively less serious condition in the Minamata
        disease case, the Tokyo district court judged that even though
        claimants only show evidence with lower probability, they may
        receive not full but discounted compensation providing that
        there is a substantial likelihood that claimants suffer from the
        disease. The court considered that it would be scientifically dif-
        ficult for victims suffering from less serious conditions to prove
        a causal link with a high probability; if the court required the
        victims to prove causation with high probability, claimants
        would have to assume too heavy a burden of proof due to lack
        of scientific evidence, which is contradictory to the concept
        of fair share of loss. This approach actually weakens the bur-
        den of proof and ensures more effective remedies for claim-
        ants by reflecting the degree of probability in the quantum of
        damages.

Joint and several liability

9.87   Article 719 of the Civil Code provides for joint and several liabil-
        ity: 'If more than one person has inflicted damages on others by
        their joint tortious acts, each of them shall be jointly and sever-
        ally liable to compensate for those damages. The same shall apply
        if it cannot be ascertained which of the joint tortfeasors inflicted
        the damages.'

9.88   The courts' interpretation is that the act of each person needs to
        meet the requirements of this provision independently and that
        it is therefore necessary to have a causal link between the indi-
        vidual act and the occurrence of the damage. Recently, another
        interpretation has been advocated, and it has been met with
        increasing support, that when the act of each person has a com-
        mon relevance and there is causation between such collective acts
        and the occurrence of the damage, each of them shall be jointly
        and severally liable.

---

[67] For instance, Tokyo Minamata disease case, Judgment of Tokyo District Court,
7 February 1993, *Hanrei jiho special edition* (25 April 1993), 3.

9.89   The Nishiyodogawa cases[68] and the Kawasaki Pollution case[69] relate to air pollution caused by factories and automobiles on the highway. The district courts admit in both cases that emissions from factories have common relevance, even if these operations started at different times and even though the extent of their contribution to the occurrence of damage is not clear. The Nishiyodogawa cases went further to recognise the existence of common relevance between emission from factories and emission from automobiles based on commonality of pollutant.

9.90   In light of the nature of climate change issues, when a claimant suffering from damage caused by the adverse impacts of climate change brings an action seeking compensation for the damage suffered, proving a causal link between the act of emission and the damage is one of the barriers that claimants find the most difficult to surmount. This is also true for when a claimant wants to sue the government for its failure to introduce mitigation measures sufficient to avoid climate change impacts.

9.91   In the context of climate litigation, the courts would easily admit that GHG emission collectively causes adverse impacts based on scientific findings so far. The difficulty, rather, lies in proving that the act of emission by a specific defendant and/or defendants as a group caused the damage suffered by a claimant and/or claimants as a group. Some approaches taken by the courts mentioned above, for instance joint and several liability, might prove helpful in overcoming, to some extent, such difficulties.

9.92   Climate impacts occur due to accumulated acts by many all over the world and over time. Besides, the damage is in general caused not by a single factor of climate change, rather by a complex of multiple factors. Therefore, it is practically difficult, if not

[68] For the First Nishiyodogawa case, Judgment of the Osaka District Court, 29 March 1991, *Hanrei jiho* 1383, 22; for the Second to Fourth Nishiyodogawa cases, Judgment of the Osaka District Court, 5 July 1995, *Hanrei Times* 889, 64. On 29 July 1998, both the plaintiffs and defendants agreed a compromise recommended by the Osaka High Court.
[69] The First Kawasaki Pollution case, Judgment of Yokihama District Court, Kawasak Branch, 25 January 1994, *Hanrei jiho* 1481, 19. For the actions against thirteen private companies, a compromise between the plaintiffs and these defendants was reached on 25 December 1996 while for the actions against the government and the Metropolitan Highway Public Corporation a compromise was reached on 20 May 1999.

impossible, to single out a portion of damage directly attributable to climate change and to prove a causal link between the act
of emission and the damage caused by it. The approach of compensation in proportion with probabilities might play a role in
mitigating this burden of proof and in ensuring better remedies.
However, since proving some level of probabilities would still not
be scientifically easy, compensation might be considerably dis-
counted even with this approach.

Injunction

9.93   Injunctions have an important role to play in preventing environmental pollution and damage. Although there is no explicit
provision on injunction in the Civil Code, courts have reviewed
requests and issued injunctive orders in some cases based on real
rights and in other cases based on personal rights.

9.94   In cases on tort liability, the courts consider that the act should
be unlawful, which is one of the requirements for liability to be
admitted. In determining the unlawfulness of the act, the courts
make use of the balance of interest test especially by balancing
the nature of the interest which was violated and the tort: if the
nature of the interest which was violated is serious and exceeds
the limit tolerable by the victim, it is regarded as unlawful.[70] In
the case of injunctions, the Supreme Court places particular
importance on the nature of and probability of damage as well
as the public nature of activities causing damage, as observed
in its judgment in the National Route 43 case.[71] This judgment
also recognised that a higher level of unlawfulness is required for
an injunction compared to one required for compensation since
injunctive order might suspend the act in question and likely
cause serious damage to the defendant.

9.95   Injunctions have the potential to play a powerful role in climate
protection: for instance, injunctions could result in the suspension or limitation of those GHG emitting activities of large emitters that are likely to cause climate change. The difficulty lies in
the need to show 'unlawfulness': if the activities in question are
considered public in nature and/or if the damage in question is

---

[70] Oda, *Japanese Law* (see n. 1 above), pp. 197–8.
[71] National Route 43 case, Judgment of the Supreme Court, 7 July 1996, *Minshu* 49(7), 1870.

regarded as not significant, the courts would not order an injunction. However, the courts have reconfirmed in several cases that where there is a high probability of damage to human health, even if the activities in question are of a public nature, injunctive relief should be provided.[72]

9.96   The question of whether or not a request for an abstract injunction, for instance seeking to limit pollutants below a certain level, may be admitted is also an important question in the context of climate litigation. In terms of climate change, as the sources of pollution are quite numerous and diverse and claimants do not often have the necessary information, it is difficult for claimants to specify the exact content of the injunction they are seeking for each defendant in order to achieve their expected outcome. While judgments differ from court to court, the courts in general appear reluctant to admit such injunctions.

(D)   Other law

Review by independent administrative commission

9.97   The Environmental Dispute Coordination Commission ('EDCC') is an administrative commission established on 1 July 1972, by integrating the Land Coordination Commission and the Central Pollution Examination Commission under Article 3 of the National Government Organisation Act.

9.98   The EDCC enjoys quasi-judicial powers for settling environmental disputes.[73] The major roles of the EDCC are as follows: (i) settling environmental disputes quickly and justly through conciliation, mediation, arbitration and adjudication (Environmental Dispute Settlement System); and (ii) seeking coordination between mining, quarrying or gravel-collecting industries and the public interests (Land-use Coordination System).

9.99   Decisions of the commission can be subject to judicial review by courts but the court is bound by the facts determined by the commission as long as the facts are based on substantial evidence.

---

[72] For instance, National Route 43 case, *ibid.* and Nagoya nanbu air pollution case, Judgment of Nagoya District Court, 27 November 2000, *Hanrei jiho* 1746, 3.
[73] See www.soumu.go.jp/english/eo.html.

9.100   The EDCC environmental dispute settlement system provides a quicker, cheaper, and access-friendly means to settle disputes, especially common ones such as disputes relating to pollution. However, in the case of climate change, as a number of emitters exist all over the world, it would be a challenge for the EDCC to deal with such global issues if a climate-related complaint about large emitters is brought.

Human rights

9.101   As mentioned above, the Constitution contains a list of human rights, which includes the right to life (Article 13) and the right to maintain the minimum standards of wholesome and cultured living (Article 25), but this has no reference to a right to the environment. In practice, the courts have provided compensation and ordered injunctive relief on the basis of personal rights, the legal basis of which are Articles 13 and/or 25. Recently, the right to live in peace, based on these two provisions of the Constitution, has been invoked by claimants as grounds for compensation and injunctive relief. The right to live in peace is understood as providing an added value in that it extends the scope of interests protected by law, which means grounds of civil litigation, to non-pecuniary injury to life.

9.102   Japan is a Party to various international human rights conventions including the International Covenant on Civil and Political Rights. Although Japan has not yet ratified the optional protocol to ICCPR that recognises the Committee's competence to receive and consider communications from individuals who claim to be victims of violation of rights provided for in the covenant, Japan is expected to ratify it in the near future. Once ratified, interpretations by the Committee could influence the acts of the government as well as the courts.

Criminal law

9.103   The Criminal Code enacted in 1907[74] does not have special provisions on the environment.

---

[74] The Criminal Code, 1907. See www.japaneselawtranslation.go.jp/law/detail/?id=1960&vm=04&re=01&new=1.

9.104 Most environmental legislations, including climate-related laws such as the 1998 Law and the 1979 Act, contain penalties for non-compliance. The objective of these provisions is to ensure compliance with and to realise the outcomes of these legislations.

9.105 Experiences of severe environmental pollution have led to the enactment of the Act on Punishment of the Crime of Causing Pollution Harmful to Human Health, 1970 ('the 1970 Act'). The objective of the 1970 Act is to punish a person for having caused a risk to public health or for intentionally or negligently emitting substances hazardous to human health in the course of operations in factories or installations.

9.106 The 1970 Act has three features. First, the Act penalises a person for having caused a risk, not injury, to public health. Second, it punishes not only the person having caused such a risk but also the legal person. Third, the Act contains provisions that allow a presumption of a causal link between hazardous substances and the risk that occurred without clear evidence of causation.

9.107 The Supreme Court has in the past interpreted the term 'operations' narrowly, attracting criticism that it would reduce the effectiveness of the Act.[75] Nevertheless, the provisions on presuming a causal link and on punishment of a legal person would be helpful in case the government decides to hold illegal emitters responsible.

Public trust/global commons

9.108 The Japanese legal system does not recognise the concept of a public trust. However, in the actions for judicial review and for tort liability, sometimes claimants have invoked the concept of the right of nature and have given nature the status of a claimant. For instance, in the Amaminokurousagi case,[76] the claimants, on behalf of amaminokurousagi, also known as the Amami rabbit or *Pentalagus furnessi*, and a couple of other species that have their habitat in the area, brought an action for revoking a licence granted for forest development. The claimants argued that they

---

[75] Daito tessen enso gas funsyutsu case, Judgment of the Supreme Court, 23 September 1987, *Keishu* 41(6), 255.
[76] Amaminokurousagi case, Judgment of Kagoshima District Court, 22 January 2001.

were entitled to standing on behalf of these species. The court rejected this concept while admitting that the concept of right of nature has raised serious questions of the current legal system, the basis of which is to protect the interests of individual natural and legal persons.

Competition/anti-trust law

9.109   The Law on Prohibition of Private Monopoly and Ensuring of Fair Trade ('the Anti-Monopoly Law')[77] was enacted in 1947, while Japan was still under the occupation of the Allied forces. Under such circumstances, the Anti-Monopoly Law was heavily influenced by the US antitrust legislations. In the same year, based on the Law, as the organ to implement the Anti-Monopoly Law, the Fair Trade Commission ('FTC'), an independent administrative commission, was established.

9.110   The Anti-Monopoly Law has the goal to promote free and fair competition, to stimulate creative initiatives by entrepreneurs, to enhance business activities, to increase the level of employment and the real income of the people, and thereby to ensure the interests of consumers and to promote the democratic and social development of the national economy.[78] With a view to achieving this goal, the Law prohibits private monopolisation.[79] It also regulates various types of combinations of companies in order to prevent the excessive concentration of economic power.[80] Companies are prohibited from acquiring shares, which result in a substantial restraint of competition.[81] Unreasonable restraint of trade starting with cartel and unfair trade practices is also prohibited.[82]

9.111   In the context of climate change, in March 2010 the FTC issued an interim report on issues under competition policy relating to the use of market mechanisms to address climate change,[83]

---

[77] The Law on Prohibition of Private Monopoly and Ensuring of Fair Trade (the Anti-Monopoly Law), 1947. See www.japaneselawtranslation.go.jp/law/detail/?id=1929&vm=04&re=01&new=1.
[78] Article 1 of the Anti-Monopoly Law.
[79] Article 2.5, *ibid.*   [80] Articles 9.1 and 9.2, *ibid.*
[81] Articles 10.1 and 15, *ibid.*   [82] Articles 3 and 19.9, *ibid.*
[83] Fair Trade Commission, *Interim Report on Issues under Competition Policy Relating to Use of Market Mechanisms to Address Climate Change*, March 2010. See www.jftc.go.jp/pressrelease/10.march/10033102.pdf.

focusing on the national emissions trading scheme. The report raises some issues which are likely to violate the Anti-Monopoly Law: for instance, it would be the case if business persons collectively decide on the amount of production and of supply in light of each reduction target; on means to achieve the target; on when and to what extent increased carbon price would be added to the price of products and services.

Public international law

9.112 International law concluded by Japan is in effect part of the Japanese legal system without the need for transposing it into national law.

9.113 There is no case so far in which principles of international environmental law such as sustainable development have been directly applied.

9.114 However, in several cases, claimants have invoked the application of international treaties, for instance the Convention on Biological Diversity ('CBD') as the additional ground for illegality in the actions for revocation of administrative disposition,[84] in actions for tort liability and in citizen actions.[85] In most cases, courts have decided that provisions of CBD and agreements on protection of migratory birds require parties only to make efforts to take appropriate measures without requiring them to take specific measures and therefore the act in question does not violate these treaties.

9.115 In the Grampus Purchase case, the Nagoya District Court decided that the CBD would not apply to an act by a private person but the objective and effect of the Convention might be taken into account when interpreting 'public order' provided for in the Civil Code.[86] The court did not admit the possibility of direct application to an act by a private person but did admit the possibility of indirect application of an international environmental agreement.

9.116 In the context of climate change, in case a company emits excessive GHG, against which a person wants to get an injunctive

---

[84] Kenodo Hachioji Junction case, Judgment of Tokyo District Court, 31 May 2005.
[85] Wajiro Higata Umetate case, Judgment of Fukuoka District Court, 31 March 1998.
[86] Judgment of Nagoya District Court, 7 March 2003.

order by the court to stop such emissions, by way of indirect application above, the court might decide on whether or not the act is unlawful not only based on national legislations but also by taking into account the objectives and commitments of the FCCC. Conditions and circumstances in which the court indirectly applies international law are not necessarily clear: much depends on the discretion of the courts.

(E)   Practicalities

Founding jurisdiction

9.117   The Code of Civil Procedure, 1996,[87] provides for rules covering jurisdiction. An action shall be subject to the jurisdiction of the court that has jurisdiction over the location of the general venue of the defendant.[88] The general forum is determined by his/her domicile, by his/her residence if he/she has no domicile in Japan or his/her domicile is unknown, or by his/her last domicile if he/she has no residence in Japan or his/her residence is unknown.[89] The general venue of a juridical person or any other association or foundation shall be determined by its principal office or business office, or by the domicile of its representative or any other principal person in charge of its business if it has no business office or other office.[90]

9.118   The general venue of a foreign association or foundation shall be determined by its principal office or business office in Japan, or by the domicile of its representative or any other principal person in charge of its business assigned in Japan if it has no business office or other office in Japan.[91]

9.119   The general venue of a State shall be determined by the location of a government agency that represents the State in a suit.[92]

9.120   Actions relating to a tort may be also filed with the court that has jurisdiction over the place where the tort was committed.[93]

---

[87] The Code of Civil Procedure, 1996. See www.japaneselawtranslation.go.jp/law/detail/?id=1940&vm=04&re=01&new=1.
[88] Article 4.1 of the Code of Civil Procedure.   [89] Article 4.2, *ibid.*
[90] Article 4.4, *ibid.*   [91] Article 4.5, *ibid.*
[92] Article 4.6, *ibid.*   [93] Article 5(9), *ibid.*

Enforcement

9.121   The Civil Enforcement Act, 1979,[94] regulates the enforcement of judgments by the courts. There are different procedures for monetary and non-monetary claims.

Ancillary order

9.122   The Law on Civil Interim Measures, 1989,[95] provides for two types of interim measures aiming to secure the enforceability of judgment by the courts. The first type of measures is an order of provisional seizure which may be issued to preserve the property to carry out compulsory execution for a claim for payment of money.[96] The second type is an order of provisional disposition, (i) to preserve the property or (ii) to establish or maintain the legal relationship between parties in dispute.[97]

Public interest litigation

9.123   Traditionally, standing for actions is granted to those who have a legitimate interest in the subject matter. While there is no system similar to class actions in US law, there is a system of representative action, in which a representative who pursues actions is selected by those wishing to participate in actions and in which all parties should be specified.[98]

Costs/funding

9.124   A defeated party shall bear court costs.[99] All costs except court fees should be paid in advance of the proceedings. In the context of environmental litigation, costs of witnesses and of expert opinions are essential, which makes litigation costly.

---

[94] The Civil Enforcement Act, 1979.
[95] The Law on Civil Interim Measures, 1989. See www.japaneselawtranslation.go.jp/law/detail/?id=1875&vm=04&re=01&new=1.
[96] Subsection 2 of the Law on Civil Interim Measures.
[97] Subsection 3, *ibid*.
[98] Oda, *Japanese Law*, pp. 411–412.
[99] Article 61 of the Civil Procedure Code.

Obtaining information

9.125 Under the Act on Access to Information Held by Administrative Organs, 1999, any person may request the disclosure of information held by the government and its organs. Upon such request, in principle, the government needs to disclose information it holds. The government may refuse the request for disclosure only if the case comes under one of the reasons provided for in the Act.

9.126 The problem is that the Act does not apply to information held by a local authority. Disclosure of such information depends on whether or not the local authority has local regulations for disclosure of information and on the procedure and conditions such regulations require.

9.127 The Civil Procedure Code of 1996 was amended in 2001. Since then in civil proceedings the holder of the document in question may not refuse to submit the document in the cases specified in the Act, such as where a party personally possesses the document that he/she has cited in the suit; and where the document has been prepared in the interest of the party who offers evidence or with regard to the legal relationships between the party who offers evidence and the holder of the document.[100]

9.128 The Code of 1996 strengthens the power of the court to order submission of documents in the proceedings. The court, when it finds that a petition for an order to submit a document is well-grounded, shall make an order to the effect that the holder of the document should submit the document pursuant to conditions and procedures provided for in the Code.[101]

Conclusion

9.129 Both in judicial review and in civil litigation, Japanese case law demonstrates a clear trend towards better environmental protection and more effective remedies for victims. In judicial review, standing has been a challenge for actions to be filed. With flexible interpretation by courts, standing in judicial review cases has expanded to cover persons other than the addressees of the administrative disposition.

---

[100] Article 220, *ibid.*   [101] Article 223.1, *ibid.*

9.130   In civil litigation, causation and the collective and combined
        nature of pollution which relates to several and joint liability have
        been barriers for victims of environmental damage to obtain-
        ing remedies. Courts and scholars have tried to overcome such
        barriers and to introduce new methods and approaches such
        as epidemiological evidence and discounted compensation in
        proportion with probabilities to lighten the burden of proof for
        claimants.

9.131   Nevertheless, because of the nature of climate change, courts will
        face further difficulties in dealing with climate litigation. Among
        the challenges courts will face are: how to deal with 'damage'
        since it is difficult to distinguish damage caused by climate
        change from that due to other factors; how to treat the uncer-
        tainty surrounding causation; and to whom standing should be
        granted in which categories of actions.

9.132   As for standing, in light of the nature of the interest in climate
        protection, standing should be more flexible in judicial review.
        One of the options is to expand the scope of Citizen Actions, for
        instance, to national budgetary and financial acts; another is to
        provide a standing to NGOs and environmental groups acting
        for the public interest of climate protection.

9.133   Placing clear and specific obligations on the government, local
        authorities and large emitters, starting with emission-reduction
        obligations, is essential to realising aggressive GHG reductions.
        It is also necessary to strengthen judicial review by the courts.

9.134   For compensation for damage caused by climate impacts, some
        innovative ideas and schemes might be useful to explore, for
        instance, a compensation fund or insurance scheme. This could
        be funded by levying a charge on those who emit more than they
        are permitted to. The fund could pay for restoration and rehabili-
        tation of the damaged area, and offer damages to those affected.
        For more effective remedies, it is necessary both to vitalise the
        means of litigation and to elaborate regulatory schemes that pro-
        vide effective remedies for victims.

Africa and the Middle East

10

Egypt

DALIA FAROUK AND LAMIAA YOUSSEF

(A)   Introduction

The Egyptian legal system

10.01   Egypt has a civil code system and there is no binding doctrine of precedent. However, judgments of higher courts are persuasive. The sources of Egypt's laws in order of priority are legislation, custom, the principles of Islamic Sharia, and equity.[1]

10.02   The Egyptian judicial system is divided into two main types of courts, the ordinary judiciary and the State Council judiciary. There are also several other specialised courts and judicial organs. The courts generally work in a three-tier system. In the ordinary judiciary, these are the Courts of First Instance, the Courts of Appeal and, for points of law but not of fact, the Court of Cassation. In the State Council, these are Administrative Courts, the Administrative Judiciary, and the Supreme Administrative Court. Historically, the courts in Egypt have been slow and – with the exception of the higher courts – not very sophisticated. Seeking redress through the courts could therefore be a lengthy process with uncertain outcomes.

10.03   Egypt does not recognise class actions. However, any person who can prove personal direct interest in a matter deliberated before a court of law may intervene in the case and join with either party. This applies in both public law and private law litigation.

The authors would like to thank the staff at Habi Center for Environmental Rights ('HCER'), especially Mr Mahmoud Al Qadi and Ms Fatma Sayed, for the information on the environmental and climate change cases handled by HCER in lower courts, which is not published. The authors would also like to thank Mr Tamer Mabrook, a blogger, for an interview on the facts of his case involving industry defamation claims.

[1]   Article 2(2) of the Civil Code.

The governmental stance on climate change

10.04   Egypt signed the United Nations Framework Convention on
          Climate Change ('FCCC') on 10 November 1994. It also signed
          the Kyoto Protocol, on 15 March 1999. Being a non-Annex I
          country, Egypt did not take any steps to issue specialised legis-
          lation on climate change. However, it does have various pieces
          of environmental legislation which in many cases overlap with
          climate change issues.

10.05   Despite being a non-Annex I country, Egypt took steps to address
          climate change on a policy level. It launched programmes aim-
          ing at capacity building and procurement of various studies for
          implementation of the FCCC.[2] However, despite the number of
          policies and studies, these are not being translated into legally
          binding regulations nor implemented on the ground so as to pro-
          vide real action in combating climate change.

10.06   In terms of policies, Egypt prepared and submitted two com-
          munications under the FCCC, which triggered various useful
          studies and strategies relating to climate change. In terms of
          regulatory bodies, Egypt formed an inter-ministerial National
          Climate Change Committee in October 1997[3] and restructured
          it in 2007.[4]

10.07   In 2000, Egypt adopted a National Strategy for Solid Waste
          Management that aims to eliminate the uncontrolled accumula-
          tions of solid waste. Under this strategy, solid waste is treated as
          a natural resource. The strategy has been implemented but not
          with much success.[5]

10.08   The real progress made by Egypt is in the energy sector, where
          the country has taken concrete steps. This progress is largely
          motivated by the energy crisis in Egypt rather than concerns over
          climate change. However, such policies contribute to combating

---

[2] See www.eeaa.gov.eg.
[3] Article 1 of the Prime Minister's Decree no. 2883 (1997).
[4] See www.giswatch.org/country-report/2010-icts-and-environmental-sustainability/
    egypt.
[5] See www.ncbi.nlm.nih.gov/pubmed/19712653; http://pdf.usaid.gov/pdf_docs/
    PDACA202.pdf; and www.metap-solidwaste.org/fileadmin/documents/country_data/
    SWM_Egypt_A4.pdf.

climate change since the energy sector is Egypt's largest contributor to emissions.

10.09   Egypt also reorganised the Supreme Council for Energy in 2006 by the Decree of the Prime Minister no. 1395 for the year 2006. The Supreme Council for Energy developed the National Energy Efficiency Strategy and oversees its implementation.

10.10   A major player in the energy efficiency scheme is the New and Renewable Energy Authority ('NREA'), established in 1986 to develop and introduce renewable energy technologies to Egypt on a commercial scale. From 1995 to the present, the President allocated to NREA by Presidential Decree several pieces of government land for establishment of wind farms in the Zaafarana area in the West Suez Gulf;[6] in the Rowaysat area in the Matrouh Governorate;[7] and in Beni Suef, Menya, and Assiut;[8] as well as land for the establishment of a Solar Thermal Power Plant in the Kuraymat area in the Giza Governorate.[9] The NREA aims at covering 20 per cent of generated electricity by renewable energy by the year 2020.[10]

---

[6] Presidential Decree no. 400 for the year 1995, published in the Official Gazette on 28 December 1995 and, later, Presidential Decree no. 168 for the year 2009, published in the Official Gazette on 4 June 2009. This wind farm has been implemented in several stages in cooperation with Germany, Denmark, Spain and Japan. Most of it has been completed and operating since August 2010. See Annual Report of 2010 on www.nrea. gov.eg/arabic1.html for more information. Other areas in Zaafarana are currently in the last stages of implementation. They involve a 120 MW wind farm in cooperation with Denmark and Japan. Another area that will produce 200 MW is planned for implementation in Al Zayt Gulf in cooperation with Germany and the World Bank. See www.nrea. gov.eg/arabic1.html.

[7] Presidential Decree no. 399 (2006), Official Gazette, 30 November 2006.

[8] Presidential Decree no. 319 (2009), Official Gazette, 17 September 2009. The NREA is currently studying with Japan the establishment of a 200 MW wind farm in the third area allocated by this decree west of the Nile under the Assuit Governorate. The first phase is scheduled to be completed by December 2011 and the second phase in January 2013.

[9] Presidential Decree no. 212 (2003), Official Gazette, 21 August 2003. The station has been established with consultancy and funding from the Global Environmental Fund (GEF) and the World Bank and through consultancy and contracting contracts with Spanish, Japanese and Egyptian consultants. The President has also approved a 9.4 billion Japanese Yen loan from Japan International Cooperation Agency (JICA) to be used in this project, by Decree no. 69 for the year 2009. See www.nrea.gov.eg/english1.html for more information.

[10] See www.nrea.gov.eg/english1.html.

10.11   Fuel switching from liquid fuel oil to natural gas is also a major
         component of the Egyptian energy policy[11] and will help reduce
         GHG emissions.[12] Fuel switching is currently being applied in
         electricity generation, industry, residential sectors, and public
         and private transport.[13]

10.12   On 14 March 2005, the Minister of Environmental Affairs estab-
         lished the Designated National Authority of Clean Development
         Mechanism by Decree no. 42 for the year 2005. Egypt is deemed
         to be 'among the leading countries in Arab States region in terms
         of the number of registered CDM projects and a developed pipe-
         line of prospective projects'.[14] These exceed twenty-five projects
         in different stages of validation. Nevertheless, this number is still
         deemed to be 'far below the country's overall potential for CDM
         projects in energy and industry sectors'.[15]

*Industrial and natural resources (emissions sources
and energy mix)*

10.13   Egypt's Second National Communication submitted on 7 June
         2010 under the FCCC (the 'Second Communication') provides
         that 'fossil fuels; petroleum products and natural gas represent
         the main sources for the primary energy ... Renewable energy
         sources currently include hydropower, representing about 11 per
         cent of energy production in Egypt for 2006/07'.

10.14   In the fiscal year 2008–9, Egypt's reserves of oil and oil conden-
         sates were estimated to be about 4.4 billion barrels and its proven
         reserves of natural gas were about 77.2 trillion cubic feet.[16] In
         spite of this, experts believe that 'Egypt's share of these reserves,
         after its foreign partners take their share, may be fully depleted
         by the beginning of 2020'.[17]

---

[11] See www.moee.gov.eg/Arabic/fr-main.htm.
[12] See www.naturalgas.org/environment/naturalgas.asp.
[13] See www.moee.gov.eg/Arabic/fr-main.htm.
[14] UNDP Climate Change Risk Management Programme for Egypt www.undp.org.
      eg/Portals/0/Project%20Docs/Env_Pro%20Doc_Climate%20change%20Risk%20
      Management.pdf.
[15] *Ibid.*
[16] See www.egyptoil-gas.com/read_article_international.php?NID=1560.
[17] Hussein Abdallah, former First Undersecretary of the Ministry of Petroleum to *Al Masry
      Al Youm* Newspaper on 7 May 2010, available in English at www.almasryalyoum.com/
      en/news/petroleum-expert-egypt-oil-and-gas-may-dry-2020.

10.15   Egypt's National Greenhouse Gas Inventory reveals that 'estimated total GHG emissions in 2008 are about 288 $MtCO_2e$'.[18] The Second Communication provides that the energy sector (61%) is the primary contributor to emissions of GHGs in Egypt, followed by agriculture (16%), industrial processes (14%) and then the waste sector (9%). According to the Second Communication, Egypt's share in the total world GHG emissions in 2000 was 0.58%.

National climate change risks

10.16   Egypt identified the most vulnerable sectors to climate change as being (i) agriculture and food security, (ii) coastal zones, (iii) aqua-culture and fisheries, (iv) water resources, (v) human habitat and settlements, (vi) tourism, and (vii) human health.[19]

The Egyptian Constitution

10.17   The 1971 Egyptian Constitution[20] does not include explicit Articles dealing with climate change or the right to a healthy and safe environment. In 2007, Article 59 of the Constitution was amended to state: 'The protection of the environment is a national duty and the law shall regulate the necessary measures to preserve a healthy environment.'[21] This language does not give rise to an explicit duty on the State to preserve a healthy environment and is still relatively new and as yet to be interpreted by courts in legal proceedings. However, taking into consideration how other similar clauses have been interpreted, such as Article 33 (see below), one cannot rule out that the courts will deem this Article to provide such duty on the part of the State, its public bodies, as well as private persons.

---

[18] Second Communication, p. xix.

[19] See Second Communication; David Sterman, *Climate Change in Egypt: Rising Sea Level, Dwindling Water Supplies,* July 2009 at www.climate.org/topics/international-action/ egypt.html; Shardul Agrawala *et al., Development and Climate Change in Egypt: Focus on Coastal Resources and the Nile*; Produced for the OECD, 2004; and Mohammad Saber, *Environmental Consequences of Global Change in Egypt* (The International Geosphere-Biosphere Programme's Global Change Newsletter No. 70, December 2007), p. 16, at www.igbp.net/documents/NL_70-5.pdf.

[20] Amended on 22 May 1980; 26 May 2005; and 29 March 2007.

[21] Originally, this Article 59 related to the preservation of socialist gains. Until this amendment in 2007, the Constitution did not provide any clause in relation to the environment.

10.18   Constitutional provisions do not create on their own dir-
        ect obligations on individuals, but merely an obligation on
        the State to issue laws that apply constitutional principles.
        However, some clauses were used in various private law and
        public law litigations in relation to standing. In these litiga-
        tions, the court recognised the existence of direct personal
        interest by the claimant (as required by Law no. 13 for the year
        1968 regarding Civil and Commercial Procedures (the 'CCP'))
        on the basis of some constitutional clauses giving rights to citi-
        zens. These litigations did not relate to climate change; how-
        ever, there have been some relating to environmental issues to
        which an analogy might be made.

10.19   An example of this is the courts' interpretation of Article 33 of
        the Constitution. Article 33 states that 'Public property shall
        have its sanctity. Its protection and support shall be the duty
        of every citizen in accordance with the law.' Public property
        is defined by Article 30 of the Constitution[22] as 'the property
        of the State and of the public juristic persons'. This Article
        has been interpreted by courts as giving standing to citi-
        zens in litigation against public and private bodies involving
        harm to, or misuse of, public property.[23] In the environmen-
        tal context, the Administrative Judiciary, in a preliminary
        judgment,[24] accepted standing of environmental NGOs based
        on Article 33 of the Constitution.[25] The case was raised by the
        Habi Center for Environmental Rights ('HCER'), an Egyptian
        NGO, against the Minister of Water Resources requesting the
        annulment of his decision to demolish a part of the River Nile
        to establish an artificial island, arguing harm to the water
        environment. The court stated that 'public property has its
        sanctity and its protection is a duty on every Egyptian. It is
        no doubt that one of the means of such protection is resort-
        ing to the judiciary to annul administrative decisions that

---

[22] Amended in 2007.
[23] Judgment in the cases nos. 30953 and 31314 for the year 56j, Supreme Administrative
     Court, issued on 14 September 2010.
[24] A preliminary judgment is a judgment that does not settle the merits of the dispute but
     which settles preliminary questions that are needed for the dispute to continue, such as
     issues of standing or delegation of an expert to deliver a technical report on one aspect
     of the dispute.
[25] Case no. 18948 for the year 56j, the Administrative Judiciary, Third Circuit.

affect these public monies'.[26] Accordingly, Article 33, and by analogy Article 59 after its amendment, will give standing in any climate change claim under public or private law, where there will be harm to public property or to the environment in general – such as cases involving a sea level rise causing coastal erosion, or increased salinity of water causing deterioration of drinking-water quality, or harm to fisheries.

10.20   In the context of striking down legislation, constitutional review in Egypt is a subsequent review of annulment. This means that conformity to the Constitution is checked in relation to issued legislation rather than a draft law, a policy, or an administrative decision; and it is only made after such legislation is approved and issued by Parliament. There are no precedents for unconstitutionality of a legislation based on environmental arguments, because, before 2007, there was no constitutional clause addressing the environment. However, it is expected that this amendment will give rise to constitutional litigation on environmental issues. It is doubtful that climate change constitutional litigation will follow in the absence of an explicit clause on climate change.

10.21   Constitutional review may only be exercised by the Supreme Constitutional Court in relation to an existing dispute between litigants in a lower court of law. Litigants may not raise initial cases directly to the court but have to obtain permission from the lower court which is reviewing the original dispute.

10.22   There is a requirement of direct personal interest. A constitutional claim is only acceptable if adjudication in the constitutional claim will have a direct effect on the claim in the original case. Litigants may not submit constitutional claims or defences 'for academic or ideological purposes; nor for the purposes of protecting idealist values or expressing personal opinion; nor for purposes of affirming the rule of law against violations of its substance that do not relate to the claimant; nor to express an opinion in a matter which did not cause [personal] harm to the claimant, even if it inspires general attention'.[27]

---

[26] The case is still pending before the court. A judgment has not been given yet on the merits of the case.

[27] Ezz El Din Al Danasory and Abdel Hameed Al Shawarby, *The Constitutional Lawsuit* (Alexandria: Monsha't Al Maaref Publishers, 2001), p. 45.

The 'Environmental Law'

10.23   Egypt does not have a legislation governing climate change and
         is not committed to reduce its GHG emissions under any inter-
         national conventions. However, Egypt's principal environmen-
         tal law, Law no. 4 for the year 1994 regarding the Environment
         (the 'Environmental Law'), provides some clauses which regu-
         late maximum permitted emissions of individual establishments
         subject to the law. It does not regulate emissions on a national
         level. However, it states in Article 34 that 'the aggregate pollu-
         tion resulting from all the establishments in one area must be
         within the limits determined by law'. Annex 5 of the Executive
         Regulation of the Environmental Law determined such limits;
         however, the Environmental Law did not provide a definition for
         the 'area' to be used in such determination. In practice, this rule
         has not been followed (see the discussion below of the Talkha
         Fertilizer Company case).

10.24   Establishments subject to the provisions of the Environmental
         Law are liable to ensure that emissions or leakages of air pollut-
         ants do not exceed the maximum levels permitted by laws and
         decrees in force and determined in the Executive Regulation.[28]
         Pollutants subject to the maximum levels regulated by the
         Executive Regulation include some of the GHGs such as sulfur
         dioxide, nitrogen oxides and carbon monoxide.[29] In addition, it
         is prohibited to use machines, engines or vehicles with exhaust
         emissions exceeding the limits set by the Executive Regulation
         of the Environmental law.[30] Sanctions for violations may range
         from administrative penalties (such as closure of the business
         or suspension of the violating activity) to criminal liability (that
         varies from fines up to a maximum of EGP 500,000 and impris-
         onment) or civil liability (removal of the impact of the violating
         activity or compensation to the administrative authority for the
         costs of removal).

10.25   The Environmental Law established the Egyptian Environmental
         Affairs Agency ('EEAA'), which is the primary agency responsible

---

[28] Article 35 of the Environmental Law.
[29] Annex 6 of the Executive Regulations of the Environmental Law.
[30] Article 36 of the Environmental Law.

for implementation of the Environmental Law.[31] It regulates all kinds of pollution and provides for environmental licensing requirements.

10.26 Under the Environmental Law, polluting industries (including the oil industry, companies operating in the electricity generating industry, industrial establishments, quarries and mines, and any other entity which may, in the opinion of the licensing authority, have an impact on the environment)[32] must conduct an environmental impact assessment ('EIA') and apply for an operating license from the licensing authority, which may not be issued except after consultation with the EEAA.[33] Such establishments are expected to keep a register of the impact of their activities on the environment.[34] The EEAA is authorised to follow up on entries in the register to ensure that they conform to the facts; to take samples as required; and to conduct appropriate tests to determine the impact of the establishment's activities on the environment and the extent of its compliance with the law.[35]

10.27 The Environmental Law does not provide for a duty to conduct consultations with NGOs and local communities. However, Article 19 delegated to the EEAA the power to determine the procedures and requirements of the EIA. The *Guide to Policies and Procedures Regarding the EIA* (the 'Guide') was indeed prepared by the EEAA and is constantly updated. It is not published in the Official Gazette but is deemed to be an executive regulation because it was issued based on an express delegation in the Environmental Law. The Guide provides for a consultation meeting with local communities and concerned NGOs as part of the EIA in relation to Type C establishments. In practice, such consultations are not uniformly held.

10.28 The legal authority of the Guide is not above controversy. It has not been proven beyond reasonable doubt that such Guide binds the EEAA itself to conform to its procedures. The consequences

---

[31] *Ibid.*, Article 2.
[32] Article 11 of the Executive Regulation of the Environmental Law and Annex 2 of the Executive Regulation.
[33] Articles 19 and 23 of the Environmental Law.
[34] *Ibid.*, Article 22. [35] *Ibid.*

of the EEAA choosing to remove the consultation requirement in its next update are also unclear; could NGOs prevent it from doing so? The legal authority of the Guide is currently under scrutiny in court.[36] The case relates to the Talkha Fertilizer factory. The Ministry of Environment originally objected to the project because, during the EIA, it was claimed that the level of emissions in the Talkha area were so high that even if emissions of the factory itself do not violate individual limits, the area will be harmed by an additional factory.[37] The factory was later granted a permit. HCER challenged the administrative decision in the State Council judiciary based on the failure of the EEAA to conduct proper consultations with the local communities. The case is still pending and the court will determine as part of its review whether the Guide is binding on the EEAA as well as the consequences of the failure to hold consultations.

10.29   Article 103 of the Environmental Law states that every citizen and NGO concerned with environmental protection shall have the right to report any violation of the Environmental Law. Furthermore, Article 65 of the Executive Regulation provides that every citizen and NGO concerned with environmental protection shall have the right to resort to the competent administrative or judicial agencies for the purpose of applying the provisions of the Environmental Law and its Executive Regulation. These Articles have been used in litigation under public law, private law and criminal law.

10.30   The majority of environmental cases are being brought under the Environmental Law, and are likely to continue being so. While no cases have been argued on the basis of climate change, there have been violations which caused air pollution and were of a type which contributed to climate change, that have been taken to court on the basis of air pollution regulations. These cases were mainly brought under the section dealing with air pollution in the Environmental Law. Claims brought under the Environmental Law include: (i) claims in the State Council judiciary against public bodies forcing them to act according to the Environmental Law; and (ii) claims under private and criminal

---

[36] Case no. 9218 for the year 64j, the Administrative Judiciary, Third Circuit.
[37] See www.hcer.org/node/232.

laws against private persons for violation of the rules of the Environmental Law.

10.31   An example of the first type of these claims is case no. 1898 for the year 57j before an administrative court. The case was raised by an NGO against the Minister of the Interior for his failure to issue an executive decree to implement emission limits of vehicles set by the Executive Regulation of the Environmental Law. The claim has been denied and is currently being appealed before the Supreme Administrative Court under case no. 4918 for the year 53j. There are more successful precedents in the context of environmental rights. In the verdict in cases nos. 7814 for the year 54j, 9090 for the year 54j, and 1771 for the year 55j (all issued on 2 May 2002 in the First Circuit of the Alexandria Administrative Judiciary), the standing of several environmental NGOs was accepted, based on Article 103 of the Environmental Law and Article 65 of the Executive Regulation. The case related to a decision by the Governor of Alexandria to allocate a part of Lake Mariout to an investor to demolish and build a structure thereupon. Fishermen, NGOs and other public figures challenged the decision and won.

10.32   The majority of claims against private persons under the Environmental Law are raised by the EEAA for violations of the Environmental Law. However, the courts accepted intervention by NGOs in such EEAA claims on the basis of Article 103 of the Environmental Law and Article 65 of its Executive Regulation. Examples are the criminal case no. 1575 for the year 2005 in Tebbin Criminal Court[38] and the criminal case no. 5329 for the year 2008 in Basatin Partial Court.[39]

10.33   To date, these litigations have succeeded in establishing standing in court and in forcing public and private persons to abide

---

[38] This was a criminal claim raised by EEAA against the National Cement Company in Helwan relating to violations of the Environmental Law. Several NGOs intervened in the case joining the claimant, EEAA. The court accepted the intervention, and these NGOs submitted a civil claim. The criminal case was later settled between EEAA and the company, and the civil claim was dismissed accordingly.

[39] The case is now registered under a new no. 3825 for the year 2009, Criminal First Instance Court of South Cairo. It relates to a criminal claim raised by EEAA for transport and possession of dangerous medical wastes. Here again, the court accepted the intervention of environmental NGOs. The case is still pending.

by the law, but have not succeeded in establishing a right to
compensation. Nor had they attempted to do so. In these litigations, the claimants did not request compensation but merely
cessation of the environmental violations. HCER are currently
attempting to do so in a case concerning the violation by the
Governor of Kafr El Sheikh of the Environmental Law in relation to refuse handling. Article 38 of the Executive Regulation
of the Environmental Law prohibits open-air burning of solid
waste. The waste collection points managed by the Kafr El
Sheik Governorate systematically burn refuse in the open air.
HCER raised the case no. 1 for the year 2005 Environmental
in Kafr El Sheikh Court to establish the existence of a violation. The court appointed an expert to determine (i) whether
garbage was being burnt, and (ii) who was harmed by this. It is
important to note that even though burning of solid waste constitutes 9 per cent of Egypt's emissions, arguments in the case
did not include any arguments on climate change but the claim
was based on air pollution. The expert established the violation
and determined the people affected to be those inhabiting the
houses in the direction of the wind. The court is still reviewing
the compensation claim and it still remains to be seen how the
court will identify those harmed by the violation and quantify
the harm.

The 'Natural Reserves Law'

10.34   Law no. 102 for the year 1983 regulating Natural Reserves ('NRL')
prohibits any act, action or activity that may cause deterioration of the natural environment or that may cause air pollution of the natural reserves in any form.[40] It is also prohibited
to exercise, without the prior approval of EEAA, any activity or
conduct any experiments in the areas surrounding the natural
reserves if such acts would have an impact on the environment
of the natural reserve.[41] Sanctions vary from fines to imprisonment.[42] Moreover, the violator shall be liable for the removal
or the repair expenses that are determined by EEAA and shall
have equipment or tools used in the commission of the offence
confiscated.[43]

---

[40] Article 2 of the NRL.   [41] *Ibid.*, Article 3.
[42] *Ibid.*, Article 7.   [43] *Ibid.*, Article 7(3).

10.35   Article 5 of NRL grants environmental NGOs the right to resort to administrative and legal authorities to bring legal actions for the implementation of the provisions of the NRL.

10.36   This law may be used in climate change claims where natural reserves are being affected.

(B)   Public law

Overview

10.37   This section addresses the process whereby decisions of public bodies may be reviewed by the courts. The legal principles discussed herein form part of Egyptian Administrative Law. Judicial review of decisions of public bodies that are deemed to be equivalent to is handled by the Supreme Constitutional Court under a different framework, discussed above.

10.38   Attempts to force the government to act or to stop it from acting in climate change matters should be brought in the State Council judiciary under public law. Claims to stop government action in the context of environmental issues have usually not been raised by industry, but by environmentalists trying to stop the government from violating environmental laws.

10.39   There are several types of administrative claims. The most important is the Annulment Case which relates to the cancellation of final administrative decisions. This is the type of case which has been used in environmental claims and which will likely be used in climate change litigation. Thus, we limit our review to this particular case.

10.40   Here again, there is not much significant litigation in relation to climate change, but there are some recent attempts in environmental rights. Most of these examples have been mentioned above in the section on the Environmental Law. In this section, we set out the general principles of public law claims which also apply to administrative claims against public bodies raised pursuant to the Environmental Law.

Justiciability

10.41   There are some categories of decisions and acts issued by public bodies that may not be subject to judicial review in the State

Council. These include: sovereign acts;[44] executive regulations issued pursuant to laws;[45] decisions issued by certain bodies having a judicial nature such as decisions of public prosecutors and police inspectors issued as part of a judicial process;[46] and circulars of public bodies that do not exceed powers given to such bodies by law.[47] The government's decision whether to regulate climate change is likely to be deemed a sovereign act which is not actionable in courts.

Standing

10.42   The claimant must establish a personal direct interest in the claim for the case to be allowed. However, the State Council judiciary has adopted a wide interpretation of the claimant's interest, based on the principle of legality, which has resulted in easier access to judicial process than in the ordinary courts. The court recognised a personal interest for electing citizens in relation to elections; candidates to a public office; property owners in relation to planning decisions; residents of a town and members in municipalities; as well as citizens in relation to decisions affecting the interest, health or future of all citizens.[48]

10.43   A climate change claim raised by any citizen would be accepted by the State Council judiciary as having sufficient personal direct interest.

Existence of an administrative decision

10.44   There must be an administrative decision. An administrative decision is defined as 'the declaration by the administration of its will, binding to others on the basis of its authority laid down by laws and regulations, with the purpose of creating a specific legal status, provided that it is possible, lawful and motivated by the pursuit of public interest'.[49]

---

[44] Article 11 of Law no. 47 for the year 1972 concerning the State Council (the 'State Council Law').

[45] Dr Fathy Fikry, *A Brief on the Annulment Case According to the Court Rulings*, enlarged edition (Cairo: People Printing Company, 2009), p. 37.

[46] *Ibid.*, p. 73.   [47] *Ibid.*, p. 108.   [48] *Ibid.*, p. 170.

[49] Case no. 1042 for the year 9j, Supreme Administrative Court, issued on 12 February 1966.

10.45   The failure of the administrative authority to take a decision
         which it must take is considered a negative decision that is
         actionable.[50] The law must require the administration to take
         such a decision. On this basis, the Administrative Judiciary
         refused a claim relating to the annulment of the negative deci-
         sion of the administration refraining from transferring all fac-
         tories outside residential areas. The court stated that laws and
         regulations, including the Environmental Law, do not oblige
         the administration to do so.[51] Negative decisions form the
         majority of decisions in public interest litigation and would
         also be the relevant type of decisions in the climate change
         context.

10.46   Two characteristics of a decision that may be annulled are rele-
         vant in this context. First, the decision must be issued by a pub-
         lic law person (including public universities and professional
         syndicates). Some private law persons are treated like public
         law persons if their activities are deemed to relate to a public
         utility, such as private universities. Accordingly, a case simi-
         lar to the UK precedent *Dimmock*[52] could be brought up under
         Egyptian law even if against a private university. Second, the
         decision must be final and not subject to any ratification by a
         higher authority. Preparatory procedures by public bodies such
         as recommendations, policy studies and investigations are not
         deemed to be administrative decisions subject to annulment.[53]
         Pursuant to this characteristic, the results of public consulta-
         tions of the EIA will not be deemed a final decision that may be
         challenged.

10.47   The Annulment Case must be raised within sixty days from the
         date of knowledge of the administrative decision, by way of notice
         or publication in the Official Gazette or administrative circulars
         or by way of actual knowledge. This time limit does not apply
         in relation to negative decisions or decisions with continuing
         consequences.

---

[50] Article 10 of the State Council Law; and Dr Fathy Fikry, n. 45 above, p. 224.
[51] Case no. 32975 for the year 61j, Administrative Judiciary, First Circuit, issued on 24
      November 2009.
[52] [2007] EWHC 2288 (Admin); See Ch. 17, para. 17.16.
[53] Dr Fathy Fikry, n. 45 above, p. 104.

Grounds for judicial review

10.48   Pursuant to Article 10(14) of the State Council Law and judicial precedents, there are four categories of reasons based on which an administrative decision could be challenged. These are (i) incompetence; (ii) procedural and formal defects; (iii) unlawfulness; and (iv) abuse of power.

10.49   The second and third of these grounds have been used in the context of environmental rights. For example, failure of the administrative authority to hold consultations in relation to an EIA before issuing a permit will be deemed a procedural defect, even if the results of such consultations do not bind the administrative authority.[54] Failure of the administrative authority to abide by the Environmental Law will fall under the category of unlawfulness of a decision.

(C)   Private law

Overview

10.50   This section covers the legal principles governing a climate liability claim raised by one private person against another private person. It deals with claims raised by persons harmed by climate change against persons accused of causing climate change, usually industrial establishments.

10.51   There have been no attempts to take climate change claims to court under private law. However, there have been some attempts to raise environmental claims relating to pollution and other environmental issues. These may be taken as guidance to determine the appropriate legal basis for climate change claims under private law, although it may be more difficult to prove causation and harm in climate change related proceedings than in a case involving environmental violations.

10.52   Tortious liability is governed by Articles 163–178 of the Civil Code. Generally, tort liability under Egyptian law is based on fault. However, there are instances where compensation will be awarded on a 'non-fault' basis.

---

[54] See Dr Fathy Fikry, n. 45 above, p. 277 for similar analysis.

Liability on a fault basis

10.53   According to Article 163, any person who commits a fault which causes damage to another person shall be liable for damages. Examples of claims which would fall under this category include claims raised by private individuals or NGOs or members of local communities against industrial projects that fail to abide by legal regulations of GHGs, or possibly against farmers for burning rice hay, causing health issues to surrounding individuals.

10.54   The claimant has to establish fault. Fault means 'a breach of a legal obligation to observe due care towards others, by deviating from the behaviour of the reasonable man'.[55] The law does not require that the act constituting the fault violates a statutory text. In fact, scholars specifically state that 'an employer is not relieved from his negligence because he has satisfied all the requirements imposed by administrative authorities, if it is found that such requirements are not enough to protect third parties; and that such employer failed to take other precautions called for by the necessity of protecting people. Requirements imposed by laws and regulations are minimum thresholds for necessary precaution'.[56] In addition, in other contexts, courts have declared that 'The grant of permission for the establishment and operation of a factory does not amount to a cause beyond the claimant's control which relieves the claimant from its responsibility for causing harm to others.'[57]

10.55   Despite the above, defendants may still argue that current Egyptian laws and regulations regarding the environment may be deemed as a ceiling to the environmental rights that could be claimed in court. If the Environmental Law regulates maximum emission levels of certain gases, and if the respondent did not exceed such limits, it would be difficult for the claimant to establish fault or a deviation from the conduct of the reasonable man. This is because the assumption is that the limits determined by law

[55] Abdel Razaq El Sanhoury, *Al Wasit in the Civil Code, Sources of Obligation*, Pt II, Vol. II (Dar Al Nahda Publishers, 1981), p. 1094.
[56] Ezz El Din Al Danasory and Abd El Hameed Al Shawarby, *Civil Liability in the Light of Jurisprudence and the Judiciary*, Vol. I (Alexandria: Monsha't Al Maaref Publishers, 2004), p. 77.
[57] Cassation Case no. 622 for the year 44j, issued on 22 June 1977.

are limits within which emissions are not harmful. This assumption is reinforced by the language of the preamble to Annex 6 of the Executive Regulation of the Environmental Law determining the maximum levels of emissions. The preamble states that the gases covered by the Annex will 'result in damage to public health or to animals or plants or materials or properties, or may interfere with humans' daily life, and would thus be deemed air pollution *if* the emissions from such pollutants result in concentrates that exceed the maximum levels permitted in outer air'.

10.56   The question is more difficult in relation to GHGs, on which the Environmental Law is silent. Here again, there is still ground to say that because the subject of emissions is regulated by the Environmental Law, gases left unspecified are intended not to be prohibited by the legislator. This argument is reinforced by the fact that the FCCC and Kyoto Protocol have not prevented non-Annex I countries from continuing to emit GHGs; and hence an argument could be made that these conventions authorised such emission. These questions have yet to be taken to court.

Liability on a non-fault basis

10.57   Article 178 of the Civil Code stipulates that 'anyone who guards things, guarding of which requires special care … is responsible for the damage caused by such things, unless he proves that damage has occurred as a result of an alien reason to which he did not contribute'.

10.58   The liability of the 'guardian of things' is a strict liability under which a person is deemed liable for damage that has occurred although no fault could be attributed to his side. For this purpose, a 'guardian' need not be the owner, the possessor or the beneficiary of the 'thing', but is the person with actual independent control over the thing.[58] Here the fault is assumed. In order to avoid liability, the defendant must prove a foreign cause. In some cases, owners of factories were deemed as guardians of the equipment of the factory and liable for compensation for harm caused by such equipment regardless of fault or legal compliance.[59]

---

[58]   El Sanhoury, n. 55 above, p. 1524 ff.
[59]   Cassation Case no. 622 for the year 44j, n. 57 above.

Definition of damage/harm

10.59   The difficulty in climate change claims arises from the nature of harm caused by climate change. For one thing, the harm does not materialise immediately but in the long term. The more difficult issue is scalability. While in a pollution case it is easy for local communities to establish that the effect of the pollution materialises in their local community and thus prove harm, in climate change cases the harm is dispersed on a global level and it is difficult to prove that the defendant is primarily responsible for the long-term harm that is caused by many contributors around the world. A civil claim will not be accepted by the court unless the claimant proves actual harm.

10.60   Egyptian law does not recognise the concept of 'material increase in risk' or a similar concept as an appropriate measure or criterion for damage. There is a requirement that the damage be actual and not anticipated. This means that the harm must have actually been realised or will definitely be realised in the future.[60] Accordingly, future harm is only actionable if the claimant can establish that it will occur beyond any doubt.

10.61   The claimant must also be the person actually harmed by fault of the respondent. The claimant is 'the harmed, every harmed, and no one but the harmed'.[61] This imposes a great difficulty in the context of climate change litigation because of the time lag between the fault and the harm. For example, under Egyptian law, if scientific tests prove that water pollution will lead to an increase in the rate of kidney failure, this does not give grounds to every person who drinks from this polluted water to raise a claim based on the threat to his/her health. Only persons who actually suffer kidney failure and who can establish causation between the polluted water and their illness will be awarded damages.

10.62   Egyptian law recognises the concept of assumed damage, but only in limited cases. For example in relation to interest, the law provides that interest will be awarded for failure to pay on time without the need to establish harm.[62] The assumption of damage in relation to interest is an exception to the general rule which

[60] El Sanhoury, n. 55 above, p. 1201.
[61] *Ibid.*, p. 1277.   [62] Article 228 of the Civil Code.

provides that damage must be actual. In the context of climate change, a similar test must establish an assumption of damage. Otherwise, if the general principles of tort apply on climate change claims, civil liability will be impossible to establish. If actual damage cannot be proved by the claimant, the court will refuse to award damages to the claimant. Legislative intervention in this context is imperative.

10.63   If the fault causes harm to many persons, each individual will have the right to raise an independent claim for the specific harm he/she suffered.[63] This is regardless of whether each harm was independently caused directly by the fault or whether the harms were caused serially (meaning that the fault caused harm to X and the latter's harm caused another harm to Y). If the fault causes harm to a group of persons who do not constitute a legal personality, for example immigrants inhabiting a specific location, each individual may not represent the others in a claim.

Causation

10.64   Generally, in fault based liability, the claimant proves fault and damage only. If the respondent wants to establish lack of causation, he/she has to establish the existence of a cause beyond his/her control (pursuant to Article 165 of the Civil Code) which alone resulted in the harm (by proving *force majeure* or the claimant's fault or the fault of a third party); or establish that his/her fault is not the 'effective' cause of the harm.

10.65   If the fault is committed by several persons, we must distinguish between the case where the fault is the same or similar by all the respondents; and where only one fault is effective.

10.66   Article 169 of the Civil Code provides for a rule in case the fault is equally or similarly committed by several persons. It states that 'When several persons are responsible for an injury, they are jointly and severally responsible to make reparation for the injury. The liability will be shared equally between them, unless the judge fixes their individual share in the damages due.' Accordingly, if they are deemed jointly liable, the claimant may

---

[63] El Sanhoury, n. 55 above, p. 1284.

request 100 per cent of the damage from any of them and the respondent will have a right of recourse against the others. In order for multiple wrongdoers to be deemed jointly liable, three conditions must be fulfilled: (i) each one must have committed a fault; (ii) each fault must have caused the harm; and (iii) the harm caused by each fault must be the same harm.[64] The third of these conditions will be difficult to establish if we apply the general principles governing damage in tort liability (see below). For this condition to be satisfied in the context of climate change, the harm for all persons needs to be a threat to health or land or safety, but not the different physical or fiscal harm specific to each claimant.

10.67   On the other hand, jurisprudence and the judiciary accept the theory of the 'effective cause'. Accordingly, in the climate change context, a factory causing huge amounts of emissions could be deemed as an effective cause of climate change; but not an owner of a vehicle.

Available remedies

10.68   Damages are the primary means of compensation in tort liability. The person at fault is liable for both foreseeable and non-foreseeable direct losses. Indirect losses are not compensated for, even if they were foreseeable. A loss of profits is not always deemed an indirect loss under Egyptian law. If a claimant proves that his loss of profit is a direct consequence of harm, such claimant will be awarded compensation for such loss. A loss is deemed direct if it is a natural consequence of the fault which the tortfeasor could not have avoided by exerting reasonable effort.[65]

10.69   The judge may order specific performance if the claimant requests this. In such case he/she may 'as compensation, order a return to the original state or order the execution of a specific act relating to the unlawful act'.[66] Examples of this include removal of the equipment or activity causing climate change or ordering the publication in newspapers of the criminal verdict against a party in cases of defamation as a compensation for moral damage.

---

[64] *Ibid.*, p. 1290.   [65] Article 221 of the Civil Code.
[66] Article 171(2) of the Civil Code.

(D)   Other law

Criminal law

10.70   Criminal sanctions are used under public law and private law and have been referred to where relevant in the above sections. However, we provide here a section on possible claims against environmental activists for slander and defamation.

10.71   In general, activists, including lawyers and advocacy groups, face huge practical and legal hurdles in carrying out their work, including access to information, dealing with public authorities, and navigating the court system. However, due to recent legal developments, activists may also face legal liability for their activism.

10.72   Trust Chemical Industries ('TCI'), a chemicals company manufacturing caustic soda, chlorine and hydrogen and located in Port Said,[67] sued in 2008 a blogger and an ex-employee for publishing photographs allegedly showing that the company had dumped hazardous materials in Lake Manzala. The blogger also reported harsh working conditions in the factory. TCI sued for defamation and the court fined the blogger and required him to pay damages to TCI.[68] Reports state, however, that the blogger tried to obtain an order for closure of the factory through the courts and lost.[69] The blogger raised this latter case in an ordinary court (rather than the State Council judiciary) and lost for lack of jurisdiction. The blogger did not pursue the case. Lower court verdicts are not published; accordingly, it is difficult to understand the reasoning of the court. There are many specific circumstances in this case that might have informed the court's decision. It is, however, the first verdict of this type and may influence future litigation in this regard.

Public trust – does Egyptian law recognise this doctrine?

10.73   The Egyptian legal system does not recognise the concept of trusts of private property as known in the common law system.

---

[67] See www.sanmargroup.com/Chemicals/TCI/TCI main.htm.
[68] See http://en.rsf.org/egypt-tamer-mabrouk-is-the-first-blogger-26–05–2009,33140.
[69] *Ibid.*

However, recent interpretation of constitutional clauses may lead to the establishment of a quasi public trust concept in relation to public property. Courts are beginning to recognise that Article 30 of the Constitution, as amended in 2007 (which states that 'Public property is the property of the people and it is represented in the property of the State and of the public legal persons'), read in conjunction with Article 33 discussed above, gives right to a similar doctrine. The Supreme Administrative Court recently stated that:

> [these Articles] mean that public property is owned in common by the people with all its individuals. This gives every citizen and member of this people a right in this property. In fact, [such citizen] has a duty to defend such right in accordance with the law, by following the procedures, licenses and tools determined by the law to guarantee such protection, including resorting to court to issue a judicial verdict that is deemed to be the exequatur by which such protection is realised.[70]

This argument is likely to be used even more in future cases on environmental issues, especially with the addition of a constitutional clause in 2007 making the protection of the environment a national duty.

(E) Practicalities

Enforcement

10.74 The enforcement methods provided by the CCP include seizure of property (movable or immovable) and of cash. Separate proceedings must be filed for enforcement of a judgment. Egypt is a signatory to the New York Convention ('NYC'), and therefore a valid arbitral award is enforceable without retrial of the merits if it fulfils the conditions of the NYC and the Law of Arbitration in Civil and Commercial Matters no. 27 of 1994.

10.75 Egyptian courts will not recognise a judgment of any foreign court unless there is reciprocal recognition of judgments of Egyptian courts, or if there is a treaty between the two countries. Egypt concluded treaties for reciprocal recognition of awards with a very few countries, including Italy and some Arab countries.

---

[70] Cases nos. 30953 and 31314 for the year 56j, n. 23 above.

10.76   Designated[71] employees of the EEAA, and its branches in the governorates, shall have the capacity of judicial officers vested with the power to effect seizures in order to prove the commission of crimes in violation of the provisions of the Environmental Law or the decrees issued in implementation thereof.[72] These employees shall have the right to enter establishments; to carry out a periodic follow-up on the environmental registers of establishments; and to take the necessary samples and conduct appropriate tests to verify the establishment's impact on the environment.[73]

Public interest litigation

10.77   Public-interest litigation is very prevalent in Egypt, most evidently in relation to Islamic public order and political rights. Individuals – mostly lawyers – and NGOs lead the efforts in such litigation. However, the majority of public-interest issues are fought outside courts by civil society through public demonstrations. For example, in relation to the Canadian company E-Agrium's fertilisers factory in Ras Al-Barr, Damietta, local society and NGOs won through public demonstrations, preventing the plant from being constructed.[74] Although a case has been raised by the local residents,[75] the dispute was resolved by the government before the issuance of a verdict, under pressure from public opinion.[76]

Litigation costs

10.78   Theoretically, the unsuccessful party pays the cost of the claim including attorney's fees.[77] In practice, each party covers its litigation costs. The actual amounts ordered by the courts are symbolic and represent but a fraction of the actual costs.

---

[71] By a decree of the Minister of Justice in agreement with the Minister of Environmental Affairs.
[72] Article 102 of the Environmental Law.
[73] *Ibid.*, Article 5; and Article 18 of the Executive Regulation.
[74] See http://weekly.ahram.org.eg/2008/902/eg9.htm for information on the dispute.
[75] Case no. 55826 for the year 62j, before the Administrative Judiciary, First Circuit, issued on 29 December 2009.
[76] See www.merip.org/mero/mero102109.html.
[77] Article 184(1) of the CCP.

Obtaining information

10.79   There is no explicit national legislation that regulates the right to access information. By contrast, there are several laws that limit the access to information of the State relating to the higher policies of the State or to national security.[78]

10.80   The Environmental Law does not provide for a right for the public to obtain information. It only provides for an obligation on the EEAA to publish regular reports on the environmental indicators.[79] The EEAA regularly does so.[80]

10.81   Egypt is a signatory to the International Convention on Civil and Political Rights (the 'CCPR'), which provides, in Article 19, for the right to access information subject to restrictions in the law. It is doubtful that this Article will give rise to a right to information in a court claim. In a case relating to consumer rights,[81] the court referred to the CCPR, but based its verdict on an express right to information in the Consumer Protection Law no. 67 of 2006 rather than the CCPR. A similar provision does not exist under the Environmental Law.

10.82   In the course of litigation, the claimant has the right to oblige his/her opponent to submit any document which will affect the claim if there is any law that requires the submission of such documents to any administrative authority upon its request. The Environmental Law gives the EEAA the right to access the records and information related to the effect of the institution's activities on the environment (such records are obligatory under the Environmental Law), and hence the claimant will have the right to require assigning an expert to examine the necessary records and information. Moreover, a claimant or the

---

[78] Such as Law no. 121 of 1975 regarding the Preservation of Official Documents of the State and Regulating their Publishing, and the Presidential Decree no. 472 of 1979 regarding the System for the Preservation of Official Documents of the State and Regulating their Publishing and Use. These laws deem such information to be confidential for a period that may not exceed fifty years, after which access may be given through the National Archives according to its rules.

[79] Article 5 of the Environmental Law.

[80] See www.eeaa.gov.eg/arabic/main/achivements.asp.

[81] Case no. 8450 for the year 44j, the Administrative Judiciary, Economic and Investment Circuit, issued on 17 February 2001.

court can call for witnesses to give testimony but they must be willing to attend. There is no way to oblige witnesses to attend against their will.

10.83   Outside the course of litigation, a request to establish the status of the case may be requested from the court. Based on such request, the court assigns an expert to examine the case and submit a report to the court.

Sovereign immunity

10.84   There is no explicit legislation in relation to State sovereign immunity. Egyptian public bodies do not enjoy sovereign immunity from civil proceedings. Any party has the right to bring a legal action against public bodies and has the right to enforce any final judicial verdict issued by an Egyptian competent court or an arbitration panel against them.

10.85   In some cases, public bodies refuse to enforce a judgment. In this case, the litigator raises a criminal claim against the officer in question pursuant to Article 123 of the Egyptian Penal Code no. 58 of 1937. Threatened by imprisonment, the public officer implements the judicial verdict.

10.86   As a general principle, the assets of the Egyptian government are divided into public assets and private assets. Public assets are any fixtures or movables, owned by the government or public bodies, and allotted for public interest, such as water or electricity utilities. Public assets cannot be attached and are immune from seizure. In theory, private assets may be attached. In practice, they may be difficult to locate.

(F)   Conclusion

10.87   Because there is no legislation on climate change, climate change litigation is scarce in Egypt. The few litigations that have been raised were dressed in arguments relating to air pollution and environmental rights and not climate change. Claims under public law have higher success rates because they usually only relate to annulment of an administrative decision. Claims involving compensation, whether brought under public or private law, will likely fail because of the requirements of actionable damage under Egyptian law. Without legislative intervention in the context of climate change, success would, in our opinion, be impossible.

11

Israel

ISSACHAR ROSEN-ZVI

(A) Introduction

The Israeli legal system

11.01　Israel is a representative democracy with a parliamentary system. The Prime Minister serves as head of government and the Knesset serves as Israel's legislative body. The President is the head of State, but this role is mostly symbolic.

11.02　The Israeli legal system has its roots in the British Mandate on Palestine. The British, who ruled Palestine between 1917 and 1948, replaced many of the legal rules and institutions that were in place during the Ottoman era, infusing the legal system with significant common law elements.[1] This common law system was carried over into Israeli statehood and continues to evolve through new laws and doctrines, many of which have been imported from foreign legal regimes. The major source of influence, originally England, is now the United States.

The governmental stance on climate change

11.03　Israel ratified the FCCC in May 1996 and the Kyoto Protocol in March 2004. However, despite its being a developed country and a large per-capita greenhouse gas ('GHG') emitter,[2] Israel was classified as a non-Annex I country, probably due to its insignificant

---

[1] Assaf Likhovski, *Law and Identity in Mandate Palestine* (Chapel Hill: The University of North Carolina Press, 2006), p. 23.

[2] US Department of Energy, Carbon Dioxide Information Analysis Center (CDIAC), 'Carbon Dioxide Emissions (CO_2), Metric Tons of CO_2 Per Capita'. According to this survey, in 2007 Israel was located at the thirty-fifth place in terms of per capita emissions. Available at http://data.un.org/Data.aspx?d=MDG&f=seriesRowID%3A751.

contribution to overall universal GHG emissions.[3] As a result, Israel is currently not bound to reduce GHG emissions or to otherwise take measures to combat climate change under the Kyoto Protocol. Nonetheless, in the past few years the Israeli government has passed several decisions designed to combat climate change and prepare Israel for a post-Kyoto agreement, which would most likely require Israel to reduce GHG emissions.

11.04　　Major government decisions on climate change include: the August 2008 decision to establish a five-year (2008–12) investment programme for renewable energy;[4] the September 2008 decision to increase energy efficiency, with the aim of bringing about 20 per cent savings in anticipated electricity consumption by 2020;[5] the January 2009 decision that established targets and mechanisms for the promotion of renewable energy, with the aim of generating 10 per cent of Israel's electricity from renewable sources by 2020;[6] and the June 2009 decision to establish a directors-general committee to prepare a climate change policy to formulate an adaptation and mitigation plan.[7]

11.05　　At the 2009 Copenhagen Summit, Israel's President, Mr Shimon Peres, announced that 'Israel will make best efforts to reduce its CO_2 emissions by 20 per cent in 2020 compared to a business as usual scenario'.[8] This mitigation goal was later endorsed by the Minister of Environmental Protection in a letter to the secretariat of the FCCC.[9] Following the Copenhagen Summit, in March 2010 the government established an inter-ministerial committee to formulate a national action plan ('NAP') for the reduction of GHG emissions in accordance with the declared targets.[10] In November 2010, the government adopted the NAP formulated by the inter-ministerial committee.[11] The NAP sets the emission

[3] M. Yanai, J. Koch and U. Dayan, 'Trends in CO_2 Emissions in Israel – an International Perspective', *Climatic Change*, 101 (2010), 555–63, at 557 (Israel's contribution to global emissions is less than 0.5 per cent).
[4] Government Decision No. 3954 (21 August 2008).
[5] Government Decision No. 4095 (18 September 2008).
[6] Government Decision No. 4450 (29 January 2009).
[7] Government Decision No. 474 (25 June 2009).
[8] Ministry of Environmental Protection, 'Climate Change: High on Israel's Agenda', *Israel Environment Bulletin* (September 2010), 29.
[9] *Ibid.*　　[10] Government Decision No. 1504 (14 March 2010).
[11] Government Decision No. 2508 (28 November 2010).

reduction target at 13 $MtCO_2e$ below BAU scenario for 2020. It also allocates 2.2 billion NIS in the years 2011–20 for its implementation, with 539 million NIS of this sum allocated in the years 2011–12.

Clean Air Act 2008

11.06   In 2008, the Knesset passed the Clean Air Act ('CAA'), which entered into force on 1 January 2011. The CAA was designed primarily to 'improve air quality as well as to prevent and reduce air pollution'.[12] However, it defines 'pollutant' as, inter alia, 'a material whose presence in the air causes or may cause … climate or weather change', and it defines 'air pollution' as 'the presence of a pollutant in the air'.[13] Thus the CAA serves also as a regulatory tool to combat climate change.[14]

11.07   The CAA prohibits any 'person' (including corporate entities) from causing 'strong or unreasonable air pollution'.[15] For pollutants listed in Annex I, the Act requires the Minister of Environmental Protection ('the Minister') to establish 'ambiance standards', a deviation from which would be considered 'strong or unreasonable air pollution'. Unfortunately, many GHGs, such as CO_2, HCFCs and methane, are not listed in Annex I. Nonetheless, since the CAA defines those GHGs as 'pollutant[s]', the Minister has to make a determination (either through an ordinance or otherwise) as to what levels of their presence in the air is considered 'strong or unreasonable air pollution'.

11.08   The CAA further requires the government to approve, within one year of the day the Act enters into force (i.e., 1 January 2012), a perennial NAP for the advancement of the Act's goals, which would include national and regional targets for the reduction of air pollution as well as methods and mechanisms for achieving these targets.[16] The CAA also requires local governments to

---

[12] CAA, para. 1.   [13] *Ibid.*, para. 2.

[14] Ministry of Environmental Protection, 'Coping with Climate Change in Israel', *Special Issue: UN Copenhagen Climate Change Conference* (December 2009), p. 8. For an excellent and comprehensive analysis of climate-related requirements in the CAA, see David Schorr, 'Has the Reduction of Greenhouse Gas Emissions Law already been Enacted?', *Hukim – Journal on Legislation*, 3 (2011), 241 (Hebrew).

[15] CAA, para. 3.   [16] *Ibid.*, para. 5.

take measures to prevent and reduce air pollution created in their jurisdiction.[17] Since 'air pollution' results, inter alia, from the emission of GHGs into the atmosphere, both the NAP and the actions taken by local governments would have to include GHG reduction.

11.09 The nucleus of the CAA deals with the regulation of 'stationary emission sources' ('SES') defined as 'any facility … that emits pollutants into the air or that cause[s] or may cause pollutants to be emitted into the air'.[18] The Act divides such sources into two categories: heavily polluting SESs, including the energy, chemicals, metal production and processing, and mineral industries, which are prohibited from operating without an emission permit; and the rest of the SESs, which need only a business license. For the first category, the CAA delineates an extensive permitting process, which includes an application with wide disclosure requirements, environmental impact statements, and public participation.[19] The Act also instructs that the decision whether or not to issue a permit should be based on its compatibility with the NAP and its impact on the ability to realise the NAP's goals.[20]

11.10 The CAA also regulates 'mobile emission sources', which include the transportation sector, which is responsible for more than 20 per cent of total GHG emissions. The Act instructs the Minister to adopt ordinances that would prevent and reduce air pollution (which includes GHG emissions, as discussed above) from mobile emission sources, taking into account the standards adopted in other developed countries and the relevant EU Directives.[21] Thus, in setting the standards for Israel, the Minister must take into account the standards recently adopted by both the EU and the USA for regulating CO_2 emissions from light-duty vehicles.[22]

---

[17] *Ibid.*, para. 9.   [18] *Ibid.*, para. 2.
[19] *Ibid.*, paras. 17–34.   [20] *Ibid.*, para. 20(b)(4).
[21] *Ibid.* paras. 35–8.
[22] Regulation (EC) No. 443/2009 of the European Parliament and of the Council of 23 April 2009 setting emission performance standards for new passenger cars as part of the Community's integrated approach to reduce CO_2 emissions from light-duty vehicles. Available at http://eur-lex.europa.eu/LexUriServ/LexUriServ.do?uri=OJ:L:2009:140:0001:0015:EN:PDF; US EPA, *Light-Duty Vehicle Greenhouse Gas Emission Standards and Corporate Average Fuel Economy Standards* (7 May 2010).

Industrial and natural resources (emissions sources and energy mix)

11.11   Israel is a developed country. Based on the nominal gross domestic product, its economy was in 2008 the forty-first largest in the world. In 2010 Israel joined the OECD. The major industrial sectors include metal products, electronic and biomedical equipment, gas and oil refinement, chemicals, water and transport equipment. Israel is rather poor in natural resources and it therefore depends on imports of petroleum, coal, food, uncut diamonds and production inputs. Recently, however, Israel has discovered large gas reserves off its coast.

11.12   In 2008, electricity generation was responsible for more than 54 per cent of total GHG emissions in Israel.[23] Almost all electricity generation in Israel is coal-, fuel oil- or gas-fired. Coal is the main source (around 60 per cent) for electricity generation. Since 2005 there has been a move towards replacing fuel oil with natural gas. One characteristic of the Israeli electricity sector is rapid expansion in demand for electricity. It is expected that demand for electricity will double by 2030.[24]

11.13   The following details the main sources of GHG emissions in Israel as of 2005: energy consumption by domestic, commercial and public premises: 34%; industry (mainly chemical, cement, gas and oil refinement): 30%; transportation: 18%;[25] waste disposal: 8.5%; and agriculture: less than 3%. It is expected that in a BAU scenario, and in the absence of mitigation action, Israel's GHG emissions would double from 71 $MtCO_2e$ in 2005 to 142 $MtCO_2e$ in 2030. This rapid growth is primarily due to Israel's high growth in population and GDP per capita.[26]

---

[23] Danny Rabinowitch and Carmit Lubanov, 'Climate Justice in Israel', *The Association of Environmental Justice in Israel – Position Paper no. 1* (2010), p. 5.

[24] McKinsey & Company, *Greenhouse Gas Abatement Potential in Israel: Israel's GHG Abatement Cost Curve* (2009), p. 37 ('McKinsey Report').

[25] In 2008 transportation accounted for more than 20 per cent of total GHG emissions. *See* Rabinowitch and Lubanov, n. 23 above, p. 8.

[26] McKinsey Report (see n. 24 above).

National climate change risks

11.14   Israel is vulnerable to many climate change related problems due to its diversity of geographic features relative to its small size. As a coastal State on the eastern shore of the Mediterranean Sea, and with its Coastal Plain hosting 70 per cent of its population, Israel may be adversely affected by sea level rise. It is estimated that a rise of one metre in sea level would cause a loss of between 50 and 100 metres of coastal areas and the destruction of the coastal cliffs and many archaeological heritage sites.[27]

11.15   Climate change is also likely to have a detrimental effect on Israel's hydrology. According to scientific studies, climate change would decrease significantly the level of precipitation in Israel's southern area, moving the desert lines northwards (already, one-half of Israel's territory is desert). Reduction in overall precipitation combined with increased rainfall intensity could increase soil erosion, surface runoff and salinisation and would lead to accelerated desertification. This desertification would have detrimental effects on Mediterranean ecosystems, biodiversity, agriculture and water supply, which could fall to 60 per cent of current levels by 2100. Furthermore, sea-level rise may salinate the Coastal Aquifer, one of Israel's main water sources. Further depletion and contamination of water resources in the region, which already suffers from an acute water shortage, could potentially worsen the geo-political conflict in the Middle East.[28]

11.16   Delayed rainfall, increased evaporation and greater frequency and intensity of heatwaves lead to lower soil moisture, which increases the risk, as well as the frequency and intensity, of

---

[27] P. Alpert, 'The Effects of Climatic Changes on the Availability of Water Resources in Israel' in T. Watanabe (ed.), *Proceedings of the Kick-off Workshop for the Research Project on the Impact of Climate Change on Agricultural Production System in Arid Areas* (ICCAP, 2002), pp. 8–13. Decrease of precipitation would also affect the northern part of the country thus increasing the water problem. See R. Samuels, A. Rimmer, A. Hartmann, S. Krichak and P. Alpert, 'Climate Change Impacts on Jordan River Flow: Downscaling Application from a Regional Climate Model', *Journal of Hydrometeorology*, 11(4) (2010), 860–79.

[28] An analogy could be found in a recent UNEP report arguing that the massacre in Darfur was a result of an ongoing struggle over the natural resources that are vanishing due to climate change.

woodland fires. In December 2010 Israel suffered the worst woodland fire in its history. This fire caused the destruction of more than 50 km² of forested area (5 million trees) in the Carmel Forest, the deaths of 44 people and the evacuation of 17,000 from their homes. Climate change is likely to increase the frequency of such fires.

11.17   Climate change may also increase the risk of vector-borne diseases. The degradation of the water resources would likely cause water-related epidemics such as malaria, cholera, dysentery, West-Nile virus and Giardia.[29]

(B)   Public law

Overview

11.18   Climate change litigation would likely be brought mostly under administrative law. One reason is the many grounds for judicial review of administrative decisions. Another reason is the many hurdles that would confront litigants under private law.

11.19   This section addresses the process whereby decisions of public authorities may be reviewed by the courts. The legal principles form part of Israeli administrative law, and judicial review cases are generally brought in either the Administrative Court or the High Court of Justice ('HCJ').

Justiciability and standing

11.20   Threshold barriers to litigation, the most important of which are justiciability and standing, and which inhibit actions against public authorities in other common law jurisdictions (such as the United States, England and Canada), do not exist in Israel. Since the 1980s the scope of the justiciability doctrine – the limits upon legal issues over which a court can exercise its judicial authority – was narrowed by the Supreme Court to such an extent that almost any matter, including the signing of peace treaties, is considered justiciable.[30] Clearly, administrative decisions and

---

[29] Ministry of Environmental Protection, 'Vulnerability and Adaptation to Climate Change', *Israel Environment Bulletin*, 24 (2001).
[30] HC 910/86, *Ressler v. Minister of Defence*, 42(2) PD 441 (1988).

actions with regards to climate change would be considered justiciable.[31]

11.21 Similarly, the Supreme Court nullified the standing requirement with regard to petitions of a public nature, which include petitions against environmental harms. While in other jurisdictions petitioners must demonstrate sufficient connection to and harm from the action challenged in order to have standing, in Israel a petitioner merely must demonstrate that the public at large (or part thereof) will likely be harmed by the administrative decision or action.[32] Since climate change has a harmful impact on the public at large, any 'public petitioner' would have standing.

General grounds for judicial review

11.22 Administrative decisions and actions that raise issues relating to climate change can be challenged on many grounds. These grounds fall under three categories: competency, procedural impropriety, and unreasonableness.

Competency

11.23 Competency is the authority of an administrative body to deal with and make pronouncements on certain matters. An important doctrine that the Court inferred from the bestowal of competency upon an administrative body is the lasting obligation of such a body to consider whether to exercise its authority.[33] Administrative bodies are not allowed to leave their authority untouched, but are obligated to use the discretion vested in them and decide whether the circumstances require them to exercise their authority.[34] In the climate change context, a litigant could use this doctrine to challenge the inaction of an appropriate administrative body with respect to implementing regulations concerning climate change.

---

[31] Yoav Dotan, *Administrative Guidance* (Nevo Press, 1996), pp. 178–85.
[32] HC 6492/08 *SAL Educational Projects Association* v. *Commander of IDF Forces in the West Bank* (Delivered on 14 January 2010).
[33] HC 297/82 *Berger* v. *Minister of Interior*, 37(3) PD 29 (1983).
[34] Daphne Barak-Erez, *Administrative Law*, 2 vols. (Israeli Bar Publishing, 2010), Vol. I, p. 201.

Procedural impropriety

11.24   Courts can intervene in administrative decisions or actions whenever the administrative bodies fail to apply the required procedures. The procedural obligations are either prescribed by the HCJ in its rulings or mandated by legislation dealing with specific issues; Israel has no general Administrative Procedure Act. The basic procedural steps required by the court are to collect all relevant information, to conduct serious deliberation (which includes considering and evaluating different alternatives), and lastly to reach a reasoned decision which is subject to judicial review.[35]

11.25   Administrative bodies are also required under the Freedom of Information Act 1998 to disclose information to the public upon request, and when environmental matters are concerned, the law obliges the authorities to make the information public on a dedicated website, even in the absence of a request.[36]

Unreasonableness

11.26   Courts have discretion to intervene in decisions of administrative bodies if and when they find that such decisions are unreasonable. The unreasonableness doctrine is premised on the obligation of an administrative body to take into account matters that a statute requires the body to consider either expressly or by implication from the purpose of the statute; the obligation can also be implied from the general purposes of the legal system.[37] Moreover, even when the administrative decision-maker took into account all relevant matters, the court can still set aside a decision for failing to attribute the proper weight to a certain consideration. Although generally the weight to be attributed to relevant matters is within the discretion of the authorised administrative bodies, this discretion is subject to a ruling by the court that the weight given to one or more of the relevant considerations radically exceeds the proper weight that should be attributed to it.[38] In the climate change context the unreasonableness

---

[35] *Berger*, n. 33 above.

[36] Freedom of Information Act, 1998, para. 6A.

[37] HC 6163/92 *Eisenberg* v. *Minister of Building and Housing*, 47(2) PD 229 (1993) (Implied general obligation); HC 5016/96 *Horev* v. *Minister of Transportation*, 51(4) PD 1 (1997).

[38] Barak-Erez, n. 34 above, Vol. II, p. 723.

doctrine can be exercised whenever an administrative body fails to take into consideration or to give enough weight to the impact of a certain decision or action on the increase of GHG emissions levels.

Specific grounds for judicial review

Clean Air Act

11.27 As discussed above, the Israeli CAA imposes on the Minister numerous duties, among them: (i) to make determinations as to the maximum authorised levels of GHGs emitted into the atmosphere; (ii) to approve a NAP that includes, inter alia, methods and mechanisms for the reduction of GHG levels; (iii) to take into account the impacts of climate change in issuing permits or business licenses to 'stationary emission sources'; and (iv) to regulate 'mobile emission sources' in a way that reduces air pollution (including GHG emissions). Local governments are also required to reduce the levels of GHG emitted in their jurisdiction. Any failure by these administrative bodies to comply with the duties owed under the CAA could be challenged in court under each of the legal grounds discussed above.

Government decisions

11.28 The Israeli government has issued several governmental decisions (each a 'GD') that tackle directly or have bearing on climate change (see paras. 11.04 and 11.05 above). GDs are executive orders. The normative status of such decisions can vary based on the legal authority upon which they are given, their content, and their level of specificity. If the legal authority to decide on the matter at hand is given not to the government but to another administrative body, then a GD would be considered a recommendation lacking any authoritative power. If, on the other hand, the government has the legal competence in the matter at hand, then a GD can have the status of either mandatory regulation or administrative guidance, depending on its content and level of specificity.[39] The more general the content of a GD is, the more likely it would be considered an administrative guidance;

---

[39] Dotan, n. 31 above, p. 106.

likewise, the more specific and operative a GD is, the more likely it would be considered a mandatory regulation.

11.29   Since the GDs that deal with climate change, either directly or indirectly, are issued under the residual competence of the government, and since their content is quite concrete and operative, specifying targets, timetables and in some cases even budgetary sources, it is reasonable to assume that they would be interpreted by the courts as mandatory regulation. In such a case, the government would be bound by the commitments it undertook in these GDs. It is noteworthy that thus far courts have been quite reluctant to enforce GDs on the government (probably due to political considerations), though such enforcement is not without precedence.[40]

Planning law

11.30   The Planning and Construction Act, 1965 mandates, in certain circumstances specified in the Act itself as well as in the regulations issued under it, the preparation of an Environmental Impact Assessment ('EIA') and submission of it to the planning committee. The committee is required to take the EIA's findings into consideration when deciding whether to approve the plan, to refuse approval or to make amendments to it.[41] One circumstance in which an EIA is required is when the execution of the plan is bound to have 'a significant impact on the environment'.[42]

11.31   In a recent decision, the Supreme Court bolstered the status of EIAs.[43] Planning committees have discretion in deciding whether to require an EIA and what should be included in it. The Court held, however, that the committees' discretion is constrained by the general administrative law doctrines, including unreasonableness, especially due to the potentially detrimental and irreversible impact of planning decisions on the environment and on human health and quality of life. Thus, the larger the planned project is and the more harmful its projected effects are, the more

---

[40] HC 8397/06 *Eduardo* v. *The Minister of Defence* (delivered on 29 May 2007).
[41] Planning and Construction Act, paras. 76C(4), 119C; Planning and Construction Regulation (Environmental Impact Assessments) 2003 ('EIA Regulation').
[42] EIA Regulation, para. 2.
[43] HC 9409/05 *Adam Teva Vadin* v. *National Planning Committee for National Infrastructures* (delivered on 24 October 2010).

unreasonable it would be not to require an EIA that reviews alternatives to the proposed plan, including the 'zero alternative', namely, the possibility of not executing the plan at all. It is possible, therefore, that a proposed plan which is projected to have a substantial impact on GHG emissions would be considered as having 'a significant impact on the environment' and thus would require the submission of an EIA that considers different alternatives to the proposed plan including the 'zero alternative'. Having said that, it should be noted that the case law to date deals only with impacts on the 'environment' which are either local or national in scope, and it is thus unclear whether the courts would be willing to extend the interpretation of the 'environment' in the statute to the global environment.

11.32   The CAA makes this implicit obligation more explicit. An 'impact on the environment' which requires the submission of an EIA is defined in the EIA Regulation as including the 'abating or reducing [of] existing environmental nuisances'.[44] The definition of 'environmental nuisance' refers, inter alia, to the definition of 'air pollution' in the Abatement of Environmental Nuisances (Civil Action) Act 1992, which in turn refers to the definition of 'air pollution' in the CAA.[45] Moreover, the CAA mandates that in the framework of permitting SESs (including power plants, large industrial plants, refineries and refuse-disposal sites), the EIA must include a chapter on the impact of the proposed SES on 'air pollution'.[46] Since 'air pollution', as defined in the CAA, includes the emitting of GHGs into the atmosphere, the law explicitly requires planning institutions to demand the submission of an EIA whenever a proposed plan is projected to have an impact on climate change, and to take its findings into consideration when deciding whether to approve a plan or issue a permit.

Examples in practice

11.33   Very few attempts have been made so far to challenge administrative bodies for failing to take into account the impact of their

---

[44] EIA Regulation, para. 1.
[45] CAA, para. 88 (amending the Abatement of Environmental Nuisances (Civil Action) Act, para. 1).
[46] CAA, paras. 23 and 18.

decisions on climate change. None has succeeded. One such attempt is the case *Adam Teva Vadin* v. *Government of Israel*.[47] The case, filed prior to the CAA coming into force, deals with a decision by the National Planning Committee for National Infrastructures to proceed with the planning of two new coal-fired power plants. The petitioners argued that the planning should not proceed without performing a full review and acquiring the relevant data with regard to the following: (i) the projected impact on the public health both generally and in the area; (ii) the projected levels of GHG emissions from the power plant and their implication on Israel's capability in the future to meet its potential obligations under the FCCC to reduce GHG emissions; and (iii) the alternatives to coal-fired power plants, which could equally serve the energy needs of Israel.

11.34   The petition is based on several legal grounds. The first is that the decision is unreasonable. The petitioners argued that the planning committee failed to consider or give enough weight to the fact that the power plant, if approved, would increase Israel's CO_2 emissions by more than 10 per cent. This result would obstruct Israel's probable future commitment to reduce its GHG emissions under a successor protocol to the Kyoto Protocol and would conflict with the mandate in the September 2008 GD for an increase in energy efficiency. The second is that the decision was founded on improper factual grounds thus breaching procedural obligations. One of the relevant uncollected facts is the external costs of additional GHG emissions into the atmosphere. The third ground is that the EIA was improperly executed for failing both to consider the increase in GHG emissions and to review less harmful alternatives to the two coal-fired power plants.

11.35   The Court did not reject the petition but recommended that it be withdrawn until the planning committee issued its final decision regarding the proposed plan. The petitioners accepted the Court's recommendation and withdrew their petition.

11.36   Another case that challenges an administrative body's decision due to its impact on climate change is *Adam Teva Vadin* v.

---

[47]   HC 5811/08 *Adam Teva Vadin* v. *Government of Israel* (delivered on 17 July 2008).

Minister for National Infrastructures.[48] The petition deals with a
decision by the Minister for National Infrastructures to license
an oil shales project in the Adolam region, an area of high environmental sensitivity. One of the legal grounds on which the
petition is based is that the administrative decision contradicts
the government's declared position as reflected in both the GDs
that promote renewable energy and increase energy efficiency,
and the President's declaration at the Copenhagen Summit. The
case is still pending.

Constitutional law

11.37   Israel has no formal constitution. Its constitutional building-
        blocks are made of Basic Laws. In the early 1990s, the Knesset
        enacted two basic laws – Basic Law: Human Dignity and Liberty;
        and Basic Law: Freedom of Occupation. These basic laws protect
        fundamental human rights, including the right to life, bodily
        integrity and dignity, the right to property and the freedom of
        occupation. In 1992, the Supreme Court declared that these basic
        laws marked the starting point of a 'Constitutional Revolution',
        elevating these laws to a constitutional level and bestowing on
        courts the power of judicial review.[49] The Supreme Court read
        into the Basic Laws several cardinal human rights that were not
        expressly included – the right to equality, freedom of speech and
        freedom of religion – by seeing them as directly derived from the
        right to dignity.

11.38   Despite this expansive interpretation, the Supreme Court has
        thus far refused to recognise the existence of a constitutional
        right to adequate environment, limiting any constitutional
        claim with regard to the environment to instances in which a
        person's health or life are clearly endangered.[50] Since the Court
        refused to recognise the existence of a constitutional right to
        decent environment, it is unlikely that it would strike down

---

[48]   *Adam Teva Vadin* v. *Minister for National Infrastructures* (petition for an order nisi) (on
       file with the author).
[49]   Guy E. Carmi, 'A Constitutional Court in the Absence of a Formal Constitution? On the
       Ramifications of Appointing the Israeli Supreme Court as the Only Tribunal for Judicial
       Review', *Connecticut Journal of International Law*, 21 (2005), 67–91.
[50]   HC 4128/02 *Adam Teva Vadin* v. *Prime Minister of Israel*, 58(3) PD 503 (2004).

legislation that is likely to have a negative impact on climate change.

(C)   Private law

Overview

11.39   This section addresses the different private law causes of action that one private legal person can bring against another to seek remedies for damages resulting from climate change. No private law claim that is based on allegations of actual or anticipated damages from climate change has been filed in Israel to date. Due to the many difficulties a plaintiff would face in establishing liability, it is not anticipated that such a claim would be filed in the near future.

11.40   The traditional causes of action which are likely to be employed in the climate change context, if and when its impact becomes more severe, are in nuisance, breach of statutory duty and negligence. These torts are found in the Tort Ordinance, 1968, which is a codification of the common law torts introduced by the British into the law of Mandate Palestine in 1947. It is, therefore, unsurprising that Israeli tort law was very much influenced by English tort law. New causes of action were created by the CAA, which also broadened the scope of existing causes of actions under the Abatement of Environmental Nuisances (Civil Action) Act and the Class Action Act.

Nuisance

11.41   Nuisance doctrine is divided into private and public nuisance. Private nuisance occurs when one legal person behaves or conducts its business in a manner that unduly interferes with the reasonable use or enjoyment of land by another person.[51] For the purpose of climate change related claims, private nuisance is less significant as it deals with the interference of one person with another person's enjoyment of his/her land and it is therefore too narrow in scope and would probably not be construed as encompassing GHG emissions, which by themselves are not harmful to adjacent

---

[51] Tort Ordinance, para. 44.

land. Moreover, so far as 'air pollution' (including GHG emissions) is concerned, the tort of private nuisance became immaterial with the enactment of the Abatement of Nuisances Act, and later the Abatement of Environmental Nuisances (Civil Action) Act, which deal specifically with 'strong or unreasonable air pollution', as recently amended and redefined by the CAA. Public nuisance, on the other hand, is more relevant for our purposes.

Public nuisance

11.42   Public nuisance is an unlawful act or omission the effect of which is to endanger the life, safety, health, property or comfort of the public, or to obstruct the public in the exercise of a right common to all subjects.[52] Very few actions in public nuisance have ever been brought in Israel.

11.43   One significant procedural limitation in applying this tort is that generally only the Attorney General can bring a claim in public nuisance. A private Party can bring an action only if he/she suffered particular damage above that suffered by the public at large, which in the climate change context could be very difficult. Moreover, the private Party must also show that the alleged nuisance endangers the public or obstructs the public's exercise of its rights in some way.[53] It is therefore very likely that any action in public nuisance brought in the climate change context would be brought by the State and that the targets of such suits would be large industrial GHG emitters.[54]

Breach of statutory duty

11.44   Breach of statutory duty – also called 'negligence per se' – contains the following elements: (i) the defendant breached a duty imposed by a statute; (ii) the statute is intended to protect the particular plaintiff, the class to which the plaintiff belongs

---

[52] *Ibid.*, para. 42.
[53] Daniel Fish, *Environmental Law in Israel* (Mishpatim Publishing, 2000), pp. 82–5.
[54] In the USA such actions in public nuisance have been brought by states and local governments against electric power companies and large automobile manufacturers. See *Connecticut* v. *American Electric Power*, 406 F Supp 2d 265 (SDNY, 2005); *People of the State of California* v. *General Motors* (NDcal, 17 September 2007).

or the public as a whole; (iii) the plaintiff suffered a damage as a result of the breach; (iv) the damage was the kind of damage that the statute was intended to prevent; and (v) the statute does not indicate that the legislature did not intend the statutory breach to give rise to a civil action.[55] The Supreme Court has broadened the scope of the tort in practice by interpreting many statutes as giving rise to civil claims.[56]

11.45 Liability for breach of statutory duties for climate change related damages may arise under the CAA. The Act makes any violation of its provisions an actionable tort.[57] Thus, the CAA clearly indicates that it was intended to protect the interests not only of the State but also of individuals. If an individual suffers climate change related damages (discussed below) as a result of a violation of the CAA by either the State or private Parties (i.e., industries regulated under the statute), a reasonable interpretation would be that such damages are of the type the statute was intended to prevent. Since, as mentioned, the statute explicitly makes any violation of its provisions a tort, defendants could not plausibly argue that the legislature did not intend the breach of the statute to give rise to a civil action. Therefore, all the elements of the tort would be satisfied; however, to establish liability the plaintiff would also have to prove 'damages', 'foreseeability' and 'causation' as under the tort of negligence (discussed below).

Negligence

11.46 In order for a plaintiff P to establish liability against defendant D for negligence, P must prove the following: (i) D owed P a 'duty of care' (both notional and concrete), which required D to adhere to a certain standard of conduct; (ii) D breached that duty of care; (iii) P suffered 'damages'; (iv) those damages were 'caused' by D's breach of his/her duty; and (v) the damages suffered by P were 'foreseeable'.[58] Negligence doctrine is very complex and contains many intricacies.[59] The discussion here will focus only on issues

---

[55] Tort Ordinance, para. 63.

[56] Ariel Porat, 'Tort Law' in A. Shapira and K. C. Dewitt-Arar (eds.), *Introduction to the Law of Israel* (Kluwer, 1995), p. 135.

[57] CAA, para. 70.   [58] Tort Ordinance, para. 35.

[59] Porat, n. 56 above, pp. 128–35.

that are important or raise particular difficulties in the climate change context.

Who may be sued?

11.47 The most likely defendants in Israel are (i) large producers of fossil fuels and gas (such as oil refineries and natural gas companies) and (ii) heavy users of fossil fuels, fuel oil, coal and gas that cause GHG emissions, including large industries and power generators. Even though many other corporations and all individuals emit GHGs into the atmosphere, they are not potential defendants because the *de minimis* doctrine protects them from liability.[60]

11.48 Unlike other common law countries, in Israel the Supreme Court has found public authorities liable in negligence, both in the exercise of executive or operational powers and in the exercise of policymaking authority. In one case, the Court held the State liable in negligence for not repairing highways and ordered it to pay damages to people injured while using such highways.[61] In another case, it imposed liability on a municipality for the improper weighing of policy considerations with regard to the allocation of its scarce resources.[62] Recently, the Court held Mekorot, Israel's public water company, liable in negligence due to over-salination of the water it supplied, which caused damages to a flower grower.[63] Thus, it is likely that the courts would be willing to hold public bodies liable in negligence for climate change related damages occurring due to failure to execute their administrative powers or even for improper policymaking.

Duty of care and foreseeability

11.49 When examining liability in negligence the first step is to determine whether there was a duty of care between the particular D and the particular P with regard to the actions which were actually taken and in relation to the damage which was actually suffered by P. The scope of the duty of care is limited to foreseeable damages only. This could prove to be a difficult element to

[60] Tort Ordinance, para.4.
[61] CA 144/60 *State of Israel* v. *Hauati*, 16 PD 209 (1962).
[62] CA 73/86 *Sternberg* v. *City of Bnei Brak*, 43(3) PD 343 (1989).
[63] CA 10078/03 *Shatil* v. *Mekorot* (delivered on 19 March 2007).

establish in the climate change context. Foreseeability is both factual and normative. The factual question is whether D *could* have foreseen that the action it carried out is of the type of actions that may result in the type of damages suffered by P. The normative question is whether D *should* have foreseen that the action it carried out is of the type of actions that may result in the type of damages suffered by P.[64] In other words, the question is what damages are reasonably foreseeable as a result of D's actions and which plaintiffs are within the zone of foreseeable risk to such damages. Moreover, in Israel there is a specific statutory defence for damage occurring due to an irregular natural cause that a reasonable person could not have foreseen, and the results of which could not have been prevented through reasonable care.[65]

11.50   In the climate change context, questions would arise as to what are the foreseeable risks of climate change and whether they are sufficiently established scientifically. Another relevant inquiry would be about when the adverse effects of the activities that increased GHG emissions became sufficiently well known so as to establish liability. It is noteworthy that when bodily injuries are involved, P is required to establish only that the *type* of damages he suffered as a result of D's actions are reasonably foreseeable, but not that the extent of the damages was foreseeable. It is unclear whether this ruling also applies to property damages.

What damages are compensable?

11.51   The damages that may be caused by climate change are diverse, including destruction of shores and buildings as a result of sea level rise, loss of life and property as a result of extreme weather events such as floods and fires, loss of fertile agricultural land as a result of enhanced desertification, and death as well as health problems resulting from climate change related diseases.

11.52   Israeli courts readily afford a remedy not only for physical damages, namely bodily injuries and injuries to property, but also for pure economic damage that results from P's negligence.[66] Pure economic damage is a financial loss suffered by P as a result of

---

[64] Porat, n. 56 above, pp. 128–35.
[65] Tort Ordinance, para. 64(1).
[66] HP 106/54 *Weinstein* v. *Kadima*, 8 PD 1317 (1954).

the negligent action of D, absent any damage to P's body or property. Thus, it would be easier to bring an action in negligence for climate change related damages in Israel than in other common law countries which are more reluctant to compensate for pure economic loss. For example, a hotel chain that suffers from a sharp rise in vegetable prices as a result of climate change related floods that ruined all the vegetables in the fields would be able to bring a claim for compensation in negligence against large GHG emitters.

Causation

11.53   A difficult hurdle posed before any claim in negligence arising in the climate change context is establishing causation. The Israeli law of causation is based on the *sine qua non* test – causation between D's action and damage to P is established if the damage to P would not have occurred in the absence of D's action. Nevertheless, for cases in which the *sine qua non* test fails systematically, such as damages that could have been effected by more than one cause, the Court applied other tests that are more favourable to injured Parties, such as the 'material cause' or 'sufficient cause' tests. Generally, the Israeli Supreme Court tends to look for ways, sometimes very creatively, to compensate injured Parties when they believe such compensation is merited.[67]

11.54   A second issue in the climate change context would be the apportionment of liability for damages among the myriad of emitters that are globally diffused. The Israeli Supreme Court has addressed a similar situation in which several tortfeasors acted separately, each of them caused a substantial portion of the damage, but it was impossible to determine what portion each of the tortfeasors caused; in this case the Court held each of the tortfeasors liable.[68] When the damage suffered by P was bodily injury the Court held each tortfeasor liable for the full damage, whereas when property damages were involved the Court demonstrated willingness to apportion liability among the tortfeasors.[69] In the climate change context, it would be, of course, impossible to hold each tortfeasor liable to the full damage of each of the multitude of

[67] Porat, n. 56 above, p. 146.
[68] FH 15/88 *Melech* v. *Kornheuser*, 44(2) PD 89 (1990).
[69] CA 304/68 *Genosar* v. *Dhabra*, 23(1) PD 366 (1969).

injured Parties; a court would probably apportion liability based on some criteria, the most likely of which is market share.[70]

11.55   Another problem would be to distinguish tortious from non-tortious damages. While it is clear that D's conduct (emitting GHGs) creates risks to a large number of people, and in some cases those risks materialise and cause damages, each P would not be able to prove by the preponderance of the evidence that the damages he/she suffered occurred as a result of D's negligent conduct (such as climate change related extreme weather events) rather than as a result of natural events (such as non-climate change related extreme weather events) which would have happened regardless of D's conduct. Since this problem recurs for each and every P, it would be impossible to establish causation and to hold tortfeasors liable for their negligent conduct.

(1) Woodland fires are an example of this problem. Some fires occur naturally, and in many such cases nobody can or should be held liable for the fire-related damages. Other fires happen as a result of climate change.[71] Delayed rainfall and increased evaporation increase the frequency and intensity of woodland fires; in these situations, P would argue that D should be held liable for the fire-related damages that were caused as a result of D's negligent conduct (emitting GHGs). However, D would argue that the specific fire that injured P occurred naturally and would have occurred regardless of D's negligent conduct; thus no causation was established and no liability can be imposed on D. This argument could be raised by each D and for every fire event; therefore, no tortfeasor would ever be held liable for its negligent conduct.

(2) In a recent decision, the Israeli Supreme Court came up with an innovative solution to this problem, though in an *obiter dictum*. In *Carmel Hospital* v. *Malul*,[72] the Court ruled that in situations where a tortfeasor creates recurring risks to a large group of people and where there is a

---

[70] For market share liability (MSL) in the USA, see *Sindell* v. *Abbott Laboratories*, 26 Cal 3d 588 (1980). For an indication that the Israeli Supreme Court is inclining to adopt MSL, see DNA 4693/05 *Carmel Hospital* v. *Malul* (delivered 29 August 2010).

[71] Thomas W. Swetnam, 'Fire History and Climate Change in Giant Sequoia Groves', *Science*, 262 (1993), 885–9.

[72] *Carmel Hospital* v. *Malul* (see n. 70 above).

systemic bias that prevents plaintiffs from proving in the preponderance of the evidence that *in their case* the risk materialised and caused them damage, then in all the cases a different rule of 'statistical-based compensation' would apply. This rule specifies that the tortfeasor would be held liable only for the damages that, based on statistical evidence, result from its negligent conduct. The Court specifically mentioned environmental pollution cases as falling under this category.

New civil causes of action

Clean Air Act

11.56 First, the CAA makes any unlawful actions or omissions under it an actionable tort and applies the Tort Ordinance to them.[73] Second, an Annex to the Abatement of Environmental Nuisances (Civil Action) Act 1992 specifies a list of NGOs that are responsible for environmental protection ('environmental NGOs'). The CAA instructs that various governmental bodies and the environmental NGOs can bring a civil action under the CAA, provided that if the cause of action is an injury suffered by a person, that person consented to the suit.[74] Third, when the tortfeasor is a corporation, the CAA imposes liability for the corporation's actions and omissions on any active functionary and high-level employee, unless they can prove that the tortious act or omission has been done without their knowledge and that they took all reasonable measures to prevent it.[75]

11.57 Since the CAA imposes many obligations on corporations, both procedural and substantive, any unlawful act or omission relating to climate change that ends up causing a damage is actionable. An expansive interpretation of the statute would also allow a private Party to file for an injunction, even if no injury has taken place as a result of an unlawful act or omission under the CAA. The ability to obtain an injunction is subject to the restrictions on the ability to issue an injunction specified in the Tort Ordinance.[76]

---

[73] CAA, para. 70.   [74] *Ibid.*, para. 71.
[75] *Ibid.*, para. 72.   [76] *Ibid.*, para. 74.

Abatement of Environmental Nuisances
(Civil Action) Act

11.58   The Abatement of Environmental Nuisances (Civil Action) Act
        allows any person who was injured or may be injured by an
        'environmental nuisance' (or an environmental NGO acting in
        the interest of such a person) to petition the court for an injunc-
        tion to abate the nuisance, to repair any damage and to restore
        the environment to its status quo ante.[77] The definition of 'envir-
        onmental nuisance' contains, inter alia, 'air pollution' and refers
        to the definition in the Abatement of Nuisances Act, 1961.[78] In
        the past, the definition of 'air pollution' in the Abatement of
        Nuisances Act referred to 'any strong or unreasonable air pol-
        lution, including pollution by smoke, gases, fumes, dust and the
        like'.[79] The CAA amended the definition of 'air pollution' in the
        Abatement of Nuisances Act to incorporate the definition of this
        term in the CAA, which as discussed above, refers to any 'material
        whose presence in the air causes or may cause ... climate or wea-
        ther change'.[80] The result is that the Abatement of Environmental
        Nuisances (Civil Action) Act can now be used by any person who
        is injured by climate change related practices.

11.59   A weakness of the Abatement of Environmental Nuisances
        (Civil Action) Act is that the remedies that can be sought under
        it are restricted to injunctions. Thus, this statute does not pro-
        vide a relief for any damages suffered as a result of an 'environ-
        mental nuisance'. However, the Class Action Act, 2006 provides
        a remedy. Under this Act, a class action can be brought against
        an 'injurer' in relation to an 'environmental nuisance'. For the
        definition of both these terms, the Act refers to the Abatement of
        Environmental Nuisances (Civil Action) Act.[81] Since the defin-
        ition of 'environmental nuisance' includes climate change related
        injuries, such nuisances are actionable under the Class Action
        Act. It is noteworthy that the State can be sued under the Class
        Action Act as a direct 'injurer', but it cannot be sued for fail-
        ing to supervise, regulate or enforce legal obligations on private
        injurers.[82]

---

[77] Abatement of Environmental Nuisances (Civil Action) Act, para. 2.
[78] *Ibid.*, para. 1.   [79] Abatement of Nuisances Act, 1961, para. 4.
[80] CAA, para. 2.   [81] Class Action Act, Annex II, para. 6.
[82] Class Action Act, para. 3(a).

Statute of Limitation

11.60   Limitation law mandates that an action in tort must be brought
within seven years of the accrual of the cause of action, which is,
in most cases, the time of the occurrence of the damages happening. If the tort is a continuous one, the cause of action accrues as
long as the tort continues. When latent damages are involved, the
cause of action is deferred to the day when the plaintiff found out
about it, but no more than ten years from the accrual of the cause
of action.[83]

(D)   Conclusion

11.61   Climate change litigation in Israel is in its infancy. A handful of
cases raising climate change related claims have been brought
before the courts, and the few that were brought are all in public
law. It is, however, quite likely that with the intensification of climate change related damages and as the impacts become more
severe, we shall see more and more such claims in both public
and private law, particularly if no significant international agreement is reached. This chapter provided some grounds for climate
change related claims in Israel.

---

[83] Tort Ordinance, para. 89.

12

Kenya

PATRICIA KAMERI-MBOTE AND COLLINS ODOTE

(A) Introduction

The Kenyan legal system

12.01   The Republic of Kenya is a constitutional democracy whose primary sources of law are enumerated in Section 3 of the Judicature
Act[1] and the Constitution promulgated in August 2010 following a referendum. As a former British colony, Kenya's legal system has drawn heavily on the English and Indian legal systems.
Under the Judicature Act, the sources of Kenyan law are: (i) the
Constitution; (ii) Acts of Parliament including subsidiary legislation; (iii) specific Acts of the Parliament of the United Kingdom;
(iv) English statutes of general application in force in England on
12 August 1897; (v) the substance of common law and doctrines
of equity; and (vi) African customary law. The common law, doctrines of equity and statutes of general application are applicable
in 'so far only as the circumstances of Kenya and its inhabitants
permit and subject to such qualifications as those circumstances
may render necessary'. African customary law is applicable in
'civil cases in which one or more of the parties is subject to it or
affected by it, so far as it is applicable and is not repugnant to justice and morality or inconsistent with any written law'.

12.02   The Constitution is 'the supreme law of the Republic'.[2] It recognises 'the general rules of international law'[3] as well as 'any treaty

The authors gratefully acknowledge the research assistance of Wilson Kamande.

[1] Chapter 8, Laws of Kenya, available at National Council for Law Reporting, www.
kenyalaw.org.
[2] Article 2(1), *Constitution of Kenya* (2010) (Republic of Kenya, *Constitution of Kenya*,
Government Printer, August 2010, available at National Council for Law Reporting,
www.kenyalaw.org).
[3] *Ibid.*, Article 2(5).

or convention ratified by Kenya' as forming part of the law of Kenya.[4] 'Any law, including customary law, that is inconsistent with the Constitution is void to the extent of the inconsistency, and any act or omission in contravention of the Constitution is invalid.'[5]

12.03   The Constitution provides for two categories of courts: superior courts and subordinate courts. The superior courts consist of the Supreme Court, the Court of Appeal, the High Court and other courts established pursuant to the Constitution with the status of the High Court.[6] Subordinate courts include the Magistrates courts, the Kadhis' courts, the Courts Martial and other courts or local tribunals as may be established by an Act of Parliament.[7] The Constitution has mandated the establishment of a land and environment court with the status of the High Court to hear and determine disputes relating to '… the environment and the use and occupation of, and title to, land'.[8] Currently, there is a land and environment division of the High Court which was established in 2007.

Government stance on climate change

12.04   Kenya signed the FCCC in 1992, ratified it in 1994 and ratified the Kyoto Protocol in February 2005. Kenya is a non-Annex I country and is as such not legally bound to reduce its greenhouse gas ('GHG') emissions under the Kyoto Protocol. However, Kenya has placed high national importance on issues of climate change; for example, the draft National Environment Policy 2008 addresses climate change.[9] The draft policy recognises climate change as a cross-cutting theme involving many ministries within the government and touching on all aspects of the country's socio-economic fabric. To give climate change a higher profile at the national level and to help in addressing climate-related issues in respect to relevant ministries, a

---

[4] *Ibid.*, Article 2(6).   [5] *Ibid.*, Article 2(4).
[6] *Ibid.*, Article 162(1) and (2).
[7] *Ibid.*, Article 169(1).   [8] *Ibid.*, Article 162(2).
[9] Government of Kenya, Ministry of Environment, *Draft National Environment Policy* (2008), p. 44 (on file with the author).

coordination unit was established in the Prime Minister's office in 2009.[10]

National Climate Change Response Strategy

12.05   In April 2010, the government published the National Climate Change Response Strategy ('NCCRS'), which was developed by the Ministry of Environment and Mineral Resources to address the increasing impacts of climate change in the country and to take advantage of any arising opportunities, for example from carbon trade and transition to a green economy. The strategy proposes 'climate smart' development and climate change 'proof' solutions necessary for the attainment of Vision 2030 goals.[11] The NCCRS is expected to be operationalised within an integrated framework anchored on the FCCC and complementary to the United Nations Convention to Combat Desertification and the Convention on Biological Diversity.[12]

Draft Climate Change Bill 2010

12.06   The draft Climate Change Bill 2010 is the first proposed legislation that aligns with the objectives of the National Climate Change Response Strategy of providing a framework for nationwide actions for mitigating and adapting to changing climate, for development under the changing climate and for combating the impacts of climate change in various sectors of the economy.[13]

12.07   The draft Bill proposes far-reaching recommendations on mitigation and adaptation, governance of climate change programmes, technologies to be adopted, public participation and dissemination of information to the public. The Bill would require the government to prepare and publish a public engagement strategy setting out the steps it intends to take to inform

---

[10] See P. Kameri-Mbote and R. Okello-Orlale, *Environment Sector Gender Analysis: Successes, Challenges, Opportunities and Necessary Interventions* (report prepared for DANIDA (2009). On file with the author).

[11] Government of Kenya, *National Climate Change Response Strategy* (April 2010), p. 17. See www.environment.go.ke/images/final%20complete%20nccrs%202010.pdf. Government of Kenya, *Vision 2030* (2008), spells out Kenya's development aspirations in the next twenty years and specifically seeks to transform the country from a developing to a medium-income economy by the year 2030. It has political, economic and social pillars which have been broken down into goals and objectives for the attainment of the Vision.

[12] NCCRS (see n. 11 above).   [13] Draft Climate Change Bill, 2010, Section 3.

the public about climate change programmes specified in the Bill and also to encourage the public to contribute to the achievement of the objectives of those programmes.[14] The Bill would also mandate the formulation, implementation, publication and regular update of national climate change programmes in relation to: adaptation and mitigation; education and awareness, including integration in the school curriculum; assessment of vulnerability and climate change threats; capacity building in strategic climate change sectors; and research, development and technology transfer.[15]

12.08   The Bill also proposes the establishment of a National Clean Energy Development Mechanism Authority as envisaged under the Kyoto Protocol.[16] The proposed Authority would include representatives from the Ministries of Environment, Foreign Affairs, Finance, Planning, Energy, Agriculture, Trade and Industry, and Tourism. It would have regulatory functions,[17] capacity building functions,[18] and technology transfer functions.[19]

12.09   Under the Bill, public bodies would be required to exercise their functions in delivering climate change programmes in the most sustainable way possible.[20] The government would have the power to impose duties on public bodies relating to climate change.[21]

Industrial and natural resources (emissions sources and energy mix)

12.10   Kenya is classified as a developing country with, in 2010, a real GDP growth rate of 4.5%, a population growth rate of 2.6% and a per capita GDP growth rate of 0.9%.[22] Kenya has a complex

[14] *Ibid.*, Section 4(1)(a) and (b).
[15] *Ibid.*, Section 8.   [16] *Ibid.*, Section 24(1).
[17] *Ibid.*, Section 25(1).   [18] *Ibid.*, Section 25(2)(a)–(c).
[19] *Ibid.* Section 25 promotes transfer of environmentally safe and sound technology which furthers the objective of sustainable development taking into account local knowledge and circumstances; and encourages the trading or banking of CERs earned from CDM projects as marketable commodity.
[20] *Ibid.*, Section 31(1).   [21] *Ibid.*, Section 31(2).
[22] Kenya National Bureau of Statistics/World Bank (2009).

climate, with wide variations across the country and strong sea-
sonality. Temperatures vary widely between the coastal strip, the
arid and semi-arid lands and the temperate highland plateau.
Only 17% of the land is arable. Most of Kenya's 39 million people
live in the fertile and high-potential agricultural areas, and about
20% of the country's population and 50% of its livestock are in
the arid and semi-arid areas.

12.11   Kenya's natural endowments are limited. It lacks major exploit-
able mineral resources. Kenya's natural flora and fauna are
among the country's most valuable assets.[23] The national economy draws heavily on climate-sensitive sectors: agriculture and
nature-based tourism.[24] Individual livelihoods are also largely
based on climate-sensitive activities such as agriculture and livestock rearing.

12.12   Land use change accounts for the greatest source of emissions. As reliance on biomass and hydroelectric power sources
is reduced, Kenya's developing economy will demand more
from alternative energy sources, which may result in increased
emissions.[25] Thus, GHG emissions in Kenya could double by
2030.[26]

National climate change risks

12.13   Kenya already experiences extreme weather events such as periodic floods and droughts. Recent major droughts occurred in
1998–2000, 2004–05 and 2009. Major floods occurred in 1997–8
and 2006. All of the climate model scenarios show increases in
mean annual temperature in future years; the mid-range emission scenario shows a rise of almost 1° C by 2030 and around
1.5° C by 2050. However, the range across all the models is considerably wider, with projections from 1 to 3.5°C by the 2050s.[27]
These changes are likely to impact agricultural production and
pasture productivity.

---

[23] NCCRS (see n. 11 above), p. 30.   [24] *Ibid.*, p. 8.
[25] *Ibid.*, p. 39.   [26] NCCRS (see n. 11 above).
[27] Stockholm Environment Institute, *Economics of Climate Change in Kenya* (Project
Report, 2009, hereinafter 'SEI Project Report').

12.14   Kenya's coastline has diverse flora and fauna. The coral reefs –
        which buffer the coastline against waves – mangrove forests
        and other marine resources as well as low-lying tourist facilities
        are at risk from the predicted sea level rise, which may lead to
        submergence of parts of the Kenyan coast.[28] Kenya is a water-
        scarce country with uneven water distribution. Climate change
        effects on precipitation are likely to alter the availability of water.
        Further, climate change will have substantial effects on forest
        cover in Kenya, which had decreased to less than 2 per cent by
        2005. This has implications for water availability as water catch-
        ment areas are destroyed.

12.15   Climate change will also negatively impact Kenya's key eco-
        nomic sectors: agriculture, tourism, livestock, horticulture,
        fisheries and forestry. In 2006, agriculture directly contributed
        26% to Kenya's GDP and a further 27% through other sectors;
        tourism and fisheries contributed 10% and 0.5% respectively.[29]
        Wildlife deaths have been reported and fisheries are likely to be
        affected by rising temperatures. The production of major cash
        crops such as tea has also declined. Aggregate models indicate
        that additional net economic costs (on top of existing climate
        variability) could be equivalent to a loss of almost 3% of GDP
        each year by 2030.[30] An initial fiscal estimate of Kenya's imme-
        diate needs for addressing current climate conditions as well as
        for preparing for future climate change is $500 million annually,
        starting from 2012.[31]

12.16   Climate change will affect food security as floods and droughts
        lead to the loss of productive assets. Famine cycles have short-
        ened from every twenty years in 1964 to yearly in 2009 due to
        extreme climatic variations. There are also indirect contributions
        through destruction of physical and social infrastructure such as
        roads and bridges during storm events.[32] This affects the trans-
        portation of food across the country.

---

[28] NCCRS (see n. 11 above), p. 32.   [29] *Ibid.*, p. 34.
[30] SEI Project Report (see n. 27 above).   [31] *Ibid.*
[32] NCCRS (see n. 11 above), p. 38. See SEI Project Report (n. 27 above) and IGAD, *Climate
     Change and Human Development in Africa: Assessing the Risks and Vulnerability of
     Climate Change in Kenya* (Malawi and Ethiopia Human Development Report 2007/2008).
     Occasional Paper, Human Development Report Office, IGAD Climate Prediction and
     Applications Centre (ICPAC).

(B)   Public law

Overview

12.17   Judicial review is a process of control over public bodies by which a court reviews the legality of a public body's actions. The purpose of judicial review was expressed in *R* v. *Secretary of State for Transport ex p. LB Richmond*[33] as ensuring that government is conducted within the law. A court exercises judicial review by examining whether the decision has been made in accordance with the law. That is, the scope of judicial review is not the merits of the decision but rather the decision-making process followed by the public body in reaching the decision.[34] Thus, judicial review can ensure that an individual is given fair treatment by the authority to which he/she has been subjected.

12.18   Through judicial review, a court could quash a decision (*certiorari*), stop unlawful action (prohibition), require the performance of a public duty (*mandamus*), declare the legal position of the litigants (declaration), order monetary compensation and maintain the status quo (a stay).[35] Judicial review is used to challenge public bodies exercising regulatory functions for failure to act or for taking an improper action (e.g. one outside the jurisdiction of the public body). This is a possible avenue for climate change litigation under the draft Climate Change Bill with respect to the proposed duties of public bodies to: (i) undertake programmes for adaptation and mitigation; (ii) report on progress towards implementation of programmes; (iii) prepare a land-use strategy; (iv) promote energy efficiency; and (v) prepare and implement waste prevention and management plans.[36]

12.19   The legal regime for judicial review proceedings in Kenya is the Law Reform Act[37] and Order 53 of the Civil Procedure Rules, 2010.[38] Section 8(2) of the Law Reform Act empowers the High

---

[33] No. 3 [1995] Env. LR 409.

[34] *Supreme Court Practice*, 1997, vol. 53/1–14/6.

[35] Albert Mumma, 'The Continuing Role of Common Law in Sustainable Development' in C. O. Okidi *et al.*, *Environmental Governance in Kenya: Implementing the Framework Law* (Nairobi: East African Educational Publishers, 2008), pp. 90–109, at p. 92.

[36] Part III of the Draft Climate Change Bill (see n. 13 above).

[37] Chapter 26 of the Laws of Kenya (see n. 1 above), sections 8–10.

[38] Chapter 21 of the Laws of Kenya (see n. 1 above).

Court to make an order of *mandamus*, prohibition or *certiorari* in any case in which the High Court in England is empowered to do so by virtue of section 7 of the Administration of Justice (Miscellaneous Provisions) Act, 1938 of the United Kingdom. The procedure for judicial review is provided by Order 53 of the Civil Procedure Rules. It requires that the applicant seek leave of the court before filing the application. Leave is only granted if the court considers that the applicant has 'sufficient interest' (or *locus standi*) in the matter in issue. Judicial review could be a tool for litigating climate change cases when a public body has made a decision that has negative impacts on the environment and is either outside the ambit of the powers of the body or is made without regard to procedural requirements. Thus if, for example, a public body is required to regulate the use of efficient energy options, one could challenge the manner in which that power is exercised.

Justiciability and standing

12.20   Justiciability refers to the amenability of a matter for judicial determination. It requires that an actual and substantial controversy be present before a decision can be rendered.[39] Any litigation, including climate change related, must satisfy the justiciability test; thus, not every complaint will be accepted for judicial determination. Under the traditional test for justiciability, a complainant must demonstrate that the defendant's actions caused harm resulting in personal or proprietary damage to the complainant. Further, the complainant must demonstrate that this damage was specific to her/him and greater than that suffered by the public. Most climate change actions would not be able to sustain this test and thus would be non-justiciable.

12.21   Many environmental cases in Kenya in which plaintiffs brought actions on behalf of the general public have been lost due to the courts holding that the plaintiffs lacked *locus standi*. This restrictive view of *locus standi* is best demonstrated by the Kenyan case of *Wangari* v. *Kenya Times Media Trust*.[40] However,

---

[39] *Metropolitan Life Ins. Co.* v. *Kinsman*, 747 NW 2d 653.
[40] HCCC No. 5403 of 1989 reported in 1 KLR (E&L) 164–74 where the renowned Kenyan Nobel Laureate, Professor Wangari Maathai, brought a suit in her capacity as coordinator

the requirement for 'sufficient interest' has been simplified by the enactment of the 2010 Constitution and Environmental Management and Co-ordination Act ('EMCA').[41] Article 70 of the Constitution and Section 3 of EMCA grant every person in Kenya the *locus standi* to sue in any environment-related matter. Courts in Kenya have in recent years also upheld the rights of individuals to bring cases to courts without having to demonstrate personal injury and loss.[42] It follows, therefore, that the most important justiciability issues for climate change litigation are determining the impact of the action complained about and demonstrating causation.

Grounds for judicial review

12.22   Section 8(2) of the Law Reform Act limits the High Court of Kenya to issue the writs of *mandamus*, prohibition, or *certiorari* only in the circumstances that the High Court in England is empowered to issue such writs. In England, the various grounds for judicial review that have developed over time are best expressed in the court's decision in *Council for Civil Service Unions* v. *Minister for the Civil Service*: the only grounds for judicial review are illegality, irrationality and procedural impropriety.[43] However, within these broad established categories, many more specific grounds for judicial review have evolved.

Ultra vires

12.23   Public bodies may only act within the powers that they have been given by law. Those powers are often specified in legislation. A

---

of the Green Belt movement seeking to restrain the defendants from constructing a multi-storey building in a public recreation area known as Uhuru Park situated in the centre of Nairobi City, the capital of Kenya. However, the case was struck out on the basis that Wangari Maathai lacked *locus standi*.

[41] Act no. 8 of 1999.

[42] See, e.g., *Samson Ole Reya* v. *Attorney General*, 1 KLR (E&L), 2006, 761–70. The plaintiffs brought a suit against the government arguing that the decision to introduce a weed, known as *prosopis Juliflora*, in 1983 to their area ostensibly to curb desertification had interfered with their right to a clean environment due to the invasive nature of the weed. Amongst the objections raised to the suit by the defendants was that the applicants lacked *locus standi*. However the court rejected this objection, holding that with the enactment of EMCA, an action could only be dismissed if it was shown that it was frivolous, vexatious or an abuse of the court process.

[43] [1985] AC 374.

public body is not allowed to act without authority or beyond those powers. Engaging in such conduct is termed 'ultra vires' and can either be substantive or procedural. Procedural ultra vires occurs when a public body fails to follow required procedure while substantive ultra vires occurs when a public body exercises power beyond its limits. In *Anisminic Ltd* v. *Foreign Compensation Commission*, the court held that public bodies would be ultra vires if they attempted to decide a case that was outside their area of control or if they made errors of law in their decision-making process.[44] In *Re Racal Communications*, the court held that *any* 'error of law' is a ground for review as an illegality; that is, there is no need to prove that the error was ultra vires.[45] Numerous cases have been decided by the Kenyan courts dealing with the issue of acting ultra vires. In *Mohammed Zafar Niaz Chaudry & Waheed* v. *The Permanent Secretary Ministry of Education*, the applicants as officials of the Islamia Madrasa Society challenged the decisions of the Permanent Secretary of the Ministry of Education to cancel the licence for a school run by the applicants and then to issue another licence which changed the nature and size of the population of the school.[46] The court granted the orders sought by the applicants on the grounds that the actions of the Permanent Secretary were ultra vires: only the Minister for Education could exercise such powers unless he had expressly delegated the powers through a gazette notice, which in this case he had not.

Exercising a power for the wrong purpose

12.24   Where an authority or public body is given power for a certain purpose, it is not expected to act outside the purpose. The purpose might be explicit or implicit. In either case, the authority is not allowed to exercise a power for some other purpose than the one for which it was granted.

Principles of natural justice

12.25   The principles of natural justice are also described as 'procedural fairness'. They apply at first glance to all administrative

---

[44] [1968] APP LR 12/17.   [45] [1980] APP LR 07/03.
[46] High Court at Nairobi, Misc. App. No. 76 of 2006.

decision-making situations. However, they only bind administrative bodies where a judgment is being made that may have the effect of interfering with an interest of the individual. They do not apply when general policy, for example, is being determined.[47]

12.26   There are two key components to natural justice: fair hearing and bias rules. The fair hearing rule is derived from the maxim *audi alteram partem* (hear the other side). All those affected by the decision should be given a chance to state their case and be heard and thus no party should be condemned unheard. The bias rule requires impartiality on the part of the decision-maker. The test is whether a fair-minded observer might reasonably apprehend that the decision-maker might not bring an impartial mind to the resolution of the question. The principle has been upheld in the majority of the judicial review cases in Kenya. In the 1997 case of *Mirugi Kariuki* v. *Attorney General*, the court quashed the decision of the Attorney General to deny the applicant the right to be represented by a Queen's Counsel in a case where he had been charged with treason.[48] The Attorney General made this decision summarily without hearing the applicant. The court held that this action should have been arrived at only after hearing the applicant in accordance with the rules of natural justice. This position was upheld in *Obed Nthiwa* v. *Commissioner of Cooperative Development* where the court quashed the decision of the Commissioner to suspend the applicant as a member of the central management committee of a cooperative society without giving him an opportunity to be heard.[49] The court held that the action was ultra vires and against the rules of natural justice.

Fettering discretion

12.27   Where a public body is vested with discretion to make a certain decision or act in a certain way, it is supposed to exercise the discretion within the law. The public body should not fetter that discretion by, for example, adopting an overly rigid policy or set

---

[47] Fiona L. McKenzie, *Grounds of Review, The Law Handbook*, available at www.lawhandbook.org.au/handbook/ch21s02s06.php.
[48] Civ. App. No. 70 of 1997.
[49] Misc. App. No. 462 of 2006 reported in eKLR [2007].

of guidance or by agreeing to act in accordance with the decision of another public body.[50]

12.28　There have been no climate litigation matters brought before Kenyan courts. The new Constitution and the amended Civil Procedure Rules dictate an overriding objective regarding litigation: the determination of disputes without undue delay and without undue regard to technicalities and formalities of procedure. Courts are bound to give effect to this overriding objective in interpreting the legislative provisions, and parties and their advocates are obliged to assist the court in furthering this objective. The court is expected to take the following factors into account in furthering the overriding objective: (i) the just determination of proceedings; (ii) the efficient disposal of the business of the court; (iii) the efficient use of available judicial and administrative resources; (iv) the timely disposal of the proceedings at a cost affordable to the parties; and (v) the use of suitable/appropriate technology. This provides a good context for climate change actions that may be brought to Kenyan courts in the future.

Public interest litigation

12.29　Litigation is a useful tool for vindicating rights and resolving disputes between parties. While traditional litigation largely focuses on disputes between two private entities based on personal or proprietary damage, the nature of environmental issues is such that they are not readily amenable to private litigation. Because environmental rights are more easily characterised as public rights than as private rights, the concept of public interest litigation has emerged as an avenue for protecting environmental rights. Through public interest litigation, public-spirited individuals can bring suits to enforce rights and provide relief to wide sections of society.

12.30　In Kenya, the concept of public interest litigation is relatively new.[51] Neither citizens nor courts have embraced the concept.

[50] For a discussion of the exercise of discretion in the Kenyan context, see P. L. O. Lumumba, *An Outline of Judicial Review in Kenya* (University of Nairobi, 1999), pp. 58–83.

[51] M. O. Makoloo, B. O. Ochieng and C. O. Oloo, *Public Interest Environmental Litigation: Prospects and Challenges* (Nairobi: ILEG, 2007), p. 60.

The legal framework has also been largely unsupportive to public interest litigation due to restrictive laws on *locus standi*. However the new Constitution provides a legal framework supportive of public interest litigation through its relaxation of the rules of *locus standi*: it gives everyone the right to bring an action on violation of environmental rights without proof of loss or damage.[52] The pervasive nature of climate change and the effects it has on wider sections of society make it a particularly promising area for the use of public interest litigation to ensure relief to victims of climate change.

Constitutional and framework environmental law

12.31   The recognition and guarantee of human rights within a country's legal system provide a basis for protecting the environment and ensuring a clean and healthy environment. While many constitutions do not expressly mention climate change or address climate change related issues,[53] the discourse of rights generally and the right to life in particular has developed worldwide to an extent that many courts now appreciate that the provisions on the right to life in a country's constitution can be used to deal with environmental degradation.[54]

12.32   On 4 August 2010, Kenyans held a referendum and voted for a new Constitution which has heralded a new dawn in the

---

[52] *Constitution of Kenya*, 2010, n. 2 above.

[53] See D. Badrinarayana, 'India's Constitutional Challenge: A less Visible Climate Change Catastrophe' in B. J. Richardson *et al.* (eds.), *Climate Law and Developing Countries: Legal and Policy Challenges for the World Economy* (Edward Elgar, 2009), pp.63–83, discussing using the Constitution in India to litigate climate change issues despite there being no mention of climate change in the Indian Constitution.

[54] For a discussion of cases in Asia and Latin America see generally B. J. Preston, 'The Role of the Judiciary in Promoting Sustainable Development: The Experience of Asia and the Pacific', *Asia Pacific Journal of Environmental Law*, 9 (2), (3) (2005), 109–211. See also D. Tackacs, 'The Public Trust Doctrine, Environmental Human Rights, and the Future of Private Property', *New York University Environmental Law Journal*, 16 (2008), 711. In the East African context the constitutional provisions on right to life have also been interpreted to include right to a clean and healthy environment. For a discussion of these cases see P. Kameri-Mbote and C. Odote, 'Courts as Champions of Sustainable Development: Lessons From East Africa', *Sustainable Development Law and Policy*, 10(1) (2009), 31 available at www.wcl.american.edu/org/sustainabledevelopment/documents/ SDLP_09Fall.pdf?rd=1.

country's governance framework.[55] The new Constitution has
made great strides forward in the environmental field including, for the first time in the country's history, the right – in
the Bill of Rights – to a clean and healthy environment.[56] This
is a marked improvement from the position under the old
Constitution, which did not even mention the word environment in its provisions.[57] The new Constitution recognises the
importance of environmental management to the country's
governance, pointing out in its Preamble that the environment
is the country's heritage and as such the people of Kenya are
'determined to sustain it for the benefit of future generations'.[58]
Additionally, the Constitution puts sustainable development
at the centre of all governance processes and decisions in the
country by identifying it as a national value and principle of
governance.[59]

12.33   The constitutional fundamental human right to a clean and
healthy environment expressly includes the right to 'have the
environment protected for the benefit of the present and future
generations'[60] and to 'have obligations relating to the environment fulfilled'.[61] The government is required to:

> (a) ensure sustainable exploitation, utilisation, management and con-
> servation of the environment and natural resources, and ensure equit-
> able sharing of accruing benefits; (b) work to achieve and maintain a
> tree cover of at least ten per cent of land area of Kenya; (c) protect and
> enhance intellectual property in, and indigenous knowledge of, bio-
> diversity and the genetic resources of the communities; (d) encourage
> public participation in the management, protection and conservation
> of the environment; (e) protect genetic resources and biological diver-
> sity; (f) establish systems of environmental impact assessment, envir-
> onmental audit and monitoring of the environment; (g) eliminate
> processes and activities that are likely to endanger the environment;

[55] *Constitution of Kenya*, 2010 (see n. 2 above).
[56] *Ibid.*, Section 42.
[57] See generally J. B. Ojwang., 'The Constitutional Basis for Environmental Management'
in C. Juma and J. B. Ojwang (eds.), *In Land We Trust: Environment, Private Property and
Constitutional Change* (Nairobi and London: Initiative Publishers and Zed Books, 1996),
pp.39–60. See also C. O. Okidi, 'Concept, Structure and Function of Environmental
Law' in C. O. Okidi *et al.* (eds.), *Environmental Governance in Kenya: Implementing the
Framework Law* (Nairobi: East African Educational Publishers, 2008), pp. 3–60, at p. 18.
[58] See *Constitution of Kenya*, 2010, n. 2 above, at Preamble.
[59] *Ibid.*, Section 10.   [60] *Ibid.*, Section e 42(a).   [61] *Ibid.*, Section 42(b).

and (h) utilise the environment and natural resources for the benefit of the people of Kenya.[62]

12.34   The right to sue in environmental matters is constitutionally guaranteed. Article 70(1) categorically provides:

> If a person alleges that a right to a clean and healthy environment recognised and protected under Article 42 has been, is being or is likely to be, denied, violated, infringed or threatened, the person may apply to a court for redress in addition to any other legal remedies that are available in respect to the same matter.

Article 70(2) empowers a court to 'make any order, or give any directions it considers appropriate'. Furthermore, the Constitution restates, albeit in different words, the provisions of EMCA that 'an applicant does not have to demonstrate that any person has incurred loss or suffered injury'.[63]

12.35   These constitutional provisions are supported by the framework environmental law, the EMCA,[64] which, in addition to recognising in almost similar terms to the Constitution the right to a clean and healthy environment,[65] provides principles of environmental law to govern public bodies in making decisions on the management of the environment and to govern courts in their consideration of environmental cases. These principles, based on internationally agreed general principles of environmental law, include the following: (i) the principle of public participation in development of policies, plans and processes for the management of the environment; (ii) the cultural and social principles traditionally applied by any community in Kenya for the management of the environment and natural resources in so far as the same are relevant and are not repugnant to justice and morality or inconsistent with any written law; (iii) the principle of international cooperation in the management of environmental resources shared by two or more countries; (iv) the principle of inter-generational equity; (v) the polluter pays principles; and (vi) the precautionary principle.[66]

---

[62] *Ibid.*, Section 69(1).   [63] *Ibid.*, Section 70(3).
[64] See EMCA, n. 42 above.   [65] *Ibid.*, Section 3(1).
[66] *Ibid.*, Section 3(5). See also A. Angwenyi, 'An Overview of the Environmental Management and Coordination Act' in C. O. Okidi *et al.* (eds.), *Environmental Governance in Kenya: Implementing the Framework Law* (Nairobi: East African Educational Publishers, 2008), pp. 142–82.

12.36   The result of these constitutional and legislative stipulations is a basis for citizen action and demand for the legal protection of those environmental rights. Even before the adoption of the new Constitution, the Kenyan judiciary had already ruled that citizens in Kenya had a right to a clean and healthy environment. In the landmark case of *Peter K. Waweru* v. *Republic*,[67] twenty-three property owners in Kiserian, a small town in Kenya, had been charged under the country's Public Health Act[68] with the twin offences of discharging raw sewage into a public water source and the environment and failing to comply with a statutory notice from a public health authority. The applicants filed a constitutional reference arguing that the charge violated their constitutional rights because the authorities improperly discriminated against them by charging only them with unlawful conduct in which all land-owners in the town had engaged. The court agreed with the applicants and discharged them. The court then discussed the implications of their action for sustainable development and for environmental management. It held that the actions were against the right of the residents of the areas to a clean and healthy environment.[69] Thus although the criminal charges against them were unconstitutional for being discriminatory, the original acts complained about were injurious to the environment. Consequently the court ordered remedial action to be taken by government agencies to ensure that the offending action ceased.

12.37   The *Waweru* case has provided a sound jurisprudential basis for the Kenyan courts in addressing environmental cases. Judges have pointed out that the right to life can be threatened by many things. It is thus arguable that a court could consider that climate change threatens the right to life and the right to a clean environment. Such an argument, however, will require that evidence clearly establish that climate change related activities can be demonstrated as having impacts on the environment. A plaintiff could refer to the huge body of literature demonstrating that climate change is real and is negatively impacting societies.[70]

---

[67] 1 KLR (E&L) 677–700.
[68] Chapter 242 of the Laws of Kenya (see n. 1 above).
[69] See n. 36 above, p. 687.
[70] Jennifer Kilinski, 'International Climate Change Liability: A Myth or Reality?', *Journal of Transnational Law and Policy*, 18(2) (2009), 378–418, at 378. See also the assessment

12.38   The precautionary principle is useful in situations where there is a lack of full scientific certainty by nevertheless allowing for the establishment of liability and thus for remedial action. The principle acts by reversing the rules on the burden of proof. The principle was used successfully in the Pakistan case of *Shehla Zia* v. *Wapda*.[71] In Kenya, the precautionary principle has been applied in *Sam Odera and Others* v. *The National Environmental Management Authority and EM Communications*, a challenge to NEMA's issuance of an environmental impact assessment licence to a company that wanted to set up a telecommunications mast in a residential area.[72] The case demonstrates the country's recognition of the precautionary principle as a useful basis for determining the appropriate outcome in an environmental case and could be invoked as precedent in climate change litigation in Kenyan courts. In addition to referencing the *Odera* case, a plaintiff litigating a climate change related claim could refer to the inclusion of the precautionary principle within the FCCC.

(C)   Private law

12.39   Private law actions can be brought by private persons against other private persons for private injuries.[73] The causes of action in private law are trespass, nuisance, the Rule in *Rylands* v. *Fletcher* and negligence. The remedies for their redress are an award of damages, injunction and declaratory judgments.[74]

Trespass

12.40   As developed under the common law, trespass is related to invasion or unlawful intrusion that interferes with one's person or property. Its more common use in modern times relates to land. This makes it relevant to climate change actions in a country like Kenya where land-based actions are a big factor in climate

---

report for the 4th Inter-Governmental Panel on Climate Change ('IPCC'), 2007, available at www.ipcc.ch/pdf/assessment-report/ar4/syr/ar4_syr_spm.pdf. See also the US case of *Massachusetts* v. *Environmental Protection Agency* 549 US (2007).

[71] PLD 1994 SC 693.
[72] High Court, Misc. Civ. App. No. 400 of 2006.
[73] *Gouriet* v. *Union of Post Office Workers* [1978] AC 435.
[74] Mumma (see n. 35 above).

change.[75] An action in trespass can be brought either by the owner of the land or any lawful occupier of the land against anyone who interferes with the right of ownership or possession. The interference is required to be direct and physical and not an indirect interference. Trespass thus seeks to protect the right of an occupier to enjoy his/her land without unjustifiable interference.[76]

Nuisance

12.41 Nuisance was traditionally the most common cause of action asserted at common law. Nuisance is defined as the interference with the use and enjoyment of land belonging to another. The interference requirement limits the availability of the cause of action to owners and occupiers of land. There are two types of nuisance: private nuisance and public nuisance.

12.42 Private nuisance is defined as a continuous, unlawful and indirect interference with the use or enjoyment of land, or some right over or in connection with it. To succeed in an action for private nuisance, the claimant must prove that there was a continuous interference over a period of time with his/her use or enjoyment of land. The claimant must also prove that the defendant's conduct was unreasonable, thereby making it unlawful. The applicable rule is *sic utere tuo ut alienum non laedas* ('so use your own property as not to injure your neighbour's'). In determining the reasonableness of the interference, a court will consider various factors, such as locality, sensitivity of the claimant and the utility of the defendant's conduct. The claimant must further prove damage: either physical damage to the land or property upon it or otherwise injury to the claimant's health that prevents him/her enjoying the use of the land.

12.43 Public nuisance is the interference with the public's reasonable comfort and convenience.[77] It is primarily a crime, prosecuted by the Attorney General. It is only actionable as a tort if the claimant has suffered damage over and above other members of the public.

---

[75] See generally NCCRS (n. 11 above), and Draft Climate Change Bill, 2010 (n. 13 above).
[76] Mumma (see n. 35 above).   [77] UNEP Compendium, p xi.

Rule in Rylands v. Fletcher

12.44   This rule comes from the eponymous English case.[78] It creates a 'strict liability' cause of action where the claimant does not have to prove negligence in order to succeed.[79] The rule states: 'Where a person for his own purposes brings and keeps on land in his occupation anything likely to do mischief if it escapes, he must keep it at his peril, and if he fails to do so, he is liable for all damage which is a natural consequence of the escape.'

Foreseeability

12.45   Foreseeability is a prerequisite of liability under the rule in *Rylands* v. *Fletcher* and under negligence. This is the ability to see or know in advance, hence the reasonable anticipation that harm or injury is a likely result of acts or omissions.[80]

Negligence

12.46   Negligence is a cause of action that arises from the breach of a duty of care. The development of the law of negligence has been built on the foundation of identification of circumstances which give rise to a duty of care. Negligence has, from the past, been held to mean a failure to do something which a reasonable man would have done in the circumstances, or the doing of something that such a person would not have done in the circumstances.[81]

12.47   The common law only recognises a remedy for negligence where the defendant owed a duty of care to the plaintiff.[82] In order to succeed in a negligence claim, the plaintiff must prove that the defendant owed her/him a duty of care, that the defendant breached this duty, and that the breach resulted in the claimant suffering injuries/damage.[83]

---

[78] *Rylands* v. *Fletcher* (1868) LR 3 HL 330.
[79] For further discussions regarding this rule, see Ch. 17.
[80] *Cambridge Water Co* v. *Eastern Counties Leather plc* [1994] 2 WLR 53 (HL) at 101.
[81] *Blyth* v. *Birmingham Waterworks Co* (1856) 11 Ex at 784.
[82] *Thomas* v. *Quartermaine* (1887) 18 QBD 694.
[83] *Caparo Industries* v. *Dickman* [1990] 1 All ER 568.

Causation

12.48   Causation is an important ingredient in proving negligence. The plaintiff must demonstrate the link between the breach of duty and the resultant damage. For liability to arise, the plaintiff must show that the defendant's particular acts or omissions were the cause of the loss or damage sustained.[84] This has been problematic in environmental causes of action generally in Kenya and the same is likely to be the case for climate change.

12.49   The common law causes of action continue to have relevance in environmental management in Kenya by providing a basis for giving effect to various environmental rights and principles.[85] This is likely to be the case for climate change actions. Kenyan litigants have a possibility of litigating climate change cases under nuisance and negligence. However, such actions would have to grapple with the issue of causation to sustain an action.

(D)   Other laws

Criminal law

12.50   Climate change litigation, like other environmental litigation, is likely to be complex and indeterminate.[86] Criminal sanctions may be an option where civil and administrative law fail to adequately deter or remedy violations.[87]

12.51   Kenyan law provides for criminal sanctions to enforce environmental laws. EMCA specifies a general penalty of imprisonment up to eighteen months, a fine of up to 350,000 Kenya shillings (about USD 4,216[88]) or both for violation of the Act or any regulation made under the Act.[89] It also provides for liability of corporations. Furthermore, Section 145 imputes liability on the part of the directors and officers of a corporation. This imposition of liability is intended to motivate directors and officers to establish

---

[84] *Ibid.*   [85] Mumma (see n. 35 above).

[86] Patricia Kameri-Mbote, 'The Use of Criminal Law in Enforcing Environmental Law' in C. O. Okidi (ed.), *Environmental Governance in Kenya: Implementing the Framework Law* (Nairobi: East African Educational Publishers, 2008), pp. 110–25.

[87] *Ibid.*, at p. 113.

[88] Using the prevailing exchange rate of 1 USD to 83 Kenya Shillings.

[89] Section 144, EMCA (see n. 41 above).

corporate mechanisms for environmental compliance, and thus to avoid passing the cost of non-compliance to consumers or the general public. Under the draft Climate Change Bill, contravention of the provisions of the Bill would be an offence punishable on conviction through imprisonment for a term not exceeding five years or a fine not exceeding one million Kenya shillings (about USD 12,048[90]) or both.[91]

Public trust

12.52   The Kenyan judiciary has considered the idea of the public trust doctrine in the context of forestry. In *Republic* v. *Minister for Environment and Natural Resources*, the applicants sought to get the court's view on the applicability of the public trust doctrine with regard to forests. Within a context where forest cover in the country had gone down to a paltry 2 per cent and amid concerns over allocations of forest land to private actors allied to the government, there was a huge public outcry.[92] They sought writs of *certiorari* to quash the relevant government notice and prohibit the government from dealing with the forest areas in a manner detrimental to Kenya's environmental health.[93] The court granted the orders, thereby stopping the government from proceeding with the exercise until such time as the issue was fully heard and determined. Similarly in *Waweru* v. *The Republic*, the court held that the Government and its agencies are under a public trust to manage land resources, forests, wetlands and waterways in a way that maintains a proper balance between the economic benefits of development and the need for a clean environment.[94] The concept was also quoted with approval by the court in *John Peter Mureithi and Two Others* v. *Attorney General and Four Others*, a matter relating to land allegedly grabbed from a clan which had held it as trust land.[95] The court recognised the application of the

---

[90]   See n. 88 above.   [91]   Section 39, EMCA (see n. 41 above).
[92]   The concerns about the forest cover in Kenya and the impact that its loss has on future generations have resulted in the inclusion of a specific provision in the Constitution requiring the State to 'work to achieve and maintain a tree cover of at least ten per cent of the land area of Kenya'. Section 69(1)(b), *Constitution of Kenya*, 2010 (see n. 2 above).
[93]   High Court of Kenya, Misc. Civ. App. No. 421 of 2002.
[94]   *Ibid.*
[95]   Misc. Civ. App. No. 158 of 2005, reported in eKLR [2006].

public trust doctrine with respect to both trust land and public land stating that the doctrine 'had deep roots in African communities and is certainly not inherited from the Romans'.

12.53 The public trust concept has therefore been used to ensure protection of the environment, especially as regards critical ecosystems like forests and wetlands. The doctrine can be used to regulate the interest of property rightholders for the benefit of environmental conservation. In addition, the State as the public trustee over land is also under a duty to ensure that the land is not used in a manner that exacerbates climate change.

12.54 In appropriate cases, a suit can be brought against the State under the public trust doctrine. Most activities that lead to the destruction of critical ecosystems such as forests and wetlands are sanctioned by government institutions. They may be allowed after environmental impact assessments have been carried out and the National Environment Management Authority has granted a licence allowing the project proponents to proceed. The argument to be advanced in this case is that the State failed in its duty of preventing activities that result in climate change from being undertaken on a wetland, or preventing the destruction of a forest.

Regional framework

12.55 Kenya is a member of the East African Community and also of the African Union. Thus positions adopted within these fora and their legal stipulations influence Kenya's position and practice on climate change generally and climate liability specifically. In preparation for the Copenhagen Summit in December 2009, African ministers and heads of States held numerous meetings and adopted common positions on climate change issues. At the end of a meeting of the African Ministers on the Environment (AMCEN) in Nairobi from 25 to 29 May 2009, the Ministers adopted the Nairobi Declaration on the African Process for combating climate change.[96] The Declaration decried the conclusions of the 4th Inter-governmental Panel on Climate Change,

---

[96] Available at www.unep.org/roa/Amcen/Amcen_Events/3rd_ss/Docs/nairobi-Decration-2009.pdf.

especially regarding the social, economic and environmental consequences and impacts of climate change, pointing out that while Africa contributed the least to global climate change, its people were bearing the brunt of the consequences.[97]

12.56   In essence, the Declaration called for the developed countries to bear liability for causing climate change. This position has been the main African position in international negotiations on climate change and represents Africa's attitude towards climate change liability. The position also holds that the developed countries should provide funds to enable Africa to adapt to and mitigate the effects of climate change. The East African Community also adopted a position before Copenhagen[98] and has been active in discussing climate change issues amongst the five partner States.

(E)   Conclusion

12.57   Climate change is having serious negative effects on Kenya. Addressing its impacts requires the concerted efforts of many stakeholders and the use of numerous approaches and tools. Law can be used to force public institutions to act to avert climate change. It can also be used to hold those who engage in activities resulting in or aggravating climate change responsible through private actions or criminal indictments. However, determining liability for climate change is fraught with numerous hurdles.

12.58   Critical to successful litigation is the question of causation. The legal and policy framework in Kenya has only recently started to appreciate and respond to climate change issues. It does not expressly address the question of liability for climate change. However, there are several traditional legal avenues that could be creatively applied to sustain climate change related actions and prove liability successfully in courts. What will be required is innovation, reform and adoption of a multifaceted approach to the question of addressing the effects of climate change.

[97] *Ibid.*
[98] Available at www.eac.int/environment/index.php?option−com_docman.

South Africa

JAN GLAZEWSKI AND DEBBIE COLLIER

(A) Introduction

13.01   There are four main climate-determining factors in South Africa:
the northward moving cold Benguela current along its western
coast which originates in Antarctic waters; the southern flowing warm Agulhas current on the eastern seaboard originating
in the tropics; the high central plateau known as the Highveld;
and the resultant varying atmospheric conditions during winter
and summer. The authorities predict that 'by mid-century the
South African coast will warm by around 1–2ºC, and the interior by around 2–3ºC. After 2050, warming is projected to reach
around 3–4ºC along the coast, and 6–7 ºC in the interior'.[1] These
types of temperature changes will place a massive strain on an
already water-stressed nation currently dealing with problems
of poverty and unemployment, poor service delivery and low
levels of education. These problems notwithstanding, the South
African legal system itself appears well oriented to address the
legal issues that are likely to arise with the onslaught of climate
change.

Jan Glazewski B.Com., LL.B., M.A. (Cape Town), LL.M. (London), LL.D. (Cape Town),
Professor in the Institute of Marine and Environmental Law at the University of Cape
Town, Advocate of the High Court of South Africa and a member of the Cape Bar.

Debbie Collier B.A., LL.B. (Rhodes), LL.M., Ph.D. (Cape Town), Deputy Director of
the Institute of Development and Labour Law and Senior Lecturer in the Department of
Commercial Law at the University of Cape Town, Attorney of the High Court of South
Africa.

The authors wish to acknowledge the research assistance of Rebecca Browning and the
guidance of Andrew Gilder B.A., LL.B., LL.M. (Marine and Environmental Law) (Cape
Town) and Director at IMBEWU Sustainability Legal Specialists (Pty) Ltd. Responsibility
for the contents remains that of the authors.

[1] Department of Environmental Affairs, *National Climate Change Response Green Paper
2010*, GN 1083 of 2010, *Government Gazette* No. 33801, 25 November 2010, p. 7.

13.02   In April 1994 South Africa removed over 300 years of racially based government authority by adopting a democratic constitution. In doing so it transformed from a system of parliamentary sovereignty to a constitutional democracy underpinned by a progressive Bill of Rights contained in Chapter 2 of the Constitution which is now the supreme law.[2] The Bill of Rights contains, amongst other things, an environmental right.[3] Notwithstanding these developments, the historic Roman-Dutch legal system, a mixed legal system reflecting aspects of both the European civil law and the English common law traditions, was retained.[4] This system, supplemented by a growing body of statute law, is to a large extent still intact today, provided that where there is conflict with the Constitution, the offending law must give way.[5]

13.03   South Africa is a party to the UNFCCC, Kyoto Protocol and numerous other international environmental conventions and accepts the conclusions of the IPCC in its 4th Assessment Report on the warming of the climate system, that 'it is very likely that the increase in anthropogenic greenhouse gas concentrations is responsible for much of this warming trend since the mid twentieth century'.[6] South Africa has played a leading role in the various Conferences of the Parties (COPs) in maintaining the African countries' agenda, but it is also closely aligned to the other BASIC countries (Brazil, India and China) in climate change negotiations. The country will host the COP XVII in Durban in December 2011.

---

[2] Section 2 of the Constitution of the Republic of South Africa Act 108 of 1996.
[3] Section 24 of the Constitution (see (B) Public law below).
[4] The civil law component derives from Dutch occupation of the Cape of Good Hope, from around 1652, which resulted in the introduction of Roman-Dutch law to the Cape; and the common law component from the subsequent defeat of the Dutch settlers by the British. On the South African legal system and its history and development generally, see Lourens Marthinus Du Plessis, *An Introduction to Law*, 3rd edn (Kenwyn, SA: Juta, 1999); H. R. Hahlo and Ellison Kahn, *The South African Legal System and its Background* (Cape Town: Juta, 1968); and *The Union of South Africa: the Development of its Laws and Constitution* (Cape Town: Juta, 1960); Basil Edwards, *Introduction to South African Law and Legal Theory*, 2nd edn (Durban: Butterworths, 1995); and Reinhard Zimmermann and Daniel Visser, *Southern Cross: Civil Law and Common Law in South Africa* (Cape Town: Juta, 1996).
[5] Section 2 of the Constitution.
[6] Department of Environmental Affairs, *National Climate Change Response Green Paper 2010*, p. 6.

(B)   Public law

The constitutional framework

13.04   The Bill of Rights chapter of the Constitution includes an environmental right in the following terms:
'[e]veryone has the right–
(a) to an environment that is not harmful to their health or well-
being; and
(b) to have the environment protected, for the benefit of present
and future generations, through reasonable legislative and
other measures that–
   (i) prevent pollution and ecological degradation;
  (ii) promote conservation; and
 (iii) secure ecologically sustainable development and use of
natural resources while promoting justifiable economic
and social development.[7]
Subsection (iii) refers to 'sustainable development and use of natural resources while promoting justifiable economic and social
development'. This is particularly apposite as the gap between
rich and poor remains one of the underlying challenges facing
the new government. A recent OECD survey reports that South
Africa's Gini coefficient, an internationally accepted measure of
inequality, increased from 0.66 to 0.7 between the advent of democracy in 1993 and 2008.[8] It also found that while total income
poverty in South Africa has decreased slightly, it persists at acute
levels in certain racial groups.[9]

13.05   The environmental right has been embraced by the judiciary in
a number of cases. In *BP Southern Africa (Pty) Ltd* v. *MEC for
Agriculture, Conservation and Land Affairs*[10] the Court stated
that '[b]y elevating the environment to a fundamental justiciable

[7] Section 24 of the Constitution.
[8] Leibbrandt, Woolard, Finn and Argent, 'Trends in South African Income Distribution
and Poverty since the Fall of Apartheid', *OECD Social, Employment and Migration
Working Papers No. 101* (Directorate for Employment, Labour and Social Affairs, 20
January 2010), p. 10.
[9] Leibbrandt *et al.*, 'Trends in SA Income Distribution', p. 4. The report distinguishes
'income poverty', a measure of income from non-monetary benefits such as access to
water.
[10] 2004 (5) SA 124 (W).

human right, South Africa has irreversibly embarked on a road, which will lead to the goal of attaining a protected environment by an integrated approach, which takes into consideration, *inter alia*, socio-economic concerns and principles'.[11] In the same vein the Constitutional Court has affirmed that the concept of sustainable development is part of South African law, stating that:

> NEMA, which was enacted to give effect to section 24 of the Constitution, embraces the concept of sustainable development. Sustainable development is defined to mean 'the integration of social, economic and environmental factors into planning, implementation and decision-making for the benefit of present and future generations'. This broad definition of sustainable development incorporates two of the internationally recognised elements of the concept of sustainable development, namely, the principle of integration of environmental protection and socio-economic development, and the principle of inter-generational equity.[12]

13.06   The State, in its response to climate change, is therefore obliged to consider the environmental right, including the notion of sustainable development, and this opens the door to litigation in the context of climate change.

National Environmental Management Act ('NEMA')

13.07   NEMA[13] is the flagship statute of the Department of Environmental Affairs and came into force in January 1999.[14] It is a framework Act and includes both private law and public law provisions for the protection of the environment.

13.08   NEMA is underpinned by the notion of sustainable development and a set of national environmental management principles which apply to all organs of State. Sustainable development is defined as 'the integration of social, economic and environmental factors into planning, implementation and decision-making so as to ensure that development serves present and future generations'.[15]

---

[11] At 144D, as cited in J. Glazewski, *Environmental Law in South Africa*, 2nd edn (Durban: Lexis Nexis, 2005), p. 15.

[12] *Fuel Retailers Association of Southern Africa* v. *Director-General: Environmental Management, Department of Agriculture, Conservation and Environment Mpumalanga Province and Others* 2007 (6) SA 4 (CC) at para. [59] (original footnotes omitted).

[13] Act 107 of 1998.   [14] Glazewski, *Environmental Law in SA*, p. 137.

[15] Section 1.

The national environmental management principles include the preventive principle,[16] the polluter pays principle[17] and the precautionary principle,[18] which are particularly relevant to climate change and are likely to be invoked in climate change litigation.

13.09   The environmental right along with NEMA promote the State's responsibility to consider not only ecological factors in environmental decisions, but also the socio-economic factors as contained in Chapter 2 of the Constitution.[19] NEMA also provides guidelines for administrators when making administrative decisions[20] and provides for the formulation of environmental implementation plans and environmental management plans by certain national government departments and provinces.[21] These would be expected to include climate change considerations.

The duty of care requirement

13.10   NEMA also elaborates the common law principles of delict, central to this chapter and discussed in (C) Private law below, by introducing a statutory duty of care requirement which echoes that of the English law of tort discussed in Chapter 17. Section 28 places a duty of care on every person who causes, may cause or has caused significant pollution or degradation of the environment to take reasonable measures to prevent such pollution or degradation from occurring, continuing or recurring, or in the event that such harm is authorised by law or cannot reasonably be avoided or stopped, to minimise and rectify such pollution or degradation of the environment.[22]

13.11   The issue of the retrospective application of section 28 is an important one, as much damage is due to historical practices. In *Bareki NO and Another* v. *Gencor Ltd and Others*[23] it was held that section 28 does not have retrospective application. This hurdle to liability was however subsequently removed by section 12 of the National Environmental Laws Amendment Act[24] which now explicitly provides for the retrospective application of section 28.

---

[16] See sections 2(4)(*a*)(ii); 2(4)(*a*)(iii); and 2(4)(*a*)(viii).
[17] See section 2(4)(p).   [18] See section 2(4)(*a*)(vii).
[19] Glazewski, *Environmental Law in SA*, p. 138.
[20] *Ibid.*, p. 139.   [21] *Ibid.*, p. 143.
[22] Section 28(1).   [23] 2006 (1) SA 432 (T).
[24] Act 14 of 2009.

13.12   Section 28 is a general provision, and the duty it imposes could apply to both State and private persons. The section imposes a special statutory duty of care, the standard being the duty to take 'reasonable measures'. If the necessary steps are not taken, the Director General or provincial head may direct such persons to take certain measures, including assessing and evaluating the impact of specific activities, and then report back.[25] Furthermore, the Minister of Environmental Affairs may recover costs expended by the State when taking reasonable measures to remedy the situation[26] in the event of a failure to comply with a directive.

13.13   Section 28 enhances the possibility of successful climate change litigation. In a private law dispute (see (C) Private law below), section 28 is likely to assist a plaintiff to persuade the court of the wrongfulness of the defendant's conduct, which is an important hurdle that the plaintiff must overcome in establishing liability in the context of climate change litigation.

Administrative law

13.14   With the advent of a Bill of Rights, South Africa took the opportunity to codify its vast body of administrative law principles in section 33, which states that:

> everyone has the right to administrative action that is lawful, reasonable and procedurally fair. Everyone whose rights have been adversely affected by administrative action has the right to be given written reasons.

13.15   Section 33 goes on to enjoin the necessary legislation to give effect to the right which resulted in the enactment of the Promotion of Administrative Justice Act[27] ('PAJA') in 2000. The PAJA is now the primary pathway to judicial review of administrative action in South Africa,[28] although certain administrative action may be reviewable under a particular statute where a provision enables it.

---

[25] Section 28(4).   [26] Section 28(7).   [27] Act 3 of 2000.
[28] C. Hoexter, *Administrative Law in South Africa* (Cape Town: Juta & Co, 2000), p. 114.

Access to information

13.16   The Promotion of Access to Information Act[29] ('PAIA') gives effect
to section 32 of the Constitution which states that 'everyone has
the right of access to any information held by the State; and any
information that is held by another person and that is required
for the exercise or protection of any rights'. In *Trustees, Biowatch
Trust* v. *The Registrar: Genetic Resources*[30] (although PAIA was
not yet operative) the court, within the framework of the constitutional right to information, held that citizens are entitled to
information regarding genetically modified organism ('GMO')
related activities including information relating to (existing and
pending) GMO permits, risk assessment and compliance with
public participation requirements. This right of access to information is affirmed by the provisions in PAIA. Some information,
such as trade secrets, need not be disclosed.[31]

13.17   This is fortified by section 31 of NEMA, titled 'Access to environmental information and the protection of whistle-blowers',
which explicitly provides that no person may be dismissed or
disciplined or otherwise prejudiced or be found liable for disclosing any information if, at the time of disclosure, the person
acted in good faith and reasonably believed that the disclosure
revealed evidence of an environmental risk. In order to be protected, the disclosure must comply with the procedure set out in
section 31.

13.18   The right to obtain information and the protection of 'whistle-
blowers' by PAIA and NEMA affords a potential plaintiff in
climate change litigation an opportunity to obtain documents
that may assist the plaintiff to establish a claim based on climate
change, and provides protection (from dismissal or other disciplinary action) to persons who disclose such information.

---

[29] Act 2 of 2000.
[30] (TPD) 2005 (4) SA 111 (T). Although largely successful in obtaining the information
sought, the Biowatch Trust was saddled with the award of a costs order against them,
which they successfully appealed in *Biowatch Trust* v. *Registrar, Genetic Resources and
Others* 2009 (6) SA 232 (CC) (see (F) Practicalities below).
[31] For the limits on the duty to disclose see for example *Transnet and Another* v. *SA Metal
Machinery Company* 2006 (6) SA 285 (SCA).

Planning for GHG-intensive and energy-related activities

13.19   South Africa has an extensive set of planning laws at national,
          provincial and local spheres of government that directly or
          indirectly have, or potentially have, an impact on climate
          change considerations. At national level these include: the Local
          Government: Municipal Systems Act,[32] which among other
          things provides for Integrated Development Plans ('IDPs') that
          can potentially incorporate climate change considerations; and
          the relatively recent Energy Act,[33] which among other things
          aims to 'ensure effective planning for energy supply, transporta-
          tion and consumption; and [to] contribute to sustainable devel-
          opment of South Africa's economy'.[34] Chapter 5 of NEMA read
          with extensive regulations made under it provides for environ-
          mental assessment,[35] which in theory should take into account
          greenhouse gas emissions in considering development propos-
          als. South Africa also has electricity generation and nuclear-
          related legislation in place at national level.[36] The government has
          recently released a report entitled *Integrated Resource Plan for
          Electricity: 2010 to 2030* which among other things sets out the
          future energy mix between various sources including nuclear,
          renewable energy and coal-based sources.[37]

Atmospheric pollution

13.20   The Preamble to the National Environmental Management:
          Air Quality Act[38] acknowledges that 'atmospheric emissions of
          ozone-depleting substances, greenhouse gases and other sub-
          stances have deleterious effects on the environment both locally
          and globally'. Among the objectives of the Act is to 'give effect to
          section 24(b) of the Constitution [the environmental right quoted
          above] in order to enhance the quality of ambient air for the sake
          of securing an environment that is not harmful to the health and
          well-being of people'.[39]

---

[32] Act 32 of 2000.   [33] Act 34 of 2008.   [34] Section 2(k), (l).
[35] R543 to R 547, *Government Gazette* No. 33306, 18 June 2010.
[36] Electricity Act 41 of 1987; Nuclear Energy Act 46 of 1999; and National Nuclear Energy
      Regulator Act 47 of 1999.
[37] Final Report dated 25 March 2011.
[38] Act 39 of 2004.   [39] Section 2(b).

13.21   The Act requires the establishment of a national framework
         'for achieving the objects of this Act' within two years of this
         section taking effect.[40] A National Framework for Air Quality
         Management was tabled during September 2007 and refers to
         greenhouse gases and climate change amongst other things.[41] No
         person may conduct certain listed activities without an atmos-
         pheric emission licence,[42] and various conditions can be laid
         down in this regard including the requirement that the holder of
         the licence must specify any greenhouse gas emissions that may
         be generated.[43]

13.22   Several cases[44] illustrate the application of the constitutional
         right to an environment that is not harmful in the context of air
         pollution. Although not directly concerned with liability for cli-
         mate change, these decisions may assist the plaintiff to establish
         liability in climate change litigation.

                    Liability in the event of a disaster

13.23   The Disaster Management Act[45] seeks to prevent and reduce the
         risk of disasters (such as those caused by extreme weather phe-
         nomena), and carefully carves out the responsibilities of national,
         provincial and local government in the management of disasters.
         These responsibilities include the establishment of disaster man-
         agement centres. The Act however expressly indemnifies the des-
         ignated Minister, the national, provincial or municipal disaster
         management centres or their employees or other persons exercis-
         ing a duty in terms of the Act from liability for anything done in
         good faith in terms of the Act.[46]

13.24   Section 30 of NEMA also provides for the control of an emer-
         gency incident, described as an unexpected sudden occurrence,

---

[40] Section 7(1).
[41] GN 1138, *Government Gazette* No. 30284, 11 September 2007, para. 2.4.1.
[42] Section 22.   [43] Section 43(1)(l).
[44] See for example *Minister of Health and Welfare* v. *Woodcarb (Pty) Ltd and Another* 1996
     (3) SA 155 (N); *Hichange Investments (Pty) Ltd* v. *Cape Produce Company (Pty) Ltd t/a
     Pelts Produce* 2004 (2) SA 393 (ECD); *Tergniet and Toekoms Action Group and Others*
     v. *Outeniqua Kreosootpale (Pty) Ltd and Others* (23 January 2009) Case No. 10083/2008
     (CPD); and *Nature's Choice Properties (Alrode) (Pty) Ltd* v. *Ekurhuleni Municipality* 2010
     (3) SA 581 (SCA).
[45] Act 57 of 2002.   [46] Section 61.

such as a major emission, and prescribes certain duties which, if not performed by the responsible person, will amount to an offence that may result in a fine or imprisonment on conviction.

13.25   In addition, the National Water Act[47] imposes specific obligations on the town planning authorities to indicate floodlines in township layout plans. The Act provides that no person may establish a township unless the layout plan shows, to the satisfaction of the local authority, the line indicating the maximum level likely to be reached by floodwaters on average once in every one hundred years.[48] It is predicted that plaintiffs will rely on these statutory obligations in bringing actions for property damage such as coastal properties affected by rising sea levels as a result of climate change.

Enforcement mechanisms

13.26   The legislature has crafted an elaborate legal framework to encourage compliance and ultimately enforce environmental laws. Key innovations include the 2003 NEMA amendments which enabled the appointment of environmental management inspectors ('EMIs') (known locally as the 'Green Scorpions'), whose task it is to monitor and enforce compliance with South Africa's environmental laws. EMIs have been granted extensive powers to inspect and seize, to investigate certain activities and to enforce the law through the use of compliance orders.[49] EMIs are likely to play an important role in the near future in 'policing' activities that, in contravention of the law, may ultimately contribute to climate change.

13.27   Although a clear improvement on the prior framework, the current regime is criticised for being 'fragmented': it is said that 'environmental compliance and enforcement mechanisms remain scattered across many different laws, which are in turn administered by an array of national, provincial and local authorities'.[50] As a result 'duplication, confusion, bureaucracy

[47] Act 36 of 1998.   [48] Section 144. See also section 145.
[49] See section 31B–L.
[50] A. Paterson and L. Kotzé (eds.), *Environmental Compliance and Enforcement in South Africa: Legal Perspectives* (Cape Town: Juta, 2009), p. 371.

and inaction continue to frustrate effective ... environmental compliance and enforcement in South Africa'.[51] The current challenge is to harness the opportunities of the extended platforms for enhancing compliance and enforcement and to address the identified weaknesses.

13.28 In line with the constitutionally embedded principles of cooperative government,[52] in the event of a dispute or disagreement between different bodies of government concerning the exercise of a public function that may significantly affect the environment, NEMA provides for any Minister, Member of the (provincial) Executive Council ('MEC') or Municipal Council to refer such a dispute to conciliation. In addition, provision is made for such a dispute to be arbitrated or for an investigation to be instituted.

13.29 The opportunities for a private party, including a civil society organisation, to seek redress from the State for the State's failure to comply with environmental law is much assisted by the provisions of the Constitution and NEMA on the issue of standing to sue (see para. 13.36 below). This opens up possibilities to halt activity that is harmful to the environment or to seek remediation for environmental damage from the State.

13.30 Short of litigation (which may take the form of a common law action or an application to compel an authority to perform a statutory duty), NEMA expressly provides that 'anyone may request the Minister, a MEC or Municipal Council to appoint a facilitator to call and conduct meetings of interested and affected parties with the purpose of reaching agreement to refer a difference or disagreement to conciliation in terms of this Act ...'.[53] This provides an innovative mechanism for interested parties to seek the resolution of disputes about environmental damage and climate change without having to resort to litigation.

13.31 The State enforcement of environmental laws is achieved through both traditional command-and-control mechanisms, such as criminal and administrative sanctions,[54] and alternative

---

[51] *Ibid.*   [52] Chapter 3 of the Constitution.

[53] Section 17(2), NEMA.

[54] See Kidd, 'Chapter 10 – Criminal Measures' in Paterson and Kotzé, *Environmental Compliance and Enforcement in SA*; and Winstanley, 'Chapter 9 – Administrative Measures', *Ibid.*

measures that encourage and reward compliance, such as voluntary compliance and incentive based measures.[55]

13.32   Various criminal sanctions are provided for in the legislative
framework for the protection of the environment, including
innovative sanctions such as compensation orders, forfeiture,
remediation and the revoking of licences.[56] However, establishing criminal liability presents substantial challenges (both in
terms of resources and in terms of law, such as the higher burden
of proof in criminal cases) and it would seem that, in principle,
criminal law mechanisms are intended to be invoked only as a
measure of last resort.

13.33   It should also be noted that a private person may institute
and conduct a private prosecution in respect of 'any breach or
threatened breach of any duty, other than a public duty resting
on an organ of state ... where that duty is concerned with the
protection of the environment and the breach of that duty is an
offence'.[57]

13.34   Numerous administrative measures may serve as effective, and
less expensive, alternatives to the imposition of criminal sanctions. These include measures such as directives, abatement and
compliance notices, and the withdrawal of licences or permits.[58]
In addition, NEMA makes provision for administrative penalties
where an application is made for rectification in the case of the
unlawful commencement of a listed activity without the required
authorisation.[59]

13.35   In summary, enforcement in South Africa falls largely upon the
traditional command-and-control approaches, although the
recent past has seen efforts to complement these with the so-
called voluntary compliance measures, such as self-regulation
codes,[60] and with incentive-based measures, such as tax benefits

---

[55] See Lehmann, 'Chapter 11 – Voluntary Compliance Measures' and Paterson, 'Chapter 12 –
Incentive-based Measures', *Ibid.*
[56] Section 34, NEMA.
[57] Section 33(1), NEMA.
[58] See Winstanley, 'Chapter 9 – Administrative Measures' in Paterson and Kotzé,
Environmental Compliance and Enforcement in SA.
[59] Section 24G(2A), NEMA.
[60] See Lehmann, 'Chapter 11 – Voluntary Compliance Measures' in Paterson and Kotzé,
Environmental Compliance and Enforcement in SA.

and subsidies.[61] The availability of such measures may inform the manner in which a complainant in a climate change dispute seeks redress.

Standing to sue

13.36 Prior to the enactment of the Constitution, a considerable obstacle encountered by persons wishing to enforce and implement environmental laws was the requirement of legal standing to sue.[62] The Constitution has relaxed the standing requirement and now allows concerned citizens or non-governmental agencies to bring actions when the environment is harmed or potentially threatened.[63] This is done by way of section 38 of the Bill of Rights, which confers standing on persons listed in the section to litigate (including the pursuit of class actions)[64] when a right in the Bill of Rights has been infringed or threatened.[65] Plaintiffs may use this provision to enforce their environmental rights.[66] In addition, Part 3 of Chapter 7 of NEMA also includes a provision relating to standing to enforce environmental laws.[67] These

---

[61] See Paterson, 'Chapter 12 – Incentive-based Measures', *Ibid.*

[62] Glazewski, *Environmental Law in SA*, p. 120.

[63] On the role played by NGOs in environmental law litigation generally, see for example *Earthlife Africa (Cape Town)* v. *Director-General, Department of Environmental Affairs and Tourism and Another* 2005 (3) SA 156 (C) and *Biowatch Trust* v. *Registrar, Genetic Resources and Others* 2009 (6) SA 232 (CC).

[64] On class actions generally see *Permanent Secretary, Department of Welfare, Eastern Cape, and Another* v. *Ngxuza and Others* 2001 (4) SA 1184 (SCA).

[65] Section 38 states that '[t]he persons who may approach a court are–
(a) anyone acting in their own interest;
(b) anyone acting on behalf of another person who cannot act in their own name;
(c) anyone acting as a member of, or in the interest of, a group or class of persons;
(d) anyone acting in the public interest; and
(e) an association acting in the interest of its members'.

[66] See for example the discussion on standing to sue in *Wildlife Society of Southern Africa* v. *Minister of Environmental Affairs and Tourism* 1996 (3) SA 1095 (Tk) and in *Minister of Health and Welfare* v. *Woodcarb (Pty) Ltd* 1996 (3) SA 155 (N), although decided under the Interim Constitution.

[67] Section 32 of the NEMA provides that:
'(1) Any person or group of persons may seek appropriate relief in respect of any breach or threatened breach of any provision of this Act ... or of any provision of a specific environmental management Act, or of any other statutory provision concerned with the protection of the environment or the use of natural resources–
(a) in that person's or group of person's [sic] own interest;
(b) in the interest of, or on behalf of, a person who is, for practical reasons, unable to institute such proceedings;

sections empower the State to act on behalf of citizens to enforce their rights when their environmental rights are infringed or threatened, and NGOs to initiate litigation or to join in the plaintiff's action as *amici* (friends of the court) in matters in which they have an interest.[68]

13.37   The increasing concern with the environmental and health effects of decades-long mining activity has resulted in, amongst other things, the formation of environmental public interest law groups such as the Centre for Environmental Rights established during 2010.[69]

Public law remedies

13.38   NEMA, along with the specialised suite of environmental statutes, contains various remedies for those in contravention of their provisions. On conviction of a listed offence, NEMA empowers the court to order an award of damages, compensation or a fine and to order that remedial measures be undertaken.[70] In addition, provision is made for the cancellation of permits[71] and the forfeiture of items[72] on conviction of an offence. Provision is also made for liability of an employer in respect of the conduct of its employees[73] and for the liability of a director where the director has failed to take reasonable steps to prevent the commission of an offence.[74]

13.39   An interesting innovation introduced in 2003 provides for a court to order that a sum of money, up to a quarter of a fine imposed by the court, 'be paid to the person whose evidence led to the conviction or who assisted in bringing the offender to justice'.[75] This provides an incentive for 'bounty hunting' of offenders who unlawfully damage the environment.

(c) in the interest of or on behalf of a group or class of persons whose interests are affected;

(d) in the public interest; and

(e) in the interest of protecting the environment.'

[68] See Feris, Chapter 6 'Environmental Rights and *Locus Standi*' in Paterson and Kotzé, *Environmental Compliance and Enforcement in SA* (see n. 50 above), pp. 148–50.

[69] See www.cer.org.za, accessed on 2 March 2010.

[70] Section 34(3).   [71] Section 34C.   [72] Section 34D.

[73] Section 34(5).   [74] Section 34(7).   [75] Section 34B.

(C) Private law

13.40   At the heart of issues around liability for climate change is the South African law of delict,[76] which 'is primarily concerned with the circumstances in which one person can claim compensation from another for harm that has been suffered'.[77] The genealogy of the South African law of delict 'stretches from the Twelve Tables in Roman Law to the Bill of Rights in our Constitution'.[78]

13.41   While in certain jurisdictions (e.g. the English legal system) a number of separate delicts (or torts) are recognised, the approach in South Africa is one of general principles or requirements that determine delictual liability.

13.42   The starting point is that: '*damage (harm) rests where it falls*, that is, each person must bear the damage he suffers (*res perit domino*)'.[79] In order to hold somebody else liable for damage in the law of delict the aggrieved party must prove the five elements of a delict, namely: an act or omission; wrongfulness; fault; causation; and harm (loss).

(1) Act or omission (conduct)

13.43   'In order to constitute a delict, one person … must have caused damage or harm to another person … by means of an *act* or *conduct*.'[80] Generally this requires a positive act or an omission (the failure to act).

13.44   Where the conduct is an omission, which is likely to be the case in many instances of damage caused by a failure to act on climate

---

[76] Referred to as the Law of Tort in English common law systems (see (C) Private law in Ch. 17). This section draws on a report titled *The Law of Delict and Climate Change: Legal Implications for the City Council of Cape Town* (February 2011), by Collier and Glazewski.

[77] Loubser and Midgley (eds.), *The Law of Delict in South Africa* (Oxford University Press, 2009), p. 4.

[78] *Ibid*. The pillars of the law of delict have been described as the *actio legis Aquiliae* (an action of patrimonial damage to person or property), the *actio iniuriarum* (an action for *solatium* for injury to personality), and the action for pain and suffering (for impairment of bodily or physical-mental integrity). Neethling and Potgieter, *Neethling, Potgieter, Visser: Law of Delict* (Durban: LexisNexis, 2010), p. 5.

[79] Neethling and Potgieter, *Law of Delict*, p. 3.

[80] *Ibid*., p. 25.

change, the courts are more reluctant to find the defendant liable
for the resultant harm because of the potential of indeterminate
liability and the plaintiff may be required to establish that the
defendant had a legal duty (or 'duty of care' as it is commonly
known in the English law of tort) to prevent harm. This is an
aspect of wrongfulness, which is core to establishing delictual
liability.

(2)   Wrongfulness

13.45   Wrongfulness is concerned with whether the social, economic
and other costs associated with imposing liability can be justified,
or, stated differently, whether it is reasonable to impose liability.[81]
For example, in cases of pure economic loss, if a multiplicity of
claims is likely to result if liability is imposed or there is a possibility that the plaintiff could incur indeterminate liability, the
court is unlikely to find the defendant liable.[82] The enquiry into
wrongfulness might also focus on the infringement of a right or
the breach of a duty, particularly in the case of an omission.

13.46   The complexities of the wrongfulness enquiry in the context of
environmental damage, particularly where the damage is caused
by the user of a product as opposed to the manufacturer, are illustrated in *Natal Fresh Produce Growers' Association and Others
v. Agroserve (Pty) Ltd and Others*[83] where the plaintiff sought an
interdict that would prohibit the defendants from manufacturing
and distributing (duly registered) hormonal herbicides in South
Africa. These herbicides are transported through water and air and
are deposited on, and cause damage to, fresh produce (on the evidence, specifically in the Tala Valley area in KwaZulu Natal). The
court was of the view that the manufacture of the herbicides was
not rendered unlawful merely because the use of the herbicides by
certain third parties resulted in damage to the plaintiffs. The court
upheld an exception to the plaintiff's plea, maintaining that:

> [i]t may be that the use [of the herbicides] cannot take place with-
> out the manufacture and distribution, so that the manufacture and

---

[81] Du Bois *et al.*, *Wille's Principles of South African Law* (Cape Town: Juta Law, 2007),
pp. 1098–9.
[82] *Ibid.*, p. 1106.   [83] 1990 (4) SA 749 (N).

distribution can be regarded as a *causa sine qua non* of the use, but that is not sufficient to saddle the manufacturers with legal responsibility of the conduct of the users.[84]

13.47   It should be noted however that the decision in *Natal Fresh Produce Growers' Association and Others* v. *Agroserve (Pty) Ltd and Others* precedes the adoption of the Constitution and NEMA. Today the outcome may well have been different in light of the environmental right and NEMA's implementation of the preventive, polluter pays and precautionary principles.

13.48   In exercising its discretion in deciding whether or not conduct is wrongful, the court is informed by notions of public policy and the 'legal convictions of the community'. Public policy is informed by the spirit, purport and objects of the Bill of Rights.[85] In the context of damage (injury, loss of life or damage to property) caused by climate change, the constitutional rights most likely to be invoked include rights relating to bodily integrity, property and to the environment. Thus, in *Hichange Investments (Pty) Ltd* v. *Cape Produce Co. (Pty) Ltd t/a Pelts Products*,[86] in a consideration as to what is 'significant' pollution, which, if found to exist, would afford the plaintiff a particular cause of action, the court expressed the view that 'in the light of the constitutional right a person has to an environment conducive to health and well-being, I agree with the view expressed in Glazewski in *Environmental Law in South Africa* … that the threshold level of significance will not be particularly high'.[87]

13.49   Whether or not the defendant will be liable for harm caused by omissions, by negligent misstatements,[88] and harm which takes the form of pure economic loss[89] will often depend on whether the plaintiff is able to prove wrongfulness. In other words, harm caused in these cases is generally not prima facie wrongful.

---

[84] At 755–6.

[85] Section 39(2) of the Constitution. See the decision in *Carmichele* v. *Minister of Safety and Security* 2001 (4) SA 938 (CC). See also Du Bois *et al.*, *Wille's Principles of SA Law*, p. 1101.

[86] 2004 (2) SA 393 (E).   [87] At 414–5.

[88] In this case the court will consider factors such as the existence of a contractual or similar relationship between the parties.

[89] Although such claims were largely denied prior to 1979, this position has been relaxed as a result of the decision in *Administrateur, Natal* v. *Trust Bank van Afrika Bpk* 1979 (3) SA 824 (A).

13.50   To be liable in the case of an omission, which is a likely scenario in the context of climate change, the court, in addition to considering policy issues such as the possibility of indeterminate liability, generally requires the existence of some other factor which indicates that the harm is actionable.[90] These factors include:[91]

- preceding positive conduct that has created a new source of danger;[92]
- control of a dangerous thing or situation;[93]
- existence of a special relationship between the parties;[94]
- an obligation to act in terms of common law or statute – consider for example the duty of care imposed by section 28 of NEMA (see para. 13.10 above) which may well be invoked in the context of climate change litigation; useful to the plaintiff in such a case is the principle that an act or omission in violation of a statutory provision is prima facie wrongful;[95]
- obligations which arise out of a particular office. [96]

---

[90]   In other words, the defendant will be liable in respect of an omission where there is a legal duty in the circumstances to act. *Minister van Polisie* v. *Ewels* 1975 (3) SA 590 (A).

[91]   See Du Bois *et al.*, *Wille's Principles of SA Law*, pp. 1113–7; Neethling and Potgieter, *Law of Delict*, pp. 58–71; and Loubser and Midgley, *The Law of Delict in SA*, pp. 217–9.

[92]   Before the (minority) decision in *Silva's Fishing Corporation (Pty) Ltd* v. *Maweza* 1957 (2) SA 256 (A), prior conduct was an 'indispensable' requirement for liability for omissions. The courts now accept that, in the absence of prior conduct, other factors may nonetheless be sufficient to establish liability. Neethling and Potgieter, *Law of Delict*, pp. 58–9.

[93]   Visser refers to the classic example where 'a landowner or occupier of rural land neglects to control a fire not started by him or herself and the fire then spreads and causes damage on a neighbouring property' (*Minister of Forestry* v. *Quathlamba (Pty) Ltd* 1973 (3) SA 69 (A)), in Du Bois *et al.*, *Wille's Principles of SA Law*, p. 1114.

[94]   In *Silva's Fishing Corporation (Pty) Ltd* v. *Maweza* 1957 (2) SA 256 (A) the relationship involved a boat owner and the crew that was contracted to operate the boat. Neethling and Potgieter, *Law of Delict*, p. 69.

[95]   *Ibid.*, p. 76.

[96]   *Ibid.*, p. 70. Some authors point out that there is some authority that delictual liability may arise where the defendant has created an impression or an expectation which the plaintiff may reasonably rely on. The idea is that: '[w]here one party acts in reasonable reliance on the impression created by another party that the latter will protect the person or property of the former, a legal duty rests upon the party creating the impression to prevent prejudice to the party acting in reliance on that impression'. As translated from Neethling and Potgieter, 'Deliktuele aanspreeklikheid weens 'n late: 'n nuwe riglyn vir die regsplig om positief op te tree?', *Tydskrif vir die Suid-Afrikaanse Reg*, 4 (1990), 763 at 766. See also *Compass Motors Industries (Pty) Ltd* v. *Callguard (Pty) Ltd* 1990 (2) SA 520 (W). However this is not a well-tested and established principle of the South African law of delict.

13.51　In some cases several factors may be at issue.[97] It is also recognised that 'the situations in which there will be liability for omissions are constantly evolving'[98] and that constitutional values have an important role to play in this regard.

13.52　In determining wrongfulness for an omission, a distinction is made between individuals and public bodies, and 'the threshold at which the harm caused by the omissions of public bodies will be held to be wrongful' is lower than that for individuals.[99]

13.53　Constitution values and imperatives play an important role in determining liability for omissions by public bodies. In *Van Duivenboden*[100] and *Carmichele*[101] the constitutionally embedded notion of public accountability was raised as an aspect of wrongfulness. In certain circumstances where a public authority is involved there may be a constitutional duty to act, making *accountability* (the ability to justify one's actions) a pivotal enquiry when determining liability of public authorities.[102]

13.54　The law recognises various defences excluding wrongfulness, such as authority and consent to a harmful act, which may be raised in the context of climate change litigation.

(3)　Fault (intention/negligence)

13.55　As a general rule, fault (either intention (*dolus*) or negligence (*culpa*)) is required for delictual liability.[103]

13.56　Intention may take one of three forms: *dolus directus* where the wrongdoer intends the harmful consequence of his conduct;

---

[97] The decision in *Minister van Polisie* v. *Ewels* 1975 (3) SA 590 (A) illustrates this. The case involved the assault of an ordinary citizen in a police station by a policeman not on duty, in the presence of other policemen who failed to prevent the assault. Neethling indicates that the duty to prevent the assault 'may be deduced from the statutory duty to prevent crime, from the special relationship between policeman and citizen, as well as from the public office occupied by the policemen'. Neethling and Potgieter, *Law of Delict*, p. 72.

[98] Du Bois *et al.*, *Wille's Principles of SA Law*, p. 1114 (footnotes omitted).

[99] *Ibid.*, p. 1113.

[100] *Minister of Safety and Security* v. *Van Duivenboden* 2002 (6) SA 431 (SCA).

[101] 2001 (1) SA 489 (SCA) and the 2001 (4) SA 938 (CC) decisions.

[102] Du Bois *et al.*, *Wille's Principles of SA Law*, p. 1115.

[103] Neethling and Potgieter, *Law of Delict*, p.123. South African law recognises limited instances of strict liability (see *ibid.*, pp. 357–75).

dolus indirectus where the wrongdoer intends one unlawful consequence, knowing that this will result in additional consequences and the aggrieved party is seeking compensation for harm caused by the additional consequences; and *dolus eventualis* where the wrongdoer, while pursuing a particular consequence, does not desire, but does foresee the possibility, of a further consequence causing harm for which the aggrieved party seeks compensation.[104]

13.57　In the absence of an intention to cause harm, the defendant may still be liable if the defendant acted *negligently*. The formula for *negligence* is stated in *Kruger* v. *Coetzee*:[105]
'For the purposes of liability *culpa* arises if–
(a) a *diligens paterfamilias* [a reasonable person] in the position of the defendant–
　(i) would foresee the reasonable possibility of his conduct injuring another in his person or property and causing him patrimonial loss; and
　(ii) would take reasonable steps to guard against such occurrence; and
(b) the defendant failed to take such steps.'[106]

13.58　The reasonable person 'is not an exceptionally gifted, careful or developed person; neither is he underdeveloped, nor someone who recklessly takes chances or who has no prudence'.[107] Where the wrongdoer causes harm while engaged in an activity that requires a certain level of expertise (e.g. medical surgery) the test for negligence is that of the reasonable expert (e.g. the reasonable surgeon).[108] Grossman makes the point that '[a]t the level of expert knowledge, potential climate change defendants have likely known of the climate-changing risks of their products for quite some time'.[109]

13.59　Once foreseeability has been established, the question arises 'whether the reasonable person would have taken steps to

[104] *Ibid.*, pp. 127–8; Du Bois *et al.*, *Wille's Principles of SA Law*, p. 1129; and Loubser and Midgley, *The Law of Delict in SA*, pp. 106–7.
[105] 1966 (2) SA 428 (A).　　[106] At 430.
[107] Neethling and Potgieter, *Law of Delict*, p. 135.　　[108] *Ibid.*, p.139.
[109] David A. Grossman, 'Warming Up to a Not-So-Radical Idea: Tort-based Climate Change Litigation', *Columbia Journal of Environmental Law*, 28(1) (2008), at 48 (original footnotes omitted).

prevent the damage'.[110] This entails a number of considerations, including: the seriousness of the damage that may materialise as a result of the defendant's conduct; the purpose or utility of the defendant's conduct; and the cost of taking precautionary measures.[111]

13.60   Liability for negligence may be limited through contractual and statutory mechanisms. Mechanisms to limit liability will however be interpreted restrictively and will be subject to constitutional scrutiny.

13.61   In the context of climate change litigation, it is likely that most defendants have some knowledge of the possible negative consequences that may arise from their actions although they may not have the direct intention to cause harm through global warming. Intention in the form of *dolus indirectus* or *dolus eventualis* may therefore be at issue, or if not *dolus*, then negligence.

(4)   Damage

13.62   The law of delict aims to compensate persons who have suffered loss as a result of damage caused by the defendant. Damage is described as '… the detrimental impact upon any patrimonial or personality interest deemed worthy of protection by the law'.[112]

13.63   Determining patrimonial loss as a result of damage to property can be a relatively easy exercise achieved by 'comparing the market value of the property before it was damaged to the market value thereafter'.[113]

13.64   In the context of climate change 'property damages could include lost coastal land, buildings, structures, infrastructures, and agriculture'.[114] It has also been observed that sea level rise plaintiffs may have a claim 'based on the *present* costs of *preventing* future harms'.[115] This would include the cost of building sea walls, raising land and relocating structures.[116]

---

[110]   Neethling and Potgieter, *Law of Delict*, p. 145.
[111]   *Ibid.*, pp. 146–7.   [112]   *Ibid.*, p. 212.
[113]   Du Bois *et al.*, *Wille's Principles of SA Law*, p. 1136 (footnotes omitted).
[114]   Grossman, 'Tort-based Climate Change Litigation', at 16.
[115]   Grossman, 'Tort-based Climate Change Litigation', at 17.
[116]   *Ibid.*, at 18.

13.65   As a general principle, an aggrieved party may not claim for loss
         which he or she could reasonably have prevented. Furthermore,
         where harm has resulted from a multitude of causes, the law pro-
         vides for the apportionment of damages. It may also happen that
         the plaintiff has contributed to the loss suffered. Such contribu-
         tory negligence is governed by the Apportionment of Damages
         Act,[117] section 1(1)(a) which states that where any person suf-
         fers damages that are partly his own fault and partly the fault of
         another person, the damages claim shall be reduced by the court
         to such extent as the court may deem just and equitable having
         regard to the degree in which the claimant was at fault in relation
         to the damage.

13.66   Where potential harm is envisaged, the interdict (see para. 13.81
         below) provides a useful remedy for a plaintiff seeking to prevent
         such harm from materialising.

                            (5)   Causation

13.67   The defendant must have caused the harm for which the plaintiff
         seeks redress. Generally both 'factual' and 'legal' causation are
         required in order to establish liability.

13.68   The method for determining factual causation is the *conditio sine
         qua non* test – the 'but for' test, which 'entails that one mentally
         eliminates the wrongful conduct which one suspects was the
         cause of the harm and that one then asks what probably would
         have happened if lawful conduct had been substituted for the
         conduct which had been eliminated'.[118]

13.69   Linking factual causation to a particular defendant in the case of
         harm caused by climate change, which is the result of a multitude
         of factors (many greenhouse gas emitters), does present a chal-
         lenge. It has been said however that 'it need be established only
         that the defendant's conduct was *one* of the antecedents which
         jointly amount to the cause of the harm, not that it was the only
         or even the main cause of the harm'.[119] Furthermore, '[a] plaintiff
         is not required to establish the causal link with certainty, but only

[117]   Act 34 of 1956.
[118]   Du Bois *et al.*, *Wille's Principles of SA Law*, p. 1117 (footnotes omitted).
[119]   *Ibid.*, p. 1118.

to establish that the wrongful conduct was probably a cause of the loss, which calls for a sensible retrospective analysis of what would probably have occurred, based upon the evidence and what can be expected to occur in the ordinary course of human affairs rather than an exercise in metaphysics'.[120]

13.70　Decisions about factual causation turn on an enquiry of probabilities.[121] In other words if a 'greater than 50 per cent chance' that the conduct caused the harm is established, the requirement for causation is met and the fact that there are a multitude of causes is a factor that will then be taken into account in assessing the damages to be awarded to the plaintiff.[122]

13.71　An argument is made that 'the studies and models such as those the IPCC relied upon provide a solid basis for arguing that a general causal link exists between greenhouse gas emissions, climate change, and effects such as sea-level rise, thawing permafrost, and melting sea ice – all probably beyond the "more likely than not" standard used in the legal arena'.[123] The difficulty however, as stated above, is the multiple sources of greenhouse gas emissions. As a result, causation, in its traditional formulation, is likely to constitute a stumbling block in establishing liability for climate change. This is confirmed in Chapter 17 on English law, which considers the use, such as has occurred in the case of harm caused by exposure to asbestos from different sources, of the notion of 'material increase in risk' as a possible alternative approach to causation. It would appear too that the South African courts may be persuaded to deviate from the *conditio sine qua non* test where it is appropriate to do so.[124]

13.72　The notion of legal causation entails a normative enquiry on the premise that it would be unfair if the defendant were required to compensate the plaintiff for 'the endless chain of harmful consequences which his act may have caused'.[125] The defendant will therefore not be liable for damages that are too remote.

---

[120] Nugent JA in *Minister of Safety and Security* v. *Van Duivenboden* 2002 6 SA 431 (SCA) at 449, cited in Du Bois *et al.*, *Wille's Principles of SA Law*, p. 1118.
[121] *Ibid.*, p. 1120.　[122] *Ibid.*
[123] Grossman, 'Tort-based Climate Change Litigation', at 23.
[124] See *Minister of Safety and Security* v. *Van Duivenboden* 2002 6 SA 431 (SCA) and the discussion in Du Bois *et al.*, *Wille's Principles of SA Law*, pp. 1118–20.
[125] Neethling and Potgieter, *Law of Delict*, p. 187.

Consider for example the unsuccessful plaintiff's claim in the *Natal Fresh Produce Grower's Association* case (see para 13.46 above).[126]

13.73   In determining legal causation, South African courts have adopted a flexible approach which entails weighing up various factors, 'such as reasonable foreseeability, directness, the absence or presence of a *novus actus interveniens*, legal policy, reasonability, fairness and justice'.[127]

13.74   As mentioned earlier, the South African approach to delictual liability is one of general principles rather than separate delicts or torts, although over time certain principles have crystallised around common forms of liability. In the context of climate change liability, product liability and nuisance are two such forms worthy of further reflection.

Product liability

13.75   Harm caused by a defective product is generally presumed to be wrongful. Although strict liability for defective products was rejected by the courts,[128] this is likely to change now that the Consumer Protection Act ('CPA'),[129] which introduces a form of strict liability and became operative in March 2011, is in force.

13.76   In the context of climate change, the notion of product liability claims would likely focus on the liability for harm caused by the manufacturers (rather than users) of products that emit greenhouse gases. These include car manufacturers and utilities such as electricity suppliers who use fossil fuels in electricity generation. The difficulty which plaintiffs would face include the elements of wrongfulness and causation as the decision in the *Natal Fresh Produce Growers' Association* case[130] (see paras. 13.46 and 13.72 above) illustrates.

---

[126] In this case however the decision turned on whether or not the defendant's conduct could be regarded as wrongful.

[127] *OK Bazaars (1929) Ltd* v. *Standard Bank of South Africa Ltd* 2002 (3) SA 688 (SCA), cited in Du Bois *et al.*, *Wille's Principles of SA Law*, p. 1130.

[128] See *Wagener* v. *Pharmacare Ltd; Cuttings* v. *Pharmacare* 2003 (4) SA 285 (SCA).

[129] Act 68 of 2008.   [130] 1990 (4) SA 749 (N).

13.77   The CPA may assist the plaintiff in that it introduces a statutory
        form of liability for harmful products.[131] The CPA establishes
        liability for damage caused by goods. Producers, importers, dis-
        tributors or retailers of any goods are each liable for any harm
        caused.

Nuisance and neighbour law

13.78   Cases of nuisance and neighbour law may give rise to an inter-
        play of principles of property law and the law of delict. Nuisance
        typically involves 'forms of *unreasonable* use of land by one
        neighbour at the expense of another'.[132] Nuisance claims, using
        the principles of delict, are however not restricted to neighbours,
        and are generally concerned with an act or omission that incon-
        veniences another's right of use and enjoyment.[133]

13.79   The principle *sic utere tuo ut alienum non laedas* underpins
        neighbour law and means that one should only use one's prop-
        erty so that it does not harm others. For example, a plaintiff could
        sue a car manufacturer or a State-owned enterprise for harm to
        his property if such an enterprise utilises its property unrea-
        sonably and wrongfully.[134] A public nuisance concerns an act or
        omission that offends, threatens or inconveniences the public at
        large.[135] Remedies for both public and private nuisance claims
        may include damages and/or an interdict.

Private law remedies

13.80   In private law proceedings, the typical remedies which a plaintiff
        might seek as a result of unlawful harm to person or property are
        damages (see (4) Damage above) and/or an interdict.

13.81   An interdict may take the form of either a mandatory or a pro-
        hibitory interdict, which may be either interim or final. The

---

[131]   Cf. sections 55, 56, 60 and 61 of the Act.
[132]   Neethling and Potgieter, *Law of Delict*, p. 121 (original footnote omitted).
[133]   See for example *Verstappen* v. *Port Edward Town Board* 1994 (3) SA 569 (D) and *Minister of Health and Welfare* v. *Woodcarb (Pty) Ltd* 1996 (3) SA 155 (N).
[134]   Neethling and Potgieter, *Law of Delict*, pp. 117–24.
[135]   See *Diepsloot Residents' and Landowners' Association and Another* v. *Administrator, Transvaal* 1994 (3) SA 336 (A).

requirements that entitle the applicant to seek a final interdict are '(a) a clear right; (b) an injury actually committed or reasonably apprehended; and (c) the absence of similar protection by any other ordinary remedy'.[136] The court's discretion whether or not to award a final interdict is limited and will depend on whether or not an alternative remedy (for example damages) is adequate.[137]

13.82   While there is to date no climate change litigation per se on which to comment, the discussion clearly demonstrates the evolving nature of the private law principles which renders the law capable of adapting to new scenarios and threats of harm. There are concerns, however, about whether the principles are capable of adapting quickly and adequately enough. It has been said that 'the principal objections to the law of delict as an effective tool in environmental compliance relate to problems of proof and the fact that the essential elements of the Aquilian action sit uncomfortably in context of environmental pollution or degradation'.[138]

(D)   Other law

The protection of human rights

13.83   In addition to an environmental clause, the Bill of Rights provides for the right to life,[139] and the right to healthcare, food and water, and social security in certain circumstances.[140] These rights may ultimately impose a burden on the State if they are successfully invoked in circumstances of hardship brought about by the effects of climate change.

13.84   The Bill of Rights also recognises, in section 25, that '[n]o one may be deprived of property except in terms of law ... and no law may permit arbitrary deprivation of property'. Furthermore, the section provides that '[p]roperty may be expropriated only in terms of law ... (a) for a public purpose or in the public interest; and (b) subject to compensation ...'. As a result, the State, should

---

[136] *Setlogelo* v. *Setlogelo* 1914 AD 221 at 227.
[137] Harms, *Civil Procedure in the Superior Courts* (Durban: LexisNexis, 2010), para. A5.2 ('Interdicts').
[138] Summers, 'Chapter 13 – Common-Law Remedies for Environmental Protection' in Paterson and Kotzé, *Environmental Compliance and Enforcement in SA*, p. 358.
[139] Section 11.   [140] Section 27.

it seek to regulate (restrict) property rights in order to mitigate the hazards of climate change, will, if challenged, be required to demonstrate that any deprivation of property is not arbitrary. In the event that a deprivation of property amounts to an expropriation, the State will also be required to compensate for the loss of property.[141]

The public trust doctrine in South African law

13.85　In South Africa the notion of *public trust* is explicitly used in statutes with reference to water,[142] minerals[143] and the environment.[144] In so far as the environment is concerned, NEMA provides that 'the environment is held in public trust for the people, the beneficial use of environmental resources must serve the public interest and the environment must be protected as the people's common heritage'.[145]

13.86　The public trust doctrine, in effect, places a responsibility on the State to regulate harmful behaviour that may contribute to climate change.

(E)　Regional arrangements and 'soft' law

13.87　South Africa is a party to the 1992 Treaty of the Southern Development Community ('SADC'), a regional economic cooperation agreement. Although the Treaty does not refer specifically to climate change, among its objectives are that the fifteen member countries '… coordinate, harmonise, and rationalise their policies and strategies for sustainable development in all areas of human endeavour…',[146] and agree to cooperate in areas of natural resources and environment.[147] In the same vein South Africa has been an active participant in the New Partnership for Africa's

---

[141] On the use of the terms 'deprivation' and 'expropriation', see *First National Bank of SA Ltd t/a Wesbank* v. *Commissioner, South African Revenue Service; First National Bank of SA Ltd t/a Wesbank* v. *Minister of Finance* 2002 (4) SA 768 (CC) at para. [57]; and see generally the discussion in A. J. van der Walt, *Constitutional Property Law* (Cape Town: Juta Law, 2005), pp. 180–91.

[142] See section 3 of the National Water Act 36 of 1998.

[143] See the Preamble to the Mineral and Petroleum Resources Development Act 28 of 2002.

[144] See section 2(4)(*o*) of the National Environmental Management Act 107 of 1998.

[145] Section 2(4)(*o*).　　[146] Preamble.　　[147] Art 21(3)(e).

Development ('NEPAD'), which includes an environmental component. This initiative has been carried forward by the African Ministerial Conference on the Environment ('AMCEN') with the support of the African Union ('AU'). As regards climate change, South Africa has been at the forefront of leading the African agenda through NEPAD in climate change negotiations including the various Conferences of the Parties (COPs).

(F)   Practicalities

13.88   The South African legal system provides a comprehensive framework for potential climate change litigants to obtain relevant environmental information, with protection for whistleblowers, and to pursue a variety of remedies in a number of fora.

13.89   On the question of jurisdiction, section 19 of the Supreme Court Act[148] empowers a court to take jurisdiction over persons residing within a particular area and over causes of action arising within that area. A plaintiff seeking recourse in the South African courts where the defendant does not reside in South Africa is required to attach property to confirm jurisdiction. This may present practical difficulties for the plaintiff. In addition, in terms of the Prescription Act,[149] most debts prescribe after a lapse of only three years, requiring legal action to be commenced soon after the damage is suffered.

13.90   Public interest litigation received a major boost when the decision in *Biowatch Trust* v. *Registrar, Genetic Resources, and Others*[150] was handed down by the Constitutional Court. Although Biowatch, an environmental watchdog, had been successful in the court a quo in an application for access to certain information on genetically modified organisms, the Court had made an adverse costs award against Biowatch on the basis of 'inept requests for information'. The Constitutional Court, however, found that the action of the High Court 'was demonstrably inappropriate on the facts, and unduly chilling to constitutional litigation in its consequences'.[151] The Court reversed the decision of the High Court

---

[148] Act 59 of 1959.   [149] Act 68 of 1969.
[150] 2009 (6) SA 232 (CC).   [151] At para. [60].

and ordered the relevant governmental authorities to pay the costs incurred by Biowatch.

(G)   Conclusion

13.91   The above survey shows that South Africa has in place a broad array of laws which apply to the climate change phenomenon. These are by and large of an anticipatory and regulatory nature in that the legislature has put in place an imposing body of statutes and regulations to prevent activities which directly or indirectly contribute to climate change. These range from statutes regulating exploitation of natural resources, to planning laws, to laws combating various forms of waste generation and pollution control.

13.92   As regards potential liability for the climate change phenomena, the point of departure for a plaintiff will be the delictual principles outlined above. While the fault requirement may be met, we suggest that any plaintiff may be hard pressed to overcome the other requirements, in particular causation. Nevertheless the increasing array of public laws and norms may result in the bar being lowered in this regard.

13.93   It is suggested that before we see litigation around the effects of climate change in South Africa, we are more likely to see the courts applying their minds to more immediate environmental problems such as the phenomenon of acid mine drainage, the consequences of which are coming to the fore.

Europe and Eurasia

14

European Union Law

LUDWIG KRÄMER

(A) Introduction

The European Union legal system

14.01　The European Union ('EU') is a regional integration organisation consisting at present of twenty-seven European Member States that have transferred part of their sovereignty to the EU. The EU is based on international treaties – the Treaty on European Union ('TEU') and the Treaty on the Functioning of the European Union ('TFEU') – and its power to act is laid down in the various provisions of these treaties; there is no 'common law' applicable to it. In this regard, the EU is similar to a civil law country.

14.02　A number of specific features distinguish the EU from traditional international organisations. First, the TEU and TFEU address not only the relations between the Member States and the EU institutions, but also establish rights and obligations for individuals. Second, though legislative decisions in climate change matters are taken by majority vote in the European Parliament – whose members are directly elected – and the Council, which consists of the governments of the twenty-seven Member States, the adoption of legislation on climate change is only possible on the basis of a proposal by the European Commission. The Commission oversees the application of EU law in the Member States, and has the duty to act in the general interest of the EU rather than in the interest of the individual Member States.

14.03　The Court of Justice of the EU, consisting of a General Court ('GC') (formerly the Court of First Instance) and the European Court of Justice ('ECJ'), has the duty to ensure the correct application of EU law. Its judgments are binding on all public authorities, both at EU and at Member State level. When a question of EU law becomes relevant in a case before a national court, that court may ask the European Court for an interpretation, and where there is no judicial remedy under national law against a decision of the national court, that court is obliged to make a request to the ECJ for an interpretation of the relevant EU law provision.

14.04   The competence to adopt environmental legislation, including legislation on climate change, is shared between the EU and the Member States. When EU legislation is adopted, Member States are not only obliged to implement it, but they must not adopt provisions or practices that contradict EU provisions, though in the case of legislation based in the environmental provisions of the TFEU they may maintain or introduce more stringent national provisions than those provided by the European rules.

Constitutional/principal environmental/ human rights law

14.05   The TEU lays down as objectives of the EU, among others, 'sustainable development' and 'a high level of protection and improvement of the quality of the environment'.[1] The TFEU sets out that '[e]nvironmental protection requirements must be integrated into the definition and implementation of the Union policies and activities, in particular with a view to promoting sustainable development'.[2] Articles 191–193 TFEU, which specifically address environmental policy, state explicitly that the EU's environmental policy shall contribute to 'combating climate change'.[3]

14.06   The EU is not yet a member of the European Convention on Human Rights and Fundamental Freedoms of 1950, but its accession is now required under Article 6(4) TEU, which states that the provisions of the Convention 'shall constitute general principles of the Union's law'. In 2000, the EU adopted a separate Charter on Fundamental Rights,[4] which now has the same legal value as the EU Treaties, though in the case of the United Kingdom and Poland, a Protocol to the Lisbon Treaty states that the Charter does not create justiciable rights in those countries except in so far as they have created such rights under national law.

---

[1] Article 3(3), TEU.   [2] Article 11, TFEU.
[3] Article 191(4), TFEU .   [4] OJ, C 364, 18.12.2000, p. 1.

14.07   There is no comprehensive EU climate change legislation. The EU has signed and ratified the Kyoto Protocol, which imposes a reduction by 2012 of 8 per cent of the EU's greenhouse gas ('GHG') emissions from 1990 levels. At the time, the EU agreed to an internal, legally binding 'burden-sharing'[5] system, which provided for differentiated obligations for the – at that time fifteen – Member States.[6] Another binding burden-sharing agreement was decided in 2009 among the now twenty-seven Member States,[7] which aimed at reducing the EU's GHG emissions by 20 per cent by the year 2020, compared to 2005 levels.[8]

Trading with emission allowances

14.08   The main EU instrument to address the reduction of the emission of GHGs is Directive 2003/87[9] establishing a scheme for GHG emission allowance trading (the 'EU ETS').[10] The Directive provides larger industrial installations with tradable allowances for the emission of carbon dioxide (CO_2). When an installation does not require the use of all the allowances it has obtained, it can sell them; by the same token, when its emissions are likely to emit more CO_2 than its allowances levels permit, it can buy

---

[5] Council Decision 2002/358/EC of 25 April 2002 concerning the approval, on behalf of the European Community, of the Kyoto Protocol to the United Nations Framework Convention on Climate Change and the joint fulfillment of commitments thereunder, OJ L 130, 15.5.2002, pp. 1–3.

[6] The reduction/increase percentages were fixed as follows: Belgium –7.5%; Denmark –21%; Germany –21%; Ireland +13%; Greece +25%; Spain +15%; France 0%; Italy –6.6%; Luxembourg: –28%; Netherlands: –6%; Austria: –13%; Portugal: +27%; Finland: 0%; Sweden: +4%; United Kingdom –12.5%.

[7] Decision 406/2009/EC, of 23 April 2009 on the effort of Member States to reduce their greenhouse gas emissions to meet the Community's greenhouse gas emission reduction commitments up to 2020, OJ L 140, 5.6.2009, pp. 136–48.

[8] The reduction/increase percentages were fixed as follows: Belgium –15%; Bulgaria +20%; Czech Republic +9%; Denmark –20%; Germany –14%; Estonia +11%; Ireland –20%; Greece –4%; Spain –10%; France –14%; Italy –13%; Cyprus –5%; Latvia +17%; Lithuania +15%; Luxembourg –20%; Hungary +10%; Malta +10%; Netherlands –16%; Austria –16%; Poland +1%; Portugal +1%; Romania +19%; Slovenia +4%; Slovakia +13%; Finland –16%; Sweden –17%; United Kingdom –16%.

[9] A Directive is a legally binding instrument, addressed to EU Member States. It obliges them as to the result to be achieved, but leaves to the national authorities the choice of form and methods (Article 288 TFEU).

[10] Directive 2003/87/EC of 13 October 2003 establishing a scheme for greenhouse gas emission allowance trading within the Community and amending Council Directive 96/61/EC, OJ L 275, 25.10.2003, pp. 32–46.

allowances on the market. Installations which participate in the trading system need not respect the requirement of using the best available techniques for limiting their CO_2 emissions. However, Member States may be able to impose national CO_2 performance standards on installations even though they are covered by the emissions trading Directive.[11] The distribution of allowances follows national allocation plans that must be established by the Member States and approved by the Commission.

14.09   This Directive has been amended and strengthened several times, most recently to include aviation activities in the EU ETS;[12] and as of 2013, the total number of EU emission trading allowances will be reduced by 1.74 per cent each year.[13] Furthermore, the percentage of allowances to be auctioned will increase from 2013. Whilst in the energy sector all allocation will be auctioned from 2013, the percentage of allowances to be auctioned will vary from sector to sector.

Alternative energies

14.10   Directive 2009/28, which has replaced earlier EU legislation, aims to ensure that, by 2020, at least 20 per cent of total energy consumption in the EU will stem from renewable energy sources.[14] To that end, each Member State is to reach a specific percentage level of energy consumption from renewable

---

[11] Directive 2010/75/EU of 24 November 2010 on Industrial Emissions repeats the formulation in the Integrated Pollution Prevention and Control (IPPC) Directive that where emissions of greenhouse gases covered by the emissions trading regime are involved, a permit may not include emission limit values for direct emissions of greenhouse gases unless necessary to prevent significant local pollution (Article 9). But Preamble 10 then provides that 'In accordance with Article 193 of the Treaty on the Functioning of the European Union (TFEU), this Directive does not prevent Member States from maintaining or introducing more stringent protective measures, for example greenhouse gas emission requirements, provided that such measures are compatible with the Treaties and the Commission has been notified.'

[12] Directive 2008/101/EC of 19 November 2008 amending Directive 2003/87/EC so as to include aviation activities in the scheme for greenhouse gas emission allowance trading within the Community, OJ L 8, 13.1.2009, pp. 3–21.

[13] Directive 2009/29/EC of 23 April 2009 amending Directive 2003/87/EC so as to improve and extend the greenhouse gas emission allowance trading scheme of the Community, OJ L 140, 5.6.2009, pp. 63–87.

[14] Directive 2009/28/EC on the promotion of the use of energy from renewable sources, L 140, 5 June 2009, pp. 16–62.

sources, with the levels varying according to (i) earlier efforts by the individual Member States, (ii) the possibilities to fulfil the objective, and (iii) considerations of equity.[15] Furthermore, each Member State is obliged to ensure that, by 2020, 10 per cent of its energy consumption in the transport sector comes from renewable energy sources. A further Directive passed in 2009 addresses the mixing of bio-fuels with petrol and diesel,[16] and contains detailed sustainability requirements, applicable to both the areas within the EU and third countries, about bio-fuel generation; the Commission must report every two years on whether the relevant third countries are complying with these requirements.

Other measures

14.11   The EU has adopted a non-binding target of increasing energy efficiency by 20 per cent by 2020. In order to reach that objective, the European legislators adopted a Directive on the eco-design of energy-using products;[17] a work programme elaborated under this Directive[18] provides for the fixing of energy standards for fifty-seven product groups (computers, television sets, light bulbs, refrigerators etc.) to be progressively adopted by way of an accelerated legislative procedure. A further Directive[19] from 2006 requires the creation and development of national action

---

[15] By 2020, the following percentages shall have to be reached: Belgium 13%; Bulgaria 16%; Czech Republic 13%; Denmark 30%; Germany 18%; Estonia 25%; Ireland 16%; Greece 18%; Spain 20%; France 23%; Italy 17%; Cyprus 13%; Latvia 40%; Lithuania 23%; Luxembourg 11%; Hungary 13%; Malta 10%; Netherlands 14%; Austria 34%; Poland 15%; Portugal 31%; Romania 24%; Slovenia 25%; Slovakia 14%; Finland 38%; Sweden 49%; United Kingdom 15%.

[16] Directive 2009/30/EC of 23 April 2009 amending Directive 98/70/EC as regards the specification of petrol, diesel and gas-oil and introducing a mechanism to monitor and reduce greenhouse gas emissions and amending Council Directive 1999/32/EC as regards the specification of fuel used by inland waterway vessels and repealing Directive 93/12/EEC, OJ L 140, 5.6.2009, pp. 88–113.

[17] Directive 2009/125/EC of 21 October 2009 establishing a framework for the setting of ecodesign requirements for energy-related products (Text with EEA relevance), OJ L 285, 31.10.2009, pp. 10–35.

[18] See Communication from the Commission to the Council and the European Parliament – Establishment of the working plan for 2009–2011 under the Ecodesign Directive, COM/2008/0660 final, COM(2008) 660.

[19] Directive 2006/32/EC of 5 April 2006 on energy end-use efficiency and energy services and repealing Council Directive 93/76/EEC, OJ L 114, 27.4.2006, pp. 64–85.

plans on energy efficiency and fixes a non-binding target of a 9 per cent increase in energy efficiency to be reached by 2015.

14.12   A Directive on energy efficiency of buildings was adopted in 2002 and reviewed in 2010,[20] and provides for measures to increase the energy efficiency of not only new buildings and apartments, but also of existing buildings and apartments that undergo major restoration. Such buildings must comply with minimum performance requirements and require an energy performance certificate that must be passed on to any future buyer. The Directive also puts in place a methodology for calculating the energy performance of buildings.

14.13   European rules passed in 2009 concerning passenger cars put into circulation within the EU stipulate that these may not emit more than 130 grams CO_2 per kilometre; there is an intention to further lower this standard by 2020 to 95 grams per kilometre.[21] This obligation is to be phased in between 2012 and 2015. Less stringent limit values have been set for light commercial vehicles, though not for trucks.[22]

14.14   The EU has adopted a considerable number of legally binding measures in the agricultural, energy, transport and industrial sectors to reduce energy consumption, increase energy efficiency, promote the generation and use of energy from renewable sources, and to reduce the emission of GHGs.[23]

14.15   Additional EU provisions that have some relevance for climate change litigation deal with the environmental impact assessment

[20] Directive 2010/31/EC of 19 May 2010 on the energy performance of buildings, OJ L 153, 18 June 2010, pp. 13–35.

[21] Regulation 443/2009 of 23 April 2009 setting emission performance standards for new passenger cars as part of the Community's integrated approach to reduce CO_2 emissions from light-duty vehicles, OJ L 140, 5.6.2009, pp. 1–15.

[22] Regulation 595/2009, OJEU 2009, L 188, p. 1.

[23] See in particular Directive 2003/96 restructuring the Community framework for the taxation of energy products and electricity, OJEU 2003, L 283 p. 51; Directive 1999/94 relating to the availability of consumer information on fuel economy and CO_2 emissions in respect of the marketing of new passenger cars, OJEU 1999, L 12, p. 16; Regulation 842/2006 on certain fluorinated greenhouse gases, OJEU 2006, L 161, p. 1; Directive 2006/40 relating to emissions from air conditioning systems in motor vehicles, OJEU 2006, L 161, p. 12; Directive 2009/31 on the geological storage of carbon dioxide, OJ 2009, L 140, p. 114; Regulation 1005/2009 on substances that deplete the ozone layer, OJEU 2009, L 286, p. 1.

of certain public and private projects, the environmental assessment of plans and programmes, industrial emissions, and with access to information, participation in decision-making and access to justice in environmental matters.

14.16   The environmental liability Directive[24] is not likely to play a significant role in climate change litigation. Indeed, this Directive only applies to certain activities which are listed in an Annex. Such activities must have damaged natural habitats, fauna or flora species, the water or the soil. However, the Directive only applies to damage 'caused by pollution of a diffuse character, where it is possible to establish a causal link between the damage and the activities of individual operators' (Article 4(4)). In practice, such a causal link is almost impossible to establish.

The EU institutions' stance on climate change

14.17   From the very beginning of the discussions for an international agreement on climate change, the EU has favoured efficient and effective measures against climate change. It signed and ratified the UN Convention on Climate Change 1992 and stabilised its CO_2 emissions by 2000 at the level of 1990. At the Kyoto Conference in 1997, the EU favoured the adoption of strict measures to reduce overall GHG emissions by 2012. It signed and ratified the Kyoto Protocol, which provided for a reduction of EU GHG emissions by 8 per cent (compared to 1990 levels). Its measures intended to implement these commitments are described above. The EU committed itself on several occasions to achieving the objective of limiting the global average temperature increase to not more than 2°C above pre-industrial levels, and has always favoured, on an international level, the adoption of more efficient measures to fight climate change.

14.18   At the Copenhagen Conference in 2009, the EU offered to reduce its emissions by 30 per cent (compared to 2005 levels) by the year 2020, provided that similar commitments were made by other developed countries and economically more advanced developing countries; this commitment had already been laid down in

---

[24] Directive 2004/35 on environmental liability with regard to the prevention and remedying of environmental damage, OJ 2004, L 143, p. 56.

EU legislation.[25] When the negotiations in Copenhagen for an international agreement failed, the EU Member States opposed a unilateral EU commitment to a 30 per cent reduction in emissions, but stuck to the original reduction plan of 20 per cent.

EU risks from climate change

14.19   Most of the impacts of climate change risk have repercussions within the EU, as the EU territory covers such a large geographical area.[26] The main consequences include an increased risk of coastal and river floods, droughts, loss of biodiversity, threats to human health, and damage to economic sectors, such as forestry, agriculture and tourism.

14.20   At present, temperatures are forecasted to rise everywhere, with southern Europe having to face tropical temperatures and more frequent heatwaves. Should, however, a change in the ocean currents lead to the disappearance of the Gulf Stream that provides Europe with a warm, mitigated climate, the average temperatures might fall considerably and change the EU's climate drastically. A rise in sea levels would threaten large coastal areas and create problems for countries such as The Netherlands or coastal zones which lie at present below sea level. Droughts will occur more frequently, and desertification and soil erosion are likely to progress with greater speed than currently. Southern Europe in particular will be confronted with greater water scarcity than at present. Together with more frequent droughts and changing precipitation levels, there will be considerable impact on crops and changes in the biological diversity, while more tropical diseases will spread across Europe.

14.21   The consequences of a changing climate for the EU are difficult to assess because the EU is an affluent region and measures will be undertaken to mitigate the effects of climate change. These include dike construction, irrigation projects, water transfer, changes in production methods in agriculture, different approaches to the construction of buildings, changes in

---

[25] Decision 406/2009 (see n. 7 above).
[26] See European Environment Agency, *Impacts of Europe's Changing Climate* (EEA Briefing 3/2008, Copenhagen, 2009).

energy-saving and energy-efficiency measures, and changes in tax legislation and working methods. The agricultural sector will request more State aid, and other sectors are likely to rely heavily on public financial and/or economic support. It seems clear that the effects of climate change will not favour market freedom, but rather interventionist measures, in Europe.[27]

14.22   Mitigation measures and their impact as well as State intervention are likely to be largely adopted at regional (Member State) level, as the impact of climate change will vary considerably from one Member State to another.

Existing industries and natural resources

14.23   The EU's primary energy production relies on various types of sources: nuclear energy (28.4%), coal and lignite (22.0%), natural gas (19.7%), renewable sources (16.3%) and crude oil (13.6%).[28] The EU depends on imports for 54.8% of its energy. There is no internal EU energy market per se; the use of the different energy sources varies greatly from one Member State to another, as do the tax provisions and public measures to promote renewable energy and increased energy efficiency.

14.24   Though EU policy decisions and legislative measures promote renewable energies and greater energy efficiency, Member States frequently take decisions in this area according to their specific national energy situation. At present, about half of the EU Member States turn to nuclear energy, while several Member States strictly object to it – though as a result of the climate change discussions, these positions are changing. Nuclear energy is, in most countries, not a competitive industry, but relies on

---

[27] See for paras. 14.20 and 14.21, European Environment Agency, *Impact of Europe's Changing Climate – 2008 Indicator-based Assessment* (EEA Report 4/2008, Copenhagen, 2008); European Environment Agency, *Climate Change and Water Adaptation Issues* (EEA Technical Report 2/2007, Copenhagen, 2007); European Environment Agency, *Adapting to Climate Change in Europe – SOER 2010 Thematic Assessment*; *Mitigating Climate Change – SOER 2010 Thematic Assessment*; *Understanding Climate Change – SOER 2010 Thematic Assessment* (Copenhagen, 2010); Umweltbundesamt (Germany), *Impacts of Climate Change and Water Resources – Adaptation Strategies for Europe* (Dessau, 2008).

[28] See Eurostat, *Eurostat Yearbook 2010* (Luxembourg, 2010), p. 555. The figures refer to 2007.

direct and indirect State aid to remain viable. Coal remains an important source of energy in several Member States (Poland, Spain, Germany), and is also important for social (employment) reasons, though it is not competitive with imported coal. Current EU policy seeks to phase out State aid for coal by 2018.

(B)   Public law litigation

14.25   The EU is an international regional integration organisation with specific characteristics, so most litigation in the area of climate change concerns the relationship of the EU and its Member States. A first series of European court cases addressed the division of power between the EU and Member States in climate change matters. In a second series, the European courts had to intervene to decide on the validity of EU legislative acts or specific decisions on climate change. A third series of court decisions concerned the enforcement of the application of EU climate change law in Member States. Actions brought by private persons against the EU have mainly concerned individual decisions taken by the European Commission.

14.26   Actions for damages will be discussed in (C) Other EU law provisions below, although it is questionable whether actions brought against the EU also form part of public law.

Court decisions on the allocation of powers between the
EU and its Member States

14.27   The division of powers between the EU and its Member States and any related disputes concern the EU and its Member States. Due to the nature of such disputes, private individuals are not normally involved in the same. As Member States, meeting in Council, decide – together with the European Parliament – on legislative measures, disputes as to allocation of powers are infrequent. In climate change questions, only one set of acts has, until now, been the subject of litigation.

14.28   In one case, the Commission considered the national allocation plan ('NAP') under the emissions allowances Directive, submitted by Poland, to be incompatible with the conditions of Directive 2003/87 and reduced the annual quantity of emission allowances by around 25 per cent. Poland asked the GC to annul the Commission's decision.[29]

14.29 The Court found that the Commission had exceeded its powers by using an assessment method of its own, thereby reaching different results than Poland had done. The Court held that the drawing up of a NAP was a matter which fell within the competence of the Member States and that the Commission only had limited powers to oversee the Member States' relevant decisions. The Court annulled the Commission's decision.

14.30 In case T-263/06 involving Estonia, where the Commission again had objected to the NAP for much the same reasons as in the case concerning Poland, the Court came to the same conclusion[30] for similar reasons. The Commission then appealed both cases[31] and these are currently pending. It is likely that other such cases brought by Member States against the Commission[32] will not be decided by the Court before the appeal procedure has ended.

14.31 Member States have also obtained victories against the Commission in two other cases concerning Directive 2003/87, where the respective competences were in question. In case T-178/05,[33] the question was raised whether a Member State, after having submitted its NAP plan to the Commission, was entitled to amend it and increase the overall amount of allocations it distributed. When the United Kingdom ('UK') did so, the Commission rejected the amendments as inadmissible. However, the Court held that it followed both from the wording of the Directive and from the general structure and objectives of the system which it established that the Commission could not restrict a Member State's right to amend its NAP and annulled the Commission's decision. The Commission later rejected the amendments proposed by the UK for a second time, but for different reasons,[34] and the UK then decided not to challenge the Commission's decision.

[29] GC, case T-183/07, *Poland* v. *Commission*, ECR 2009, p. II-3395.
[30] GC, case T-263/07, *Estonia* v. *Commission*, ECR 2009, p. II-3463.
[31] See ECJ, case C-504/09, *Commission* v. *Poland*; case C-505/09, *Commission* v. *Estonia*.
[32] GC, cases T-194/07, *Czech Republic* v. *Commission*; T-368/07, *Lithuania* v. *Commission*; T-483/07, *Romania* v. *Commission*; T-499/07, *Bulgaria* v. *Commission*.
[33] GC, case T-178/05, *United Kingdom* v. *Commission*, ECR 2005, p. II-4807.
[34] Commission, Decision C(2006) 426 of 22 February 2006.

14.32   In another case, Germany had submitted to the Commission a
        NAP which provided for the possibility of some later amend-
        ments to take account of economic development in Germany.
        The Commission rejected the provisions on ex-post adjustments
        as inadmissible, stating that a NAP could not be subsequently
        amended. When Germany applied to the GC,[35] the Court pro-
        ceeded to a literal, historical, contextual and teleological inter-
        pretation of the relevant provisions of Directive 2003/87. It came to
        the conclusion that the Directive did not prohibit Member States
        from ex-post adjustments. Furthermore, the Court held that the
        Commission had erroneously considered that the German provi-
        sions discriminated in favour of new market entrants, and that
        the Commission had not sufficiently justified its decision to
        prohibit certain ex-post adjustments.

The validity of EU legislation

14.33   Actions on the compatibility of EU climate change legislation
        with the EU 'constitution' (the EU Treaties), with general prin-
        ciples of EU law or with public international law are mostly
        brought by companies or private individuals. Member States –
        as members of the Council – are also co-legislators in climate
        change matters, but do not appear as applicants to the courts,
        although they would have standing for actions against an EU
        legislative act.

14.34   The first decision on climate change issues concerned the request
        for a preliminary ruling that had been referred to the ECJ by an
        Italian court.[36] In that case, an Italian company claimed damages
        from a customer who defended himself with the argument that
        the purchase contract was invalid because it contradicted an EU
        regulation on the ban of the ozone-depleting substance hydro-
        chlorofluorocarbon ('HCFC'). The Italian court wanted to know
        whether the ban of HCFC was in conflict with provisions and
        principles of EU law, in particular as substances with a higher
        global-warming potential had not been prohibited.

---

[35] GC, case T-374/04, *Germany* v. *Commission*, ECR 2007, p. II-4431.
[36] ECJ, case C-341/95, *Bettati*, ECR 1998, p. I-4355. The ECJ confirmed this finding in a par-
      allel case, decided on the same day, case C-284/95, *Safety Hi-Tech*, ECR 1998, p. I-4301.

14.35   The ECJ examined whether the ban was compatible with the objective to protect the environment, whether it ensured a high level of protection and whether it took into account the available scientific and technical data. It also examined the compatibility of the ban with the provisions on the free circulation of goods and the proportionality principle, with competition law, with State aid provisions and with the requirement of sincere cooperation between the EU and Member States. The Court concluded that the HCFC ban was in full compliance with EU law.

14.36   In climate change matters, a French company brought a case before French courts, contesting the validity of Directive 2003/87 on GHG emission allowance trading.[37] The French court asked the ECJ whether this Directive was valid in light of the principle of equal treatment,[38] in so far as it makes the allowance trading scheme applicable to installations in the steel sector without extending its scope to the aluminium and plastics industries.

14.37   The ECJ held that the chemical sector covered a large number of installations. Its inclusion into the scheme would have made the management of the scheme more difficult and increased the administrative burden. As the EU institutions introduced the scheme by way of a step-by-step approach, applying it in the beginning only to some installations and economic sectors, they were entitled to take the view that the complete exclusion of the chemical sector from the scheme outweighed the advantages of including some larger chemical installations. As regards the non-ferrous metal sector, the Court concluded that the amount of direct emissions from that sector – 16.2 million tonnes of CO_2 in 1990 – was so different from that of the steel sector – with 174.8 million tonnes of CO_2 emissions – that, in view of the step-by-step approach, the EU legislature was entitled to treat the two sectors differently, without having to take into consideration the indirect emissions attributable to the different sectors. The ECJ held that the validity of Directive 2003/87 did not contain a discrimination of the steel sector.[39] The Court explicitly mentioned, though, that the emission allowances trading scheme was a new

[37] Directive 2003/87 (see n. 10 above).
[38] Conseil d'Etat, aff. No. 287110, Décision of 8 February 2007.
[39] ECJ, case C-127/07, *Arcelor and Others*, ECR 2008, p. I-9895.

instrument in EU law and that the EU legislature had a considerable degree of discretion, in particular during the initial stages of the use of that instrument, to differentiate between the industrial sectors. These remarks leave it open as to whether the Court might, in a future case, not find an unjustified different treatment of industrial sectors.

14.38   The French company also tried to directly question the validity of Directive 2003/87 before the GC. However, the Court found that the Directive was of a general nature and that the applicant was not individually and directly affected by its adoption, as required by Article 263(4) TFEU. Consequently, it declared the action to be inadmissible.[40]

14.39   Directive 2003/87, as amended by Directive 2008/101,[41] was also the subject of a preliminary request referred to the ECJ by a British court in a case introduced by the Air Transport Association of America and a number of US airline companies. The British court posed the question as to whether the inclusion of aviation activities within the EU ETS was compatible with customary international law, the Chicago Convention on International Civil Aviation of 1944, the Open Skies Agreement[42] and the Kyoto Protocol.[43] The decision is pending; a judgment is expected by the end of 2011 or in 2012.

The enforcement of EU climate change provisions in the Member States

14.40   Actions in relation to the enforcement of EU climate change provisions in the EU Member States are, in practice, exclusively commenced by the European Commission. It is true that Article 259 TFEU provides that a Member State that considers another Member State to have failed to fulfil an obligation under the Treaties may bring the matter before the ECJ. However, this

---

[40] GC, case T-16/04, *Arcelor v. European Parliament and Council*, judgment of 2 March 2010.
[41] Directive 2008/101 (see n. 12 above).
[42] This probably refers to the Community Air Service Agreement, concluded between the United States and the EU on 2 March 2007. However, this was not specified in the published and publicly available documents.
[43] ECJ, case C-366/10, introduced on 22 July 2010.

provision has, until the end of 2010, never been used in the environmental sector; and in other areas of EU policy, its application is extremely rare,[44] as Member States largely prefer to let the Commission take action against a Member State.

14.41 The Commission is entitled to take legal action against a Member State when it considers that the relevant Member State has failed to fulfil an obligation under EU law.[45] It has discretion in this regard that is not controlled by the ECJ. Private individuals may not bring an action against the Commission for failing to act or for damages when the Commission has failed to take any action. In the past, all such actions brought by private persons against the Commission have been unsuccessful. The decision by the ECJ is a declaratory judgment; no sanction is foreseen, except that the Court may, on the Commission's request, impose a lump sum or penalty payment, when a Directive was not transposed into national law.[46] When a Member State does not comply with a judgment of the Court issued under Article 258 or 259 TFEU, the Commission may, under Article 260 TFEU, bring a second case against that Member State and ask for financial sanctions.[47]

---

[44] See Court of Justice, case 141/78, *France* v. *United Kingdom*, ECR 1979, p. 2923; case C-145/04, *Spain* v. *United Kingdom*, judgment of 12 September 2006.

[45] See Article 258 TFEU: 'If the Commission considers that a Member State has failed to fulfil an obligation under the treaties, it shall deliver a reasoned opinion on the matter after giving the State concerned the opportunity to submit its observations.

If the State concerned does not comply with the opinion within the period laid down by the Commission, the latter may bring the matter before the Court of Justice of the European Union.'

[46] See Article 260(3) TFEU: 'When the Commission brings a case before the Court pursuant to Article 258 on the grounds that the Member State concerned has failed to fulfil its obligation to notify measures transposing a directive adopted under a legislative procedure, it may, when it deems appropriate, specify the amount of the lump sum or penalty payment to be paid by the Member State concerned which it considers appropriate in the circumstances.

If the Court finds that there is an infringement it may impose a lump sum or penalty payment on the Member State concerned not exceeding the amount specified by the Commission ...' This provision has only been in force since 1 December 2009.

[47] See Article 260(2) TFEU: 'If the Commission considers that the Member State concerned has not taken the necessary measures to comply with the judgment of the Court, it may bring the case before the Court after giving that State the opportunity to submit its observations. It shall specify the amount of the lump sum or penalty payment to be paid by the Member State concerned which it considers appropriate in the circumstances.

If the Court finds that the Member State concerned has not complied with its judgment it may impose a lump sum or penalty payment on it.'

Until the end of 2010, such sanctions were imposed in four environmental[48] and in a number of other cases.

14.42   In climate change matters, the Commission brought a court action against Italy and Finland for failure to transpose Directive 2003/87 on the emission allowances trading scheme into their national legal order by the deadline specified in the Directive; for Finland, this action was limited to the province of Aaland. The Court stated in both cases that the Directive had not been transposed in time.[49] Furthermore, the Court found in two cases[50] that Luxembourg had not met the transmission deadline for the necessary information on the actual GHG emissions, required under Decision 280/2004.[51] Luxembourg then had to take the necessary measures to comply with its obligations.

14.43   Overall, it should be noted that the Commission has limited itself until now to taking court action against a Member State when EU legislation had not been transposed into national law or when data had not been transmitted to the Commission. It has not taken action against Member States when the climate change provisions of EU law had been incorrectly applied, for example when GHG emissions had increased in contravention of Decision 2002/358[52] or Member States had been too generous in allocating ETS allowances.[53] One can only speculate as to the reasons for

---

[48]   See Court of Justice, cases C-387/97, *Commission* v. *Greece*, ECR 2000, p. I-369 (€20,000 per day); C-278/01, *Commission* v. *Spain*, ECR 2003, p. I-14141 (€624.000 every six months); C-304/02, *Commission* v. *France*, ECR 2005, p. I-6263 (lump sum of €20 million and €57.6 million every six months); C-121/07, *Commission* v. *France*, ECR 2008, p. I-9159 (lump sum of €10 million).

[49]   ECJ, cases C-122/05, *Commission* v. *Italy*, judgment of 18 May 2006; C-107/05, *Commission* v. *Finland*, judgment of 12 January 2006.

[50]   ECJ, cases C- 61/07, *Commission* v. *Luxembourg*, judgment of 18 July 2007; C-390/08, *Commission* v. *Luxembourg*, judgment of 14 May 2009.

[51]   Decision 280/2004, OJEU 2004, L 49, p. 1.

[52]   For example, according to Decision 2002/358 (see n. 5 above) Belgium should have reduced its greenhouse gas emissions until 2012 by 7.5 per cent; until 2005, it had only reduced them by 0.7 per cent. Denmark should reduce greenhouse gas emissions by 21 per cent until 2012; until 2005, it had reduced them by 8.7 per cent. Spain was allowed to increase its emissions by 15 per cent; until 2005, it had increased them by 53.1 per cent. See for details L. Krämer, 'Klimaschutzrecht in der Europäischen Union', *Revue Suisse du Droit International et Européen*, (2010), 311.

[53]   In a letter of 17 March 2004, the Commission had stated that this practice constituted unjustified State aid, since the undertakings could sell the surplus allowances and retain the proceeds of the sale; such an advantage could seriously distort competition. The letter is mentioned in GC, case T-387/04, *ENBW Energie Baden-Württemberg* v. *Commission*, Order of 30 April 2007, ECR 2007, p. II-1195, para. 23.

the Commission's passivity and it is questionable as to whether this passivity is compatible with the Commission's obligation to 'ensure the application of the Treaties, and of measures adopted by the institutions pursuant to them' and to 'oversee the application of Union law under the control of the Court of Justice of the European Union'.[54]

Action by private persons against individual decisions by the European Commission

14.44 Private undertakings have tried in a number of cases to challenge the decisions taken under Directive 2003/87[55] by the European Commission concerning the NAPs of Member States and the allocations made to the individual undertakings.

14.45 In case T-489/04,[56] the GC concluded that the decision as to how many allocation allowances, including allowances to individual undertakings, were to be distributed was taken by the individual Member States and not by the Commission. The Member States only had to respect the overall ceiling fixed by the Commission. Individual undertakings were therefore not directly and individually affected by the Commission's decision and thus had no standing.

14.46 On appeal from the applicant, the ECJ confirmed these findings.[57] It held that the Commission's decision 'was not such as to directly affect the legal situation of the appellant and was therefore not of direct concern to him'.[58] Subsequently, all applications by undertakings against the Commission's decisions regarding NAPs have been considered inadmissible. The reasoning of the GC has varied slightly: either the applicants were considered not to be *individually* concerned,[59] or they were considered not to be *directly* concerned.[60]

---

[54] Article 17(1), TEU.   [55] Directive 2003/87 (see n. 10 above).

[56] GC, case T-489/04, *US Steel Kosice* v. *Commission*, Order of 1 October 2007.

[57] ECJ, case C-6/08P, *US Steel Kosice* v. *Commission*, Order of 19 June 2008.

[58] *Ibid.*, n. 68.

[59] GC, cases T-130/06, *Drax Power and others*, Order of 25 June 2007; T-28/07, *Fels-Werke and others* v. *Commission*, Order of 11 September 2007; T-241/06, *Buzzi Unicem* v. *Commission*, Order of 27 October 2008.

[60] GC, cases T-13/07, *Cemex UK* v. *Commission*, Order of 6 November 2007; T-193/07, *Górazde Cement* v. *Commission*, Order of 23 September 2008; T- 195/07, *Lafargue Cement* v. *Commission*, Order of 23 September 2008; T-196/07, *Dyckerhoff* v. *Commission*, Order of

14.47   In case T-387/04,[61] the applicant argued that the German NAP
         contained elements of State aid, as it included an over-allocation
         of trading allowances to some undertakings. As a competi-
         tor of those undertakings, it was individually affected by the
         Commission's decision which constituted an authorisation of
         the NAP and State aid elements; and since the NAP did not give
         the German authorities any discretion in distributing the allow-
         ances otherwise, it was also directly affected by the decision.

14.48   The Court held that the Commission's decision did not con-
         stitute an authorisation of the NAP, but a mere review; the
         Commission had thus not authorised any eventual State aid con-
         tained in the NAP. The annulment of the Commission's decision
         on the German NAP would thus not procure any advantage to
         the applicant and the Court, therefore, declared the application
         inadmissible.

14.49   In 2010, a Spanish undertaking brought an action against the
         Commission's decision[62] to authorise Spain to pay compensation
         to undertakings in respect of the additional costs borne by those
         electricity producers who, as a result of public-service obligation,
         had to ensure that a part of their production used domestic coal.
         The applicant argued that this decision infringed provisions on
         the internal market, competition and environmental protection,
         in that it promoted the operation of installations which increase
         the level of gas emissions into the atmosphere: this constituted a
         breach of the prohibition on allocating new free emission allow-
         ances. The case is pending.

General assessment of EU public law litigation

14.50   A general look at the public law litigation on climate change issues
         at EU level reveals that most of the litigation takes place between
         the EU institutions and the EU Member States. This concerns the

---

23 September 2008; T-197/07, *Grupa Ozarów* v. *Commission*, Order of 23 September 2008;
T-198/07, *Cementownia 'Warta'* v. *Commission*, Order of 23 September 2008; T-199/07,
Cementownia Odra v. *Commission*, Order of 23 September 2008; T-203/07, *Cemex
Polska* v. *Commission*, Order of 23 September 2008; T-208/07, *Belchatów* v. *Commission*,
Order of 20 October 2008.

[61] GC, case T-387/04 (see n. 53 above).
[62] GC, case T-484/10, *Gas Natural Fenosa* v. *Commission*.

allocation of power, the validity of EU legislative provisions and the enforcement of EU legislation in the Member States. National courts may, via the preliminary court procedure, provoke a judgment by the ECJ as to the validity of EU legislation. In substance, though, the ECJ is very reserved in this regard and does not easily annul EU (climate change) legislation because it takes the view that the EU legislature benefits from a large amount of discretion as to the provisions which it adopts.

14.51   The European Commission oversees the transposition of EU climate change legislation into the national legal order of the Member States as well as the formal requirements linked to that, such as the drawing up of plans or the transmission of reports or data to the Commission. However, it is reserved to look into the practical application of the provisions within the Member States. For example, larger infrastructure and industrial installation projects must, before they are authorised, be the subject of an environmental impact assessment which also shall examine the direct and indirect effects of the project on the climate.[63] Until now, the Commission has never examined if, and to what extent, national assessments comply with this requirement.

14.52   Practically all activities by the EU institutions belong to the sphere of public law. There is thus no room for private law litigation concerning climate change issues. This also includes action for damages.

14.53   Private persons and undertakings are mostly barred from access to the EU courts by virtue of the provision of Article 263(4) TFEU which gives them standing only when they are directly and individually affected by a legislative act or a specific decision. In practice, they only have the possibility to question the validity of EU climate change *legislation* by bringing an action to a national court and asking that court to make a reference to the Court of Justice for a preliminary ruling. As almost all *specific decisions* by the EU Commission are addressed to Member States, judicial

---

[63]   Directive 85/337, OJEU 1985, L 175, p. 40, Article 3: 'The environmental impact assessment will identify, describe and assess in an appropriate manner, in the light of each individual case ... the direct and indirect effects of a project on the following factors:- human beings, fauna and flora, soil, water, air, climate and landscape ...'

action against such a decision is also barred. Actions before the EU courts appear only to be possible where a breach of State aid rules is invoked, as in such cases competition within the EU could be distorted. However, no such case has yet been decided by the EU courts.

14.54   Article 340(2) TFEU addresses the non-contractual[64] liability of the EU, and reads: 'In the case of non-contractual liability, the Union shall, in accordance with the general principles common to the laws of the Member States, make good any damage caused by its institutions or by its servants in the performance of their duties.' Article 340(3) TFEU extends this obligation to the European Central Bank. The action may be addressed against any action of an institution, including legislative measures. Omissions to act may also be challenged.

14.55   In order to be admissible, an action for compensation of damage must indicate to which unlawful conduct of an EU institution the action relates, why the applicant considers that there is a causal link between the conduct and the damage, and the nature and the extent of that damage.[65] The EU courts have a tendency to be relatively generous with regard to the admissibility of actions under Article 340(2) TFEU.

14.56   By contrast, the requirements for an action to succeed are rather strict. As regards the unlawful conduct of the EU institutions, the rule of law which is breached must intend to confer rights on individuals.[66] Furthermore, the breach of the rule of law must be sufficiently serious. This is the case when the institution in question manifestly and gravely disregarded the limits of its discretion; where only reduced or no discretion is granted, the mere infringement of EU law is sufficient.[67] The system is one of strict liability; therefore, the concept of negligence is not relevant in this context.

---

[64] According to Article 340(1) TFEU, contractual liability of the EU 'shall be governed by the law applicable to the contract in question', and shall not be discussed here.

[65] See GC, cases T-138/03, *Abad Pérez and Others* v. *Commission*, ECR 2006, p. II-4857, para. 44; T-16/04 (see n. 40 above), para. 132.

[66] ECJ, cases C-352/98P, *Bergaderm and Goupil* v. *Commission*, ECR 2000, p. I-5291; C-198/03P, *Commission* v. *CEVA and Pfizer*, ECR 2005, p. I-6357; GC, case T-16/04 (see n. 40 above).

[67] GC, case T-16/04 (see n. 40 above).

14.57 In *Arcelor* v. *European Parliament and Council*,[68] the GC assessed whether the EU institutions, by adopting Directive 2003/87, committed a sufficiently serious breach of a rule of law by exceeding the limits of the broad discretion which they enjoyed under the present Articles 191 and 192 TFEU. The Court examined successively the applicant's right of property, the freedom to pursue an economic activity, the principles of proportionality, equal treatment and legal certainty, and the freedom of establishment. It held that the applicant had not proven that any of these legal provisions or principles had been breached. Until the end of 2010, this was the only case concerning non-contractual liability which had been brought in front of an EU court.

(C)   Other EU law provisions

14.58 **Human rights**. EU law does not grant an individual right to a clean environment. The Charter on Fundamental Rights only provides that '[A] high level of environmental protection and the improvement of the quality of the environment must be integrated into the policies of the Union and ensured in accordance with the principle of sustainable development.'[69] Until now, this provision has not been used in the context of an action on climate change issues before EU courts; it is unclear how the provision will be interpreted by European courts.

14.59 **Constitutional rights**. The TFEU lists, as mentioned above, the fight against climate change as one of the policy objectives of the EU's environmental policy. Environmental policy objectives were used by the ECJ to underpin interpretations of EU law provisions, but were never used to justify an action without any specific rule of law supporting the action.

14.60 **Supply chain regulation**. Recent EU legislation prohibits the placing on the market of timber harvested in contravention of the applicable legislation in the country of harvest.[70] One of the declared objectives of this Regulation is to reduce illegal logging, which has been declared 'responsible for about 20% of global CO_2

---

[68]   *Ibid.*
[69]   Charter of Fundamental Rights of the European Union, OJEU 2000, C 364, p. 1, Article 37.
[70]   Regulation 995/2010, OJ EU2010, L 295, p. 23.

emissions'.[71] No cases have yet come in front of the court on such matters.

14.61   **Criminal law**. Under the allocation of competences in the EU, criminal law cases are not brought to EU courts, but rather are exclusively the jurisdiction of national courts.

(D)   Soft law

14.62   The only instrument of dispute resolution other than the EU courts at EU level is the European Ombudsman. The Ombudsman is empowered to receive complaints from natural or legal EU persons concerning instances of maladministration of the EU institutions or bodies. He examines such complaints, reports on them and gives recommendations or reports on his conclusions.[72] His recommendations are not binding.

14.63   Until now, the Ombudsman has not looked into issues of climate change, though he has dealt with some complaints regarding access to NAPs for GHG emission allowance trading. His influence in dispute settlement is generally rather limited.

(E)   Practicalities

14.64   The provisions on standing before the EU courts do not differentiate between EU citizens and residents and other residents. However, such a differentiation may follow from specific provisions of EU law. For example, according to Article 15 TFEU, 'any citizen of the Union and any natural or legal person residing or having its registered office in a Member State' shall have a right of access to documents of the Union institutions and bodies.

14.65   The judgments of the ECJ and the GC are enforceable by law. Enforcement is governed by the rules of civil procedure in the Member State in the territory of which it is carried out.[73]

14.66   Actions brought before the EU courts do not have suspending effect. However, the courts may order that application of the

---

[71] *Ibid.*, Recital 3.   [72] See for details Article 228 TFEU.
[73] Articles 280 and 299 TFEU.

contested act be suspended. The courts may also, in cases before them, prescribe any necessary interim measures.[74]

14.67　The ECJ has categorically denied that the public interest in a particular lawsuit could overcome the requirement laid down in Article 263(4) TFEU, that a person must be directly and individually affected by the contested act. Environmental organisations do not therefore have standing in environmental issues, unless a decision is addressed to them.[75] The new provision of Article 263(4) TFEU, according to which actions against a regulatory act which does not entail implementing measures only require a direct concern, may lead in future to some softening of the courts' very restrictive interpretation of Article 263(4).

14.68　A decision as to the cost of the litigation is given in the judgment or order which closes the proceedings. The general rule is that the unsuccessful party shall be ordered to pay the necessary costs if they have been applied for in the successful party's pleadings.[76]

14.69　Regulation 1049/2001[77] is concerned with access to documents held by EU institutions and bodies. Its wording is, like Article 15 TFEU on which it is based, relatively liberal. However, in practice, EU institutions and bodies make large use of the exceptions provided for in that Regulation and are not really committed to principles of an open society and of transparency, though there is a slow evolution for the better. There are no specific provisions on access to information in the course of litigation.

14.70　In environmental matters, the Aarhus Convention on Access to Information, Participation in Decision-making and Access to Justice in Environmental Matters applies. It has been ratified by the EU[78] and is, at least as regards access to information, part of EU law. Its provisions prevail over those of Regulation 1049/2001.[79] The right of access to information under the

---

[74]　Articles 278 and 279 TFEU.

[75]　See the landmark decision of the ECJ, case C-321/95P, *Greenpeace and Others* v. *Commission*, ECR 1998, p. I-651.

[76]　Rules of procedure of the ECJ, OJ EU 2010, C 177, p. 1, Article 69; Rules of procedure of the GC, OJEU 2010, C 177, p. 37, Article 87.

[77]　Regulation 1049/2001, OJ 2001, L 145, p. 43.

[78]　Decision 2005/370; see also Regulation 1367/2006, OJEU 2006, L 264, p. 13 which implements the Aarhus Convention.

[79]　See Regulation 1049/2001 (see n. 77 above), Article 2(6).

Convention is considerably broader and the exceptions to this right are considerably narrower, though neither the EU institutions nor the EU courts are as yet accustomed to applying the Aarhus Convention. However, in a recent important case[80] the ECJ has held that the provisions of the Convention 'now form an integral part of the legal order of the European Union', and that in any area covered by EU environmental law, national courts have a duty to interpret its national law and procedural rules as far as possible to be consistent with the access to justice provisions of the Convention. Neither the EU institutions nor the Member States and their Governments enjoy immunity from legal action at EU level. The ECJ has pronounced, as of the end of 2010, more than 600 judgments against Member States in environmental matters. The judgments are accepted and, generally, measures are taken to comply with them.

(F) Conclusion

14.71   The EU succeeded in adopting strong and far-reaching climate change legislation which is binding on all twenty-seven Member States, without a significant amount of court litigation. Its policy commitments, which already take into consideration the time-frame leading up to the year 2050, were reached by consensus and did not really raise objection by public authorities, private operators and public opinion. Climate change policy within the EU is based on the consensus of society; concerns have been voiced that the reduction of GHG emissions and the replacement of fossil fuels by renewable energy is not advancing quickly enough. Litigation is likely to increase when the Commission tries to enforce the legally binding targets of 2020, and when it is likely to become apparent that some EU Member States will not be able to comply with their obligations.

14.72   Litigation initiated at EU level in favour of more drastic adaptation or mitigation measures is unlikely to increase in the future. Indeed, neither the human rights provisions nor the EU rules on environmental policy allow representatives of civil society or environmental or human rights organisations to bring such

---

[80] Case C-240/09, *Lesoochranárske zoskupenie VLK v. Ministerstvo životného prostredia Slovenskej republiky*, 8 March 2011.

actions to the EU courts. In particular, the requirement that an applicant normally must be *directly and individually* concerned by a piece of legislation or a measure is a very strong barrier of access to EU courts. At present, applicants will be asked to apply to the national courts. The national courts will have to decide within the legislative framework set by the EU, without being able to challenge it themselves, as the ECJ alone decides on the validity of EU legislation; and the ECJ will only very exceptionally question the decisions by the EU legislature.

14.73 At present, most of the litigation at EU level will be initiated by private undertakings that want less climate change legislation and less action. In view of the political and societal consensus on the necessity to fight climate change, their chances of significantly influencing this fight via litigation appear to be rather limited.

Germany

HANS-JOACHIM KOCH, MICHAEL LÜHRS
AND RODA VERHEYEN

(A)   Introduction

15.01   Section A of this chapter provides an overview of the German
legal system and facts and figures relevant to climate change.[1]
It also gives an overview of German climate change policy and
the legal instruments that have been introduced to combat global warming. Given Germany's membership of the EU, it should
be noted that there will inevitably be a certain degree of overlap
with the chapters in this volume relating to other EU Member
States. The section does not cover German measures to deal with
the effects of climate change. Section B focuses on public law,
with a particular focus on how to: (i) enforce existing law (including through the adoption of climate-friendly discretionary
decisions); (ii) make existing law stricter; and (iii) force the government to legislate. Section C looks at private law in the field of
climate change, focusing on tort law and possible causes of action
as there is no case law on the subject to date. Section D focuses on
information law. Section E provides a brief conclusion.

The German Legal System

15.02   As a member of the EU, Germany must abide by EU law. The country is a federal constitutional democracy and its Constitution or
'Basic Law' (*Grundgesetz, GG*) has played a major role in political
and legal developments since its creation after World War II. It
contains a set of basic human rights (Articles 1–20 GG). While
there is no specific 'environmental right', the State has expressed

---

[1] Status as of 10 March 2011. Subsequent changes have not been processed.

an aim to protect the environment in Article 20a GG. The basic rights are well entrenched in the German legal system as a whole, but there is no distinct area that could be termed 'Human Rights Law'. Rather, every administration, court and legislator is directly bound to give effect to the basic rights. The rights even regulate relationships between private persons or entities to a certain degree.[2]

15.03 Germany has a civil legal system. Strictly speaking, all law derives from the legislators, the parliaments and local decision-making bodies at various levels: federal (*Bund*), state (*Land*), regional (*Landkreis*) and municipal (*Gemeinde*). In practice, however, the German higher courts' interpretations of the law serve as an additional authority. The country has a well-established process for scrutinising the actions of its legislators. The Federal Constitutional Court (*Bundesverfassungsgericht*, *BVerfG*) makes decisions nullifying or calling for stricter laws relatively frequently.

15.04 German climate policy is derived from federal policy, with specific federal policy plans shaping legislation. This is true despite the fact that the GG confers upon the Federal Government no general legislative power to deal with the environment or climate protection.[3] The German states bear a great degree of responsibility in terms of law enforcement, including for federal law (Article 83 GG). Many states have developed their own climate change strategies, or at least strategies concerning the levels of CO_2 emissions.

15.05 The judicial system is subdivided into two branches that deal with administrative and civil/criminal matters respectively. The first branch consists of administrative courts (*Verwaltungsgerichte*, *VG*), which deal with any kind of judicial review of public actions or decisions. There is then generally resort to a

---

[2] Third-Party Effect (*Drittwirkung*): BVerfG (Lüth-Decision), 15 January 1958, 1 BvR 400/51.

[3] For the federal level to legislate, it must be granted the relevant power in the GG. The respective legislative powers are expressly provided for in the GG in themes: air pollution control, noise abatement, waste management, nature conservation or water supply (see Article 74 (1) Nos. 24, 29, 32 GG). Climate is not explicitly mentioned, but can also fit under the power to enact 'law relating to economic affairs' (Article 74 (1) No. 11 GG).

higher administrative court (*Oberverwaltungsgerichte, OVG*). The federal high administrative court in Leipzig (*Bundesverwaltungsgericht, BVerwG*) will normally be available in the last instance, to decide issues of law only and not issues of fact. Criminal/civil matters are dealt with by district courts (*Amtsgericht, AG*), with resort to the higher district courts (*Oberlandesgericht, OLG*) and, in the last instance, the federal court in Karlsruhe (*Bundesgerichtshof, BGH*).

15.06   In all branches and instances there is the possibility of resort to the BVerfG to argue non-compliance with basic rights or other rules contained in the GG.

Emission sources and energy mix

15.07   Germany is currently the seventh biggest greenhouse gas ('GHG') emitter worldwide.[4] Overall German emissions in 1990 amounted to 1232 Mio. t CO_2-e.[5] This figure included industry in the former German Democratic Republic, which collapsed after German reunification in 1990. In 2008, emissions were down to 958 Mio. t CO_2-e (amounting to a reduction of 22.2%), and in 2009 emission had decreased to 878 Mio. t CO_2-e (an overall reduction of 28.7%).[6]

15.08   GHG emissions in Germany are primarily caused by energy generation (80.6%), industrial processes (10.9%) and agriculture (6.9%). Industry's share of final energy consumption is 28%, private households 25.6% and the transport sector 30.3%. In 2007, Germany's primary energy needs were met by the following sources: petroleum (34%), natural gas (22%), hard coal (14%), lignite (11%), nuclear energy (11%) and renewables (7.2%).[7] By 2010, the share of renewable energy had increased to 10.3%.[8]

---

[4] See Tables 2 and 3 in *The Climate Change Performance Index 2011* by Germanwatch and Climate Action Network Europe (CAN), December 2010, available at www.germanwatch.de.

[5] Federal Environmental Agency (UBA), *National Inventory Report for the German Greenhouse Gas Inventory 1990–2008* (2010), p. 53 (Table 1), available at www.unfccc.int.

[6] UBA, Press Release 13/2010.

[7] *Fifth National Report of the Government of the Federal Republic of Germany* ('Fifth National Communication'), p. 9, available at www.unfccc.int.

[8] See Federal Ministry for the Environment, '*Erneuerbare Energien in Zahlen*', 2010 (reference year 2009), available at www.erneuerbare-energien.de.

15.09 As well as undertaking major discussions about the future of nuclear power, Germany is experiencing a wave of applications for new coal power plants. In 2008, forty-three new fossil-fired plants (> 20 MW) were either being built or were in the planning/licensing phase. Of these, about twenty-five were large, new coal-fired plants.[9] Some of these plants have now been abandoned. In March 2011, however, a new 2,100 MW coal plant by the river Elbe in Brunsbüttel was granted a licence in accordance with the Federal Emission Control Act (BImSchG).[10]

15.10 Energy resources in Germany are limited to coal, lignite and natural gas; however, large offshore wind parks have been granted support and are currently being developed. NGOs and expert bodies such as the German Advisory Council on the Environment ('SRU') contend that German energy demand could be met entirely by renewable sources by the year 2050.[11]

Climate protection legislation

15.11 Climate change law in Germany has become a highly elaborate and complex subject.[12] It is mostly derived from regulatory law (*Ordungsrecht*), and is set out in terms of distinct 'do's and don'ts'. Only industrial emissions are regulated through an economic instrument – the emissions trading scheme. Despite the many statutes and regulations (whether of EU or domestic origin), it has been said that federal legislators are not doing enough to deal with the problems of climate change.[13] Legally, this question must be judged against the overarching goal of protecting the environment stated in Article 20a GG, as well

---

[9] Sachverständigenrat für Umweltfragen (SRU), '*Wege zur 100% erneuerbaren Stromversorgung*', Jan. 2011, p. 183 ff (see www.umweltrat.de); Verheyen, 'Die Bedeutung des Klimaschutzes bei der Genehmigung von Kohlekraftwerken und bei der Zulassung des Kohleabbaus', ZUR 2010, p. 403.

[10] Landesamt für Landwirtschaft, Umwelt und ländliche Räume Schleswig Holstein, Medien-Information, Landesamt für Landwirtschaft, Umwelt und ländliche Räume erteilt erste Teilgenehmigung für SWS-Kohlekraftwerk in Brunsbüttel, 1 March 2011.

[11] See n. 9 above.

[12] Koch, '*Climate Change Law in Germany*', *JEEPL*, 7(4) (2010), 411; and 'Klimaschutzrecht – Ziele, Instrumente und Strukturen eines neuen Rechtsgebiets' in Gesellschaft für Umweltrecht (eds.), *Dokumentation der 34. wissenschaftlichen Fachtagung in Leipzig 2010, 2011* (forthcoming).

[13] For an overview, see Verheyen, n. 9 above.

as against the State's obligation to protect its citizens (mainly based on the right to life and health under Article 2 GG). Article 20a GG aims to protect the natural basis of life. There is no doubt that climate protection, though not specifically referred to, is covered by this provision – a view which has been upheld by the BVerwG.[14]

15.12   Article 20a GG has been criticised for not conferring explicit law-making duties on the State, and there is now a petition to explicitly include climate protection in the GG.[15]

Mitigation targets

15.13   Germany has always been a frontrunner in terms of setting climate targets and in contributing to the international negotiations on the subject.[16] However, there is still a reluctance to adopt legally binding targets such as those in the UK instead of merely sectoral targets. The first political goal set in Germany was to reduce emissions to 25% below 1990 figures by 2005. This was not achieved. Under the agreement between EU States to share the burden of implementing the Kyoto Protocol, Germany has committed to reducing its GHG emissions to 21% below 1990 levels between 2008 and 2012.[17] Germany is on target to fulfil this commitment. The 'Meseberg Energy and Climate Programme' of 2007[18] sets out how Germany will achieve the 2007 EU targets. This programme still contains the framework for federal climate policy. Overall, Germany has committed to reducing GHG emissions to 40% below 1990 levels by 2020.

---

[14] BVerwG, 25 January 2006, 8 C 13/05, BVerwG, 23 November 2005, 8 C 14/04.

[15] Official website of the German Bundestag, www.bundestag.de (search for 'Klimaschutz als Staatsaufgabe' and 'Petitionsausschuss' which is the responsible body for petitions from the general public).

[16] Verheyen, in Koch and Caspar (eds.), *Klimaschutz im Recht* (1997), p. 7.

[17] Council Dec. 2002/358/EC of 25 April 2002, OJ 2002, L 130, p. 1; Dec. 406/2009/EC of 23 April 2009, OJEU L 140, p. 136.

[18] Bundesregierung, 'Das Integrierte Energie- und Klimaprogramm der Bundesregierung', Meseberg (August 2007); Bundesregierung, 'Bericht zur Umsetzung der in der Kabinettsklausur am 23/24' (August 2007), in *Meseberg beschlossenen Eckpunkte für ein Integriertes Energie- und Klimaprogramm* (December 2007); UBA, *Wirkung der Meseberger Beschlüsse vom 23.08.2007 auf die Treibhausgasemission in Deutschland im Jahr 2020* (October 2007); SRU, *Umweltgutachten 2008*, marginal no. 102 ff.

15.14 There are several sectoral climate targets contained in legal provisions, such as: (i) the aim to increase the share of renewable electricity to 30% by 2020 (§ 1 para. 2 EEG);[19] (ii) the aim to increase the share of renewable energy in heating by 14% by 2020 (§ 1 para. 2 EEWärmeG);[20] and (iii) the aim to increase the percentage share of high-efficiency combined heat and power ('CHP') plants in electricity and heat generation from 12% to 25% (§ 1 KWKG).[21] The prevailing view is that these targets are not enforceable in the courts.[22]

Emission Trading Scheme

15.15 The EU Emissions Trading Scheme ('ETS') has been established in Germany through the Federal Greenhouse Gas Emissions Trading Act ('TEHG'),[23] the Federal Allocation Act ('ZuG') 2007,[24] the National Allocation Plan I of 31 March 2004,[25] the ZuG 2012[26] and National Allocation Plan II[27] of 28 August 2006. It covers approximately 1,650 installations in Germany.[28]

15.16 The ETS has given rise to many disputes in the courts, with operators challenging allocation decisions made by the German Emissions Trading Authority ('DEHSt').[29] Operators have argued that the establishment of the ETS has infringed basic rights such as the right to property (Article 14 GG), the right

---

[19] Erneuerbare Energien Gesetz, BGBl I 2008, p. 2074, last amended on 11 August 2010, BGBl I, p. 1170.

[20] Erneuerbare Energien Wärmegesetz, BGBl I 2008, p. 1628, last amended on 15 January 2009, BGBl I, p. 1804.

[21] Law on the Conservation, Modernisation and Development of Combined Heat and Power ('KWKG') of 19 March 2002, BGBl I 2002, p. 1092, last amended on 25 October 2008, BGBl I 2008, p. 2101.

[22] Salje, *EEG Kommentar*, 5th edn (2009), § 1, p. 140; Müller, Oschmann and Wustlich, *EEWärmeG Kommentar* (2010), §1, marginal no. 2, 3.

[23] Of 8 July 2004, BGBl I 2004, p. 1578; last amended on 16 July 2009, BGBl I 2009, p. 1954.

[24] Of 26 August 2004, BGBl I 2004, p. 2211; last amended on 22 December 2004, BGBl I 2004, p. 3704.

[25] See www.bmu.de/english/emissions_trading/national_allocation_plan/doc/5894.php, 31 March 2004.

[26] Of 7 August 2007, BGBl I 2007, p. 1788.

[27] See www.bmu.de/emissionshandel/downloads/doc/36957.php dated 28 June 2006.

[28] See Koch, 'Immissionsschutzrecht' in Koch (ed.), *Umweltrecht*, 3rd edn (2010), § 4, marginal comment 135 ff.

[29] See Kobes and Engel, *'Der Emissionshandel im Lichte der Rechtsprechung'*, NVwZ 2011, pp. 207, 269.

to freedom of occupation (Article 12 GG) and the principle of equal treatment (Article 3 GG). The courts have, nonetheless, consistently upheld the ETS.[30]

Legislation on energy efficiency

15.17   In general there is still great potential for measures that increase energy efficiency, especially since the majority of industrial facilities in Germany (including those for electricity generation) are not covered by any specific energy efficiency requirements at all. While energy efficiency is still required for industrial installations under § 5 para. 1 1st sentence Nr. 4 Federal Emission Control Act ('BImSchG'), this provision has effectively been suspended for all installations covered under the ETS (§ 5 para. 1 4th sentence, which was introduced in conjunction with the TEHG).[31]

15.18   Regulatory requirements do play a significant role in increasing energy efficiency in the building sector. An example of this is the Energy Saving Act ('EnEV'),[32] which applies to buildings. The KWKG helps to expand heat networks and contains an obligation to connect CHP, to accept and to purchase the electricity and heat produced by these installations (§§ 4–8 KWKG).[33]

15.19   With regard to motor vehicles, the EU has set binding targets for CO_2 emissions from new vehicles (Regulation 443/2009).[34] This Regulation has not yet been implemented into German law. In respect of product efficiency requirements, German law

---

[30]   See BVerwG, 30 June 2005, 7 C 26/04 and BVerfG, 14 May 2007, 1 BvR 2036/05 which did not accept the appeal against the BVerwG decision. For further discussion of the many disputes arising from the implementation of the TEHG, see Frenz, 'Gleichheitssatz und Wettbewerbsrelevanz bei BVerfG und EuGH – Das Beispiel Emissionshandel', DVBl 2010, p. 223 with references. See also the DEHST website at www.dehst.de.

[31]   For a critique see SRU, *Umweltgutachten* (2008), para. 164 ff and Verheyen, n. 9 above.

[32]   Of 24 July 2007, BGBl I 2007, p. 1519, last amended on 29 April 2009, BGBl I 2009, p. 954. See further Vogel, *'Einige ungeklärte Fragen zur EnEV'*, BauR 2009, p. 1196; and Schlarmann and Maroldt, *'Energieeinsparverordnung und Energieausweis in der Praxis'*, BauR 2009, p. 32.

[33]   See n. 21 above.

[34]   Regulation (EC) No. 443/2009 of the European Parliament and the Council of 23 April 2009 on setting emission performance standards for new passenger cars as part of the EU's integrated approach to reduce CO_2 emissions from light-duty vehicles, OJ L 140, p. 1.

essentially follows EU rules. For example, Germany has transposed the EU Eco-design Directive of 2005.[35]

Legislation on renewable energy

15.20   The EEG is the core instrument supporting renewable energy
generation.[36] At the heart of the EEG are two fundamental obligations placed on electricity grid operators. First, they must give
priority to feeding in, transmitting and distributing renewably
generated energy (§§ 5 para. 1 and 8 para. 1, first sentence, No.
1 of the EEG 2008); and second, they must pay a guaranteed
price designed to promote the use of renewable energy, which is
not yet market-ready. The feed-in tariffs are initially paid for by
grid system operators and electricity supply companies through
an elaborate vertical and horizontal compensation mechanism,
although the costs are in the end borne by consumers. This regulatory model has proven extremely effective,[37] and the ECJ has
classified this instrument as compliant with EU law.[38]

15.21   The Renewable Energy Heat Act contains, inter alia, a statutory
obligation to cover a percentage of heat demand from renewable
energy sources.[39]

15.22   A key factor in promoting renewable energy involves encouraging greater use of biofuels and biogas.[40] However, the general
attempt to support biogas has resulted in conflict surrounding
the level of land use required.[41] The biogas installations also

---

[35]   Directive 2005/32/EC of 6 July 2005, OJ L 121, p. 29, amended by Directive 2009/125/EC
of 21 October 2009, OJ L 285, p. 10.
[36]   See above, n. 19 above; Verheyen *et al.*, www.futurepolicy.org/fileadmin/user_upload/
PACT/Laws/Germany_legal_analysis.pdf (English summary); Prall and Ewer, 'Umweltschutz im deutschen Energierecht' in Koch (ed.), *Umweltrecht*, 3rd edn (2010), § 9.
[37]   See the Bundesregierung (German government), '*Konzept zur Förderung, Entwicklung
und Markteinführung von geothermischer Stromerzeugung und Wärmenutzung*', dated
13 May 2009, BT-Drs. 16/13128.
[38]   ECJ, 13 March 2001 (C 379/98, 2001, I–2099).
[39]   See n. 19 above.
[40]   Regulation on Requirements for sustainable production of Biofuels, BGBl I 2009, p.
3182, last amended on 22 June 2010, BGBl I 2010, p. 814. See also for supporting measures: Ordinance on Access to Gas Supply Grids of 25 July 2005, BGBl I 2005, p. 2210, last
amended on 17 October 2008, BGBl I 2008, p. 2006; Ordinance on Fees for Access to Gas
Supply Grids of 25 July 2005, BGBl I 2005, p. 2197, last amended on 17 October 2008,
BGBl I 2008, p. 2006.
[41]   SRU, *Klimaschutz durch Biomasse* (2007), marginal no. 105 ff, 150.

cause controversy because of the fumes and odours they generate, and in a growing number of cases community groups and
environmental organisations have opposed permits for these
plants.[42]

15.23   One of the main political issues in respect of renewable fuels
         concerns the use of biofuels in cars. The EU has prescribed a
         10 per cent share of biofuels in the transport sector (Directive
         2009/28/EG, Article 3 para. 4). This requirement has already
         been implemented in part.[43]

Planning law

Climate change in impact assessments

15.24   Germany has largely implemented the EU Directives on EIAs and
         strategic environmental assessments ('SEAs')[44] through the Act
         on Environmental Impact Assessment ('UVPG').[45] In Germany,
         an EIA or SEA is a separate procedure which is integrated into
         the actual licensing or planning procedure (§ 2 para. 1 UVPG).
         It can only be challenged in the context of an action against the
         actual licence or plan, and its outcome does not preempt the out-
         come of the licensing or planning procedure in any way.

15.25   The EIA must look at the environmental impact of a project. As
         stated in the administrative guidance to the EIA ('UVPVwV'),[46]
         all impacts 'relevant to the decision' must be assessed. As the cli-
         mate is expressly mentioned as factor in § 2 para. 1 Nr. 2 UVPG,
         there should be no doubt that this includes the global climate.[47]
         However, there is to date no court case explicitly concurring
         with this opinion. In practice, EIAs and SUPs tend to include
         global climate effects, even though there is no acknowledged

---

[42] See BVerwG, 21 December 2010, 7 B 4/10 (on planning law and licencing of such plants) and VGH München, 13 December 2010, 4 CE 10.2839 (dealing with a municipal-level referendum regarding the location of a biogas plant). See in general Nies, 'Aktuelle Entwicklungen der Rechtsprechung zu Tierhaltungs- und Biogasanlagen', AUR 2010, p. 292.

[43] Law on biofuel quota of 18 December 2006, BGBl I 2006, S. 3180, last amended 15 July 2009, BGBl I 2009, S. 1804 and 36. Verordnung zur Durchführung des Bundes-Immissionsschutzgesetzes, 29 January 2007, BGBl I 2007, p. 60.

[44] EIA, Directive 85/337/EEC and its amendments; and SEA, Directive 2001/42/EC.

[45] Of 24 February 2010, BGBl I 2010, p. 94.

[46] Of 18 September 1995, GMBl, p. 671.

[47] Würtenberger, 'Der Klimawandel in den Umweltprüfungen', ZUR 2009, p.171.

methodology.[48] The problem lies essentially with defining the impacts or effects of a given project on the climate, given that this is a cumulative problem and that impacts on the regional scale are still relatively uncertain.

15.26   In urban planning, 'climate protection requirements' must be considered at all times (§ 1 para. 5, 2nd sentence of the Federal Building Code ('BauGB')).[49] Thus, the municipalities should make a level-specific, municipal contribution to climate change mitigation.[50] This has been expressly recognised in BVerwG judgments.[51] Moreover, specifically designated areas must, under § 9 para. 1 No. 23b BauGB, when constructing buildings, implement 'certain building measures … to allow the use of renewable energy and particularly solar energy'. Under § 11 para. 1 No. 4 BauGB, municipalities may agree on 'the use of district networks, combined heat and power plants and solar energy facilities to provide heat, cooling and electricity supplies'.[52]

15.27   § 35 para. 1 BauGB sets out a simplified procedure under which a facility designed to use wind energy, hydropower or biogas may be approved as a development project conducted in the undesignated outlying area.[53] Furthermore, climate protection should be considered in land-use planning at the regional and even state level (§ 2 Nr. 6 Spatial Planning Act, 'ROG').[54]

Revenue and tax law

15.28   Most of Germany's climate law is now no longer based on economic instruments. The fundamental instrument aimed at

---

[48] See on this, in the context of coal-fired power plants, Verheyen, n. 9 above, p. 406 ff.
[49] Baugesetzbuch of 23 September 2004, BGBl I, p. 2414, last amended on 31 July 2009, BGBl I, p. 2585.
[50] See Koch and Hendler, *Baurecht, Raumordnungs- und Landesplanungsrecht*, 5th edn (Boorberg, 2009), § 14 marginal no. 39, and Ingold and Schwarz, '*Städtebau- und Energiefachrecht*', NuR 2010, p. 308.
[51] BVerwGE 118, S. 33 (41); 125, S. 68 (73); see also the decision by the Competition Senate at the BGH: BGHZ 151, 274 at 285.
[52] See further Mitschang, '*Die Belange von Klima und Energie in der Bauleitplanung*', NUR 2008, p. 601; '*Die Belange von Klima und Energie in der Raumordnung*', DVBl 2008, p. 745.
[53] See Koch and Hendler, n. 50 above, § 25, marginal no. 79.
[54] See BGBl I 2008, p. 2986, 22 December 2008. This provision also calls on states and regions to safeguard natural sinks as well as storage spaces for greenhouse gases.

reducing CO_2 emissions is the eco tax (Eco Tax Act 2000).[55] This brought in taxation on electricity and increased taxation on fossil fuels, while also simultaneously decreasing tax on labour and amending existing legislation such as the Fossil Fuel Tax Act. The eco tax was strongly resisted by industry, which argued that it infringed basic freedoms of the GG as well as the principle of equal treatment (Article 3 GG). However, it was declared fully lawful by the BVerfG.[56]

15.29   As of 1 January 2011, a special aviation tax applies for all flights from Germany.[57] Levies vary depending on the distance covered by the specific flight as well as the number of passengers. This tax has been criticised on the grounds that aviation now also falls within the ETS. It is also still disputed whether the tax itself infringes the GG.[58]

National climate change risks

15.30   Mean air temperature increased in Germany by 0.9°C between 1901 and 2006, while annual rainfall increased by approximately 9 per cent from the beginning of the nineteenth century, and the 1990s were the warmest decade of the twentieth century. In 2008, the Federal Cabinet approved the 'German Strategy for Adaptation to Climate Change'.[59] This Adaptation Strategy predicts a number of possible outcomes resulting from climate change, inter alia: (i) more instances of extreme precipitation leading to flooding; (ii) winter flooding due to a decrease in snowfall and therefore snowpacks as a result of warmer winters; and (iii) frequent low-water phases during dry summer periods, which will affect cooling-water availability and ecological health and increase erosion as well as the risk that pollutants, waste fertilisers and waste pesticides will find their way into ground and surface waters.[60]

---

[55] See BGBl I, p. 378, 24 March 1999.
[56] BVerfG, 20 April 2004, 1 BvR 905/00.
[57] See BGBl I 2010, p. 1885, 9 December 2010.
[58] Eilers and Hey, 'Haushaltskonsolidierung ohne Kompetenzgrundlage', DStR 2011, p. 97.
[59] Bundesregierung, 'Deutsche Anpassungsstrategie an den Klimawandel', 17 December 2008, at www.bmu.de/klimaschutz/downloads/doc/42783.php.
[60] Text partly taken from the Fifth National Communication: see n. 7, p. 183.

15.31   A recent major study on the legal implications of climate change
        shows that adapting to the impact of climate change will necessi-
        tate major alterations in coastal protection law, spatial and other
        planning law enforcement mechanisms, as well as requiring legal
        tools to tackle uncertainty.[61] This is a growing area of law, and
        one which may provide fertile ground for future lawsuits.

(B)   Public law

15.32   This section discusses the ways in which court challenges may
        improve and strengthen climate protection. While the climate
        protection instruments referred to above are often challenged by
        those they target, as seen with the challenges against the alloca-
        tion of certificates under the emissions trading regime, there is
        still relatively little case law challenging the legislative or admin-
        istrative decisions on climate grounds. This is partly due to the
        standing restrictions that have always governed German admin-
        istrative law and have been upheld by the judiciary. These restric-
        tions essentially bar all general climate considerations from
        judicial review, while also generally allowing those to whom cli-
        mate regulation is addressed (mostly operators and industry) to
        sue at all instances. As this seems about to change, there is a need
        to reconsider possible cases for judicial review. In this context, as
        mentioned above, constitutional law contains the legal basis for
        using climate protection arguments in administrative courts.

The constitutional context

15.33   Article 20a GG states that, 'mindful also of its responsibility
        toward future generations, the State shall protect the natural
        bases of life by legislation and, in accordance with law and just-
        ice, by executive and judicial action, all within the framework of
        the constitutional order'. As the climate system is undoubtedly
        a natural resource vital to survival and development, climate
        protection is covered by this provision,[62] even though, strictly
        speaking, protection of the natural systems will not include,

---

[61] Cf. Reese, et al., *Rechtlicher Handlungsbedarf für die Anpassung an die Folgen des Klimawandels* (UBA-Berichte, 2010), with English summary at www.uba.de.

[62] BVerwG (see n. 14).

for instance, protection of infrastructure threatened by climate change. Furthermore, it is clear from the wording that this 'aim' is different from a traditional human rights obligation. As such, it is difficult to assess what climate change mitigation obligations arise directly from the GG. The literature on constitutional law contains a wide range of proposals, including a general prohibition against allowing the environmental situation to worsen[63] and an obligation for energy policy to promote renewable energy before all other energy sources.[64] There is as yet no case law confirming the precise application of Article 20a GG with respect to climate change. Interestingly, however, the BVerfG recently nullified a regulation on cages for laying hens on the basis (inter alia) that this regulation violates Article 20a GG, thus accepting Article 20a GG as a 'firm' yardstick against which to measure federal law.[65] Moreover, in the context of the commercial release of genetically modified organisms, the BVerfG emphasised the special duty of care of the legislator in the face of scientific uncertainty.[66]

15.34   In general, Article 20a GG appears to place all State authorities, including the legislature, under an obligation to engage in proactive climate change policy. This must be viewed in close conjunction with the duties of protection derived from the basic human right to life and health (Article 2 GG). The BVerfG has not *excluded* the possibility that an individual could rely directly on Article 20a[67] – thus indirectly placing Article 20a GG in the vicinity of other human rights covered by the GG. The personal freedoms and guarantees provided in the GG include not only a protection of the rights of individuals against State intervention, but also an obligation on the legislator to protect and promote the holders of basic rights.[68] This is particularly relevant where

---

[63] See Murswiek, '*Staatsziel Umweltschutz – Article 20a GG*', NVwZ 1996, p. 222, 226; Waechter, '*Umweltschutz als Staatsziel*', NuR 1996, p. 321, 327; Petersen, '*Staatsziel Umweltschutz – Chance oder Leerformel?*', Jahrbuch Umwelt und Technikrecht, vol. 58 (2001), pp. 59, 76.

[64] Gärditz, '*Einführung in das Klimaschutzrecht*', JuS 2008, p. 324, 327.

[65] BVerfG, 12 October 2010, 2 BvF 1/07.

[66] BVerfG, 24 November 2010, 1 BvF 2/05.

[67] BVerfG, 10 November 2009, 1 BvR 1178/07, Leitsatz 5b: 'it can be left open whether …'.

[68] Isensee, 'Das Grundrecht als Abwehrrecht und als Schutzpflicht' in Isensee and Kirchhof (eds.), *Handbuch des Staatsrechts der Bundesrepublik Deutschland*, 3rd edn, vol. V (2007), § 111.

the 'environment-reliant' basic legal concepts of life, physical integrity (Article 2 GG) and property (Article 14 GG) are threatened by private users' environmental impacts. As such, the State also has an objective constitutional responsibility, for example to take action against health-damaging air pollution and noise from industrial facilities and motor vehicles by introducing adequate statutory regulations. This also applies in respect of the wide-ranging threats to people's health and property which would arise from significant changes in the climate. Examples include the threat of flooding or water scarcity caused by periods of drought.

15.35   Article 1 GG may also in some instances be interpreted as assigning the State a responsibility to protect against risks arising from negative impacts on the environment. Under Article 1 GG, 'Human dignity shall be inviolable. To respect and protect it shall be the duty of all state authority.' A State obligation to secure an 'ecological subsistence level' may be inferred from these guarantees.[69] If the international community fails to meet the 2°C target, then the scope of the resulting threats will be such that measures to mitigate them could well be necessary to secure the 'ecological subsistence level' arising from Article 1 GG in conjunction with Article 2 GG.

15.36   However, the main obstacle faced by a judicial review of a law or a decision taken by an authority arguing that it insufficiently protects the climate (and thus for example the right to life/health) is that the State's obligation to protect as set out in Article 20a GG and Articles 1 and 2 GG gives the State broad scope in terms of 'assessing, evaluating and structuring'.[70] Only when the State's failure to comply breaches the 'subsistence level' requirement is it deemed to have breached the constitutional duty to protect.[71] This is the reason why major cases on environmental pollution have been lost in court. An example is long-range air pollution, where forest owners argued that emission standards had to be tightened by the legislator to protect their property (Article 14

---

[69] Höfling, in Sachs (ed.), *Grundgesetz*, 4th edn (2007), Article 1, marginal no. 31.
[70] See BVerfG, 14 January 1981, 1 BvR 612/72 (aviation noise).
[71] On the obligation of the State not to fall short of minimum requirements, see BVerfG, 28 May 1993, 2 BvF 2/90. See further Koch, in Koch (ed), *Umweltrecht*, 3rd edn (2010), p. 178 ff.

GG);[72] another is ground-level ozone, with individuals arguing
that the emission control standards enacted by the government
violated their right to health (Article 2 GG),[73] and yet another is
aviation noise (again Article 2 GG).[74] This, however, is a dynamic
concept. If, for example, the concept of emission budgets is elaborated further, it is possible to conceive a case which forces the
administration to do more to achieve a certain climate protection
aim or target, or to generally argue that (as in the case for waste or
agriculture) nothing is being done or (as in the case of transport)
far too little is being done. Who could bring such cases, and how
they would work is discussed in the next section.

Judicial review law

Overview

15.37   Public law is considered to be all law that applies between the
State and citizens (private persons or legal entities). Article 19
para. 4 GG guarantees that the judiciary will scrutinise actions
by the State with respect to the individual. The main group of
cases in climate change law will be those challenging a particular administrative decision (*Verwaltungsakt, VA*), allowing a particular industrial installation, airport or road to be built. In these
cases, the lawsuit would attack that administrative act – an action
for annulment (§ 42 para. 1 Administrative Court Procedures
Code, 'VwGO'[75]). If one considers that an administrative decision must be taken, an action for engagement would be eligible,
i.e. the authority ordered by the court to take a certain decision
(§ 42 para. 2 VwGO). For such an action to be successful, the
plaintiff will have to show that the law affords him a specific right
to the desired behaviour, for example in protecting his interests
in property or health. For the whole system of judicial review it is
decisive to determine whether the subject matter is a VA or not.[76]

---

[72] BVerfG, 14 September 1983, 1 BvR 920/83. See also the civil law side of this in BGH, 10 December 1987, Az.: III ZR 220/86.

[73] BVerfG, 29 November 1995, 1 BvR 2203/95.

[74] BVerfG, 14 January 1981, 1 BvR 612/72.

[75] BGBl I 1991, 686, 19 March 1991, last amended by law of 22 December 2010, BGBl I, p. 2248.

[76] The term is defined in § 35 of the Administration Procedural Code, BGBl I 2003, p. 102, dated 23 January 2003.

There are also similar types of suits addressing actions by the public authorities that are not decisions binding certain individuals, but simply constitute activities 'in reality'.

15.38   However, courts will also – under certain circumstances – scrutinise the lawfulness of statutes or regulations. In particular, state and municipal law can be challenged taking a 'norm control action' (§ 47 VwGO). In the climate context this is relevant for land-use plans, for spatial planning acts on state or regional level, but also for all other law enacted by the states as long as the respective state law allows the norm control action.

15.39   Depending on the case, there is also the option of directly challenging federal law before the BVerfG, either by an individual (Article 93 para. 1 Nr. 4a GG) or by a public body such as the federal parliament or parts of it, a government or parliament of a state, etc. Such cases are governed by the procedural code for the BVerfG (BVerfGG),[77] and not the VwGO. Any court can refer a case for a direct opinion to the BVerfG (Article 100 GG) if it sees a conflict with the basic laws of the GG.

15.40   In administrative matters, it will normally be necessary to argue the case with the authority on a higher level before going to court (see §§ 69 ff VwGO), especially if a VA is not granted, or a decision negatively affects the individual. It will be this last decision that is the subject matter of the judicial review.

15.41   Generally speaking, a lawsuit will be successful if (i) it is procedurally eligible – this includes standing of the plaintiff; and (ii) it can be shown that the challenged act or omission by a public body violates material law *and* (normally; exceptions will be discussed below) the 'subjective right' of the plaintiff (§ 113 para. 5 VwGO), including rights granted directly by the GG. This last requirement is of high importance for all judicial reviews taken in the context of climate change. It means that even if on the proced ural level standing can be shown, there might still be no review of the substantive law (say, compliance with a target such as in § 1 EEG to achieve 30 per cent renewable energy by the year 2020)

---

[77] Of 11 August 1993, BGBl I 1993, 1473, last amended on 22 December 2010, BGBl I, p. 2248.

because the failure to achieve this target will not affect the plaintiff's rights.

15.42   The VwGO (§§ 42, 43) foresees essentially the following possible actions: (i) annulment of a VA; (ii) obligation of a public authority to enact a VA; (iii) obligation to omit a certain type of behaviour; (iv) obligation to undertake a certain type of behaviour; and, in the case of norm control actions, (v) nullify a statute or regulation. Due to the separation of powers, the court can revoke VAs, but not 'make' them itself.

Grounds for judicial review (*Klagegründe*)

15.43   Generally, a judicial review can be based on any of the following grounds: (i) action or decision not in compliance with the applicable legal provision(s); (ii) unlawful exercise of discretion; (iii) procedural errors; or (iv) unconstitutionality of the applicable provision or law.

15.44   Ground (i). Generally, a decision will have to be in accordance with the legal framework and have a firm legal basis. If the rule in question simply stipulates legal criteria for a certain type of decision and does *not* afford discretion, the case will revolve around the facts and whether these fulfil the legal criteria. The court's role is straightforward: it can offer its own finding of facts and legal interpretation, and, in particular, give a different interpretation of the specific legal criteria, an example in the context of climate change being in relation to a permit to run a major power station (governed by §§ 5, 6 BImSchG) which does not afford discretion.

15.45   Provisions that afford authorities a margin of appreciation are an exception to this rule. In such cases, due to the complexity and special circumstances of the law in question, an authority will be afforded room to manoeuvre, and the courts will not intervene even if the matter in question is one of interpreting the law and factual circumstances. This heavily criticised concept is now widely applied in nuclear safety law,[78] on genetically modified organisms[79] and in nature conservation, especially species protection law.[80]

[78]   BVerwG, 19 December 1985, 7 C 65/82.
[79]   BVerwG, 15 April 1999, 7 B 278/98.
[80]   BVerwG, 9 June 2010, 9 A 20/08.

15.46   Ground (ii). If the rule in question affords discretion to the author-
         ities, the case will – in addition to testing whether the purely legal
         criteria are met – revolve around whether or not discretion was
         exercised in a lawful way.

15.47   While there are some differences in theory between the types of
         discretion offered (simple discretion in nature protection law,
         planning discretion in road building, management discretion
         in water law), the method of scrutiny applied by the courts is
         very similar. The task given to the authority is to weigh interests
         against each other and then come to a 'justly weighed' conclu-
         sion. The courts will therefore scrutinise whether the authority
         has (i) actually exercised its discretion; (ii) gathered and assessed
         all relevant information; (iii) not taken into consideration facts or
         interests that the applicable law did not intend to be considered;
         and (iv) not acted outside its discretion.[81] A similar test is applied
         in cases of planning or management discretion, with the general
         obligation being to weigh all interests in a 'just' manner[82] and to
         ensure that conflicts arising from the project are solved by the
         decision itself.[83]

15.48   Ground (iii). As a rule of thumb, non-compliance with the rules
         of procedure and form will not lead to the annulment of a deci-
         sion, especially with respect to planning decisions. This is already
         stated in the Administrative Procedure Act ('VwVfG')[84] and
         specified in many other provisions.

15.49   Ground (iv). At any stage of a court procedure the plaintiff can
         argue that the applicable provision in law violates one or several
         of the basic (human) rights or other rules of the Constitution.
         An example of the former would be a provision in federal law
         which regulates flight noise but in an insufficient manner and in
         conflict with Article 2 para. 2 GG (health protection).[85] Another
         example would be the proposed climate protection law of the

---

[81] See Kopp and Ramsauer, 'VwVfG', *Kommentar*, § 40, No. 58.
[82] BVerwG, 14 February 1975, IV C 21.74.
[83] BVerwG, 23 January 1981, 4 C 68/78.
[84] § 46 VwVfG: 'The repeal of an administrative act … may not be claimed only because it
      was taken in violation of regulations on the procedure, the form or the local jurisdiction,
      if it is evident that the error has not influenced the decision as such.'
[85] See n. 70 above.

state of Nordrhein-Westphalia, which has been criticized for falling outside the state's jurisdiction.[86]

Standing

15.50 Standing has traditionally been a major hurdle for all actions
relating to the environment. German legal tradition has rejected
popular actions and remains focused on protecting the *rights of
individuals*, not providing a judicial review of all actions or omissions by public authorities.[87]

15.51 § 42 para. 2 VwGO stipulates that plaintiffs will only have standing if they demonstrate that the act or omission that is challenged
in court relates to their 'subjective rights'. In practice, this means
the plaintiff must find a provision in the given law which protects
the interests of the plaintiff (*drittschützend*), not just the interests
of society as a whole,[88] and make a cursory case that this 'subjective right' is violated by the public authority or lawmaker. On
the whole, many laws, especially those relating to the protection
of nature or containing precautionary measures or policies, will
not be deemed to be *drittschützend*, while noise and air pollution
provisions will be.

15.52 A notable exception is the norm control action. The plaintiff can
challenge the statute or regulation on the basis of all applicable
law, regardless of whether this confers any specific rights or interests on the plaintiff. This is one reason why, for example, resist-
ance against coal-fired power plants has focused on challenging
the land-use plans enacted by the municipalities.

15.53 It must be reiterated that neither standing nor the scope of
judicial scrutiny is an issue for the addressee of a decision, for
example the operator of a plant. He can basically argue all substantive law. This situation has led to some provisions in federal
and state law introducing a limited type of class action, i.e. limited

---

[86] Schink, '*Regelungsmöglichkeiten der Länder im Klimaschutz*', UPR 2011, p. 91.
[87] Koch, '*Verbandsklage im Umweltrecht*', NVwZ 2007, p. 369; SRU, *Rechtsschutz für die
Umwelt – Die altruistische Verbandsklage ist unverzichtbar* (2005).
[88] There is such a wealth of case law on this issue, that looking at individual rules with
respect to whether they are meant to protect the plaintiff (*drittschützend*) or not cannot be covered here. See for a summary Ramsauer, in Koch (ed.), *Umweltrecht*, 3rd edn
(2010), p. 142 ff.

standing provisions for NGOs,[89] the most important one being § 64 Federal Nature Protection Act ('BNatSchG'), introduced only in 2002. However, standing is limited to major projects such as road construction, landfill sites and specific decisions related to nature protection.[90]

15.54 In transposition of the Aarhus Convention and EU Directive 2003/35, the Federal Environmental Appeals Act ('UmwRG') of 2006 now allows suits by environmental NGOs in a broader context, namely for all projects requiring an EIA. However, this option has been restricted to breaches of rules: (i) protecting the environment; and (ii) affording rights to individuals. This limitation, in turn, has been criticised[91] for not being in compliance with the Aarhus Convention of 1998 and EU Directive 2003/35. After decisions by some German courts to the effect that the UmwRG is consistent with EU law,[92] the Münster OVG referred the matter to the ECJ for a preliminary ruling.[93] The ECJ's ruling is still pending, but some conclusions can be drawn on the basis of the opinion of the Advocate General in *Sharpston*,[94] with which the ECJ is likely to concur. In essence, the Advocate General argues that the implementation of Directive 2003/35 in German law is insufficient, that NGOs can rely directly on this Directive to seek access to courts and, in this context, are:

> permitted to argue that there has been an infringement of *any environmental provision relevant* to the approval of a project, including provisions which *are intended to serve the interests of the general public alone* rather than those which, at least in part, protect the legal interests of individuals.[95]

---

[89] These must be officially registered and show that they have as their main purpose the protection of the environment (§ 3 Federal Environmental Appeals Act of 7 December 2006, BGBl I 2006, p. 2816).

[90] Some states still retain their own nature protection acts which contain some additional standing provisions. These cannot be dealt with in detail here.

[91] See Berkemann, '*Umwelt-Rechtsbehelfsgesetz auf dem gemeinschaftsrechtlichen Prüfstand*', NordÖR 2009, p. 336; Gellermann, '*Europäisierte Klagerechte anerkannter Umweltverbände*', NVwZ 2006, p.7; Koch (see n. 87 above).

[92] OVG Schleswig, 12 March 2009, 1 KN 12/08, OVG Lüneburg, 7 July 2008, 1 ME 131/08, but see also OVG Lüneburg, 10 March 2010, 12 ME 176/09.

[93] OVG Nordrhein-Westfalen, 5 March 2009, order for reference to the ECJ, 8 D 58/08.AK.

[94] Case C-115/09, Opinion of 16 December 2010.

[95] *Ibid.*, para. 95 (emphasis added).

15.55   This would mean that – at least in the context of projects that must undergo an EIA – NGOs would in future be able to argue 'objective' law in court, not being restricted to either law that protects only the environment in certain procedures (§ 64 BNatSchG) or provisions that afford – in the German terminology – *Drittschutz* to individuals.[96] In terms of climate protection, this could make a decisive difference.

Other procedural aspects of judicial review

15.56   In judicial review law, if factual matters are disputed, it is the court's responsibility to assess the facts and even investigate itself in cases where the plaintiff has not submitted enough evidence (see § 86 para. 1 VwGO). In practice, however, it will be necessary for the plaintiff to argue both facts and law to the most detailed level.

15.57   Court costs are normally not excessive in Germany. They are calculated on a fixed legal basis applying the value of the claim in question as set by the court (§ 52 para. 1 of the Court Cost Act ('GKG')).[97] To guide court discretion, a detailed table has been issued by judges,[98] which is not binding but will almost always be applied. For example, this table stipulates that actions taken by NGOs will normally be fixed at €15,000 – even if this case was taken against a major road-building project of a value of several million Euros. This would then result in a fee of €242, which would – in accordance with the GKG – automatically be multiplied by three for actions commenced in an administrative court (by four for actions commenced in a high court), resulting in moderate court costs of €726 or €968, respectively. In addition, attorney fees would arise. There is no obligation to appear with an attorney in a first instance court. This obligation only arises in the higher courts (see § 67 VwGO). Attorney fees would also depend on the value of the claim. In the example given above, a first instance case would cost around €1,700 plus tax

---

96 Note however that there is some uncertainty in this regard because the Advocate General has not taken a position as to whether this scope of access to court should only apply to EU law or to national rules as well.

97 Of 5 May 2004, BGBl I 2004, p. 718, last amended on 22 December 2010, BGBl I, p. 2248.

98 The currently applied version of this is the *Streitwertkatalog 2004*, available at www.justiz.nrw.de/BS/Hilfen/streitwertkatalog.pdf.

etc. in accordance with the Attorney Fee Act ('RVG').[99] However, given that these fees would not cover real costs, attorneys operate mostly on the basis of fee agreements. As a general rule, the defeated party bears all the costs of the case.

State aid/competition law

15.58 Municipalities, which hold major property interests, also have civil law options to enforce climate protection aims. For example, the *Börnsen* municipality won its case against an oil trading association which had challenged, under competition law, contracts under which property buyers were obliged to use the electricity and heat generated by the municipality's own CHP plant in housing to be built on the relevant property.[100]

Other cases

OECD complaints

15.59 The OECD *Guidelines for Multinational Enterprises* ('the Guidelines')[101] contain a set of rules which can be applied to improve climate protection, aimed at multinational enterprises operating in or from adhering countries. These Guidelines are said to be 'voluntary' in that they do not constitute public or private international law; however, they are to some extent institutionalised with national contact points ('NCP')[102] administering a complaint procedure. The NCPs are to support the implementation of the Guidelines, to inform the public about them and to handle complaints as specified in the 'Procedural Guidance' to the Guidelines. NCPs should offer a 'forum for discussion to resolve conflicts and problems arising from the implementation of the Guidelines',[103] and anyone claiming an interest can bring a

---

[99] Of 5 April 2004, BGBl I 2004, p. 718, last amended on 22 December 2010, BGBl I, p. 2300.

[100] BGH, 9 July 2002, KZR 30/00.

[101] Version of 2000, available at www.oecd.org/dataoecd/56/36/1922428.pdf. A revision is currently on the way which will lead to a new, 2011 version.

[102] The German NCP is based at the German Federal Ministry of Economics and Technology.

[103] See for more detail Verheyen, *'Transparency and the OECD-Dispute Settlement Process'* (Germanwatch, 2009), at www.germanwatch.org; and OECD Watch, 'Guide to the OECD guidelines for multinational enterprises' complaint procedure, at www.oecdwatch.org.

claim for breaches of the Guidelines. In terms of substantive law, the environment chapter (Chapter V) of the Guidelines contains general as well as quite specific obligations, such as to 'establish and maintain a system of environmental management', including the collection and evaluation of adequate and timely information regarding the environmental, health, and safety impacts of the enterprise's activity (V.1.a), disclosure of risks arising from its activities (III.1.) and obligations to refrain from deceptive marketing practices (VII.4).

15.60   The first climate-related complaint was launched against Volkswagen in 2007, on a number of substantive points.[104] It was turned down by the NCP, on the basis that no violation of the Guidelines had been found. A second climate-related complaint was brought in 2009, against Vattenfall, a Swedish-based energy company.[105] This complaint was also turned down. In both cases, the NCP argued that the particular conduct of the company was not forbidden by law, and that climate protection considerations were essentially policy led.

15.61   One major problem with the Guidelines is that there is currently no procedure in place for requesting judicial review of an NCP decision. The NCP argues that there is no entitlement to a complaint procedure, as it is only engaged as a mediator, i.e. that its rejection of a complaint is not a formal administrative decision which can be challenged in court. The counter-argument is that, even if the Guidelines are not binding on companies, States are under an obligation to open up a procedure to interested parties and so to provide a complaint procedure. Under the GG, any activity by a public authority with a bearing on public interests must be challengeable.

Justification of climate-related protest

15.62   An issue of growing importance – especially since the *Kingsnorth* ruling (see Chapter 17) – is whether NGO actions such as mounting chimneys or blocking access to plants can

---

[104] See www.germanwatch.org/corp/vw-besch-e.pdf.
[105] See www.greenpeace.de/fileadmin/gpd/user_upload/themen/klima/OECD-Beschwerde.
pdf.

be legally justified where it is for the public good. This has been argued under § 227 BGB (Emergency Aid) and §§ 228, 904 BGB (State of Necessity) in defence against claims for financial damages in the context of a Greenpeace action against lignite mining.[106] However, the court, while acknowledging that climate change is a major issue, rejected the notion that private action could be warranted to stop lignite mining.

(C) Private law

15.63 In Germany, no direct climate liability claims have yet been made. Commentators from some law firms have expressed views that are very sceptical as to the chances of success of such claims;[107] and debate has now started[108] also as to whether such claims would be covered by standard liability insurance.[109]

15.64 The subject matter of this section is climate liability in the narrow sense. It therefore deals only with statutory claims that allow proceedings to be brought against the direct or indirect originators of climate change. The presentation follows the respective common law torts which do not exist in German law in this form but will help the non-German reader to navigate this area. The tort of 'negligence' (see 15.65) is followed by claims arising from 'private nuisance' (see 15.88) and 'strict liability' (see 15.97). We show that substantial potential lies in cases where the owner of a coastal property claims costs for increasing coastal protection infrastructure from, for example, operators of large coal-fired power plants; similarly, claims for damages after a major storm flood.

---

[106] LG Aachen, 16 March 2006, 1 O 126/05. Upheld by the BGH, 17 December 2007, VI ZR 216/06.A. For an action against nuclear power, see LG Dortmund, 14 October 1997, Ns 70 Js 90/96.

[107] Spieth and Hamer, *'Potential liabilities arising from climate change'* (Freshfields Bruckhaus Deringer client briefing, 2009), p. 3; and Chatzinerantzis and Herz, *'Climate Change Litigation – Der Klimawandel im Spiegel des Haftungsrechts'*, NJOZ 2010, p. 594–8.

[108] Responding to Chatzinerantzis and Herz, *ibid.*, Frank, *'Climate Change Litigation – Klimawandel und haftungsrechtliche Risiken'*, NJOZ 2010, p. 2296–300.

[109] Lach and Morbach, *'Versicherungsschutz für CO_2-Haftungsklagen'*, VersR 2011, pp. 52–4.

Negligence

15.65   The fundamental rule of the German law of delict – § 823, para.
1 BGB (German Civil Code) – provides a damages claim for loss
of, or damage to, a legally protected good (e.g. property) that is
attributable to a person who is at least negligent. There is an obvious similarity to the common law concept of 'negligence'. The
differences will become apparent in the discussion of the individual conditions of liability that are discussed below.

Factual causation

15.66   As in common law jurisdictions, German law has a two-fold test
for causation. A distinction is made between the question of causal
relationship in the logical or scientific sense between the action
and the loss (causation) and the further question of whether it is
justified to hold the person who has caused the loss responsible
(accountability).[110] It is recognised that causation in the logical or
scientific sense is determined according to the so-called *conditio
sine qua non* formula (the 'but for test'). According to this test,
an event is to be viewed as a cause if, without it, the result, in its
specific form, would not occur.[111] The act of an offender is therefore still a cause even if it in itself could not result in the damage
but only in combination with the actions of another (so-called
cumulative causation).[112] In spite of this simple and attractive
definition, German legal literature considers that questions of
causation belong to the biggest problems of environmental liability law.[113] The defendants in climate liability trials also see their
best chances of defence in this area.[114]

Causation by innumerable (ubiquitous) emission sources

15.67   Defendants will like to emphasise the similarity between climate change related damage and the forest damage caused by the

---

[110] Staudinger and Kohler, *Kommentar zum Bürgerlichen Gesetzbuch mit Einführungsgesetz
und Nebengesetzen*, vol. 3, *Sachenrecht, Umwelthaftungsrecht* (2010), Introduction, marginal no. 159.

[111] BGH, 4 July 1994, II ZR 126/93, marginal no. 15.

[112] BGH, 20 November 2001, VI ZR 77/00, marginal no. 9; Staudinger and Kohler (see n. 110
above), Introduction, marginal no. 172.

[113] Staudinger and Kohler (see n. 110 above), Introduction, marginal no. 156, with further
references.

[114] Chatzinerantzis and Herz (see n. 107 above), 596.

so-called 'acid rain'[115] that initiated a broad debate on liability law in Germany in the 1980s. At the time it was accepted that air pollutants with a large-scale effect, particularly the sulphur dioxide and nitrogen oxide emissions from a very large number of larger and smaller sources (power stations, industrial plants, heating and traffic), had damaged a considerable part of the German tree population. The polluters, however, escaped liability because it was impossible to attribute the loss of a particular forest owner to one or more specific polluters.[116]

15.68   But in the case of GHG, unlike the forest damage example, there is no similar causation problem if, as we assume here, it can be shown that the gases are distributed evenly into the atmosphere and therefore that every molecule that is emitted, irrespective of where it actually comes from, contributes at least marginally to the greenhouse effect and thereby to the rise in temperature and its consequences.[117]

Burden of proof

15.69   As a rule, it is the claimant who carries the burden of proof in relation to the cause of the damage. For some groups of cases, however, the law eases the evidential burden, even as far as a reversal of the burden of proof. This is the case when the defendant breaches a protective or safety duty or (this forms a sub-category of such cases) exceeds specified emission limits.[118] The causation presumption is explained here as the procedural consequence of a reasoning that lies at the basis of the substantive law. Underpinning a limit or protective duty is always[119] the expectation that, in case of breach, there will be a considerable increase in the likelihood of specific damage occurring.[120] This expectation is attributed to the effect of a rebuttable presumption for the causation of the types of damage that with increased probability result from the given breach of duty.[121]

---

[115] *Ibid.*, 597.   [116] BGH, 10 December 1987, III ZR 220/86, marginal. no. 13.

[117] Frank (see n. 108), p. 2298. See also Verheyen, *Climate Change Damage in International Law* (Martinus Nijhoff, 2005), p. 248 ff.

[118] BGH, 17 June 1997, VI ZR 372/95, marginal no. 11; BGH, 2 April 2004, V ZR 267/03, marginal no. 37.

[119] This interpretation might not be valid for precautionary limits.

[120] Staudinger and Kohler (see n. 110 above), Introduction, marginal no. 267.

[121] *Ibid.*, marginal. no. 265, with further references.

15.70   It seems plausible that this argument applicable to emission limits could be applied to establish a prima facie causal relationship
between GHG emissions and the increased global mean temperature due to the anthropogenic greenhouse effect. This link is not
only implied by the German legislator, but explicitly recognised
in statutes. For example, the legislator assumes that GHGs have
a 'potential to raise the temperature of the atmosphere' that can
be calculated precisely (§ 3 para. 4 TEHG). The 'aim' of 'slow-
ing down the anthropogenic greenhouse effect and contributing
towards the reduction of atmospheric GHGs levels' was set as
early as 2007 in the Federal Allocation Act 2007 for Greenhouse
Gas Emission Permits (see para. 15.15 above).[122]

Standard of proof

15.71   § 286 ZPO (Civil Procedure Act) defines the applicable standard
of proof: a disputed fact may only be accepted as proven by the
judge when he or she is 'persuaded' of the 'truth' of the submission. 'Persuasion' does not, however, require incontrovertible certainty. It is rather the case that the judge is permitted and indeed
must, in the poetic words of the Federal Judges, 'be satisfied with
a degree of certainty that is sufficient to subdue doubt for life's
practical purposes, but without eliminating it completely'.[123] The
actual level of probability of causation by the defendant in a particular case must be high enough for no reasonable doubts to
remain.

15.72   It is not to be expected within the foreseeable future that the
courts will follow the view held in legal literature that in order
to prove causation it is generally sufficient that the court is persuaded of predominant probability.[124] It could however prove to
be helpful that the objective content of the basic rights (see 15.34
above) is to be taken into account in establishing requirements
for evidence.[125] It therefore seems perceivable that the courts

---

[122] Explanatory Statement accompanying the draft of the ZuG 2007, BT-Drs. 15/2966, p. 15.
[123] BGH, 17 February 1970, III ZR 139/67, marginal no. 72.
[124] Prütting, *Münchener Kommentar zur Zivilprozessordnung*, 3rd edn (2008), § 286, marginal no. 47.
[125] BVerfG, 27 January 1998, 1 BvL 15/87, marginal. no. 37; Prütting, *ibid.*, § 286, marginal no. 129.

would lower the standard of proof in cases where the difficulties in providing evidence are due not to the circumstances of the particular case but to the limits of 'human knowledge', especially if otherwise it would not be possible to ensure the effective protection of fundamental rights.

Chances to prove causation

15.73   As for the chances to prove causation in court we will have to distinguish between the various stages of the causal chain. The first part of the chain from emissions to the resultant global warming can most likely be evidenced with the research results published in the IPCC Assessment Reports; it is even possible that a court will recognise a causation presumption for this part (see para. 15.70 above). But it will be much more difficult to prove the second link in the causal chain, namely that specific losses are caused by the effects of the global rise in temperature. This is because, as is emphasised often enough by those who are sceptical as regards the establishment of liability,[126] in particular as regards extreme weather events, according to the present state of scientific knowledge it can only be shown that these occur more frequently or severely as a result of climate change; not, however, that climate change related circumstances have had an effect on a *specific* event. However, cases are conceivable in which this connection could be proven. In particular, sea-level rise, including in its regional dimension, could at least partially be attributable to anthropogenic climate change. Since the risk of storm floods depends on the sea level, GHG emissions would be manifest in every storm flood damage, at least as a contributing factor. Therefore, a claim related to storm-surge events was recently given good prospects of success.[127]

Increase of risk and liability

15.74   In spite of those prospects, there remain many case groups in which only an increased risk can be established. This situation raises the question as to whether establishing a cause that is only probable can lead to liability. In Germany, in light of the so-called acid rain cases, there was broad debate on this, particularly in

---

[126] Chatzinerantzis and Herz (see n. 107 above), p. 593.
[127] Frank (see n. 108 above), pp. 2296–7.

the 1980s, which focussed on, among other matters, the concept of 'pollution share liability' as developed by US law.[128] Its application to the acid rain cases was considered because it was not possible to show *whose* sulphur dioxide emissions had resulted in specific damage. This problem does not exist in respect of CO_2 emissions if it is possible to assume that every emission contributes marginally to climate change (see 15.68 above). What is problematic here is much rather the question as to whether climate change has contributed to a particular loss *at all*. These two constellations differ in that in the first case other *anthropogenic* emissions are an obstacle to the proof of causation whereas in the second case it is the conceivable cause of *natural* influences that are.

15.75   In German legal literature advocates of liability on the basis of probability are primarily in favour of the first of the two case groups in which the class of possible perpetrators can be determined and natural influences are excluded as far as possible.[129] In the second case group, liability is sometimes considered to be desirable *de lege ferenda*,[130] but only very few commentators hold the view that liability is already provided for by the current state of the law, for example by analogous application of §§ 830 para. 1 s. 2, 254 BGB.[131] The courts have not recognised an increased risk or an 'endangering impact' on the environment as material grounds for liability, not even in exceptional cases, but have viewed these circumstances, in a case of the first category, at best as a starting point for a (rebuttable) presumption: this has happened on the basis of a rule that covers impact on waterpaths but not on the air (§ 89 Water Management Act ('WHG')).[132] Affirmation by the German courts of liability on the basis of probability is barely to be reckoned with in the future.

---

[128] Staudinger and Kohler (see n. 110 above), Introduction, marginal nos. 165–7 for references.

[129] *Ibid.*, marginal no. 202 for references.

[130] Köndgen, *Überlegungen zur Fortbildung des Umwelthaftpflichtrechts* (UPR, 1983), pp. 345–56, at p. 347; Reiter, *Entschädigungslösungen für durch Luftverunreinigungen verursachte Distanz- und Summationsschäden* (ESV, 1998), p. 129 ff.

[131] Seyfert, *Mass Toxic Torts: Zum Problem der kausalen Unaufklärbarkeit toxischer Massenschäden* (Duncker & Humblot, 2004), p. 110 ff.

[132] BGH, 22 November 1971, III ZR 112/69, marginal no. 27.

Legal causation/accountability

15.76 To be held accountable for a loss, established case law requires: (i) adequate causal connection; and (ii) that the loss (in terms of its type and the way in which it has arisen) is covered by the scope of the liability rule. Adequacy is affirmed if the occurrence of the relevant type of loss, when viewed retrospectively and in objective terms, was not completely improbable, or if its probability was 'increased by more than only an insignificant amount'.[133] In contrast to common law practice, legal causation does not depend on whether it is reasonable to hold the relevant offender liable. The courts cannot therefore spare the relevant offender on the basis of a 'sympathetic' balancing of interests.

15.77 It appears almost impossible that a loss could be considered too improbable and therefore 'inadequate', given that all the types of loss for which there is potentially a claim have been the subject of discussions of the characteristic consequences of climate change for years. This is all the more so given that the minimum probability is required in respect of the loss itself, not in respect of the specific, possibly atypical causal chain of events.[134] All loss that arises from damage to property or health comes within the scope of § 823 para. 1 BGB, even if it is brought on by complex atmospheric processes. This is because the protective function of this basic rule of the law of delict is not limited to particular dangers or particular ways in which danger arises.

15.78 Particular conditions for accountability apply in cases of indirect causation in which the loss only arises on subsequent action by a third party. The indirectly responsible party will only be liable if his/her contribution breached a duty to protect the general public (a so-called *Verkehrssicherungspflicht* or safety duty).[135] The contents of the safety duty depend on the recognised dangers and on the preventative measures that are technically available and economically reasonable for the indirectly responsible party. It is up to the civil courts to rule on the existence of the duty and in doing so they may take public law provisions into consideration.

---

[133] Palandt and Grüneberg, *Bürgerliches Gesetzbuch*, 70th edn (2011), introduction to § 249, marginal. nos. 24–7.
[134] *Ibid.*, marginal no. 27, with references.
[135] Palandt and Sprau, *Bürgerliches Gesetzbuch*, 70th edn (2011), § 823, marginal no. 45.

A safety duty of this type also applies when putting products into circulation.[136] Of particular importance among the indirect initiators of climate change are motor vehicle manufacturers, where emissions are produced only when the motor vehicles are used by the buyer. An option would be to impose a duty of care on manufacturers that would entail taking constructive measures to reduce the CO_2 emissions of the vehicles they produce. The fleet target in Regulation (EC) No. 443/2009 (see 15.19 above) comes to mind as a possible standard.

Illegality/lack of justification

15.79   If particular behaviour causes damage in an attributable way, its unlawfulness will be 'indicated' by the application of § 823 para. 1 BGB. That means that the relevant behaviour is to be viewed as unlawful even in the absence of a finding of a breach of duty unless, exceptionally, grounds for justification arise. Such grounds can arise, in particular, from certain duties to tolerate infringements of one's rights, because if someone must tolerate an infringement, this can logically be interpreted as an intervention right of the beneficiary; that is, as a justification to intervene. Emissions-related damage must be tolerated where prescribed by the legislature on the basis of the prevailing interest in the activity causing the emissions. The types of emission that come within this bracket include emissions arising from customary use of land or from the operation of a licensed factory.

Justification by customary land use

15.80   A landowner need only tolerate damage that is either 'insignificant' (§ 906 para. 1 BGB) or, to the extent that it arises from the customary use of another property, cannot be avoided by measures that are reasonable in terms of cost (§ 906 para. 2 1st sentence BGB). If these conditions are satisfied there will be no liability in delict as there will be no illegality.[137] The first justification will never apply to a case that seriously comes into consideration for a liability claim because the significance threshold is generally exceeded in cases of damage to property or to health.[138] The second justification, however, is a serious possibility.

---

[136]   Staudinger and Kohler (see n. 110 above), Introduction, marginal nos. 59–61.
[137]   BGH, 18 September 1984, VI ZR 223/82 (Kupolofen), marginal no. 18.
[138]   Palandt and Bassenge, *Bürgerliches Gesetzbuch*, 70th edn (2011), § 906, marginal no. 17.

15.81   § 906 para. 2 1st sentence BGB must, in the first instance, be considered applicable to GHG emissions if it is to have any exculpatory
effect. Applicability in this situation might be challenged by the
argument that the provision has been systematically integrated
into the law concerning the interests of neigbours contained in
the BGB. This is why it is said to be applicable to emissions that
have an effect within a limited geographic sphere, i.e. an area
with a radius of up to 50 km only.[139] This would be an argument
against the application of § 906 BGB to GHG emissions as these
gases only give rise to liability for their adverse effects after they
have, in the first instance, had an effect on a worldwide scale,
i.e., after they have contributed to the increase of the total global
GHG volume. It is not, however, compatible with the objective
of this provision to exclude long-range effects from the scope of
its application. This is because the legislator wanted, with § 906
BGB, to make a general decision under which circumstances the
interests of the landowner in protecting the land take a back seat
to the interest of another owner in using it, i.e. the legislator has
created a generalised definition of property that is not genuinely
of a neighbour-law nature.[140] This interpretation is also backed by
the preparatory documents for the BGB.

15.82   As GHG emissions are likely to be considered a customary land
use, the exclusion of tortious liability for damages to the land
belonging to a claimant still hinges on the fact that the effects
were not preventable through economically reasonable measures
(which will be discussed below).

Justification by licences

15.83   Generally, tortious liability is excluded by a pollution control
licence that has been issued to a factory as a result of an administrative procedure that has involved the participation of the
public. This is because, according to § 14 sentence 1 BImSchG, a
licence imposes a duty to tolerate the effects of the operation (see
15.79 above). An emission licence issued according to § 4 TEHG
(see 15.15 above) that accompanies the pollution control licence

---

[139] Reiter (see n. 130 above), p. 57; Marburger, 'Zur zivilrechtlichen Haftung für
Waldschäden' in Breuer, Kloepfer, Marburger and Schröder (eds.), *Waldschäden als
Rechtsproblem*, vol. 2 (UTR, 1986), p. 109 ff. at p. 116.
[140] Säcker, *Münchener Kommentar zum BGB*, 5th edn (2009), § 906, marginal no. 1.

as a separate legal act, can, by contrast, not have an exculpatory effect because the TEHG does not impose a duty to tolerate.[141]

Fault/responsibility

15.84   In contrast to common law, the legal provisions as to liability for negligent and intentional actions are brought together in § 823 BGB. As no relevant legal differences are evident in the case of an intended action, the only issue of interest is the allegation of negligence. Negligence is defined in § 276 para. 2 BGB as the failure to exercise reasonable care. The standard of reasonable care is not to be determined on an individual, but rather on an objective, basis considering which behaviour can be expected of a particular group of people (for example, that of ordinary factory operators). A person has not acted with reasonable care when he/she has not undertaken necessary and reasonable action to avoid a foreseeable danger.

15.85   In terms of foreseeability it must be noted that the BGH has acknowledged that an action is not to be considered negligent if a competent expert has confirmed that no significant risk will arise from it.[142] But since the moment that the IPCC Reports documented the scientific consensus that there is a high probability of anthropogenic causation of climate change and of certain types of damages arising from it, the emitters of GHGs should have been unable to refer to 'experts' who tell them the contrary. Moreover, licences that have been granted by the authorities would speak against a finding of negligence as long as there are no special circumstances that make a special care reasonable. This view is supported where the permitted action constitutes a threat to the general public,[143] which unquestionably can be said about climate change. But it is not clear how the courts would find if the defendant were able to show that being the only one to perform mitigation measures would put his business at risk for survival.

Reimbursable damages

15.86   According to § 823 para. 1 BGB, only those damages are eligible for compensation that result from the infringement of the

---

[141] Staudinger and Kohler (see n. 110 above), Introduction, marginal no. 54.
[142] BGH, 8 July 1971, III ZR 67/68, NJW 1971, p. 1881, at p. 1882.
[143] Palandt and Sprau (see n. 135 above), § 823, marginal no. 43.

interests protected by that provision such as life, health and property. Liability for pure economic loss is found under § 823 para. 2 BGB which applies if the defendant has infringed a so-called protective law (*Schutzgesetz*). A protective law is a general regulation the purpose of which is the protection of individuals and not just the general public. Even certain types of factory licences that impose requirements in favour of a distinguishable group of people are – together with the legal basis for the licence – recognised as a protective law. In spite of this, it is not easy to find a protective law applicable to GHG emitters, as § 5 para. 1 sentence 4 BImSchG does not allow imposition of any emission limits (see 15.17 above).

15.87   At least § 14 sentence 1 BlmSchG, which provides a claim to economically justifiable precautionary measures against the consequences of emissions (see 15.94 below), is likely to be considered a protective law because this legal character has been recognised for injunctive relief under § 1004 BGB,[144] which is replaced by § 14 sentence 1 BlmSchG, if a pollution control licence has been granted. As long as, for example, an emitter who is required to take precautionary measures against floods of river banks or in coastal areas disregards these measures, he is liable for the loss in value of the land as far as it can be proven that this loss in value is a result of the increased risk of flooding, as well as, as the case may be, for the increase in insurance premiums.

Private nuisance

15.88   German civil law stipulates that anyone can demand that interferences with his/her property be ceased as long as there is no overriding interest in the activity from which the interference originates. But GHG emitters will, as a rule, be able to show an overriding interest (see 15.90 below). In such a case the endangered property owners can rely on a claim for protective measures (instead of one for injunctive relief): these measures can be performed either at the source of the interference, for example by reducing emissions (see 15.91 below), or at the location of the potentially damaging effect, for example by increasing the

---

[144] BGH, 20 November 1992, V ZR 82/91, marginal no. 33.

height of a dyke (see 15.94 below). If protective measures cannot reasonably be expected of the person causing the interference, compensation can be considered for the interference that must be accepted by the affected party (see 15.96 below). The order of available remedies – injunctive relief, protective measures, financial compensation – shows an obvious parallel to 'private nuisance' cases in common law jurisdictions.

Claim for termination of greenhouse gas emissions

15.89   According to § 1004 para. 1 BGB, any person can demand the cessation of an activity that creates a concrete danger of an interference with his/her land. For example, a court might have to examine a claim by a coastal landowner who fears her land could be flooded by a storm surge, that a GHG emitter cease its activity. The claimant would have to show that the increase of the risk of flooding caused by the local sea level rise is not only insignificant.

15.90   In practice it will, however, be almost impossible to require a cessation of emission activity. As there is a lot of support for the argument that the emission of GHG is to be considered a customary use of land, an injunction is precluded according to § 906 para. 2 1st sentence BGB if the threatening flood cannot be prevented by economically reasonable measures. Even if the flood could be prevented, in cases where installations have been granted a pollution control licence, an injunction is precluded according to § 14 1st sentence (first half) BImSchG.

Claim for abatement of emissions

15.91   A person who does not have a right to cessation of operations because of a pollution control licence can make a claim for the abatement of emissions under § 14 1st sentence (second half) BImSchG if this is technically possible and economically reasonable to require of the operator. The measure of reasonableness is the financial capability of an average business of that particular type, though the limit of reasonable investment is surpassed if the operator would no longer attain a fair level of income from the operations. How close the operator must come to this limit depends especially on which damages are likely to occur without the sought protective measures.

15.92   It is expected that the defendant will object and argue that even very large abatements would not bring appreciable advantages to the claimant and all others affected. According to § 275 para. 2 BGB the stark disproportionality of costs and benefits leads a claim to fail. But abatement measures of a single operator could however miss the point. This becomes apparent when the situation is compared to a claim for cessation of emissions: if a high number of interferers contribute in an insignificant way to an (in totality) significant interference, the affected person can demand cessation of his contribution from each and every interferer without having to sue them in one and the same claim.[145] Consequently, it would be decisive whether the *totality* of the emission abatement measures that would be considered reasonable to impose on the emitters would lead to an appreciable improvement of the situation for those affected by the emissions.

15.93   Nevertheless, it seems that such a claim will not likely be successful. This is because a court would be forced to analyse *for every emitter* the extent to which abatement measures could be reasonably imposed on him and then to set the total costs of all measures in proportion to the amount of avoided damages *for every person* affected by climate change. This Herculean task could – at least from a psychological point of view – easily lead a court to decide that such a case is lacking justiciability.

Claim for safety measures (especially against flooding)

15.94   Given that, under a claim based on § 14 1st sentence BImSchG, it would always be for the operator to choose the course of action to remedy the risk of damage, it would not be possible to claim a particular protection measure. However, the claimant would be free to name his/her measure of priority, given that issues of technical possibility and economic feasibility could only be judged against a distinctly defined measure. In particular with regard to economic feasibility, measures at the place of the pending damage (passive protection measures) would likely be more successful than a claim for reducing emissions. This can be exemplified with a case of coastal property owners raising a claim for erecting dykes to a level which ensures that the risk of floods will be equal

---

[145]   Palandt and Bassenge (see n. 138 above), § 906, marginal no. 29.

to that without climate change and the ensuing rise in sea levels (locally).

15.95   The first obvious advantage is that there could be no doubt that the measure would actually remedy the damage/risk of damage, which could be doubted if only a fraction of global emissions is omitted. Secondly, the costs and benefits of such measures could be specified precisely: building costs on the one hand, and on the other the reduced risk of flooding for all goods and valuables that can be found in the threatened coastal area. Thirdly, the economic burden placed on the defendant would be much more adequate than in the case of an action calling for emission reductions. His/her obligation would be limited to a share of the building costs for the dyke, the share being defined by the defendant's own share of emissions based on global emissions. It seems, after all, plausible to hold a defendant liable only for 'his share' of the damaging factor,[146] this also being applicable to protection measures. Given that even large power plant operators only contribute a small fraction of global GHG emissions, their share of the building costs would also be small.

Claim for financial compensation

15.96   In as far as the affected person is unable to assert a right to protective measures because they are not considered economically reasonable to impose on the emitter, a claim for compensation according to § 906 para. 2 2nd sentence BGB can be considered. This provision affords damages for the special burden a property owner must accept, if he cannot stop the activity affecting him because of the predominant public interest (*Aufopferungsentschädigung*). Given this special situation, full damages will not be awarded, but – as in the case of expropriations for the public interest – only limited compensation.[147] In this way, coastal property owners could be compensated for damages due to storm floods that they must otherwise accept. It would only be consistent to award them – even before the damage has occurred – a compensation for the decreased value of the property (due to the increased flood risk).[148] This reasoning is

---

[146] *Ibid.*, § 1004, marginal no. 26.   [147] *Ibid.*, § 906, marginal no. 27.
[148] Frank (see n. 108 above), p. 2298.

based on an understanding of § 906 para. 2 2nd sentence BGB as including distant or cumulative damages such as those resulting from climate change.

Strict liability

15.97 § 1 UmweltHG (Environmental Liability Act) grants a strict liability right to compensation for cases in which – as a consequence of acts affecting the environment – a human being is killed, his/her health is compromised or a thing is damaged. The definition of environmental impact includes the emission of (greenhouse) gases (§ 3 UmweltHG). The right does not require the emission to be illegal, and can thus be used against emitters who have a pollution control licence. Only factory operators who are included on an annex to the law are subject to such strict liability. The list includes all of the largest GHG emitters. The liability is limited to a maximum amount of €170 million (§ 15 UmweltHG) per incident. No liability arises in relation to damages that were caused before 1 January 1991 (§ 23 UmweltHG).

15.98 The application of the UmweltHG could only be problematic on two grounds, which have been raised by scholars:[149] (i) The legislator did not want to establish liability for such distant and cumulative damage, including for climate-impact damage. A closer look at the preparatory materials for the statute reveals, however, that these types of damages were not to be excluded from liability per se, but only insofar as they cannot be attributed to a particular polluter.[150] In the case of climate damages, polluters (or their share of emissions) can be identified. (ii) It has been argued that the preventive aim of the statute would be undermined if liability would apply to an activity which is not preventable (as a CO_2-free economy is not currently conceivable). This can be countered by the fact that the legislator has prescribed a compensation duty (as in the case of § 906 para. 2 2nd sentence BGB, see 15.96 above) even though the damage could not be prevented with economically reasonable expense. Some argue that

---

[149] Chatzinerantzis and Herz (see n. 107 above), p. 597 ff.
[150] Explanatory statement accompanying the draft of UmweltHG, BT-Drs. 11/7104, pp. 16, 29.

this type of compensatory duty would override the UmweltHG, but the majority view is that both concepts apply in parallel.[151]

(D)   Information law

15.99   Generally, information law is of great importance to climate protection in increasing transparency and knowledge.

Claims for information against public authorities

Environmental Information Act

15.100   Germany implemented the EU access to information require-ments into national law mainly through its Environmental Information Act (*Umweltinformationsgesetz* ('UIG'))[152] and the associated state laws. There have been many cases brought under the UIG involving climate-relevant data and information. The first obviously climate-related case (in 2006) was a claim made by the NGO Germanwatch against the German Export Credit Agency Hermes AG, requesting information about the CO_2 impact of the export credit guarantees granted to German com-panies for investment abroad.[153] The defendant, the German Ministry of Economy, was of the opinion that data on CO_2 emis-sions of installations supported by export credit guarantees were not environmental information and thus not covered by the obligation in § 4 para. 1 UIG to make available information on the environment. This opinion was not shared by the court. Therefore, as part of a settlement, the information was made available in as much as it was available to Hermes AG.

15.101   In the wake of the ETS there is now also a growing body of case law concerning claims made by industry to receive information about allocation permits granted to competitors. This jurispru-dence shows that, even in the context of competitors request-ing information, the requests must normally – with only few

---

[151] Kohler, '*Duldungspflichtabhängige Aufopferungshaftung als Grenze der Umweltge-fährdungshaftung*', NuR 2011, p 7.

[152] Of 22 December 2004, BGBl I 2004, p. 3704.

[153] See VG Berlin, 10 January 2006, 10 A 215/04, NVwZ 2006, p. 850. See also Mecklenburg and Verheyen, '*Informationen über Exportförderung als Umweltinformation*', NVwZ 2006, p. 781.

exceptions – be granted. In one case decided on appeal by the BVerwG the court ruled that the term 'emissions' as part of the definition of 'environmental information' also encompasses information about the actual allocation volume.[154]

Consumer information

15.102 There have been a number of cases based on obligations stemming from EU Directive 1999/94/EG relating to the availability of consumer information on fuel economy and CO_2 emissions in respect of the marketing of new passenger cars[155] and the corresponding German Regulation (PKW-EnKV) in conjunction with the general prohibition against misleading advertising (§§ 3, 4 UWG).[156] Directive 1999/94 contains specific requirements for display and advertising of CO_2 emissions from cars. As the wealth of cases shows, these are not always complied with. A concerted action led by the NGO Deutsche Umwelthilfe, acting as a consumer organisation with standing in accordance with EU and German law, has shown most major car producers to be non-compliant.[157]

15.103 There have also been cases barring companies from using climate-related arguments to boost the popularity of their products. For example, the LG Berlin granted injunctive relief on the basis of §§ 3, 6 para. 2 Nr. 4, 8, 12 UWG to a major producer of wind power stations who challenged an advertisement campaign by an institute for nuclear power (Deutsches Atomforum e.V.).[158] The institute had displayed windmills next to nuclear power stations with the slogan '*Klimaschützer unter sich*' (literally: 'Climate Protectors amongst themselves') in posters and ads. This was deemed to be comparative advertising by way of

---

[154] BVerwG, 24 November 2009, 7 C 2/09. See also OVG Berlin-Brandenburg, 8 May 2008, 12 B 24.07.
[155] Amended by Directive 2003/73/EC, OJ L 12, 18 January 2000, p. 16.
[156] Law against unfair competition, 3 March 2010, BGBl I 2010, p. 254.
[157] See OLG Stuttgart, 30 September 2010, 2 U 45/10; BGH, 4 February 2010, I ZR 66/09; LG Stuttgart, 37 O 1/11 KfH; LG Frankfurt, 3–12 O 53/10 and 3–08 O 82/10; OLG Hamm, I-4 U 151/10; LG Hanau, 6 O 25/10; LG Braunschweig, 22 O 2152/09; LG Köln, 84 O 9/2011 (not published). See also Klinger, 'Mitteilung zum Urteil des LG Berlin vom 21. März 2006 – 102 O 97/05', ZUR 2006, p. 606; 'Mitteilung zu Urteil des LG Essen vom 08. März 2006 – 41 O 168/05', ZUR 2006, p. 605.
[158] LG Berlin, 7 December 2010, 16 O 560/10.

image transfer (from the 'good' image of windpower to the 'bad' image of nuclear power), which is generally forbidden in Germany under the UWG. The LG Berlin also granted injunctive relief against a campaign in which Vattenfall described as 'CO₂ free' a coal-firedpower station equipped with carbon capture facilities.[159]

Stakeholder information

15.104   There have been efforts to use general company law provisions on stakeholder rights to information about company risks in a climate context. While there are no court decisions on this issue, it seems that most large companies in Germany are currently not complying with, for example, the obligation in § 289 of the commercial code ('HGB')[160] to report on regulatory and factual climate risks.[161]

(E)   Conclusion

15.105   While courts fully acknowledge the importance of climate protection in Germany, there is relatively little case law actually enhancing obligations to reduce emissions. This is due to legislative efforts to enforce climate protection targets through substantive law. However, it is not unreasonable to expect that, with growing evidence of the impacts of climate change, if the substantive law proves insufficient, courts will increasingly be willing to challenge authorities' decisions. Especially with standing requirements being eased in respect of NGOs, there is now real scope for claims promulgating energy efficiency in installations or based on Article 20a GG.

15.106   In terms of civil law it appears possible to claim protective measures against the impacts of climate change, or even damages; however, it is unlikely that the courts would order reductions in emissions as a remedy in a nuisance case. Many legal and factual problems remain that only the courts – in the context of concrete cases – will be able to resolve.

---

[159]   LG Berlin, 4 December 2007, 97 O 297/07.
[160]   10 May 1897, RGBl 1897, 219, last amended 1 March 2011, BGBl I 288 (Nr. 8).
[161]   Verheyen, 'Informations- und Berichtspflichten der deutschen börsennotierten Automobilkonzerne im Hinblick auf die durch den globalen Klimawandel und eine weitere Ölpreissteigerung hervorgerufenen Risiken' (January 2008), available at www.germanwatch.de.

16

Poland

BARTOSZ KURAŚ, MACIEJ SZEWCZYK,
DOMINIK WAŁKOWSKI, TOMASZ WARDYŃSKI,
AND IZABELA ZIELIŃSKA-BARŁOŻEK

(A) Introduction

The Polish legal system

16.01 Poland is a republic with a civil law legal system. The primary Polish legislation is its Constitution of 1997[1] ('the Polish Constitution') and the main sources of law are: (i) ratified international treaties (including the treaties concerning participation in the European Union and the secondary European legislation in the form of regulations that have direct effect in Member States); (ii) statutes (acts passed by the Parliament and executed by the President); and (iii) executive orders (issued by the Government or relevant ministers).

The governmental stance on climate change

16.02 Poland is both Party to the FCCC and a member of the European Union. Consequently its obligations related to climate change result from these two legal regimes.

16.03 There are several public authorities involved in climate change matters in Poland, including the Ministry of Environment (responsible for overall climate-related legislation), and the National Centre for Emission Balancing and Management, responsible for the maintenance and operation of the European Union Emissions Trading Scheme in Poland.

---

[1] Journal of Laws 1997, No. 78, item 483, as amended.

16.04   Studies conducted in 2009 reveal that, in the view of most Poles, climate change has become a problem. According to 73.5% of those questioned, climate change affects their everyday life. Even though the public appears to recognise both climate change and the need to counter it, 72.2% of respondents felt that there were more important issues to prioritise. The view that climate change is a natural phenomenon not requiring human intervention is held by 29.4% of those polled, although the majority (63.1%) does not share this opinion.[2]

16.05   The Polish government is also aware that climate change consequences need to be properly addressed. In December 2009, the Minister for the Environment, Maciej Nowicki, stated: 'Countries that emit the most carbon dioxide and other greenhouse gases should commit to specific obligations to reduce such emissions, whereas developing countries, in particular the least developed countries, should obtain financial, technological and organisational assistance in adapting to climate change, as well as for their rapid social and economic development. This is called for by human solidarity.'[3]

16.06   Polish commitment towards climate change challenges was specifically demonstrated during the COP14 conference that was held in Poland (in the city of Poznań) in December 2008.

Emission Allowances Trading Act 2011

16.07   The primary Polish legislation concerning greenhouse gas ('GHG') emissions is the Greenhouse Gases Emission Allowances Trading Act dated 28 April 2011[4] (the 'EATA') that implements the provisions of Directive 2003/87/EC[5] into the Polish legal system.[6]

16.08   The European Union Allowances are granted to entities running installations in line with the National Allocation Plan.

---

[2] www.cbos.pl/PL/wydarzenia/03_konferencja/klimat.pdf.
[3] www.mos.gov.pl/artykul/7_aktualnosci/10518_nowicki_wzywam_do_solidarnosci.html.
[4] Journal of Laws 2011, No. 122, item 695.
[5] Directive 2003/87/EC of the European Parliament and of the Council of 13 October 2003 establishing a scheme for greenhouse gas emission allowance trading within the Community and amending Council Directive 96/61/EC.
[6] The new legislation came into force on 21 June 2011 and it substituted the previous regulation as of 22 December 2004 (the 'former EATA').

An installation that commences activity during the settlement period is granted allowances in the form of a permit for participation in the emission trading scheme.

16.09   The entities running these installations are obliged to disclose their emission allowances and their actual level of emissions in the given year of the settlement period.

16.10   The allowances that were not applied to actual emissions remain valid for the subsequent years of a settlement period. The allowances remaining in the acount of an entity at the end of a settlement period, therefore, are replaced by the number of allowances for the subsequent period.

16.11   If an entity lacks the necessary number of allowances it will have to pay a monetary penalty.

16.12   While the European Union emission allowances are tradable, any sale contract must be notified to the national register by the relevant entity running an installation situated in Poland.

Industrial and natural resources context

16.13   The Polish economy is characterised by high energy consumption and a high coal ratio in primary fuel use (Poland holds the second place in the EU for the level of coal used in its national energy mix), which, in turn, explains the high emission rate of the Polish economy.

16.14   According to data for 2009, 55.84 per cent of electrical power production in Poland originated from coal and 33.66 per cent from brown coal. However, it should be noted that the production of energy from coal has decreased. In 2007 electrical power plants in Poland produced 93,100 GWh from coal, decreasing to 86,500 GWh in 2008, and in 2009 a further decrease took place with production at the level of 84,200 GWh.[7]

16.15   In total, heavy industry (steel, chemical and mineral industries) has an approximate 60 per cent share of the total energy

---

[7] http://edgp.gazetaprawna.pl/index.php?act=mprasa&sub=article&id=296318.

consumption by the processing industry. In recent years a percentage increase was noted in the rate of chemical and paper industry consumption. By contrast, the percentage share of the foodstuffs, textiles and machine industries decreased. The decrease in energy consumption noted in the steel industry was primarily caused by production limitations.[8]

16.16   Poland belongs to a small number of countries that have no problem with meeting Kyoto targets. The emission of GHGs in Poland decreased dramatically in the first stage of a systemic transformation from 1989–91 and subsequently stabilised at a level of approximately 30 to 35 per cent less emissions than in the base year. At the same time, however, the government forecasts that CO_2 emissions may begin to grow in the next few years as a result of rapid economic development. This may prove to be a hindrance in achieving the EU reduction goal by 2020.[9]

National climate change risks

16.17   Climate forecasts for Poland show that a temperature increase of approximately 3.0°C to 3.5°C is expected by the final decade of the twenty-first century.[10] The temperature increase will be smaller in the summer, but summers will feature lengthy periods of sunshine with frequent heatwaves punctuated by thunderstorms. This will lead to strong evaporation and possible periods of drought.

16.18   A serious threat, particularly to the Baltic Sea, is an increase in sea level. Until now, the level has increased by approximately 1.5 to 2.9 mm per year and it is estimated that it will increase by as much as 0.1 m to 0.97 m by 2080. It is estimated that 1789 km² of the coastal area is prone to flooding. If the sea level increases, Gdańsk, for example, will face danger since 880 ha of its area lies

---

[8] www.kashue.pl/materialy/opracowania/Analiza_sektorow-CL_24_08_2009.pdf.
[9] http://parl.sejm.gov.pl/WydBAS.nsf/0/C8292E9AF82C2743C12573B50050884F/$file/infos_023.pdf.
[10] www.imgw.pl/wl/internet/zz/klimat/0804_przyszlosc.html.

one metre below sea level and 1020 ha from 1 to 2.5 metres above sea level.[11]

16.19 A significant risk related not so much to climate change itself as to actions intended to prevent such change is the threat of so-called emission leakage. As Poland has high emission levels, local companies will be heavily encumbered by costs related to reduction efforts. These costs could directly affect the selection of a production location or impact on the volume of exports. According to recent studies, the introduction of an auctioning system from 2013 might lead to a situation where electrical power producers will be forced to shift some of their costs to energy consumers. This will cause an increase in production costs and may result in indirect emissions leakage (as an effect of the increase in electrical power prices).[12]

(B)   Public law

Overview

16.20 This section is intended to address the procedures through which entities (individuals, NGOs and entrepreneurs) may challenge the public authorities (including both their activity and inactivity), as well as the decisions they make concerning or involving climate change matters (including court decisions).

Grounds for judicial review

16.21 There are two distinct avenues under Polish law for challenging laws: (i) proceedings to declare legislative measures unconstitutional; and (ii) proceedings to overturn or amend an individual decision.

16.22 Laws may be subject to review, particularly to assess their conformity with the Polish Constitution as well as international treaties ratified by Poland. The Constitutional Tribunal

---

[11] www.chronmyklimat.pl/theme/UploadFiles/analiza_zmiany_klimatu_polska.pdf.
[12] www.kashue.pl/materialy/opracowania/Analiza_sektorow-CL_24_08_2009.pdf.

exercises such review at relevant bodies' requests.[13] If a given law is declared unconstitutional, it will fully or partially lose force. Moreover, a Constitutional Tribunal ruling on non-compliance with the Polish Constitution, an international treaty or a law on which a binding decision was made, constitutes grounds for an individual[14] to restart proceedings, overturn a decision or adopt another resolution through relevant proceedings.

16.23   To the extent that such a constitutional review is of an abstract nature (i.e. it does not deal with a specific factual situation), anyone whose constitutional freedoms or rights have been violated may file a complaint with the Constitutional Tribunal. Such a complaint must relate to a law's compliance with the Polish Constitution or any other legal enactment on the basis of which a court or public administrative body ultimately ruled on the complainant's freedoms or rights or on his/her duties as specified in the Polish Constitution. Although such a complaint is filed on an individual and specific basis, a decision as to the unconstitutionality of a law is effective *erga omnes*. The right of an individual to such a complaint is also likely to apply to claims for unconstitutionality of climate change related legislation.

16.24   A request by a relevant body to assess a law's constitutionality is not limited in time, whereas an individual constitutional complaint must be filed within three months of the handing-down of the legally binding, i.e. final, judgment, decision, etc.

16.25   It is possible in principle for final and binding administrative decisions (i.e. establishing rights and duties of individuals such as a permit for participation in the emission trading scheme) to be overturned through one of the following means: (i) a complaint filed by a party before an administrative court claiming illegality of a decision; or through the adoption of one of the following extraordinary procedures concerning legally binding administrative decisions: (ii) renewal of administrative proceedings (e.g. in the event that a decision was based on false evidence or as a result of an offence); or (iii) declaration by an administrative

---

[13] Such relevant bodies, authorised to apply for constitutional review of legal acts include, in particular, the President, the Speakers of both Houses of Parliament, the Prime Minister, fifty members of the Sejm (lower House of Parliament) and thirty senators.

[14] Supreme Court ruling dated 6 November 2009, I CZ 62/09, LEX No. 599746.

body of invalidity of a decision, which, for instance, was issued without legal basis or in glaring violation of the law. The final two procedures have an exceptional nature, however, and in practice a complaint before an administrative court essentially serves as a tool to abolish final administrative decisions.

16.26 A complaint may be brought before an administrative court by either the party whose rights and duties are impaired by a decision concerned (e.g. the entity running an installation), or, in particular, by anyone having a legal interest therein (e.g. the entity which may be affected by the operations of the installation), or by a prosecutor, Citizens' Rights Ombudsman, Children's Rights Ombudsman or (under certain conditions) an NGO. The appellant must file a complaint within thirty days of the handing-down of the relevant decision, whereas the prosecutor, Citizens' Rights Ombudsman and Children's Rights Ombudsman can file a complaint within six months from the date of delivery of a decision to a party in an individual case. The deadline for filing a motion to renew proceedings is one month from the date when a party learnt of the circumstances constituting the basis to renew proceedings. As to the procedure for a declaration of invalidity, a decision can be invalidated at any time unless such decision has resulted in irrevocable legal consequences. Invalidation, in some instances, is also not possible ten years after the date of service or announcement of a decision.

Grounds for liability of State Treasury for illegal activity of administrative bodies

16.27 Irrespective of the ability to overturn legislation, Polish law provides for the ability to pursue claims against the State Treasury in connection with damage incurred by an entity as a result of (i) the passing of a law, legally binding decision or judgment, (ii) failure to pass a law, judgment or decision required by law, and (iii) illegal actions or negligence in exercising public authority. If damage was caused through either the passing of or failure to pass a law, decision or judgment, remedy may be sought by means of bringing proceedings for unconstitutionality or illegality. This process may, in principle, also apply to matters involving climate change legislation or judgments.

16.28   The State Treasury is liable to compensate if the following preconditions jointly arise: (i) damage occurs (ii) which is either the consequence of an illegal action or lack of action by an authority and (iii) there is an adequate causal relationship between the damage and action by the authority.

16.29   The obligation of the public authority to act must derive from law. It cannot be derived from general axiological assumptions such as a pressing need to regulate an issue for moral or social reasons. Liability for damage caused by legislative negligence only arises if individual rights, granted by law in an obvious and unconditional manner, cannot be exercised due to the failure to adopt an appropriate law.[15]

16.30   The compensation claims noted above expire three years from the date when the injured party learnt of the damage and of the person (entity) liable to remedy it. However, this cannot be longer than ten years from the date when the event causing damage actually occurred.

Examples in practice

16.31   There are no adjudication judgments by Polish courts to date that deal with climate change liability. A small number of proceedings based on Polish climate change regulations concern the allocation of emission allowances, or allocation to new installations[16] as well as the classification of emission allowances for tax purposes.[17]

16.32   There is, however, an absence of unequivocal conditions justifying recognition of direct State liability for climate change. This is because the law does not provide for precise environmental goals that should be achieved by the State through clearly specified means and the lack of performance or improper performance of which could lead to entities' direct harm.

---

[15] See Supreme Court ruling dated 4 August 2006, III CSK 138/05, OSNC 2007, No. 4, item 63.

[16] E.g. Supreme Administrative Court judgment dated 5 November 2009, II OSK 891/09, Provincial Administrative Court in Warsaw judgment dated 18 May 2010, IV SA/Wa 356/10.

[17] E.g. Provincial Administrative Court in Wrocław judgment dated 26 March 2010, I SA/Wr 85/10.

State Treasury liability for delay in issuing a National Allocation Plan

16.33   According to the former EATA, a National Allocation Plan for the current settlement period (2008–12) should have been adopted and announced by September 2007. However, in light of the dispute pending between Poland and the European Commission[18] concerning the total number of emission allowances to be distributed in the National Allocation Plan, the National Allocation Plan was only passed on 1 July 2008,[19] therefore, after the commencement of the second commitment period.

16.34   The delayed issue of the National Allocation Plan significantly hindered plant operators from undertaking investment decisions, both in relation to the budget allocated to limit production emissions and to the purchase of missing allowances. In light of this, a compensatory liability of the State toward these operators could therefore be potentially considered.

16.35   It should nevertheless be noted that the liability on this basis may arise only if specific guarantees for individuals (or units) clearly and unconditionally arise from the primary source of law (the former EATA in this case).[20] The meaning of legislative negligence concerns those situations when 'the obligation of specific action by a public authority is specified by law and it can be determined what specific action was to be taken by a public authority to avert damage'.[21]

16.36   This scenario, however, should be treated only as a possibility. Effective pursuit of claims in this area would require a declaration of not only negligence on the part of a State body (the Council

---

[18]   On 26 March 2007 the European Commission approved the Polish National Allocation Plan, but on the condition, among others, of reducing the number of rights to 208.5 million annually (whereas Poland requested 284.6 million). The decision was the subject of a claim before a first instance court and subsequently at the European Court of Justice. Its indirect effect was a delay of nearly one year in issuing an executive regulation for the National Allocation Plan.

[19]   Order of the Council of Ministers dated 1 July 2008 on adoption of the National Plan of Allocation of Allowances for carbon dioxide emissions for years 2008–12 for the community emissions trading scheme (Journal of Laws, No. 202, item 1248).

[20]   Supreme Court ruling dated 4 August 2006, III CSK 138/2005; see Supreme Court ruling dated 6 July 2006, III CZP 37/06.

[21]   Constitutional Tribunal judgment dated 4 December 2001, SK 18/00.

of Ministers), but also the demonstrated existence of a causal link between such negligence and damage (i.e. loss or forfeited benefit) suffered by an operator of a specific installation.

Expected trends in the development of climate change challenges

16.37   Since regulations introduced to address climate change are increasingly harsh, resulting in higher limits to emissions levels and the need to incur outlays to minimise the environmental impact of high-emission projects, it appears that the number of court cases initiated by entrepreneurs might increase in the near future (especially in the post-Kyoto period, after 2012).

16.38   As noted, administrative courts already hear cases concerning the allocation of emission allowances and participation in the European Union Emission Trading Scheme. The introduction of a system of allowance auctioning might, depending on its final legal architecture, entail additional complaints of entrepreneurs citing procedural flaws relating to the method of allocation, or even questioning the constitutionality of limiting commercial freedom in this way.

16.39   Potential court proceedings could also be initiated by individuals, such as those living close to planned projects which will emit GHG. It should be pointed out that under the current legal system individuals, as well as NGOs whose scope of statutory activity encompasses the legal interests of others (e.g. environmental organisations), can under certain legally specified instances, be parties to administrative proceedings and even appeal final decisions before an administrative court.[22] Quite apart from this, as described in the section on private law (see para. 16.48 ff below), such entities may file compensation claims against investors or operators of the relevant installations.

16.40   In the case of any activity which definitely or potentially negatively impacts the environment, it is necessary, prior to obtaining an investment permit, to conduct an environmental impact

[22] See Supreme Administrative Court in Warsaw resolution dated 12 December 2005, II OPS 4/05.

assessment (EIA).[23] In principle, within the EIA procedure, the investor drafts a report, which sets out the environmental conditions of the investment. The law specifies the content of this report very generally by stating, inter alia, that it must include a description of the predicted effects on the environment caused by the planned undertaking, in particular on the surface of the earth, the climate and the landscape.[24] If it can be demonstrated that climate change should be considered as a predicted effect of a given project, a description of the climate change that an investment may cause should be an integral part of an EIA report.

16.41 Presently, the practice of the administrative bodies and entities drafting the reports does not provide for a specific requirement to draft an EIA report with consideration of a project's specific climate change effects. However, the possibility of the introduction of such a requirement in the future cannot be excluded.

Environmental administrative liability

16.42 It is possible to envisage the pursuit of climate change related claims based on the Polish law[25] implementing the environmental liability Directive.[26] The liability introduced by Directive 2004/35 encompasses both a preventive liability (prevention of damage) and restitutional liability (restoration to a previous State). Directive 2004/35 does not, however, impose a duty to provide compensatory mechanisms for the damaged party.

16.43 Polish law, similarly to the environmental liability Directive, provides for initial assumptions in relation to environmental protection and especially to prevention of environmental

---

[23] See Council Directive 85/337/EEC of 27 June 1985 on the assessment of the effects of certain public and private projects on the environment (OJ L 175, 40–8) and the Polish law implementing this Directive: the Act dated 3 October 2008 on the provision of information on the environment and its protection, public participation in environmental protection and environmental impact studies (Journal of Laws No. 199, item 1227, as amended).

[24] Article 66 (1) point 7) letter b), Journal of Laws 2008, No. 199, item 1227, as amended.

[25] Act dated 13 April 2007 on the prevention of environmental harm and its remedy (Journal of Laws No. 75, item 493, as amended).

[26] Directive 2004/35/EC of the European Parliament and of the Council of 21 April 2004 on environmental liability with regard to the prevention and remedying of environmental damage (OJ L 143/56).

damage. It applies to damage inflicted to protected natural areas and species, and to the activity of entities that use this environment and create a risk of harm thereto, in the latter case irrespective of the fault of such entity (i.e. liability on the basis of risk). Polish law contains a list of such activities and this includes most of the activities conducted on the basis of environmental permits. The environmental liability under the law implementing Directive 2004/35 is an administrative liability, which means that the administrative authorities are responsible for its application (with access to court on appeal). The remedies of injured parties to the proceedings are limited, and there are no grounds for compensation under this regime.

16.44   The law covers damage not only to protected areas and species, but also to ground and water. Damage to ground means a negative ecological, chemical or quantitative effect on water. Damage within the ambit of this law would therefore cover an activity causing an increase in water level, including sea level.

16.45   The obligation to prevent such damage applies in the event of imminent threat of environmental damage, i.e. if there is a high probability of environmental harm that can be foreseen.

16.46   Similarly to Directive 2004/35, Polish law can only be applied to environmental damage or the imminent threat of such damage, if it is possible to establish a causal link between the damage and the activities of individual operators.

16.47   In many cases, as in cases of tortious liability, it is necessary to demonstrate this causal relationship in order for an administrative body to impose a preventative or restitutional obligation. In relation to climate change litigation this is exceptionally difficult (see para. 16.48 ff below).

(C)   Private law

Basic information on tort liability

16.48   There are no examples yet in Poland of private law claims for compensation based on climate change related damage. Such claims could be pursued on the basis of present tort law, but the biggest problem would be demonstrating the causal relationship that is necessary to ascribe liability.

16.49   Basic torts that could be applied toward claims relating to climate change liability include the liability of (i) a public authority and (ii) industrial operators.

16.50   According to the basic principle of tort liability, anyone who through his/her own fault inflicts damage on another party is obliged to redress it. The basic precondition for liability is therefore the wrongdoing of the perpetrator (however in some circumstances, described below, the liability is based on risk, without any consideration of the fault of the party inflicting damage). If it were possible to prove that a factory emitting GHGs inflicted damage on somebody through culpable activity (e.g. it became impossible due to global warming to operate cold water fish breeding and the wrongdoing arose from transgression of allowable norms governing the emission of gases into the atmosphere or failure to install a legally required catalyser), and it was also possible to specify the damage, one might potentially seek compensatory damage from the perpetrator.

16.51   The concept of fault is not defined in Polish law. According to established case law, a culpable act is generally an act which is illegal, and such a term should be interpreted broadly taking into account the principles governing social existence.[27] A first defence by a company accused of contributing to climate change would be that the relevant activity is in conformity with the legally required sector permits (which in turn are compliant with the law). The potential effectiveness of such defence could only be weakened by a future ruling, e.g. deeming that actions contributing to climate change without appropriate preventative action to minimise their negative impact are illegal (irrespective of environmental permits and terms thereof).

16.52   The prevailing trend in recent years has placed greater emphasis on the subjective (the awareness and will of the perpetrator) rather than on illegality. In relation to climate change actions, such a distinction with clear non-intentional fault (negligence) would obviously have fundamental significance.

---

[27] See Supreme Court ruling dated 19 December 1979, IV CR 447/79, OSN 1980, No. 7–8, item 143, Supreme Court ruling dated 2 December 2003, III CK 430/03, OSN 2005, No. 1, item 10.

16.53   The burden of proof rests with the victim, who must demonstrate the existence and level of damage, the causal relationship and the culpable actions on the part of the perpetrator.

Who can claim?

16.54   It is currently difficult to demonstrate that certain damage suffered by an individual arose because of climate change. Once those suffering damage from climate change can demonstrate a causal relationship between the actions of a perpetrator and the damage sustained, they might be entitled to compensation based on tort law.

Who would be the defendants?

16.55   The polluters are likely to be potential defendants in litigation concerning climate change damage. Although everyone is to a certain degree responsible for climate change, in practical terms, the greater the impact by a given entity (e.g. the greater the emission of GHG), the easier it is potentially to demonstrate that the influence of such entity on the climate is sufficiently significant to ascribe liability to it. However, it is most important to demonstrate the causal relationship between the damage and the actions of the perpetrator. This might turn out to be very difficult in view of the current level of knowledge and certainty on the origins of climate change.

Liability of public authorities

16.56   As already discussed in the section on public law (see 16.20 ff above), entities exercising public authority are liable for their actions or negligence if such actions are 'inconsistent with the law'.

Issues of causation

16.57   A causal relationship constitutes the basic precondition for liability and must exist between an event that under law causes liability (e.g. emission of CO_2 into the atmosphere over permissible levels) and damage. Moreover, the causal relationship also determines the level of compensation. The perpetrator is only liable for the normal consequences of actions or negligence from which damage results. According to the prevailing concept, the term 'normal consequences' refers to a sufficient objective causal relationship whereby a specific effect is linked to the event triggering liability (the so-called necessary condition test). It must therefore be considered whether the harm would have arisen if the event constituting the basis for liability had not occurred.

Liability relating to the conduct of business

16.58 With regard to climate change related issues, the liability of a business operator running a plant powered by natural forces (steam, gas, electrical power, liquid fuels, etc.) could have a fundamental significance. The business must be based around the operation of such machines and facilities. It is not sufficient that the business operator only makes use of them for supplemental activities.

16.59 A business operator is liable, irrespective of fault, on the basis of risk of damage to persons or property caused through the operation of his business. He can only be exempt if he proves that damage occurred as a result of *force majeure* or exclusively due to the fault of the victim or a third party for whom he is not liable. The owners of mechanical means of communication (e.g. cars) and operators of businesses using or producing explosive materials are liable on the same grounds. Additionally, the same principle applies to so-called 'high-risk business', meaning a business causing a threat of industrial accident due to the types, categories and quantities of hazardous substances situated therein.[28]

16.60 Also in such a case, the basic precondition for liability is an adequate causal relationship between the function of the business and the resulting damage. According to Supreme Court

---

[28] See J. Skoczylas, 'Odpowiedzialność cywilna na podstawie ustawy – Prawo ochrony środowiska', *Przegląd Sądowy*, 4 (2003), 71 ff; and 'Odpowiedzialność za szkodę wyrządzoną środowisku – tezy do nowelizacji art. 435 k.c.', *Przegląd Sądowy*, 7–8 (2008), 5 ff.

adjudication, such liability covers, for example, damage resulting from the effects of sewage, factory smoke and gases on humans and agriculture, cattle and bees, even if an enterprise emits poisonous substances into the atmosphere at levels not exceeding established norms.[29] Liability here is therefore independent of fault and illegality.

Obligation to prevent harm

16.61   Within the framework of tort liability the law not only imposes the duty to remedy damage, but also to prevent it. Anyone, who as a result of actions by another party is at threat of damage, can demand that such party undertakes measures necessary to reverse the threatened danger, and, if necessary, to provide appropriate security. In such cases, the source of danger must be the (objectively) illegal actions of another party.

16.62   Additionally, those directly at threat of damage or who have suffered damage may ask for remedy from the entity liable for such threat or violation as well as the adoption of preventative means (particularly through the installation of facilities or equipment) of protecting against such a threat or violation. If this is not possible or is excessively difficult, they can demand the cessation of the activity causing the threat or violation. If the threat or violation concerns the environment as a common good, public authorities or NGOs can also put forward such a claim.

16.63   A separate issue (assuming that the above regulation would apply toward climate change in the future) is what methods should be recognised as necessary to reverse impending danger caused by climate change, and to restore a state consistent with the law. Again, it is necessary in such case for the victim to demonstrate an adequate causal relationship.

Civil claims arising from creation of an area of limited use

16.64   In principle, the use of a facility should not cause a transgression of environmental quality standards. However, Polish

---

[29] See Supreme Court ruling dated 7 April 1970, III CZP 17/70, OSP 1971, No. 9, item 169; Supreme Court ruling dated 9 May 2008, III CSK 360/07 (unpublished); Supreme Court ruling dated 28 November 2007, V CSK 282/07, OSNC 2008, No. 2, item 54.

environmental protection law provides exceptions to this rule on the basis of which various types of limitations to the use of property may be introduced.

16.65 For example, areas where use is restricted may be established in certain cases where environmental quality standards cannot be maintained beyond the site of a plant or other installation, despite the application of available technical, technological and organisational solutions.

16.66 A reduction in environmental quality standards on neighbouring real estate may reduce its value. For this reason, if the use of a property, on which limitations have been imposed as described, has become impossible or severely limited, a property owner may demand a buyout of the real estate or its part. An owner can also demand compensation for damage.

16.67 Areas of limited use are specially created around sewage treatment plants, municipal dumps, airports, electrical power lines and stations.[30]

16.68 Unlike the case of facilities that directly affect neighbouring properties, where the area of impact is limited (e.g. airports generating noise affecting neighbouring properties), it is difficult in the case of climate change to set the boundary of impact. Therefore, it would be difficult to create an area of limited impact, which is one precondition to pursue compensation on the basis discussed here. However, this does not exclude the pursuit of compensation on general principles.[31]

Other factors

Co-liability

16.69 If several persons are liable for harm inflicted under a tort, their liability is joint. The precondition for such a liability is a prohibited act committed by several persons (although they may be held liable on the basis of various principles and in connection with

---

[30] See, e.g., a judgment concerning the creation of a limited use area for a military airport – F-16 base: Supreme Court ruling dated 25 February 2009, II CSK 546/08, Supreme Court ruling dated 6 May 2010, II CSK 602/09, Supreme Court ruling dated 12 December 2008, II CSK 367/08.

[31] See Supreme Court ruling dated 6 May 2010, II CSK 602/09.

various events). The result of a prohibited act or acts must be a single tort. This unity of tort is determined by its indivisibility or such type of joint harmful act that there can be no distinction of damage for which specific persons are liable. Finally, a sufficient causal relationship must exist.

16.70   Polish law allows a victim to seek remedies from any jointly liable tortfeasor; and, in cases where there are several jointly liable tortfeasors, the issue of their relative contribution to the damage will be addressed by the courts. If one tortfeasor remedied the relevant damage, he/she will be entitled to claim from other jointly liable parties.

Limitation issues

16.71   Claims for damage for prohibited acts and harm to a person expire three years from the date when the victim learnt of such damage and of the party obliged to remedy it. As for property damage, the limitation statute provides that it cannot be longer than ten years from the date when the event causing the damage took place.[32]

Class action

16.72   It has recently become possible to seek compensation (among others) from tort law in group proceedings after fulfilling certain preconditions described in the Act on Group Proceedings[33] (such as, for example, the number of claimants and the unity of the event causing damage).

Remedies

16.73   The level of compensation due is set according to general rules. Remedies may be sought upon demonstration that (i) a certain event occurred that created an obligation to remedy damage (e.g. river pollution by industrial activity powered by natural forces), (ii) damage was caused, and (iii) there is a causal relationship between the event and the damage.

---

[32]   W. Dubis, 'Article 442' in E. Gniewek (ed.), *Civil Code: Commentary*, 2nd edn (C. H. Beck, 2006); Z. Radwański, 'Przedawnienie roszczeń z czynów niedozwolonych w świetle znowelizowanego art. 442 KC', *Monitor Prawniczy*, 11 (2007).

[33]   Act on Group Proceedings dated 17 December 2009 (Journal of Laws No. 7, item 44).

16.74   The law does not define damage. The case law has established various meanings to it, and the most common one sets out that damage alone is a loss to goods or legally protected interests that the victim suffered against his/her will.

16.75   Damages may be to property or to a person. In the latter case the victim's loss may be in the form of tangible or intangible damage.[34]

16.76   In the case of material damage, the Polish legal system distinguishes between the loss (*damnum emergens*) and lost benefit (*lucrum cessans*). Both types of damage should be, in principle, considered whenever compensatory liability arises. In order to determine the extent of damage, a comparison must be made of the actual assets of the victim with hypothetical ones that would exist but for the event causing harm. The material consequences of an event should also be assessed in the context of an adequate causal relationship.

16.77   The burden of proving damage rests with the victim, which is difficult in many cases. In the case of climate change, the quantum of the damage (assuming the ability to prove a causal relationship between atmospheric emissions and damage incurred) is likely to be complicated, because a quantitative appraisal of damage caused, for example, by an increase in temperature, is very difficult. For instance, many factors would have to be considered if a glacier melts as a result of a temperature increase and a ski resort becomes unusable. Changes to property value, lost benefits, and the consideration of benefits obtained, are only some of such elements (in the order of priority). In a situation where it is difficult to assess the damage a court may award an appropriate sum in a judgment at its own discretion based on consideration of the circumstances of the case.

16.78   In principle, the victim decides whether the remedy should be through restoration to a previous state or through payment of appropriate damages. Since restoration to the previous state in the case of climate change claims may prove impossible or

---

[34] See more in Z. Radwański and A. Olejniczak, *Zobowiązania – część ogólna*, 9th edn (C. H. Beck, 2010); A. Szpunar, *Odszkodowanie za szkodę majątkową. Szkoda na mieniu i osobie*, 1st edn (Branta, 1999); A. Szpunar, *Zadośćuczynienie za szkodę niemajątkową*, 1st edn (Branta, 1999).

excessively difficult, it would have to be assumed that the victim's options would be limited to compensation.

Protection of property against emissions

16.79   In addition to tort liability, protection of rights of a material nature (*actio negatoria*) could also apply in the case of climate change. In protecting the environment it is possible to use methods which protect property against emissions. Such claims of property owners, however, would primarily have a preventative nature and be intended to cease emissions. Additionally, material law provides rights to owners both of restitutional and compensatory nature: (i) to restore a status consistent with the law as well as (ii) to remedy the effects of any violations. An example of such violation would be an action that disturbs the use of neighbouring properties beyond an average level.[35] The latter might not be easy to prove for climate change related claims, as one would again have to prove the causal relationship.

(D)   Other law

Human and constitutional rights

16.80   The Polish Constitution recognises the natural environment as subject to special protection and interest on the part of public authorities. Primary law refers to the duty of the Republic of Poland to ensure freedom and human rights as well as protection of the environment through the principle of sustainable development.[36] However, the law does not specifically regulate environmental rights in the section dedicated to human freedoms and rights.[37]

16.81   The normative construction adopted in the Polish Constitution imposes a duty on public authorities to pursue a policy ensuring environmental security to present and future generations. The

[35] See Supreme Court ruling dated 28 December 1979, III CRN 249/79, OSNC 1980, No. 7–8, item 144.

[36] Article 74 together with Article 5, Polish Constitution.

[37] However, environmental protection reasons may justify limitations in the exercise of constitutional freedoms and rights. These limitations, however, cannot violate the essence of freedoms and rights. See Article 31 (3), Polish Constitution.

law directly states that environmental protection is an obligation of public authorities. This duty to care for the environment and bear liability for its deterioration is also imposed on individuals.

16.82 Despite the rather extensive regulation of principles governing environmental protection and sustainable development, no clear connection can be found in the Polish Constitution between the right to the environment and human rights.[38] This law therefore does not provide a solid basis to make such a clear connection and provide grounds for possible individual claims. It is recognised in the case law that no subjective rights can be derived from obligations of the State.[39] This position has been confirmed in a judgment of the Constitutional Tribunal[40] in which it stated that the definition of the duty of public authorities to maintain a policy ensuring environmental security entails general State policy and, therefore, it does not directly entail any subjective rights on the part of an individual.

16.83 Moreover, the constitutional norms only contain so-called 'programme norms' primarily addressed to parliament on which the speed and manner of implementation depends. Fulfilment of these measures, however, is entrusted to all public authorities, legislative as well as executive, as well as to judicial and local governmental bodies.[41]

16.84 The concept of personal interests in Polish civil law may, however, prove helpful when attempting to bring claims that arise from detrimental climate change. Personal interests are certainly intangible and are strictly related to human personality.[42] Their range is open and dynamic, thus it is possible to (flexibly) rely on them according to need.[43] A party whose personal interests have been threatened by another party's actions may demand cessation

---

[38] J. Ciechanowicz-McLean, *Prawo i polityka ochrony środowiska* (Wolters Kluwer, 2009), p. 21.

[39] B. Banaszak, *Konstytucja Rzeczypospolitej Polskiej. Komentarz* (C. H. Beck, 2009), p. 377.

[40] Constitutional Tribunal judgment dated 6 June 2006, K 23/05, OTK-A 2006, No. 6, item 62.

[41] See P. Winczorek, *Komentarz do Konstytucji Rzeczypospolitej Polskiej z dnia 2 kwietnia 1997 r.* (Liber, 2000), p. 18.

[42] M. Pazdan, 'Dobra osobiste i ich ochrona' in M. Safjan (ed.), *System prawa prywatnego. Prawo cywilne – część ogólna*, vol. I (C. H. Beck, 2007), p. 1150.

[43] *Ibid.*

of such actions. In turn, in the event of a violation, the claimant may demand that the violating party takes action to eliminate its effects. If material damage was inflicted through a violation of personal interests, the victim may demand its remedy according to the general principles provided in civil law.

16.85   The Supreme Court has found that tolerance by administrative bodies of noise levels exceeding the legally permissible limit is an illegal act that can violate the personal interests of individuals.[44] The Court supported the trend in recent judgments to recognise the right to a clean biological environment and satisfaction of aesthetic regard for natural beauty through civil law means. Consequently, the Court stated that specific obligations of administrative bodies 'may constitute a sufficient legal basis, in relation to relevant civil code regulations, for establishing claims of a civil law nature'.

16.86   Such views had already been expressed much earlier. In the 1970s, the Court stated that the human right to a clean biological environment and satisfaction of aesthetic regard for natural beauty can be protected by the relevant legal instruments related to the protection of personal interests. The Court added, however, that this is possible only if a violation of such right also constitutes a violation or threat to personal interests.[45] A somewhat different view was expressed in a Supreme Court ruling where the right to benefit from a clean environment was explicitly recognised as a personal interest within the meaning of civil law provisions.[46]

16.87   The ability to express a personal interest in the form of right to the environment is however a debatable issue. The above rulings have also met with criticism from certain legal commentators.[47]

16.88   Such criticism nevertheless does not forestall the ability to consider a subjective right to the environment, which can indeed

[44] Supreme Court ruling dated 23 February 2001, II CKN 394/00.
[45] Supreme Court ruling dated 10 July 1975, I CR 356/75 OSPiKA 1976/12, item 232 with critical remarks by S. Grzybowski.
[46] Supreme Court ruling dated 20 July 1984, II CR 5/84, PiP 1988/2, p. 142 with critical remarks by B. Kordasiewicz.
[47] See also Supreme Court ruling dated 2 April 1981, I CR 80/81 Nowe Prawo 1983/5, p. 121, OSNCP 1981/12, item 241 with critical remarks by W. Katner.

be sought on the basis of liability principles regarding violation of personal interests. The case law in relation to this is quite vast, yet the extent to which this can be applied in the context of GHG emissions and their contribution to climate change is unclear.[48]

16.89 Such a concept would nevertheless be highly attractive because it is not necessary to prove fault on the part of the obligated entity. Therefore, the obtaining of evidence is significantly facilitated. Moreover, a threat to a personal interest (and not actual violation) suffices. Such simplifications, however, do not adequately reflect the need to practically apply these measures towards environmental degradation and the unfavourable effects of climate change. The fundamental difficulty would be the proper identification of the obligated entity.

Criminal law

16.90 In principle, criminal liability in Polish law is based on the liability of natural persons. Liability of legal entities is present and specified in a separate law, but nevertheless has a specific nature. It is established under a different procedure than that provided under Directive 2008/99/EC.[49] Under Polish law, in principle, the collective entity[50] is subject to liability only if the prohibited act committed by a given representative of an entity was confirmed through a legally binding judgment convicting such representative.[51] The result, in practice, is that criminal liability of legal persons does not arise in Polish law. It can be anticipated as a result that the need to primarily determine criminal liability of

---

[48] See P. Mazur, 'Formy zbiorowe ochrony prawa osobistego do środowiska', *Państwo i Prawo*, 5 (2006), 105; W. Radecki, 'Ochrona środowiska naturalnego a ochrona dóbr osobistych' in J. St. Piątowski (ed.), *Dobra osobiste i ich ochrona w polskim prawie cywilnym. Zagadnienia wybrane* (Ossolineum, 1986), p. 233 ff; P. Mazur, 'Prawo osobiste do korzystania z wartości środowiska naturalnego, *Państwo i Prawo*, 11 (1999), 53.

[49] Directive 2008/99/EC of the European Parliament and of the Council of 19 November 2008 on the protection of the environment through criminal law.

[50] A collective entity is a specific concept under Polish criminal law and includes not only legal persons, but also organisational units without legal personality, except for the State Treasury, local self-government authorities, etc.

[51] W. Radecki, *Instytucje prawa ochrony środowiska. Geneza. Rozwój. Perspektywy* (Difin, 2010), p. 453.

a natural person will prevent the application of liability rules in relation to legal persons in the event of any acts causing detrimental climate change.

16.91   Also significant is the fact that the global and cross-border nature of climate change is a major obstacle in applying criminal regulations and the proper attribution of liability. Emissions of gases and substances will often only cause harm after accumulating from numerous sources, and that harm may only materialise in the distant future.

(E)   'Soft' law

16.92   Poland is a member of the OECD and it is, therefore, possible to submit a complaint to a national contact point[52] against actions of multinational companies violating the OECD *Guidelines for Multinational Enterprises* ('the Guidelines'), which contain a series of guidelines on proper activities by a multinational company. The scope of these guidelines includes, in particular, transparency of information, sound management systems, activities relating to corporate social responsibility as well as environmental protection. In this respect, they may concern the issue of climate change.

A complaint may be filed by Parties interested in resolving a dispute, including NGOs, trade unions and business groups.

The observance of the Guidelines is voluntary and is not subject to legal enforcement.

16.93   The filing of a complaint against a corporation violating the Guidelines leads to an eventual mediation between the Parties. If the Parties do not resolve the dispute, a mediator issues a statement and eventually makes recommendations on guideline implementation. Upon consultation with interested Parties, the mediator may publicly announce the outcome of the proceedings unless their confidential nature and the interests of all Parties dictate that they should not be made public.

---

[52] There is a national contact point in Poland at the Polish Information and Foreign Investment Agency (PAIiIZ) (see www.paiz.gov.pl).

(F) Practicalities

Finding jurisdiction

16.94   The jurisdiction of Polish courts is determined by reference to the defendant, his/her/its place of residence or ordinary presence, or registered office (if a legal person or other organisation), in accordance with the principle *actor sequitur forum rei*.[53]

16.95   This principle, on the basis of which a defendant should be sued in the courts of the country where a harmful event took place or may have taken place,[54] has key significance in relation to climate change compensation claims.

16.96   In deciding which law is applicable, a court will in particular rely on Council Regulation (EC) No. 864/2007 dated 11 July 2007 on the law applicable to non-contractual obligations ('Rome II'). Pursuant to Rome II, a plaintiff may select the law of the country in which an event giving rise to the damage took place or the law of the country where damage occurred.

16.97   For a foreign claimant from outside the EU, the choice of law is based on Polish private international law principles, and for climate change claims the applicable law is that of the country in which the event causing damage took place.

16.98   There is a series of exceptions to these regulations and their discussion exceeds the scope of this publication. Even if it is assumed that these exceptions do not apply, mere determination of the place 'where an event causing damage took place or could have taken place' may prove to be a significant challenge in the climate change context.

---

[53] Procedural regulations on the basis of which the jurisdiction of Polish courts is established (understood to be an international attribute) are found in the Civil Procedure Code of 17 November 1964 (Journal of Laws 1964, No. 43, item 296, as amended), as well as in Council Regulation (EC) No. 44/2001, Council Regulation (EC) No. 2201/2003 (of lesser interest to us due to its subject matter), and other international law provisions, including the Lugano Convention on jurisdiction and the enforcement of judgments in civil and commercial matters. International treaties, including bilateral agreements not listed here as well as Council Regulations, have priority over national code provisions.

[54] Article 5(3), Regulation 44/2001, and Article 5(3), Lugano Convention.

Public interest litigation

16.99   The concept of public interest litigation is not practised in Poland, although the law in principle allows for such litigation. Polish law provides that NGOs whose statutory aims include environmental protection can intervene in such cases, with claimant consent, to proceedings at any stage.[55] Irrespective of this right, Polish environmental protection law provides for further rights of environmental organisations.[56] They may, if an environmental threat or violation affects the common good, demand restoration from the entity responsible for such threat or violation to a state consistent with the law, as well as an undertaking of preventative measures. If this is impossible or excessively opposed, a cessation of the relevant activity giving rise to the threat of damage or violation may be sought.

Enforcement

16.100   In principle, foreign civil judgments are recognised in Polish law provided that there are no obstacles listed in specific regulations (e.g. mandatory jurisdiction of Polish courts in a case or contradiction to fundamental principles of the legal order in Poland). Each public body faced with the issue of effectiveness of a foreign judgment assesses it for the purposes of pending proceedings, although other bodies are not bound by such assessment. For this reason it is possible to put forward a motion in court to determine whether a foreign court judgment should be recognised.

16.101   In relation to arbitration court rulings, Poland is Party to the New York Convention on the recognition and enforcement of foreign arbitral awards. Court judgments and settlements concluded before, or approved by, foreign courts are subject to implementation in Poland upon issue of an enforcement clause by a Polish court.

---

[55] Article 61, para. 3, Civil Procedure Code of 17 November 1964 (Journal of Laws 1964, No. 43, item 296, as amended).
[56] Article 323 (2), Environmental Protection Law Act of 27 April 2001 (Journal of Laws 2008, No. 25, item 150, as amended).

Ancillary orders

16.102 Any party to proceedings or participant therein may apply for an injunction if a claim is rendered probable[57] and there is a legal interest in granting such injunction. Such legal interest is deemed to exist if the lack of an injunction would prevent or seriously hinder implementation of a judgment rendered in a case or in another manner prevent or seriously hinder achievement of the goal in case proceedings. An injunction may be applied for prior to, or in the course of, proceedings.

16.103 In deciding on the type of injunction the court will consider the interests of the parties: due legal protection to be provided to the entitled party but not to the extent that the injuncted party would be encumbered beyond necessity, as such an injunction could not satisfy a claim.

Costs/funding

16.104 A court usually rules on costs in a final judgment in any given instance. The losing party is under an obligation to pay, on demand, its opponent's costs; these include all costs necessary to pursue rights and prepare an effective defence including court fees and attorney remuneration limited to a level set in separate regulations. This is usually lower than the actual amount of fees agreed between lawyer and client, thus it is usually not possible to obtain full payment of professional legal services from the opponent.

16.105 In the event of only partially favourable judgment, costs are split or proportionally allocated between the parties. A court may, however, oblige one of the parties to reimburse all costs if

---

[57] According to theory, rending probable (*semiplena probatio*), understood as an alternative measure to evidence in the strict sense and which does not provide certainty, but only a probability of an assertion about some fact. It constitutes an exception to the general rule of demonstrating asserted facts in favour of the party, which the law allows in a particular case to give credence to a fact on which it relies, instead of proving it. It is exempted as a measure from the formalism of ordinary evidentiary proceedings – its aim is to speed up proceedings in the case. However, it is at the discretion of the court to decide whether the findings made on the basis of rending probable are sufficiently reliable to be considered as credible facts.

its opponent lost only an insignificant part of his/her claims or when civil law provisions do not include strict criteria to specify the amount of the claim.

16.106   The costs related to the issue of a temporary injunction in injunction proceedings are initially borne by the plaintiff, who may demand reimbursement of these costs from the defendant together with other costs of proceedings.

Receipt of information

16.107   During the course of proceedings, a court may request a party or third party to disclose a document in its possession if it contains evidence that is vital in resolving the case. This is an exception to the principle that no one is obliged to disclose a document which harms their own case, since a party cannot refuse to disclose a document on the basis that it may result in the loss of a case (although not necessarily the case in question). This exemption refers to disclosure of a privileged document, as defined in separate regulations.

16.108   In addition to court proceedings, the regulations concerning access to public information and to information on the environment and its protection are of relevance. Information can be sought from public administrative bodies on the basis of both of these regimes, and anyone can submit an appropriate request without having to demonstrate a legal or material interest in such information.

(G)   Conclusion

16.109   As discussed in this chapter, Polish law provides a number of legal avenues that allow both individuals and companies to seek satisfaction in a variety of procedural forms. However, the unusual characteristics of climate change claims make liability based on the same seem very hypothetical and uncertain at this stage. Moreover, the lack of case law in this area does not enable one to draw firm conclusions as to the future of climate change liability in Poland.

England

SILKE GOLDBERG AND RICHARD LORD QC

(A) Introduction

The English legal system

17.01   England is part not only of the United Kingdom of Great Britain
and Northern Ireland ('UK'),[1] but of the European Union, and
this dual status is important in considering its law. England is a
constitutional monarchy, but has no written constitution. It has
a common law legal system. The main sources of the law are: (i)
legislation, which may be 'primary' in the form of statutes passed
by Parliament, secondary legislation, or European legislation
in the form of Regulations, which have direct effect as a matter
of English law; and (ii) the common law to be found in decided
cases[2] and as developed by the courts using a system of precedent. The law of tort, and much administrative law, is common
law based.

The governmental stance on climate change

17.02   The Department of Energy and Climate Change ('DECC') was
created in October 2008, to bring together energy policy and climate change mitigation policy. DECC is responsible for all aspects
of UK energy policy, and for tackling global climate change on
behalf of the UK. The global challenge of climate change is now
firmly established on the political agenda of the UK.[3] The rising

---

[1] The law of England includes, for present purposes, that of Wales.
[2] Reports of most of the recent cases decided by English courts are available free on www.
bailii.org.
[3] See, for example, the establishment of the Department of Energy and Climate Change
('DECC') in October 2008 (DECC's website is available at www.decc.gov.uk/default.
aspx).

importance of addressing climate change in the UK was recently expressed in a case before the Planning Inspector,[4] who noted that:[5]

> [t]here is no dispute over the national need to address climate change and the importance attached by the Government to the role of exploiting sources of renewable energy in doing so. This is manifest from a range of publications including, for example, the Renewable Energy Strategy 2009, the Energy Act 2008 and the Climate Change Act 2008.

17.03   In September 2010, Prime Minister David Cameron stated that he wanted his Coalition Government to be the 'greenest Government ever'.[6] Although he acknowledged the UK was lagging behind its European counterparts in introducing renewable energy into its energy mix and that the current budget deficit would be a huge challenge to overcome, the Secretary of State for Energy and Climate Change Chris Huhne claimed that the UK was 'in a unique position to become a world leader in [the renewable energy] industry. [The UK] … should be harnessing our wind, wave and tidal resources to the maximum'.[7]

Climate Change Act 2008

17.04   The UK has international commitments to combating climate change and reducing greenhouse gas ('GHG') emissions. As a signatory to the Kyoto Protocol, the UK is required to reduce its GHG emissions by 12.5 per cent (below 1990 levels) in the period 2008–12[8] and although no legally binding treaty was agreed upon at the Copenhagen Conference in December 2009, the UK pushed for an international agreement to cut global emissions by 50 per cent by 2050 or on 80 per cent reductions by developed countries.[9] The European Climate Change Programme ('ECCP')

---

[4] In England and Wales, the Planning Inspectorate is in charge of appeals and related case-work under the applicable planning and environmental legislation.

[5] *Enertrag UK Ltd* v. *South Norfolk DC* (2010) PAD 13, at para. 72.

[6] 'Cameron: I want to be the greenest government ever': *The Guardian*, 14 May 2010, available at www.guardian.co.uk/environment/2010/may/14/cameron-wants-greenest-government-ever.

[7] http://blogs.ft.com/energy-source/2010/09/23/the-ft-thanet-debate-chris-huhne-on-the-future-of-offshore-wind/.

[8] http://unfccc.int/files/national_reports/initial_reports_under_the_kyoto_protocol/application/pdf/report_final.pdf.

[9] www.guardian.co.uk/commentisfree/2009/dec/20/copenhagen-climate-change-accord.

set even more ambitious targets and policies to be collectively achieved by the Member States of the European Union. The ECCP aimed to (i) cut GHG emissions by 20 per cent below 1990 levels by 2020; (ii) improve energy efficiency by 20 per cent; and (iii) increase energy from renewable sources to 20 per cent of all energy.[10]

17.05 The Climate Change Act 2008 ('CCA') set legally binding national targets. The CCA provides that it is the duty of the Secretary of State to: ensure that the net UK carbon account for the year 2050 is at least 80 per cent lower than the 1990 baseline;[11] set up the Committee on Climate Change ('CCC', an independent body established to advise the Secretary of State); and establish an emissions trading scheme.

17.06 Carbon budgets are set for five-year periods by the Secretary of State (advised by the CCC) and represent the limit of the GHG that may be emitted over that time. Last year the Government announced that the carbon budget for 2020 is 34 per cent below the 1990 baseline.[12] The CCA does not provide for any sanctions for failure to meet its target but as the targets are legally binding, the Government could be liable for judicial review. An action for judicial review allows the courts to make a declaration that the Government has failed to comply with its obligations under the CCA and exposes the Government to public criticism and loss of credibility in international negotiations.[13] Even if a direct action for judicial review based on breach of obligations imposed by the CCA is unlikely, the existence and content of the legislation are already influential in case law as illustrated by the references to it in the Heathrow Airport cases.[14]

17.07 The CCA also gave power to the Government to introduce national emissions trading schemes which led to the establishment of the mandatory Carbon Reduction Commitment Energy Efficiency Scheme ('CRC') that applies to large businesses and

[10] www.carbontrust.co.uk/policy-legislation/international-frameworks/european-union-policy/pages/europeanunionukpolicy.aspx.
[11] Section 1(1) of the 2008 Act.
[12] www.publications.parliament.uk/pa/cm200910/cmselect/cmenergy/193/19305.htm.
[13] http://uk.practicallaw.com/5-242-0025#a315662.
[14] For example *London Borough of Hillingdon* v. *Secretary of State for Transport* [2010] EWHC 626 (Admin), §§ 3, 41, 77.

public sector organisations. Under the CRC, allowances are sold by the Government at a fixed price per tonne of CO_2 or traded on a secondary market. Participants will have to surrender a number of allowances that matches their level of emissions in the relevant compliance year at the end of that year. The money raised from the auctions will be 'recycled' back to the participants according to their performance during that year thus incentivising large businesses to lower GHG emissions.[15]

Industrial and natural resources (emissions sources and energy mix)

17.08   In 2009, gas-fired generation accounted for 44 per cent of total electricity generation; coal-fired generation for 28 per cent; other renewables for 3 per cent; wind for 2.5 per cent; hydro for 1.3 per cent; and nuclear power stations for about 18 per cent.[16]

17.09   The UK has oil and gas reserves in the North Sea and although these resources are in decline, Oil & Gas UK (an industry trade body) stated[17] that the oil and gas fields could still be delivering 1.5 million barrels per day by 2020, enough to satisfy 35 per cent of UK energy demand but only if high fuel prices and tax breaks are combined to make viable a growing backlog of exploration and development projects in the North Sea.

17.10   According to figures published by the Government, the following are the main sources of GHG emissions in the UK:[18] 35 per cent comes from the power and heavy industry sectors; 20 per cent comes from workplaces; 20 per cent comes from transport; 13 per cent comes from water and space heating in domestic premises; and 11 per cent comes from farming, changes in land use and waste.

17.11   A report prepared for The Energy Intensive Users Group and the Trades Union Group[19] has stated that power and heavy industry

[15] www.decc.gov.uk/en/content/cms/what_we_do/lc_uk/crc/crc.aspx.
[16] www.world-nuclear.org/info/inf84.html.
[17] www.guardian.co.uk/business/2010/feb/24/plenty-of-north-sea-oil.
[18] http://centralcontent.fco.gov.uk/central-content/campaigns/act-on-copenhagen/ resources/en/pdf/DECC-Low-Carbon-Transition-Plan.
[19] www.eiug.org.uk/publics/WWA%20Impact%20of%20Climate%20Change%20Policies %20EIUG%20TUC%202010723.pdf.

in the UK (such as steel-making, ceramics and chemicals companies) will be most affected by the climate change initiatives, which make operations in the UK more expensive as compared to other countries.

National climate change risks

17.12   According to UK Climate Projections[20] average UK temperature has risen since the mid-twentieth century, as have average sea-level and sea-surface temperatures around the UK coast. Trends in precipitation are harder to identify, although it is thought that winters will become wetter and summers drier throughout the UK.[21] Climate change will mean the UK has an increased risk of flooding, coastal erosion, damage to essential infrastructure due to intense rain events and increased levels of UV radiation.[22]

(B)   Public law

Overview

17.13   This section addresses the process whereby decisions of public bodies may be reviewed by the courts (hence the common term 'judicial review'). The legal principles form part of English administrative law, and judicial review cases are generally brought in the Administrative Court.[23]

17.14   Because of their nature, judicial review proceedings are likely to be the most common type of legal action brought in relation to climate change issues. A number of different types of action can be envisaged: (i) review of decisions which implement or purport

---

[20] The UK Climate Projections (UKCP09) make available climate information for adaptation purposes. Funded by a number of UK ministries, including the Department of Energy and Climate Change, they carry out research in partnership with several academic and scientific institutions, including the Environment Agency Marine Climate Change Impacts Partnership (MCCIP), the Met Office, Newcastle University, Proudman Oceanic Laboratory (POL), Tyndall Centre and University of East Anglia (UEA). Further information is available at: http://ukclimateprojections.defra.gov.uk/content/view/868/531/.

[21] http://ukclimateprojections.defra.gov.uk/content/view/512/499/.

[22] www.parliament.uk/documents/post/postpn232.pdf.

[23] This section contains only the broadest summary of a very large body of law. For further detail see, for example, Michael Fordham QC, *The Judicial Review Handbook*, 5th edn (Hart Publishing, 2008).

to implement regulations directly concerning climate change; (ii) review of decisions in spheres of public body activity where it is alleged that climate change issues arise; (iii) review of decisions of public bodies in relation to private sector activity which allegedly fail to take into account climate change factors; and (iv) challenges on ancillary matters such as right to information and to protest. So for example in the first category, actions taken in purported compliance with duties owed under the Climate Change Act 2008 could be challenged. In the second category (into which the famous US case of *Massachusetts* v. *EPA* would fall) a failure by environmental government agencies to address climate change might be challenged. In the third category a whole host of decisions on planning, licensing or permitting private projects with climate change implications might be challenged, including permissions for airports, power plants or mines, or government financial support for such activities.

Grounds for judicial review

17.15   The courts do not have unfettered discretion to intervene in decisions of public bodies whenever they like, and the circumstances in which they may do so are strictly circumscribed. The court may intervene and undertake a review in three basic categories of circumstances: (i) unlawfulness of a decision; (ii) unreasonableness of a decision; and (iii) unfairness/procedural impropriety. There may be scope for review on other less well-developed grounds (such as frustration of legislative purpose, substantive legitimate expectation, or error of fact). Decisions involving Human Rights Act 1998 ('HRA') violations are susceptible to review. Where a decision is reviewed, the issue is whether it was a reasonable one and the court will not generally substitute its own views for those of the decision-maker, or undertake a broader merits review.

Other aspects of judicial reviews

17.16   The following issues are also important:
   • Generally there must be a 'decision' of a public authority, but the want of an identifiable decision is not necessarily fatal (*R* v. *Secretary of State for transport, ex p. London Borough of Richmond Upon Thames and Ors (No. 3)*[24]).

[24] [1995] Env LR 409, 413.

- A claimant must be able to show 'sufficient interest': the case law relating to interest groups (including in environmental law challenges) indicates a liberal approach where there is genuine concern (*R v. HM Inspectorate of Pollution, ex p. Greenpeace*[25]). In addition to the claimant and defendant, other 'interested parties'[26] who are directly affected (within Civil Procedure Rules ('CPR') 54.1(2)(f)) may have the right to be involved in the proceedings.
- The remedy is discretionary (*Dimmock v. Secretary of State for Education and Skills*,[27] a case where the claimant unsuccessfully sought judicial review of a governmental decision to distribute to every State secondary school in the UK a copy of Al Gore's well known film about climate change, 'An Inconvenient Truth'). A claimant may seek (under CPR 54.2, 54.3) any of the following – a quashing order, a mandatory order, a prohibiting order, an injunction, or a declaration. There can be a claim for damages, restitution or recovery of sum due (CPR 25.1) or the obtaining of alternative remedies such as obtaining a reference to the ECJ.
- Procedure generally is governed by the CPR Part 54. Timing is important (CPR 54.5): an action must be commenced promptly (this is important where other interests are affected) and in any event not later than three months after 'the ground arose'.

17.17   Costs are discretionary (*Bolton MDC v. Secretary of State for the Environment*[28]). They generally follow the event with costs liability for the unsuccessful claimant. They may include costs in favour of third parties who opposed unsuccessful challenges (*Bolton MDC*). The court may be influenced in decisions about costs by the public-interest nature of litigation and importance of issues.[29] Protection against costs exposure may be obtained (including for interest groups) by applying for a protective costs order (*Corner House Research, R (on the application of) v. Secretary of State for Trade and Industry*[30]).

17.18   The Aarhus Convention,[31] a UN Convention which the UK ratified in 2005, requires that access to justice is not barred

[25] [1994] 4 AER 329.
[26] *R v. Liverpool City Council, ex p. Muldoon* (1995) 7 Admin LR 663.
[27] [2007] EWHC 2288 (Admin).   [28] [1995] 1 WLR 1176.
[29] *R (on the application of Friends of the Earth Ltd and Anor) v. Secretary of State for Environment, Food and Rural Affairs and Ors* [2001] EWCA Civ 1950 (7 December 2001).
[30] [2005] EWCA Civ 192.
[31] Convention on Access to Information, Public Participation in Decision Making and Access to Justice in Environmental Matters, done at Aarhus, Denmark, on 25 June 1998.

by inappropriate costs rules. In August 2010 the Compliance Committee found the UK to be in breach of its obligations.[32] In December 2010 in *R (Edwards & Pallikaropoulos)* v. *Environment Agency & DEFRA*[33] the Supreme Court considered for the first time Article 9 of the Aarhus Convention, which in the EU has been implemented by Article 10a of the Environmental Impact Directive.[34] Article 9 stipulates that environmental litigation should not be 'prohibitively expensive'. In order to ascertain what costs might be considered prohibitively expensive, the UK Supreme Court made a reference to the Court of Justice of the European Union ('CJEU') regarding the correct test to be applied in relation to cost orders in environmental cases. A decision of the CJEU is expected in 2011 or early 2012.

Examples in practice

Direct and indirect challenges

17.19   Challenges directly related to climate change have to date been few. If the US trend crosses the Atlantic,[35] there may be a rise in actions both from environmental groups seeking to compel public authorities to regulate in relation to climate change and from industry seeking to prevent or curtail such regulation.[36]

17.20   Challenges may also be made against activities which contribute to climate change and their effects, such as aircraft movements, whose noise was challenged in the 'Night Flights' series of cases (including *Hatton* v. *UK*[37]). Other examples are the Heathrow third runway case (*Hillingdon LBC* v. *Secretary of State for Transport*[38])

---

[32] www.unece.org/env/pp/compliance/C2008–33/Findings/ece.mp.pp.c.1.2010.6.add.3. edited.ae.clean.pdf.

[33] [2010] UKSC 57.

[34] Council Directive 85/337/EEC of 27 June 1985 on the assessment of the effects of certain public and private projects on the environment, as amended.

[35] As frequently occurs, although the US legislation on climate change is very different from the UK legislation.

[36] Opposition by the aviation industry to the inclusion of aviation emissions in phase III of the EU ETS took the form of a challenge to certain UK regulations in relation to the relevant EU Directive in *R (Air Transport Association of America Inc)* v. *SSECC* [2010] EWHC 1554 (Admin). The matter will apparently be referred to the European Court.

[37] ECHR, 36022/97, 8 July 2003.

[38] [2010] EWHC 626 (Admin) where express reference was made by Carnwath LJ to the CCA and Government Climate Change Policy. In *Barbone* v. *Secretary of State for Transport* [2009] EWHC 463 (Admin) one of the grounds of the unsuccessful challenge to the granting of planning permission to increase capacity of Stansted airport was that it

and, in another context, *Greenpeace* v. *Secretary of State for Trade and Industry*[39] on future use of nuclear power.

17.21   Challenges may concern not climate change itself but ancillary issues (such as the right to protest against climate change and the right to inform/educate/publicise concerning climate change). There are examples of challenges *against* climate change information/protests (*Dimmock* v. *Secretary of State for Education and Skills, Heathrow Airport Ltd* v. *Garman*[40]). But in other areas, there are examples of positive challenges to defend/secure a right to protest (*Tabernacle* v. *Secretary of State for Defence*[41]).

17.22   Challenges concerning the interpretation and enforcement of EU law and international obligations may provide for a lower threshold of review or more extensive relief than purely domestic law cases (including injunctions against the Crown) (*Rockware Glass Ltd, R (on the application of)* v. *Quinn Glass Ltd and Anor*[42]).

Human rights law and judicial review

17.23   Article 8, European Convention on Human Rights ('ECHR') (right to private and family life) could potentially be engaged (as in *Hatton* – see below at para. 17.27) by climate change impacts, as might Article 1, Protocol 1, ECHR (right to peaceful enjoyment of possessions) where there is damage to or interference with property. It is conceivable that Article 2 ECHR (right to life) could be engaged if there are serious enough effects, although this seems unlikely in the UK in the foreseeable future.

17.24   Many of the ECJ's decisions are predicated on the generally applicable principles from the case of *X + Y* v. *Netherlands*[43] where the State was held liable for not preventing a human rights violation by failing to put in place adequate systems to prevent a girl from being abused. In the environmental context, the case of *López Ostra* v. *Spain*[44] proved a landmark decision. The applicants were

---

was inconsistent with Government policy on climate change. Similar arguments may be made in favour of projects such as wind turbine farms (*Derbyshire Dales DC* v. *Secretary of State for Communities and Local Government* [2009] EWHC 1729 (Admin)).

[39] [2007] EWHC 311 (Admin).   [40] [2007] EWHC 1957 (QB).

[41] [2009] EWCA Civ 23.

[42] [2006] EWCA Civ 992. See also *Cemex UK Cement Ltd* v. *DEFRA*, [2006] EWHC 3207 on the EU emissions trading regime.

[43] (1986) 8 EHRR 235.   [44] [1994] ECHR 46.

residents of Spain who complained that a waste treatment facility near their home violated their right to privacy and family security guaranteed by Article 8 of the ECHR. It was held that severe environmental pollution may infringe the Article 8(1) right, irrespective of whether health is seriously endangered. Another noteworthy case in this context is *Guerra* v. *Italy* [1998] ECHR 7 in which Article 8(1) was held to be violated by the State's failure to inform residents near a factory about the health and safety risks posed by that factory.

17.25   In claims involving alleged breaches of human rights, the claimant must be a victim of that violation.[45] Given that even codified human rights can be very uncertain in terms of their scope and crystallisation towards the individual, one must face the problem that there is no clear defined environmental right to be a victim of. The relevant ground of judicial review would appear to be irrationality in relation to governmental environmental decision-making, but this is a very hard threshold to meet given that *Wednesbury* unreasonableness[46] requires a decision so unreasonable that no reasonable authority could have come to it. In the human rights context, particularly post HRA, there is some authority to suggest that this threshold will be lowered with regard to questions of interference in human rights[47] and that where the decision interferes with human rights, the court will require substantial justification for the interference in order to be satisfied that the response fell within the range of responses open to a reasonable decision-maker. This remains to be tested in an environmental context, but given that such a trend is highly qualified by judicial emphasis of the importance of not undermining governmental authority, one can envisage that a court will be far less inclined to interfere in decision-making that does not conflict with a clearly codified right.

---

[45] Section 7(1) of the Human Rights Act 1998. The victim, with the exception of governmental organisations, can however be a non-natural person (*Österreichischer Rundfunk* v. *Austria* (35841/02), [2006] ECHR 1043).

[46] *Associated Provincial Picture Houses Ltd* v. *Wednesbury Corporation* [1947] EWCA Civ 1, at para. 230. The term '*Wednesbury* unreasonableness' derives from the principle established in this case.

[47] *R (on the application of Mahmood)* v. *Secretary of State for the Home Department* [2000] EWCA Civ 315, at para. 856 per Lord Phillips of Worth Matravers.

17.26   It is worth considering the interesting recent employment case of *Nicholson* v. *Grainger Plc.*[48] The Employment Appeal Tribunal held that the employer had discriminated against Nicholson's fundamental philosophical belief in environmental protection contrary to the Employment Equality (Religion or Belief) Regulations 2003 which defines the ground for discrimination as 'religious belief or philosophical belief' with the caveat that a philosophical belief must be akin to religion. While this may be more a case of discrimination against non-standard beliefs, it does provide an example of environmentalism being recognised by the courts from an individual's perspective.

17.27   In a domestic context, *Hatton* v. *United Kingdom*[49] held that a government scheme imposed in 1993 that altered the regulation of noise arising from night flights out of Heathrow Airport was not in violation of the Article 8 right to respect for private and family life. Until the entry into force of the Human Rights Act 1998 there was no facility in English law, for the national courts to consider whether an alleged increase in night flights was a justifiable limitation on the right to respect for the private lives of those who lived near the airport. Therefore, it was held that there had been a violation of the Article 13 right to an effective remedy.

17.28   A case of interest is the action brought in 2009 in *Platform, People and Planet* v. *Commissioners of HM Treasury*[50] where two NGOs sought to challenge the Government's actions or inactions in its capacity as major shareholder in RBS, a large bank which was part nationalised after the 2008 financial crash. Specifically it was alleged that RBS's lending practices involved support for many projects and companies which contributed to significant GHG emissions, that RBS policies contravened the Government's own policies on GHG emission, and that in formulating policies to be adopted by it as shareholder the Government failed to follow its policy, under a 'Green Book', of assessing the environmental impact of provision of funds to RBS.

17.29   The claimants alleged (i) a legitimate expectation that public funds would not be used to allow RBS to act in contravention of the public interest in mitigating climate change, (ii) failure in

---

[48] [2010] 2 All ER 253.   [49] (36022/97), (2003) 37 EHRR 28.
[50] [2009] EWHC 3020 (Admin).

drawing up the policies to take into account other so called 'Green Book' policies, and (iii) breach of Article 6 of the EHCR. The court dismissed the first and third grounds as hopeless. The second ground was also rejected (although after a lengthier discussion), on the basis that none of the materials relied upon restricted the Government's wide discretion. The case adds nothing to administrative law, neither does it provide guidance (except in relation to its own special facts) on climate change related issues which may be amenable to review, but is an example of an indirect approach in a legal challenge to the perceived problems of climate change.

Property rights and planning law

17.30   In *Arscott* v. *Coal Authority*[51] the claimant argued that the 'common enemy' rule in the law of nuisance (i.e. flood preventative action does not constitute nuisance if it results in flooding on another's land) breached Article 8 of the ECHR or Article 1 of the Protocol to the Convention for the Protection of Human Rights and Fundamental Freedoms. The court dismissed his claim stating that the 'common enemy' principle was inoffensive to those rights and struck a fair balance between the right of the occupier to do what he liked with his own land and the right of his neighbour not to be interfered with. Furthermore, the rule balanced the interests of persons whose homes and property were affected and the interests of the general public.[52] Although this case does not relate directly to climate change one can see that the principle is applicable to climate change.

17.31   Human rights issues frequently arise in planning matters, especially given the Protocol to the ECHR Article 1 right to 'the peaceful enjoyment of possessions'. Here, any environmental agenda can be both the beneficiary and the victim of the human rights argument. In *R (on the application of Littlewood)* v. *Bassetlaw District Council*,[53] one of the grounds of the Littlewoods' application for judicial review against the planning grant of a pre-cast concrete manufacturing facility close to their home was that the local authority failed to consider the impact of the development on climate change. The court held that the grant was not

---

[51] [2004] EWCA Civ 892.
[52] *Marcic* v. *Thames Water Utilities Ltd* [2004] 2 AC 42 applied.
[53] [2009] Env LR 21.

Wednesbury unreasonable as adequate environmental reports and statements were made despite climate change not specifically being dealt with.

17.32   Contrast this with *Bradford* v. *West Devon BC*[54] where the claimants appealed the refusal of planning permission for two wind turbines. The local council's decision cited the adverse effects on surrounding landscapes and the residential amenities of nearby occupiers. Although the planning inspector acknowledged the importance of the need to combat global warming, and in spite of the fact that the project would have supplied electricity to more than 1,200 homes, it was decided that the benefits were outweighed by the unacceptable harm to the character and appearance of the distinctive local landscape.

17.33   The increase of coastal erosion and inundation due to climate change may affect rights of owners of coastal property and bring them into conflict with local or national authorities who are accused of inaction or the wrong type of action.[55] There is a duty on the Crown to 'protect the realm from the inroads of the sea by maintaining the natural barriers, or by raising artificial barriers',[56] although this is not an absolute one to prevent all erosion by any means. It is also conceivable that a party dissatisfied with action on coastal defences could seek to rely on Article 1 of the First Protocol to the ECHR which protects property rights, although apart from other difficulties with such a claim there would appear to be no deprivation of property (as opposed to failure to protect property).

(C)   Private law[57]

Preliminary considerations

17.34   The possibility of private law remedies (that is where one 'private' (non-State) legal person sues another for damages or an injunction) for loss or damage caused by climate change is one that has

---

[54] [2007] PAD 45.

[55] An example of litigation in relation to coastal erosion is *Boggis* v. *Natural England* [2009] EWCA Civ 1061.

[56] *Attorney-General* v. *Tomline* 1880 14 Ch D 58.

[57] For a detailed discussion of liability under English law generally, see Giedré Kaminskaité-Salters, *Constructing a Private Climate Change Lawsuit under English Law* (Kluwer Law

generated much interest and discussion, and equal measures of excitement (for environmentalists) and alarm (for sectors of industry and their insurers).

17.35   A discussion of possible private remedies in a chapter on English law necessitates consideration of procedural law and conflict of law as well as substantive law. English law in this context is most likely to be relevant only in litigation before English courts. This is in turn likely to occur only (in simplified terms) where (i) the person sued (defendant) or one of them is domiciled in England, and/or (ii) the persons suing (claimants) are able to found jurisdiction against a foreign-based defendant in respect of damage occurring in England.[58] Even where an action is brought against a defendant domiciled in England, English conflict of law rules may require application of a different substantive law (for example when damage is suffered other than in England).[59] For this reason the laws in relation to establishing jurisdiction and in relation to applicable law are important in terms of the practicalities of private law claims.

17.36   There have been no significant private law claims in England based directly on allegations of actual or anticipated damage from climate change. It should be emphasised at the outset that the authors see no reason to suppose that one could be brought today with any realistic chances of success. This section thus focuses on potential bases for such liability. The prospect of this kind of liability being established is widely thought to become more likely if and when the impacts of climate change become more severe, especially if no satisfactory international regulatory regime is agreed. The analysis involves a consideration of the applicability of existing legal principles of tort (delict) to climate change scenarios, borrowing on discussion and actual cases in the USA and elsewhere.[60]

International, 2010), and James Burton, Stephen Tromans QC and Martin Edwards, 'Climate Change: What Chance a Damages Action in Tort?', *UKELA e-law*, 55 (2010), 22.

[58] In this section 'C' and 'D' are used where appropriate to denote claimant(s) and defendant(s).

[59] By parity of reasoning it is of course possible that English law could be applied in an action other than in England if damage was suffered in England.

[60] The main US cases (including *Connecticut* v. *AEP*, *Kivalina* v. *Exxon* and *Comer* v. *Murphy*) are discussed in Chapter 20. Whilst there are significant differences between

17.37   Whether or not 'direct' cases involving actions against emitters and similar defendants for damages for the effect of climate are successful, it is very likely that there will be much litigation against professionals, public bodies, utility companies and other categories of defendant, for damage allegedly caused or contributed to by climate change. These cases typically involve allegations that the defendant failed to factor in the effects of climate change, whether in designing buildings, planning civil engineering projects, or auditing accounts of a company exposed to climate-related risks. This type of potential for liability is of great significance not only to those directly at risk from such actions, but to their investors, lenders, insurers and professional advisers.

17.38   The two principal 'torts' under which a 'direct' climate change related claim could be brought are 'nuisance' and 'negligence'.[61] Although these sometimes overlap, they have distinct origins and are aimed at different types of conduct. Each is discussed below. Because both torts are 'common law' torts, with the principles to be found in numerous decided cases, it is regrettably difficult to summarise their scope succinctly, and impossible without reference to such cases.

What damage might be actionable?

17.39   Fundamental to any analysis is a consideration of what type of harm or damage a claimant might allege, and what type of defendant he/she may claim against. English law most readily affords a remedy in the case of 'physical' injury or damage, specifically where the claimant is injured or made ill (or killed) or his/her property is physically damaged. The law recognises the right to recover where a claimant is economically harmed, but in much more limited circumstances. As discussed in Chapter 2, some types of climate damage are (or are likely in future to be) much easier to show as 'caused' by climate change than others. Damage may include almost any kind of adverse change (hotter,

---

English and US law, there are sufficient similarities to make these cases instructive, particularly in the analyses on public nuisance and causation or 'traceability' of harm.

[61]   Although other causes of action might conceivably be invoked, such as 'product liability' claims, 'Rylands v. Fletcher' claims and conspiracy. For a consideration of these, see Kaminskaité-Salters, n. 57 above.

colder, wetter, drier, windier), and in a climate context any significant change may potentially be adverse, especially if it occurs too
quickly to allow the relevant property or ecosystem to adapt to
the change. However examples of damage in England which may
give rise to claims are (i) damage to property caused by sea level
rise, (ii) illness or disease caused by heatwaves or warmer mean
temperatures, and (iii) damage to property caused by extreme
weather events, either in isolation or by reference to increased
incidence, such as heavy rain leading to flooding, strong winds,
and damage to property due to change in precipitation patterns
(floods or shrinkage damage). Harm in terms of economic loss
alone is less likely to be actionable.

Who might claim

17.40   This depends largely on who suffers the damage referred to above.
Claimants could be individuals, corporations, NGOs/charities or
local or national governmental institutions. For various reasons
large property owners might be the most likely claimants, suing
on the basis of losses aggregated over time and/or at different locations. These could include local government bodies who may also
have a public interest in bringing claims for public nuisance.

Who might be defendants?

17.41   Turning to the question of who may be sued, the most likely targets
of any litigation are those most likely to be alleged to be 'responsible' (to use a neutral word) for climate change. One of the hurdles
for any private law claim is that virtually every individual in the
world is in some (if minute) sense 'responsible' for GHG emissions,
but the larger the organisation (usually a corporation) concerned
the more easily it may be said that its activities contribute to climate change in a sufficiently material way to attract liability. The
types of activity are likely to be those that involve energy-intensive
activities and GHG emissions or those that develop products or
services that in turn contribute to GHG emissions.

Nuisance

17.42   The paradigm case of nuisance is 'a condition or activity which
unduly interferes with the use or enjoyment of land'.[62] However

---

[62]   *Clerk & Lindsell on Torts*, 20th edn (Sweet & Maxwell, 2010), § 20–01.

nuisance is not necessarily limited to claims against defendants in respect of their use of land or by claimants in relation to use or enjoyment of their land. The definition of nuisance is complicated by a distinction between 'private' nuisance, most often taking the form of an unreasonable use of D's land affecting the use of enjoyment of the land of his neighbour, C,[63] and 'public' nuisance, which is a crime and a tort actionable in damages.[64] Although the two are not mutually exclusive,[65] for present purposes public nuisance is the more relevant, and has been the subject of a number of recent cases.[66] In summary:

(1) Public nuisance is a crime the essence of which is an act or omission the effect of which is to endanger the life, health, property, [morals] or comfort of the public, or to obstruct the public in the exercise or enjoyment of rights common to all subjects with the relevant area or sphere of operation.[67]

(2) At common law public nuisance includes a very diverse group of activities, all causing (at least) annoyance or inconvenience.[68]

(3) It is only actionable when a private individual has suffered particular damage over and above that suffered by the public generally.[69]

17.43   Thus public nuisance covers a potentially wide range of activities and, unlike private nuisance, is not limited to activities on D's property affecting C's rights in relation to his/her property. Acts which are otherwise intrinsically lawful may constitute public nuisance, although not everything which causes

---

[63] See, for example, *Hunter* v. *Canary Wharf* [1997] AC 655.

[64] *Tate & Lyle* v. *GLC* [1983] 2 AC 509.

[65] *Colour Quest* v. *Total* [2009] EWHC 540, at para. 432.

[66] *Colour Quest* v. *Total*, *ibid.*; *R* v. *Rimmington* [2005] UKHL 63; *Corby* v. *Corby Borough Council* [2008] EWCA 463.

[67] The potential width of the tort arises in part from the fact that the 'rights' referred to are not apparently positive rights in the formal legal sense, but more the right to go about one's normal daily business unperturbed.

[68] Thus *Rimmington* (see n. 66 above), § 9 includes references to 'erecting a manufactory for hartshorn, erecting a privy near the highway, placing putrid carrion near the highway, keeping hogs near a public street and feeding them with offal, keeping a fierce and unruly bull in a field through which there was a footway, keeping a ferocious dog unmuzzled and baiting a bull in the King's highway'. This list is cited in a book on climate change not so much for amusement, but to demonstrate the potential width of the tort (and crime) of public nuisance.

[69] *Clerk & Lindsell on Torts* (see n. 62 above), §§ 20–03 to 20–05.

annoyance or inconvenience to the general public is an action-able nuisance.

17.44   One of the difficulties applying the nuisance analysis to climate change damage is that unlike the classic nuisance cases involving noise, smells, smokes etc., there will be no geographic connection between C and D. This however is simply an unusual consequence of the nature of climate change rather than a fundamental requirement of nuisance.

17.45   The four key questions which would need to be addressed in any such claim would be:
(1) What was the nature of the harm or damage suffered by C?
(2) Could it be shown to be caused by D's activities?
(3) Were D's activities such as could in the circumstances amount to a nuisance (this is linked with (1) and (2))?
(4) Would a defence of statutory authority be available?

Negligence

17.46   The limits of the tort of negligence are difficult to define, but the essence of the tort is easily stated: in general terms D 'must take reasonable care to avoid acts and omissions which [he] can reasonably foresee would be likely to injure [his] neighbour',[70] and a breach of that duty will sound in damages. Whilst economic loss may in limited circumstances be recoverable, the 'damage' must generally be to C's property or person.

17.47   A preliminary question in the context of climate change liability is whether D owes any duty to C to take reasonable care, and this issue, which considers who is one's 'neighbour', is the subject of much case law.

17.48   Many attempts have been made to reformulate a universally applicable test[71] in a way which allows the law to react to new situations without opening the 'floodgates' to tort claims based on a general principle of uncertain scope. In *Caparo* a threefold test was adopted whereby a duty of care existed if and only if: (i) there

---

[70] *Donoghue* v. *Stevenson* [1932] AC 562, 580.
[71] By way of example only, see *Anns* v. *Merton* LBC [1978] AC 728 and *Caparo* v. *Dickman* [1990] 2 AC 605.

was sufficient proximity between the parties; (ii) the damage was foreseeable; and (iii) the imposition of a duty of care was just, fair and reasonable. Even this approach asks as many questions as it answers, when 'proximity' is itself an elusive concept, not used in a geographical sense, and 'just, fair and reasonable' are all almost infinitely elastic. However the 'just, fair and reasonable'[72] requirement can be used as a 'catch all' provision whereby the courts deny expansion of the tort to cover new types of conduct, on policy grounds, even where logic and first principle might be said to justify this. Broad social and economic considerations may militate against a general expansion of tortious liability, and as noted in Chapter 5, this factor has been reflected in a number of Australian decisions.[73] The pendulum has swung in some common law jurisdictions away from a 'universal' test and back towards an 'incremental' approach. This raises similar questions in a different form, as to when a court should recognise a duty in a new situation, but with the burden on the claimant to justify the existence of a duty it militates against extension of negligence to cover GHG emissions.

17.49   One of the ironies of the common law is that, despite judicial protestations of unwillingness to make decisions which are effectively policy rather than legal ones,[74] the common law nature of negligence liability allows judges to do just that. Lord Atkin's famous exposition of the 'neighbour' principle was preceded by this passage:

> The liability for negligence whether you style it such or treat it as in other systems as a species of 'culpa,' is no doubt based upon a general public sentiment of moral wrongdoing for which the offender must pay. But acts or omissions which any moral code would censure cannot in a practical world be treated so as to give a right to every person injured by them to demand relief. In this way rules of law arise which limit the range of complainants and the extent of their remedy.[75]

17.50   This sentiment has been echoed in modern times, for example by Lord Bingham who said that 'the public policy consideration

---

[72] See for example *Sutradhar* v. *NERC* [2006] UKHL 33, especially para. 32, where the House of Lords held that an English defendant was on the facts under no duty of care in respect of alleged arsenic poisoning suffered by the claimant in Bangladesh.

[73] Para. 5.54 ff.

[74] Echoed in the 'justiciability' issue raised in the US climate change cases.

[75] *Jonoghne* v. *Stevenson* [1932] AC 562, 580.

which has first claim on the loyalty of the law is that wrongs should be remedied and that very potent counter considerations are required to override that policy'.[76] In the context of such uncertainty about the scope of a duty of care, it lends credence to those who take the 'broad brush' view that whether and when a duty will be found to exist will depend on how seriously people or property are damaged in future, and how those said to be in part responsible have conducted themselves. Different possible scenarios in ten, twenty or fifty years' time may provide different answers to the question whether GHG emission is at least in some circumstances and for the purposes of the law of tort 'moral wrongdoing for which the offender must pay'.

Issues of damage

17.51   On the basis of the IPCC reports as to future trends as well as actual evidence of damage to date, there are a number of types of damage which would be recognised as qualifying for compensation in nuisance or negligence if other hurdles were overcome. These include damage to land and buildings caused by sea level rise, and damage from floods or 'extreme weather events', soil shrinkage or subsidence due to drought.[77]

17.52   A consideration which might be relevant on the issues of damage, causation, reasonable conduct or 'duty of care' is the 'net benefit' point. Put simply the question is whether, if (for example) a heatwave causes death or harm to 500 people, those 500 can claim without reference to an assertion by D which says that the same climate change means that 300 (or even 600) less people die of cold in winter, in the same or even in different locations. Another possible aspect of 'net benefit' is a temporal one; as explained in Chapter 2, climate change may make autumn floods in a specific location more likely but at the same time make spring floods in the same place less likely.

---

[76] *X (Minors)* v. *Bedfordshire CC* [1995] 2 AC 633.

[77] See para. 3.23 above. This section focuses on types of damage which are likely to occur in the UK. Other countries may suffer other types of damage (e.g. from glacier/snowpack melt, desertification etc.).

17.53   A further problem is the question of mitigation of (or adaptation
         to) damage which potentially arises in an acute form where cli-
         mate change occurs progressively over a relatively long period, in
         contrast to much damage (which is the subject of litigation) which
         happens instantly or more quickly. This issue arises in equally
         acute form in the FCCC negotiations. One of the oddities of the
         FCCC terminology is that 'mitigation' (which to an English tort
         lawyer means avoiding the damage caused by a harmful event) is
         used to describe something else (avoiding the harmful event of
         climate change itself) and what a tort lawyer would call mitiga-
         tion is called adaptation. Leaving aside such semantic issues, if it
         can be seen that C's property will be damaged in the future as a
         result of the tortious conduct of D, to what extent (i) is C entitled
         to expend money to avoid or minimise the damage and reclaim
         it from D; (ii) is C bound to expend such money to minimise the
         damage, in the context of any claim against D; and (iii) is the cost
         and value of such action measured in purely economic terms,
         or do social, cultural and human rights considerations play a
         part?[78]

Issues of causation

17.54   Any claim of this type involves at least two basic links in terms of
         the 'chain of causation': (i) Was the damage (or the event which
         caused the damage) caused by 'climate change' as opposed to
         'ordinary' weather/climate, the passage of time or something
         else? (ii) To what extent was D's conduct a contributory factor in
         this? Before considering these, more general issues in relation to
         causation need to be addressed.

'Specific causation'

17.55   The English law of causation has developed by reference to reso-
         lution of factual issues and whether the claimant can show 'on
         balance' of probabilities that damage A was caused by event B.
         Recognising that many consequences have more than one cause,
         in general it is sufficient to show that B was 'an effective cause', an

---

[78] Thus for a small island threatened by sea level rise, relocation of inhabitants may in economic terms be cheap compared to building flood/storm defences, but it may not be 'reasonable' to require the cheaper option to be taken.

undefined expression connoting a narrower test than a 'but for' test but a wider one than sole or dominant cause. When the event is 'damage' there is also the question of whether the damage is 'indivisible' or not. A house which is destroyed by an explosion may be contrasted with one which progressively crumbles over many years due to erosion or subsidence. Where the damage is divisible it may be possible to apportion different parts of it to different causes. Even in the case of indivisible damage with more than one potential cause, there are two potentially overlapping issues: one of factual inquiry (and the role of presumption or statistics in that inquiry) as to which out of several potential causes was in scientific terms a cause; and the other a legal inquiry as to which of several 'scientific' causes are sufficiently 'direct' or 'effective' to be 'legally causative'.

17.56 The traditional approach to causation may work well enough for damage directly attributable to mean temperature increase or sea level rise. These are instances of damage where the (or the main) underlying cause is on the basis of the science 'known' or provable to the requisite standard of proof – for example the emissions of a large number of GHG emitters. Here the causation problem in relation to D is not necessarily a conceptual one, because the contribution of each emitter may well be calculable, but whether as a matter of law the ascertainable contribution is sufficiently material to make it, in legal terms, a cause. The difficulty in showing the materiality (in causative terms) of the effect of the GHG emissions of any given D or group of Ds remains perhaps the most significant obstacle to private law claims. One potential way around this obstacle in the case of long-term progressive damage is to analyse it as divisible, so that a D who is (for example) 'responsible' for 1 per cent of total emissions is 100 per cent liable for 1 per cent of the damage. This may have a similar effect to apportionment of liability for indivisible damage, and issues of joint or several liability (see para. 17.63 below) but is conceptually distinct.

17.57 The traditional approach works less well for the consequences of extreme weather events ('EWEs'), which are more likely to be seen as (at least in part) 'indivisible'. Where an allegation is made that these are caused or contributed to by climate change, the likely response is that such events have always happened, and that it is impossible to tell which if any are caused or contributed to by climate change.

17.58 A possible counter-argument from C is to argue that (for example) a given type of EWE used to happen every twenty years but now happens every twelve-and-a-half, ten, or five years and thus the chance of a given event increases by 60 per cent, 100 per cent, or 200 per cent. C may rely on the acceptance by the courts that if factor X doubles (or more) the risk of event Y happening, then in some circumstances, if event Y happens, on balance of probability it is 'caused' by event X.[79] This doctrine is potentially significant for climate change claims where a 100% increase in frequency of EWEs can be said to equate to a doubling of risk, but needs however to be adopted with caution, partly to prevent the conclusion that all of the events in a given period were 'caused' by climate change and partly because as emphasised in the recent Supreme Court decision in *Sienciewicz* v. *Grief*,[80] this approach may be more appropriate where there are alternative competing causes rather than concurrent causes with cumulative effect.[81] It is however significant that analyses have been undertaken which calculate the increase attributable to anthropogenic emissions in the risk of certain EWEs happening,[82] including heatwaves and flooding.[83]

[79] And this conclusion has been accepted by the courts of appeal in some cases involving contracting illness or disease, where if the risk of an event is more than doubled by factor X, that is tantamount to proving that on balance of probability factor X has caused the event: *Novartis Grimsby* v. *Cookson* [2007] EWCA 1261, at 74, *Ministry of Defence* v. *AB* [2010] EWCA 1317, at 153, *Sienciewicz* (see n. 80 below) at 72–93 although differing views on 'doubling the risk' were expressed by different judges.

[80] [2011] UKSC 10.

[81] At para. 93. Although unnecessary to the actual decision which turned on the scope of a special rule for mesotheliomia cases, there was a wide-ranging discussion in the case about the role and relevance of statistical evidence in proof of causation.

[82] For a description of the scientific approach including the concept of Fractional Attributable Risk, see Myles Allen *et al.*, 'Scientific Challenges in the Attribution of Harm to Human Influence on Climate', *University of Pennsylvania Law Review*, 155 (2007), 1353. As the authors observe, it is essential that the lawyers and scientists agree on what the right causation question is.

[83] See for studies of this nature in relation to the 2003 European heatwave and the 2000 UK floods, the work of Allen *et al.* in, respectively, *Nature*, 421 (2003) and 470 (2011). See also Chapter 2.

A different approach – 'material increase in risk'

17.59   A further possible line of argument by C is to move away from traditional notions of proof of causation and look at epidemiological and statistical evidence to assess D's contribution to the risk of an occurrence.

17.60   English law has given some recent support to this approach albeit to a limited extent, specifically in *Fairchild* v. *Glenhaven*[84] and subsequent cases applying and considering it.[85] These cases establish that in appropriate cases it may not be necessary to prove that on balance of probability event X caused event Y in the traditional sense but rather that X gave rise to a 'material increase in risk' of Y occurring. However as these cases make clear, the conditions for application of such a principle are currently very stringent, and arise largely out of issues peculiar to the disease of mesothelioma. *Fairchild* also addresses an issue different in kind from many climate change causation issues because (i) the actual cause of the claimant's illness was known to be one (or more) fibres from one of the defendants, the problem being from which one; and (ii) mesothelioma and other diseases are discrete medical conditions caught only once by the sufferer, unlike climate change which is itself (by definition) a change in an existing state of affairs leading to a series of different weather conditions.[86]

17.61   Whilst the *Fairchild* approach could, if some of the restrictions on its application are relaxed as the law develops,[87] apply in future in a climate change context, in relation to the basic issue of materiality of contributions of specific actors to climate change as a global phenomenon, it is not necessary to invoke it and neither does it provide a solution for C on this issue.

---

[84] [2003] 1 AC 32.

[85] See *Barker* v. *Corus* [2006] 2 AC 572, *Ministry of Defence* v. *AB* [2010] EWCA 1317, *Sanderson* v. *Hull* [2008] EWCA Civ 1211, at paras 40–53, and particularly, *Sienciewicz* (see n. 80 above) at 10, also a mesothelioma case.

[86] For a more detailed discussion of *Fairchild* in a climate change context, see Kaminskaité-Salters, n. 57 above, pp. 161–172. *Sienciewicz* suggests that the 'material increase in risk' doctrine is unlikely to be extended into the general law of causation.

[87] Whilst commentators have suggested that the *Fairchild* approach could be of less restricted application than *Fairchild* itself suggests (*Clerk & Lindsell*, see n. 62 above, § 2–53), in *Ministry of Defence* v. *AB* (see n. 85 above) the Court of Appeal took a conservative view as to the likelihood of its wider application as did the Supreme Court in *Sienciewicz*.

17.62   D's argument that something actionable if done by one person is
not actionable if done by many persons where each person undertakes a small part of the action in question may be unattractive,
and English law has recognised that at least in nuisance cases what
is relevant is the cumulative effect of actions by many people, and
it is no defence for any one of them to claim he/she contributed
only minimally to that overall effect.[88]

17.63   Is a tortfeasor liable for his/her 'share' of all damage or, as
logically might be the case on a traditional analysis, only a
share of damage caused by that temperature rise attributable
to non-anthropogenic or non-tortious conduct? The ortho-
dox English law approach is that where there are several
tortfeasors[89] liable for the same damage (as would be the case
unless the damage caused by different factors could be divided
up – see para. 17.55 above) each is liable for 100 per cent of the
damage subject to a right to recover a contribution from other
tortfeasors.[90]

17.64   In a climate change context the only practical approach would
appear to be based on liability only for a proportionate share
of the damage.[91] A powerful argument by defendants is that it
is impossible to make anyone liable at all when everyone is an
emitter. This can be expressed either by saying that any contribution by an individual defendant is not 'material' or invoking a
principle similar to the US concept of 'fair traceability' between
damage and conduct. However the distribution of emissions is
highly skewed. Although quantification of 'share' of emissions

---

[88] *Thorpe* v. *Brumfitt* (1871) LR 8 CH App 650, *Pride of Derby & Derbyshire Angling
Association* v. *British Celanese* [1952] 1 AER 1326.

[89] The word 'several' is used both to mean 'many' and to mean 'several as opposed to
joint'. Climate change litigation is not concerned with joint tortfeasors (those acting
together or in concert) except possibly in the conspiracy cases as discussed more fully
in Chapter 20.

[90] However in appropriate situations the court may apportion liability for apparently indivisible damage by reference (for example) to degree of exposure to asbestos (*Barker* v.
Corus [2006] 2 AC 572). The actual result for mesothelioma cases has been reversed by
statute by s. 3 of the Compensation Act 2006, but the underlying reasoning remains
valid.

[91] In *Fairchild* the House of Lords referred to the 'market share' approach as adopted in
Sindell v. *Abbott Laboratories* 26 Cal. 3d 588 (1980), one of the US 'DES' cases. In
Sienciewicz, at para. 17, the Supreme Court endorsed an 'apportionment' approach of
liability for a share of damage in appropriate cases.

depends on methodology,[92] it is not difficult to argue that a few hundred corporations are directly or indirectly 'responsible' for significant percentages of total anthropogenic emissions.[93]

17.65   A further issue arises in relation to the time lag between emission and effect. In approximate terms, CO_2 emitted is likely to 'remain' active for climate change purposes for many years, and the time lag between emission and effect may be similarly significant. There may also be a further time lag between the change in climate itself and the resulting damage. Thus damage in year 2010 may be 'caused' by conduct many years before,[94] and, for example, Allen has referred to a time lag of perhaps a quarter of a century, as well as emphasising the importance of the TCR (Transient Climate Response) and not the more widely quoted ECS (Equilibrium Climate Sensitivity).[95]

Issues of fault and foreseeability

Negligence and fault

17.66   Whereas some tortious liability is 'strict' in the sense that it depends only on proof of harm caused to X by Y, in others Y is only liable if he has been at fault in some sense. As the name of the tort suggests, liability in negligence requires C to show that any damage was caused by a lack of reasonable care on the part of D. In nuisance, the position is less clear cut, but the essence of the tort is unreasonable use of land. This requirement presents

---

[92] Whilst it is relatively straightforward in the case of direct emitters such as power companies burning fossil fuels, it is less so for 'producers' such as oil and gas production companies or 'facilitators' such as car manufacturers, who may contend that any responsibility is that of the purchasers of their products.

[93] Although it refers to environmental damage as a whole and not just climate change damage, the October 2010 Trucost report at www.trucost.com/news_more.asp?sectionID =5&pageID=34&newsID=100 is of interest in attributing about one-third of the US$ 6.6 trillion costs of human activity in 2008 to only about 3,000 corporations. Similar exercises undertaken in connection with the US cases (referred to above) and elsewhere conclude that a relatively small number of energy corporations are 'responsible' for significant percentages of total global emissions, although much depends on methodology and the definition of attribution.

[94] With the beginning of climate change for present purposes being traced to the beginning of the industrial age, and the cause being cumulative effect since that time. In *Kivalina* the allegation is that 35 per cent of the GHG increase since pre-industrial times has occurred since 1980.

[95] Allen (see n. 82 above).

serious obstacles in the way of private law claims at the present time, due to the likely strength of D's assertion that its activities were overall reasonable, essentially meeting a market demand, and/or that there was no real alternative. These defences may however become increasingly difficult if with the passage of time the adverse effects of GHGs become clearer and the choices of alternative low-carbon technologies more practical.

Allegations of deliberate wrongful conduct

17.67   Tortious liability depends primarily on whether what D did was unreasonable, and whether he knew it was so is irrelevant. However it may be much more difficult for D to say conduct was reasonable if he actually knew that it was damaging and/or that there were viable forms of alternative conduct.

17.68   It is also possible that C may focus on not only D's conduct in relation to emissions as such, but also in relation to allegations of the dissemination of (mis)information or lobbying activities. In two of the US cases,[96] conspiracy allegations have been raised to the effect that energy sector groups conspired to suppress the truth and/or discredit opponents for the purposes of preventing regulation of GHG emission. There is of course a distinction between vigorous expression of a genuinely held view and deliberate falsehood.

Foreseeability of damage

17.69   'Foreseeability' of damage is relevant in the tort of negligence at the stage of examining the existence or scope of D's duty of care, which arises only in relation to foreseeable (types of) damage. Foreseeability is closely linked with fault or negligence in the sense of lack of reasonable care, as the content of the duty to act reasonably is limited to where the consequences of one's actions can be foreseen to be harmful. Three aspects of this are that: (i) the test is objective with the question being what is reasonably foreseeable as opposed to actually foreseen by D; (ii) it is the type and not the extent of damage which needs to be foreseeable; and (iii) what needs to be foreseeable is a risk of damage not the certainty of it. It is now established

---

[96] *Kivalina* and *Comer*.

that foreseeability of harm is also a prerequisite of recovering damages in nuisance.[97]

17.70   In factual terms there may therefore be significant focus on when the risk of adverse effects of GHGs became sufficiently well known. The complaint in the US case of *Kivalina*[98] sets out a detailed chronology of events alleged to be relevant in terms of foreseeability, starting with calculations by Arrhenius in 1896.

17.71   There exists a tort of breach of statutory duty, but this is unlikely to be relevant in a climate change context. So for example the remedy of a person alleging breach of duties imposed by the CCA would be a public law remedy of judicial review and not a claim in tort for breach of statutory duty.[99]

Issues of statutory authority and non-justiciability

17.72   A major 'threshold' issue arises as to whether, even if the requirements of tortious conduct are otherwise made out, the courts will entertain private law actions. Two overlapping reasons which may be relied upon by D are those of 'non-justiciability' and 'statutory authority'. Whilst there is a danger in relying on US jurisprudence, it is instructive to consider the arguments and decisions in the US cases where defendants have argued both that private law claims are 'non-justiciable' as raising 'political questions' and that by 'pre-Emption' or 'displacement' their actions have been authorised by Federal Regulation such as the Clean Air Act.[100] Some courts have held that climate change related claims are non-justiciable because the regulation of GHG emission is within the exclusive province of the government and/or executive and is a matter of foreign and/or national policy.[101]

---

[97] *Cambridge Water Company* v. *Eastern Counties Leather plc* [1994] 2 AC 264.
[98] www.climatelaw.org/cases/country/us/kivalina/Kivalina%20Complaint.pdf/view, para. 135.
[99] *Clerk & Lindsell*, see n. 62 above, § 9–33.
[100] In *AEP* v. *Connecticut*, the US Supreme Court held that the *Clean Air Act* displaced any federal common law rights of action, reversing the Second Circuit's decision on this issue (10-174, 2011 WL 2437011 (US June 20, 2011)).
[101] *Kivalina*, but contrast *Massachusetts* v. *EPA*, *Comer* v. *Murphy* and *Connecticut* v. *AEP*.

17.73 While the UK has its own domestic law on 'non-justiciability', this is not likely to be applicable in the context of such claims.[102] However the issue of statutory authority may be more relevant, when there is a great deal of regulation of industry under environmental and pollution control legislation, which might be said to give statutory authority to emit GHG to the extent that this is not prohibited.[103] In addition it might be argued that the CCA and Kyoto Protocol have authorised any emissions which do not involve breach of their provisions.

17.74 It would appear that none of the current legislation gives sufficiently direct authorisation to emissions to prevent an otherwise valid common law claim.[104]

17.75 In *Budden* v. *BP Oil and Shell Oil* [1980] JPL 586, the claimant alleged damages in negligence and nuisance alleging damage to health as a result of excess levels of lead in petrol. One of the grounds that the claim failed was that the lead levels were within the statutorily permitted maximum. This case may however be distinguished for present purposes in that by the statute in question Parliament could be taken to have provided for determination (by the Secretary of State under the Regulations) of a reasonable level of lead in petrol. The case was not one of statutory authority as such but rather one where the fact that

---

[102] As explained in *Berezovsky* v. *Abramovich* [2011] EWCA Civ 153, § 100: 'This can arise in two separate circumstances. The first is in a *Buttes Gas & Oil v Hammer* [1982] AC 888 type case where the court has no measurable standard of adjudication or is in a judicial no-man's land. That was the position in that case where a decision would have required consideration of the territorial claims of four different states each with its own laws. The other case arises if there is reason to suppose (usually as a result of a communication from the Foreign Office) that an investigation into the acts of a foreign state would embarrass the government of our own country.'

[103] The grant of planning permission for an activity will not necessarily provide a defence to an action in nuisance (*Wheeler* v. *Saunders* [1995] Env. LR 286), although statutory authority to construct or operate a facility does authorise the activities which that necessarily or naturally entails (*Allen* v. *Gulf Refining* [1981] AC 1001); cf. *Tate & Lyle Industries* v. *GLC* [1983] 2 AC 509 where the House of Lords held that statutory authority will not provide a defence in respect of 'more harm than was necessary'.

[104] See *Marcic* v. *Thames Water Utilities* [2004] AC 42 and *Dobson* v. *Thames Water Utilities* [2009] EWCA 28. *Dobson* involved claims in negligence and nuisance as well as under Article 8(1) of the ECHR, alleging impact of odours and mosquitoes from the operation of D's sewage treatment works.

conduct was within legal limits, provided, on those facts, a defence to a claim in tort. Furthermore the environmental pollution/control legislation does not address CO_2, the main GHG, or the issues of climate change, so an argument that a corporation acting within the terms of its licence cannot be liable in tort faces difficulties.

17.76   Further reliance could be placed on the Kyoto Protocol by defendants in States which have ratified it, if sued in respect of their post-Kyoto actions. For example an English corporation could argue that emission of CO_2 within its allocation under the National Allocation Plan ('NAP') pursuant to the EU ETS Directive[105] cannot be actionable, as the purpose of the EU ETS Directive and the relevant NAP is to help EU Member States meet their Kyoto Protocol targets. However Kyoto does not purport to legislate for safe or even reasonable maxima of emissions, and the CCA only provides broad duties on the Government to achieve a long-term objective. Thus Kyoto arguably does not provide a defence of statutory authority.

Other factors

Limitation issues

17.77   An action in tort must, if governed by English law, normally be brought within six years of the accrual of the cause of action[106] which is when the relevant damage occurred, or, in the case of progressive damage, when some damage occurred. An alternative period, under the Latent Damage Act 1986, of three years from when (in simplified terms) the claimant was or should have been aware of the right to claim, might apply. Difficult questions of limitation might apply to actions alleging damage as a result of climate change, for example as to when sufficient damage, caused by the action complained of, had occurred to trigger accrual of

---

[105] Directive 2003/87/EC of the European Parliament and of the Council of 13 October 2003 establishing a scheme for GHG emission allowance trading within the Community and amending Council Directive 96/61/EC.

[106] Limitation Act 1980, s. 2. Where the relevant substantive law is foreign law, the foreign limitation period will generally apply under the Foreign Limitation Periods Act 1984.

the cause of action, or when the claimant was fixed with relevant knowledge for triggering an alternative three-year period.

Remedies

17.78   In private law claims there are two important categories of remedy which may, depending on the facts, be sought. The first is damages, assessed on a compensatory principle of putting the plaintiff, as nearly as possible, in the position he/she would have been in but for the damage caused by the tort, subject to complex rules limiting damages to what is not 'too remote'. The second, which may be applicable in nuisance cases, is the discretionary remedy of the injunction whereby the defendant may be required to abate the nuisance.[107]

(D)   Other law

Criminal law

17.79   In 2008, the 'Kingsnorth Six', who had successfully scaled a smokestack at Kingsnorth power station in Kent and painted the name of the Prime Minister on it to draw attention to its harmful effects on the environment, avoided criminal prosecution by establishing that the 'lawful excuse' defence of Criminal Damage Act 1971, s. 5 extended to protection of other property endangered by climate change.

17.80   The protesters' defence to the charges of criminal damage was that they believed they had a 'lawful excuse' as defined in s. 5 of the Criminal Damage Act. The defence is available where there is a belief in the immediate necessity of damage to protect other property. Crucially, the belief is subjective – that is, it is immaterial whether the belief is justified, so long as it is honestly held. They successfully argued an honest belief that by damaging the property at Kingsnorth they might protect far more property globally from climate change damage (resulting from Kingsnorth's CO_2 emissions). The expert evidence supplied by the defendants included that of several leading climate change

---

[107]   This is the remedy claimed in the US case of *Connecticut* v. *AEP* (see Chapter 20, para. 20.64ff).

scientists who confirmed that climate change was a direct result of human action.

17.81   While this may appear to be unequivocal judicial acceptance of the importance of action against climate change, it is worth positing this case against that of the 'Drax 29' (post-Kingsnorth Six). The twenty-nine protesters stopped and unloaded a coal train on its way to Drax power station and were prosecuted for obstructing a train contrary to s. 36 of the Malicious Damage Act 1861.[108] This Act does not contain the 'lawful excuse' defence and the defendants instead relied on the general common law defence of necessity to avoid imminent threat of death or serious injury.[109] One can easily see how this was applied in the context of climate change related deaths; however, the judge held that the former did not offer them a defence as a matter of law, and further refused to allow all their climate change experts' evidence saying it would allow the protesters 'to hijack the trial process as surely as they hijacked the coal train'.[110]

The influence of international law on climate change liabilities in the UK

17.82   The UK is a Party to the two principal international treaties aimed at tackling the problems associated with climate change, the FCCC and the Kyoto Protocol.[111]

17.83   Against this background, one might expect international law to have exerted a strong influence on climate change liabilities within the UK. Yet, while the increased statutory regulation of this area has led to a greater willingness on parties to litigation in the UK to base submissions on domestic climate change

---

[108] *R* v. *Bard and Ors* ('*The Drax 29*') [2009] – Leeds Crown Court.

[109] *R* v. *Martin* [1989] 1 All ER 652.

[110] An interesting postscript is the collapse in January 2011 of the prosecution of six protesters against a similar power station, on the basis that one of them was an undercover police officer, whose conduct may have encouraged or provoked any criminal activity.

[111] The UK signed the FCCC on 12 June 1992, ratified the Convention on 8 December 1993, and the Convention entered into force on 21 March 1994. The UK signed the Kyoto Protocol on 29 April 1998, ratified the Protocol on 31 May 2002, and the Convention entered into force on 16 February 2005 (see the FCCC website, available at http://maindb.unfccc.int/public/country.pl?country=GB).

policy documents and regulations,[112] international law has scarcely been referred to directly by courts in the UK.[113]

17.84 Therefore, whilst several principles of international environmental law, such as the precautionary principle and the principle of sustainable development, have been given effect in the UK through several Government policy strategy documents,[114] when interpreting these principles UK courts have tended to limit themselves to domestic sources.

Standing before UK courts

17.85 In some cases, non-governmental organisations have relied on their observer status at meetings of the Parties to international environmental treaties in order to demonstrate a 'sufficient interest' to bring a case.[115] For example in *R* v. *Inspectorate of Pollution ex p. Greenpeace Ltd (No. 2)*,[116] which concerned an application for judicial review by Greenpeace challenging a variation of an existing authorisation granted by the Government to British Nuclear Fuels plc in respect of a new thermal oxide nuclear reprocessing plant, Otton J held that in order to determine whether Greenpeace had standing it was appropriate to take into

---

[112] See, for example, *R (on the application of People and Planet)* v. *HM Treasury* (2010) Official Transcript, at para. 11, where Justice Sales dismissed the submission that s. 1 of the Climate Change Act created a legitimate expectation; and *R (on the application of Hillingdon LBC)* v. *Secretary of State for Transport* (2010) Official Transcript, where Carnwath LJ held that the Secretary of State for Transport's policy support for a third runway and new passenger facilities at Heathrow Airport was not immutable and was subject to review in light of developments in climate change policy, symbolised by the Climate Change Act 2008.

[113] The only instance in which an international climate change treaty has been directly referenced is in the case of *J & A Young (Leicester) Ltd* v. *The Commissioners for Her Majesty's Revenue & Customs* (2008) Official Transcript, at para. 16, where the Kyoto Protocol was cited to explain the purpose of the Climate Change Levy (CCL): 'The objective of the CCL is to encourage energy efficiency. It is also intended to stimulate investment in energy saving equipment. The aim of the legislation is to address issues of climate change, GHG emission and pollution standards set by the Kyoto protocol.'

[114] See, for example, Department for Environment, Food and Rural Affairs ('DEFRA'), *DEFRA's Climate Change Plan*, 2010; *Climate Change: Taking Action Parts 1 and 2*, 2010; *Adapting to Climate Change: A New Approach*, 2010; and *The UK Government Sustainable Development Strategy*. See also R. Khalastchi, 'International Environmental Law in the Courts of the United Kingdom' in Anderson and Galizzi (eds.), *International Environmental Law in National Courts* (BIICL, 2003), at p. 226.

[115] On this point, see Khalastchi, *ibid.*, at pp. 225–6.

[116] *R* v. *Inspectorate of Pollution ex p. Greenpeace Ltd (No. 2)* [1994] 4 All ER 329.

account, inter alia, 'the nature of the applicant and the extent of the applicant's interest in the issues raised'.[117] In confirming that Greenpeace had sufficient interest to bring the case, Otton J in particular noted that:[118]

> Greenpeace International has […] been accredited with consultative status with the United Nations Economic and Social Council (including United Nations General Assembly). It has accreditation status with the UN Conference on Environment and Development. They have observer status or right to attend meetings of 17 named bodies including Parcom (Paris Convention for the Prevention of Marine Pollution from Land Based Sources).

17.86   In light of this and other similar cases,[119] it is conceivable that a non-governmental organisation could rely on its consultative or observer status to an international climate change treaty for the purpose of demonstrating a sufficient interest to bring an application for judicial review.

Public trust – might the doctrine be applied in the UK?

17.87   The unique nature of the problem of climate change has led to innovative thinking in relation to extending the trust concept from private property to public goods such as the environment itself or specific parts of it. The essential theory, as discussed in US jurisprudence, is that sovereign States and/or public bodies are trustees of public goods for the benefit of the beneficiaries (the public at large) who may be able to compel the trustees to ensure proper care is taken of the trust property.[120] Whilst the English law of trusts is well developed, and there are statements in early cases which might support a general principle of public trust in appropriate circumstances,[121] it is difficult to

---

[117] *Ibid.*, at para. 78.   [118] *Ibid.*, at para. 80.

[119] See, for example, *R* v. *Poole Borough Council, ex p. Beebee et al.* (Queens Bench Division, 21 December 1990), *Journal of Environmental Law*, 3 (1991), 293; and *R* v. *Secretary of State for Foreign & Commonwealth Affairs, ex p. The World Development Movement* [1995] 1 WLR 386.

[120] The foremost exponent of this doctrine in the US is Prof. Mary Wood, and references to many of her works on the subject can be found at www.law.uoregon.edu/faculty/mwood/publications.php.

[121] The case of *Robert Arnold* v. *Benajah Mundy*, Supreme Court of New Jersey, 6 N.J.L. 1, 1821, N.J. is an 1821 decision of the New Jersey Supreme Court, which cites extensively early English authority in support of the doctrine of public trust as a common law doctrine.

see this doctrine being of any practical significance in English law, especially where the statutory provisions of the CCA are in place.

Competition/anti-trust law

17.88   The EU State aid regime is the main area of competition law which has influenced climate change policy arrangements, and in turn climate change litigation developments, in the UK context. In the UK, State aid considerations figure prominently in (i) the UK Emission Trading Scheme, (ii) the Carbon Reduction Commitment Energy Efficient Scheme ('CRC'), (iii) Renewables Obligations Certificates ('ROCs') and (iv) Feed-In Tariffs.

17.89   Affected parties who believe that any of these four policy arrangements distort competition and want to challenge certain allocation rules in light of Article 107 are entitled to lodge a claim with the European Commission[122] or ask a national court to block aid. However, Commission decisions in relation to these policy arrangements and case law appear to suggest that the Commission takes a prima facie view that the allocation modes are compatible with the common market in light of the *Guidelines on State Aid for Environmental Protection*.[123] The Commission held the UK Emission Trading Scheme to be State aid but compatible with Article 107(3)(c) (Decision N416/2001). The Commission also found that the ROCs are State aid but compatible with Article 107(3) in light of the Environmental Guidelines at points 61 and 62 concerning green certificates systems in its Decision N504/2000, and further changes to the scheme in 2008 fall within the scope of the Guidelines at point 110 (Decision 414/2008). Concerning the UK FITs scheme, the Commission held this to be compatible with Article 107(3) in light of points 107 to 109 and 119 of the Environmental Guidelines.

---

[122]   The Department for Business, Innovation & Skills ('BIS') State Aid Branch has responsibility for State aid policy in the UK and provides further guidance to UK companies for lodging a complaint.

[123]   This has been suggested by commentators in relation to the case *EnBW Energie Baden-Württemberg AG*. See, for example, J. De Sepibus, *The European Emission Trading Scheme put to the Test of State Aid Rules* (Working Paper No. 2007–34, NCCR Trade Regulation, 2007).

17.90   As a result, the main competition law challenge to UK climate
         change policy has been by the Commission itself and not indi-
         vidual companies using legal action in national courts or the
         European Court of Justice ('ECJ'). These challenges have been
         structured as legal arguments that do not directly refer to consid-
         erations of anti-competitive practices, and are more procedural
         than substantive in question. For example, in Case T-178/05 the
         Commission attempted to argue that the UK's amendments to
         its national allocation plan ('NAP') under Article 9 of Directive
         2003/87, increasing the total number of allowances, are inad-
         missible. However, the ECJ found that the Commission made an
         error of law, as this rejection was not based on either the NAP's
         incompatibility with the criteria of Annex III or with Article 10
         of the Directive, which directly refer to the EU State aid rules.[124]

17.91   As a result, competition litigation is unlikely to either further or
         impede climate change policy in the UK context.

World heritage

17.92   There are twenty-eight UNESCO World Heritage Sites in the UK,
         subjecting the State to obligations to protect them under Articles
         4, 5 and 6 of the 1972 World Heritage Convention which engage
         climate change mitigation, including in relation to the Devon
         and Dorset coasts.

Liability in public international law

17.93   The potential liability of the UK as a State under public
         international law is beyond the scope of this book, and is thus
         mentioned here only very briefly for the sake of complete-
         ness. As an Annex I Party to the FCCC, the UK is subject not
         only to the vague commitments set out in Article 4(1), such as
         the obligation to promote and cooperate in the development,
         application and diffusion of technologies that control, reduce
         or prevent anthropogenic emissions,[125] but also to the slightly

---

[124] See also *Drax Power and Ors* v. *Commission of the European Communities*, where the
      applicant contended that the Commission wrongly rejected the United Kingdom
      National Allocation Plan ('NAP') for a second time following its decision in Case
      T-178/05.
[125] Article 4(1)(c), FCCC.

more stringent commitments set out in Article 4(2), such as the commitment to 'take corresponding measures on the mitigation of climate change, by limiting its anthropogenic emissions of GHGs and protecting and enhancing its GHG sinks and reservoirs'.[126]

17.94   As a Party to the Kyoto Protocol, the UK is also subject to the very specific quantified emission limitation or reduction commitments specified as a percentage of the base year or period in Annex B to the Protocol (for the UK, this is 92 per cent).[127]

17.95   A breach by the UK of its specific commitments could potentially give rise to State responsibility. Under the compliance mechanism of the Kyoto Protocol,[128] Annex I Parties can be held accountable for failures to meet emission reduction and related inventory and reporting commitments. Issues as to the compliance of Parties with the Kyoto Protocol are decided by the Compliance Committee, which consists of a facilitative branch and an enforcement branch. Whereas the facilitative branch assists Parties to the Kyoto Protocol in their compliance with advice in relation to the same, the enforcement branch determines consequences for any Protocol Party that does not meet its commitments.

17.96   In theory, a violation of binding commitments in the Protocol would entitle another Protocol Party to invoke the UK's responsibility and could bring a relevant case before the International Court of Justice. However, in practice, this is highly unlikely given the international political ramifications such an action would have.

17.97   The situation is different in relation to the FCCC, as the language of the commitments in this treaty renders them difficult to enforce. It appears that the effect of Article 14(1) of the FCCC may be limited as it does not provide for enforceable primary legal norms of international law, but only a general framework without the required specificity.

---

[126] Article 4(2)(a), FCCC.   [127] Annex B, Kyoto Protocol.

[128] A detailed description of the compliance mechanism under the Kyoto Protocol is outside the scope of this chapter. For an introduction to the topic by the FCCC, see 'An Introduction to the Kyoto Protocol Compliance Mechanism', available at http://unfccc.int/kyoto_protocol/compliance/items/3024.php, last accessed on 31 March 2011.

17.98   Consideration has also been given to the viability of actions
         between States based on the public international law principle
         of 'no harm', as a State must take measures to ensure that activ-
         ities undertaken within its territory and its jurisdiction do not
         cause adverse effects on human health and the environment in
         other States or areas beyond national jurisdiction, even when
         there is no conclusive evidence demonstrating the link between
         the activity and the effects ('precautionary principle'). However, a
         lack of available forum makes this problematic.[129]

(E)   'Soft' law

17.99   The UK is a member of the OECD and it is thus possible to bring
         a complaint before the national contact point[130] for failure of a
         multinational enterprise to comply with the OECD Guidelines
         containing recommendations for 'responsible business conduct
         consistent with applicable law'. Detailed provisions are made for
         matters such as disclosure of information and implementation of
         environmental management plans. Such complaints have been
         brought in Germany, for example against Volkswagen, the car
         manufacturer.[131] As indicated in the section on public law (see
         17.13 ff above), review of decisions of public bodies may be under-
         taken on the basis that a whole host of activities may adversely
         affect climate change or conversely on the basis that activities
         likely to cause climate change may accordingly infringe regula-
         tions for the protection of the environment generally. It is beyond
         the scope of this book to assess 'liability' in every environmen-
         tal, planning or other context which may invoke or affect climate
         change. It is clear however that because of the potential scope
         of harm from climate change, in terms of longevity, magnitude
         and variety of types of harm, there is a correspondingly long list
         of types of 'liability', both in 'hard' and 'soft' law where climate
         change is a relevant factor.

17.100   One area of law which may become increasingly relevant is in
         relation to the obligations of investors or other stakeholders

---

[129] See FIELD, *International Climate Change Litigation and the Negotiating Process*
     (Working Paper, 4 October 2010).
[130] In the case of the UK, the Department for Business, Innovation & Skills.
[131] www.germanwatch.org/corp/vw-besch-e.pdf; these are discussed in Chapter 15.

in corporations as to Socially Responsible Investment ('SRI'). Attempts to regulate activity may be made, either by reference to alleged fiduciary duties of trustees or shareholders to consider objectives wider than pure financial profit, or by reference to directors' duties under section 172(1)(d) of the Companies Act 2006. A study of this issue is beyond the scope of this chapter. In very brief summary, legal liability is unlikely to be engaged merely by corporations or their stakeholders taking a narrow view of legitimate interest in financial terms only,[132] although commercial pressure from SRI investors, lenders, insurers or international financial institutions may be very significant.

(F) Practicalities

Founding jurisdiction for a claim

17.101   The procedural rules governing the exercise of jurisdiction by an English court over a non-English domiciled defendant are complex, and there exist two parallel and potentially conflicting regimes. Where D is domiciled in the EU, the rules are governed by EU Regulation 44/2001. For present purposes the key provisions are Article 5(3) which provides for the defendant to be sued in tort in the State where 'the harmful event occurred' (a very difficult concept for climate change) and Article 6.

17.102   For D who is not EU domiciled the position is governed by the common law and the Civil Procedure Rules. 6BPD (Practice Direction 6B) 3.1(9) provides for service out of the jurisdiction on D sued in tort where the damage was sustained within the jurisdiction, or resulting from an act committed within the jurisdiction.

17.103   It is not necessarily the case that an English court will apply substantive English law in a tort claim with an international element. The relevant law will be determined by Regulation (EC) 864/2007, known as 'Rome II'. The general rule under Article 4 of Rome II is that the applicable law is that of the country in which the damage occurs, although under Article 7 for 'environmental damage or damage sustained by persons or property as a

---

[132] See for example *Cowan* v. *Scargill* [1985] 1 Ch 270.

result of such damage', C has an option to choose the law of the country in which 'the event giving rise to the damage occurred'. The Rome II regime is of potentially great significance in climate change litigation, where nationals in developing countries may allege damage suffered in those countries as a result of actions by corporations domiciled in the EU. Such corporations may be sued in their State of domicile, with the claimant able to rely on the law of his/her own State.

17.104   The most important 'ancillary' powers which the courts have are a 'freezing' order, where the defendant may be prohibited from using or dissipating funds or other assets, and a 'search' order where C's lawyers may be empowered to search the defendant's premises for documentary or other evidence where there is reason to suppose it may be destroyed without such an order.

Enforcement

17.105   Numerous enforcement mechanisms exist such as by seizure of a defendant's assets or winding up a corporation. Foreign arbitration awards can be enforced under the New York Convention,[133] or by an action on the award. Foreign judgments may be enforced (i) in the case of those from EU courts (generally) under Regulation 44/2001, and (ii) in other cases by an action on the judgment or under statutes specifically providing for enforcement.[134]

17.106   Public interest litigation is common in England. Typically this is either by determined individuals, as in the case of the celebrated 'McDonalds libel' case of *McDonalds* v. *Steel*,[135] or NGOs, environmental NGOs such as Greenpeace and Friends of the Earth (often aided by one of the numerous groups or firms of public interest lawyers), or even large/City firms acting on a pro bono basis.

---

[133] The Convention on the Recognition and Enforcement of Foreign Arbitral Awards (the 'New York Convention') of 10 June 1958, text available at www.uncitral.org/uncitral/en/uncitral_texts/arbitration/NYConvention.html, last accessed on 31 March 2011.

[134] Specifically the Administration of Justice Act 1920 and the Foreign Judgments (Reciprocal Enforcement) Act 1933.

[135] [1997] EWHC QB 366.

Litigation costs

17.107 In general in civil litigation in England, each party funds its own costs as matters progress.[136] At the conclusion of the litigation and/or at certain intermediate stages, the court may order a party who has been unsuccessful to pay at least the majority of the costs of the party who is successful in a claim or on a specific part of the proceedings. Thus the basic rule is that the loser pays and the winner recovers.

17.108 A party may in certain limited circumstances (which may include 'public interest' litigation) apply for a Protective Costs Order limiting his/her future liability for costs.

17.109 Cases can be funded by Conditional Fee Agreements ('CFAs') which in loose terms are 'no win no fee'. These are often accompanied by insurance to cover any of D's costs which C may be ordered to pay.

17.110 Class actions are not recognised as such but in practice can be run either under Group Litigation Orders ('GLOs'), under CPR Part 19 or under appropriate directions in an ordinary multi-party action.

Obtaining information

17.111 'Knowledge is power' it is said, and this is likely to apply in the climate change field, especially when one of the complaints often made is of the 'information asymmetry' in favour of industry and governments.[137]

17.112 The regulations and practices concerning (i) retention of documents and records by corporations, and (ii) accessing or disclosing the information contained in them are complex and a detailed discussion of them is beyond the scope of this book. This section governs how the law may aid ordinary research processes in obtaining information.

---

[136] State funding by way of 'legal aid' is in some circumstances available to pursue or oppose civil claims, but is unlikely to be relevant in most climate change related cases.

[137] See generally Philip Coppel, *Information Rights: Law and Practice*, 3rd edn (Hart Publishing, 2010).

Disclosure (formerly 'discovery') in civil litigation

17.113   The Civil Procedure Rules govern disclosure of documents and information in the context of actual civil proceedings. CPR Part 31 requires a party to litigation to disclose certain documents in his/her control [31.8] including those which adversely affect his/her case [31.5]. In some instances persons who are not parties to the action may be required to disclose relevant documents, and in limited circumstances pre-action disclosure may be ordered [31.16]. 'Document' is widely defined to include electronic records [CPR 31.4]. This process is only of any use in the context of existing (or sometimes contemplated) litigation.

The Freedom of Information Act 2000

17.114   This Act gives wide-ranging rights to the general public to obtain information in the possession of the Government on a broad spectrum of matters. In environmental matters the Environmental Information Regulations (see below) may be more relevant.

Other statutory/regulatory sources of information

Environmental Information Regulations 2004 (SI 2004/3391)

17.115   These give the general public the right to request environmental information from public bodies including central and local government and utility companies. Their scope, in terms of the definition of environmental information (Regulation 2), retrospective application and breadth of right to disclosure of information held, make them significant, and the list of exceptions to the obligation to disclose information is narrower than under the Freedom of Information Act. A detailed analysis of the Regulations is beyond the scope of this chapter.[138]

Companies Act 2006/Climate Change Act 2008

17.116   Section 85 of the CCA requires the Secretary of State to make, by 6 April 2012, regulations under s. 416 of the Companies Act 2006, requiring the directors' report of a company to contain information 'about emissions of GHGs from activities for which the company is responsible'.[139]

---

[138] See *Coppel, ibid.*, Ch. 6.

[139] Although of no direct relevance to English law, the US SEC guidance given in February 2010 to companies on disclosure of climate change related information in mandatory reports has been seen as highly significant.

The right to information as a human right

17.117 Attempts to use human rights instruments, whether Article 10 of the ECHR or Article 19 of the ICESCR, have generally been unsuccessful although recent ECHR cases have begun to show recognition of a right under Article 10 to access to information which, in the public interest, should be disseminated.[140] It can be argued of course that information concerning climate change is a paradigm issue of public interest.

Document retention requirements

17.118 Corporations and public bodies are under obligations of various kinds to retain documentation and records. A detailed analysis of these requirements is beyond the scope of this chapter.

Disclosure obligation

17.119 Right to Information is closely allied to obligations to disclose. Apart from the specific instances referred to above, there is increasing pressure from multiple sources on corporations and public bodies to disclose climate change related information, either publicly or to specific recipients. These include 'hard-edged' legal requirements from regulators, as well as pressure from shareholders, investors,[141] insurers, lenders and environment groups. The availability of such information is likely to lead to an increase in the attempts to use it for purposes of imposing liability (in the broadest sense) of public and private actors for climate change.

(G)   Conclusion

17.120 As with other actions or claims under English law, each climate change related action will necessarily turn on its own facts. This chapter shows that, whilst climate change has been used both as a ground for action and a defence in lawsuits and prosecutions brought in the UK, no specific regime for climate change liability

---

[140] *Matky* v. *Czech Republic* App no. 19101/03 ECHR, 10 July 2006; *Tarsasaga* v. *Hungary* App no. 37374/05 ECHR, 14 April 2009.

[141] Whether individual investors or one of the numerous groups of investors (well-known examples being those associated with the Carbon Disclosure Project and the IIGCC group) interested in climate change issues.

has developed as yet and the jurisprudence in this area is still in an early phase. However there is significant potential for the law to develop, not by quantum leaps of jurisprudence but rather by building on existing principles. This could result in the increasing imposition of liability, in respect of climate change and its consequences, in the public law, private law and human rights fields in the medium-term future.

Russia

FIONA MUCKLOW CHEREMETEFF, MAX GUTBROD,
DARIA RATSIBORINSKAYA AND SERGEI SITNIKOV

(A) Introduction

The Russian legal system

18.1   The legal system of the Russian Federation ('Russia' or 'RF')
is based on civil law principles. Its heritage lies in Soviet law
(1917–91), Russian Imperial legislation (1649–1917) and dozens of
other legal systems operating simultaneously (including the customary law of various tribes and peoples, Islamic law, Baltic law,
canon law and Judaic law), and its development has been influenced by foreign laws (such as Byzantine, Roman, Tartar, Polish,
Swedish, German, French, Italian, Dutch and Lithuanian law).[1]
The Civil Code 1994 (the 'Civil Code'),[2] which is broadly similar
to the German Civil Code, is a central piece of legislation. There
is also a substantial amount of special legislation. Whilst there is
no system of binding precedent, the higher courts have the power
to issue general guidelines, and, in practice, the decisions[3] of the
higher courts are frequently followed.

The authors would like to thank Alexey Kokorin (Head of Climate Change Programme,
WWF Russia, Moscow) for his invaluable advice and comments; also Anna Gryaznova for
her support. Statements made in this chapter by the authors do not constitute or purport to
constitute legal advice.

[1] W. E. Butler, *Russian Law*, 2nd edn (Oxford University Press, 2003) ('Butler'), Ch. 15, § 3;
see also W. Partlett, 'Reclassifying Russian Law: Mechanisms, Outcomes, and Solutions
for an Overly Politicized Field', *Columbia Journal of Eastern European Law*, 2 (2008), 1
(available at http://ssrn.com/abstract=1197762); and D. J. B. Shaw, *Russia in the Modern
World: A New Geography* (Oxford: Blackwell, 1999).

[2] Part I of the Civil Code of the RF № 51-FZ, 30 November 1994; Part II of the Civil Code
of the RF № 14-FZ, 26 January 1996; Part III of the Civil Code of the RF № 146-FZ,
26 November 2001; and Part IV of the Civil Code of the RF № 230-FZ, 18 December 2006.

[3] See www.garant.ru or information bulletins of the Supreme Arbitrary Court and
Supreme Court of Russian Federation.

18.2   The supreme source of Russian law is the 1993 Constitution of the Russian Federation (the 'Constitution').[4] The courts are guided by the Constitution and, in the event of inconsistency, constitutional provisions prevail over federal, regional and local laws.

18.3   The predominant sources of law are federal statutes, enacted by way of legislative process. Frequently such statutes are enacted as a code for given areas (for example, in forestry law, the Forest Code 2006),[5] whilst supplemental legislative acts further develop certain provisions of a code.

18.4   Russian law also includes the following sub-laws:
- *Presidential decrees* – the President has the power to enact normative and non-normative decrees, which must comply with constitutional provisions and federal laws.
- *Governmental directives* – the Government may issue directives, which have normative character.
- *Agency regulations* – agencies are permitted to enact regulations, provided these do not contradict the Constitution or any relevant codes.

18.5   Each of the eighty-three subjects (or 'Regions')[6] of the Russian Federation has its own constitution or charter, as well as legislation. According to the Constitution (Article 76) 'the laws and other legislative acts of the subjects of the Russian Federation may not contradict federal laws'. Thus, federal laws are 'superior' to regional laws.[7]

---

[4] Adopted by national vote on 12 December 1993, as amended by the Amendments to the Constitution of the Russian Federation on 30 December 2008 (№ 6-FKZ) and 30 December 2008 (№ 7-FKZ).

[5] Federal Law № 200-FZ 'The Forest Code of the Russian Federation', 4 December 2006, as amended on 22 June 2010.

[6] I.e. twenty-one Republics, forty-six Oblasts (provinces), nine Krais (territories), one Autonomous Oblast (the Jewish Autonomous Oblast), four Autonomous Okrugs (districts) and two federal cities (Moscow and St Petersburg).

[7] See further S. Nystén-Haarala, 'Mechanics to Promote Green Business in Russia', in W. Th. Douma and F. M. Mucklow (eds.), *Environmental Finance and Socially Responsible Business in Russia: Legal and Practical Trends* (The Hague: Asser Press, 2010) ('Mucklow'), p. 106; V. Leksin, 'The New Russian Federalism' in P. H. Solomon Jr (ed.), *The Dynamics of 'Real Federalism': Law, Economic Development, and Indigenous Communities in Russia and Canada* (Centre for Russian and East European Studies, University of Toronto, 2004) ('*Real Federalism*'); V. Kriukov, V. Seliverstov and A. Tokarev, 'Federalism and Regional Policy in Russia: Problems of Socio-Economic Development of Resource Territories

Governmental stance on climate change

18.6   Russia is the largest country in the world in terms of territory and
the world's third largest emitter of greenhouse gases ('GHGs')
after China and the USA, accounting for about 17.4 per cent of
global GHG emissions.[8] It has a population of approximately 142
million[9] living within a vast territory of about 17 million square
kilometres, stretching over 11 time zones. With respect to human
development, social disparities between the Regions and within
cities are pronounced. Furthermore, Russia is ranked at 146th
place (out of 180 countries) in the *Transparency 2009 Corruption
Perceptions Index*.[10]

Environmental awareness and education

18.7   Partly due to the low level of environmental awareness and
education,[11] the misconception that global warming and climate change are substantially to the benefit of Russia is common
among the Russian general public. The upsides most commonly
cited include a milder climate, the considerable decrease in
expenditure on heating, increases in crop yields and the development of the Northern Sea Route.[12] However, the Government and

and Subsoil Use' in *Real Federalism*; and M. M. Brinchuk, *Ekologicheskoe pravo*
(Uchebnik, Moskva: Vyshee obrasovanie, 2005).

[8] See F. Mucklow and W. Th. Douma, 'Environmental Finance and Socially Responsible
Business in Russia – An Introduction', above n. 7, Mucklow, p. 1; and R. Perelet,
S. Pegov and M. Yulkin, Climate Change: Russia Country Paper, *Human Development
Report 2007/2008*, 'Fighting Climate Change: Human Solidarity in a Divided World',
Human Development Report Office, Occasional Paper (Moscow: UNDP, December
2007), p. 2.

[9] However, Russia's demographic profile is considered unfavourable for the long-term economic outlook, with a falling and ageing population, low life expectancy and a declining
working-age population – L. Kekic, *Country Forecast: Russia* (Economist Intelligence
Unit, July 2010) ('EIU Russia Forecast 2010').

[10] 'EIU Russia Forecast 2010'; Transparency International, *Annual Report 2010*
(Transparency International, July 2010), p. 49.

[11] T. Guseva, 'Environmental Education and Capacity Building in Russia', above n.7,
Mucklow, p. 133.

[12] W. Douma, M. Kozeltsev and J. Dobrolyubova, 'Russia and the international climate
change regime' in S. Oberthür and M. Pallemaerts (eds.) with C. Roche Kelly, *The New
Climate Policies of the European Union: Internal Legislation and Climate Diplomacy*
(Brussels: VUB Press, 2010); and J. P. Milhone, *Russia's Fires Breathe New Life into
Climate Picture* (Carnegie Endowment for International Peace, Commentary, 16 August
2010).

NGOs[13] are trying to increase environmental awareness, including awareness of the negative effects of climate change.[14]

Governmental climate change agencies

18.8   Enforcement with respect to environmental matters falls within the jurisdiction of the Ministry of Natural Resources and Ecology ('MNR'), which is the main governmental authority responsible for environmental protection and natural resources.[15] Climate monitoring is conducted by the Global Climate and Ecology Institute of the Federal Service for Hydrometeorology and Environmental Monitoring ('Roshydromet') and the Russian Academy of Sciences ('RAS').

18.9   In 2008, Roshydromet, the governmental agency primarily in charge of climate-related matters, published a two-volume report[16] on the effects of climate change on Russia. The report confirms that warming observed on the Russian territory is above the world average, and that significant effects on socioeconomic activity can be expected. This is significant, as sceptical views on the anthropological contribution to, as well as the seriousness of, global warming have been expressed by some key Russian climatologists.

FCCC and Kyoto Protocol

18.10   Russia signed and ratified both the FCCC (on 28 December 1994) and the Kyoto Protocol (on 18 November 2004),[17] and participated in the negotiations for a new global agreement on

---

[13]   E.g. A. O. Kokorin and E. V. Smirnova, *Izmenyeniye Klimata: Posobiye dlya pedagogov starshih klassov* (Moscow: WWF Russia, 2010).

[14]   See J. D. Oldfield, A. Kouzmina and D. J. B. Shaw, 'Russia's Involvement in the International Environmental Process: A Research Report', *Eurasian Geography and Economics*, 44(2) (2003), 157–68; and W. Douma and D. Ratsiborinskaya, 'The Russian Federation and the Kyoto Protocol' in W. Douma, L. Massai and M. Montini (eds.), *The Kyoto Protocol and Beyond: Legal and Policy Challenges of Climate Change* (The Hague: Asser Press, 2007), pp. 135–45.

[15]   Municipal and local governmental responsibilities and authorities are not discussed in this chapter; see D. N. Ratsiborinskaya, 'Russian Environmental Law – An Overview for Businesses', above n. 7, Mucklow, pp. 49–50 ('Ratsiborinskaya'), regarding responsibilities and functions of the MNR.

[16]   http://climate2008.igce.ru/v2008/htm/index00.htm.

[17]   L. A. Henry and L. McIntosh Sundstrom, 'Russia and the Kyoto Protocol: Seeking an Alignment of Interests and Image', *Global Environmental Politics*, 7(4) (2007); 'Russia and the Kyoto Protocol: From Hot Air to Implementation?' in K. Harrison and L. McIntosh

climate change in Copenhagen (December 2009) and in Cancun (December 2010). Russia is an 'Annex Me' country, classified as a country undergoing the process of transition to a market economy.

18.11   In accordance with Annex B of the Kyoto Protocol, Russia must stay below 1990 GHG emission levels to comply with its Kyoto commitments.

18.12   Although the expectation was that energy consumption and emissions would continue to rise in Russia after 1990, the change in regime and subsequent economic decline resulted in a dramatic drop in GHG emissions. The income that Russia is expected to obtain from selling surplus quotas through the Kyoto Protocol's emissions trading mechanisms is seen from the Russian perspective as akin to compensation for the hardships that Russia has endured during the transition phases.[18] However, the implementation of the Kyoto mechanisms under Russian law has been slow, particularly with regard to establishing domestic rules on joint implementation ('JI').

Post 2012

18.13   Following the Copenhagen negotiations, Russia submitted its quantified emissions reduction target for 2020 of 15 to 25 per cent (with 1990 as the base year)[19] and stated that the range of its future GHG emission reductions will depend on the following conditions:

- appropriate accounting of the potential of Russia's forestry in contributing to meeting its anthropogenic emissions reductions obligations; and
- entry into undertakings on the part of all major emitters, of legally binding obligations to reduce anthropogenic GHG emissions.[20]

Sundstrom (eds.), *Global Commons, Domestic Decisions: The Comparative Politics of Climate Change* (Cambridge, MA: MIT Press, 2010); S. Agibalov and A. Kokorin, 'Copenhagen Agreement – A New Paradigm for the Climate Challenge Solution', *Vaprosi Ekonomiki*, RAN, 9 (2010).

[18] A. Moe and K. Tangen, *The Kyoto Mechanisms and Russian Climate Politics* (London: The Royal Institute of International Affairs, Energy and Climate Programme, 2000), p. 2.

[19] http://unfccc.int/files/meetings/application/pdf/russiacphaccord_app1engl.pdf.

[20] See also M. Gutbrod, S. Sitnikov and E. Pike-Biegunska, *Trading in Air: Mitigating Climate Change through the Carbon Markets* (Moscow: Infotropic, 2010) ('Gutbrod/ Sitnikov/Pike-Biegunska'), Ch. 4.

18.14   Accordingly, at COP16 and CMP6 in Cancun, the Russian negotiating team focused, amongst other points, on (i) pushing for
a new legally binding international agreement (and not for the
extension of the Kyoto Protocol); (ii) keeping Russia's status as
an economy in transition and obtaining more access to technology (and capacity building and training) for Annex I countries; and (iii) forestry/land-use, land-use change and forestry
('LULUCF').[21]

Climate change laws and policy

18.15   Russian law does not directly or specifically address climate
change liability. Nor is there any specific code or legislation
addressing climate change mitigation as such. Laws that might
be applied in climate change liability proceedings can be divided
into two categories for the purposes of this chapter:
(1) general environmental and human rights laws; and
(2) specific laws relating to the implementation of the FCCC and
the Kyoto Protocol ('Kyoto legislation').

18.16   There is no real overlap between these two categories of law. For
example, the Law on Air Protection 1999 ('LAP')[22] has not been
updated to regulate GHG emissions, nor has it been linked to
Russia's international obligation to mitigate climate change.

18.17   The discussion below offers a brief overview of the principal
environmental and human rights laws that might be applied in
climate change litigation proceedings, as well as the Kyoto legislation. However, in order to understand these laws, the role of
Soviet law will briefly be addressed.

Role of Soviet law

18.18   Under Soviet law, environmental law was administrative in
nature and the State owned almost everything (including all natural resources and means of production).[23] The law only regulated how this property was to be used and protected. The biggest

---

[21] Personal communication from Alexey Kokorin, WWF Russia, Moscow, 23 November
2010.
[22] Federal Law № 96-FZ 'On Atmospheric Air Protection', 4 May 1999, amended on
27 December 2009, № 374-FZ.
[23] Nystén-Haarala, above n. 7, Mucklow, p. 104.

emphasis was placed on natural resources, and laws were usually classified according to the type of resource being regulated (forests, water, agriculture etc.).[24] Thus, general environmental law is not viewed within a holistic 'ecology cycle' framework whereby the environment has intrinsic value, but from the perspective that the environment is valued in the context of, and understood to comprise, natural resources.

18.19 The Soviet legal system was not focused on monetary rewards or compensation. Hence, compensation and costs reimbursement were minimal during Soviet times. This has not greatly changed today, though the focus and understanding of the function of the law has altered somewhat in that monetary punishments and costs reimbursements are awarded, albeit at very low levels. However, the legal system is being reformed and modernised, though the approach to quantum has not yet been addressed.

Principal environmental laws

18.20 Principal environmental laws that might be applied in climate change proceedings are:[25]
- the Constitution;[26]
- multilateral environmental agreements (as ratified);[27]
- Environmental Protection Law ('EPL');[28]
- Water Code 2006 ('Water Code');[29]
- LAP;
- Forest Code;
- Law on Fauna 1995;

[24] *Ibid.*; and I. A. Ikonickaya, *Zemelnoe Provo Rossiiskoi Federacii* (Moscow: Iurist, 2002).

[25] Nystén-Haarala, above n. 7, Mucklow, p. 105; and see n. 15, Ratsiborinskaya; and O. Razbash, 'Russian NGOs and public participation – Legal and practical perspectives', above n. 7, Mucklow, pp. 69–83.

[26] Articles 42 ('Everyone shall have the right to a favourable environment, reliable information about its state and to restitution for damage inflicted on [his/her] health and property by ecological transgressions') and 58 ('Every citizen is obliged to protect nature and the environment, treat and carefully [preserve] the riches of nature').

[27] E.g. 1987 Montreal Protocol on Substances that Deplete the Ozone Layer to the Vienna Convention for the Protection of the Ozone Layer (both ratified, as amended); the 1992 Convention on Biological Diversity (ratified); 1973 Convention in International Trade of Endangered Species of Wild Fauna and Flora (ratified).

[28] Federal Law № 7-FZ 'On the Protection of the Environment', 10 January 2002, amended by № 374-FZ on 27 December 2009.

[29] Federal Law № 74-FZ 'The Water Code of the Russian Federation', 3 June 2006, as amended on 23 July 2008 № 160-FZ.

- Law on Subsoil Resources 1992;
- Law on Payment for Land 1991;
- Law on Environmental Expertise 1995;
- Law on Licensing of Various Functions 2001; and
- Law on the Protection of Juridical Persons and Entrepreneurs in Applying State Control 2001.

18.21   The rules on civil liability for damage to the environment are set out in the Civil Code (Part I, 1994) and in the Code on Administrative Offences 2001 (Part VIII).[30]

18.22   There is no explicit or direct provision which would enable a claimant to establish the liability of another party for causing harm or damage to the environment by emitting GHGs and so contributing to global warming or for failing to mitigate climate change. An argument might be constructed with respect to establishing liability for emitting 'harmful substances' into the atmosphere (though not explicitly GHGs).[31]

18.23   In general, it is very unlikely that the above federal environmental laws could provide a basis upon which to establish a claim for liability for contributing to (or failing to mitigate) climate change, as these laws do not directly establish a person's responsibility for mitigating climate change.

18.24   **Ownership structures**. An additional level of complexity is added to Russian environmental law due to the struggles of ownership over natural resources between the federal and regional governments.[32]

18.25   **Public trust doctrine**. The courts show no signs of embracing the public trust doctrine, as has been done in other countries of the BRIC (Brazil, Russia, India and China) group, including India.[33] It is unlikely that the courts will adopt this doctrine in the near or mid-term future.

---

[30] Federal Law № 195-FZ 'Code on Administrative Offences of the Russian Federation', 30 December 2001, as amended on 29 December 2010 ('Administrative Code').
[31] Articles 8(21) and 8(22), Administrative Code.
[32] Nystén-Haarala, above n. 7, Mucklow, p. 107.
[33] M. Wood, 'Atmospheric Trust Litigation Across the World' in K. Coghill (ed.), *Fiduciary Duty and the Atmospheric Commons* (Australia: Ashgate Publishing, forthcoming, www.law.uoregon.edu/faculty/mwood/forlawyers.php), p. 7.

Principal human rights laws

18.26 The subject of individual human rights in Russia is controversial.[34] As Bowring states, 'Russia has, like all its European neighbours, a long and complex relationship with human rights – and with the rule of law and judicial independence, which are its essential underpinnings'.[35]

18.27 Principal human rights laws that might be applied in climate change liability proceedings are:
- the Constitution;[36]
- human rights conventions (as ratified);[37]
- the EPL;[38]
- the Law 'On Guarantees of the Rights of Numerically Small Indigenous Peoples of the Russian Federation';[39]
- the Law 'On the General Principles of Organising Communities of Numerically Small Indigenous Peoples of the North, Siberia and the Far East of the Russian Federation';[40]
- the Law 'On Territories of Traditional Nature Use of Numerically Small Indigenous Peoples of the North, Siberia and Far East of the Russian Federation';[41] and
- various codes (e.g. the Land Code, the Water Code and the Forest Code) applicable to indigenous peoples' rights.[42]

[34] See J. Anaya, *Report of the Special Rapporteur on the situation of human rights and fundamental freedoms of indigenous peoples, James Anaya, on the situation of indigenous peoples in the Russian Federation*, 23 June 2010 (UNGA, A/HRC/15/37/Add.5, available at http://unsr.jamesanaya.org/PDFs/Russia%20Report%20EN.pdf) ('UNGA Report'), p. 5; *Report by Alvaro Gil-Robles on his Visits to the Russian Federation* (Council of Europe, Commissioner for Human Rights, 20 April 2005).

[35] B. Bowring, 'Russia and Human Rights: Incompatible Opposites?', *Göttingen Journal of International Law*, 1(2) (2009), 257–78, at 259.

[36] Chapter 2 (Rights and Freedoms of Man and Citizen).

[37] 1948 Universal Declaration of Human Rights (signed, not ratified); 1966 International Covenant on Civil and Political Rights (ratified, 1973; Optional Protocol ratified, 1991); 1966 International Covenant on Economic, Social and Cultural Rights (ratified, 1973); 1950 European Convention for the Protection of Human Rights and Fundamental Freedoms ('ECHR') (ratified, 1998).

[38] Article 3.

[39] Federal Law № 82-FZ, 30 April 1999, as amended on 5 April 2009.

[40] Federal Law № 104-FZ, 20 July 2000, as amended on 2 February 2006.

[41] Federal Law № 49-FZ, 7 May 2001, as amended on 3 December 2008.

[42] C. Henriksen, 'Indigenous peoples and industry. Complex co-existence in the Barents Euro-Arctic Region' in A. Staalesen (ed.), *Talking Barents: People, Borders and regional cooperation, Barents Review 2010* (Kirkenes: Norwegian Barents Secretariat, 2010), pp. 97–107, available at www.barents.no/index.php?cat=141647 ('Henriksen'), pp. 98–9;

ECHR

18.28   Under the ECHR, a private party alleging breach of the ECHR may file a suit against Russia directly. Many such cases involving Russia have been heard by the European Court of Human Rights ('ECtHR').[43] To date, there has only been one air pollution related case, namely *Fadeyeva* v. *Russia*.[44] Domestic implementation of ECtHR decisions was not straightforward until February 2010, when the Constitutional Court adopted a decision[45] which altered Article 392 of the Civil Code to the effect that ECtHR decisions must be implemented.

18.29   Despite these major steps towards incorporating human rights within domestic Russian law, the Russian Human Rights Ombudsman, Vladimir Lukin, has observed that the 'human rights situation in Russia is unsatisfactory', but that 'this is not discouraging, because building a lawful state and civil society in such a complex country as Russia is a hard and long process'.[46]

Indigenous peoples

18.30   There are over 160 distinct peoples in Russia, making it one of the most ethnically diverse countries in the world.[47] The law protects the rights of certain indigenous peoples through the Constitution, 'in accordance with the generally accepted principles and standards of international laws and the international treaties of the Russian Federation' (Article 69).[48]

See also I. Øverland, 'Indigenous Rights in the Russian North' in *Russia and the North* (University of Ottawa Press, 2009); 'Conference on Indigenous Constitutional Rights in Russia: Summary', *Indigenous Peoples Issues & Resources* (11 January 2010).

[43] E.g. Application Nos. 15339/02, 21166/02, 20058/02, 11673/02, 15343/02 *Budayeva and Others* v. *Russia* (ECHR 20–03–2008); Application Nos. 4916/07, 25924/08 and 14599/09 *Alekseyev* v. *Russia* (ECHR 21–10–2010) (see www.echr.coe.int/ECHR/EN/Header/Case-Law/Hudoc/Hudoc+database/).

[44] Application No. 55723/00, ECHR 09–06–2005.

[45] Resolution of the Constitutional Court of the Russian Federation, 26 February 2010, № 4-P 'On the Constitutionality of Clause 2 of Article 392 of the Civil Procedure Code of the Russian Federation'.

[46] V. Lukin, *The Report of the Commissioner for Human Rights in the Russian Federation for the Year 2006* (13 April 2007).

[47] Above n. 34, *UNGA Report*, p. 5.

[48] Focus is on 'small-numbered indigenous peoples of the North, Siberia and Far East' which covers about forty-six indigenous peoples of Russia (see http://base.garant.ru/181870/#1000), but does not apply to all groups (UNGA Report; and see above n. 33, Henriksen).

18.31   In 2009, the government adopted a 'Concept Paper on the Sustainable Development of the Indigenous Peoples of the North, Siberia and the Far East of the Russian Federation'.[49] It is described as an ambitious and a comprehensive document;[50] however, the effectiveness of the implementation of the laws relating to indigenous peoples' rights has been criticised.[51] With respect to climate change liability, these laws do not specifically address the adverse effects of climate change on ways of indigenous life – though they do address the right of indigenous peoples to receive compensation for damage to their traditional environment due to industrial activities. Due to environmental awareness issues, poverty and other reasons set out above, it is very unlikely that indigenous peoples will commence legal proceedings in Russian courts with the aim of establishing liability for climate change.[52]

Human rights litigation

18.32   The practice of human rights litigation in Russia is not widespread, and cases are not commonly successful. Thus, after avenues of domestic proceedings have been exhausted, legal proceedings are sometimes commenced at the ECtHR.

Other principles of law

18.33   The courts tend to be very reluctant to apply international law in the guise of 'general principles of law recognised by nations',[53] unless they have been formally incorporated into Russian law.

18.34   Whilst, in particular, Article 10 of the Civil Code gives a basis for courts to rely on the requirements of good faith, reasonableness and justice, as well as principles of equity and fairness and other general principles of law, they do so comparatively rarely. It is unlikely that this will change in the context of environmental (including climate change related) disputes.

---

[49] Decree of the Government of the Russian Federation № 132-r 'On the Concept paper on the Sustainable Development of Indigenous Peoples of the North, Siberia and the Far East of the Russian Federation', 4 February 2009.

[50] Above n. 34, *UNGA Report*, p. 8.   [51] *Ibid.*, p. 7.

[52] As regards indigenous peoples' challenges relating to implementation of their environmental rights, see O. O. Mironov, '*Экология и нарушение прав человека. Специальный доклад Уполномоченного по правам человека в Российской Федерации*' (ЭКОС-Информ. – №2. – 2003), available at www.ecoculture.ru/ecolibrary/art_18.php.

[53] Article 38(1)(c), 1946 Statute of the International Court of Justice.

Kyoto legislation

18.35   There are various legislative, policy and strategy instruments
that address climate change, and some regulations which address
particular aspects of the Kyoto Protocol. In particular, the following instruments address climate change mitigation and implement the FCCC and Kyoto Protocol provisions (directly and/or
indirectly).

18.36   **Climate Doctrine 2009**. The Climate Doctrine was adopted
in 2009 and signed by President Medvedev in early 2010.[54] The
Climate Doctrine states that its aim is to coordinate activities
to support the safe and sustainable development of the Russian
Federation, taking into account climate change. It is addressed
primarily to the Government with the aim of coordinating
its activities in the area of climate policy along the lines of the
Doctrine. The Climate Doctrine does not touch upon the subject
of liability, but concentrates on general issues of governmental
climate policy.

18.37   **Energy efficiency**. The Russian energy efficiency policy is set
out in the current 'Energy Strategy through 2030' ('Energy
Strategy').[55] The Energy Strategy makes it clear that the improvement of energy efficiency is viewed as a vital part of economic
policy[56] and envisages halving the energy intensity of Russia by
2030 (as compared to 2005). It states that the previous energy
strategy (the '2020 Energy Strategy') was adequate, but, based
on the recent successes of the 2020 Energy Strategy, proposes a
higher reduction of energy intensity in Russia, namely a 50 per
cent reduction (on average) in 2000 levels by 2020.[57]

18.38   There are various codes and laws which address energy efficiency
in Russia.[58] These are as follows.

---

[54]   Order of the RF President № 861-rp 'On the Climate Doctrine of the Russian Federation',
17 December 2009 ('Climate Doctrine').

[55]   Order of the RF Government № 1715-p 'On the Energy Strategy through 2030', 13
November 2009.

[56]   See Energy Charter Protocol on Energy Efficiency and Related Environmental Aspects
PEEREA *Russian Federation: Regular Review of Energy Efficiency Policies 2007* (Brussels:
Energy Charter Secretariat, December 2007) ('Energy Efficiency Review'), available at
www.encharter.org/fileadmin/user_upload/document/EE_rr_Russia_2007_ENG.pdf.

[57]   Decision of the RF Government № 1234-p, 28 August 2003 (ES-2020).

[58]   See *Energy Efficiency Review*, p. 17.

18.39   The Law On Energy Efficiency and Changes into Some Legislative Acts of the Russian Federation 2009 ('Energy Efficiency Law')[59] states that a person who breaches the Energy Efficiency Law may be subject to disciplinary, civil and/or administrative liability, according to the relevant legislation. Other relevant laws are the Law 'On Heat Supply' 2010,[60] as well as draft federal laws that are being developed: the draft Law 'On the Support of Renewable Energy Sources' and the draft Law 'On the Use of Alternative Types of Motor Fuels'. These legal developments on renewable energy are not discussed further here due to space constraints.

18.40   **JI Regulations 2009**. The Government adopted the following with respect to JI projects in Russia:
- Government Resolution No. 843 On Measures to Implement Article 6 of the Kyoto Protocol to the United Nations Framework Convention on Climate Change 2009;[61]
- Regulations On Implementation of Article 6 of the Kyoto Protocol to the United Nations Framework Convention on Climate Change 2009 ('JI Regulations').[62]

18.41   The JI Regulations provide the guidelines and rules relating to JI projects in Russia.[63] Sberbank (a Russian State bank) acts as the carbon units operator. It arranges the tender selections of the applications of Russian legal entities for approval of JI projects. The Ministry of Economic Development ('MED') approved the rules for tender selection of applications for JI projects.[64] However, none of the Kyoto-related laws and regulations address liability for causing (or failing to mitigate) climate change.

18.42   An attempt to establish liability for contribution to climate change could, in theory, be based upon a combination of the above two

---

[59] Federal Law № 261-FZ, 23 November 2009, as amended on 27 July 2010.
[60] Federal Law № 190-FZ, 27 July 2010.
[61] Decree of the RF Government № 843 'On Measures to Implement Article 6 of Kyoto Protocol to the United Nations Framework Convention on Climate Change', 28 October 2009.
[62] *Ibid.*
[63] Above n. 20, Gutbrod/Sitnikov/Pike-Biegunska, Ch. 3; M. Yulkin, 'Involving Russian Business in Kyoto', above n. 7, Mucklow, pp. 189–201.
[64] Order of MED № 485 'Rules for the Tender Selection of Applications for Approval of Projects Developed Under Article 6 of the Kyoto Protocol to the United Nations Framework Convention on Climate Change', 23 November 2009.

areas, of general environmental and human rights laws, and of the Kyoto legislation. However, to date no such arguments have been brought in any court, and legal proceedings are unlikely to emerge in the near-to-medium term.

18.43   Nevertheless, by issuing the Climate Doctrine and in developing the draft Plan for Russian Climate Doctrine Implementation (not public at the time of writing), Russia is now on the road to developing its climate change policy and perhaps, at a later date, specific climate change laws.

18.44   **Green investment scheme ('GIS').** There appear to be no draft regulations related to the GIS mechanism yet, though they are understood as being in preparation.

Regional initiatives

18.45   Belarus, Kazakhstan and Ukraine are said to plan to establish a carbon market with Russia. The market participants would be able to carry out JI projects and attract investment subject to the fulfilment of certain conditions. Establishment of a single market for these countries should be possible, as there is a similarly operating regional carbon market in the EU. However it is questionable whether there is a real need for this regional market, and how effective it is likely to be, without connecting it to the EU Emission Trading System ('EU ETS') market and reforming the existing system of pollution regulation in Belarus, Russia and Kazakhstan.

18.46   It is noted that in the Commonwealth of Independent States ('CIS') region, some countries are developing specific laws relating to climate change. For example, Belarus is in the process of adopting a new draft 'Law on Climate Protection', whilst Kazakhstan is in the process of adopting legislation on emissions trading.[65] These regional developments may affect the ways in which Russian law evolves in the future.

Industrial and natural resources

18.47   Russia has a wide range of natural resources, which include major deposits of oil, the world's largest natural gas reserves

---

[65] Personal communication from Alexey Kokorin, WWF Russia, Moscow, 23 November 2010.

and second largest coal reserves, many strategic minerals and timber.

18.48   Russia has inherited a large arsenal of heavy industry from Soviet times. The infrastructure is, in many instances, still in need of repair and modernisation. This has a direct effect on, in particular, the GHG emission levels of heavy industry, coal-fired electric plants and the transportation sector (especially in cities). Furthermore, Russia's energy efficiency is poor.

18.49   The consequences of heavy and partially non-modernised industry in Russia include air pollution, industrial, municipal and agricultural pollution of inland waterways and the coastline, deforestation, soil erosion, soil contamination from the improper application of agricultural chemicals, scattered areas of sometimes intense radioactive contamination, and groundwater contamination from toxic waste, poor urban solid waste management and abandoned stocks of obsolete pesticides.[66]

18.50   Despite the privatisations of the 1990s, these industries and natural resources typically remain in the ownership (or part ownership) of the Government. Foreign direct investment ('FDI') activity in Russia has meant that some of these sectors display a level of foreign ownership, too. Such industries predominantly exist within or overlap with the public sector.

18.51   The following are the main sources of GHG emissions in Russia: 83.3% from electricity and heat production; 1.1% from the residential sector; 7% from the industrial sector; 8% from transport; and 0.6% from other sectors (including agrarian sources).[67]

National climate change risks

18.52   Data published by Roshydromet show that between 1990 and 2000 the mean annual surface air temperature increased by 0.4°C, with temperatures in the Arctic rising at almost double the rate of the global average. The effects of climate change are felt in Russia in terms of milder winters, melting permafrost, changing

[66] See Central Intelligence Agency (CIA), *World Factbook: Russia* (as at September 2010), at https://www.cia.gov/library/publications/the-world-factbook/geos/rs.html.

[67] Energy Charter Protocol on Energy Efficiency and Related Environmental Aspects (PEEREA), *Russian Federation: Regular Review of Energy Efficiency Policies 2007*, p. 46.

precipitation patterns, the spread of disease and the increased incidence of drought, flooding and other extreme weather events.[68] Such effects are likely to (i) negatively affect agricultural crop yields and biodiversity, coastal populations (due to coastal erosion and flooding) and the way of life of indigenous peoples; and (ii) create increased internal migration and socio-economic and socio-political stresses.[69]

18.53   For example, the heatwave in the summer of 2010 (the hottest in recorded history) led to widespread fires and a state of emergency in seventeen states of Russia. The fires also destroyed 30 per cent of crops,[70] which led to a shortage of grain and government-imposed restrictions on the export of grain.

Climate change litigation in Russia

18.54   At the time of writing there have not been any specific cases in the Russian courts which can be classified as climate change litigation.[71]

18.55   Despite the dramatic consequences of the extreme heatwave, forest fires and intense smog conditions in summer 2010, no claimant (including government authorities) has filed a lawsuit against any company, claiming, for example, that the defendant company, by failing to cap or reduce their CO_2 (or other GHG) emissions, so contributed to climate change that this then led to increased death rates and loss of crops. Nor have there been any legal proceedings arising from loss or damage due to coastal erosion, droughts or floods, or in relation to the widespread loss of species and biodiversity, in which causation has been alleged through action or inaction in the face of climate change.

---

[68] National Intelligence Council, *Russia: Impact of Climate Change to 2030: A Commissioned Research Report* (Special Report NIC 2009–04D, April 2009), pp. 3 and 8.

[69] *Ibid.*

[70] According to the Ministry of Agriculture, this equates to 26 billion roubles (approximately US$859 million) of damage (experts' investigation in 18 Regions); see www.mk.ru/incident/news/2010/10/12/535998-za-leto-v-rossii-byilo-unichtozheno-30-posevov-zerna.html; http://en.rian.ru/russia/20100814/160200814.html; and http://en.rian.ru/russia/20100810/160134883.html.

[71] The definition of climate change litigation embraced in this chapter excludes any litigation as regards compliance with general environmental standards (as there is an array of such litigation in Russia).

Sectors at risk

18.56 The risk posed to business from climate change litigation is low, given the current absence and low likelihood of future claims. On the basis of the arguments set out below, and due to State owner-ship structures in Russia, the sectors most at risk are likely to be companies in the private sector (and perhaps foreign companies in particular) taking part in JI projects.

18.57 Under the Strategic Investments Law,[72] various sectors in Russia have been designated as 'strategic'. Areas included as strategic are those in which the performance of works influences hydromete-orological or geophysical processes. Climate change litigation is very unlikely to occur with respect to companies or other entities which are deemed to fall within such strategic sectors.

Future of climate change litigation

18.58 The risk of increased climate change litigation in the future is likely to remain low to very low. In the short and medium term, the impact of the global financial crisis, the slow economic recov-ery in Russia and the uncertain investment climate mean that the focus is more likely to be on economic development. In add-ition, 14 per cent of the Russian population is still living below the poverty line.[73] The year 2009 saw a nearly 50 per cent drop in FDI,[74] whilst Russia strongly relies on export receipts from cli-mate change related products, i.e. oil and gas, other raw mate-rials and basic manufactures including timber, metals and chemicals.[75] Furthermore, since around 2005, the role of the State in the economy has significantly increased and culminated in the aforementioned rules on State intervention in strategic sectors.[76] Thus, governmental and regulatory activities are more likely to

---

[72] Federal Law № 57-FZ 'On Procedures for Foreign Investments in Companies of Strategic Significance for National Defense and Security', 28 April 2008 ('Strategic Investments Law'); this law imposes restrictions on foreign investors seeking to buy shares or acquire control over Russian companies that are deemed strategic.

[73] United Nations Development Programme, *The National Human Development Report in Russia 2010* (Moscow: UNDP, 2010).

[74] Above n. 9, *EIU Russia Forecast 2010*, 'Russia: Foreign direct investment: Stocks and flows'.

[75] Two-thirds of Russia's export receipts come from these sectors; see above n. 9, *EIU Russia Forecast 2010*.

[76] See para. 18.57 above.

focus on facilitating the continued domestic economic recovery, trade, infrastructure investments and modernisation, as well as on attracting FDI, rather than on enabling (through legal reform) or participating in climate change litigation.

18.59   Additionally, as evidenced by the adoption of the NGO Law[77] in 2006, it is government policy to regulate the activities of NGOs. Aggressive action or litigation by NGOs, although theoretically possible, is, therefore, unlikely in the near or mid-term future.

18.60   Finally, Russian procedural rules are not favourable to claims by governmental authorities, cities, NGOs, industries suffering from global warming (e.g. fisheries, agriculture, timber and tourism), indigenous peoples or victims of natural catastrophes, based on climate change. A prerequisite for any such claim would be evidence that the 'concrete rights' ('*неотчуждаемые/основные права человека*') of the claimant had been violated,[78] and no such violation would be recognised in the case of GHG emissions or other environmental damage.

18.61   Therefore, litigation relating to climate change in Russia is more likely to take place in the context of Kyoto legislation related commercial proceedings (including with respect to contractual terms of Emissions Reduction Purchase Agreements, investment agreements for JI projects in Russia, carbon asset development agreements or services agreements), rather than focusing on a defendant's liability for contributing to climate change per se or being based upon environmental and human rights law.

(B)   Public law

18.62   Given that climate change litigation is relatively unlikely to take place in the near to mid-term future, the discussion as to who might be best placed to enforce any right or bring claims in

---

[77]   Federal Law № 18-FZ 'On Introducing Amendments to Certain Legislative Acts of the Russian Federation', 10 January 2006 (known as the 'NGO Law'), which amended the Civil Code, the Law on Public Associations 1995, the Law on Non-profit Organisations 1996, and the Law on Closed Administrative Territorial Formations.

[78]   Article 131, Civil Procedural Code 2002 ('CPC').

relation to damage (actual or anticipated) arising from climate change is primarily theoretical at present, both in the context of public and of private law proceedings.

Potential claimants

18.63 Under general environmental and human rights law or with respect to Kyoto legislation, claims alleging liability in respect of climate change could potentially be brought by:
- environment-related government agencies;[79]
- individuals;[80]
- companies;[81] or
- environmental NGOs.[82]

18.64 Given aforementioned circumstances, the environment-related regulatory agencies (local, national or governmental bodies) are the most likely parties to commence proceedings, if at all, and such proceedings are most likely to arise in the context of administrative or commercial matters.[83]

18.65 In Russia, class actions were substantially unknown in litigation practice until 19 July 2009, when the Federal Law 'On the Introduction of Changes into Some Legislative Acts of the Russian Federation'[84] was adopted. This law added Chapter 28.2 (*Claims on rights and lawful interests' protection of a group of plaintiffs*) to the Arbitration Procedural Code.[85] Under this code, a class action is only possible if there are at least five claims brought by individuals, agencies or organisations in the framework of the same action.[86] However, to date, to the authors' knowledge, no such actions have been brought in the Russian courts alleging liability for climate change.

---

[79] Article 5, EPL. [80] Article 11(2), EPL.

[81] Under Article 62(3) of the Constitution, foreign and Russian Parties are accorded equal treatment in Russian court proceedings.

[82] Article 12(1), EPL.

[83] However, in the *Khimkinskiy Forest* case, NGOs initiated the legal proceedings; see Decision of the Supreme Court of the Russian Federation of 1 March 2010, N ГКПИ09–1767 'On Dismissing the Application for Invalidation of Paragraph 1 of the Decree of the Government of the Russian Federation of 5 November 2009, N 1642-p'.

[84] Federal Law № 205, 19 July 2009.

[85] Federal Law № 95-FZ 'The Arbitration Procedural Code of the Russian Federation', 24 July 2002, as amended on 27 July 2010.

[86] *Ibid.*, Article 225(1) and (2).

Basic legal principles of public law review

18.66   Under the Constitution,[87] anyone can submit a claim to a relevant court whereby decisions, activity or inactivity by the Government or public bodies may be reviewed or challenged. The type of court to which such claims can be brought depends on the breach of rights/freedoms and the claimants concerned.

18.67   Under broader environmental and human rights laws, the following activities relating to climate change liability could potentially be subject to review by, or challenged before, the courts:
- general regulatory activity;
- planning (for GHG-intensive projects);
- permits (to emit or carry on potentially emitting activities, or approve/finance them); and
- actions taken under general public law.

18.68   In general, all basic legal environmental principles indirectly relating to the regulation of climate change issues, are summed up in Article 3 of the EPL. Thereunder, governmental and public bodies are responsible for ensuring a favourable environment and 'ecological safety'. Together with private entities and citizens, these agencies are obliged to protect the environment.

18.69   Thus, decisions, acts and failures to act on the part of governmental or public bodies may be reviewed or challenged in the courts.[88] At least in theory, there is a strong focus on procedural environmental rights, including the right to access to environmental information, the right to public participation and the right to access to justice.

Court system

18.70   The judicial system is comprised of the Constitutional Court, civil courts, *arbitrazh* courts and military tribunals.[89] Private parties and NGOs have standing in such courts. The *arbitrazh* courts have jurisdiction over proceedings involving legal entities and

---

[87]   Article 46(1) and (2).
[88]   Chapter XIV, EPL, on environmental liability.
[89]   Regarding the planned reform of the court system, see interview with V. Radchenko, Deputy President of the RF Supreme Court, at www.supcourt.ru/vscourt_detale.php?id=1528&w[]=%D0%E0%E4%F7%E5%ED%EA%EE.

business persons.[90] The civil courts will only become involved on issues concerning the recognition of decisions from foreign civil and *arbitrazh* courts or appeals against decisions by Russian arbitration courts.

Review of public decisions

18.71　The Federal Law 'On the Procedure for Reviewing Applications of the Citizens of the Russian Federation' regulates how a Russian citizen can realise his/her constitutional right to address State bodies and local government bodies and prescribes the procedures to be followed within State bodies and local government and by civil servants.[91] Despite the title, this law also covers applications and claims filed by foreign citizens and persons without citizenship (Article 1(3)). An applicant can file written and oral suggestions, claims and complaints (Article 4), and the government bodies/civil servants usually have thirty days to react to the filed application (Article 12). This law does not explicitly address areas which a party can complain about. Thus, theoretically, it could be used to request the review of the legality of the decisions of government bodies relating to environmental matters.

Planning (for GHG-intensive projects)

18.72　Generally, Russian legislation empowers individuals and entities to file applications with the courts to review the legality of acts, failures to act and decisions of governmental agencies if such action results in infringement of the rights and freedoms of a person, creates obstacles to the exercise of a person's rights and freedoms or unlawfully imposes a duty on a person or unlawfully holds him/her responsible. If so, the court may invalidate the relevant action or decision. The same principles apply to enactments concerning GHG-related activities.

Environmental permits

18.73　The permit system in Russia regulates the issuance of permits for environmental pollution. There are separate permits for airborne

---

[90] It is noted that the *arbitrazh* courts in Russia are the courts where commercial matters are heard. They differ from the courts where actual arbitration takes place (e.g. the International Commercial Arbitration Court (MKAS)).

[91] Federal law № 59-FZ, 2 May 2006, as amended on 29 June 2010.

emissions, water discharge and waste disposal, and for the handling of hazardous waste.[92]

18.74   Under the Federal Law 'On Complaining to Court About Activities and Decisions which Violate the Rights and Freedoms of Citizens',[93] a party can request the courts to review the legality of a permit or its compliance with the applicable law. The law allows the claimant to choose the body to which it turns for restoration of his/her environmental right. This can be a court as such, but also a superior governmental body, a municipal agency, a company, an organisation or a civil servant. The complaint must be dealt with within thirty days, whilst the application for judicial review must be dealt with within three months.

18.75   In addition, the Federal Law 'On the Sanitary and Epidemiological Well-being of the Population' can be used in support of challenges to permits relating to 'nature use'. According to this law, citizens have the right to a safe living environment, to full and reliable information on the use of natural resources by companies and organisations and their effects on the environment.[94]

18.76   However, usually, the review of permits is left to institutional enforcement agencies, namely the Federal Service for Supervision of Natural Resource Use ('Rosprirodnadzor') that has been given major control tasks at the federal and regional levels.[95] For each area there is a separate Rosprirodnadzor inspection department, with its own chief inspectors, competent to launch administrative cases. It should be noted that Rosprirodnadzor is not an independent agency, but a body within the MNR structure.[96]

---

[92] See Articles 3 and 30, EPL and other environmental laws and sub-laws.
[93] Federal Law № 4866–1, 27 April 1993, as amended on 9 February 2009.
[94] Article 8, Federal Law № 52-FZ 'On Sanitary and Epidemiological Well-Being of the Population', 30 March 1999, as amended on 28 September 2010, № 243-FZ.
[95] Decree of the RF Government № 717 'On introduction of changes into Government Decrees related to competences of Ministry of Natural Resources and Ecology, Federal Agency for Surveillance in the field of Nature Use, Federal Agency for ecological, technological and nuclear control', 13 September 2010.
[96] See V. Sapozhnikova, *Environmental Protection in Russia*, pp. 183–8, at www.inece.org/conference/7/vol1/Sapoz hinikova.pdf.

Enforcing and striking down legislation

18.77   The Constitutional Court has the power to strike down or annul any legislation for being illegal or invalid.

General public law actions

18.78   In practice, general public law actions almost never succeed as the courts often deem them too 'broad' and lacking in concrete interests.

Remedies under Russian law

18.79   There is no specific legislation rendering unlawful activities which impact on air quality or contribute to climate change. General norms may, however, be applied. Article 78 of the EPL, for instance, provides that a party must compensate another for environmental damage that was caused by it breaching environmental law. The definition of 'damage' includes actual expenses incurred to rehabilitate the affected environment, as well as financial damages and (expected) losses of profit. Article 79 of the EPL focuses on compensation for damage to citizens' health and property (as a result of breach of environmental legislation). Such damage is to be fully compensated and is further regulated by the Civil Code (Chapter 59).

18.80   Under Article 80 of the EPL, when legal or private persons act in breach of environmental law, citizens can claim the limitation or termination of relevant activities.

18.81   An enterprise can appeal the decisions of a government body in relation to any matter in which it believes its interests have been affected. For example, the Law 'On Ecological Expertise' provides for the possibility to challenge the results of an 'expertise' (Article 18(8)), the latter of which is an examination of project documents as regards their conformity with ecological requirements set out under Russian law. All cases are reviewed by a court of general jurisdiction, except for cases where there is an economic interest at stake. Thus, the *arbitrazh* courts can review, amongst other matters, industries' appeals against license/permit refusal. Neighbouring enterprises and other government authorities can also be involved in the process in different ways: as co-plaintiffs, co-defendants and third parties (if recognised by the court).

18.82   Private parties can challenge the decisions of government bodies on license or permit issue or refusal, if such decisions constitute breach of citizens' constitutional rights.

18.83   NGOs and the general public can, as well, bring a claim or a plea aimed at the protection of common environmental interest(s) (Articles 10 and 12, EPL).

(C)   Private law

Overview

18.84   Generally, potential claims between private parties with respect to climate change liability face similar issues to those under public law.

18.85   Individuals[97] (including individuals as participants in class actions), NGOs[98] and governmental bodies (federal, regional, local and municipal governments)[99] could potentially make a claim for climate change liability before the courts.[100] In the current general climate, however, governmental bodies are most likely to be best placed to enforce any rights or bring claims in relation to harm or damage (actual or anticipated) from climate change.

18.86   However, as set out above, it is very unlikely that such actions will take place in the near to mid-term future or that they would be successful if attempted. With respect to claims arising out of contracts (relating to JI projects or other emissions reduction projects), it is difficult to predict the timing of potential proceedings.

Possible defendants

18.87   As is the case for potential public law proceedings, possible defendants in private law proceedings are more likely to be corporations and businesses which are climate change causing industries. Given the non-litigious nature of Russian society and possibly the current political situation, it is very unlikely

---

[97] Articles 3 and 4, CPC.   [98] *Ibid.*
[99] *Ibid.*   [100] Article 22, CPC.

that the Government or governmental agencies would be made defendants in climate change proceedings. Often corporations are co-owned by the Government (in particular, in the case of corporations with national interests, e.g. gas, oil and other natural resources). Thus, the Government might become a defendant, directly or indirectly, by way of being co-owner of a given corporation.

18.88   **Corporations, lenders and banks**. In Russia, corporations and banks can be government-owned, partially government-owned or privately owned. It is unlikely that there will be a dramatic increase in climate change litigation in the oil and gas industry for the reasons set out above. In particular, as the oil and gas industry is predominantly owned (or part-owned) by the Government, the industry is unlikely to have to prepare itself for an increase in climate litigation as has happened, for example, in the USA.

18.89   **Government**. As mentioned above, the Government and governmental agencies are unlikely to be claimants or defendants in private law climate liability proceedings.

18.90   **Shareholders**. Shareholders generally cannot be held liable for the action of their companies. Whilst there have been some exceptions to this rule, in particular when shareholders consciously initiated bankruptcy of their companies, such exceptions are unlikely to be applied in case of environmental damage caused by climate change.

18.91   **Directors and officers**. Company directors' and officers' duties are subject to administrative, criminal and civil liability.[101] It is a general rule that a director of a company is responsible for his/ her decisions relating to the company's actions and operations. At the same time, the individual employees of a company have limited responsibility as they can be held liable only for the consequences of their own actions. Thus, it is unlikely that litigation (including climate change litigation) would be targeted at directors and officials of a company.

18.92   **Auditors**. There are no specific rules for holding auditors liable in relation to climate change matters. The general basis for holding

---

[101] E.g. Article 14(1), Administrative Code.

auditors liable is for breach of contract and breach of civil law connected with the negligent rendering of services. The Federal Law 'On Audit Activities'[102] provides for the responsibility of auditors for signing false reports; it also provides for the right of audit organisations/individual auditors to insure its/their responsibility for breach of the audit services contract or for causing damage to property of other parties as a result of audit activity. Additionally, the Criminal Code 1996 ('Criminal Code')[103] provides that auditors can be held responsible for economic crimes (for instance, for the illegal receipt and disclosure of classified commercial, tax or banking information) and any abuse of their authority.

18.93   **Regulators**. Whilst, frequently, the possibility of legal action against regulators for breach of duty is provided for in law, such lawsuits are not frequently brought. As a rule, the courts are unlikely to be well disposed towards such lawsuits. There is no experience in Russia with (and no clear basis for) lawsuits based upon the understanding that a regulator should have acted and has failed to do so.

18.94   **Insurers**. There is no basis in Russian law for the responsibility of insurers towards third parties. The Russian insurance market and law are still nascent and developing. Given reports that climate change risks could make emerging markets 'uninsurable',[104] it is unlikely that, in the future, Russian insurers will insure risks relating to damage caused by climate change or provide climate change cover for businesses which potentially could be held liable for contributing to or failing to mitigate or prevent climate change. If such cover were, however, to be provided, the insurance premium levels would be likely to be exorbitantly high.

Tort law

18.95   Article 1064(1) of the Civil Code allows a party to claim damages for any harm caused to property in general and Article 1065(1)

---

[102]   № 119-FZ, 7 August 2001, as amended on 30 December 2008.
[103]   Federal Law № 63-FZ 'Criminal Code of the Russian Federation', 13 June 1996, as amended on 4 October 2010 (№ 270-FZ).
[104]   businessGreen, *Climate risks could make emerging markets 'uninsurable'* (1 December 2010), at www.businessgreen.com/bg/news/1929033/climate-risks-emerging-markets-uninsurable.

of the Civil Code specifically allows claims for future damage, which is to be expected but remains uncertain. In theory, the basis for launching claims in a Russian court, based on environmental violations, is broad.

18.96 However, despite a number of catastrophes over the past few years (e.g. in coal mines or hydro plants, causing many deaths), this does not seem to have resulted in a substantial increase in tort litigation. Furthermore, compensation paid has been comparatively low. On the basis that there have been few successful tort claims in Russia, in addition to other factors mentioned in this chapter, we believe that potential claimants are not likely to engage in climate change litigation in Russia.

18.97 Legally, we believe there are two primary factors hindering the prospects for success of climate change liability claims in Russia, namely:

- For lawsuits to be successful, the causal nexus between an action of the defendant and the harm or damage incurred must be established. The courts, however, operate within the tradition that only the immediate consequences of an action are considered as a basis for a claim. This is a technical reason why parties suffering from harm or damage caused by climate change have not brought claims up to now.
- For a claim based on tort to be successful, the defendant must be unable to prove that his/her actions were not 'culpable' (Article 1064(2), Civil Code). A Russian court sets the standard for an action to be considered 'culpable' at a relatively high level. This means that to establish culpability, evidential proof is required that the defendant had reasons to believe that the harm or damage would occur as a result of his/her actions.

Damages for harm to health and the environment

18.98 The EPL guarantees the right of citizens to claim for harm to the environment (Article 12(1)). Yet in practice, such claims are rare due to the problems in providing sufficient evidence.

18.99 In addition to the problems in providing sufficient evidence for a claim, claimants will have difficulties in proving quantum. Russian law generally limits damages to property damage

(Article 15, Civil Code) – that is, damage that has a value that can be expressed in monetary terms. Thus, for example, costs for medical treatment (e.g. due to increased respiratory illnesses) are unlikely to be easily quantifiable because the State health system, in theory, affords treatment free of charge.

18.100   The same difficulties would be faced if trying to establish sufficient quantitative evidence of damages to substantiate a claim for climate change liability, e.g. with respect to proving that a defendant contributed to climate change due to excessive GHG emissions and, thus, caused damage or harm to property or health.

18.101   Punitive damages or damages for suffering, including death, are not recognised under civil law. Accordingly, the ability to claim substantial sums in compensation for actions that harm the environment (including the climate) is very limited.

18.102   The continued decay of infrastructure causes an increased (and often underestimated) likelihood of accidents occurring and could expose the following parties to a risk of claims:
- local, municipal and federal agencies that finance and build public infrastructure in vulnerable areas, as well as those that own and operate vulnerable infrastructure;
- private investors and owners of vulnerable buildings and other physical property;
- property and casualty insurers;
- creditors holding vulnerable infrastructure directly or indirectly as collateral; and
- vulnerable businesses, NGOs, households and citizens.

18.103   These parties could potentially claim the following types of damages in the context of climate change proceedings:
- ecological damage;[105]
- economic damage;[106] and
- social damage.[107]

18.104   The general framework relating to damages, compensation and remedies is set out in Chapter 59 of the Civil Code.

---

[105] Article 8(21), Administrative Code.
[106] Article 14, EPL.
[107] Article 18, Federal Law № 68-FZ 'On Protection of Population and Territories from Environmental and Man-caused emergency situations', 21 December 1994.

Remedies

18.105 A court can order the payment of compensation to a claimant for loss directly caused by a company's breach of environmental legislation – if, for example, emission levels exceed those stated in a permit, or the chemical composition of emissions differs from those which are approved and defined in the company's permit, causing loss. In order to obtain compensation, the claimant(s) must prove they were negatively affected by the emissions (for example by presenting medical statements).

(D) Other law

Competition/anti-trust law

18.106 Russian competition and anti-trust laws are quite vague and their rules are generally based on the principle of determination of a market share or activities aimed at malicious prevention or limitation of competition.[108] From this perspective, entities engaged in fair activities aimed at increasing their competitive potential (e.g. by putting in place GHG-emission reduction measures) would be very unlikely to be treated as preventing or limiting competition under Russian legislation. Similarly, it is unlikely that those companies that do not put in place GHG-emission reduction measures would be treated as acting in an uncompetitive manner under Russian law.

18.107 In any event no party, other than the Federal Anti-Monopoly Service, is able to commence anti-monopoly proceedings, including, for example, with respect to any companies operating with high GHG emissions (which might therefore obtain an unfair advantage over competing companies which have reduced their GHG emissions in accordance with government policy).

Principles of international environmental law

18.108 Attempts have been made to integrate principles of international environmental law into general environmental law, including,

---

[108] Federal Law № 135-FZ 'On Competition Protection', 26 July 2006, as amended on 29 November 2010.

indirectly, the principle of preventative action, the polluter pays principle,[109] the principle (or concept) of sustainable development[110] and the precautionary principle. However, some authors argue that, despite these trends, Russian environmental law has remained much the same since Soviet times.[111]

18.109   Practice shows that a court would refrain from adjudicating solely based on the violation of the aforementioned principles, as they are considered 'vague', 'non-concrete' – and considered 'soft law'.[112]

Criminal law

18.110   Criminal law could be invoked by the State and others against those contravening environmental laws or failing to perform public duties.

18.111   Chapter 26 of the Criminal Code addresses 'ecological crimes'. Those that could potentially be of relevance to climate change liability include:
   (1) violation of the rules for environmental protection when performing work (Article 246);
   (2) violation of the rules for handling ecologically dangerous substances and wastes (Article 247);
   (3) pollution of the atmosphere (Article 251);
   (4) destruction of critical habitats for organisms entered in the Red Book of the Russian Federation (Article 259);
   (5) destruction or damaging of forests (Article 261); and
   (6) violation of the regime of specially protected nature territories and nature objects (Article 262).

18.112   There is no direct provision under criminal law which makes it a crime for a person to cause, or to fail to mitigate, climate change.

---

[109] E.g. Article 32, LAP.

[110] Presidential Decree № 236 'Concerning the State Strategy of the Russian Federation for the Protection of the Environment and the Ensuring of Sustainable Development', 4 February 1994; Presidential Decree № 440 'Concerning the Concept for the Transition of the Russian Federation to Sustainable Development', 1 April 1996; and see 1998 draft 'Strategy for Sustainable Development'.

[111] Nystén-Haarala, above n. 7, Mucklow, p. 105.

[112] S. A. Bogoliobov, *Ecological Law* (*Экологическое право*) (Moscow: HORMA, 2001), Учебник для вузов, www.bibliotekar.ru/ecologicheskoe-pravo-1/77.htm; see also (E) 'Soft' law above, at para. 18.114 ff.

18.113 The penalties for ecological crimes include fines, confiscation of property, obligatory works, imprisonment and limitations to hold certain official positions.[113] Most criminal cases, including any ecological crimes, are tried in the district (*rayonnyy*) courts.

(E)   'Soft' law

18.114 'Soft law' is not considered a source of law, nor is it likely to be applied or referred to directly by a judge in a Russian court. Officially, 'soft law' is not recognised as a source of law in the Russian judicial system. Despite this, principles contained in 'soft law' may, in some cases, be used by scholars and judges as part of an argument relating to public policy.[114]

International institutions

18.115 It is unlikely that institutions or treaties such as the OECD, CITES, United Nations Educational, Scientific and Cultural Organization ('UNESCO') World Heritage, the Equator Principles, or the United Nations Principles of Responsible Investment would be able to assist in Russian legal proceedings, whether dispute resolution, mediation or conciliation.

European Union

18.116 In 1994, Russia and the European Union concluded a Partnership and Cooperation Agreement ('PCA').[115] Since June 2008, negotiations have been under way for a new EU-Russia Agreement, which is to replace the PCA, but are yet to be concluded.[116] The new EU-Russia Agreement will include legally binding commitments in many areas, including economic cooperation, trade, investment and energy, and will also touch on climate change. However, the current draft Agreement does not address climate change liability matters.

---

[113] Above n. 1, Butler, p. 549.

[114] G. Ginsburgs, R. Clark and F. Feldbrugge, *International and National Law in Russia and Eastern Europe* (The Hague: Kluwer Law International, 2001), p. 462.

[115] EU-Russia Partnership and Co-operation Agreement, 24 June 1994; EIF, 30 October 1997.

[116] Negotiations have seen a new push following the EU-Russia Summit, 7 December 2010 (see www.consilium.europa.eu/uedocs/cms_data/docs/pressdata/en/ec/118284.pdf).

OECD

18.117   Russia is not a member of the OECD. However, during the first half of 2011, Russia has intensified its relations with the OECD, and over time this may lead to a different regulation of climate change liability.

Liability under public international law

18.118   Russia's potential liability relating to climate change under public international law is outside the scope of this chapter. It is unlikely that Russia will be a claimant in public international proceedings concerning international climate change liability.[117] Furthermore, there is the fundamental difficulty of identifying which forum would have jurisdiction in such proceedings.

18.119   Whilst Russia borders fourteen countries and has concluded a number of bilateral and regional agreements with neighbours and former Soviet countries, few of these international agreements (including the investment treaties) deal with environmental issues. Even in relation to the existing treaties with neighbouring countries, litigation is the exception, rather than the rule. Accordingly, the potential for international climate change litigation initiated by Russia appears to be low.

(F)   Legal practicalities

Founding jurisdiction

18.120   A party not resident or domiciled in Russia can be made party to proceedings in a Russian court under Article 4 of the Federal Law 'On the Legal Status of Non-Residents in the Russian Federation' 2005.[118] Non-residents in Russia have all the rights and responsibilities of residents under the law, except insofar as is specifically stated in federal law.

---

[117]   Russia has not commenced any legal proceedings at the International Court of Justice ('ICJ'), to date. Note, however, that in August 2008, the Republic of Georgia commenced proceedings against Russia at the ICJ for violations of the 1965 Convention on the Elimination of all Forms of Racial Discrimination, in the context of Russia's interventions in South-Ossetia and Abkhazia between 1990 and August 2008 (see www.icj-cij.org/docket/index.php?p1=3&code=GR&case=140&k=4d).

[118]   Federal Law № 115-FZ, 25 July 2005, as amended on 28 September 2010.

Enforcement

18.121   This chapter does not discuss enforcement of court judgments
          in Russia as the likelihood of a court judgment being issued with
          respect to climate change liability is extremely low.

Public interest litigation

18.122   There is no widespread culture or tradition of 'public interest liti-
          gation' in Russia, in the sense of legal proceedings commenced
          with the aim of benefiting the public at large. However, numerous
          cases have been litigated concerning environmental issues, espe-
          cially relating to instances in which the defendant is alleged to
          have harmed the environment, resulting in a detrimental impact
          on others' health.

Litigation costs

18.123   Litigation is usually funded by the party making the claim. Also,
          the unsuccessful party must reimburse the other party for legal
          costs incurred due to the proceedings. Costs are, however, reim-
          bursed at very low rates, which has the effect of discouraging
          litigation.

18.124   Article 48 of the Constitution sets out that citizens of limited
          means are entitled to free legal assistance. In practice, however,
          free legal representation for those of limited means (funded by
          the Government) is not easily available, is restricted, occurs
          infrequently and is usually provided in relation to criminal
          proceedings.

Obtaining information

18.125   Although Russia does have specific provisions for access to envir-
          onmental information, there is no law relating to freedom of
          information at the federal level. Russia has signed, but not yet
          ratified, the 1998 Aarhus Convention on Access to Information,
          Public Participation in Decision-Making and Access to
          Justice in Environmental Matters. Therefore, public access to

environmental information is hindered,[119] and the mechanisms for requesting and obtaining information from the authorities are underdeveloped, while the authorities rarely proactively disseminate information on their functions and activities to the public.

18.126   Despite the practical hurdles, Article 42 of the Constitution and Article 3 of the EPL proclaim everybody's right to reliable environmental information as one of the general principles of environmental protection (repeated in Article 11(1) of the EPL). Article 5 of the EPL provides that one of the responsibilities of governmental bodies is to deliver reliable environmental information to the population. Furthermore, Article 11(2) stipulates that such information is to be reliable, timely and up to date.

Immunity

18.127   Under the Constitution, all legal persons are equal before the law (Article 19). Thus, government and public institutions do not, by law, enjoy immunity from suit.[120] This is not to be confused with parliamentary immunity, a notion from constitutional law,[121] giving private persons – deputies and senators – the privilege to enjoy immunity from prosecution for (alleged) administrative or criminal offences.[122] In general, however, it is unusual for a government or public institution to be sued in court, in particular with respect to environmental matters.

(G)   Conclusion

18.128   This chapter shows that climate change has not been used as a ground for legal actions in Russia and that climate change liability proceedings are highly unlikely in the short-to-medium term. There is no specific regime in place that would enable such litigation, and the jurisprudence in this area has yet to develop.

---

[119] Centre for Environmental Information (EcoInfoCentre), St Petersburg (see www. ecocentrum.ru).

[120] There is personal immunity of Duma Deputies, high officials (Federal law № 3-FZ, 'On the status of a Federation Council member and the status of State Duma member', 8 May 1994), as well as the President of Russia (Article 91, Constitution).

[121] Article 98, Constitution.

[122] Federal Law № 3-FZ, (see n. 120 above).

North America

Canada

MEINHARD DOELLE, DENNIS MAHONY
AND ALEX SMITH

(A) Introduction

19.01 Climate change has gradually emerged as *the* environmental issue
in the eyes of the public in Canada over the past decade. It has also
become one of Canada's great political, social and economic challenges. This chapter provides a legal perspective on climate change
developments in Canada. The chapter starts out with a brief introduction to the legal and political context for climate liability and
litigation.[1] This is followed with a selection of key public law issues
that arise in the context of climate liability and litigation. Private law
issues are then explored, followed by legal issues that do not neatly
fit within the public/private law divide. Some concluding thoughts
are offered on the potential for climate litigation in Canada.

The Canadian legal system

19.02 Canada operates under a federal system of government, with jurisdiction shared under the Constitution between the federal and
provincial governments. The municipal level of government is
not recognised constitutionally; rather, it derives its powers from
the provinces through legislation. A fourth form, aboriginal governments, arises out of aboriginal self-government agreements
between the federal and provincial governments and Canada's
aboriginal peoples, usually in the context of comprehensive land
claim agreements.[2]

---

[1] For a more detailed exploration of some of the issues raised in this chapter, see J. Terry
and A. Smith, Chapter 16: 'Litigation' in D. Mahony (ed.), *The Law of Climate Change in
Canada* (Aurora: Canada Law Book, 2010).

[2] J. B. Laskin, J. Terry and A. Smith, Chapter 3: 'Climate Change and the Canadian
Constitution' in Mahony, *ibid.*, pp. 3–22.

19.03   Aboriginal interests, however, are not only protected through the creation of aboriginal self-government. The Crown has fiduciary duties to protect the interests of aboriginal peoples, as specifically recognised under section 35 of the Constitution Act, 1982.[3] Some of these fiduciary obligations arise out of treaties between the Crown and aboriginal peoples; others arise out of unextinguished aboriginal rights.[4]

19.04   Jurisdiction over climate change is generally accepted to be shared and in some cases split between the federal and provincial governments. The exact limits of federal and provincial jurisdiction remain a matter of debate among governments and legal commentators. To date, most of the noteworthy climate legislation and regulations have been passed by provincial governments, but it is clear that both levels of government have jurisdiction to implement measures to mitigate and adapt to climate change and to resolve issues of liability. Some of these powers and responsibilities may be shared with or delegated to municipal and aboriginal governments.[5]

19.05   Outside of Québec, Canada's legal system is modelled on the common law tradition. Common law principles, such as negligence, nuisance and strict liability, are recognised and applied by courts in Canada, though their precise scope and application may differ in some respects from other common law jurisdictions. As discussed below in (C) Private law at para. 19.45 ff, one significant deviation from the common law tradition exists in the province of Québec, which has a civil code in place of common law tort principles. The Supreme Court of Canada's decisions are binding in both systems.

---

[3] Being Schedule B to the Canada Act 1982 (UK), 1982, c. 11. In Canada, as in the United Kingdom, there is no single document that embodies the Constitution (P. Hogg, *Constitutional Law of Canada* (Toronto: Thomson Carswell, looseleaf), pp. 1–3). The phrase 'Constitution of Canada' is defined in section 52(2) of the Constitution Act, 1982. It includes, most importantly, the Constitution Act, 1982 and the Constitution Act, 1867, (UK), 30 & 31 Victoria, c. 3 (formerly named the British North America Act).

[4] *Ibid.* For a detailed assessment of the Crown duty under section 35, see C. MacIntosh, 'On Obligation and Contamination: The Crown-Aboriginal Relationship in the Context of Internationally-Sourced Infringements', *Saskatchewan Law Review*, 72 (2009), 223–56.

[5] *Ibid.*

19.06   Human rights are addressed in Canada in two ways. One is
         through the Charter of Rights and Freedoms, enshrined in
         Canada's Constitution and binding on all levels of government
         in Canada.[6] The other way is through provincial human rights
         legislation, which is generally applicable to private parties such
         as employers, landlords and many others. International human
         rights have been influential in shaping the development of human
         rights in Canada.[7]

The governmental stance on climate change

19.07   Canada has ratified the FCCC and the Kyoto Protocol. However,
         there has not been a serious effort nationally to meet the FCCC
         commitment to return to 1990 levels of emissions by 2000.
         Furthermore, the Government does not seem poised to meet its
         Kyoto obligation to reduce emissions to 6 per cent below 1990
         levels by 2012. Previous federal governments developed plans
         that could have enabled Canada to meet its Kyoto obligations
         through a combination of emission reductions and purchase of
         credits, but these plans were never fully implemented.

19.08   The current majority federal government has made it clear that it
         does not intend to meet Canada's Kyoto emission reduction com-
         mitments. Opposition parties have passed two climate change
         Bills in the House of Commons, against the will of the then
         minority government, to ensure compliance. One of the Bills was
         also passed by the Senate and has come into force.[8] However, nei-
         ther Bill has had a measurable effect on government policy on
         climate change.

19.09   Most provincial governments have developed and are in the pro-
         cess of implementing climate change mitigation plans. These
         provincial plans are collectively not sufficient to get Canada to
         its Kyoto target, but they have resulted in significant reductions
         in some parts of Canada. A number of provinces are making

---

[6] The Charter is contained in sections 1–34 of the Constitution Act, 1982. Section 52 of the
Constitution Act, 1982 provides that 'The Constitution of Canada is the supreme law of
Canada, and any law that is inconsistent with the provisions of the Constitution is, to the
extent of the inconsistency, of no force or effect.'

[7] *Baker* v. *Canada (Minister of Citizenship & Immigration)*, [1999] 2 S.C.R. 817 at para. 70.

[8] *Kyoto Protocol Implementation Act*, S.C. 2007, c. 30.

serious efforts to bring emissions under control, while others are only taking limited action.[9]

19.10   Canadian scholars and most commentators generally consider Canada's current international position to be weak and view it as hindering rather than assisting efforts toward an adequate and fair global effort.[10] Canada has indicated a willingness to reduce its emissions to 17 per cent below 2005 levels by 2020. This commitment is considerably less than the average reductions from developed countries that are necessary to avoid a global average temperature increase of over 2°C.[11] It is also less than Canada's existing commitments, such as its FCCC commitment and its Kyoto obligation for the first commitment period. Finally, Canada's proposed target for the post-2012 regime is considerably weaker than the targets offered by most other developed countries.[12]

National climate change risks

19.11   Per capita greenhouse gas ('GHG') emissions in Canada are among the highest in the world – about double the average per capita emissions in developed countries. The USA and Australia are the only developed countries with higher emissions on a per capita basis. Total emissions in Canada represent about 3 per cent of global emissions, placing Canada currently seventh in total emissions per country.[13]

19.12   The costs, benefits, risks and uncertainties surrounding climate change are distributed unevenly among Canadian provinces. In Alberta, Saskatchewan and Newfoundland, fossil fuel resources are considered to be integral to the provincial economy.

[9] Those making a serious effort to reduce emissions at the time of writing include British Columbia and Ontario. For an overview of provincial efforts, see generally Mahony, n. 1 above, pp. 5–1 to 11–40.

[10] See e.g. J. Simpson, M. Jaccard and N. Rivers, *Hot Air: Meeting Canada's Climate Change Challenge* (Toronto: McClelland & Stewart Ltd., 2007), pp. 33–110.

[11] IPCC, Fourth Assessment Report (2007), available at www.ipcc.ch/publications_and_data/publications_and_data_reports.shtml.

[12] M. Doelle and J. Terry, Chapter 2: 'International Framework' in Mahony, n. 1 above, pp 2–1 to 2–28.

[13] D. Mahony and T. Dyck, Chapter 4: 'Federal Climate Change Law and Policy' in Mahony, n. 1 above, p. 4–3.

Manufacturing is a key industrial sector in Ontario, most notably the automobile industry. Manitoba, Québec and British Columbia have access to large-scale hydro power. A number of provinces have significant potential to develop wind, tidal, geothermal or solar power. These and other differences create very diverse provincial circumstances, both in terms of the economic impact of mitigating climate change and the opportunities available to achieve reductions.[14]

19.13   The combination of the division of powers between the federal and provincial governments and regional differences has contributed greatly to the complexity of implementing climate change policy in Canada. Differences in terms of energy sources, access to mitigation options, and economic dependence on fossil fuel related industries in particular have created a very complex political context for domestic mitigation efforts and for international leadership alike.[15]

19.14   Another important part of the context for climate liability and the potential for litigation in Canada is that the climate is already changing significantly in parts of the country, and based on current predictions, most parts of Canada will encounter more severe adverse effects in the future. Northern parts of the country are experiencing significant changes in temperature, precipitation and sea ice, which are affecting ecosystems and northern aboriginal populations in particular. Sea level rise and more extreme storms are major concerns in coastal areas. Reduced precipitation is a particular concern in the Prairie provinces (Alberta, Saskatchewan and Manitoba). Impacts on forests, agriculture, water supplies, species at risk and native cultures are among the many other concerns. Adaptation strategies are still in their infancy.[16]

---

[14]   See S. Bernstein, J. Brunnée, D. Duff and A. Green, 'Introduction' in Bernstein *et al.* (eds.), *A Globally Integrated Climate Policy for Canada* (University of Toronto Press, 2007), pp. 23–6.

[15]   *Ibid*, p. 24.

[16]   See Natural Resources Canada, *Climate Change Impacts and Adaptation: A Canadian Perspective* (2004), at http://adaptation.nrcan.gc.ca/perspective/pdf/report_e.pdf; *From Impacts to Adaptation: Canada in a Changing Climate* (2007), at http://adaptation.nrcan.gc.ca/assess/2007/pdf/full-complet_e.pdf; and D. Sauchyn, H. P. Diaz and S. Kulshreshtha, *The New Normal: The Canadian Prairies in a Changing Climate* (University of Regina Publications, 2010).

19.15   In conclusion, the combination of high per capita emissions, Canada's international position, its relative domestic inaction and the high potential impacts, particularly in northern regions, coastal areas and the Prairies, means that there are fairly distinct circumstances for the consideration of climate liability and the potential for litigation in Canada. This combination of high per capita emissions and high potential impacts on particular communities may create opportunities for litigation that are specific to Canada if not unique. Within this context, a range of possibilities for climate liability and litigation in Canada are considered in the following sections of the chapter.

(B)   Public law

19.16   This section addresses the ways in which Canadian courts could strike down laws or reverse government decisions related to climate change. Canadian courts will strike down laws that violate the Constitution. A law is unconstitutional if it exceeds the legislative competence of the legislature that passed it, violates the Canadian Charter of Rights and Freedoms or unjustifiably infringes aboriginal rights protected by section 35 of the Constitution Act, 1982. Canadian courts could invalidate, reverse or otherwise alter government decisions or compel government action related to climate change by means of a process referred to as judicial review,[17] which must be initiated by the application of an interested party.

19.17   Those affected by legislation or government decisions involving climate change may resort to public law climate change litigation. It could be initiated by, among others, an environmental group seeking to compel government action on GHG emissions; a provincial government seeking to challenge the validity of climate change legislation passed by the federal Parliament; an individual claiming that his/her right to security of the person is being unjustifiably compromised by governments' failure to combat climate change; or a corporation seeking to challenge the validity of government action in respect of its interests.

---

[17] See paras. 17.13–17.33 above.

Grounds for judicial review

19.18   This section reviews the substantive grounds for such court
         actions, beginning with legislative competence to pass laws in
         respect of climate change, an area that remains untested under
         the Canadian Constitution. The following sections address
         standing and costs.

Constitutional challenges based on
legislative competence

19.19   Legislative authority is divided between Canada's federal
         Parliament and the provincial legislatures by the Constitution
         Act, 1867. Legislation and its derivative regulations can be chal-
         lenged on the basis that their subject matter falls outside of the
         legislative competence of the federal Parliament or provincial
         legislature that passed the legislation. The Constitution Act,
         1867 divides legislative jurisdiction primarily by allocating the
         authority to legislate in respect of 'matters' enumerated in 'classes
         of subjects', which are regularly referred to as 'heads of power'.
         For instance, the federal Parliament has exclusive jurisdiction
         to legislate in respect of matters that fall within its 'trade and
         commerce' power,[18] while provinces have exclusive jurisdiction
         to legislate in respect of 'property and civil rights within the
         province'.[19] Any legislation that is related to climate change or
         has climate change implications could be challenged on the basis
         that the legislature did not have constitutional authority to pass
         that legislation.

19.20   The environment, which is at the core of climate-related legisla-
         tion, is not an enumerated head of power under the Constitution.
         As a practical matter, the provinces have historically been the
         more dominant force in environmental regulation, relying pri-
         marily on their enumerated authority over property and civil
         rights within a province.[20] Nonetheless, the Supreme Court of
         Canada has held that the environment is 'a diffuse subject that

---

[18] The Constitution Act, 1867, n. 3 above, s. 91(2).

[19] *Ibid.*, s. 92(13).

[20] The leading scholar on Canadian constitutional law has described property and civil
      rights as 'by far the most important of the provincial heads of power' (Hogg, n. 3 above,
      p. 21–1.

cuts across many different areas of constitutional responsibility, some federal, some provincial',[21] and that environmental protection is a 'fundamental value in Canadian Society'.[22] The Court has recognised the 'all-important duty of Parliament and the provincial legislatures to make full use of the legislative powers respectively assigned to them in protecting the environment'.[23] These powers are to be interpreted in a manner that 'is fully responsive to emerging realities and to the nature of the subject matter sought to be regulated.'[24]

19.21   Federal authority to regulate climate change may therefore be rooted in an enumerated head of federal power,[25] or Parliament's residual power 'to make laws for the peace, order, and good government of Canada', or some combination of these powers.[26] If Parliament passed far-reaching climate change legislation, its constitutionality might be challenged by, among others, provincial governments seeking to protect, widen or clarify the scope of their legislative authority.

19.22   Jurisdictional challenges are becoming more likely as governments advance more initiatives related to climate change. The outcomes of such challenges will depend 'on how statutory schemes are constructed and the particular language used', and until the courts consider such legislation, constitutionality will remain 'at least somewhat speculative'.[27]

Constitutional challenges based on protected individual rights

19.23   Canadian courts will strike down legislation that violates the individual rights protected by the Charter of Rights and Freedoms.

---

[21] *R* v. *Hydro-Québec*, [1997] 3 S.C.R. 213 at p. 286.
[22] *Ontario* v. *Canadian Pacific Ltd.*, [1995] 2 S.C.R. 1031 at para. 55, affirmed in *114957 Canada Ltée (Spraytech, Société d'arrosage)* v. *Hudson (Town)*, [2001] 2 S.C.R. 241 at para. 1.
[23] *R* v. *Hydro-Québec*, [1997] 3 S.C.R. 213 at p. 267
[24] *Ibid.*
[25] Possibilities include the criminal law, trade and commerce or sea coast and inland fisheries powers.
[26] *Friends of the Oldman River Society* v. *Canada (Minister of Transport)*, [1992] 1 S.C.R. 3 at p. 81.
[27] A. Lucas, 'Legal Constraints and Opportunities: Climate Change and the Law' in H. G. Coward (ed.), *Hard Choices: Climate Change in Canada* (Waterloo: Wilfred Laurier University Press, 2004), p. 179.

Thus far, courts have not held that any government legislation related to climate change violates individuals' Charter rights.[28]

19.24   One of the sections of the Charter likely to be considered in the context of climate change litigation is section 7, which provides that everyone has 'the right to life, liberty and security of the person and the right not to be deprived thereof except in accordance with the principles of fundamental justice'.[29] Because climate change has the potential to endanger safety, legislation that threatens (or, conversely, fails to protect) individual Canadians from such effects could theoretically be challenged under section 7 of the Charter.

19.25   As the law currently stands, a section 7 analysis requires a finding that there has been a deprivation of the right to life, liberty or security of the person, as well as finding that the deprivation is contrary to the principles of fundamental justice.[30] Almost without exception, the rights protected by section 7 have been connected to the criminal law. The Supreme Court of Canada has, however, split on whether section 7's guarantee of life and security of the person is engaged by a prohibition against contracting for private health insurance in the context of excessive waiting times for treatment in the public system.[31] By analogy, section 7 rights may eventually be found to be engaged by government

---

[28]   Federal and provincial environmental assessment approvals are prerequisites for the construction of many high-emitting facilities and infrastructure projects, such as oil sands extraction facilities, coal-fired power plants, and new roads. It has been suggested that government approvals arguably permit the private conduct that contributes to CC, and that CC effects experienced by plaintiffs may therefore qualify as 'state-sponsored environmental harm' (L. M. Collins, 'An Ecologically Literate Reading of the Canadian Charter of Rights and Freedoms', *Windsor Review of Legal and Social Issues*, 26 (2009), 7–48 at 18); 'Tort, Democracy and Environmental Governance: Crown Liability for Environmental Non-Enforcement', *Tort Law Review*, 15 (2007), 107–26; and D. N. Scott, 'Confronting Chronic Pollution: A Socio-Legal Analysis of Risk and Precaution', *Osgoode Hall Law Journal*, 46(2) (2008), 293–343.

[29]   Constitution Act, n. 3 above, at s. 7.

[30]   *R* v. *Beare*, [1988] 2 S.C.R. 387 at para. 28.

[31]   *Chaoulli* v. *Québec (Attorney General)*, [2005] 1 S.C.R. 791 at para. 102. Three judges of the court, including the Chief Justice of Canada, held that 'because patients may be denied timely health care for a condition that is clinically significant to their current and future health, s. 7 protection of security of the person is engaged' (*ibid.*, at para. 123). Where the lack of timely healthcare can result in death, the same was held to be the case with respect to section 7's protection of life. One of the seven judges on the panel did not rule on this issue.

legislation in respect of climate change that endangers the lives or the security of the person of Canadians. It must be emphasised that this is not currently the state of the law, but development of this branch of the 'living tree' that is the Constitution would not necessarily be at odds with Canada's constitutional tradition.[32]

19.26   A further extension of the section 7 jurisprudence would involve the recognition of a positive right, constitutionally requiring action on the part of the State, to a natural environment devoid of the dangers to life and security of the person posed by climate change.[33] It is somewhat difficult to envisage an appropriate fact scenario or to predict whether such a right would be recognised in the context of climate change litigation.

19.27   In addition to empowering courts to strike down legislation, the Charter provides that anyone whose rights or freedoms have been infringed or denied may apply to a court of competent jurisdiction to obtain such remedy as the court considers appropriate and just in the circumstances,[34] including awarding monetary damages.[35]

---

[32] The Constitution of Canada has been held to be a 'living tree' that changes with time (*Edwards* v. *Canada (Attorney General)*, [1930] A.C. 124). Charter rights can evolve in the face of changing circumstances (L. Arbour and F. LaFontaine, 'Beyond Self-Congratulation: The *Charter* at 25 in an International Perspective', *Osgoode Hall Law Journal*, 45(2) (2007), 239–75).

[33] See *Ontario* v. *Canadian Pacific*, [1995] 2 S.C.R. 1031 at para. 55; and *R* v. *Hydro-Québec*, [1997] 3 S.C.R. 213 at para. 124. As was noted in Justice Arbour's dissenting opinion in *Gosselin* v. *Québec (Attorney General)*, 'the grammatical structure of s. 7 seems to indicate that it protects two rights: a right, set out in the section's first clause, to "life, liberty and security of the person"; and a right, set out in the second clause, not to be deprived of life, liberty or security of the person except in accordance with the principles of fundamental justice' ([2002] 4 S.C.R. 429 at para. 340). The majority of the Court in *Gosselin* held that the first clause of section 7 does not impose a positive obligation on the State to protect the security of the person by, in that case, guaranteeing adequate living standards to those without other adequate sources of income. Chief Justice McLachlin, writing for the majority, was nonetheless careful to leave open the possibility that the development of the 'living tree' that is the Constitution might one day result in section 7 being 'interpreted to include positive obligations' (*ibid.*, at para. 82). The door is thus ajar, at least in theory, to the judicial recognition of positive constitutional obligations on the State to protect individuals' life and security of the person.

[34] Constitution Act, 1982, n. 3 above, at s. 24(1).

[35] See *Canada (Attorney General)* v. *Hislop*, [2007] 1 S.C.R. 429 at para. 81; and *Doe* v. *Metropolitan Toronto (Municipality) Commissioners of Police* (1998), 39 O.R. (3d) 487 (Ont. S.C.) at para. 205.

Constitutional challenges based on aboriginal rights

19.28   Section 35 of the Constitution Act, 1982 recognises and affirms
the existing aboriginal and treaty rights of the aboriginal peoples of Canada.[36] The recognition of aboriginal treaty rights does
not amount to a guarantee of those rights; the Supreme Court of
Canada has held that aboriginal rights can be infringed where
the infringement is justified with reference to a broad range of
'compelling and substantial' legislative objectives.[37] The test for
justification of an infringement is that 'a legislative objective
must be attained in such a way as to uphold the honour of the
Crown and be in keeping with the unique contemporary relationship, grounded in history and policy, between the Crown
and Canada's aboriginal peoples'.[38]

19.29   One of the more important implications of constitutionally protected treaty rights is the obligation to consult with aboriginal
peoples before decisions are made respecting aboriginal lands.[39]
Aboriginal peoples could therefore challenge federal or provincial climate change legislation that has an impact on aboriginal
lands if that legislation unjustifiably infringed constitutionally
recognised treaty rights or if the government, in making the legislation, failed to meet its duty to consult with aboriginal peoples.

19.30   Beyond the duty to consult, section 35 has the potential to reveal
substantive duties on the Crown with respect to climate change
mitigation, adaptation and liability. The starting point for any
such legal argument is that under section 35 the Crown owes a
fiduciary duty to aboriginal peoples in Canada.[40] The scope of the
Crown's duty was first explored by the Supreme Court of Canada
in *R* v. *Sparrow*[41] and has since been elaborated in a trilogy of

---

[36] The aboriginal rights thus recognised and affirmed are those that had not been extin-
guished by legislation as of the proclamation into force of the Constitution Act, 1982 on
17 April 1982. Rights subsequently acquired through land claims agreements (which are
later day treaty rights by another name) are also protected by section 35.

[37] *R* v. *Sparrow*, [1990] 1 S.C.R. 1075 at p. 1113.

[38] *Ibid.*, at para. 1110.

[39] *Haida Nation* v. *British Columbia (Minister of Forests)*, [2004] 3 S.C.R. 511 at para. 10; and
Taku River Tlingit First Nation v. *British Columbia (Project Assessment Director)*, [2004] 3
S.C.R. 550 at para. 21.

[40] The Crown's fiduciary duty in respect of aboriginal lands surrendered to the Crown was
first recognised in *Guerin* v. *The Queen*, [1984] 2 S.C.R. 335 at p. 376.

[41] [1990] 1 S.C.R. 1075.

cases: *R* v. *VanderPeet*,[42] *R* v. *Smokehouse*[43] and *R* v. *Gladstone*.[44] This jurisprudence establishes that among the aboriginal rights to be protected by the Crown under section 35 are the rights to natural resources and cultural rights. Many of the resources that aboriginal peoples rely on for sustenance, culture and to earn a modest livelihood are threatened by climate change, especially for aboriginal peoples in northern Canada.

19.31   Given the Crown's duty to protect these aboriginal rights, the most straightforward legal argument for a substantive duty concerning climate change would be to establish the existence of a duty to avoid actions that would worsen the impacts of climate change on aboriginal rights. Whether section 35 goes further to impose a legal obligation on the Crown to take action to prevent or minimise the impacts of climate change is an interesting and as of yet unanswered legal question. An extension of the latter approach to the Crown's duty would be a responsibility to assist with adaptation to climate change and potential liability for the resulting impacts to vulnerable aboriginal peoples. Among the steps that could be required to comply with such a duty are active mitigation of emissions in Canada, the pursuit of international agreements for effective mitigation and assistance with adaptation. The case law in this area is still relatively new, making any firm prediction about its future direction difficult.[45]

Judicial review of regulatory decisions

19.32   In Canada, statutes enacted by the federal and provincial legislatures have created administrative authorities with powers to regulate, including matters related to climate change. As an example, new industrial projects require a variety of approvals from regulators, which often involve environmental assessments by specialised boards, commissions, tribunals or government officials. Depending on the nature of the project, it may require

---

[42] [1996] 2 S.C.R. 507.   [43] [1996] 2 S.C.R. 672.   [44] [1996] 2 S.C.R. 723.

[45] For an overview of the issues involved in pursuing this kind of legal argument in the context of a case study on mercury contamination of country foods, see C. MacIntosh, 'On Obligation and Contamination: The Crown-Aboriginal Relationship in the Context of Internationally-Sourced Infringements', *Saskatchewan Law Review*, 72 (2009), 187–220. See also P. Macklem, 'Aboriginal Rights and State Obligations', *Alberta Law Review*, 36 (1997–1998), 97–116.

approval from both federal and provincial authorities. Where governing legislation does not validly prohibit it, affected parties can apply to have these decisions judicially reviewed.[46] Applicants can in this way challenge regulatory decisions with climate change implications before the courts.

19.33   Regulatory decisions challenged on judicial review are afforded considerable deference by Canadian courts, largely on the basis that specialised regulatory bodies have expertise of a kind that courts do not possess. As a general matter, Canadian courts conducting judicial reviews of regulatory decisions are primarily concerned with ensuring that regulators act within the scope of their delegated authority, interpret the law correctly and do not make decisions based on erroneous assessments of the relevant facts.

19.34   The test applied by a court in evaluating a regulatory decision is called the standard of review. There are two standards of review that have been elaborated in the case law across a broad range of circumstances: correctness and reasonableness.[47] The 'reasonableness' test is generally applied to fact-finding and questions of law within the 'particular expertise' of the tribunal,[48] while the 'correctness' test is generally applied to questions of law 'outside the adjudicator's specialised area of expertise.'[49] Government decisions can also be reversed or set aside on the basis that they violate procedural fairness.[50]

19.35   The most conceptually straightforward type of judicial review involves a challenge to the validity of a regulatory decision. Environmental groups recently brought such a challenge to a panel's recommendation that a major development in the Alberta oil sands receive environmental approval from the federal Department of Fisheries and Oceans. The panel had concluded, among other things, that the mitigation measures proposed by the project's proponents would make significant adverse

---

[46] The remedies available on judicial review include orders of *certiorari* and *mandamus*, injunctions and damages (D. P. Jones and A. S. de Villars, *Principles of Administrative Law*, 5th edn (Toronto: Carswell, 2009), pp. 10–13).

[47] *Dunsmuir* v. *New Brunswick*, [2008] 1 S.C.R. 190 at para. 34.

[48] *Ibid.*, at para. 54.

[49] *Toronto (City)* v. *C.U.P.E.*, [2003] 3 S.C.R. 77 at para. 62

[50] Jones and de Villars, n. 46 above, p. 392.

environmental effects unlikely. On judicial review, the Federal Court of Canada held that the panel's decision was not reasonable, because it had not provided a rationale for this conclusion.[51] The court remitted the matter back to the panel and required that the panel explain how the project's proposed mitigation measures would reduce GHG emissions to a level of insignificance. The panel subsequently articulated why it was not concerned about the environmental impact of the project, and the project proceeded.[52]

19.36   In an appropriate legislative context, an applicant can seek, on judicial review, to compel a government to regulate. Judicial reviews of this kind have been brought in relation to climate change, notably in the US case of *Massachusetts* v. *Environmental Protection Agency*.[53] In Canada, a comparable remedy was sought by the applicants in *Friends of the Earth* v. *Canada (Minister of the Environment)*.[54] This judicial review was brought under provisions of the Kyoto Protocol Implementation Act (the 'KPIA'), including a section requiring the Minister of the Environment to make regulations within 180 days that would 'ensure that Canada fully meets its obligations' under the Kyoto Protocol.[55] The KPIA was a private members Bill supported by all opposition parties in a minority Parliament. It was the government's stated policy that Canada should not attempt to meet its obligations under the Kyoto Protocol because doing so would severely damage the Canadian economy. The Federal Court of Canada held that it was not the intention of Parliament to create a justiciable duty to regulate, and expressed doubt that the Court had 'any role to play in controlling or directing the other branches of government in

---

[51] *Pembina Institute for Appropriate Development* v. *Canada (Attorney General)*, 2008 FC 302 at paras. 73 and 79.

[52] In the meantime, however, the Federal Court's remittance of the decision invalidated another required approval and may have delayed its development.

[53] 549 U.S. 497 (2007). The United States Supreme Court held that Section 202(a)(1) of the Federal Clean Air Act, 42 U.S.C. § 7521(a)(1) required the Environmental Protection Agency to formulate a judgment as to whether certain emissions 'may reasonably be anticipated to endanger public health or welfare'. The Court further held that if the EPA concluded there was an endangerment, the EPA was required to make regulations in respect of those emissions.

[54] 2008 FC 1183, aff'd by 2009 FCA 297, leave to appeal to the Supreme Court of Canada refused, [2009] S.C.C.A. No. 497.

[55] S.C. 2007, c. 30, s. 7(1)(a).

the conduct of their legislative and regulatory functions' outside of the constitutional context.[56] The Court was clearly mindful of the fact that the Members of Parliament in the opposition who passed the KPIA had the remedy of defeating the Government and bringing about an election if they so chose, and this political reality appears to have informed the Court's construction of the statute. The Court also appears to have been influenced by the absence of an effective remedy that would actually lead to compliance with Canada's Kyoto obligations.

19.37   A somewhat similar potential challenge relates to section 166 of the Canadian Environmental Protection Act.[57] Among other obligations, the section requires the Minister to act when the Minister has reason to believe that a substance released from a source in Canada contributes to air pollution that violates an international agreement. The section would appear to create obligations on the Minister, if a sufficient link could be established between a source and Canada's violation of the Kyoto Protocol.[58] Issues of standard of review and justiciability similar to the *Friends of the Earth* case would undoubtedly arise if such a case were to be brought forward.

Standing: who may challenge the constitutionality of legislation?

19.38   In order to have standing to challenge the constitutionality of legislation, a person in Canada 'need only to show that he is affected by it directly or that he has a genuine interest as a citizen in the validity of the legislation and that there is no other reasonable and effective manner in which the issue may be brought before the Court'.[59]

---

[56] 2008 FC 1183 at para. 40.   [57] S.C. 1999, c. 33.

[58] Another similar remedy is provided by the Ontario Environmental of Bill of Rights, 1993 S.O. 1993, c. 28, s. 61(1) and (2), which creates a right to apply to the Environmental Commissioner for a review of a new or existing 'policy, Act, regulation or instrument of Ontario' in order to protect the environment. This legislation imposes an obligation on government ministries to respond meaningfully to such applications.

[59] *Canadian Council of Churches* v. *Canada (Minister of Employment and Immigration)*, [1992] 1 S.C.R. 236 at p. 250, affirming *Minister of Justice of Canada* v. *Borowski*, [1981] 2 S.C.R. 575. It is not clear whether and to what extent persons outside Canada can have standing to challenge the constitutionality of legislation.

19.39   Corporations can have standing to challenge legislative compe-
         tence. While corporations have sometimes been granted stand-
         ing to challenge the constitutionality of offences with which they
         have been charged, this does not necessarily mean that they can
         benefit from a finding that the provisions violate a natural per-
         son's constitutional rights.[60]

19.40   In certain circumstances, public interest organisations can chal-
         lenge legislation on the grounds that it violates the Charter of
         Rights and Freedoms.[61] Plaintiffs seeking public interest stand-
         ing to bring a Charter challenge must show they are raising a ser-
         ious issue about the validity of the impugned legislation, that the
         plaintiff has a genuine interest in the legislation's validity, and
         that there is not another reasonable and effective way to bring the
         issue before the court. The courts, however, prefer to give stand-
         ing to individuals (natural or corporate) and so will deny public
         interest standing if it can be shown on a balance of probabilities
         that a private litigant will challenge the legislation.[62]

19.41   Organisations that are not parties to litigation involving Charter
         issues, but whose concerns may be affected by its outcome, can
         seek standing in the litigation as a friend of the court. To be rec-
         ognised as a friend of the court, an organisation must show that
         its intervention will not prejudice the parties, offer a different
         perspective, and result in relevant and useful submissions that
         will help the court to fairly decide the issues before it.[63]

Costs

19.42   In Canada, the general rule concerning costs is that the suc-
         cessful party in litigation is entitled to recover litigation costs
         from the unsuccessful party, but the amount recovered is

---

[60] See *Irwin Toy Ltd.* v. *Québec (Attorney General)*, [1989] 1 S.C.R. 927 at para. 95; and *R* v. *Wholesale Travel Group Inc.*, [1991] 3 S.C.R. 154 at paras. 167 and 172.

[61] See e.g. *Downtown Eastside Sex Workers United Against Violence Society* v. *Canada (Attorney General)*, 2010 BCCA 439 at para. 70.

[62] *Canadian Council of Churches* v. *Canada (Minister of Employment and Immigration)*, n. 59 above, at p. 252. The Court stressed that 'the recognition of the need to grant public interest standing in some circumstances does not amount to a blanket approval to grant standing to all who wish to litigate an issue'.

[63] *Pinet* v. *Penetanguishene Mental Health Centre (Administrator)*, 2006 CanLII 4952 (ON S.C.) at para. 35.

subject to rules and the discretion of the court.[64] Some of the factors that can be considered by courts in assigning costs include the apportionment of liability, the complexity of the proceeding, the importance of the issues and the conduct of the parties.[65]

19.43 In Charter cases, the court can also consider the public interest in its determination regarding costs. Even an unsuccessful plaintiff may be awarded costs because he/she is 'fulfilling a civil responsibility' by bringing to the court's attention a serious matter that he/she believes impacts on 'the human rights of the members of the community'.[66] Furthermore, there are avenues available in Canada for advanced cost awards in appropriate circumstances.[67]

(C) Private law

19.44 This section addresses private litigation related to climate change that could be brought in Canada. Private law, as it is

---

[64] In Ontario, for instance, section 131(1) of the Courts of Justice Act, R.S.O. 1990, c. C.43 provides that, subject to the court's Rules of Civil Procedure, R.R.O. 1990, Reg. 194, the costs of a proceeding or a step in a proceeding 'are in the discretion of the court, and the court may determine by whom and to what extent the costs shall be paid'. Some courts, including Ontario's, assign maximum amounts recoverable per hour on a rising scale based on the number of years the billing lawyer has been practising law. These maximum amounts can be considerably less than the amounts actually paid to counsel. In circumstances where the conduct of an unsuccessful party warrants it, costs may be awarded at a higher level. In Ontario, the higher costs scale, 'substantial indemnity costs', are one-and-a-half times the amount of regular 'partial indemnity' costs (Rules of Civil Procedure, R.R.O. 1990, Reg. 194, Rule 1.03(1)). In the Federal Court costs can be set with reference to a tariff table, but the Court retains 'full discretionary power over the amount and allocation of costs' (Federal Courts Act, R.S.C. 1985, c. F-7, s. 400(1) and (4)). For an example of the Federal Court disregarding the tariff amount, see *Air Canada* v. *Toronto Port Authority and Porter Airlines*, 2010 FC 1335 at paras. 14–16.

[65] See Rules of Civil Procedure, n. 64 above, Rule 57.01.

[66] *Grushman* v. *Ottawa (City)*, [2000] O.J. No. 4884 (QL) (Div. Ct.) at para. 7. See also *Schachter* v. *Canada*, [1992] 2 S.C.R. 679 at para. 106; *Allman* v. *Northwest Territories (Commissioner)*, [1983] N.W.T.R. 231 at p. 321; *Valpy* v. *Ontario (Commission on Election Finances)*; and *Canadian Association for Children, Youth and the Law* v. *Canada (Attorney General)*, [2004] 1 S.C.R. 76 at para. 69.

[67] It is generally recognised that courts have discretion to grant such orders under appropriate circumstances to litigants acting in the public interest. For a detailed discussion of the issue of costs in Canada, see C. Tollefson, 'Cost in Public Interest Litigation: Recent Developments and Future Directions', *Advocates Quarterly*, 35 (2009), 181–200.

understood here, 'is concerned principally with the mutual rights and obligations of individuals', including corporations.[68] The private law actions considered in this section arise primarily in tort, but also in the context of securities law. Tort law in Canada is common (or judge-made) law, while securities law is shaped by legislation. This section also discusses the possibility of actions under the public trust doctrine.

Tort litigation

19.45   Outside of Québec, where the Civil Code of Québec governs,[69] Canadian tort law is rooted in English common law. Certain English tort cases remain important, and in recent decades the influence of American jurisprudence has increased. However, the general trend has been towards increased Canadian judicial independence in this area, with the main features of Canadian tort law being shaped by the Supreme Court of Canada.[70]

19.46   The Supreme Court has held that one of the goals of tort law is to create 'a disincentive to risk-creating behaviour',[71] and this quasi-regulatory aspect of tort law could prove significant if a court concluded in the right circumstances that climate change was not adequately regulated. Climate change tort litigation actions could be brought in negligence, conspiracy, strict liability, or public or private nuisance.[72] Such actions would raise common issues in respect of standing, causation, proximity and damages. Defendants could include oil sands developers, power companies and other large industrial emitters, including federal and provincial governments.

---

[68] S. Waddams, *Dimensions of Private Law: Categories and Concepts in Anglo-American Legal Reasoning* (Cambridge University Press, 2003), p. 1. Private law also includes 'government agencies in many of their relations to citizens' (*ibid.*). An example of a private law action involving government would be a claim brought by a government agency against a company for breach of contract.

[69] The source of civil liability in Québec is the broadly worded duty not to cause injury established by Article 1457 of the Civil Code of Québec. The principles that inform the Article 1457 analysis in Québec are substantially similar to the principles that inform the common law analysis that is applied in the rest of Canada, and in both contexts the Supreme Court of Canada's decisions are binding.

[70] The decisions of the Supreme Court of Canada are binding on all Canadian courts.

[71] *Resurface Corp. v. Hanke*, [2007] 1 S.C.R. 333 at para. 6.

[72] For nuisance and negligence, see Chapter 17 at 17.42–17.50.

19.47   Plaintiffs in climate change tort litigation could include Inuit and
         First Nations groups; property owners suing under class action
         legislation to recover for damage to property that they believe is
         due to climate change attributable to major emitters of GHGs;
         public interest litigants concerned about the environmental con-
         sequences of climate change; or even the Crown in its capacity of
         parens patriae.[73]

Tort actions

Negligence: the *Anns* test in Canada[74]

19.48   The tort of negligence imposes liability for harm caused as a result
         of unreasonable acts or omissions.[75] Negligence is the primary
         means by which Canadian courts have recognised new forms of
         tort liability since the House of Lords' 1932 decision in *Donoghue*
         v. *Stevenson*.[76] The categories of negligence are never closed, and
         as a result of its evolving and expanding nature, negligence is the
         most important tort in Canadian society.[77] Negligence would
         likely be pleaded in most climate change tort actions.

19.49   The test for negligence in Canada requires that there be a duty of
         care owed by the defendant to the plaintiff, and that the defend-
         ant failed to meet the requisite standard of care. To determine
         whether there was a duty of care, a court must apply the two-
         stage *Anns* test as it has been developed by the House of Lords
         and subsequently elucidated by the Supreme Court of Canada.
         In stage one, a prima facie duty of care arises if the plaintiff can
         establish foreseeability and proximity; that is, the court deter-
         mines whether the harm that occurred was a reasonably fore-
         seeable consequence of the defendant's act. The Supreme Court

---

[73] In *British Columbia* v. *Canadian Forest Products Ltd*, [2004] 2 S.C.R. 74 the Court characterised the Crown's *parens patriae* jurisdiction as follows: 'Since the time of de Bracton it
has been the case that public rights and jurisdiction over these cannot be separated from
the Crown. This notion of the Crown as holder of inalienable "public rights" in the environment and certain common resources was accompanied by the procedural right of the
Attorney General to sue for their protection representing the Crown as *parens patriae*'
(*ibid.*, at para. 76).

[74] In *Cooper* v. *Hobart*, [2001] 3 S.C.R. 537, the Supreme Court of Canada unanimously held
that the *Anns* test remained the law in Canada despite its abandonment by the House of
Lords: see Chapter 17 at 17.46–17.50.

[75] For a general discussion of negligence principles, see Chapter 17 at 17.46–17.50.

[76] [1932] A.C. 562.

[77] L. Klar, *Remedies in Tort* (Toronto: Carswell, looseleaf), 16.I-37, §2.

has held that 'The proximity analysis involved at the first stage of the *Anns* test focuses on factors arising from the *relationship* between the plaintiff and the defendant.'[78] In stage two, the court looks at 'whether there are residual policy considerations outside the relationship of the Parties that may negative the imposition of a duty of care'.[79]

To establish foreseeability in the context of an action related to climate change, the court will be called upon to determine 'whether the plaintiff is so closely and directly affected by the emissions or other acts of the defendant that the defendant ought reasonably to have the plaintiff in contemplation as being affected by those acts'.[80]

To establish proximity,[81] a plaintiff can show that the case falls into one of the existing categories of negligence that recognise proximity.[82] If the plaintiff's case does not fall into an existing category of negligence, then a relationship of proximity can be established by showing that the law of negligence should be extended to recognise a newly proposed category of negligence based on the relationship existing between the plaintiff and the defendant. In this way, the proximity analysis allows for the expansion of the categories of negligence 'to meet new circumstances and evolving conceptions of justice'.[83]

19.50   Where a duty of care is established, the plaintiff must also show that the defendant failed to meet the standard of care applicable in the circumstances. The Supreme Court of Canada has characterised the standard of care as follows:

> a person must exercise the standard of care that would be expected of an ordinary, reasonable and prudent person in the same circumstances.

---

[78] *Cooper* v. *Hobart*, n. 74 above, at para. 30.

[79] *Ibid.*

[80] Terry and Smith, n. 1 above, at p. 16–6. For a general discussion of foreseeability, see 17.66–17.71.

[81] Proximity is 'a broad concept which is capable of subsuming different categories of cases involving different factors' (*Canadian National Railway Co.* v. *Norsk Pacific Steamship Co.*, [1992] 1 S.C.R. 1021, cited in *Cooper* v. *Hobart*, n. 74 above, at para. 35). The focus on the proximity analysis is 'on the relationship between alleged wrongdoer and victim: is the relationship one where the imposition of legal liability for the wrongdoer's actions is appropriate?' (*Hill* v. *Hamilton-Wentworth Regional Police Services Board*, [2007] 3 S.C.R. 129, at para. 23).

[82] *Cooper* v. *Hobart*, n. 74 above, at para. 23.

[83] *Hill* v. *Hamilton-Wentworth Regional Police Services Board*, n. 81 above, at para. 25.

The measure of what is reasonable depends on the facts of each case, including the likelihood of a known or foreseeable harm, the gravity of that harm and the burden or cost which would be incurred to prevent the injury. In addition, one may look to external indicators of reasonable conduct, such as custom, industry practice, and statutory or regulatory standards.[84]

Each of these factors could be relevant in negligence actions brought in respect of climate change and influence the standard of care applicable.

19.51   A negligence claim in respect of climate change could be based on an existing or new category of negligence. No claim for damages resulting from climate change has been brought under an existing category of negligence, and no new category of negligence based on climate change has been argued to date before Canadian courts. Establishing proximity, which to some extent is an exercise in results-oriented reasoning on the part of courts, would likely be a crucial challenge for any claimant seeking a remedy for negligent contribution to climate change.

Conspiracy

19.52   The test for proving the tort of conspiracy requires agreement between two or more persons, an unlawful activity, the intent or likelihood that the unlawful activity would cause damage, and actual damage.[85] The tort of conspiracy has not been pleaded in respect of climate change before Canadian courts, but such claims have been brought, so far without success, in the United States.[86] Proving all elements of the tort could be challenging, but if proven, planned and deliberate wrongful conduct may lead to the imposition of punitive damages.[87]

Private nuisance

19.53   Nuisance is 'the unreasonable interference with the use of land'.[88] In a decision of the Supreme Court of Canada under Québec civil

---

[84]   *Ryan* v. *Victoria (City)*, [1999] 1 S.C.R. 201 at para. 28.
[85]   *Cement LaFarge* v. *B.C. Lightweight Aggregate*, [1983] 1 S.C.R. 452 at pp. 471–2.
[86]   *Native Village of Kivalina* v. *ExxonMobil*, Case No. CV-08–1138, filed 26 February 2008; *Comer* v. *Murphy Oil USA*, No. 07–60756 (5th Cir., 16 Oct 2009).
[87]   See *Whiten* v. *Pilot Insurance Co.*, [2002] 1 S.C.R. 595, at para. 113.
[88]   *St Lawrence Cement* v. *Barrette*, [2008] 3 S.C.R. 392 at para. 77 (see also Chapter 17 at 17.42–17.45).

law, the court held that 'nuisance is a field of liability that focuses on the harm suffered'[89] and that no-fault liability 'furthers environmental protection objectives' and 'reinforces the application of the polluter-pays principle'.[90] An advantage of suing in nuisance rather than negligence is that plaintiffs would not need to establish that the defendant owed a duty of care and failed to meet the standard of care. No private nuisance claims have been brought in Canada in respect of damages allegedly due to climate change.

19.54   Private nuisance may be well-suited to environmental class actions.[91] In a recent Ontario trial of the common issues in an environmental class action, the Ontario Superior Court of Justice ruled that plaintiffs had a cause of action in private nuisance arising from the defendant's contamination of the soil on the plaintiffs' property.[92] A similar action could be brought in respect of climate change.

Strict liability

19.55   Strict liability will be imposed when the 'non-natural use of land' leads to the 'escape' of something that causes harm. The Supreme Court of Canada has held that non-natural use is 'a flexible concept that is capable of adjustment to the changing patterns of existence',[93] but it is not clear how it would be applied in the context of climate change litigation.[94]

Public nuisance

19.56   The tort of public nuisance allows the Crown, as *parens patriae*, to sue for relief from interferences with 'the exercise of clear public rights, such as navigation, fishing or access to roads or

---

[89] *Ibid.*   [90] *Ibid.*, para. 80

[91] Class actions allow a class of plaintiffs to proceed against a defendant on issues common to the class, and are governed by legislation. See e.g. Ontario Class Proceedings Act, 1992, S.O. 1992, c. 6. In order for a class to be certified under this legislation the court must conclude that a class action is the preferable procedure for resolving common issues, which is determined with reference to the 'three accepted goals of a class proceeding: judicial economy, access to justice and behaviour modification' (*Pearson* v. *Inco Ltd., et al.*, 2006 CanLII 913 (ON C.A.) at para. 25, leave to appeal to the S.C.C. refused 265 D.L.R. (4th), vii).

[92] *Smith* v. *Inco*, 2010 ONSC 3790 (certified as *Pearson* v. *Inco*).

[93] *Tock* v. *St. John's Metropolitan Area Board*, [1989] 2 S.C.R. 1181 at p. 1189.

[94] See also 17.66.

waterways'.[95] The relief sought is generally injunctive relief: for instance, a defendant could be ordered to stop blocking a public highway.[96]

19.57 While the Supreme Court of Canada has characterised public nuisance as 'a poorly understood area of the law',[97] it has also characterised *parens patriae* as 'an important jurisdiction that should not be attenuated by a narrow judicial construction'.[98] The court has also suggested in *obiter dicta* that by suing in public nuisance, provincial governments may be able to win injunctive relief or compensation in respect of environmental damage to public lands.[99]

19.58 No public nuisance suits in respect of climate change have been brought in Canada, but such suits have been brought in the United States.[100]

Issues of causation[101]

19.59 The usual test for causation is the 'but for' test: the plaintiff would not have suffered damages but for the actions of the defendant.[102] Canadian courts will rely on a different test for causation, the material contribution test, where the following criteria are

---

[95] B. Bilson, *The Canadian Law of Nuisance* (Toronto: Butterworths, 1991), at p. 46. A public nuisance can include 'any activity which unreasonably interferes with the public's interest in questions of health, safety, morality, comfort or convenience' (*Ryan* v. *Victoria (City)*, [1999] 1 S.C.R. 201 at para. 52).

[96] For a general discussion of public nuisance, see 17.42–17.45.

[97] *Ryan* v. *Victoria (City)*, n. 95 above, at para. 52.

[98] *British Columbia* v. *Canadian Forest Products*, [2004] 2 S.C.R. 74 at para. 76.

[99] *Ibid.*, at para. 81.

[100] See *American Electric Power Co.* v. *Connecticut*, 564 U.S. (2011), in which the Supreme Court of the United States dismissed an action brought by several states and others to compel several large electric utilities to reduce their greenhouse gas emissions on the grounds that the emissions constituted a public nuisance. The court, which divided 4–4 on the issue, affirmed the Second Circuit court's decision that at least some of the plaintiffs had standing to bring their claim, but unanimously held that the US *Clean Air Act* and the US Environmental Protection Agency's implementation of that Act displaced any federal common law right to seek an abatement of emissions. Similarly, in *Comer* v. *Murphy Oil USA, Inc.*, No. 07–60756 (5th Cir., 16 October 2009), a class action brought by residents and property owners who had suffered damage as a result of Hurricane Katrina, the Fifth Circuit of the US Court of Appeals held that the plaintiffs had standing to assert a public nuisance claim. The *Comer* litigation is ongoing.

[101] For a broader discussion of issues of causation, see Chapter 17, paras.17.54–17.65.

[102] *Athey* v. *Leonati*, [1996] 3 S.C.R. 458 at para. 14.

met: it must be impossible for reasons outside of the plaintiff's control for the plaintiff to prove causation under the 'but for' test, and the plaintiff's injury must be within the 'ambit of the risk' created by the defendant's breach of the defendant's duty of care to the plaintiff.[103] Futhermore, a material contribution giving rise to liability must be beyond the *de minimus* range.[104]

19.60   Because of the varying nature of weather in most cases it would be very difficult to prove causation of damages related to climate change under the 'but for' test. It is possible that courts could attribute causation to emitters on the basis of the 'material contribution' test.[105]

Joint and several liability v. market share liability

19.61   While it can be argued that virtually all members of modern industrial societies are implicated in climate change, virtually no individuals and only a relatively small number of corporations are likely to be the target of climate change tort actions. Some might suggest that in these circumstances it would be unfair to make the likely targets of such litigation jointly and severally liable for the damage done to plaintiffs by industrial society as a whole. The market share theory of liability, which has been adopted in the United States,[106] presumes that a defendant's 'contribution to the aggregate risk of harm should approximate the defendant's output'.[107] In addition to benefiting defendants by limiting their liability to their market share, market share liability also allows plaintiffs who have suffered loss to avoid the 'tortfeasor identification problem'[108] that can arise in cases of highly fungible products such as generic drugs or perfectly fungible causal agents such as GHG emissions. Market share liability has not been adopted

---

[103]   *Resurface Corp.* v. *Hanke*, [2007] 1 S.C.R. 333 at para. 25.

[104]   *Athey* v. *Leonati*, n. 102 above, at para. 15.

[105]   In certain cases it is sufficient to prove on the balance of probabilities that the negligence of the plaintiff contributed to the injury, rather than proving that the harm would not have occurred but for the negligent act of the defendant (*Myers* v. *Peel County Board of Education*, [1981] 2 S.C.R. 21 at p. 35).

[106]   See *Sindell* v. *Abbot Laboratories* (1980), 607 P.2d 924 (Calif.).

[107]   D. J. Grimm, 'Global Warming and Market Share Liability: A Proposed Model for Allocating Tort Damages among CO2 Producers', *Columbia Journal of Environmental Law*, 32 (2007), 209–50, at 215.

[108]   *Ibid.*, p. 216.

by Canadian courts, and it is unclear what position they would take on this issue.

Limitation issues

19.62 Tort liability generally falls within provincial jurisdiction over property and civil rights.[109] Limitation periods are governed by provincial limitations legislation, which sets out different limitation periods in different circumstances and for different actions. These can differ significantly from province to province and must be consulted in light of the circumstances of a proposed claim.[110]

Securities litigation

19.63 Securities are subject to provincial jurisdiction,[111] and there can be variation in the law from province to province on fine points, but the main features of the law are largely the same across Canada.[112]

19.64 Securities litigation involving climate change is likely to be limited to claims that issuers have breached their timely disclosure obligations under provincial securities laws. Issuers of securities are required to make full, true and plain disclosure of all material facts related to securities before they are issued to the public and to report all material changes thereafter.[113] As a result, issuers of securities may be required to consider risks related to climate change and discuss them in their disclosure filings.[114] If management fail to do so, shareholders can bring a suit against the issuer and the directors and officers of the issuer.

---

[109] Constitution Act, 1867, n. 3 above, s. 92(13).

[110] In Ontario, for instance, no limitation is placed on environmental claims that have not been discovered (Limitations Act, 2002, S.O. 2002, c. 24, s. 17).

[111] This may change. Canada is one of the few jurisdictions in the world not to have a national securities regulator, and the Supreme Court of Canada recently heard a reference from the federal government respecting its ability to regulate securities: In the Matter of a Reference by Governor in Council concerning the proposed Canadian Securities Act, as set out in Order in Council P.C. 2010–667 (26 May 2010).

[112] Canadian securities law is to some extent influenced by American jurisprudence, but also differs from American securities law in important respects.

[113] See, for example, section 56(1) and the definition of 'material change' in section 1 of the Ontario Securities Act, R.S.O. 1990, c. S.5.

[114] The Ontario Securities Commission's National Instrument 51–102, *Continuous Disclosure Obligations*, requires issuer's management to discuss known trends, demands,

The public trust doctrine

19.65   The public trust doctrine, which is rooted in Roman law, has come to play a significant role in US environmental law. It is based on the principle that the public has a right to use particular natural resources and the Government should maintain them for that purpose. In Canada, its influence has, until recently, been limited to jurisdictions that have taken steps to enshrine aspects of the principle in environmental statutes.[115] In 2004, however, the Supreme Court of Canada appears to have opened the door to the common law public trust doctrine in Canada.[116] While it did not apply the public trust doctrine in the case, it suggested that there would be no legal barrier to the use of the doctrine in an appropriately pleaded case. Since then, the Prince Edward Island Court of Appeal has also recognised this possibility by allowing a claim based in part on the public trust doctrine to proceed.[117]

19.66   To date, there have not been any cases that have considered the substance of a public trust claim. This makes it impossible to predict what the scope of the doctrine might be in Canada. In the short term, therefore, initiating climate change litigation under the public trust doctrine in Canada is fraught with risk and uncertainty. In other jurisdictions, the doctrine was initially applied to public rights to navigation, water rights and water access. Only gradually has the doctrine been applied beyond these traditional subject matters. As the case law develops, it will become clear whether the doctrine follows a similar path, or whether it is immediately applied to a broad range of assets and resources considered to be held in the public trust.[118]

commitments, events or uncertainties that are reasonably likely to affect the issuer's business: Form 51–102F1, Part 2, Item 1.2. In some circumstances this would require management to discuss potential damages to the corporation's assets due to CC.

[115]   For example, the Yukon has included the public trust in its environmental statute; see *Environment Act* S.Y. 1991, c.5, s.7.

[116]   See *British Columbia* v. *Canadian Forest Products Ltd*, [2004] 2 S.C.R. 74. This is in contrast to the situation in England: see the proximity analysis involved at the first stage of the test in England, at Chapter 17, para. 17.48.

[117]   See *Prince Edward Island* v. *Canada (Minister of Fisheries and Oceans)*, 2006 PEISCAD 27.

[118]   J. V. DeMarco *et al.*, 'Opening the Door for Common Law Environmental Protection in Canada: The Decision in *British Columbia* v. *Canadian Forest Products Ltd*', *Journal of Environmental Law and Practice*, 15 (2005), 233–55. See also A. Gage, *Asserting the Public's Environmental Rights* (Vancouver: BC Continuing Legal Education Society,

(D)   Other issues

The role of public international law

19.67   Public international law has been very influential in shaping
environmental law in Canada. International law influences
domestic law in a variety of ways. Customary international law
is generally accepted to be directly binding in Canada. This
means customary international law can directly shape common
law developments in Canada and it can affect the application of
legislation. International treaties require implementation to be
binding.

19.68   All sources of international law can be used as interpretive tools,
regardless of the source or the state of implementation. With
respect to legislation, for example, international law is recognised to be part of a contextual approach to interpreting legislation, in part based on a rebuttable presumption that legislation is
designed to be in compliance with Canada's international obligations. Many international principles and commitments have in
fact been incorporated directly into domestic legislation. Soft law
principles, such as precaution, polluter pays, public participation
and environmental impact assessment, are all reflected in environmental legislation at the federal and provincial levels.[119]

The role of climate change in environmental
assessment processes

19.69   The consideration of climate change in the environmental assessment ('EA') of projects in Canada is still in its infancy. Only
gradually has climate change been recognised as a possible environmental effect in federal and provincial EA processes. Many

---

2008). For a discussion of movements to consider the atmosphere as part of the public trust, see also M. C. Wood, 'Atmospheric Trust Litigation', in W. C. G. Burns and
H. M. Osofsky (eds.), *Adjudicating Climate Change: Sub-National, National, and Supra-
National Approaches* (Cambridge University Press, 2009), available online at www.law.
uoregon.edu/faculty/mwood/forlawyers.php.

[119]   H. M. Kindred, 'The Use and Abuse of International Legal Sources by Canadian Courts:
Searching for a Principled Approach' in O. E. Fitsgerald (ed.), *The Globalized Rule of
Law: Relationships between International and Domestic Law* (Toronto: Irwin Law Inc.,
2006).

processes are still designed around the concept of the significance of the effects of a single project in isolation from the impacts of other projects, though most EA processes in Canada do consider the concept of cumulative effects in some form. Guidance on how to incorporate climate change considerations into EA has been developed in cooperation between federal and provincial EA agencies.[120] Whether existing EA regimes are sufficient to ensure a meaningful consideration of climate change remains to be seen.

19.70   One interesting legal question in this regard is how the significance of GHG emissions is to be determined. Should it be considered in absolute terms by looking at the total emissions of a project? Should it be considered in relative terms, such as the emissions of the project compared to best available technology (BAT) or the lowest available GHG emissions per unit of product or service to be delivered? In the latter case, would the relevant standard be the BAT within an industry sector such as the oil sands, or the lowest GHG emissions option for meeting the need that the project is designed to meet?[121]

GHG emissions as 'releases' under provincial legislation

19.71   Some provincial environmental statutes contain general provisions prohibiting the release of a substance that may cause an adverse environmental effect. Releases specifically authorised under an approval are typically exempt from these prohibitions.[122] For activities that involve significant releases of GHG emissions that are not specifically authorised, these sections open the door to possible prosecutions, including the possibility of private prosecutions. Private prosecutions can be brought

---

[120] See Federal-Provincial-Territorial Committee on Climate Change and Environmental Assessment, *Incorporating Climate Change Considerations in Environmental Assessment: General Guidance for Practitioners* (Ottawa: Canadian Environmental Assessment Agency, November 2003), available online at www.ceaa.gc.ca/default. asp?lang=En&n=A41F45C5-1.

[121] See T. Kolby, 'The Canadian Environmental Assessment Act and Global Climate Change: Rethinking Significance', *Alberta Law Review*, 47 (2009), 161–83. See also N. J. Chalifour, 'Case Comment: A (Pre)Cautionary Tale about the Kearl Oil Sands Decision', *McGill Journal of Sustainable Development Law and Policy*, 5 (2009), 251–87.

[122] Nova Scotia Environment Act, SNS 1994–95, c. 1, ss. 67 and 68.

by individuals in Canada; however they can be taken over by government prosecutors at the discretion of the responsible Attorney General.[123]

Climate change and species at risk

19.72 Climate change is predicted to significantly increase the number of species at risk. Canada currently has legislation at the federal and provincial levels designed to identify and protect species at risk. The process in most jurisdictions involves a scientific listing process with some level of political oversight. Once listed, most species-at-risk legislation in Canada affords protection to the listed species in the form of prohibitions against interference with the species and its critical habitat. This means, for property owners and proponents of activities with the potential to interfere with the recovery of a species at risk, that the ability to continue to engage in the activity may be curtailed either directly through government action or indirectly as a result of judicial review applications brought by individuals or organisations concerned with the protection of species at risk.[124]

Greenwashing

19.73 Another area of potential litigation relates to so-called 'greenwashing' efforts by companies which claim that either the company as a whole or some of its products or services are more climate-friendly than they actually are. There are at least three possible litigation options available in cases of such false claims. First, greenwashing could constitute a negligent misrepresentation under tort law. Second, in situations where the statement is made to induce a person into purchasing a product or service, greenwashing may also constitute an innocent or fraudulent misrepresentation under contract law. Third, false statements about the climate change record of a company or its products or services could run afoul of anti-competition laws under the Competition Act.[125]

---

[123] K. Ferguson, 'Challenging the Intervention and Stay of an Environmental Private Prosecution', *Journal of Environmental Law and Practice*, 13 (2004), 153–94.

[124] For an overview of the federal Species at Risk Act ('SARA'), see K. Smallwood, *A Guide to Canada's Species at Risk Act* (Vancouver: Sierra Legal Defence Fund, 2003).

[125] Competition Act, R.S., 1985, c. C-34, ss. 36 and 52.

Citizen submissions under NAAEC

19.74   The North American Free Trade Agreement's ('NAFTA') citizen submission procedure is a key component of the North American Agreement on Environmental Cooperation ('NAAEC'), the environmental side agreement to NAFTA. Under Article 14 of the NAAEC, any resident of Canada may file a submission claiming that Canada 'is failing to effectively enforce its environmental laws'. Assuming that the submission complies with the procedural requirements in Article 14(1), the NAAEC Secretariat then considers whether the submission warrants requesting a 'response' from Canada.

19.75   Criteria considered include whether the matter deserves 'further study' and whether the submitter has pursued 'private remedies' available under Canadian law. Once the Secretariat has received and considered the response from Canada, it may then recommend to the Council that a 'factual record' be prepared. When completed, the factual record is delivered to the Council, which then decides whether to release some or all of its contents to the public.

19.76   The utility of this mechanism is limited by two key factors. One is that there are only limited environmental laws in Canada dealing with climate change. The second limitation is that while the process brings important public attention to failure to effectively enforce laws, it does not require countries to remedy the problem.[126]

Petitions to the Commissioner for Sustainable Development

19.77   Another avenue available outside the court system in Canada to encourage the federal government to effectively implement and enforce its environmental laws is the petition process offered by the Commissioner for Sustainable Development ('CSD'). The

---

[126] See Commission for Environmental Cooperation, *A Guide to Articles 14 and 15*, available online at www.cec.org/Page.asp?PageID=122&ContentID=1388; and J. Gardner, *Discussion Paper: Analysis Articles 14 and 15 of the NAAEC Council's Emerging Conflict of Interest* (28 April 2004), at www.cec.org/Storage/56/4831_Discussion-paper-28%20 Apr_en.pdf, p. 7.

process is open to anyone concerned about the effective implementation or enforcement of federal environmental laws. Once a petition is filed, the Commissioner will ask the federal department or agency responsible to respond to the questions raised in the petition. The department or agency is required to respond, but no further action is required. Issues raised elsewhere in this chapter, such as compliance with section 166 of CEPA, could be the subject of a petition under this process.

(E)   Conclusion

19.78   Climate change litigation in Canada is in its infancy, which means there are still many opportunities to explore the extent of liability in the context of public and private law. Particularly as the federal and provincial governments take on more responsibilities to address climate change, there will be more potential for litigation aimed at ensuring accountability. Some areas explored in this chapter, such as tort law and judicial review, already have well-developed foundations. Others, including aboriginal rights, Charter challenges and public trust cases, are based on less-entrenched principles. In the end, the success of any climate litigation will turn on the factual basis that can be established. While it is unlikely that Canada will compete with the US in terms of the number and range of climate cases, climate litigation in Canada is clearly on the rise.

20

United States of America

MICHAEL B. GERRARD AND GREGORY E. WANNIER

(A)   Introduction

20.01   The prospect of carbon liability in the United States is a relatively recent phenomenon. It is only in the last decade that US environmental lawyers and policy-makers have begun to turn their attention to climate change, as climate-related litigation has surged, government action on several fronts has begun, and climate change has generally been recognised as a factor to consider in decision-making across the economy. This chapter lays out existing options to establish liability for greenhouse gas ('GHG') emissions along legislative, regulatory and judicial channels.

The United States legal system

20.02   The United States of America ('USA') was founded as a constitutional democracy. Its primary document is the US Constitution, which establishes the absolute rules for how the federal government functions. It has a three-part system: the bicameral legislature (House of Representatives and the Senate, which together form the Congress) passes legislation; the President signs and implements such laws; and the federal court system, guided by the Supreme Court, determines the legality of federal (and some other) activities. In order to execute the law, the President relies heavily on a federal bureaucracy of administrative agencies, which utilise their technical expertise to implement congressional mandates through regulations and thereby create a set of legal rules subsidiary to statutes (laws). In addition to this, federal courts work in a common law system, and so are able to set laws through judicial decision-making.

20.03   The Constitution also lays out the USA's strong federalist struc-
         ture, whereby power is apportioned between the national gov-
         ernment and its several states. States are given broad power, via
         the 10th Amendment, over all policy areas not explicitly granted
         to the federal government or prohibited. The federal government
         has power via the Constitution's Commerce Clause to legislate
         on any policy issue that affects interstate commerce, effectively
         giving it power over GHG emissions (which have effects beyond
         a single state). In the absence of comprehensive federal activity,
         however, some states have begun to adopt climate-related laws.

Constitutional and major statutory rights

20.04   The Constitution does not explicitly grant a right to environmen-
         tal protection. However, it is famously concise, and so this should
         not be read as showing hostility to environmental protection. The
         major environmental statutes in effect today also do not include
         explicit language on substantive rights: instead, they speak of
         'primary goals'. The Constitution confers the right to 'due pro-
         cess', and numerous federal and state statutes confer procedural
         rights.

Federal stance on climate change

Major international treaties

20.05   The USA has ratified the United Nations Framework on Climate
         Change. On the eve of the 1997 Conference of the Parties in
         Kyoto, the US Senate, by a vote of 95–0, adopted a resolution
         opposing ratification of any climate treaty that did not impose
         binding obligations on the rapidly developing economies com-
         parable to those to be imposed on the USA.[1] Though President
         William Clinton and Vice President Albert Gore supported
         the Kyoto Protocol and the USA became a signatory before the
         Clinton Administration left office, they did not submit it to
         Senate for ratification, knowing that it would be defeated. When
         George W. Bush became President in January 2001, he explicitly
         repudiated the Kyoto Protocol. His successor, Barack Obama,
         who was inaugurated in January 2009, supports US participation

---

[1] S. Res. 98, 105th Cong. (1997).

in international climate negotiations, but he has presented no climate treaty to the Senate for ratification. By way of context, it is useful to bear in mind that the USA is also not a signatory to the UN Conference on Law of the Sea,[2] which also would have binding effect; however, it often adopts domestic legislation that carries out the substantive terms of multinational environmental agreements.

20.06   The USA is among the States that have associated themselves with the Copenhagen Accord, and also endorsed the agreements reached at Cancun. As such, it has taken on commitments to contribute to a potential $100-billion-per-year climate action fund to be given by developed countries to developing countries.[3] It has also been involved with much of the institutional structuring that has occurred at both meetings, including agreeing in principle: to contribute to a $100-billion-per-year climate fund that the developed world has collectively pledged to establish by 2020; to help accelerate transfers of relevant green technologies;[4] and individually to reduce emissions around 17 per cent below 2005 levels by 2020, 'in conformity with anticipated US energy and climate legislation, recognising that the final target will be reported to the Secretariat in light of enacted legislation' (and with further reductions thereafter).[5] However, neither of these agreements includes any binding limits on emissions or other legally binding international commitments, and the legislation that was then anticipated was never enacted.

Negotiating position

20.07   The current national Administration under President Obama recognises the severity of climate change and has committed to reducing the country's GHG emissions. Obama has pledged to battle GHG emissions, and has said that the USA is 'determined' to take action.[6] The President has also taken steps to

---

[2] United Nations Convention on the Law of the Sea, 10 December 1982.
[3] Copenhagen Accord, paragraph 8, 18 December 2009, FCCC/CP/2009/L.7 18.
[4] *Ibid.*
[5] Letter from Todd Stern, United States Special Envoy for Climate Change, to Yvo de Boer, Executive Secretary, United Nations Framework Convention on Climate Change (28 January 2010), available at http://unfccc.int/files/meetings/cop_15/copenhagen_accord/application/pdf/unitedstatescphaccord_app.1.pdf.
[6] Barack Obama, 'Remarks by the President at United Nations General Secretary Ban Ki-Moon's Climate Change Summit' (22 September 2009); available at www.un.org/wcm/

begin regulating GHG emissions in the executive branch based on existing authorities, especially the Clean Air Act of 1970.

20.08   A strongly partisan atmosphere currently prevails in Washington. President Obama is a Democrat, as is a majority of the Senate. The House of Representatives was controlled by the Democrats until January 2011. The House passed a comprehensive climate Bill in June 2009 based on an economy-wide cap-and-trade system, but the Bill died in the Senate, whose current rules require affirmative votes of sixty of its one hundred members to enact legislation. The Republicans took control of the House in January 2011, and their leadership is strongly opposed to climate regulation and is attempting to block President Obama's efforts. The next national election will be in November 2012; whether President Obama is re-elected, and the composition of the House and the Senate, will be determined then. Meanwhile, this political situation has hampered the President's ability to make climate-related commitments in the international arena.

Industrial and natural resources (emissions sources and energy mix)

20.09   The USA has been the largest energy consumer in the world according to the Energy Information Administration ('EIA'), using 94.6 quadrillion British Thermal Units (qBTUs) of energy in 2009.[7] However, its use is almost identical to China's use over the past few years,[8] and the International Energy Agency ('IEA') has calculated that China overtook the USA in total consumption in 2008.[9] Over a third of this energy usage is from petroleum (35.3 qBTUs), largely in the transportation and industrial sectors. Another 20 to 25 per cent each comes from natural gas and coal, with coal primarily going to satisfy electricity needs and natural gas fairly split among industrial and residential heating, and

webdav/site/climatechange/shared/Documents/USA.pdf ('We understand the gravity of the climate threat. We are determined to act. And we will meet our responsibility to future generations.').

[7]   ENERGY INFO. ADMIN., U.S. DEPT. OF ENERGY, DOE/EIA-0384(2009), 2009 ANNUAL ENERGY REVIEW 37 (2010) ('EIA 2009 ENERGY REPORT').

[8]   Energy Information Administration, China Energy Data, Statistics and Analysis – Oil, Gas, Electricity, Coal, available at www.eia.doe.gov/cabs/China/Profile.html.

[9]   Jing Yang, 'China's Energy Consumption Rises', *WALL ST. J.*, 28 February 2011.

electricity generation. Under 10 per cent of energy needs are met each by nuclear power (which exclusively creates electricity), and by renewable sources (used mostly for electricity but also across other sectors). See Figure 20.1 for a graphical summary of energy sources and end-uses in the US economy.

20.10   The electricity market itself is dominated by coal, which provides about half of the national market. Natural gas and nuclear power also comprise about 20 per cent each. Natural gas is surging in importance, however, and will account for over half of all installed capacity from 2011–14.[10] This leaves renewable sources as constituting 11 per cent of the market.[11] Traditional hydropower provides over three-quarters of renewable electricity, largely in the northwest and northeast but also scattered across the south.[12] Biomass is mostly used for non-electric heating, but is also a reasonably important source of electricity, while the remaining resources constitute less than 10 per cent of the renewable market each. Among these, wind power is the fastest-growing source of electricity, and is on track to outpace all power sources except natural gas in new installed capacity in 2011.[13] However, this number is forecast to drop off from 2012–14 in the face of regulatory uncertainty.[14]

20.11   Although transportation and electricity together use about two-thirds of the USA's energy, industrial activities and residential/commercial uses are also important, and are fuelled largely by petroleum and natural gas resources. Heavy manufacturing is an important part of the US economy, particularly in the midwest and parts of the south,[15] while the northeast and

---

[10] ENERGY INFO. ADMIN., U.S. DEPT. OF ENERGY, 2009 ELECTRIC POWER ANNUAL 18, tbl. 1.4 (2010) ('EIA 2009 POWER REPORT').

[11] Ibid.

[12] ENERGY INFO. ADMIN., U.S. DEPT. OF ENERGY, 2009 RENEWABLE ENERGY CONSUMPTION AND ELECTRICITY PRELIMINARY STATISTICS, tbl. 3 (2010).

[13] EIA 2009 POWER REPORT, above n. 10, at 18 tbl. 1.4.

[14] Ibid.

[15] U.S. DEPT. OF COM., MANUFACTURING IN AMERICA: A COMPREHENSIVE STRATEGY TO ADDRESS THE CHALLENGES TO U.S. MANUFACTURERS (2004); Econ Post, State economies where manufacturing is number 1 industry, at http://econpost.com/industry/state-economies-where-manufacturing-number-1-industry; see generally National Association of Manufacturers, Manufacturing By State, at www.nam.org/ResourceCenter/State-Manufacturing-Data/Manufacturing-by-State.aspx.

midwest use large amounts of natural gas for space-heating requirements.[16]

National climate change risks

20.12   The USA faces several threats from a changing global climate. These dangers can be categorised into temperature disturbances, rising sea levels, water-supply shifts, and more extreme storm fronts. Most of the USA has seen a constant increase in heat-wave incidence since 1950 (although still below 1930s surges).[17] Rising sea levels affect much of the US eastern seaboard and Gulf Coast region, including large swathes of Florida, and the major cities of New York, Boston and New Orleans.[18] Water supplies have tended in the past fifty years to tighten in the south and southwest, while increasing in the north and northeast.[19] This will be particularly problematic in the southwest, where water supplies will be further strained as winter snow packs melt earlier and thereby provide less water runoff.[20] Meanwhile, more precipitation has led to more numerous and extreme precipitation events in the northeast,[21] and could contribute to increased flooding.[22] This precipitation in the northeast will help contribute to more severe snowstorms in the winter, while the Gulf Coast region could see a higher incidence of tropical storms and hurricanes.[23] Meanwhile, more intense wave activity has already begun to erode coastlines along the Pacific northwest, and in the South Atlantic.[24]

---

[16] ENERGY INFO. ADMIN., U.S. DEPT. OF ENERGY, A LOOK AT RESIDENTIAL ENERGY CONSUMPTION IN 1997 (1997); ENERGY INFO. ADMIN., U.S. DEPT. OF ENERGY, 2001 RESIDENTIAL ENERGY CONSUMPTION SURVEY: HOUSEHOLD ENERGY CONSUMPTION AND EXPENDITURES TABLES, tbl. 1 (2002).

[17] U.S. CLIMATE CHANGE SCI. PROG. & SUBCOMM. GLOBAL CHANGE RESEARCH, WEATHER AND CLIMATE EXTREMES IN A CHANGING CLIMATE: REGIONS OF FOCUS: NORTH AMERICA, HAWAII, CARIBBEAN, AND U.S. PACIFIC ISLANDS 37–42 (2008) ('CCSP REPORT').

[18] U.S. GLOBAL CHANGE RESEARCH PROG., NAT'L OCEANIC & ATMOSPHERIC ADMIN., GLOBAL CLIMATE CHANGE IMPACTS IN THE UNITED STATES 149–50 (2009) ('GCRP REPORT').

[19] CCSP REPORT, above n. 17, at 43.   [20] GCRP REPORT, above n. 18, at 139.

[21] CCSP REPORT, above n. 17, at 46–8.   [22] GCRP REPORT, above n. 18, at 135.

[23] CCSP REPORT, above n. 17, at 53–62, 73–5; GCRP REPORT, above n. 18.

[24] Ibid., at 68–73.

20.13   These impacts have already affected communities in the Gulf region, and in Alaska, which has led to climate litigation (see para. 20.63 below). In addition, crop and livestock production is particularly at risk from water stresses,[25] the health industry could be strained by new tropical and waterborne diseases and increased heat stress,[26] and numerous ecosystems, which provide valuable services to society, are severely threatened.[27]

(B)   Public law

Overview

20.14   Judicial activity on climate-related issues is a relatively recent phenomenon: the USA has seen a large surge in recent litigation activity, from only one climate-related case brought in 2003, to over a hundred cases in 2010.[28] During the presidency of George W. Bush (January 2001 to January 2009), most climate-related litigation was brought by environmental groups seeking to force GHG regulation, and challenging specific projects on GHG-related grounds. Since Barack Obama took office in January 2009, there has been a surge of litigation brought by industry and by states that oppose regulation, seeking to stop the federal regulatory activity instituted by the Obama Administration.

Types of judicial review

Statutory challenges

20.15   One way to attempt to block federal action is to challenge an underlying statute that grants certain powers. In such a challenge, a plaintiff alleges that a given law violates the provisions of the Constitution (i.e. it is unconstitutional). Constitutional challenges to the text of environmental statutes (as opposed to their enforcement) have rarely succeeded. States are also subject to challenges based on lack of constitutional authority. In particular, the Dormant Commerce Clause prohibits states from interfering purposefully or excessively in interstate commerce. Plaintiffs seldom succeed in such challenges.

---

[25] GCRP REPORT, above n. 18, at 71–8.
[26] *Ibid.*, at 89.   [27] *Ibid.*, at 79–88.   [28] See Fig. 20.2 below.

20.16   This type of constitutional challenge is not relevant today at the federal level with respect to climate, largely because there is no national climate change law to challenge. Most federal activity on climate change has occurred under the auspices of the Clean Air Act, a statute that is generally accepted as constitutional today. At the state level, there has been more activity, most notably in California under Assembly Bill 32 ('AB 32'), which established a comprehensive climate regulatory regime for that state. However, challenges to AB 32 have thus far been limited to its implementation, and not to the authority of the statute itself.

Regulatory challenges

20.17   Many of the statutes enacted by Congress authorise federal agencies to adopt regulations implementing them. If the underlying statute is deemed constitutional, parties may also challenge those regulations which have been passed pursuant to those statutes. The agencies must follow the Administrative Procedure Act, which requires the agencies to publish draft regulations, provide explanatory background information, invite public comment, and then publish the final regulations. At that point, the regulations may be challenged in federal court by anyone who will be adversely affected by them. Interested parties may also petition agencies to adopt regulations, and sue the agencies if they fail to do so.

20.18   These challenges will generally allege that the regulation goes against the text or intent of its underlying statute, or that proper procedures were not followed, or (less commonly) that applying the statute in a particular way is unconstitutional. Within the set of federal administrative challenges, they can be national in scale, based on statutory interpretation; or more local and project-based, based on both statutory and regulatory interpretation.

Grounds for judicial review

Clean Air Act

Statutory basis

20.19   The Clean Air Act of 1970 ('CAA') is by far the most important basis for climate regulation, and by extension carbon emissions liability. The main section, for regulation of stationary sources, was designed to achieve certain standards of air pollution necessary to protect the public health and welfare. The basic design for most pollutants is that the Environmental Protection Agency ('EPA') is entrusted to set National Ambient Air Quality Standards ('NAAQS'), which represent the safe concentration of a variety of pollutants.[29] States are then required to establish State Implementation Programs ('SIPs'), subject to EPA approval, to achieve these NAAQS. If the SIP does not satisfy the EPA, it may instead impose a Federal Implementation Plan ('FIP') on that state. All major emission sources must get Title V permits that delineate emissions allowances for individual facilities based on state or applicable federal requirements. In addition, major new emissions sources are subject to New Source Review ('NSR'), under which technology standards are set depending on whether the area is in attainment with NAAQS.[30] These standards are also determined by states, subject to EPA approval. The EPA may also set nationwide technology standards under the New Source Performance Standard program.

20.20   The CAA has an entirely different section for the regulation of motor vehicles. The EPA may directly regulate motor vehicle emissions. These rules supersede state motor vehicle standards, except that the State of California may promulgate its own standards, subject to EPA approval, and other states may adopt the California standards.[31]

20.21   For a pollutant to be subject to CAA requirements, it must first be deemed by the EPA to endanger the public health and welfare. Once so listed, a pollutant will become subject to various CAA provisions, depending on the EPA's subsequent regulations.

---

[29] 42 U.S.C. § 7409 (2006). The original goal was for such standards to be met by 1975, although later amendments (in 1977 and 1990) pushed back this date.

[30] If the area where a new facility is being built is not in attainment, then the facility is subject to Non-Attainment ('NA') standards, which require that the technology used result in the Lowest Achievable Emissions Rate ('LAER'). If the area is in attainment, or if a NAAQS has not yet been set, then the facility need only reach the Prevention of Significant Deterioration ('PSD') standards, which are the Best Available Control Technology ('BACT'); a less stringent requirement than LAER. 42 U.S.C. §§ 7470–509 (2006).

[31] 42 U.S.C. § 7543 (2006).

20.22 Finally, the ability to sue under the CAA is given both to the EPA to enforce compliance with its regulations, and to members of the public, either to enforce compliance with the statute, or to challenge the EPA's failure to undertake any non-discretionary duty.[32] This is the so-called 'citizen-suit' provision of the Act, and allows private individuals to sue the Government or private actors (facility managers) who may violate the Act.

Regulatory activity

20.23 In 2007 the US Supreme Court issued a seminal decision, *Massachusetts* v. *EPA*, finding that the EPA could not decline to regulate GHGs purely for reasons of policy or expedience; it had to make a real determination of whether these gases contribute to global climate change, which is a threat to public health and welfare. This led to some limited EPA activity where the EPA began researching ways it could regulate GHGs; but no major regulation occurred until President Obama took office and appointed Lisa Jackson as the new EPA Administrator in 2009.

20.24 Under Administrator Jackson, the EPA has issued four major and interrelated climate regulations, which together impose a national system of carbon liability on regulated sectors. In order to justify any regulatory activity, the EPA first had to issue an Endangerment Finding, which determined that GHG emissions from moving vehicles are 'reasonably likely' to threaten public health and welfare, and thus certified six GHGs as pollutants subject to the CAA. Next, the Vehicle Tailpipe Rule sets GHG emission standards for Light Duty Vehicles under the moving source regulatory provisions in the CAA.

20.25 The final two rules work in conjunction to regulate stationary sources. First, the Timing Rule, or Reconsideration Decision, interprets the Clean Air Act's language to conclude that the Vehicle Tailpipe Rule will also mandate that stationary sources be subject to technology standards. The Tailoring Rule then

---

[32] 42 U.S.C. § 7604 (2006); see 42 U.S.C. § 307 (2006) for a summary of which courts will hear different cases; generally, national regulations must be challenged in the District of Columbia Circuit Court of Appeals, while other actions will be heard in regional federal courts.

limits these regulatory requirements to emitters of 100,000 tons of CO_2 equivalent (CO_2e) per year. This limitation was deemed to be necessary because the CAA normally applies to facilities emitting 250 or more tons per year, but given the volume of GHG emissions emitted compared to other pollutants, this is an unreasonable number.[33] These national rules went into effect on 2 January 2011 (except the Endangerment Finding, which was already in effect).

Current and recent litigation

20.26   The largest set of climate litigation currently underway relates to the EPA's recent national climate regulations under the CAA. Over ninety individual cases have been filed against the four rules listed above, from more than thirty-five distinct parties. Just two of these parties have called for more stringent regulation (those from the Sierra Club and the Center for Biological Diversity).[34] The cases split roughly evenly among challenges to the four major EPA regulations (listed above). Because these challenges are to the EPA's national implementation of the CAA, they are in the District of Columbia Circuit Court of Appeals (the 'DC Circuit'). The Court will hear these challenges in 2011 or 2012. The Court has denied a motion to stay implementation of the EPA's regulations pending decisions on these challenges.

20.27   The DC Circuit tends to be deferential to administrative actions that are well-documented and well-explained in the record, but it also tends to strike down rules that are contrary to the plain words of a statute. Under this light, the Endangerment Finding and the Tailpipe Rule may be in good shape, especially since the motor vehicle industry, the industry that is directly affected by the Tailpipe Rule, has accepted it. But the Tailoring Rule is on shakier ground because on its face its numerical thresholds differ

---

[33] Endangerment and Cause or Contribute Findings for Greenhouse Gases under Section 202(a) of the Clean Air Act, 74 Fed. Reg. 66, 496 (15 December 2009); Light-Duty Vehicle Greenhouse Gas Emission Standards and Corporate Average Fuel Economy Standards, 75 Fed. Reg. 25,324 (7 May 2010); Reconsideration of Interpretation of Regulations That Determine Pollutants Covered by Clean Air Act Permitting Programs, 75 Fed. Reg. 17,004 (2 April 2010); Prevention of Significant Deterioration and Title VI Greenhouse Gas Tailoring Rule, 75 Fed. Reg. 31, 514 (3 June 2010).

[34] Much of the information compiled here and below can be accessed from the CCCL Climate Litigation Chart, available at www.climatecasechart.com.

from those in the statute, and the fate of the Timing Rule seems to be linked to that of the Tailoring Rule.

Clean Water Act

Statutory basis

20.28   Although the CAA is the main source of regulatory activity (and by extension, litigation), several other statutes provide possible angles to address climate change and establish carbon liability. The Clean Water Act ('CWA'), passed in 1972, provides for the regulation of pollutants into waterways. One portion of the statute functions by requiring states to set Water Quality Standards subject to EPA approval under §303(c). Once established, states must promulgate lists (under §303(d) of the CWA) of waterways that fail to meet these standards.[35] These lists form the basis for eventual development of Total Maximum Daily Loads ('TMDLs'), which set acceptable pollutant levels for certain waterways and open the door for water quality-based effluent limitations designed to preserve these TMDLs, under the National Pollutant Discharge Elimination System ('NPDES').[36] All of these actions must be approved by the EPA.

20.29   The CWA has a citizen suit provision similar to that in the CAA; any adversely affected party may sue a private actor for violating statutory or regulatory mandates, or the EPA itself for failing in its duties to administer the statute.[37]

Regulatory activity

20.30   Although water regulation does not generally relate to climate, the EPA issued a memorandum on 15 November 2010, asking twenty-three coastal states and five coastal territories to seriously consider ocean acidification problems (which have been directly linked to GHG levels in the atmosphere[38]) in their future monitoring activities under the CWA.[39] The EPA noted that all coastal

---

[35] 33 U.S.C. § 1313 (2006).   [36] *Ibid.*, § 1311, 1342 (2006).

[37] *Ibid.*, § 1365 (2006).

[38] European Project on Ocean Acidification, Ocean Acidification and Its Impact on Marine Life, at http://oceanacidification.wordpress.com/2009/01/19/ocean-acidification-and-its-impact-on-marine-life.

[39] Envtl. Prot. Agency, Memorandum on Integrated Reporting and Listing Decisions Related to Ocean Acidification (2010); Clean Water Act, s. 303(d): Notice of Call for Public Comment on 303(d) Program and Ocean Acidification, 75 Fed.

states already have established appropriate pH ranges of 6.5 to 8.5 for their ocean areas, and that states 'should' list waters that do not meet these criteria on their §303(d) lists. The EPA has not pushed hard here, and its actions thus far focus on data collection, suggest rather than mandate, and are self-consciously subsidiary to efforts under the CAA.[40] However, recognition of ocean acidification may open the door for future action under the CWA. Much of the states' administration of the CWA is subject to federal approval, so the EPA could enforce its views. Further, EPA guidance under the CWA sets a maximum of eight to thirteen years before TMDLs should be developed for all bodies of water placed on a §303(d) list. The EPA's efforts to gather data on the federal level, and help individual states in this regard, could give a boost to these activities; the more states know about this issue the sooner they may find themselves compelled to address it. As such, the EPA 'recognizes that the §303(d) program under the CWA has the potential to complement and aid in [CAA climate regulation efforts]'.[41]

NEPA

Statutory basis

20.31   The National Environmental Policy Act, enacted in 1970, aims to influence federal agencies' decision-making process by requiring that they consider the environmental ramifications of their actions. Agencies must issue Environmental Impact Statements ('EISs') for major federal actions significantly affecting the environment.[42] This is a procedural requirement without substantive bite. The NEPA applies to almost all discretionary actions of federal agencies, including permit approvals of private facilities. Several courts have ruled that

---

Reg. 13, 537 (22 March 2010). The action stems at least in part from a settlement reached earlier in the year with the Center for Biological Diversity (CBD), which had challenged the EPA's earlier refusal to require that Washington State consider ocean acidity as a threat to its coastal water systems. Press Release, Center for Biological Diversity, 'Legal Settlement Will Require EPA to Evaluate How to Regulate Ocean Acidification under Clean Water Act' (11 March 2010), available at www.biologicaldiversity.org/news/press_releases/2010/ocean-acidification-03–11–2010.html.

[40] ENVTL. PROT. AGENCY, QUESTIONS AND ANSWERS ON OCEAN ACIDIFICATION AND THE CLEAN WATER ACT 303(D) PROGRAM (2010).

[41] *Ibid.*, at 3.   [42]   42 USC § 4332(2) (2006).

GHG emissions are appropriate topics for consideration under the NEPA.[43]

20.32   To help implement the NEPA, Congress also established the Council on Environmental Quality ('CEQ') within the Executive Office of the President (not within the EPA).[44] Under the NEPA, the CEQ is charged with adopting regulations to guide agency actions and to help determine what must be done to satisfy NEPA standards.

20.33   Several states have also passed their own statutes similar to the NEPA designed to accomplish the same goals for state agencies. Among the more notable such statutes are the California Environmental Quality Act ('CEQA') and New York's State Environmental Quality Review Act ('SEQRA').[45] The CEQA in particular has more substantive bite than the NEPA.

Regulatory activity

20.34   On 18 February 2010, the CEQ issued a draft guidance document requiring that agencies consider the direct and indirect GHG emissions resulting from their contemplated actions, as well as the effect of climate change itself on their projects.[46] The guidance sets a threshold for when GHG emissions should be considered, noting emissions of 25,000 metric tons or more might be 'an indicator that a quantitative or qualitative assessment may be meaningful to decision makers and the public'.[47] Although it has received public comments on the draft, the CEQ has so far yet to issue a final guidance.[48]

---

[43]   See, e.g., *Center for Biological Diversity* v. *National Highway Traffic Safety Administration*, 538 F.3d 1172 (9th Cir. 2008); *Mid States Coalition for Progress* v. *Surface Transportation Board*, 345 F.3d 520 (8th Cir. 2003).

[44]   42 USC § 4342 (2006).

[45]   Cal Pub. Res. Code §21,000 *et seq.* (West, 1970); N.Y. Envtl. Conserv. Law §§ 3–0301(1)(b), 3–0301(2)(m) and 8–0113 (McKinney, 1995).

[46]   Counc. Envtl. Quality, Memorandum for Heads of Federal Departments and Agencies: Draft NEPA Guidance on Consideration of the Effects of climate Change and Greenhouse Gas Emissions (2010).

[47]   *Ibid.*

[48]   Council on Environmental Quality, 'New Proposed NEPA Guidance and Steps to Modernise and Reinvigorate NEPA', available at www.whitehouse.gov/administration/eop/ceq/initiatives/nepa.

Current and recent litigation

20.35   Unlike other major environmental statutes, the NEPA has no citizen suit provision: instead, challengers can bring claims as outlined by the Administrative Procedure Act ('APA').[49] Numerous NEPA cases have concerned climate change impacts; a total of forty-four such cases had been brought as of March 2011 under the NEPA.[50] As above, several leading decisions have invalidated environmental impact reviews for failing to consider climate change.[51] States have been a heavy area of litigation activity as well: another thirty-five challenges were filed to state NEPA equivalents, with the large majority of these challenges (about 80 per cent) filed in California under the CEQA.[52]

20.36   This litigation has also targeted international activity. In particular, one NEPA lawsuit was brought against two federal corporations, the Overseas Private Investment Corporation ('OPIC') and the Export-Import Bank ('Ex-Im'), based on their failure to consider the impact of GHG emissions of over $32 billion in financing and political risk insurance they had provided to several fossil fuel projects around the world. In settling the case, both entities pledged to consider GHG emissions and release more information in the future. They also each established $250 million funds to finance clean technology projects.[53]

ESA

Statutory basis

20.37   The Endangered Species Act of 1973 ('ESA') was passed to ensure preservation of biodiversity. Under the ESA, two federal bureaux [54] are responsible for listing plant and animal species as endangered (facing possible extinction), or threatened

---

[49]   5 U.S.C. § 706 (2006).   [50]   See Fig. 20.2 below.

[51]   See, e.g., *Center for Biological Diversity* v. *National Highway Traffic Safety Administration*, 538 F.3d at 1172; *Mid States Coalition for Progress* v. *Surface Transportation Board*, 345 F.3d at 520.

[52]   See below, Fig. 2.

[53]   *Friends of the Earth* v. *Mosbacher* (N.D. Cal. 2007), Interlocutory appeal denied (September 2007) (settled February 2009), available at www.foe.org/pdf/Ex-Im_Settlement.pdf, www.foe.org/pdf/OPIC_Settlement.pdf; see also Press Release, Friends of the Earth, 'Landmark Global Warming Lawsuit Settled' (6 February 2009).

[54]   The Fish and Wildlife Service ('FWS') and National Marine Fisheries Service ('NMFS').

('likely to become an endangered species within the foreseeable future'),[55] without taking economic considerations into account.[56] Once a species is listed, the Secretary of the Interior or Commerce must determine its critical habitats, as well as a recovery plan for the species as a whole (including setting certain restrictions on activities within the habitat).[57] Endangered species are additionally protected from any projects that would constitute a 'taking' (harming individuals in the population).[58] However, there are a number of exceptions, most commonly for projects where developers take steps to 'minimize or mitigate' their detrimental impact on a given listed species; a comprehensive permitting programme exists for projects impacting critical habitat.[59]

20.38   The ESA has a citizen suit provision under which adversely affected parties may sue private actors or the Government for violating statutory or regulatory mandates.[60]

Regulatory activity

20.39   The past few years have seen a large debate about the role of the Polar Bear, which may face extinction primarily due to climate change, in the ESA's structural protections. This debate has revolved around three key agency decisions. First, during the Administration of President George W. Bush, the Department of Interior listed the Polar Bear as a 'threatened species' on 14 May 2008.[61] Six months later, it issued a 'special rule' stating that this listing could not be used to impose permitting requirements based on GHG emissions outside Alaska.[62] Importantly, this 'special rule' only applies to the Polar Bear so long as it is listed as a 'threatened' (and not 'endangered') species. Under the Obama Administration, the Department of the Interior continues to

---

[55] 16 U.S.C. §§ 1532(6), (19) (2006).   [56] *Ibid.*, §§ 1533(a)–(b) (2006).
[57] *Ibid.*, §§ 1533(c), (f) (2006).   [58] *Ibid.*, § 1538(a) (2006).
[59] *Ibid.*, §§ 1539(a) (2006).   [60] *Ibid.*, §§ 1540(g) (2006).
[61] Determination of Threatened Status for the Polar Bear (Ursus Maritimus) Throughout Its Range, 72 Fed. Reg. 28, 212 (15 May 2008) (the 'Listing Rule'); see also Press Release, 'Secretary Kempthorne Announces Decision to Protect Polar Bears under Endangered Species Act' (14 May 2008), available at www.fws.gov/home/feature/2008/polarbear012308/pdf/DOI_polar_bears_news_release.pdf.
[62] Endangered and Threatened Wildlife and Plants; Special Rule for the Polar Bear, 50 CFR pt. 17 (2008), available at http://alaska.fws.gov/pdf/pb4d.pdf.

stand by its original rulings,[63] but it has also designated critical habitat for the Polar Bear.

Current and recent litigation

20.40   Both of the above 2008 rules were immediately challenged in federal court on two fronts: by environmentalists who argue that the Polar Bear should be listed as endangered and that the 'special rule' is invalid; and by industry groups who challenged that the Polar Bear should not be listed at all and that the special rule arbitrarily excludes Alaska.[64] These challenges are currently pending.[65]

20.41   Some have argued that the ESA might be used to combat GHG emissions. However, the structure of the ESA is generally seen as ill-suited for this purpose.[66] The ESA focuses on harm to individuals and populations in limited regions, and can stop development within or affecting critical habitats, but the greatest damage to the habitat of the Polar Bears, for example (that of shrinking sea ice), comes from projects originating outside the Arctic, over which it would be much more difficult, both administratively and politically, to impose ESA permitting requirements.

SEC

20.42   On 8 February 2010 the Securities and Exchange Commission ('SEC') issued a Guidance that clarified climate disclosure obligations for US public companies. It noted that companies should report effects on their business from four sources: (i) the impact of legislation and regulation; (ii) the impact of international accords; (iii) indirect consequences of regulation or business trends; and

---

[63] Allison Winter, 'Interior will Keep Bush's Polar Bear Rule', GREENWIRE, ENVT. & ENERGY REP., 8 May 2009.

[64] Lawrence Hurley, *Obama Admin Explains 'Threatened' Listing for Polar Bears*, GREENWIRE, ENVT. & ENERGY REP., 23 December 2010.

[65] A federal court recently asked EPA to clarify its listing decision to help the judicial review process, holding that EPA's previous stated reasons were insufficient. *In re: Polar Bear Endangered Species Act Listing and 4(d) Rule Litigation*, 2010 WL 4363872 (D.D.C. 2010). Arguments over the 'special rule' will be heard after the listing decision is resolved.

[66] Bryan Walsh, 'Polar Bears: Protected, but Not Safe', *TIME*, 14 May 2008; Holly Doremus, 'Polar Bear Politics: Listing Polar Bears Won't Do Much, But We Should Do It Anyway', *SLATE*, 17 January 2008; see also J. B. Ruhl, 'Climate Change and the Endangered Species Act – Building Bridges to the No-Analog Future', *B.U.L. REV.*, 88 (2008), 1.

(iv) physical impacts of climate change.[67] This guidance has had some effect: only 17 of the 151 companies examined in the study that filed a 2009 10-K failed to mention climate change at all.[68] Most disclosures focused on the impact of legislation and regulation; only a third to half of companies discussed the other three topics, with climate impacts being the least-discussed factor that businesses considered in their operations.[69] In 2008 the Attorney General of New York launched an investigation of the securities disclosures of several coal-burning electric utilities, but there has been no other litigation against companies concerning GHG disclosures in securities filing.[70]

Barriers to judicial review

20.43 Although multiple avenues exist to potentially challenge government and other activities for violating statutory provisions, there are also several barriers to such review. The principal barriers are laid out below.

Constitutional standing

20.43A One of the principal restrictions on litigation is termed 'standing'. The United States Constitution confers jurisdiction over 'cases' and 'controversies', and this has been interpreted to mean that a plaintiff must show a 'concrete and particularized' injury-in-fact, which must be 'actual or imminent, not conjectural or hypothetical'.[71] This injury must be to the litigants directly, and not merely to the environment at large.[72] In addition, the injury must be shown to result fairly directly from the challenged activity ('causation'), and court action here must be able to remedy litigants' injuries in some palpable way ('redressability').[73]

---

[67] Sec. & Exch. Comm'n, *Commission Guidance Regarding Disclosure Related to Climate Change*, 75 Fed. Reg. 6, 290 (8 February 2010).

[68] For more information on corporate SEC disclosures, see Columbia Law School, Climate Change Securities Disclosures Resource Center, at www.law.columbia.edu/centers/climatechange/resources/securities#catalog.

[69] *Ibid.*

[70] Felicity Barringer and Danny Hakim, 'New York Subpoenas 5 Energy Companies', *N.Y. Times*, 16 September 2007.

[71] *Lujan* v. *Defenders of Wildlife*, 504 U.S. 555 (1992).

[72] *Friends of the Earth, Inc.* v. *Laidlaw*, 528 U.S. 167, 181 (2000).

[73] *Lujan*, above n. 71; *Steel Co.* v. *Citizens for Better Environment*, 523 U.S. 83 (1998).

20.44   Injury-in-fact may present a difficult barrier for parties seeking to address widespread rather than localised conditions. Environmental groups often base challenges on injuries suffered by particular members and their property. Companies and industry groups opposed to environmental regulations have less difficulty because they typically can show specific economic injury.

20.45   The global and cumulative nature of anthropogenic climate change pose challenges for plaintiffs attempting to link particular emissions (such as those from a set of power plants or even an entire industrial sector) to a particular weather event (such as a hurricane). When emissions abatement is sought, it can also be difficult to show redressability – i.e. that abating specific emissions will itself have a discernible effect on the climate.[74]

20.46   The case for environmental standing was helped by the 2007 *Massachusetts* v. *EPA* decision in the Supreme Court, where the Court held by a 5–4 decision that the Commonwealth of Massachusetts had standing to challenge the EPA's failure to regulate GHG emissions from vehicles. In this decision, the Court acknowledged that 'The harms associated with climate change are serious and well recognized'.[75] It also noted that contribution to an injury may be sufficient to ground standing: the defendant need not be the sole contributor to the petitioner's harm to be held responsible for its activities ('small incremental steps' also justify judicial review).[76] In that case, Massachusetts alleged that its coastline was being harmed as a result of climate change. Additionally, redressability is satisfied so long as a judicially mandated change would 'slow or reduce' the stated injury (the injury does not have to disappear entirely).[77] However, the longer-term impact of this ruling remains uncertain: the Court noted specifically that states are 'entitled to special solicitude in [the Court's] standing analysis'.[78]

Prudential standing

20.47   After establishing constitutional standing, litigants must also demonstrate prudential standing within the particular statute at

---

[74]   CCSP REPORT, above n. 17, at 53–68.
[75]   *Massachusetts* v. *E.P.A.*, 549 U.S. 497, 521 (2007).
[76]   *Ibid.*, at 523–4.   [77]   *Ibid.*, at 525.   [78]   *Ibid.*, at 520.

issue. This test examines whether or not the interest alleged is 'arguably within the zone of interests to be protected or regulated by the [statutory provision] or constitutional guarantee in question'.[79] Importantly, the test is 'not meant to be especially demanding', excluding only those whose interests are 'marginally related to or inconsistent with the purposes implicit in the statute'.[80]

20.48   Prudential standing requirements should not present a barrier to most existing challenges, which are primarily brought either by environmental interests or by regulated parties (states and industry). Instead, where this test has been applied in the environmental context it has eliminated tangential interests that indirectly benefit or lose from market changes caused by the regulation.[81]

Ripeness and finality

20.49   In addition to showing that they are the right parties to sue, litigants must also show that they are not suing too early. The ripeness doctrine seeks to 'prevent the courts, through avoidance of premature adjudication, from entangling themselves in abstract disagreements over administrative policies … [until their] effects [are] felt in a concrete way'.[82] In such an inquiry, courts consider (i) 'the fitness of the issues for judicial decision' and (ii) 'the hardship to the parties of withholding court consideration'.[83] A case may be considered 'fit' for a court when the issue presented is purely legal, and there is relatively little utility from observing practical applications of the challenged activity.[84] This is less likely to be true when the agency retains considerable discretion in how to apply

---

[79] *Assoc. of Data Processing Service Orgs. (ADPSO)* v. *Camp*, 397 U.S. 150, 153–4 (1970); *Bennett* v. *Spear*, 520 U.S. 154, 175–6 (1997); *National Credit Union Admin.* v. *First Nat. Bank & Trust Co.*, 522 U.S. 479 (1998).

[80] *Honeywell Intern. Inc.* v. *E.P.A.*, 374 F.3d 1363 (D.C. Cir. 2004) (quoting *Clarke* v. *Securities Industry Ass'n*, 479 U.S. 388, 399 (1987)).

[81] *Hazardous Waste Treatment Council* v. *Thomas*, 885 F.2d 918 (D.C. Cir. 1989).

[82] *Nat'l Park Hospitality* v. *Dep't of the Interior*, 538 U.S. 803 (2003).

[83] *Abbott Laboratories* v. *Gardner*, 387 U.S. 136, 149 (1967).

[84] For applications of this test, see *Cement Kiln Recycling* v. *E.P.A.*, 493 F.3d 207, 216 (D.C. Cir. 2007) ('When a challenge to an agency document … turns only on whether the document on its face … purports to bind both applicants and the Agency with the force of law-[sic]the claim is fit for review.'); *Miller* v. *Brown*, 462 F.3d 312 (4th Cir. 2006); *Texas* v. *U.S.*, 497 F.3d 491 (5th Cir. 2007).

a new rule. When examining 'hardship', the emphasis is often on whether the petitioners face an imminent choice of expensive compliance or penalised non-compliance with a regulation.[85]

20.50   The finality requirement is related to ripeness, and limits judicial review to final agency actions, where the decision-maker has reached a definitive conclusion to take the harm-causing action ('an agency rule, order, license, sanction, relief' or equivalent).[86] To be final, an action must mark 'the consummation of the agency's decision-making process'; and it must determine 'rights or obligations' from which 'legal consequences' will flow.[87]

Exhaustion

20.51   Litigants must exhaust administrative channels before they can seek judicial review. If there is an opportunity to submit comments on a proposed rule, for example, they must do so. This requirement helps ensure that agencies are aware of objections before they take final action, and protects them against ambush.

Mootness

20.52   Finally, a challenge may become moot, and therefore no longer be appropriate for judicial resolution, where the alleged injury is no longer felt. However, the Supreme Court has held that a lawsuit does not become moot simply because a polluter has ceased polluting, if it could thereafter resume its original activities.[88] Mootness may also bar actions that seek to prevent an irreparable injury (such as the destruction of a forest), and the injury takes place before a final decision is rendered (at least if plaintiffs did not seek a preliminary injunction to block the action).

Remedies

Injunctive relief

20.53   The available remedies for a lawsuit depend on the nature of the challenge and the identity of the defendant. As discussed below,

---

[85] *Nat'l Park Hospitality Ass'n* v. *Dept. of Interior*, 538 U.S. 803 (U.S. 2003); *Lujan* v. *Nat'l Wildlife Fed.*, 497 U.S. 871, 892 (1990); see also *Abbott Labs*, 387 U.S. at 136, for application of this test.
[86] 5 U.S.C. § 704 (2006).
[87] *Bennett* v. *Spear*, 520 U.S. 154, 177–8 (1997).
[88] *Friends of the Earth, Inc.* v. *Laidlaw Environmental Services, Inc.*, 528 U.S. 167 (2000).

the United States Supreme Court rejected a claim for injunctive relief in a case, *American Electric Power* v. *Connecticut*, that concerned the power of the federal courts to direct electric utilities to reduce their GHG emissions. The decision was a narrow one, however, based entirely on the conclusion that the Clean Air Act has directed the EPA to regulate GHGs, leaving no remaining role for injunctive actions under the common law.

20.54   If a statute is declared to be unconstitutional on its face, it is not automatically stricken from the code but it may become ineffective. If a court declares an agency regulation to be invalid, it may vacate the rule, or it may instead choose to allow the rule to remain in effect while the agency corrects the defects. Some courts have run a two-part test to determine whether to vacate the EPA's rules: 'the seriousness of the order's deficiencies … and the disruptive consequences of an interim change'.[89] Particularly, where a 'rule has become so intertwined with the regulatory scheme that its vacatur would sacrifice clear benefits to public health and the environment', courts may choose merely to remand regulations.[90]

20.55   If a litigant successfully demonstrates that an agency has improperly failed to undertake some mandatory activity, as occurred in *Massachusetts* v. *EPA* in 2007,[91] the court will ordinarily direct the agency to take that action. Specific time limits are usually not imposed, but the litigants may return to court to seek redress for unreasonable delays.

Litigation costs

20.56   In the USA, each party to litigation typically bears its own fees and costs; there is no general 'loser pays' rule. However, several statutes provide that prevailing plaintiffs may receive attorney's fees. The CAA, CWA, and ESA explicitly allow fees to be granted to successful petitioners in citizen suits where 'appropriate'.[92] Such fee awards have been a significant source of financing for some environmental litigation. The NEPA does not have a similar

---

[89] *Allied-Signal, Inc.* v. *Nuclear Regulatory Comm'n*, 998 F.2d 146, 150–1 (D.C. Cir. 1993); see also *North Carolina* v. *EPA*, 550 F.3d 1176 (D.C. Cir. 2008) (reducing to a remand an earlier vacatur issued in *North Carolina* v. *EPA*, 531 F.3d 896 (D.C. Cir. 2008)).

[90] *North Carolina*, 550 F.3d at 1178–9.

[91] *Mass.* v. *EPA*, 549 U.S. at 497.

[92] 42 U.S.C. § 7607 (2006); 33 USC § 1365 (2006); 16 U.S.C. § 1540 (2006).

provision, but successful plaintiffs can claim these fees under the Equal Access to Justice Act.[93] Except under extraordinary circumstances, unsuccessful plaintiffs are not liable for defendants' legal fees.

Energy litigation activity

20.57   As the largest source of US GHG emissions, energy projects, and particularly electricity power plants, have become a large source of litigation. In particular, the Sierra Club, a US environmental NGO, is leading a coordinated litigation campaign by environmental groups to challenge all new coal-fired power plants.[94] These campaigns utilise administrative procedures and litigation to challenge several aspects of these facilities under a wide array of legal theories: GHG emissions, conventional air pollutant emissions, cooling water discharges, ash disposal, land acquisition, railway lines to carry fuel, public utility commission approvals, and others. Similarly, the environmental community is litigating against coal mining activities, especially focusing on mountaintop removal. Many of these challenges have been successful.[95] The litigation costs and judicial uncertainty, coupled with possible GHG regulations, have created a major cloud of uncertainty over all proposed coal-fired power plants.

20.58   There are also a significant number of legal challenges to renewable energy projects. These lawsuits are not coordinated, however, and not based on any unifying principle. Instead they arise from local parties protesting aesthetic harms (wind farms have been particularly challenged as being unsightly),[96] or from

---

[93] 5 U.S.C. § 504 (2006).

[94] Sierra Club, 'Stopping the Coal Rush', at www.sierraclub.org/environmentallaw/coal.

[95] Sierra Club, 'Stopping the Coal Rush', Plant List, at www.sierraclub.org/environmental-law/coal/plantlist.aspx.

[96] The most prominent of these controversies concerned the proposed 'Cape Wind' project off the coast of Massachusetts, which has been a target of litigation. Kim Geiger, 'First U.S. Offshore Wind Project Faces Lawsuit', L.A. TIMES, 26 June 2010; Beth Daley, '6 Groups File First Suit to Halt Wind Farm', BOS. GLOBE, 26 June 2010. However, this project was issued its permit to begin construction on 7 January 2011. DEPT. OF ARMY, PERMIT NO. NAE-2004–388, CAPE WIND ASSOCIATES, available at www.nae.usace. army.mil/projects/ma/CapeWind/permit.pdf; DEPT OF ARMY RECORD OF DECISION, APPLICATION NO. NAE-2004–388, CAPE WIND ASSOCIATES, available at www.nae.usace. army.mil/projects/ma/CapeWind/ROD.pdf.

environmentalists concerned with other environmental harms (certain large solar projects may pose a threat to desert ecology, and some wind projects have been alleged to threaten a species of endangered bats, for example).[97] Although this local litigation does not target the industry as such, it can be a significant problem for specific projects. As such, some have argued that a federal statute should be passed to pre-empt such litigation (along the lines of the federal law that inhibits local laws against telecommunications towers).[98] There has been no recent legislative action to enact this statute, however.

(C)   Private law

Overview

20.59   In addition to challenging specific governmental actions, interested parties may also attempt to utilise the US's private law system as a springboard to provide a basis for climate-relevant complaints. There are relatively few legal mechanisms available here, largely because the USA does not constitutionally or statutorily recognise a right to a non-polluted environment. However, several lawsuits have been brought that explore the use of these theories.

20.60   Attempts to base carbon liability in private causes of action could be displaced by climate legislation, or possibly by regulation or perhaps even the possibility of regulation under existing law (principally the CAA). However, even without such displacement, such lawsuits face multiple challenges, as described below.

Bases for liability

20.61   These claims sound in tort, which is defined as 'a civil wrong ... for which a remedy may be obtained'.[99] Two kinds of tort theories have been advanced in the climate change context – public

---

[97] See, e.g., *Animal Welfare Institute* v. *Beech Ridge Energy LLC*, 675 F. Supp.2d 540 (D. Md. 2009).

[98] Federal Telecommunications Act of 1996, 47 U.S.C. § 253 (2006).

[99] *Black's Law Dictionary*, 9th edn. (2009) at 1626.

nuisance and fraudulent misrepresentation (the latter, linked with conspiracy).

Public nuisance

20.62   Public nuisance on the national level is a common law injury, defined not by any national statute, but by the courts. On the state level, it can be either court-defined or legislated. The basic test for this (applicable in federal law, although it may vary slightly from state to state) is an 'unreasonable interference with a right common to the general public'.[100] This definition includes significant interference with the public health, safety, morals, peace, or comfort, as well as conduct 'of a continuing nature' that is detrimental to a public right.[101] However, this test is infamously malleable, and so courts often decide what constitutes a nuisance on a case-by-case level.[102] The right interfered with must be common to the public as a class, and not merely a right held by one person or even a group of citizens;[103] although the harm must remain individualised.[104] Under the common law, public nuisance is a no-fault tort, meaning that no maliciousness or negligence need be shown to establish liability.

20.63   In the USA, state courts have a long history of applying common law public nuisance doctrine to compensate pollution victims in the absence of sufficient environmental protections.[105] The federal court system has also done so under federal common law since before the turn of the twentieth century.[106] This doctrine has

---

[100]   RESTATEMENT (SECOND) OF TORTS § 821A (1979).

[101]   *Ibid.*, § 821B.

[102]   *Lucas* v. *South Carolina Coastal Council*, 505 U.S. 1003, 1055 (1992) (J. Blackmun, dissenting) ('one searches in vain … for anything resembling a principle in the common law of nuisance').

[103]   RESTATEMENT (SECOND) OF TORTS § 821C(2)(c) (1979) (allowing a citizen to sue 'as a representative of the general public').

[104]   *Ibid.*, § 821C(1).

[105]   Bruce Yandle, *Common Sense and Common Law for the Environment: Creating Wealth in Humming Bird Economies* (Rowman and Littlefield, 1997), pp. 88–89; Tom Kuhnle, 'The Rebirth of Common Law Actions for Addressing Hazardous Waste Contamination', *Stan. Envtl. L.J.*, 15 (1996), 187, 193. For a modern example, see *United States* v. *Hooker Chems. & Plastics Corp.*, 722 F. Supp. 960, 963–70 (W.D.N.Y. 1989) (this case is better known as the 'Love Canal Case', which involved toxic dumping by a chemicals company leading to major health concerns in a neighbouring community).

[106]   *Baltimore & P. R. Co. v Fifth Baptist Church*, 108 U.S. 317 (1883) (applying equitable common law norms to impose liability for private nuisance); *Missouri* v. *Illinois*, 180 U.S.

been used by private and governmental parties (particularly state governments[107]) to control pollution that is beyond their legislative control. However, federal common law nuisance actions are designed only to address gaps where neither state law, nor federal legislation or regulations, apply.[108] In particular, 'separation-of-powers concerns create a presumption in favor of pre-emption of federal common law whenever it can be said that Congress has legislated on the subject'.[109] Courts have also tended to limit liability to the direct owners of properties that cause harm, even if the original toxic pollutants arrived from elsewhere.[110]

Public nuisance has become the largest source of climate-relevant private litigation today. In total, four major cases have been filed claiming that various parties have caused a public nuisance through their GHG emissions.[111] *California* v. *General Motors Corp.*, involving the State of California suing a group of car companies for money damages resulting from GHG emissions, was dismissed and is concluded.[112] *Comer* v. *Murphy Oil*

208, 241 (1901) (compelling one state to restrict activities that imposed a 'public nuisance' on another).

[107] See, e.g., *State of Ga.* v. *Tennessee Copper Co.*, 206 U.S. 230 (1907) (granting the state of Georgia an injunction preventing emissions from plants located across the border in the state of Tennessee).

[108] *City of Milwaukee* v. *Illinois*, 451 U.S. 304, 314 n. 7, 315 (1981) (noting that 'if state law can be applied, there is no need for federal common law' and that '[w]here Congress has so exercised its constitutional power … courts have no power to substitute their own [judgment]'); see also *Diamond* v. *Gen. Motors Corp.*, 97 Cal. Rptr. 639, 642–6 (Ct. App. 1971) (denying a public nuisance claim because 'plaintiff is simply asking the court to do what the elected representatives of the people have not done: adopt stricter standards … and enforce them').

[109] *Matter of Oswego Barge Corp.*, 664 F.2d 327, 335 (C.A.N.Y. 1981).

[110] *City of Bloomington* v. *Westinghouse Electric Corporation*, 891 F.2d 611, 614 (7th Cir. 1989).

[111] *Connecticut* v. *Am. Elec. Power Co., Inc.*, 582 F.3d 309 (2nd Cir. 2009) rev'd No. 10-174, 2011 WL 2437011 (U.S. 2011); *Comer* v. *Murphy Oil USA*, 585 F.3d 855, 860 (5th Cir. 2009) (discussing the relevant threshold issues), *vacated*, *reh'g granted en banc*, 598 F.3d 208 (5th Cir. 2010), *appeal dismissed*, 607 F.3d 1049 (5th Cir. 2010) (dismissing the case due to lack of quorum); *Native Vill. of Kivalina* v. *ExxonMobil Corp.*, 663 F. Supp. 2d 863 (N.D. Cal. 2009); *People of State of California* v. *Gen. Motors Corp.*, 2007 WL 2726871 (N.D. Cal. 2007). Another case, where a private citizen sued state and federal government environmental agencies for allowing GHG emissions, was quickly dismissed: *Korsinsky* v. *U.S. E.P.A.*, 2005 WL 2414744 (S.D.N.Y. 2005).

[112] *Cal.* v. *GM*, 2007 WL at 15–49. California subsequently withdrew its appeal to the 9th Circuit, citing advancements made by the Obama Administration as having satisfied its concerns. Motion for Appellee, No. 07–16908 (9th Cir. 2009) (motion to withdraw appeal).

seeks damages from a large group of GHG emitters for injury caused by Hurricane Katrina, which was allegedly intensified by global warming. This case was dismissed after a rather convoluted appellate history, in which the court granted en banc review and vacated the panel decision, and then lost a quorum for en banc review but left the panel decision vacated.[113] *Native Village of Kivalina* v. *ExxonMobil Corp.* is a suit by an Alaskan village against a group of GHG emitters for the cost of relocating; it was dismissed by the trial court and is now under appeal before the Ninth Circuit.[114] Most importantly by far, on 20 June 2011 the Supreme Court ruled in *American Electric Power* v. *Connecticut.* That decision is discussed in detail below.

American Electric Power *v.* Connecticut

20.64   By way of background, in 2004, at a time when environmentalists were frustrated at the refusal of Congress and President George W. Bush to regulate greenhouse gases (GHGs), two suits were brought against six electric power companies that run fossil fuel plants in a total of twenty states. One suit was brought by eight states and New York City; the other suit was brought by three land trusts. The plaintiffs in both cases claimed that the GHGs from the power plants constitute a common law nuisance, and they asked the court to issue an injunction requiring the plants to reduce their emissions.

20.65   In 2005, Judge Preska of the US District Court for the Southern District of New York dismissed the cases on the grounds that they raise non-justiciable political questions.[115] The Second Circuit heard oral argument in June 2006. As the third anniversary of that argument passed, the Second Circuit's long delay in deciding became one of the great mysteries in climate change law. Meanwhile, the Supreme Court issued the landmark decision in *Massachusetts* v. *Environmental Protection Agency*, and later one of the three members of the panel that heard the arguments in the *Connecticut* case was elevated to the Supreme Court – Judge Sotomayor. Finally in September 2009 the two remaining

---

[113]   *Comer*, 585 F.3d at 860. This appeal to the Supreme Court was dismissed on 10 January, 2011. *Comer*, 607 F.3d, *cert. denied* (U.S. Jan. 10, 2011) (No. 10–8168).

[114]   *Kivalina*, 663 F. Supp. at 869.

[115]   *Connecticut v. Am. Elec. Power Co.*, 406 F.Supp.2d 265 (S.D.N.Y. 2005).

members of the panel issued the decision – Judge McLaughlin, an appointee of the first President Bush, and Judge Hall, appointed by the second President Bush.[116]

20.66   The Second Circuit decision was a major win for the plaintiffs. First, the panel found that the case was perfectly justiciable and did not raise political questions as that concept has been interpreted by the Supreme Court.[117] Second, though it did not need to, the panel found not only that the states had standing to sue – which was already known from the *Massachusetts* decision – but also that the private land trusts had standing because they alleged that their property was being harmed by climate change.[118] This would potentially open the courthouse doors to broad classes of people and entities beyond states. Third, the panel found that the federal common law of nuisance applied, and that it had not been displaced by the Clean Air Act and EPA actions under that statute.[119] Thus the Second Circuit remanded the case to the district court for further proceedings.

Supreme Court decision

20.67   Eight justices participated in the deliberations of *AEP*; Justice Sotomayor was recused. The decision was unanimous, 8–0, and was written by Justice Ginsburg. The decision reversed the Second Circuit and found that the federal common law nuisance claims could not proceed.[120] The sole reason was that the Clean Air Act, as interpreted in *Massachusetts*, gave the EPA the authority to regulate greenhouse gases, and the EPA was exercising that authority. This displaced the federal common law of nuisance. The Court declared, 'Congress delegated to EPA the decision whether and how to regulate carbon-dioxide emissions from power plants; the delegation is what displaces federal common law.'[121] Thus it is not for the federal courts to issue their own rules.

20.68   This may be the most intriguing paragraph in the opinion: 'The petitioners contend that the federal courts lack authority to adjudicate this case. Four members of the Court would hold that at least

---

[116] *Connecticut*, 582 F.3d at 309.
[117] *Ibid*. at 321.   [118] *Ibid*. at 332.   [119] *Ibid*. at 371.
[120] *Connecticut*, 2011 WL 2437011 at 4.
[121] *Ibid*. at 10.

some plaintiffs have Article III standing under *Massachusetts*, which permitted a State to challenge EPA's refusal to regulate greenhouse gas emissions; and further, that no other threshold obstacle bars review. Four members of the Court, adhering to a dissenting opinion in *Massachusetts*, or regarding that decision as distinguishable, would hold that none of the plaintiffs have Article III standing. We therefore affirm, by an equally divided Court, the Second Circuit's exercise of jurisdiction and proceed to the merits.'[122]

20.69   Though unnamed in the opinion, clearly the four justices who find standing, and no other obstacles to review, are Justices Ginsburg, Breyer, Kagan and Kennedy. The four who disagree are Chief Justice Roberts and Justices Scalia, Thomas and Alito. The Ginsburg group thus apparently rejects the political question defense as well as the standing argument. Should another case come up on which Justice Sotomayor was not recused, there might be a 5–4 majority to allow climate change nuisance litigation, but for the Clean Air Act displacement. So this aspect of the Supreme Court decision did not set precedent in the technical sense, but it may give an indication of how the Supreme Court as presently constituted would rule in another case where states sued on public nuisance grounds about GHGs, but where displacement was not operating.

20.70   On the other hand, the paragraph quoted above (when considered in conjunction with *Massachusetts*) may hint that Justice Kennedy believes that only states would have standing. Thus there might be a 5–4 majority against any kinds of GHG nuisance claims (and maybe other kinds of GHG claims) by non-states.

State claims left unresolved

20.71   The Court explicitly did not decide whether the Clean Air Act pre-empts state public nuisance litigation over GHGs. Thus some plaintiff group will probably press state common law claims, perhaps on the remand in *AEP* v. *Connecticut*. The defendants would certainly argue that the Clean Air Act displaced state common law nuisance claims as well. The plaintiffs would no doubt counter that the Clean Air Act has provisions that explicitly say that

---

[122]   *Ibid.* at 7.

common law claims are not pre-empted, at least by certain parts of the Clean Air Act.[123] In the next volley, the defendants would quote Justice Ginsburg's statement in *AEP* that 'judges lack the scientific, economic, and technological resources an agency can utilize in coping with issues of this order … Judges may not commission scientific studies or convene groups of experts for advice, or issue rules under notice-and-comment procedures'.[124] Where this ball stops, only time can tell.

20.72   It is also possible that plaintiffs will forum shop – they will look for the district or the circuit where they are most likely to prevail in their non-pre-emption argument.

20.73   Pressing state common law nuisance claims will raise several additional complications. One of them is which state's law will apply. If relief is sought against a particular facility, it might well be the law of the state where the facility is located. The Fourth Circuit recently considered common law nuisance claims against facilities in several states in a case concerning conventional air pollutants, not GHGs. The court found that the laws of the states where the plants were located specifically allowed the activities – in other words, the facilities were operating pursuant to and in compliance with state permits – and therefore nuisance actions were precluded.[125] If the same doctrine applied to the defendants' facilities in a new case about GHG, the plaintiffs would face a tough burden in proving that the plants were not operating in accordance with state law.

20.74   Another complication with state common law nuisance claims is that some states would act to bar such claims. On 17 June 2011, Governor Rick Perry of Texas signed a Bill providing that companies sued for nuisance or trespass for GHG emissions would have an affirmative defense if those companies were in substantial compliance with their environmental permits.[126]

20.75   Since the *AEP* opinion was based entirely on displacement by congressional designation of EPA as the decision-maker on GHG

---

[123]   42 U.S.C.A § 7604(e).
[124]   *Connecticut*, 2011 WL 2437011 at 11.
[125]   *N. Carolina, ex rel. Cooper* v. *Tennessee Valley Auth.*, 615 F.3d 291 (4th Cir. 2010).
[126]   SB 875 (to be codified at Tex. Water Code Ann. § 7.257).

regulation, if Congress takes away EPA's authority to regulate GHGs but does not explicitly bar federal common law nuisance claims, these cases will come back. Thus this interestingly changes the political dynamic a bit – success by opponents of GHG regulation in their efforts to take away EPA's authority could swiftly bring back the common law claims, unless they are also able to muster enough votes to go further and explicitly pre-empt the federal and state common law claims.

Damages vs injunctive relief

20.76   Another question left open is whether the Supreme Court's decision bars all federal common law nuisance claims, or only those like *AEP* that sought injunctive relief. This particular question may be litigated very soon, perhaps in the two other public nuisance cases for GHGs that are currently pending. *Village of Kivalina* v. *Exxon Mobil* was put on hold pending the decision in *AEP*, but now that the case is off hold the plaintiffs are arguing that *AEP* affects only suits for injunctive relief, not their own suit for money damages. Meanwhile, *Comer* v. *Murphy Oil* was re-filed on 27 May 2011 after its procedurally convoluted dismissal (see para. 20.63 above); it, too, is seeking money damages, not an injunction.

20.77   None of these cases has come close to the merits. There has been no discovery in any of them, or litigation of such difficult issues as how a district court would determine what is a reasonable level of GHG emissions from a myriad of industrial facilities, or (in the cases seeking money damages) what defendants would be liable, what plaintiffs would be entitled to awards, what defendants would have to pay what share of the award, and what plaintiffs would enjoy what share of the award. Among the other issues that would have to be addressed are extraterritorial jurisdiction over foreign entities; the impossibility of attributing particular injuries to particular defendants; and the effect of the fact that most of the relevant emitting facilities were presumably operating in accordance with their governmentally issued emissions permits.

20.78   Everything else aside, *AEP* appears to be a reaffirmation of EPA authority. That is shown by two things. First, the language of the decision itself is quite strong on EPA's power under the Clean Air

Act. For example, the Court stated: 'It is altogether fitting that Congress designated an expert agency, here, EPA, as best suited to serve as primary regulator of greenhouse gas emissions.'[127] Second, Justices Alito and Thomas wrote a concurring decision saying the opinion assumed that *Massachusetts* governed and could not be distinguished; they did not necessarily agree with it, but no party had raised that issue.[128] But, perhaps significantly, Chief Justice Roberts and Justice Scalia did not join in that concurrence. Therefore its seems that there may now be a 7–2 majority in favour of keeping *Massachusetts* and its finding that the EPA has strong authority to regulate GHGs under the Clean Air Act. This, in turn, may have somewhat strengthened the EPA's hand in the multiple litigations now pending in the US Court of Appeals for the District of Columbia Circuit challenging the EPA regulations.

Fraudulent misrepresentation and conspiracy

20.79 Attempts have also been made to hold GHG emitters liable by accusing them of fraudulent misrepresentation to the government and public for private gain. There is no federal cause of action for this, but most states have their own causes of action, and utilise some version of the following test: 'One who: 1) fraudulently makes a misrepresentation of fact, opinion, intention, or law; 2) for the purpose of inducing another to act or to refrain from action in reliance upon it; 3) is subject to liability to the other in deceit for pecuniary loss caused to him; 4) by his justifiable reliance upon the misrepresentation.'[129] Most states add that if the statement is 'material', or if the party making the representation has reason to know that the plaintiff is likely to regard it as important in making a decision, then the reliance need not be justifiable.[130] To be actionable, a fraudulent misrepresentation generally must concern fact rather than mere opinion, judgement, expectation, or probability.[131]

20.80 An attempt could be made to utilise the conspiracy claim as an alternative basis for liability for climate misinformation

---

[127] *Connecticut*, 2011 WL 2437011 at 11.   [128] *Ibid.* at 13.

[129] RESTATEMENT (SECOND) OF TORTS § 525 (1979) (element demarcation added).

[130] *Ibid.* (case citations).   [131] *Ibid.* (Comment d).

campaigns. There is a federal conspiracy statute that addresses attempts to defraud the US government, but it only applies to federal offences.[132] However, conspiracy has also been defined in the federal common law, as 'a combination "of two or more persons who, by some concerted action, intend to accomplish some unlawful objective for the purpose of harming another which results in damage"'.[133] Generally, conspiring parties must have 'reached a unity of purpose or a common design and understanding, or a meeting of the minds in an unlawful arrangement'.[134] Several states also have their own (similar) conspiracy rules.

20.81   Plaintiffs have used fraudulent misrepresentation and conspiracy claims in the past as part of an effort to hold industries accountable for alleged attempts to misdirect scientific research on an important issue for financial gain. The most famous example comes from a series of lawsuits against the tobacco industry.[135] Although none of these cases ever reached a decision on the merits, the industry eventually agreed to a $206 billion settlement with all plaintiffs.[136] In addition, the federal government filed a suit under the Racketeer Influenced and Corrupt Organizations Act ('RICO').[137] The Government successfully established legal fault in that case, but the remedies were limited to injunctive relief (no damages were awarded).[138]

20.82   Attempts to impose similar liability for funding bad climate science face significant hurdles. The plaintiffs in the tobacco case

---

[132] 18 U.S.C. § 371 (2006).

[133] *Vieux* v. *E. Bay Reg'l Park Dist.*, 906 F.2d 1330, 1343 (9th Cir. 1990).

[134] *Gilbrook* v. *City of Westminster*, 177 F.3d 839, 856 (9th Cir. 1999) (*en banc*) (quotation omitted).

[135] *Cipollone* v. *Liggett Group, Inc.*, 505 U.S. 504 (1992) (protesting efforts to prevent releases of data); see generally Douglas N. Jacobson, 'After *Cipollone v. Liggett Group, Inc*: How Wide Will the Floodgates of Cigarette Litigation Open?', *Am. U.L. Rev.*, 38 (1989), 1021, 1023; Hanoch Dagana and James J. White, 'Governments, Citizens, and Injurious Industries', *N.Y.U. L. Rev.*, 75 (2000), 354, 363.

[136] Tucker S. Player, 'After the Fall: The Cigarette Papers, the Global Settlement, and the Future of Tobacco Litigation', *S.C. L. Rev.*, 49 (1998), 311; Arthur B. LaFrance, 'Tobacco Litigation: Smoke, Mirrors and Public Policy', *Am. J. L. & Med.*, 26 (2000), 187.

[137] 18 U.S.C. § 1962 (2006).

[138] *United States* v. *Philip Morris USA, Inc.*, 449 F. Supp. 2d 1 (D.D.C. 2006), order clarified, 477 F. Supp. 2d 191 (D.D.C. 2007); see generally Civil Division, United States Department of Justice, Tobacco Litigation, at www.justice.gov/civil/cases/tobacco2/index.htm ('DOJ Tobacco Litigation Listing'). Appeals on both sides were unsuccessful.

had very strong facts using (by then) uncontroversial science, and still only succeeded after certain insider revelations.[139] Climate science is much more complicated, and in the USA particularly it is much more controversial; scientists still exist, though overwhelmingly outnumbered, who question fundamental aspects of the scientific basis for climate change, which could undermine attempts to label any one party as 'hiding the truth'. To establish liability in climate cases, litigants might have to prove that these companies believed climate change presented dangers, and nonetheless began a coordinated industry effort to obfuscate the facts. They then might have to show that this obfuscation actually hurt them; or that the Government's climate regulation efforts were significantly affected by reliance on corporate-funded climate research.[140] Finally, given that the nature, sources and impacts of climate change are subjects of vigorous political debates in the USA, attempts to impose liability for advocacy in one direction or the other raise important issues under the free speech and free press clauses of the First Amendment to the US Constitution.

20.83   Two GHG lawsuits have raised such conspiracy claims: *Comer* and *Kivalina*. *Comer* additionally made a fraudulent misrepresentation claim under Mississippi state law. As with the public nuisance cases, none of these claims have been heard on the merits: in *Kivalina*, this claim was dismissed with the public nuisance claim without discussion; and *Comer*'s two claims were separated out from public nuisance early on and dismissed as a 'generalised grievance'.[141]

Barriers to judicial review

20.84   Before even reaching the merits of these tort theories, plaintiffs would have to overcome several barriers to judicial review, as summarised below.

---

[139] Insiders gave accounts of industry meetings developing strategies to mislead the public and active manipulation of datasets. Richard Ausness, 'Conspiracy Theories: Is There a Place for Civil Conspiracy in Products Liability Litigation?', *Tenn. L. Rev.*, 74 (2007), 383, 384–5. See also 'DOJ Tobacco Litigation Listing', above n. 138.

[140] These findings are context-specific elements of fraud, which is defined legally as '[a] knowing misrepresentation of the truth or concealment of a material fact to induce another to act to his or her detriment'. *Black's Law Dictionary*, 9th edn (2009), 731.

[141] *Comer*, 585 F.3d at 868 (quoting *Allen* v. *Wright*, 468 U.S. 737 (1984)).

Constitutional standing

20.85   Standing here is similar to the standing question discussed above under the statutory claims; the test is essentially the same. Unsurprisingly then, many of the concerns with establishing standing (particularly looking at causation of climate change and redressability if emissions are reduced) are similar. As with public litigation, plaintiffs will need to demonstrate a real, tangible harm being protected. This makes property owners, and particularly states (in light of *Massachusetts* v. *EPA* and its 'special solicitude' for states), best suited to bring a case for private nuisance.

20.86   Particular issues arise with causation associated with fraudulent misrepresentation. The chain of causation is even more attenuated, as plaintiffs may not only have to show that GHG emissions led to their particularised injuries, but also that alleged conspiracies to misinform the Government and public actually affected policy.

Political question doctrine

20.87   The political question doctrine is a court-created doctrine that prevents courts from hearing cases that may interfere with the proper functioning of the other two federal branches. The classical form of the political question doctrine has its origins in *Marbury* v. *Madison*, a foundational court decision that in 1803 introduced the idea that the court system should limit itself to resolving cases involving individual rights and injuries: '[q]uestions, in their nature political, or which are, by the constitution and laws, submitted to the executive, can never be made in this court'.[142] Courts have applied this doctrine not just in the face of clear jurisdictional conflict, but also where needed to preserve the legitimacy of the judiciary, or to avoid conflict with other branches of government.[143] In either case, the goal is generally to 'restrain the Judiciary from inappropriate interference' with the other branches' affairs.[144] Where applied, the political

---

[142] *Marbury* v. *Madison*, 5 U.S. 137, 170 (1803).
[143] Rachel Barkow, 'More Supreme than Court? The Fall of the Political Question Doctrine and the Rise of Judicial Supremacy', *Col. L. Rev.*, 102 (2002), 237, 253–5.
[144] *United States* v. *Munoz-Flores*, 495 U.S. 385, 394 (1990).

question doctrine generally follows a multi-factor test laid out in *Baker* v. *Carr*.[145]

20.88 Public nuisance claims for GHGs are particularly vulnerable to allegations that insufficient judicial tools exist to resolve many important questions, including what level of emissions qualifies something as a public nuisance; how to deal with the fact that the challenged actions (such as extracting oil and coal, and building automobiles) were not only lawful but were encouraged by the Government over a period of many years; how to apportion damages that resulted from the activities of millions of companies all over the world for a period of more than a century; and how to distribute money damages, when the victims number in the billions, are all over the world, and include many who are deceased and many more who are unborn. However, as noted above, the Supreme Court in *American Electric Power* split 4–4 on whether the political question doctrine impedes common law nuisance claims for GHGs, and most observers believe that if Justice Sotomayor had not been recused from that case, she would have sided with the plaintiffs, leading to a 5–4 majority rejecting the political question doctrine in this context.

Causation

20.89 All common law tort claims, whether federal or state, require a showing that the alleged wrong actions in fact caused plaintiffs' harm (cause-in-fact), and that the wrong actions are sufficiently related to the injury to be legally recognised as responsible (proximate cause). As with the foundational torts, causation inquiries vary from state to state, and so there is no unified standard. However, most states utilise some variation of this bifurcation,

---

[145] *Baker* v. *Carr*, 369 U.S. 186, 217 (1962) (laying out a test of six factors, any one of which is sufficient to justify avoiding judicial resolution: '[1] [A] textually demonstrable constitutional commitment of the issue to a coordinate political department; [2] a lack of judicially discoverable and manageable standards for resolving it; [3] the impossibility of deciding without an initial policy determination of a kind clearly for non-judicial discretion; [4] the impossibility of a court's undertaking independent resolution without expressing the lack of the respect due coordinate branches of government; [5] an unusual need for unquestioning adherence to a political decision already made; or [6] the potentiality of embarrassment from multifarious pronouncements by various departments on one question'.).

explained below. For both of these inquiries, the plaintiff will generally bear the burden of proving causation.[146]

20.90   Factual causation is established when 'the harm would not have occurred absent the conduct'.[147] However, the defendant need not be the sole cause: if multiple actors, acting independently, each could have caused this harm, then any of them can be considered the factual cause.[148] The courts have yet to decide whether these black letter doctrines apply in the climate change situation, with its millions of potential defendants, dispersed over time and space.

20.91   Legal causation limits liability to 'harms that result from the risks that made the actor's conduct tortious'.[149] Put another way, a party is only liable for expected harms from their bad conduct. Where the action is intentional or reckless, this liability extends even to harms that were unlikely.[150] Conversely, if the action is merely negligent, then trivial contribution to a larger event that actually caused the injury will not establish liability. The standard of care to be applied retroactively to historic GHG emitters is very much an open question.

(D)   Other law

State laws

20.92   As stated above, the USA is a federalist system; individual states have the power to set their own laws and policies in many areas. Many states have done so, with commitments to reduce their GHG emissions into the future.

20.93   California in particular has led the way in climate policy, most notably with its passage of Assembly Bill 32 ('AB32') in 2006, which commits California to achieving 1990 levels of emissions by 2020. To implement this programme, the California Air Resources Board ('CARB') is empowered to take a wide variety of measures, most notably a cap-and-trade programme, but also including new building codes, clean energy financing measures,

---

[146]   RESTATEMENT (THIRD) OF TORTS: PHYSICAL & EMOTIONAL HARM § 28 (2010).
[147]   *Ibid.*, § 26.   [148]   *Ibid.*, § 27.
[149]   *Ibid.*, § 29.   [150]   *Ibid.*, § 33.

grid restructuring, clean vehicle rules, and other measures that would inevitably impose liability across the economy.[151] California's cap-and-trade programme is scheduled to take effect in 2013.

20.94 Other than California, no states have active plans to implement cap-and-trade programmes. The State of New Mexico's Environmental Improvement Board approved a cap-and-trade system on 2 November 2010, but the incoming governor fired the entire Board on 5 January 2011, and attempted to prevent the cap-and-trade rule from being published.[152] This action was in turn overturned by the New Mexico Supreme Court, but the situation there remains in flux.[153]

Regional laws

20.95 In addition to individual state activities, three groups of states have also joined forces to establish cap-and-trade systems that have the potential to impose emission limitations within their boundaries. In the northeast, the Regional Greenhouse Gas Initiative ('RGGI') comprises nine states,[154] caps power sector emissions at 10 per cent below 2005 levels by 2018, and has a functioning market in place to accomplish this.[155] RGGI has the only mandatory cap-and-trade system for GHGs now operating in the USA. In the west, the Western Climate Initiative ('WCI') has brought together eleven US states and Canadian provinces[156] and has a goal of reducing 2005 emissions by

---

[151] For more information on specific plans, see California Air Resources Board, 'Climate Change Program', at www.arb.ca.gov/cc/cc.htm.

[152] Margot Roosevelt, 'New Mexico Threatens a U-Turn on Environmental Regulations', *L.A. Times*, 5 January 2011.

[153] Press Release, N.M. Envtl. Law Ctr., 'NMELC Wins Supreme Court Victory' (26 January 2011), available at http://nmenvirolaw.org/index.php/site/pressreleases-more/nm_supreme_court_orders_records_administrator_to_print_rules.

[154] Connecticut, Delaware, Maine, Maryland, Massachusetts, New Hampshire, New York, Rhode Island and Vermont. Additionally, Pennsylvania and the Canadian Provinces of Québec, New Brunswick and Ontario are observers. New Jersey was a full member, but the governor recently withdrew from the programme; however, New Jersey's implementing legislation has yet to be repealed.

[155] See Regional Greenhouse Gas Initiative, CO_2 Budget Trading Program, at www.rggi.org/home.

[156] WCI includes seven US states (Arizona, California, Montana, New Mexico, Oregon, Utah and Washington) and four Canadian provinces (British Columbia, Manitoba,

15 per cent by 2020, though it is not scheduled to go into effect until 2012 (with full implementation in 2015)[157] and, except for California, state action remains uncertain. Finally, the midwest established the Midwestern Greenhouse Gas Reduction Accord ('MGGRA') with seven states and provinces,[158] which has set an 18 to 20 per cent reduction goal below 2005 levels by 2020,[159] though very little activity has occurred to date. All three regions also include several observers. However, the November 2010 election brought Republican opponents of climate regulation to power in certain states, which is leading several of these states to consider dropping out.[160]

20.96   If the federal government were to adopt comprehensive climate legislation, these regional agreements would likely be folded into the national programme. Otherwise, any federal laws or regulations could either ignore the regional programmes (leaving them relatively intact), or they could pre-empt these programmes via the Supremacy Clause, which holds that the United States Constitution and federal statutes are 'the supreme law of the land'.[161]

Criminal law

20.97   Criminal liability in the USA is founded on violations of federal or state statutes. No existing or foreseeable statute makes it a crime to emit GHGs. Criminal liability could attach for the filing of false reports with the Government, but no such charges have been brought related to GHGs.

Public trust

20.98   Some scholars have suggested that public trust principles present an opportunity for judges to hold governments accountable for

Ontario and Québec). Additionally, six Mexican states, six additional US states, and four additional Canadian provinces, are observers. Arizona's membership does not include participation in WCI's cap-and-trade programme.

[157] See Western Climate Initiative, at www.westernclimateinitiative.org.

[158] Six US states (Illinois, Iowa, Kansas, Michigan, Minnesota and Wisconsin) and one Canadian province (Manitoba). Observers include Indiana, Ohio, South Dakota and the Province of Ontario.

[159] See Midwest Greenhouse Gas Reduction Accord, at www.midwesternaccord.org.

[160] See Fig. 3 for a graphical depiction of the states involved in each of these three initiatives.

[161] U.S. Const. art. VI, cl. 2.

their emissions. Public trust doctrine in the environmental context holds that governments necessarily hold all of their natural resources in trust for their citizens, and as such carry a fiduciary duty to preserve these resources for present and future use.[162] Under such a hypothetical 'atmospheric trust' theory, the atmosphere could be characterised as a national asset, which would then impose upon the Government an obligation to prevent waste to that asset.[163] Citizens could bring a suit either as a beneficiary of that trust, based on harms (health impacts etc.) felt from the Government's failure to preserve the property; or as co-tenants of the trust, for failure by the Government to pay to preserve the property.[164]

20.99   In May 2011 several lawsuits were filed simultaneously in states around the country based on the public trust doctrine and GHGs. These cases raise some of the same issues of separation of powers and judicial competence as are present in *American Electric Power*, but these issues will presumably be litigated under the new lawsuits.

International law

Treaty liabilities

20.100 The USA has been and continues to be reluctant to subject itself to international laws in the environmental field. As stated above, it has not ratified the Kyoto Protocol or UNCLOS. It also withdrew recognition of the International Court of Justice's ('ICJ') general jurisdiction in 1985, following a decision with which it disagreed.[165] The USA continues to grant specific jurisdiction to the ICJ in certain circumstances, and under certain treaties. Also, US courts often follow treaty mandates even when such treaties

---

[162] See Jan S. Stevens, 'The Public Trust: A Sovereign's Ancient Prerogative Becomes the People's Environmental Right', *U.C. Davis L. Rev.*, 14 (1980), 195.

[163] Mary Wood, 'Atmospheric Trust Litigation' in William C. G. Burns and Hari M. Osofsky (eds.), *Adjudicating Climate Change: Sub-National, National and Supra-National Approaches* (New York: Cambridge University Press, 2009), p. 99.

[164] *Ibid.*

[165] Letter from George P. Schultz, Secretary of State, United States, to Javier Perez de Cuellar, Secretary General, United Nations (7 October 1985) (referring to Department Statement, Dept. of State, 'U.S. terminates acceptance of ICJ compulsory jurisdiction' (7 October 1985)), reprinted in *I.L.M.*, 24 (1985), 1742.

lack binding effect.[166] However, a treaty can impose mandatory treaty authority over the US court system, meaning that judges must abide by the provisions of the treaty in interpreting the law, only '[i]f the treaty contains stipulations which are self-executing, that is, require no legislation to make them operative'.[167] The USA is not currently a Party to any environmental treaties that would impose such a binding obligation with respect to GHG emissions.

20.101   The country is a Party to the FCCC and, as noted above, has endorsed the Copenhagen and Cancun agreements. No FCCC-specific claims have been brought forward in any US tribunal to date.

Foreign judgments

20.102   The USA is relatively friendly to recognising and enforcing foreign judgments.[168] However, it does not do so on the basis of any treaties; instead recognition is governed by state law, on three separate bases. First, the Uniform Foreign Money Judgment Recognition Act of 1962 grants enforceability to judgments 'granting or denying recovery of a sum of money' other than taxes, penalty, or familial support, unless the foreign court used faulty procedure.[169] It is recognised by thirty states.[170] Second, the Uniform Foreign-Country Money Judgments Recognition Act of 2005 updates the 1962 law by clarifying certain points, and adding a statute of limitations.[171] This update has been recognised by thirteen states.[172] Importantly, several of the forty-three states above have included reciprocity requirements on foreign states to take advantage of these Acts.[173] Nineteen states do not recognise

---

[166]   Janet Koven Levit, 'Does Medellin Matter?', *FORDHAM L. REV.*, 77 (2008), 617, 624–5.

[167]   *Medellin* v. *Texas*, 552 U.S. 491, 505–6 (2008) (quoting *Whitney* v. *Robertson*, 124 U.S. 190, 194 (1888)).

[168]   Lucien Dhooge, '*J. Aguinda v. ChevronTexaco*: mandatory grounds for the non-recognition of foreign judgments for environmental injury in the United States', *J. TRANSNAT'L L. & POL'Y*, 19(2) (2009).

[169]   Unif. Foreign Money-Judgments Recognition Act (1962) 13 U.L.A. 261, §§ 1(2), 3, 4 (West, 1986).

[170]   Dhooge, above n. 168, at 3.

[171]   National Conference of Commissioners on Uniform State Laws, Summary of the Uniform Foreign-Country Money Judgments Recognition Act, at www.uniformlaws. org/ActSummary.aspx?title=Foreign-Country, Money Judgments Recognition Act.

[172]   Dhooge, above n. 168, at 3.   [173]   *Ibid.*, at 27.

either Act, but rely on the comity doctrine. This doctrine holds that '[n]o sovereign is bound … to execute within his dominions a judgment rendered by the tribunals of another state; [but rather is free] to give effect to it or not, as may be found just and equitable'.[174] The result of these three different types of recognition is that the law of recognition of foreign judgments remains uncertain.[175]

20.103   As this is written, Ecuador is pursuing civil litigation against Chevron for oil contamination. The case was originally brought in the US courts but then dismissed on *forum non conveniens* grounds.[176] Proceedings then took place in Ecuador, and that country's courts awarded a judgment for the plaintiffs of $9 billion in damages against Chevron.[177] However, Chevron had alleged various improprieties in the conduct of that litigation, including successfully subpoenaing documents related to potential tampering with judicial independence;[178] and at its request a US federal court on 7 March 2011 issued a preliminary injunction against the enforcement in the US courts of any judgment rendered by the courts of Ecuador in this litigation.[179]

OECD

20.104   The USA is a member of the OECD and it is thus possible to bring a complaint if a business fails to comply with the OECD Guidelines calling for 'responsible business conduct consistent with applicable law'. Such a complaint might look similar to one brought in Germany, as described in Chapter 17 at para. 17.99.[180]

---

[174] *Hilton* v. *Guyot*, 159 U.S. 113, 166 (1895); see also *Dhooge*, above n. 168, at 24, n. 143.

[175] Ronald A. Brand, 'Enforcement of Foreign Money-Judgments in the United States: In Search of Uniformity and International Acceptance', *Notre Dame L. Rev.*, 67 (1991), 253, 255 (referring to this area of law as being in an 'unreduced and uncertain condition').

[176] *Aguinda* v. *Texaco, Inc.*, 142 F. Supp. 2d 534 (S.D.N.Y. 2001), aff'd, 303 F.3d 470 (2d Cir. 2002).

[177] Simon Romero and Clifford Krauss, 'Ecuador Judge Orders Chevron to Pay $9 Billion', *N.Y. Times* (14 February 2011).

[178] *In re Application of Chevron Corp.*, 709 F. Supp. 2d 283 (S.D.N.Y. 2010), aff'd sub nom. *Chevron Corp.* v. *Berlinger*, 629 F.3d 297 (2d Cir. 2011).

[179] *Chevron Corp.* v. *Donziger*, 2011 WL 778052 (S.D.N.Y. 2011).

[180] Germanwatch, 'Complaint against Volkswagen AG under the OECD Guidelines for Multinational Enterprises (2000) – Request to the German National Contact Point (Federal Ministry of Economics and Technology) to initiate the procedures for the

(E)   Practicalities

Jurisdiction

Domestic activities

20.105   In order to hear a case, a federal court must have both personal jurisdiction (over the parties to the suit) and subject-matter jurisdiction (over the subject of the suit). Personal jurisdiction ensures that the party being sued has significant ties with the USA that justify bringing them to US courts. This has historically protected some foreign-run companies, although having business within the USA would be enough to ground jurisdiction. Subject-matter jurisdiction can come either if the question presented is primarily based on federal laws (federal-question jurisdiction), or if the litigants come from multiple states and have put over $75,000 at issue (diversity jurisdiction).[181] Most of the litigations detailed above have federal-question jurisdiction, because they are based on federal statutes or federal common law. *Comer* v. *Murphy Oil* relied instead on diversity jurisdiction.

20.106   If the federal court does not have jurisdiction, then claims must be brought under state courts; and indeed, many cases of national significance are litigated in state courts. Also, even if a federal court has jurisdiction, parties may still bring their claims in state courts unless federal law provides exclusive jurisdiction to federal courts. This exclusive jurisdiction is provided for in most of the main environmental statute citizen provisions, including the CAA, CWA and ESA.

Foreign activities

20.107   Jurisdiction over foreign activities by US entities is primarily established by the Alien Tort Claims Act ('ATCA'), passed with the first Judiciary Act in 1789. This act says quite simply that '[t]he [federal] district courts shall have original jurisdiction of any civil action by an alien for a tort only, committed in violation of the law of nations or a treaty of the United States'.[182]

---

solution of conflicts and problems in the implementation of the Guidelines' (7 May 2007), available at www.germanwatch.org/corp/vw-besch-e.pdf.

[181]   See 28 U.S.C. §§ 1330–69, 1441–52 (2006).

[182]   28 U.S.C. § 1350 (2006).

20.108 The ATCA was used heavily in the mid-1990s to hold corporations liable for contributing to human rights violations by foreign governments.[183] These lawsuits never resulted in an actual monetary judgment, but did yield several large settlement payments.[184] However, in 2010 an appellate court ruled in *Kiobel* v. *Royal Dutch Petroleum* that corporations cannot be held liable under the ATCA.[185] This case has garnered widespread attention, and will likely be appealed to the Supreme Court.[186] However, the decision also explicitly leaves room for officers of corporations to be sued in their individual capacities if they 'purposefully aid and abet' a violation of international law.[187]

20.109 Looking at climate litigation, this Act is limited in at least two ways. First, it only applies to treaties and customary law that the USA recognises, which explicitly excludes, for example, any climate liability established by the Kyoto Protocol. Second, the Supreme Court has expressed 'great caution' in allowing cases to be brought under the ATCA,[188] and specifically has limited its applicability to violations recognised in 1789, and some reasonable number of new claims of similar character and specificity as that original list.[189] These limitations would make it very difficult to use the ATCA as a jurisdictional hook to impose carbon liability.

Enforcement

20.110 The USA has a strong history of enforcing domestic judicial decisions, giving its judicial system a particularly large amount of power in the overall government structure. There is also a strong culture of enforcing existing statutory obligations; most relevant federal statutes (including all but one listed above) have citizen suit provisions that allow individuals to sue for enforcement of these laws.

---

[183] John B. Bellinger III, 'Will Federal Court's *Kiobel* Ruling End Second Wave of Alien Tort Statute Suits?', *WASH. L. FOUND. L. BACKGROUNDER*, 25(34) (2010), 1, 2.

[184] *Ibid.*, at 2.

[185] *Kiobel* v. *Royal Dutch Petroleum Co.*, 621 F.3d 111 (2nd Cir. 2010).

[186] Bellinger, above n. 183, at 3.

[187] *Kiobel*, 621 F.3d at 122.

[188] *Sosa* v. *Alvarez-Machain*, 542 U.S. 692, 728 (2004).

[189] *Ibid.*, at 725.

Obtaining information

20.111   The Freedom of Information Act ('FOIA'), passed in 1966, is the most effective source of information on government activities. This Act requires federal agencies to make available to the public any agency rules, orders, records and opinions, with limited exceptions (mostly pertaining to national security, staff issues and ongoing litigation).[190] To accomplish this, they must set in place procedures for any party to petition for such information, and must respond to all requests within twenty business days (though this deadline is often missed).[191] In addition, each state has its own version of the FOIA, which can be used for those agencies. Although delays are not uncommon in this process, it has been a key source of information in environmental litigation efforts.

20.112   In addition, discovery rules during litigation mandate access to all relevant non-privileged documents by both parties. The USA has a strong discovery process, which will prove useful if any private law claims (particularly conspiracy claims) are allowed to move forward (discovery is normally unavailable during the pendency of a motion to dismiss.) However, administrative litigation rarely gets to discovery beyond the FOIA because those cases are almost all based on record review, and administrative records are automatically disclosed.

Government immunity from litigation

20.113   The national government is technically immune from litigation unless it consents to the lawsuit.[192] However it has waived this sovereignty for most tort claims,[193] and this immunity does not extend to challenges to legislative or regulatory actions. State governments are immune from suits by citizens of other states and foreigners under the 11th Amendment. In addition, the Supreme Court has read the 'structure of the original Constitution' as providing sovereign immunity against lawsuits brought by citizens

---

[190]   5 U.S.C. § 552(b) (2006).
[191]   5 U.S.C. § 552(a)(6) (2006).
[192]   *Gray* v. *Bell*, 712 F.2d 490, 507 (D.C. Cir. 1983).
[193]   28 U.S.C. § 1346(b) (2006).

of their own state.[194] However, several exceptions exist; most notably, state officers can be sued for unconstitutional acts,[195] although only injunctive relief is available.[196] Also, states can be sued by other states, the federal government, or for other specific charges. The main effect of these rules is that (absent certain contractual waivers) states cannot be sued for damages in federal courts, though injunctive relief remains available. States may be sued for damages in state courts.

(F) Conclusion

20.114   Carbon liability in the USA is characterised by the absence of comprehensive climate legislation on the federal level. Given this absence, the primary relevant federal activity will be the EPA's continuing efforts to apply the CAA to problems of climate change and GHG emissions. Meanwhile, several states and groups of states have also stepped into this gap to make emission reduction commitments in various policy forums, and establish regional cap-and-trade markets. The recent group of private lawsuits claiming damages based in public nuisance and/or conspiracy to misinform the public are similarly enabled by this lack of legislative activity, although they face serious challenges in a court system that has largely been reluctant to step into this policy gap. (See para. 20.64 above for The United States Supreme Court's decision in *American Electric Power* v. *Connecticut*.)

20.115   The Congress that was elected in November 2010 will clearly not enact a programme of climate regulation, and many of its members are attempting to block the EPA's efforts to utilise its existing statutory authority over GHGs. The congressional and presidential elections of November 2012 will determine the course of US climate regulation in the years to follow. Whatever the outcome of these elections, it is likely that the courts will continue to play a central role.

---

[194] *Alden* v. *Maine*, 527 U.S. 706 (1999).
[195] *Ex parte Young*, 209 U.S. 123 (1908).
[196] *Edelman* v. *Jordan*, 415 U.S. 651 (1974).

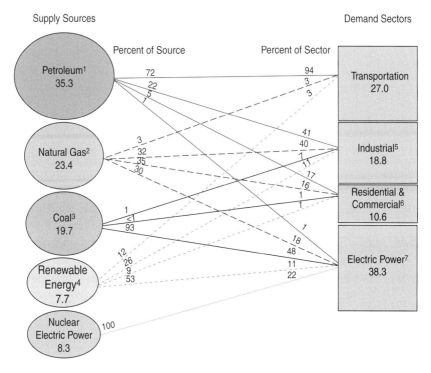

Figure 20.1[197]   Graphical summary of energy sources and end-uses in the US economy

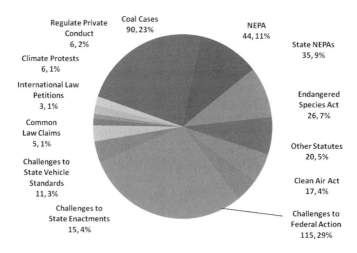

Figure 20.2a[198]   Types of climate cases filed (393 total cases as of 11 March 2011)

[197]   EIA 2009 ENERGY REPORT, above n. 7, at 37.
[198]   Figs. 20.2a and 20.2b courtesy of Arnold & Porter LLP; more detail available at www.
ClimateCaseChart.com.

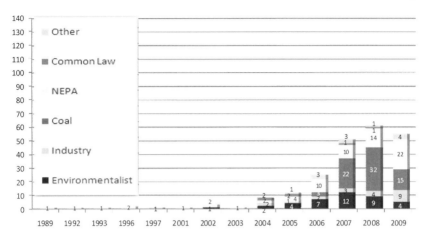

Figure 20.2b   Climate litigation: filings (X axis: year; Y axis: number of cases)

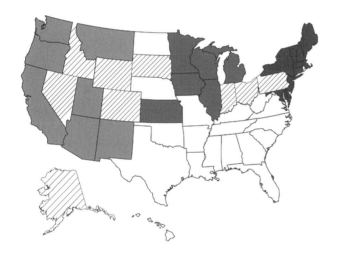

■ Regional Greenhouse Gas Initiative & TCI

■ Midwest GHG Reduction Accord

■ Western Climate Initiative

▨ Regional Initiative "Observer" States

Figure 20.3[199]   Regional initiatives

[199] Ivan Gold and Nidhi Thakar, 'A Survey of State Renewable Portfolio Standards: Square Pegs for Round Climate Change Holes?', *WILLIAM & MARY ENVTL. L. & POL'Y REV.*, 35(1) (2010), 183, 229. Map reprinted courtesy of Ivan Gold, Perkins & Coie, LLP.

Central and South America

21

Brazil

YANKO MARCIUS DE ALENCAR XAVIER AND
PEDRO LUCAS DE MOURA SOARES

(A)   Introduction

The Brazilian legal system

21.01   The legal system of Brazil is, unlike common law systems, based on codified law, which in turn is based on the Federal Constitution of 1988. However, the influence of Anglo-American law is nonetheless considerable, as is the importance of the law created by the jurisprudence of Brazilian courts, which supplements written law.

21.02   Brazil is divided into twenty-seven states, which in turn are divided into municipalities. Although each state has its own Constitution, the legislative and administrative powers of each member of the Federation, especially as regards certain areas, is given by the Federal Constitution of 1988, by which each state is bound.

21.03   The basic principles that are spelled out in the Constitution of the Federal Republic of Brazil of 1988 include human dignity, which underpins the exercise of all other constitutional rights and the boundaries of which extend far beyond the wellbeing of the individual. For present purposes, the fact that this constitutional principle encompasses the right to an ecologically balanced environment, as set out in Article 225 of the Constitution is of particular interest. Since this right is underpinned by the principle of sustainable development, it is tied to a responsibility to treat the environment as a legacy left by past generations and to be passed on to future generations for them to enjoy equal access to, and quality and benefits, of natural resources.

21.04   In addition to these principles which are directly relevant to the environmental and legal implications of climate change, other less directly relevant principles nonetheless guide the Brazilian government in relation to climate change. These include the principles of priority of human rights, defence of peace, and cooperation among peoples for human progress, all set out in Article 4 of the Constitution.

The governmental stance on climate change

21.05   While the environment can be protected by domestic law and constitutional law, academics correctly point to 'the transactional nature of environmental protection and the universal nature of the needs of environmental protection'.[1] And it is in this transnational and global respect that Brazil is actively participating in the defence of environmental values.

21.06   In terms of Brazil's international engagement, it is worth mentioning that Brazil is a member of the United Nations Environment Programme's Governing Council and of the Sustainable Development Commission that operates under the auspices of the Economic and Social Council of the United Nations. Brazil has also made efforts to modify its environmental legislation in order to put into practice the commitments undertaken under the United Nations Convention Framework on Climate Change ('UNFCCC'), to which it is a Party, as well as the Kyoto Protocol, by transposing both treaties into domestic legislation.[2] Brazil's efforts to give its international commitments national effect is also reflected in legislation such as Law No. 12.187/2009 on National Policy on Climate Change, discussed at para. 21.13 below.

21.07   Under the Cancun Agreements, the Brazilian government has made a significant commitment to reducing greenhouse gases by

---

[1] D. Dimoulis and L. Martins, *Teoria Geral dos Direitos Fundamentais* (São Paulo: Editora Revista dos Tribunais, 2007), p. 96.

[2] The Framework Convention was adopted by Congress by way of Legislative Decree No. 1, on 3 February 1994, and ratified on 28 March 1994 and promulgated by Decree No. 2652 of 1 July 1998. The Kyoto Protocol, in turn, was endorsed by Congress by way of Legislative Decree No. 144 of 20 July 2002, and ratified on 23 August 2002 and promulgated by Legislative Decree No. 5445 of 12 May 2005.

pledging to cut the same by between 36.1 per cent and 38.9 per cent below its projected emissions in 2020.[3]

Industrial and natural resources context

21.08   Brazil has an abundance of water resources and most of its energy capacity comes from hydropower. Hydropower represents almost 50 per cent of renewables.[4] As for other renewables, the energy generated from waste sugar cane should reach up to 4,500 MW. Further, there is currently around 417 MW of installed wind-power capacity in Brazil, with an additional 442 MW under construction and 441 projects near conclusion, creating a total wind power capacity of around 13,000 MW. Finally, in 2008, the National Development Bank ('BNDES') financed 47 renewable energy projects worth $5.7 million.[5]

21.09   Regarding oil reserves, according to the latest statistics from the Brazilian Petroleum *Natural Gas and Bio Fuels Statistical Yearbook*,[6] as of 31 December 2009 there were 404 blocks in the exploration phase, 61 in development and 313 fields in the oil production phase and yielding 711.9 million barrels in 2009.[7]

21.10   The monoculture of sugar cane remains prominent in eastern Brazil, both in the north but above all in the southeast. There is a monoculture of soybeans in mid-western Brazil. In addition, large-scale cattle breeding predominates in the midwest, with subsistence farming in the northeast, making agriculture and cattle breeding another significant component of the Brazilian economy.

National climate change risks

21.11   However, the economic outlook is worrisome with regard to the economic activities mentioned above in the event of further

---

[3] *Compilation of information on nationally appropriate mitigation actions to be implemented by Parties not included in Annex I to the Convention*, Note by the secretariat, FCCC/AWGLCA/2011/INF.1, p. 8.
[4] MERCOSUR, *Las energías renovables en el ambito del Mercosur, sus estados asociados y en el escenario internacional: su dimensión estratégica, productiva, ambiental y económica*, (Montevideo, 2009), p. 1.
[5] *Ibid.*, p. 11.
[6] Agência Nacional de Petróleo, *Anuário Estatístico Brasileiro do Petróleo, Gás Natural e Biocombustíveis 2010* (Rio de Janeiro: ANP, 2010).
[7] *Ibid.*

accelerated climate change, especially given that one can already see the consequences that climate change has had: floods in large cities like São Paulo, Rio de Janeiro among others; droughts in northern and southern Brazil, accompanied by the death of animals in the fields; and fires in the midwest due to low air humidity and the increase in temperatures, resulting in the death or displacement of wild animals.

(B)(1)   Public law: the role of the State in the mitigation of climate change

21.12   In order to try to mitigate the adverse effects of climate change, the federal, state and municipal governments have made efforts to adopt legislative instruments that protect the environment and reverse these effects. Article 23, section VI of the Federal Constitution of 1988 sets out the shared competences of the Federation, States, Federal Districts and municipalities to 'protect the environment and combat pollution whatever its form'. Moreover, the protection of the environment also appears in the Federal Constitution as a general principle of economic activity (Article 170, VI).

21.13   Brazil recently implemented measures that are emblematic of the struggle against global warming, promoting sustainable development in a variety of areas. An important instrument was the proclamation of Law No. 12.187/2009, creating the National Policy for Climate Change.[8] This initiative consists in the creation of a domestic legal institution that, in conjunction with other international instruments[9] signed by Brazil, will not only establish guidelines and jurisdictional instruments, but will also outline principles to guide public policies in combating global warming. Thus the Brazilian government aims to pursue the mitigation of global warming in line with sustainable development, so as to promote economic growth, eradicate poverty and reduce social inequalities. The national climate change policy that was enacted by the Federal Government is based on these legal principles. According to Article 3 of the National Policy on Climate Change,

---

[8] Brazilian Law on the National Policy on Climate Change, No. 12.189/2009.
[9] UNFCCC, Kyoto Protocol, COP15.

the implementation of the aforementioned law must respect the principles of precaution and prevention, citizen participation, sustainable development and common responsibilities. It is also worth noting that the principle of sustainable development, either explicitly or in its policy goals, is reiterated throughout the text. One example is Article 4, section I, which provides that the National Policy on Climate Change aims to reconcile social and economic development with the protection of the climate system, demonstrating Brazil's commitment to promoting economic growth without compromising environmental considerations. The law in question represents an advance in Brazilian legislation compared to the previous situation. Furthermore, it reflects international developments, evidencing an effort on the part of the Brazilian government to adopt domestic standards in order to implement, or even anticipate, international commitments.

21.14   New legal instruments were also developed at the subnational levels, designed to mitigate regional climate change. An example is Law No. 3.135 of 5 June 2007, which established the Policy on Climate Change, Environmental Conservation and Sustainable Development of the State of Amazonas. This law, like the aforementioned National Policy on Climate Change, is guided by the principles of precaution, prevention, common responsibility, sustainable development, participation, transparency and information, as well as national and international cooperation. Its ultimate goal is the creation of instruments (economic, tax and market instruments), including those that enable the execution of projects to reduce emissions from deforestation, clean energy, and net emissions of greenhouse gases, inside or outside the Kyoto Protocol's clean development mechanism.[10]

21.15   The Amazonian policy also includes the promotion of actions to increase environmental awareness of traditional communities, poor communities and students from State schools with respect to the impact and consequences of climate change. Certification seals will be instituted for public and private entities that develop projects related to climate change, environmental conservation

---

[10]   P. Lavratti and V. B. Prestes (eds.), *Direito e mudanças climáticas [recurso eletrônico]: inovações legislativas em matéria de mudanças climáticas*' (São Paulo: Instituto O Direito por um Planeta Verde, 2010), p. 118.

and sustainable development in the State of Amazonas. Action plans that contribute to mitigating the adverse effects of climate change will be elaborated and included in general and sectorial State planning.[11]

21.16   Although Brazil is not obliged to fulfil the emissions goals established by the Kyoto Protocol, it has sought to reassess its policies so as to accord with the international objective of reducing greenhouse gas emissions. Among the measures adopted, the use of clean and renewable energy stands out, in light of the fact that Brazil holds a leading position in the production of ethanol and related technologies in addition to being a country with excellent prospects for agri-business. In this context, another instrument created by the Federal Government to mitigate climate change is the National Programme of Biodiesel Production ('PNPB').

21.17   The PNPB is the rebirth of a programme that was originally not very successful – the Vegetable Oil Production Plan for Energy Purposes ('PRO-OLEO'). Due to a lack of technology at the time, the programme failed and the use of petroleum diesel was maintained. The PNPB consists of an inter-ministerial programme whose primary purpose is the sustainable economic, technical and environmental implementation of biodiesel production, with a focus on regional development and social inclusion. It is characterised by the focus on small rural communities alluding to one of the fundamental objectives of the Federal Republic of Brazil, set out in Article 3, § 3, III, of the Constitution, which is to 'reduce social and regional inequalities'. A further constitutional basis of the PNPB is described in Article 170 of the 1988 Constitution, which enshrines an overarching principle of the Constitutional Economic Order that is subject to the principles of social justice.

21.18   Furthermore, promoting competitive prices in the international market generates employment and income, diversifies the energy matrix and motivates research to improve biodiesel quality and expand the national fuel supply capacity. Substituting part of the imported oil-derived diesel remains an objective of the PNPB, promoting, above all, the environmental gains from

---

[11]   *Ibid.*

this substitution, as there are significant reductions in the release of sulphur and other particles into the environment. To create a production incentive, Law No. 11.097/2005 increased the percentage of biodiesel added to diesel oil sold to final consumers throughout the country from 2 per cent to 5 per cent.

21.19 Besides playing an instrumental role in the establishment of public policies to control climate change, Brazil's biofuel programme looks to a number of other socioeconomic objectives.[12] It is also worth pointing out that, although the biofuel programme entails damage or impact at the local level, there are significant global benefits. In this context, it is worth recalling that, among other things, Article 13 of Law No. 11.116/2005 which provides for the inclusion of biofuels in Brazil's energy policy also falls within the national strategy for mitigating climate risk.[13]

(B)(2) Public law: judicial review and climate change

21.20 Judicial review has become an important tool in implementing the right to an ecologically balanced environment that is guaranteed by Article 225 of the Brazilian Federal Constitution. An example of this type of implementation is the use of an extraordinary appeal (*Recurso Extraordinário*) in order to achieve environmental protection, a feature enshrined in Article 102, III of the Constitution. The Brazilian Constitutional Court – the Supreme Court – decides constitutional disputes brought against decisions of a court of lower instance. An extraordinary appeal can be used to declare unconstitutional any legal provisions that rank below Article 225 of the Constitution and which contravene the same. Rules that hamper the implementation and effectiveness of Article 225 may also be subject to a special appeal and may be annulled.

21.21 Other constitutional actions, such as injunctions (*Mandado de Injunção*), provided in Article 5, subsection LXXI of the Brazilian Federal Constitution of 1988, can also be used as instruments of environmental protection. An injunction is granted where the

---

[12] R. S. R. Sampaio, 'Biocombustíveis no Contexto da Regulação do Risco Climático no Brasil', available at www.planetaverde.org/artigos/arq_12_06_47_16_09_10.pdf, p. 11.
[13] Brasil Lei No. 11.116/2005, Art. 13.

absence of regulations precludes the exercise of constitutional rights and freedoms and of the prerogatives inherent to nationality, sovereignty and citizenship.

21.22   According to a literal interpretation of Article 5, at first glance it appears that the relief following a successful injunction is individual in nature. However, leading academics suggest that the injunction may be collective. Having analysed the function and purpose of this constitutional action, we conclude that even if the object of the injunction is the protection of an individual right, it can be used as an instrument of collective protection where the injunction benefits a large group of persons.[14] Therefore, this instrument could be used where it is determined that, due to public authorities' inaction, the absence of regulatory standards makes it impossible to enjoy the right to an ecologically balanced environment.

21.23   It is worth highlighting that, as these examples suggest, it is not only the pollution caused by the State or another entity that may give rise to environmental liability. The omission of the constitutional duty to protect the environment (lack of control, lack of compliance with rules when granting environmental licences, inadequate installation or maintenance of waste disposal and sewage treatment systems) can also give rise to liability. The failure of the State to monitor and/or control the occurrence of environmental damage becomes all the more serious by virtue of its constitutional duty.[15] Thus, the Brazilian Constitutional Court is in fact a body that is responsible for ensuring the implementation of public policies when faced with the inaction of government bodies, especially as regards the protection of the environment.

21.24   Another instrument available is the direct action of unconstitutionality by omission (*Ação Direta de Inconstitucionalidade por Omissão*). This instrument can be used when a constitutional norm appears to protect a given right, but in practice depends

[14] F. Didier Jr., *Ações Constitucionais*, 4th edn (Salvador: Jus Podium, 2009).
[15] T. Fensterseifer, 'A responsabilidade do estado pelos danos causados às pessoas atingidas pelos desastres ambientais ocasionados pelas mudanças climáticas: uma análise à luz dos deveres de proteção ambiental do estado e da correspondente proibição de insuficiência na tutela do direito fundamental ao ambiente', p. 17, available at www.mp.ro.gov.br/c/document_library/get_file?uuid=f24433ad-986d-467b-a649-8ce573dfd6a8&groupId=41601.

on a regulation by a given public entity that remains inoperative. Thus, in order to ensure the effectiveness of constitutional norms, an action is commenced to declare the unconstitutionality of the norm that is not directly enforceable. The same applies with respect to constitutional norms that deal with environmental matters. In order to promote the effectiveness and enforcement of environmental standards, these rules are equally susceptible to direct actions of unconstitutionality by omission.[16]

(C)   Private law: environmental liability and climate change

21.25   The duty to compensate damage results from a breach of a legal obligation (in our case, the duty to preserve the environment). Hence, liability is contingent on the existence of an unlawful act.[17]

21.26   The focus of civil liability has shifted in recent times, becoming increasingly concerned with compensating the victim of unjustly suffered harm and less with punishing the person who committed the breach. It is for criminal law to impose punishment where the perpetrator of damage should be held criminally responsible, while it is for the civil law to address the victim's situation.

21.27   However, it is also worth noting that there is a parallel trend of expansion of liability so as to allow for the compensation of all damage. Hence, besides the original and primary function of civil liability (i.e. the reparation of material loss and compensation of immaterial loss), civil liability has also come to acquire punitive and deterrent functions. Perhaps this last function is most relevant to the present study, precisely because the damage from climate change manifests itself in the future, so that prevention is of critical importance.

21.28   The basis for imposing civil liability on those causing environmental damage is found in Article 225, § 3 of the Constitution. It provides that 'the conduct and activities considered harmful to the environment shall subject the offender, individuals or legal entities, to criminal and administrative sanctions, regardless of the obligation to repair the damage caused'.

---

[16]   J. J. G.Canotilho, J. R. M. Leite, *Direito Constitucional Ambiental Brasileiro* (São Paulo: Saraiva, 2007), pp. 343–9.

[17]   S. C.Filho, *Programa de Responsabilidade Civil*, 8th edn (São Paulo: Atlas, 2009), p. 2.

21.29   From a policy perspective, environmental liability should be a regime of strict liability. In other words, it should arise under Article 927 of the Brazilian Civil Code, which affirms the obligation to compensate damage regardless of fault when the activity that gives rise to the damage entails an inherent risk of harming others. If a risk or danger to others is introduced into society, the perpetrator will be liable for the damage resulting. Regarding climate change, the biggest challenge involves identifying the causes of climate change. Brazilian law focuses on identifying the author of the immediate damage and has not yet regulated the identification of future environmental damage.

21.30   Developing this tradition of strict liability, Article 14 § 1 of Law No. 6938 of 1981 provides that 'notwithstanding the application of the penalties provided in this article, the polluter is required, regardless of fault, to repair or indemnify the damage caused to the environment and to third parties as a result of its activities ...'.

  With the enactment of Law No. 6938 of 31 August 1981, strict liability for environmental damage was clearly established. As a result, a vast and relatively new normative field emerged, specifying how this liability will attach to an operator once it has been verified that a harmful incident has occurred and has caused degradation of the environment. According to Brazilian legal scholars, this strict liability regime represents the best way to meet society's needs and to help ensure through civil liability that present and future generations can enjoy a healthy environment and ecologically balanced world.[18] To prove liability in these cases, one dispenses with the need to prove intention, recklessness and negligence, focusing instead on the causal link between the conduct of the polluter and the environmental damage in question.[19] The rationale for this approach is that what is being protected are high-value goods in which the entire community has an interest, and whose degradation or even destruction would cause disruptive consequences for

---

[18] E. Milaré, 'O Ministério Público e a responsabilidade civil do profissional nas atividades modificadoras do meio ambiente', *Revista dos Tribunais*, 623 (1987), 31; and in R. Stoco, *Tratado de Responsabilidade Civil*, 6th edn (São Paulo: Editora Revista dos Tribunais, 2004), p. 840.

[19] A. Rizzardo, *ibid.*, p. 700.

present and future generations.[20] From a climate change perspective, these legal developments highlight the importance of studying the implications for the fuel industry, given the enormous potential of liability for irreversible damage to the environment, requiring a rapid and effective response in the event of accidents.

21.31   Furthermore, Article 4, section VII of Law No. 6938 of 1981 imposes the application of the 'polluter pays' principle in the event of environmental damage, asserting that the polluter and the perpetrator will be under the obligation to restore and/or indemnify for the damage caused to the environment as a result of the use of environmental resources for economic purposes.

21.32   Overall, the regime of strict liability constitutes a major step in achieving the effective protection of the environment. Only strict liability can guarantee that those engaged in activities that generate risks to the environment will actually take appropriate remedial action in the event of damage.

21.33   Even though there have been considerable legislative developments in the area of environmental protection, it is still difficult to establish liability in the case of environmental damage and to address large-scale environmental incidents, as is illustrated, for example, by oil spills at sea.

Difficulties in applying a civil liability regime to environmental damage

21.34   Strict civil liability in relation to oil pollution originating from ships was put in place by the enactment of Decree No. 79,437 of 28 March 1977, which implemented the International Convention on Civil Liability of 1969 for Damage Caused by Oil Pollution. The 1977 Decree was modified by Decree No. 83540 of 4 June 1979, and provides that shipowners, whether they be natural or legal persons, are liable for pollution by oil discharges from their ships. However, this liability is limited in its quantum despite the system of compulsory insurance being established in order to effectively protect the reparation of the loss.

---

[20] P. A. L. Machado, *ibid.*, 322–3.

21.35   Even with these laws in place, there is a tendency to hold lengthy court proceedings on the topic of civil liability for environmental damage as a result of long discussions that are raised in the preliminary discussions. This shows that civil liability is, in contrast to preventive measures which are more effective,[21] a purely reactive mechanism unable to bring about environmental protection.

21.36   Despite Brazil's environmental laws having been noted as some of the more 'advanced' in the world, more efficient mechanisms for the prevention of environmental damage are still required. The main issue in this respect is that these laws are essentially structured on the principle of responsibility, or equivalent compensation, with liability being deemed only after the damage occurred. As part of the search for an equivalent compensation, the lawsuits turn into long disputes, which do not allow for quick and satisfactory results for the truly disadvantaged, thus favouring the perpetrators of the damage.[22]

21.37   Thus, we can only conjecture about what the ambit of civil liability for damage caused to the environment must be for it to be able to respond to promote the development of activities that prevent the occurrence of environmental harm.

Environmental protection as responsibility of private entities and public authorities

21.38   The responsibility for environmental and ecological protection lies both with the Government as well as the private sector. Thus, it could be argued that the State should be held jointly responsible for damages caused to the environment and may be asked to account for these losses individually and collectively.[23]

21.39   This liability may occur when the State does not exercise its supervisory power, which it is bound to exercise in light of a binding administrative decision. So if the Government fails to exercise its policing and supervisory duties, it will be liable alongside the

---

[21] P. B. Antunes, *ibid.*, 245–6.
[22] P. B. Antunes, *ibid.*, 246.   [23] R. Stoco, *ibid.*, 246.

relevant private entities for any damage caused as a result of this failure.[24]

21.40   The central tenet of environmental law in Brazil is that a pollutor, be it a natural or legal person, including public authorities, should be held liable for any damage caused. Furthermore, many authors argue that the Government can always be joined to any claim which ultimately aims to repair the environment. Given that if it is not directly responsible for having caused the damage, it will at least be jointly and severally liable through one of its agents as a result of an omission of a duty to monitor and prevent such damage from occurring. This fact demonstrates that it is ultimately the State's responsibility to pursue those who directly cause environmental damage.[25]

21.41   The State will be reimbursed for its spending on environmental preservation by the relevant tortfeasor. This provision enables rapid responses and effective action against environmental degradation as well as the prevention of climate change as part of a search for an ecologically balanced environment, favouring the total compensation for damage, or even a reduction of any future damage that could be aggravated by delays in reparations.

Jurisdictional instruments for controlling climate change

21.42   The Brazilian legal system provides legal instruments both for public and private entities in order to achieve environmental protection. The first instrument we will discuss is 'Public Civil Action'.

21.43   Public Civil Actions for liability resulting from environmental damage are an important legal mechanism the application of which is set out in Law No. 7.347/85. This mechanism is a procedural tool designed to protect the interests of individuals, such as

---

[24] This is the understanding of Rui Stoco which is exemplified by the situation through cases in which the industry is not authorised (business licence) to exercise the activity, or when there is no prior survey by health authorities. R. Stoco, *ibid.*, p. 840.

[25] E. Milaré, *A ação civil pública e a Tutela jurisdicional dos interesses difusos* (São Paulo: Saraiva, 1984), p. 76; and see n. 18 above.

the right to an ecologically balanced environment, contained in Article 225 of the Constitution. Prior to the introduction of this procedure, there was no instrument that matched today's scope of the Public Civil Action, which is only available to defend the environment against administrative decisions of the State.

21.44   As such, Public Civil Actions are an instrument of the Brazilian legal system in the realm of procedural law, which ensures the implementation of Article 225 by providing, if successful, for pecuniary compensation or the specific performance of an obligation to act or not act.[26]

21.45   Although it is mainly the Public Prosecutor who has standing to bring this type of action to protect the environment in accordance with Article 129 III of the Brazilian Constitution, Article 5 of the Law on Public Civil Action provides that foundations and associations may also have standing. However, the stand-out feature of this legislation is the possibility that the law provides for promoting environmental protection by popular participation. Article 6 of the Law of Public Civil Action states that anyone can, and in some cases should, trigger a report of the (Public Prosecutor), providing them with necessary information about the facts that constitute the object of action.

(D)   Other laws/rights

21.46   The problems resulting from global warming and climate change play an important role in the international agenda and contributed to the creation of international organisations which address such issues. Climate change does not only affect States on the basis of their territory. We can also observe a multitude of human rights violations which we outline below.

21.47   In this limited context, the international community is united in its efforts to change the present situation. In 2005 the Complementação Energética Regional entre os Estados Partes do Mercosul e Paises Associados was signed among Member States of the MERCOSUR and Associated Countries.[27] In its Preamble,

---

[26] Brazil Law No. 7.347/85, Art. 3. A civil action may have as its object the condemnation of money or the fulfilment of obligations to do or not to do.

[27] www2.mre.gov.br/dai/complementacaoenergetica.htm.

the Agreement highlights the rights of people to access to energy and energy cooperation between States.

21.48   The agreement brings a new perspective to existing multilateral agreements. While it recognises the right of States to administer their energy resources in a sovereign manner, it also provides for the gradual development of integration and energy security at regional level, aimed at economic, social and sustainable development. In turn, the aim of this agreement is to improve production, transportation and distribution systems and marketing of energy in order to reduce transaction and exchange costs amongst States so as to ensure a fair and reasonable valuation of these resources, thereby strengthening the processes of development in a sustainable manner.[28]

21.49   Lastly, one of the most important provisions with regard to the issue of climate change and global warming is the encouragement of the rational and efficient use of conventional energy. This goal encompasses energy efficiency, conservation of the environment, renewable energy and harmonisation of safety standards and quality. Such standards would be achieved through the technical improvements of each Member State, the use of best practices, and institutional capacity building of each State.

21.50   However, the treaty does not stipulate any deadlines or pre-set goals or clearly defined objectives. The treaty is drafted using clauses with no binding or mandatory character, allowing for interpretation according to the principles of gradualism and flexibility.

21.51   In 2009, the Declaration of Manaus was signed by the States that share the Amazon Basin.[29] This new Declaration represents another effort by Brazil in the fight against global warming. According to Brazilian President Luiz Inácio Lula da Silva, this Declaration would serve as a basis for negotiations in Copenhagen.[30]

---

[28] According to Article 1 of the Treaty.
[29] www.itamaraty.gov.br/sala-de-imprensa/notas-a-imprensa/2009/11/26/declaracao-de-manaus-reuniao-de-cupula-dos-paises.
[30] www.bbc.co.uk/portuguese/noticias /2009 /11/091126 _manaus_clima_pc_np.shtml.

21.52   The States which are Party to this Declaration support the goal established by the United Nations to reduce 40 per cent of global emissions of greenhouse gases by 2020. The Declaration of Manaus reaffirms existing support for maintaining the proposed monetary contribution of between 0.5 per cent and 1 per cent of GDP of developed countries for tackling climate change in developing countries.[31]

21.53   There are many questions surrounding the issue of global warming and amongst such diverse aspects surrounding current discussions about the environment, one question is often neglected – that of environmental refugees[32] and internally displaced persons.[33] These people, though not in the media limelight, are potentially the greatest victims of environmental disasters and climate change on our planet.

21.54   The exponential growth of global warming has caused sea levels to steadily increase. In addition to deficits widely reported by international media, these increases have also led to the creation of new legal questions which are still not resolved.

21.55   The increase in sea levels has generated sensitive changes in the fundamental structures of some States, like the enormous change in borders in Bangladesh. According to predictions from environmentalists, these changes may result in 20 to 25 per cent of the country disappearing in the next few years as a consequence of

[31] www.itamaraty.gov.br/sala-de-imprensa/notas-a-imprensa/2009/11/26/declaracao-de-manaus-reuniao-de-cupula-dos-paises.
[32] Environmental refugees are those who, due to imbalances in the natural environment which cause significant changes that are unsustainable in the environment, leave their countries in search of a new place to live with their families which hosts them and gives them subsidies in order to develop a life similar to the one they once had in their country of origin. P. L. M. Soares, 'Refugiados ambientais: a construção de um novo conceito e suas implicações à luz do Direito Internacional' in Jahyr-Philippe Bichara *et al.*, *Realidades – Organizações Internacionais e Questões da Atualidade* (Natal: Editora da UFRN, 2008), p. 187.
[33] Coming from the English term, internally displaced persons are those who suffer from the same pattern of harassment or problems listed in the 1951 Convention, the 1967 Protocol and the Cartagena Declaration of 1984, without, however, leaving the territory of their country, but in a state of flight or migration, requiring therefore protection. This term can also be used to refer to victims of disasters caused by humans, which leaves them in a similar position to that of refugees already mentioned in the referred documents: International Law Commission, Fifty-eighth Session, *Expulsion of Aliens*, (Geneva, 2006), pp. 110–24.

an increase in sea levels.[34] Or, in the case of Tuvalu, with a small land mass and a maximum elevation of only five metres above sea level, there is not just the threat of the diminishment of the State's borders, but the imminent threat of extinction of the entire State by the disappearance of one of its fundamental attributes: the territory.

21.56   With respect to Brazil, the right to property and housing has been violated particularly in coastal communities, exemplified by cases relating to the northeast – the communities of the Icarai in Fortaleza[35] and the city of Branquinha, in the state of Alagoas.[36] In these places, global warming has caused water levels to rise sharply, threatening coastal communities, destroying their homes or making it impossible to live in these areas, creating homeless families and potentially internally displaced persons in the Brazilian territory.

21.57   There have also been large fires in the interior of Brazil, specifically in the midwest and some parts of the southeast. According to the magazine *New Environment*, in 2010 about 260,000 hot spots were recorded by the Space Research Institute. Out of these, more than 70,000 were confirmed as fires, which represents an increase of 185 per cent compared to 2009.[37]

21.58   These catastrophic effects of climate change (including major floods and severe drought) have caused a widespread exodus from one region to another in Brazil, providing evidence of the existence of internally displaced persons in Brazil as a result of environmental disasters which are a direct result of global warming and climate change in general.

21.59   Climate change is constant and even though these aforementioned provisions are unshakable, it has rendered them unachievable and additionally impedes the enjoyment of other rights, such as the right to health, which is enshrined as a social right of the Brazilian Constitution. Global warming and climate change

[34] www.bbc.co.uk/portuguese/forum/ story/2007/11/071102_bangladeshnovo.shtml.
[35] diariodonordeste.globo.com/materia.asp?codigo=794687.
[36] www.correiodopovo-al.com.br/v3/municipios/4727-Fotos-mostram-Branquinha-antes-depois-chuvas-destruidoras.html.
[37] S. Queimada, *Revista Novo Ambiente, desenvolvimento com equilíbrio*, 1(4) (2010), 13 (available at www.revistanovoambiente.com.br/revista/default.php?nac=17).

have caused severe changes, leading to the emergence of micro-climates in major cities, such as the existence of heat islands in São Paulo, causing its residents to suffer from heatstroke, thermal discomfort and aggravation of respiratory diseases from high temperatures.[38]

21.60   Such incidents are also found in the study of micro-climates in slums conducted by the Faculty of Public Health, São Paulo, USP.[39] The study affirms the higher incidence of hospitalisations for pneumonia in infants, bronchitis and asthma attacks, which are diseases related to atmospheric factors, correlating with warmer micro-climates such as those in the slums. As a result, it can be concluded that the violation of the right to health is a reflection and consequence of global warming.

21.61   Finally, in cases of drought in the Pantanal and the Amazon region, there are various violations of Article 225 of the Constitution and all other international rights which are equivalent to it.

21.62   In 2010, the levels of the rivers of the Amazon Basin at some sections were very close to the lowest levels ever recorded.[40] As for the Pantanal, the situation is also critical and can be considered the worst since 1972.[41]

(E)   Conclusion

21.63   One can make the following observations from the preceding study on the impact of climate change in Brazil and its repercussions in the legal system:

21.64   In terms of regional effects, according to the Economic Survey of Climate Change in Brazil,[42] the regions that will suffer most from climate change will be the Amazon and the northeast. This allows us to draw a much more serious background against

---

[38] H. Ribeiro and E. N. Silva, 'Alterações da temperatura em ambientes externos de favela e desconforto térmico', *Revista de Saúde Pública*, 40(4) (2006) (available at www.scielo.br/scielo.php?script=sci_arttext&pid=S0034-89102006000500016).

[39] *Ibid.*

[40] www1.folha.uol.com.br/cotidiano/817477-nivel-do-rio-negro-baixa-mais-e-ja-e-a-2-maior-vazante-em-108-anos.shtml.

[41] www.olhardireto.com.br/noticias/exibir.asp ?edt=33&id=127683.

[42] J. Marcovitch, *Economia da Mudança do Clima no Brasil: custos e oportunidades* (São Paulo: IBEP Gráfica, 2010).

which to assess the effects of climate change, considering that the two regions which are most vulnerable with regard to social and economic factors are the north and northeast.[43]

21.65   According to the study, the increase in temperatures could reach 7°C to 8°C in 2100, which would result in the desertification of the Amazon as around 40 per cent of forest cover will be eliminated and replaced by a desert biome.

21.66   In the northeastern region rainfall could decrease by between 2 to 2.5 mm per day by 2100, causing severe crop losses throughout the region, with a 25 per cent reduction in capacity for grazing beef cattle. In other regions of Brazil, such as the southeast, there is a real prospect that the Paraíba River, which traverses the states of Rio de Janeiro, São Paulo and Minas Gerais, could have a 90 per cent reduction in flow by 2100.

21.67   The Economic Survey of Climate Change in Brazil also suggests that there will be a significant adverse impact on the energy sector if the pace of climate change does not slow down. One of the consequences would be that the system of hydroelectric power generation might cease to be reliable with a possible reduction of around 30 per cent in power generation – again with the greatest impact on electricity supply in the most vulnerable regions of Brazil.

21.68   Finally, it is estimated that between 130 and 200 billion Brazilian Reals would be lost as a result of an increase in sea levels and extreme environmental incidents in Brazilian coastal areas by 2100.

21.69   All the same, this cataclysmic picture can be reversed. And we can already see this in Brazil, even only through isolated individual projects. There is a growing trend to apply principles such as sustainable development in the decisions of the judiciary and actions of the executive.[44] This is possibly influenced by foreign jurisprudence which has been making new advances in environmental protection,[45] and we believe that Brazil is moving towards

[43] *Ibid.*
[44] See, for instance, STF. AD In 3540 MC/DF. Tribunal Pleno. Min. Rel: Celso de Mello. Date of Judgment 1 September 2005, published on 3 February 2006.
[45] The European Court of Human Rights, in recent rulings, has brought about an innovation by using the evolutionary interpretation of the European Convention on Human

the use of modern mechanisms such as those already observed in other countries.[46] However, much remains to be done in this area.

21.70   Moreover, the 2009 Law on National Policy on Climate Change can be seen as an instrument of progress, revealing a new governmental attitude in relation to environmental preservation.

21.71   The Government is sourcing around 417 MW of energy from wind power, and 442 MW from capacity under construction and 441 projects nearing completion. These latest efforts add to the existing wind-energy network of around 13,000 MW. In 2008, BNDES financed numerous projects for renewable energy, amounting to about US$ 5.7 million investment for a total of 47 projects.

21.72   Brazil's economy has grown over the years, and its environmental preservation policies have matured in an overall effort to integrate these policies together with the right to economic development. However, much remains to be done so that we can realise the right to an ecologically balanced environment and the principle of sustainable development, so that climate change will not interfere with the success of future generations.

Rights, of 1950, by using its provisions to safeguard the right to environment. We can see this in the cases *Lopez Ostra* v. *Spain*, *Moreno Gomez* v. *Spain*, *Hatton and Others* v. *UK*, *Fadaieva* v. *Russia*, *War and Others* v. *Italy*, which had placed the right to the environment as the foundation of the right to private and family life, referring to Article 8 of the 1950 Convention, in the cases *Öneryildiz* v. *Turkey* and *LCB* v. *United Kingdom*, with focus on Article 2 of the 1950 Convention, the European Court of Human Rights addressed the right to a balanced environment and quality as the foundation of the right to life itself, whereas in *Mc Ginley and Egan* v. *UK*, *Roche* v. *UK*, *Steel and Morris* v. *UK Clubs* and *Voids Aizsardzības* v. *Latvia*, the European Court considered, basing its reasoning on Article 10 of the Convention, which deals with the right to freedom of expression in order to guarantee freedom of expression and the right to environmental information itself. Silva, José Antonio Tietzmann e, 'A efetividade do Direito Internacional do Meio Ambiente: a jurisprudência da Corter Europeia de Direitos Humanos' in Ana Flávia Barros-Platiau and Marcelo Dias Varella (eds.), *A efetividade do Direito Internacional Ambiental* (Brasília: UNICEUB, UNITAR e UnB, 2009), pp. 293–316.

[46] Brazil is advancing the use of new principles and new interpretations of environmental law, as well as the instruments of public and private law that we have discussed throughout this chapter. The tendency is that Brazil now has a jurisprudence as advanced as the European courts, such as the ECtHR.

Mexico

JOSÉ JUAN GONZÁLEZ MARQUEZ

(A)   Introduction

The Mexican legal system

22.01   Mexico is a federal democratic republic consisting of thirty-one
states and the federal district of Mexico City, and governed by a
civil law system. The main sources of law are (i) the Constitution,
which is written; (ii) international treaties signed by the executive
with the ratification of the Senate; (iii) federal laws passed by
the federal Congress; (iv) state laws passed by state congresses;
(v) judicial decisions; and (vi) jurisprudence.

22.02   The constitutional reform of 1987 established a concurrent jurisdiction system according to which the federal and state governments share the power to legislate on environmental matters.[1]
Furthermore, in 1999 the federal Constitution was amended to
recognise both the right of people to a healthy environment and
the principle of sustainability.[2] Notwithstanding the concurrent
jurisdiction system, it is generally assumed that Article 27 of the
federal Constitution, which regulates the property system that
governs waters, land and natural resources, remains the main
foundation for Mexican environmental law.

22.03   Based on the above-mentioned constitutional principles, a complex system of federal and state environmental laws has been
passed in Mexico. Most of this environmental legislation has
been built on the command-and-control approach. Hence environmental issues, and specifically climate change problems, are
generally addressed from the perspective of administrative law.

---

[1] Official Gazette of Federation, 19 August 2004.
[2] *Ibid.*, 4 December 2000.

However, in cases of damages caused by climate change, private law – civil liability – could also be applicable.

22.04   Nevertheless, applying administrative law and private law to the restoration of climate change damage could present serious problems, as this chapter illustrates.

The governmental stance on climate change

22.05   In Mexico, no specific ministry has been created to deal with climate change. However, under Article 32-bis of the Organic Act of Federal Public Administration,[3] the Ministry of Environment and Natural Resources must conduct national public policies on climate change and protection of the ozone layer. Furthermore, under Article 33 of the Act, the Ministry of Energy must regulate and promote the development and use of alternative sources of energy.

22.06   The Mexican government ratified the Kyoto Protocol and has since created a number of bodies to implement it. In January 2004, an Executive Ordinance created the Mexican Inter-Ministerial Committee for Emission-Reduction Projects and Green House Gas Capture.[4] This Committee was designated as the National Authority for CDM projects under the Kyoto Protocol. In 2005, another Executive Ordinance replaced the Committee with the Inter-Ministerial Commission on Climate Change (the 'Commission').[5]

22.07   The Commission has the power, among others, to approve projects for emission reduction and carbon sequestration in accordance with the Protocol. The Commission is composed of representatives of the Ministries of Foreign Affairs; Social Development; Environment and Natural Resources; Energy; Economy; Agriculture, Rural Development, Fisheries and Alimentation and Communications and Transport.

22.08   Article 10 of the 2005 Executive Ordinance that created the Commission established the Advisory Committee for Climate Change, which includes climate change experts from the

---

[3] *Ibid.*, 29 December 1976, as amended on 17 June 2009.
[4] *Ibid.*, 23 January 2004.   [5] *Ibid.*, 25 June 2005.

social, private and academic sectors who are appointed by the President.

22.09 Additionally, on 15 February 2005 a group of public and private institutions[6] signed an agreement to create the Energy Sector Committee for Climate Change. The Committee's objective is to coordinate the energy sector actions regarding climate change with the Ministry of Environment.[7]

Climate change laws

22.10 Air pollution has been a constant concern for the Mexican government. At the beginning of the twentieth century, the air pollution issue was addressed only from the perspective of private law. For example, the Federal Civil Code of 1928 prohibited the construction of chimneys in close proximity to neighbouring/adjacent properties. It also prescribed minimum distances at which chimneys had to be set back from adjoining properties.

22.11 The Government then began to address pollution as a public health issue. This resulted in the enactment of the Regulation for Dangerous, Disgusting and Unhealthy Industrial or Commercial Facilities of 1940, which provided that the air emissions from such facilities should be channelled through chimneys of a certain height and should not exceed a certain concentration of pollutant particles.

22.12 In 1971, the Federal Act to Control and Prevent Pollution was enacted. Like the 1940 regulation, this law focused on the effects of air pollution on human health. The Act prohibited the emission or discharge of pollutants in concentrations that can affect human life and health, flora and fauna, and natural resources in general. This law provided that all sources of pollution (industries and vehicles) must have a license granted by the Federal

---

[6] The Ministry of Energy, the Mexican Institute of Petroleum, the State-owned oil company PEMEX, the Federal Commission of Electricity, the Light and Power Company of the Center (which no longer exists), the National Commission for Energy Savings, the Regulatory Commission of Energy, the Institute for Electric Research and the Fund for Energy Savings.

[7] See Ubaldo Inclán Gallardo, 'Mercado de bonos de carbon y sus beneficios potenciales para proyectos en México, and Comision Intersecretarial para el Cambio Climático', *Reporte de Actividades de la SENER en materia de cambio climático 2005–2006*, available at www.semarnat.gob.mx/temas/cambioclimatico/Documents/enac/reporte.

Environmental Authority and must comply with the limits of pollutant emissions established by the regulations. A regulation under this Act established the parameters of emissions from pollutant sources and many standards were developed to regulate the emissions of (i) solid particles, (ii) humidity, (iii) SO_2, (iv) CO_2, (v) CO, (vi) oxygen present in combustion gases, and (vii) SO_3, among other gases.[8]

22.13   The Federal Act for Environmental Protection of 1982 replaced the Act of 1971 but did not introduce any fundamental changes. However, when it came into force, new standards related to air pollution emissions were also approved.

22.14   In 1988, the Ecological Equilibrium and Environmental Protection General Act ('LGEEPA') changed the Government's approach to dealing with air pollution. LGEEPA focuses not only on air pollution's effects on human health but also on the protection of the environment as a whole, including natural resources. According to LGEEPA, the biggest industrial sources of air pollution come under federal jurisdiction whereas vehicle and medium- and small-sized industrial and commercial sources of air pollution come under local jurisdiction.

22.15   However, neither LGEEPA nor state environmental law establishes specific obligations to reduce pollutant emissions; they only require industrial sources to control them. Furthermore, neither LGEEPA nor state environmental law refers specifically to climate change mitigation and adaptation issues. The only instruments aimed at controlling air pollutant emissions under the Act are, in the case of industrial sources, the licensing system for operation granted by the Minister of Environment and Natural Resources and, in the case of mobile sources (that is to say, vehicles), the 'hoy no circula' programme. Under this programme, those vehicles whose emissions surpass the applicable emission limits established by Mexican Official Norms (standards) may not be operated for one day each week.

22.16   As this brief survey illustrates, the Mexican environmental law system does not yet provide a sufficient foundation for an

---

[8] See Official Gazettes of Federation, 4 March 1974; 27 June 1974; 2 August 1976; 6 September 1979; 17 June 1980 and 8 August 1980.

appropriate policy on climate change issues. Recently, however, a group of senators from the government party proposed a Bill for a Climate Change Act. Approval of the Bill is still pending. Article 1 of the Bill states the Act's objectives to be promoting adaptation to and mitigation of climate change and contributing to sustainable development.[9] The Bill establishes the general criteria for policies on mitigation and adaptation, the national system for climate change and the instruments of this system.

22.17   In order to create a national system for climate change, the Bill proposes to establish a National Commission on Climate Change[10] that would be in charge of formulating and implementing national climate change policy,[11] as well as a Climate Change Council that would function as a consultative and evaluative institution and would comprise members representing civil society, private corporations and academic organisations. Among the instruments for climate change mitigation and adaptation, the Bill would establish a Green Fund, a National Register of Emissions and a Market of Carbon Emissions.

22.18   In regard to liability, the Bill merely states in Article 57 that '[t]he public employees regulated by this law who do not comply with its provisions shall be punished with an administrative sanction'.[12] However, the Bill does not specify the form or content of such an administrative sanction.

22.19   A number of legislative steps have also been taken at the state levels. In November 2010, the State of Veracruz passed the Act of Mitigation and Adaptation of Climate Change Effects.[13] In December 2010, the State of Chiapas[14] and the federal district of Mexico City[15] both passed Acts for climate change

---

[9] The full text of the Bill is available at www.bionero.org/sociedad/iniciativa-de-ley-general-de-cambio-climatico-para-mexico.

[10] According to the Bill, this Commission will replace the Commission on Climate Change created in 2005.

[11] Currently such functions are for the Inter-ministerial Commission on Climate Change.

[12] Translated by the author from the text available at www.bionero.org/sociedad/iniciativa-de-ley-general-de-cambio-climatico-para-mexico.

[13] Available at www.ordenjuridico.gob.mx/Documentos/Estatal/Veracruz/wo55538.pdf.

[14] Available at www.cambioclimaticochiapas.org/portal/descargas/nuestro_trabajo/ley_adaptacion_mitigacion_ccch.pdf.

[15] Available at www.partidoverde.org.mx/pvem/2010/11/ley-de-cambio-climatico-del-df-ejemplo-para-ejecutivo-federal/.

adaptation. Similar to the Bill for the federal Climate Change Act, these new state acts create public institutions in charge of climate change policy and green funds to support such policies. However, none of the legislation incorporates provisions regarding liability.

Industrial and natural resources (emissions sources and energy mix)

22.20   In Mexico, combustion of fossil fuels to produce energy generates 61% of the country's total CO_2 emissions. The remainder of the CO_2 emissions comes from land use change (14%), management of waste (10%), agriculture (8%) and industrial processes (7%).[16] Thus, energy efficiency is one of the important Mexican strategies for climate change mitigation.[17] Energy efficiency actions yielded a reduction of energy consumption of 12,558 GWh (equivalent to 10.2 million tonnes of CO_2) in 2009.[18]

National climate change risks

22.21   Mexico is responsible for no more than 1.6 per cent of the world's total fossil fuel-based carbon emissions, placing it thirteenth in the rank of emitter countries.[19] However, because of its geographical conditions, Mexico is very vulnerable to climate change.[20] Every state in the Mexican Federation is confronted with at least one considerable threat from climate change effects.[21]

---

[16] See National Plan of Development, Official Gazette of Federation, 31 May 2007, available at http://dof.gob.mx/.

[17] See Mexican Special Programme for Climate Change 2009–2010, Official Gazette of Federation, 28 August 2009, pp. 8–9.

[18] Mexico Fourth National Communication to United Nations Framework Convention on Climate Change, available at http://unfccc.int/resource/docs/natc/mexnc4s.pdf.

[19] See Mexican Special Programme for Climate Change 2009–2010, Official Gazette of Federation, 28 August 2009.

[20] Adrian Fernández et al., 'Cambio Climatico y Acciones para enfrentarlo' in Ninfa Salinas Sada and Yolanda Alaniz (eds.), Temas Selectos de Medio Ambiente (Mexico: Cámara de Diputados, 2011), pp. 121–80.

[21] Mexico is among the countries with high vulnerability because 15% of its national territory, 68% of its population and 71% of its GDP are highly exposed to risk of adverse direct impacts of climate change.

22.22   According to the National Institute of Ecology,[22] there are ten especially vulnerable sectors, including agriculture,[23] health[24] and water.[25] Forty million Mexicans living in extreme poverty conditions are particularly vulnerable to climate change.[26] This applies mainly in the northern parts of the country, where water scarcity is a central issue, and in the southern parts of the country, where tropical storms cause extensive damage to crop and livestock production.

(B)   Public law

Overview

22.23   Climate change damage could implicate an administrative agency decision[27] because, under both Mexican federal and local environmental law, public agencies are in charge of authorising and regulating public and private activities that generate greenhouse gas ('GHG') emissions.[28] The federal Constitution holds that all decisions of public agencies must be issued in writing by a competent authority and must state the legal grounds and justification for the relevant action. In addition, all public agency decisions must comply with the requirements set up by Article 3 of the federal Act of Administrative Procedure. Thus, an administrative

---

[22]   See the website of the National Institute of Ecology, available at http://www2.ine.gob.mx/cclimatico/edo_sector/sector/sector.html.

[23]   It is expected that, by 2030, over-exploitation and pollution of aquifers will make all irrigation districts economically unsustainable and that, by 2050, there will be a reduction of 5 to 29% in the ability of the soil to produce corn and other cereals.

[24]   The risk of death from heat impacts will increase during the following years and some areas will be more vulnerable to diseases such as dengue or paludism as well as gastro-intestinal infections. The effects will mostly be borne by children and old people.

[25]   From 2020 to 2050 the medium summertime temperature will increase by between 1 and 3°C, and precipitation will decrease by 5 to 10% annually, diminishing the availability of water.

[26]   According to official data, the areas most vulnerable to climate change are the States of Baja California, Sonora and Sinaloa, the basin of the 'Rio Lerma' and the south of the country.

[27]   See José Juan González, 'Mexico' in Kurt Deketelaere, 'Environmental Law', *International Encyclopedia of Law* (Kluwer Law International, 2009), pp. 183–203.

[28]   The main authorisation in this regard is the environmental impact authorisation that may be granted by federal or state environmental authorities.

decision that violates these constitutional or legal requirements may be challenged in the local or federal administrative courts.

Grounds for judicial review

22.24   The circumstances in which administrative courts may review decisions of public agencies are strictly limited to the following situations:

(1) the decision has been issued by an incompetent authority;

(2) it lacks a specific object, that is to say it does not produce any legal effect;

(3) it contradicts the public trust protected by the applicable law;

(4) it has not been issued in writing or lacks the signature of the competent authority;

(5) it lacks foundation[29] and motivation;[30]

(6) it has been issued without complying with applicable procedural rules;

(7) it has been issued with a mistake as to its object, cause or motivation;

(8) it has been issued on the basis of bad faith or violence;

(9) it does not identify the issuing authority;

(10) it has been issued with an error regarding the relevant file, document or persons; or

(11) it does not specify the date or place of issuing.[31]

Other aspects of judicial review

22.25   While procedure is generally governed by the federal Act of Administrative Procedure, it is complemented by provisions under LGEEPA.

22.26   Judicial review can only occur where there has been a 'decision' by a public authority.

---

[29] Foundation is defined as the expression of all specific legal provisions that support the administrative authority resolution.

[30] Motivation means that the administrative authority is obliged to express legal arguments that support why a specific legal provision is applicable to the specific case decided by the authority.

[31] Article 3 of the federal Act of Administrative Procedure.

22.27　The only possible remedies resulting from a successful judicial review are (i) to nullify the decision, (ii) to oblige the administrative agency to issue a new decision, or (iii) to restart the decision-making process from where a violation occurred. In the field of administrative law, there is no remedy for damage, although judicial revision could halt activities that represent a risk of damage. For instance, when a court nullifies an environmental impact authorisation, the project cannot be built or operated.

Standing

22.28　A claimant must be able to show 'sufficient interest', that is, must have legal standing to file an action in court. Generally, administrative law only grants standing to those who were parties to the administrative decision-making process, i.e. the petitioner and the Government.

22.29　However, in the case of environmental authorities' decisions, Article 180 of LGEEPA (as amended in 2006 and 2011)[32] is more broad, granting legal standing to 'individuals or communities that could be affected by … works or activities' that are contrary to law and that 'cause or could cause damage to the environment, natural resources, wildlife or public health'.[33]

22.30　This generous standing rule enables civil society organisations to stop activities that could cause climate change by filing an action in the administrative courts.

22.31　No challenges directly related to climate change have been brought under this rule. However, cases in the field of environmental protection more generally illustrate the application of this provision. For instance, in 1996 a non-governmental organisation called 'Pro San Luis Ecologico' filed an *amparo* action (injunction) to challenge the Environmental Impact Assessment Authorisation issued by the Ministry of Environment and Natural Resources to a Canadian mining company established in the state of San Luis Potosi. The court considered that the administrative authority had made many mistakes when

---

[32]　Official Gazettes of Federation, 13 December 1996 and 28 January 2011.
[33]　Translated by the author from the text of the Act, available at www.diputados.gob.mx/ LeyesBiblio/ref/lgeepa.htm.

authorising the project and therefore ordered the nullification of the authorisation.[34]

Human rights law and judicial review

22.32   Article 4 of the federal Constitution establishes the right of Mexicans to a healthy environment. Thus, public agencies' decisions, laws or plans that violate this right may be directly reviewed by the federal courts via the filing of an *amparo* action (injunction). However, the 'Amparo Act' grants standing to file an action only to those people directly affected by the decision, law or plan. Consequently, other parties interested in filing an *amparo* action to enforce Article 4 of the Constitution must have previously filed an administrative action in accordance with Article 180 of LGEEPA. In addition, the scope of any resulting judicial decision is limited to those who filed the claim. Judicial decisions in *amparo* trials cannot provide remedies for damages.

22.33   Notwithstanding the above legislative limitation on filing *amparo* actions, the Supreme Court of Justice issued a decision that construed standing more broadly. In 1996, the NGO 'grupo de los cien' filed an *amparo* action (injunction) challenging an administrative agreement issued by the Ministry of Environment and Natural Resources that exempted a number of small- and medium-sized industries from the requirement to conduct environmental impact assessments. At that time, LGEEPA had not yet been amended to grant legal standing to third parties to challenge administrative decisions. However, the Court reasoned that because Mexico had signed the Rio Declaration, which included a commitment to protect the right of people to a healthy environment as a human right, individuals or NGOs therefore had standing to file legal actions necessary to protect this right.[35] In June 2011, Articles 103 and 107 of the Mexican Constitution were modified to allow NGOs to file *amparo* actions in defence of the human right to a healthy environment. It is expected that the Amparo Act will be amended to broadly recognise legal standing as well (see Official Gazette of Federation, 10 June 2011).

---

[34] A brief explanation of this issue may be found at www.newgold.com/Theme/NewGold/files/CSP%20Fact%20Sheet%20June%202010.pdf.

[35] An excellent analysis of this case is available in Lucio Cabrera Acevedo, *El amparo protector del derecho al ambiente y de otros derechos humanos* (Mexico: Porrua, 2000).

Property rights and planning law

22.34   Property rights are protected under the federal Constitution. Article 27 of the Mexican Constitution recognises that the original property of the lands and waters of the Mexican territory was vested in the Nation. The Article also recognises that natural elements such as waters and lands may be situated on private property. However, Article 27, paragraph 3 establishes that, for reasons of environmental protection, the nation shall at all times have the right to impose on private property such limitations as the public interest may demand.

22.35   Hence, Article 27, paragraph 3 of the Constitution grants the executive branch (i.e. the Mexican President or state governors) the power to limit the exercise of property rights by individuals. Ordinances on territory, urban planning and protected natural areas are examples of limitations imposed by the nation on private property with the aim of preserving ecological balance as well as to mitigate negative effects of climate change by protecting, through these instruments, natural carbon sequestration. Similar limitations on the use of private property could be established to avoid the emission of GHGs. Conversely, disobeying the provisions established by ecological ordinance or urban plans as well as protected natural areas declarations could contribute to climate change damage because stored carbon might be released due to deforestation and environmental degradation.

(C)   Private law

Preliminary considerations

22.36   The civil liability regime could provide a remedy for damage caused to people or the environment and resulting from emissions generated by activities either conducted or authorised by private or public parties.

22.37   Mexican private law recognises two types of liability: fault liability and strict liability. Fault liability is based on three elements: damage, fault (improper behaviour) and a link of causation between that conduct and the damage. Strict liability shares the elements of damage and causation but does not require proof of fault. Because strict liability is linked to dangerous activities, i.e. those involving a considerable level of risk, it has the potential to be applied to environmental, and therefore climate change, damages.

22.38   Most Mexican environmental laws envisage the application of civil liability to remedy environmental damages. For instance, Article 203 of LGEEPA (as amended in 1996) asserts that all persons contaminating or deteriorating the environment or affecting natural resources shall be responsible and shall be forced to repair the resultant damage in accordance with the Civil Code.

22.39   Similarly, Article 96 bis-1 of the Waters Act provides that individuals or corporations that illegally discharge waste waters that cause contamination in a receiving body shall assume the responsibility of repairing the environmental damage caused.

Who might claim?

22.40   While in administrative law standing is limited to those directly affected by the administrative decision, under the Code of Civil Procedure, standing is limited to those individuals or corporations directly affected by the damage.[36] However, environmental laws have changed these rules for certain contexts. For example, the Wildlife Act holds in Article 107: 'Any person or corporation may denounce to the Attorney General Office for Environmental Protection damage to wildlife or its habitat without demonstrating that it has been personally or directly affected by such damages. The Attorney General Office for Environmental Protection shall carefully evaluate the file and when it proceeds, it will file an action for such damages under strict and solidary liability.'[37]

22.41   Article 17 of the federal Constitution recently was amended to provide that the federal Congress must pass laws regulating class actions.[38] Such laws shall establish the matters where class action is available, the judicial procedures and the mechanisms for damage restoration. Such legislation has been submitted to Congress but its approval is still pending. When approved, the resulting Act will be applicable to the field of environmental protection and therefore to actions concerning damage due

---

[36] See Francisco Cornejo Certucha, 'Interés Jurídico' in *Diccionario jurídico* (Mexico: UNAM, 1992), pp. 1777–79.

[37] See Jose Juan Gonzalez Marquez, *La responsabilidad por el Daño Ambiental. El paradigma de la reparación* (Mexico: UAM-Porrua, 2002), pp.195–205.

[38] The reform was published in the Official Gazette of the Federation on 29 July 2010.

to climate change. However, the constitutional reform did not change the rules on standing established by the Federal Act of Administrative Procedure, the Civil Code or the various environmental laws. The reform just allows those who have standing to file an action to do so through a class action.

Who might be defendants?

22.42   Even though there has been no case on this question, those responsible for GHG emissions may be civilly liable for climate change damage under the general principles of the Mexican legal system.

Issues of causation

22.43   In the Mexican legal system, the victim must prove that the damage has already occurred and that such damage is the consequence of the defendant's conduct. Proving this link of causation would be one of the main challenges in applying civil liability to climate change damage.[39]

22.44   The first problem lies in proving the evidence of climate change. Such proof would necessarily involve complex science that is not as common or familiar to the courts as are evidentiary issues in cases involving traditional civil damages. Secondly, a plaintiff would have to prove that climate change is the consequence of human conduct. Thirdly, a plaintiff would have to prove which specific human conduct caused climate change. Finally, the plaintiff would have to prove that climate change has produced the civil damages, that is to say damage to persons or their properties.

22.45   To avoid the problems of proving the link of causation in cases of environmental damage, Mexican environmental laws channel liability to a specific entity. For instance Article 151 of LGEEPA (as amended in 1996) holds:

> Liability for management and final disposition of hazardous waste falls upon those who generated the waste. Where the generators have hired out the management services and final disposition of the waste to companies authorized by the Secretary and where the waste has been given to these companies, liability for these companies' operations will be independent from the liability of the generators.[40]

---

[39] See José Juan González Marquez, n. 37 above, pp. 167–82.
[40] Translated by the author from the text published in the Official Gazette of the Federation on 13 December 1996.

22.46   However, at the federal level, there is no specific causation rule applicable to damage resulting from climate change.

'Specific causation'

22.47   By contrast, two state environmental laws have established heterodox principles to avoid problems related to causation by inverting the burden of proof. According to the environmental laws of the State of Colima and the federal district of Mexico City, when an industrial facility situated close to the place where damage has occurred has the capacity of producing the damage, there is a rebuttable presumption that the facility is liable.

Other factors

Limitation issues

22.48   According to Article 1934 of the Federal Civil Code, a civil action for damages must be brought within two years of the accrual of the cause of the damage. LGEEPA (as amended in 1996) modifies this term to five years. In the context of climate change, however, calculating the limitation period might be challenging because climate change damage could be generated by a series of acts that occur at different times and that do not have enough autonomy to establish a defining moment. In addition, climate change damage might not become evident until many years after its causes occurred.

22.49   The jurisprudence of the National Supreme Court of Justice may resolve such issues. Decisions of the Court have consistently established that the limitation term must be computed from the time that the cause stops producing damaging effects rather than from the time that the cause arose. The Court was moving in this direction by 1956, when it held in an injunction trial that 'when damage is not caused from a singular act but results from a continuous sequence of events whose combinations produce the damage, the term to file the action must be computed from the time such process has concluded'.[41]

---

[41] This judicial decision is available at *Judicial Journal of the Federation*, 5ª época, tomo CXXVIII, 295, Tercera Sala.

22.50   This rule was later legislated locally by Mexico City's
        Environmental Protection Act.[42]

Remedies

Remedies in judicial review proceedings

22.51   Given that the outcome of successful judicial review proceedings
        is to modify decisions issued by public agencies, it is not possible
        to obtain a physical remedy for climate change damage through
        this route. However, through judicial review it is possible to
        stop those activities that could represent a risk of damages. For
        instance, when the court nullifies an environmental impact
        authorisation, the project cannot be built or operated.

Remedies in civil liability procedure

22.52   In general, according to Article 1915 of the Federal Civil Code,
        restoration of damage must consist of the re-establishment of
        the previous condition or, when re-establishment is impossible,
        the payment of an economic compensation. However, Mexican
        environmental laws stress the priority of remediation over eco-
        nomic compensation. For instance, Article 152-bis of LGEEPA
        (as amended in 1996) provides:

> When generation, management or final disposition of dangerous
> waste or materials results in soil pollution, those responsible for the
> operation will carry out the necessary actions to recover and to re-
> establish the conditions of the soil, so as it can be designated to some
> of the activities foreseen in the applicable programme of urban devel-
> opment plans or of ecological zoning plans for such soil or area.[43]

22.53   In regard to damages caused to wildlife or their habitats, Article
        108 of the Wildlife Act provides:

> The restoration of the damage in the case of liability for damage to
> wildlife and their habitats will consist in the re-establishment of the
> conditions previous to the commission of this damage and, if the
> re-establishment is impossible, in the payment of an economic com-
> pensation which will be dedicated, according to the regulation of

---

[42] Mexico City's Environmental Protection Act was published in the Official Gazette of
Mexico City on 13 January 2000.

[43] Translated by the author from the text published in the Official Gazette of the Federation
on 3 July 2000.

this Act, to the development of programmes, projects and activities linked to the restoration, conservation and recovery of species and populations, as well as to the diffusion of wildlife protection, to qualification of people in charge of enforcing the law and to monitoring programmes to verify compliance with the Wild Life Act.[44]

22.54   In contrast, Article 136 of the Forest Act prioritises the payment of economic compensation over ecological restoration. In cases of damage caused to forest resources, to the environment, to ecosystems or their components, the responsible party must provide the corresponding compensation.

22.55   Finally, although the Waste Act does not establish the obligation to repair environmental damage, it allows for the restoration of soils polluted by hazardous wastes in Articles 78 and 79, which respectively provide:

> Article 78. The Secretary, in coordination with the Secretary of Health, shall issue the Mexican official norms for the characterisation of polluted places and shall evaluate the risks to the environment and public health that derive from them in order to determine, in function of the risk, the restoration actions that proceed.
>   Article 79. The regulation on land use and the programmes of ecological classification and of urban development shall be considered when determining the level of remediation of polluted places with hazardous waste, based on the risks that will be avoided.

(D)   Other law

Criminal law

22.56   Although criminal law does not have the objective of damage restoration, modern criminal environmental laws may nevertheless contribute to this aim by adapting traditional principles of criminal law.[45]

22.57   Title 25 ('Crimes against the environment and environmental management') of the Federal Criminal Code contains the provisions in relation to environmental crimes. The Title contains five

---

[44] Translated by the author from the text published in the Official Gazette of the Federation on 13 December 1996.
[45] See Candido Conde-Pumpido, 'Introducción al delito ecológico' in Juan Terradillos Basoco, *El delito ecológico* (Valladolid: Trotta, 1992), pp. 25–45.

chapters, four of which classify twenty types of criminal conduct related to technological and dangerous activities, biodiversity, bio-safety and environmental management, whereas the fifth chapter contains general provisions related to innovative penalties and precautionary measures to be adopted by judges when an environmental criminal act is committed. According to Article 415, it is criminal behaviour to commit or authorise a discharge into the atmosphere of pollutant gases, smoke or dusts that may cause damage to natural resources, flora, fauna, ecosystems or the environment.

22.58   The criminal punishment consists of imprisonment from one to nine years and an administrative fine equivalent to one thousand daily minimum salaries. However, Article 421 of the Federal Criminal Code directs that, apart from these sanctions, those polluting the atmosphere may be obliged to carry out the necessary actions to re-establish the conditions of the affected natural elements to the state in which they were before the relevant crime was committed.

22.59   Generally, holding a person criminally responsible requires a complex process. In accordance with the Mexican Constitution and the Federal Code of Criminal Procedure, in order to indict someone for a criminal violation, the prosecution must acquire enough evidence to prove all of the elements of the specific crime charged as well as the probable participation of an individual in the commission of the crime.

22.60   The elements of environmental pollution crimes are: (i) a specific action, such as the emission of pollutants into the atmosphere; (ii) a result, such as the harm to public health, natural resources, wildlife, water quality or ecosystems; and (iii) the violation of an environmental statute, regulation or legal standard, such as the discharge of pollutants into a river in a quantity that exceeds the statutory limits. Failure to obtain a regulatory permit or introducing a hazard into the environment may also be considered elements of a crime in some cases.

22.61   Under Mexican law, to indict a person for the commission of an environmental crime the Government must present evidence sufficient to demonstrate that the person either purposely harmed the environment or possessed knowledge that such harm was possible. Under current regulations, criminal negligence is not sufficient for an indictment for the commission of an environmental crime.

The influence of international law on climate change liabilities in Mexico

22.62   Mexico is Party to the two principal international treaties aimed at tackling the problems associated with climate change, the United Nations Framework Convention on Climate Change ('FCCC') and the Kyoto Protocol.[46] However, since Mexico did not assume any GHG emissions reduction commitment, these treaties have not had any impact on domestic litigation.

Public trust – might the doctrine be applied in Mexico?

22.63   The public trust doctrine governs the property regime of natural resources. This doctrine prevents private ownership of air, flora and fauna. Furthermore, even where private ownership of forest land is allowed, the doctrine allows the nation to impose serious limitations on property rights in order to prevent forest degradation. The doctrine provides the foundation for the powers of the Ministry of the Environment to compel trustees to ensure that proper care is taken of the natural resources and their use or exploitation.

World heritage

22.64   There are twenty-seven UNESCO World Heritage sites in Mexico. Articles 4, 5 and 6 of the 1972 World Heritage Convention, which engage climate change mitigation, obligate the Mexican government to protect these sites. Most of these sites have been declared to be natural protected areas under LGEEPA, and thus they contribute to CO_2 sequestration and to the prevention of emissions from deforestation and degradation.

---

[46]   See the FCCC website, at http://maindb.unfccc.int/public/country.pl? country=MX.

Liability in public international law

22.65 As mentioned, Mexico is not an Annex I Party to the FCCC and as such is subject only to the general commitments set out in Article 4(1), such as the obligation to develop the national inventory of anthropogenic emissions and the obligation to promote and cooperate in the development, application and diffusion of technologies that control, reduce or prevent anthropogenic emissions. As a result, State responsibility for violation of the Convention is highly unlikely.

(E) 'Soft' law

OECD

22.66 Mexico is a member of the OECD and it is thus possible to bring a complaint before the national contact point for failure of a multinational enterprise to comply with the OECD Guidelines containing recommendations for 'responsible business conduct consistent with applicable law'. However, there is no case that illustrates this possibility.

(F) Practicalities

Founding jurisdiction for a claim

22.67 Under the Federal Code of Civil Procedure, Mexican courts have personal jurisdiction where the defendant's legal domicile is in the country or where the damage occurs in Mexican territory, without taking into account the nationality of the defendant but under the condition that the damage is the result of non-compliance with a Mexican law. [47]

Enforcement

22.68 Mexico is a Party to the North American Free Trade Agreement ('NAFTA'). Under the Environmental Side Agreement to NAFTA, the North American Agreement on Environmental

---

[47] See Article 24 paragraph IV of the Federal Code of Civil Procedure.

Cooperation ('NAAEC'), residents of Mexico who consider that the Mexican government does not comply with Mexican environmental laws may file an action called a 'petition of information' to request that the NAAEC Secretariat investigate whether there is a case of non-enforcement. This has been the main mechanism used by citizens to force public agencies to protect the environment during recent years. Although none of the cases investigated by the NAAEC Secretariat so far has related to climate change, such petitions may well occur in the future.[48]

Litigation costs

22.69   Generally, in civil litigation in Mexico each party funds its own costs as matters progress. At the conclusion of the litigation and only if the interested party includes a petition in that regard in its complaint, the court may order an unsuccessful party to pay at least the majority of the costs of the party who is successful in a claim or on a specific part of the proceedings. Thus the basic rule is that the loser pays and the winner recovers.

Obtaining information

22.70   Access to climate change justice supposes access to information.[49] The right to access to environmental information is recognised by Mexican legislation in four different ways.

22.71   Firstly, access to information is considered by the Mexican Constitution as a human right. In this way, Article 8 of the Mexican Federal Constitution provides:

> Public officials and employees shall respect the exercise of the right of petition, provided it is made in writing and in a peaceful and respectful manner; but this right may only be exercised in political matters by citizens of the Republic. Every petition shall be replied to in writing by the official to whom it is addressed, and said official is

---

[48] For information on the submission process and a record of petitions, see the section on citizen submissions on enforcement matters, available at www.cec.org.

[49] Paulo Affonso Leme Machado, *Direito á informação e meio ambiente* (Brazil: Malheiros, 2006), pp. 94–5.

bound to inform the petitioner of the decision taken within a brief period.[50]

22.72   Secondly, under LGEEPA, any person can claim access to environmental information in the context of an environmental impact assessment. In that regard, Article 34 of the Act states that once the Ministry of Environment has received an environmental impact assessment request all information pertaining to it is available for public consultation.

22.73   Thirdly, Articles 159, 159 bis-1 and 159 bis-2 of the Act require the environmental authority to gather, systematise and make accessible to the public environmental information, whereas Article 159 bis-3 gives the people the right to access information.

22.74   Finally, in 2002 the Federal Act of Transparency and Access to Information ('Access to Information Act') was passed by the federal Congress.[51] According to Article 1, the Act has the objective of guaranteeing to people the right to access information that governmental offices possess. This Act also created the Federal Institute for Access to Information as an autonomous entity in charge of promoting the right to access to information that governmental offices possess. Thus, this Act provides more comprehensive access to information on environmental matters than does LGEEPA.

22.75   When public authorities do not grant access to information as provided for in the Constitution and the Access to Information Act, relevant parties may file an *amparo* action (injunction) in order to force the authorities to disclose the requested information.

Disclosure (formerly 'discovery') in civil litigation

22.76   According to Article 134 of the Federal Code of Civil Procedure, under the request of any party the judge may require the government offices to disclose any document or piece of information that is relevant to prove the action.

---

[50] Translated by the author from the text published in the Official Gazette of the Federation on 5 February 1917, as amended in 2010, available at www.diputados.gob.mx.
[51] Official Gazette of the Federation, 11 July 2002.

Document retention requirements

22.77 According to LGEEPA, corporations and public bodies are under various obligations to retain documentation and records specifically regarding air pollutant emissions. For instance, all industrial sources of pollution are required to elaborate their own inventory of pollutant emissions and annually report it to the Ministry of Environment.

Disclosure obligation

22.78 Rights to information are closely allied to obligations to disclose. In that regard, in Mexico there is a constant pressure from civil society to compel corporations and government to disclose information not only through available legal procedures but through political action as well.

(G) Conclusion

22.79 Although Mexican environmental laws refer indirectly to climate change issues, no specific rules on climate change liability have been passed yet. Mexico's civil liability system appears to be applicable to climate change damage. However, a number of problems, such as proving the link of causation, standing to sue, time limitations to file an action, and the availability of a suitable remedy, must be solved in order to hold a defendant liable and for a plaintiff to obtain a remedy.

22.80 From the perspective of public law, administrative courts may issue a decision ordering the cessation of those activities that are causing or may cause climate change damage. But they are not empowered to order the restoration of damage already caused.

22.81 Finally, criminal law has been amended to encompass so-called environmental crimes, including provisions that criminalise specific types of air pollutant emissions. However, establishing criminal liability is also complicated, firstly because it requires the Attorney General to conduct a very careful investigation aimed at proving (i) all the elements of the criminal behaviour described by the Criminal Code, and (ii) the probable participation of the person in the commission of the crime; and, secondly, because the remedy does not consist directly in restoration.

Although a number of state climate change laws have been passed and a Bill for a federal climate change law is under discussion, none of these items includes specific provisions on climate change liability.

Thus, unless a fundamental reform is passed by Mexican Congresses (state and Federal), establishing climate change liability remains a difficult challenge.

SELECTED RESOURCES

Australia

Bates, G., *Environmental Law in Australia*, 7th edn (LexisNexis Butterworths, 2010).

Bonyhady, T. and Christoff, P. (eds.), *Climate Law in Australia* (The Federation Press, 2007).

Durrant, N., *Legal Responses to Climate Change* (The Federation Press, 2010).

Lyster, R. (ed.), *In the Wilds of Climate Law* (Australian Academic Press, 2010).

Peel, J., 'Climate Change Litigation' in *Climate Change Law and Policy in Australia* (LexisNexis Butterworths, 2009).

Preston, B., 'Climate Change Litigation' (paper presented at the 'Climate Change Governance after Copenhagen' conference, Hong Kong, 4 November 2010).

Smith, J. and Shearman, D., *Climate Change Litigation: Analysing the Law, Scientific Evidence and Impacts on the Environment, Health and Property* (Presidian Legal Publications, 2006).

China

China, People's Republic of, The Constitution of the People's Republic of China 1982.

China's Climate Change Policies and Actions (Beijing, 2007), available at www.gov. cn/zwgk/2008–10/29/content_1134378.htm.

Dongmei, Guo, *Research on Legal Systems for Addressing Climate Change* (Beijing: Law Press, 2010).

Haifeng, Deng, 'Review on Administrative Command and Control Approach in Environmental Law', *Hebei Law Science,* 23 (2005).

Law of the PRC on Environmental Protection 1989.

Law of the PRC on the Promotion of Clean Production 2002.

Law of the PRC on Energy Conservation 2007.

Law of the PRC on Circular Economy Promotion 2008.

Mingyuan, Wang, *Theory on Clean Production* (Beijing: Tshinghua University Press, 2004).

National Development and Reform Commission, *The PRC Initial National Communications on Climate Change*, available at www.ccchina.gov.cn/en/ NewsInfo.asp?NewsId=7111.

The Information Office of the State Council, *White Paper: China's Efforts and Achievements in Promoting the Rule of Law*, available at www.scio.gov.cn/zfbps/ndhf/2008/200905/t307866_2.htm.

The State Council, *National 12th Five-Year Plan*, available at http://news.sina.com.cn/c/2010–10–27/204721364515.shtml.

Wenxian, Zhang, *Research on Category for Philosophy of Law* (Beijing: China University of Political Science and Law Press, 2001).

Zitai, Zhang, 'Legal Approaches to Climate Change Adaptation', *Global Law Review*, 5 (2008).

India

Divan, Shyam and Rosencranz, Armin, *Environmental Law and Policy in India: Cases, Materials and Statutes*, 3rd edn (Delhi: Oxford University Press, 2001).

Ministry of Environment and Forests, Government of India, *Climate Change Negotiations: India's Submissions to the UNFCCC* (2009), available at http://moef.nic.in/modules/about-the-ministry/CCD/.

Ministry of Environment and Forests, Government of India, Indian Network for Climate Change Assessment, *Climate Change and India: A 4X4 Assessment – A Sectoral and Regional Analysis for 2030s* (2010).

India: Greenhouse Gas Emissions 2007 (2010).

Prime Minister's Council on Climate Change, Government of India, *National Action Plan on Climate Change* (2008), available at www.pmindia.nic.in/Pg01–52.pdf.

Rajamani, L., 'India and Climate Change: What India Wants, Needs and Needs to Do', *India Review*, 8(3) (2009), 340–74.

'Public Interest Environmental Litigation in India: Exploring Issues of Access, Participation, Equity, Effectiveness and Sustainability', *Journal of Environmental Law*, 19(3) (2007), 293–321.

'The Right to Environmental Protection in India: Many a Slip between the Cup and the Lip?', *Review of European Community and International Environmental Law*, 16(3) (2007), 274.

Singh, G. P., Aradhe, Alok, Jain, M. P. and Jain, S. N., *Principles of Administrative Law*, 6th edn (Nagpur: LexisNexis Butterworths Wadhwa, 2010).

Singh, G. P. (Justice), Ratanlal and Dhirajlal, *The Law of Torts*, 26th edn (Nagpur: LexisNexis Butterworths Wadhwa, 2010).

Indonesia

Bappenas, *Indonesian Climate Change Sectoral Roadmap (ICCSR); Scientific Basis: Analysis and Projection of Sea Level Rise and Extreme Weather Event* (2010).

Indonesian Climate Change Sectoral Roadmap (ICCSR); Sektor Pertanian (2010).

Bedner, Adriaan, *Administrative Courts in Indonesia: A Socio-Legal Study* (Kluwer Law International, 2001).

Djojodirdjo, Moegni, *Perbuatan Melawan Hukum* (Jakarta: Pradnya Paramita, 1982).

Government of Indonesia, *National Action Plan Addressing Climate Change (NAPACC)* (2007).

    National Action Plan Reduction of Green House Gas Emission, draft paper (2010).

Indonesian Centre for Environmental Law, *Research on Climate Friendly Legal Framework on Forestry Sector* (forthcoming).

Nicholson, David, *Environmental Dispute Resolution in Indonesia* (Leiden: KITLV Press, 2009).

Pompe, Sebastiaan, *The Indonesian Supreme Court: a Study of Institutional Collapse* (2005).

Santosa, Mas Achmad, *Role of Governance in Addressing Climate Change* (unpublished paper prepared for Democratic Governance Unit, UNDP-Indonesia, 2010).

Japan

Abe, Y. and Awaji, T. (eds.), *Environmental Law*, 3rd edn (Yuhikaku, 2006).

Gresser, J., Fujikura, K. and Morishima, A., *Environmental Law in Japan* (The MIT Press, 1981).

Kitamura, Y., *Environmental Law* (Kobundo, 2011).

Oda, H., *Japanese Law*, 3rd edn (Oxford University Press, 2009).

Otsuka, T., *Environmental Law*, 3rd edn (Yuhikaku, 2010).

Otsuka, T. and Kitamura, Y., *Case Book on Environmental Law*, 2nd edn (Yuhikaku, 2010).

Egypt

Agrawala, Shardul *et al.*, *Development and Climate Change in Egypt: Focus on Coastal Resources and the Nile* (produced for the OECD, 2004).

Al Danasory, Ezz El Din and Al Shawarby, Abdel Hameed, *The Constitutional Lawsuit* (Alexandria: Monsha't Al Maaref Publishers, 2001).

    Civil Liability in the Light of Jurisprudence and the Judiciary, vol. I (Alexandria: Monsha't Al Maaref Publishers, 2004).

Egypt's Second National Communication submitted on 7 June 2010 under the UNFCCC, available at http://unfccc.int/resource/docs/natc/egync2.pdf.

El Sanhoury, *Al Wasit in the Civil Code, Sources of Obligation*, part II, vol. II (Dar Al Nahda Publishers, 1981).

Dr Fikry, Fathy, *A Brief on the Annulment Case According to the Court Rulings*, enlarged edn (Cairo: People Printing Company, 2009).

Saber, Mohammad, 'Environmental Consequences of Global Change in Egypt', *The International Geosphere-Biosphere Programme's Global Change News Letter*, 70 (2007), available at www.igbp.net/documents/NL_70–5.pdf.

Sterman, David, *Climate Change in Egypt: Rising Sea Level, Dwindling Water Supplies* (2009), available at www.climate.org/topics/international-action/egypt.html.

UNDP Climate Change Risk Management Programme for Egypt, available at www.undp.org.eg/Portals/0/Project%20Docs/Env_Pro%20Doc_Climate%20change%20Risk%20Management.pdf.

Israel

Alpert, P., 'The Effects of Climatic Changes on the Availability of Water Resources in Israel' in Watanabe, T. (ed.), *Proceedings of the Kick-off Workshop for the Research Project on the Impact of Climate Change on Agricultural Production System in Arid Areas* (ICCAP, 2002).

Barak-Erez, Daphne, *Administrative Law*, 2 vols. (Israeli Bar Publishing, 2010).

Dotan, Yoav, *Administrative Guidance* (Nevo Press, 1996).

Fish, Daniel, *Environmental Law in Israel* (Mishpatim Publishing, 2000).

McKinsey & Company, *Greenhouse Gas Abatement Potential in Israel: Israel's GHG Abatement Cost Curve* (2009).

Ministry of Environmental Protection, 'Coping with Climate Change in Israel', *Special Issue: UN Copenhagen Climate Change Conference* (December 2009).

'Vulnerability and Adaptation to Climate Change', *Israel Environment Bulletin*, 24 (2001).

Porat, Ariel, 'Tort Law' in Shapira, A. and Dewitt-Arar, K. C. (eds.), *Introduction to the Law of Israel* (Kluwer, 1995).

Rabinowitch, Danny and Lubanov, Carmit, 'Climate Justice in Israel', *The Association of Environmental Justice in Israel – Position Paper no. 1* (2010).

Schorr, David, 'Has the Reduction of Greenhouse Gas Emissions Law already been Enacted?', *Hukim – Journal on Legislation*, 3 (2011), 241 (Hebrew).

Kenya

Angwenyi, Anne, 'An Overview of the Environmental Management and Coordination Act', in Okidi, C. O. *et al.* (eds.), *Environmental Governance in Kenya: Implementing the Framework Law* (Nairobi: East African Educational Publishers Ltd, 2008), pp. 142–82.

Government of Kenya, *National Climate Change Response Strategy* (2010).

Draft Climate Change Bill (2010).

Vision 2030 (2008).

IGAD, *Climate Change and Human Development in Africa: Assessing the Risks and Vulnerability of Climate Change in Kenya, Malawi and Ethiopia*, Human Development Report (Human Development Report Office, IGAD Climate Prediction and Applications Centre (ICPAC), 2007/08).

Juma, C. and Ojwang, J. B. (eds.), *In Land We Trust: Environment, Private Property and Constitutional Change* (Nairobi and London: Initiative Publishers and Zed Books, 1996).

Kameri-Mbote, Patricia, 'The Use of Criminal Law in Enforcing Environmental Law', in C. O. Okidi (ed.), *Environmental Governance in Kenya: Implementing the Framework Law* (Nairobi: East African Educational Publishers Ltd, 2008), pp. 110–125.

Kameri-Mbote, Patricia and Odote, C., 'Courts as Champions of Sustainable Development: Lessons From East Africa', *Sustainable Development Law and Policy Law Journal*, 10(1) (2009), 31.

Lumumba, P. L. O., *An Outline of Judicial Review in Kenya* (University of Nairobi, 1999).

Makoloo, M. O., Ochieng, B. O. and Oloo, C. O., *Public Interest Environmental Litigation: Prospects and Challenges* (Nairobi: ILEG, 2007).

McKenzie, Fiona L., 'Grounds of Review', *The Law Handbook*, available at www.lawhandbook.org.au/handbook/ch21s02s06.php.

Mumma, Albert, 'The Continuing Role of Common Law in Sustainable Development' in Okidi, C. O. *et al.*, *Environmental Governance in Kenya: Implementing the Framework Law* (Nairobi: East African Educational Publishers Ltd, 2008), pp. 90–109.

Okidi, C. O., 'Concept, Structure and Function of Environmental Law' in Okidi, C. O. *et al.* (eds.), *Environmental Governance in Kenya: Implementing the Framework Law* (Nairobi: East African Educational Publishers Ltd, 2008), pp. 3–60.

Republic of Kenya, Constitution of Kenya (2010).

Stockholm Environment Institute, *Economics of Climate Change in Kenya*, Project Report (2009).

South Africa

Du Bois, F. and Glazewski, J., 'The Environment and the Bill of Rights' in *Bill of Rights Compendium* (Durban: LexisNexis, 2004), 2B, pp. 1–89.

Du Bois, F. (ed.) *et al.*, *Wille's Principles of South African Law*, 9th edn (Cape Town: Juta & Co., 2007).

Glazewski, J., *Environmental Law in South Africa*, 2nd edn (Durban: LexisNexis, 2005).

Hahlo, H. R. and Kahn, E., *The South African Legal System and its Background* (Cape Town: Juta & Co., 1968).

Hoexter, C., *Administrative Law in South Africa* (Cape Town: Juta & Co., 2007).

Loubser and Midgley (eds.) *et al.*, *The Law of Delict in South Africa* (Cape Town: Oxford University Press, 2009).

Neethling and Potgieter, *Neethling, Potgieter, Visser: Law of Delict*, 6th edn (Durban: LexisNexis, 2010).

Paterson, A. and Kotzé, L. (eds.), *Environmental Compliance and Enforcement in South Africa: Legal Perspectives* (Cape Town: Juta Law, 2009).

Soltau, F., *Fairness in International Climate Change Law and Policy* (Cambridge University Press, 2009).

Strydom, H. and King, N. (eds.), *Fuggle and Rabie's Environmental Management in South Africa*, 2nd edn (Cape Town: Juta Law, 2009).

European Union

Bothe, M. and Rehbinder, E., *Climate Change Policy* (Utrecht: Eleven International, 2005).

Carlane, C. P., *Climate Change Law and Policy: EU and US Approaches* (Oxford University Press, 2010).

Freestone, D. and Streck, C., *Legal Aspects of Carbon Trading* (Oxford University Press, 2009).

Krämer, L., 'Klimaschutzrecht der Europäischen Union', *Revue Suisse du Droit International et Européen*, 20(3) (2010), 311.

Oberthür, S. and Pallemaerts, M. (eds.), *The New Climate Change Policies of the European Union* (Brussels: VUB Press, 2010).

Peeters, M., *Met recht naar klimaatbescherming* (Groningen: Europa Law Publishing, 2009).

Rodi, M. (ed.), *Emissions Trading in Europe: Initial Experiences and Lessons for the Future* (Berlin, 2008).

Schulze-Fielitz, H. and Müller, T. (eds.), *Europäisches Klimaschutzrecht* (Baden-Baden: Nomos, 2009).

Tabou, A.-S., *La mise en oeuvre du Protocole de Kyoto en Europe: interactions des contrôles international et communautaire* (Paris: La documentation francaise, 2010).

Winter, G., 'The climate is no commodity: Taking stock of the emissions trading system', *Journal of Environmental Law*, 22(1) (2010), 1.

Germany

Chatzinerantzis and Herz, 'Climate Change Litigation – Der Klimawandel im Spiegel des Haftungsrechts', NJOZ (2010), 594–98.

Frank, 'Climate Change Litigation – Klimawandel und haftungsrechtliche Risiken', NJOZ (2010), 2296–2300.

Koch, 'Climate Change Law in Germany', *Journal of European EEPL,* 7(4) (2010).

(ed.), *Umweltrecht,* 3rd edn (2010).

Koch and Hendler, *Baurecht, Raumordnungs – und Landesplanungsrecht,* 5th edn (2009).

Landmann, Rohmer and Rehbinder, *Umweltrecht,* 58th edn, vol. III (BImSchG, 2010).

Sachverständigenrat für Umweltfragen (SRU), *Wege zur 100% erneuerbaren Stromversorgung* (2011), available at www.umweltrat.de.

Staudinger and Kohler, *Kommentar zum Bürgerlichen Gesetzbuch mit Einführungsgesetz und Nebengesetzen,* vol. 3, *Sachenrecht, Umwelthaftungsrecht* (2010).

Poland

Constitutional Tribunal judgment dated 6 June 2006, K 23/05, OTK-A 2006, No. 6; see http://parl.sejm.gov.pl/WydBAS.nsf/0/C8292E9AF82C2743 C12573B50050884F/$file/infos_023.pdf

Mazur, P., 'Formy zbiorowe ochrony prawa osobistego do środowiska', *Państwo i Prawo,* 5 (2006).

'Prawo osobiste do korzystania z wartości środowiska naturalnego', *Państwo i Prawo,* 11 (1999).

Radecki, W., 'Ochrona środowiska naturalnego a ochrona dóbr osobistych' in J. St. Piątowski (ed.), *Dobra osobiste i ich ochrona w polskim prawie cywilnym. Zagadnienia wybrane* (Ossolineum, 1986).

Skoczylas, J., 'Odpowiedzialność cywilna na podstawie ustawy – Prawo ochrony środowiska', *Przegląd Sądowy,* 4 (2003).

'Odpowiedzialność za szkodę wyrządzoną środowisku – tezy do nowelizacji art. 435 k.c.', *Przegląd Sądowy,* 7–8 (2008).

Supreme Court ruling dated 25 February 2009, III CSK 546/08; see www.cop14. gov.pl/files/Polacy_o_zmianach_klimatu.pdf

England

Books and journal articles

Allen, Myles *et al.,* 'Scientific Challenges in the Attribution of Harm to Human Influence on Climate', *University of Pennsylvania Law Review,* 155 (2007).

Anderson, Michael and Galizzi, Paolo (eds.), *International Environmental Law in National Courts* (BIICL, 2003).

Burton, James, Tromans QC, Stephen and Edwards, Martin, 'Climate Change, What Chance a Damages Action in Tort ?', *UKELA, e-law,* 55 (2010), 22.

Clerk & Lindsell on Torts, 20th edn (Sweet & Maxwell, 2010).

Fordham QC, Michael, *The Judicial Review Handbook*, 5th edn (Hart Publishing, 2008).

Kaminskaité-Salters, Giedré, *Constructing a Private Climate Change Lawsuit under English Law: A Comparative Perspective* (Kluwer Law International, 2010).

Case law

Arscott v. *Coal Authority* [2004] EWCA Civ 892.

Barbone v. *Secretary of State for Transport* [2009] EWHC 463 (Admin).

Boggis v. *Natural England* [2009] EWCA Civ 1061.

Bradford v. *West Devon BC* [2007] PAD 45.

Dimmock, Heathrow Airport Ltd v. *Garman* [2007] EWHC 1957 (QB).

Dobson v. *Thames Water Utilities* [2009] EWCA 28.

Enertrag UK Ltd v. *South Norfolk DC* (2010) PAD 13, at para. 72.

Fairchild v. *Glenhaven* [2003] 1 AC 32.

J & A Young (Leicester) Ltd v. *The Commissioners for Her Majesty's Revenue & Customs* (2008).

London Borough of Hillingdon v. *Secretary of State for Transport* [2010] EWHC 626 (Admin).

Marcic v. *Thames Water Utilities* [2004] AC 42.

Nicholson v. *Grainger Plc* [2010] 2 All ER 253.

Platform, People and Planet v. *Commissioners of HM Treasury* [2009] EWHC 3020 (Admin).

R (Edwards & Pallikaropoulos) v. *Environment Agency and DEFRA* [2010] UKSC 57.

R (on the application of Friends of the Earth Ltd and Anor) v. *Secretary of State for Environment, Food and Rural Affairs and Ors* [2001] EWCA Civ 1950.

Sienciewicz v. *Grief* [2011] UKSC 10.

Tabernacle v. *Secretary of State for Defence* [2009] EWCA Civ 23.

Russia

Agibalov, S. and Kokorin, A., 'Copenhagen Agreement – A New Paradigm for the Climate Challenge Solution', *Vaprosi Ekonomiki*, RAN, 9 (2010).

Anaya, J., *Report of the Special Rapporteur on the situation of human rights and fundamental freedoms of indigenous peoples, James Anaya, on the situation of indigenous peoples in the Russian Federation*, UNGA, A/HRC/15/37/Add.5, (2010), available at http://unsr.jamesanaya.org/PDFs/Russia%20Report%20EN.pdf.

Bogoliobov, S.A., *Ecological Law (Экологическое право)* (Moscow: HORMA, 2001), Учебник для вузов, available at www.bibliotekar.ru/ecologicheskoe-pravo-1/77.htm.

Butler, W. E., *Russian Law*, 2nd edn (Oxford University Press, 2003).

Consultant, Russian law search engine, available at www.consultant.ru.

Douma, W., Kozeltsev, M. and Dobrolyubova, J., 'Russia and the International Climate Change Regime' in Oberthür, S. and Pallemaerts, M. (eds.) with Roche Kelly, C., *The New Climate Policies of the European Union: Internal Legislation and Climate Diplomacy* (Brussels: VUB Press, 2010).

Douma, W. Th. and Mucklow, F. M. (eds.), *Environmental Finance and Socially Responsible Business in Russia: Legal and Practical Trends* (The Hague: Asser Press, 2010), in particular: Mucklow, F. and Douma, W. Th., 'Environmental Finance and Socially Responsible Business in Russia – An Introduction'; Ratsiborinskaya, D. N., 'Russian Environmental Law – An Overview for Businesses'; Nystén-Haarala, S., 'Mechanics to Promote Green Business in Russia'; Yulkin, M., 'Involving Russian Business in Kyoto'; Guseva, T., 'Environmental Education and Capacity Building in Russia'.

Douma, W. and Ratsiborinskaya, D., 'The Russian Federation and the Kyoto Protocol' in Douma, W., Massai, L. and Montini, M. (eds.), *The Kyoto Protocol and Beyond: Legal and Policy Challenges of Climate Change* (The Hague: Asser Press, 2007), pp. 135–45.

Garant, Russian law search engine available at www.garant.ru.

Gutbrod, M., Sitnikov, S. and Pike-Biegunska, E., *Trading in Air: Mitigating Climate Change Through the Carbon Markets* (Moscow: Infotropic, 2010).

Henry, L. A. and McIntosh Sundstrom, L., 'Russia and the Kyoto Protocol: From Hot Air to Implementation? in Harrison, K. and McIntosh Sundstrom, L. (eds.), *Global Commons, Domestic Decisions: The Comparative Politics of Climate Change* (Cambridge, MA: MIT Press, 2010).

Kekic, L., *Country Forecast: Russia* (Economist Intelligence Unit, July 2010).

Millhone, J. P., 'Russia's Fires Breathe New Life into Climate Picture', Carnegie Endowment for International Peace (Commentary, 16 August 2010), available at www.carnegieendowment.org/2010/08/16/russia-s-fires-breathe-new-life-into-climate-picture/4ls.

Oldfield, J. D., Kouzmina, A. and Shaw, D. J. B., 'Russia's Involvement in the International Environmental Process: A Research Report', *Eurasian Geography and Economics* 44(2) (2003), 157–68.

Perelet, R., Pegov, S. and Yulkin, M., Climate Change: Russia Country Paper, Human Development Report Office, *Human Development Report 2007/2008,* 'Fighting Climate Change: Human Solidarity in a Divided World' (Moscow: UNDP, 2007), available at http://hdr.undp.org/en/media/HDR_20072008_EN_Overview.pdf.

Canada

Bernstein *et al.* (eds.), *A Globally Integrated Climate Policy for Canada* (Toronto: University of Toronto Press, 2007).

Chalifour, Nathalie, 'Making Federalism Work for Climate Change: Canada's Division of Powers over Carbon Taxes', *NJCL,* 22 (2009), 119.

Crowley, Paul, 'Inuit Defend their Human Rights against Climate Change' in Berger, S. and Saxe, D., *Environmental Law: The Year in Review* (Aurora: Canada Law Book, 2008), p. 39.

Doelle, Meinhard, *From Hot Air to Action? Climate Change, Compliance and the Future of International Environmental Law* (Toronto: Carswell, 2005).

Doelle, Meinhard and Mahony, Dennis, 'A Shift in the Legal Climate: The Emergence of Climate Change as a Dominant Legal Issue across Canada' in Berger, S. and Saxe, D., *Environmental Law: The Year in Review* (Aurora: Canada Law Book, 2008), p. 1.

Elgie, Stewart, 'Kyoto, the Constitution and Carbon Trading: Waking a BNA Bear (or Two)', *Review of Constitutional Studies,* 13 (2007), 67–129.

Elwell, Christine and Boyle, Grant, 'Friends of the Earth v the Minister of Environment: Does CEPA 166 Require Canada to Meet its Kyoto Commitments?', *JELP,* 18 (2008), 254–77.

Grimm, D. J., 'Global Warming and Market Share Liability: A Proposed Model for Allocating Tort Damages among CO2 Producers', *Columbia Journal of Environmental Law,* 32 (2007), 209–50.

Hsu, Shi-Ling, 'A Realistic Evaluation of Climate Change Litigation Through the Lens of a Hypothetical Lawsuit', *U. Colo. L. Rev.,* 79 (2008), 701–66.

Lucas, A., 'Legal Constraints and Opportunities: Climate Change and the Law' in Coward, H. G. (ed.), *Hard Choices: Climate Change in Canada* (Waterloo: Wilfred Laurier University Press, 2004).

Mahony, D. (ed.), *The Law of Climate Change in Canada* (Aurora: Canada Law Book, 2010).

Simpson, J., Jaccard, M. and Rivers, N., *Hot Air: Meeting Canada's Climate Change Challenge* (Toronto: McClelland & Stewart Ltd, 2007).

Wood, M. C., 'Atmospheric Trust Litigation' in Burns, W. C. G. and Osofsky, H. M. (eds.), *Adjudicating Climate Change: Sub-National, National, and Supra-National Approaches* (Cambridge University Press, 2009).

United States of America

Burns, William C. G. and Osofsky, Hari M. (eds.), *Adjudicating Climate Change: Sub-National, National, and Supra-National Approaches* (New York: Cambridge University Press, 2009).

Connecticut v. *American Electric Power,* 582 F.3d 309 (2nd Cir. 2009) cert. granted, 131 S. Ct. 813 (U.S. 2010); *American Electric Power* v. *Connecticut* (10-174, 2011 WL 2437011 (US June 20, 2011)).

Dhooge, J. Lucien, 'Aguinda v. ChevronTexaco: Mandatory Grounds for the Non-Recognition of Foreign Judgments for Environmental Injury in the United States', *J. Transnat'l L. & Pol'y,* 19 (2009).

Energy Info. Admin., U.S. Dept of Energy (DOE/EIA-0384(2009)), *2009 Annual Energy Review* (2010).

Gerrard, Michael B. (ed.), *Global Climate Change and U.S. Law* (American Bar Association, 2007).

Massachusetts v. E.P.A., 549 U.S. 497, 521 (2007).

North Carolina v. EPA, 531 F.3d 896 (D.C. Cir. 2008).

The Clean Air Act, 42 U.S.C. 7401–7671q (2004).

U.S. Climate Change Sci. Prog. & Subcomm. Global Change Research, *Weather and Climate Extremes in a Changing Climate: Regions of Focus: North America, Hawaii, Caribbean, and U.S. Pacific Islands* (2008).

U.S. Global Change Research Prog., Nat'l Oceanic & Atmospheric Admin., *Global Climate Change Impacts in the United States* (2009).

Brazil

Agência Nacional de Petróleo, *Anuário Estatístico Brasileiro do Petróleo, Gás Natural e Biocombustíveis 2010* (Rio de Janeiro: ANP, 2010).

Canotilho, José Joaquim Gomes and Leite, José Rubens Morato (eds.), *Direito Constitucional Ambiental Brasileiro* (São Paulo: Saraiva, 2007), pp. 316–20.

Didier Jr, Fredie, *Ações Constitucionais*, 4th edn (Salvador: Jus Podium, 2009).

Dimoulis, Dimitri and Martins, Leonardo, *Teoria Geral dos Direitos Fundamentais* (São Paulo: Editora Revista dos Tribunais, 2007), p. 96.

Filho, Sérgio Cavalieri, *Programa de Responsabilidade Civil*, 8th edn (São Paulo: Atlas, 2009), p. 2.

International Law Commission, 58th session, *Expulsion of Aliens* (Geneva, 2006), pp. 110–24.

Lavratti, Paula and Prestes, Vanêsca Buzelato (ed.), *Direito e mudanças climáticas* [*recurso eletrônico*]: *inovações legislativas em matéria de mudanças climáticas* (São Paulo: Instituto O Direito por um Planeta Verde, 2010), p. 118.

Machado, Paulo Affonso Leme, *Direito Ambiental Brasileiro*, 8th edn (São Paulo: Malheiros Editores, 2000), pp. 322–23.

Marcovitch, Jacques (coord.), *Economia da Mudança do Clima no Brasil: custos e oportunidades* (São Paulo: IBEP Gráfica, 2010).

MERCOSUR, *Las energías renovables en el ambito del Mercosur, sus estados asociados y en el escenario internacional: su dimensión estratégica, productiva, ambiental y económica* (Montevideo, 2009), p. 11.

Nunes, Cíntia Bezerra de Melo Pereira, 'Integração Energética no Mercosul e o Acordo Marco Sobre Complementação Energética' in Bichara, Jahyr-Philippe *et al.* (eds.), *Realidades – Organizações Internacionais e Questões da Atualidade* (Natal: Editora da UFRN, 2008), p. 75.

Ribeiro, Helena and Silva, Edelci Nunes da, *Alterações da temperatura em ambientes externos de favela e desconforto térmico* (Revista de Saúde

Pública, ISSN 0034–8910), available at: www.scielosp.org/scielo.php? pid=S0034–89102006000500016&script=sci_arttext.

Silva, José Antonio Tietzmann e, 'A efetividade do Direito Internacional do Meio Ambiente: a jurisprudência da Corter Europeia de Direitos Humanos' in Barros-Platiau, Ana Flávia and Varella, Marcelo Dias (ed.), *A efetividade do Direito Internacional Ambiental* (Brasília: UNICEUB, UNITAR e UnB, 2009), pp. 293–316.

Soberania, Queimada, *Revista Novo Ambiente: desenvolvimento com equilíbrio*, 1(4) (2010), 13.

Mexico

Acevedo, Lucio Cabrera, *El amparo protector del derecho al ambiente y de otros derechos humanos* (Mexico: Porrua, 2000).

Carlos, Gay García (ed.), *México: una visión hacia el siglo XXI. El cambio climático en México* (Mexico: Instituto Nacional de Ecología, Universidad Nacional Autónoma de México, US Country Studies Program, 2000).

Conde-Pumpido, Candido, 'Introducción al delito ecológico' in Basoco, Juan Terradillos, *El delito ecológico* (Valladolid: Trotta, 1992).

Fernández, Adrian *et al.*, 'Cambio Climatico y Acciones para enfrentarlo' in Sada, Ninfa Salinas and Alaniz, Yolanda (eds.), *Temas Selectos de Medio Ambiente* (Mexico: Cámara de Diputados, 2011).

González, José Juan, 'Mexico' in Kurt Deketelaere, 'Environmental Law', *International Encyclopedia of Law* (Kluwer Law International, 2009).

Hildreth, Richard G. *et al.*, *Climate Change Law: Mitigation and Adaptation* (Thomson Reuters Business, 2009).

Machado, Paulo Affonso Leme, *Direito á informação e meio ambiente* (Brazil: Malheiros, 2006).

Marquez, Jose Juan Gonzalez, *La responsabilidad por el Daño Ambiental. El paradigma de la reparación* (Mexico: UAM-Porrua, 2002).

Martínez, Julia (ed.), *Cambio climático: una visión desde México* (Mexico: Instituto Nacional de Ecología, Secretaría de Medio Ambiente y Recursos Naturales, 2004).

Richardson, Benjamin *et al.*, *Climate Law and Developing Countries: Legal and Policy Challenges for the World Economy* (Edward Elgar, 2009).

INDEX